M000096950

Tricks of the Graphics Gurus

Tricks of the Graphics Gurus

Dick Oliver
Scott Anderson
Bob Zigon
James McCord
Spyro Gumas

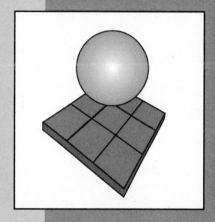

SAMS
PUBLISHING

A Division of Prentice Hall Computer Publishing
11711 North College, Carmel, Indiana 46301 USA

To our children:

Erica Oliver, age 1
Blake William Anderson, age 0.5
Brook Elizabeth Anderson, age 0.5
"Baby" Zigon, age 0
Danielle Zigon, age 4
Jamie McCord, age 3
Josh McCord, age 6
Alexandra Gumas, age 1
Andrew Gumas, age 3

Copyright © 1993 by Sams Publishing

FIRST EDITION

All rights reserved. No part of this book shall be reproduced, stored in a retrieval system, or transmitted by any means, electronic, mechanical, photocopying, recording, or otherwise, without written permission from the publisher. No patent liability is assumed with respect to the use of the information contained herein. Although every precaution has been taken in the preparation of this book, the publisher and authors assume no responsibility for errors or omissions. Neither is any liability assumed for damages resulting from the use of the information contained herein. For information, address Sams Publishing, 11711 N. College Ave., Carmel, IN 46032.

International Standard Book Number: 0-672-30308-6

Library of Congress Catalog Card Number: 92-82107

96 95 94 93   4 3 2 1

Interpretation of the printing code: the rightmost double-digit number is the year of the book's printing; the rightmost single-digit, the number of the book's printing. For example, a printing code of 93-1 shows that the first printing of the book occurred in 1993.

Composed in AGaramond and MCPdigital by Prentice Hall Computer Publishing

Printed in the United States of America

Trademarks

All terms mentioned in this book that are known to be trademarks or service marks have been appropriately capitalized. Sams Publishing cannot attest to the accuracy of this information. Use of a term in this book should not be regarded as affecting the validity of any trademark or service mark.

Publisher
Richard K. Swadley

Associate Publisher
Jordan Gold

Acquisitions Manager
Stacy Hiquet

Development Editor
Dean Miller

Editors
Fran Hatton
Hugh Vandivier
Joe Williams

Editorial Coordinators
Bill Whitmer

Editorial Assistants
Sharon Cox
Molly Carmody

Technical Reviewer
Bruce Graves

Marketing Manager
Greg Wiegand

Cover Designer
Kathy Hanley

Director of Production and Manufacturing
Jeff Valler

Production Manager
Corinne Walls

Imprint Manager
Kelli Widdifield

Book Designer
Michele Laseau

Production Analyst
Mary Beth Wakefield

Proofreading/Indexing Coordinator
Joelynn Gifford

Graphics Image Specialists
Tim Montgomery
Dennis Sheehan
Sue VandeWalle

Production
Mitzi Foster Gianakos
Dennis Clay Hager
Carla Hall-Batton
Howard Jones
Sean Medlock
Mike Mucha
Juli Pavey
Angela M. Pozdol
Linda Quigley
Michelle Self
Tonya Simpson
Suzanne Tully
Barbara Webster
Dennis Wesner
Donna Winter
Alyssa Yesh

Indexers
Suzanne Snyder
John Sleeva

Overview

Part VI: Appendices

Contents

Introduction

The Secrets Revealed

Whether you're a novice computer user or an advanced programmer, today's graphics-oriented PCs require that you explore and understand a dazzling array of graphics techniques and technologies. You don't need a PhD in math or visual arts to work with sophisticated computer graphics, but you may need some friendly, expert guidance. That's what this book is all about.

Real-World Graphics

Most books about graphics are written by academics in academic language, laden with cryptic formulas and hobbly-gobbly source code snippets ported from some UNIX workstation. When you actually run the programs in those books (if software is included at all), you may find the real-world performance less than thrilling.

You won't spot any university profs in the author list of this book. Instead, I've assembled a team of real-life "graphics gurus" willing to reveal the secrets of their trade in plain English even your kids will understand. The extensive source code and ready-to-run programs we include seldom take a textbook approach to the graphics problem at hand. We'd rather give you code specifically optimized for your computer, with as many wild and crazy speedup tricks and algorithmic shortcuts as we could find. We figured that beginners and practiced programmers alike would rather skip past the mathematical theories and see how the pros really do this stuff.

Who are these gurus? I, **Dick Oliver**, am your host throughout most of the book. I wrote the world's leading 3-D fractal design software, *Fractal Grafics 3D,* and several other graphics programs and books. **Scott Anderson** authored the fastest, easiest to use animation program for the PC, *FantaVision.* He also writes books and software to show you that most coveted of graphics effects, "morphing." **Bob Zigon** does hardware design for TrueVision, the leading high-end graphics hardware company and writes his own state-of-the-art graphics software for kicks. **James McCord** is the acclaimed author of a growing list of Windows programming reference books. **Sypro Gumas** is a professional programmer who created the popular VSA256 and TIFF256 graphics programming libraries. All of us share the uncanny ability to write in ordinary English almost as comfortably as we can write in C.

In a nutshell, we do this stuff all day, every day. We know how hard it can be, and how easy it can be when you don't need to discover all the pitfalls yourself. Most of us have thousands of customers using our software, and some of us don't get a paycheck unless those customers say, "Wow!"

We thought you might like to see some "Wows," too.

On a more humble note, computer graphics is a gargantuan, rapidly growing field, and every chapter in this book should by all rights be a thousand-page book of its own. None of us feel that we've said as much about each topic as we would like to, and a hundred more example programs beg to be written. Readers with plenty of time on their hands and cash in their pockets should drop this book and pick up 15 separate Sams titles, one for each subject in the table of contents. (See the Sams Publishing order form in the back of this book.) Be sure to go buy a cartload of graphics software to go with them.

But you might wish there was a way to get a solid grounding in state-of-the-art graphics without buying and reading a whole bookshelf and hard disk full of pulp, print, and programs. If so, you've come to the right place.

Oodles of Software

You don't need a C compiler to explore the 30 graphics programs that accompany this book because ready-to-run EXE files for each program are included. C programmers (or aspiring C programmers) won't be disappointed, though. The disks also contain over 18,000 lines of working C source code—all of it optimized for 286, 386, and 486 computers and all of it commented and complete. Of course, the disks include several spectacular graphics images, too.

The SVGA image viewer, the POLYRAY ray-tracer, and the VESA/TIFF graphics libraries are shareware and require a small registration fee to the authors if you continue to use them. All other software on the disks—covering every graphics category from stereoscopic 3-D animation to scientific visualization—is yours to explore or expand without any fee beyond what you paid for this book. By special arrangement with Cedar Software, you can also order several full-blown graphics applications and mesmerizing animations for just $5 per disk (to cover materials and shipping/handling) with the Cedar Software order form in the back of this book.

How to Use This Book

You can read this book by itself or use the accompanying programs to explore the world of graphics as you go. Special **You Can Do It** sections guide you through step-by-step examples of how to use each program.

Less technical readers can easily skip over the **Math Behind the Magic** and **Working Code** sections, whereas true techie-types can skip the English and head straight for the C.

If you aren't familiar with terms such as *bitmap, resolution, true color, VGA, VESA*, and *palette-based video mode*, be sure to read Chapter 1 before you tackle any of the others. Programmers should also read about the TransGraphics system in Chapter 2 before exploring the **Working Code** sections in the rest of the book. Otherwise, don't feel obligated to read the book in order—jump right to the section that intrigues you most and check out the others later. Just be aware that some chapters do occasionally refer to examples given in previous chapters.

You Can Do It: Installing the Software

This book includes two high-density (1.44M) 3 1/2-inch disks. On the Cedar Software order form in the very back, you can request high-density (1.2M) 5 1/4-inch disks for a $5 handling fee. Low-density (360K or 720K) disks are not available—there's just too much software to fit on them.

All the software is compressed into *archive* files, and you must install it to a hard drive before you can use it. You don't need to install all the software at once, however. With the INSTALL program, you can select which archives to decompress to your hard drive, and you can always go back and decompress others later.

If you don't wish to install all the software at once, I recommend that you install the TG.LZH and SVGA.LZH archives first. They contain the fun MOIRE program discussed in Chapter 1, the TransGraphics source code used by other programs throughout the book, and a shareware program for viewing images with VGA and Super VGA cards.

To install the disks, you must install each one separately. Here's the procedure:

1. From the DOS prompt, change to the drive that contains the installation disk. For example, if the disk is in drive A:, type A: and press Enter.

2. Type INSTALL and press Enter.

   A menu screen appears, which gives the choice of installing all the software on this disk or installing individual choices of software. The amount of space required for each set of files appears on the left.

3. If you have enough free space on your hard drive, I recommend you install all the software on each disk by selecting "Install entire disk." That way, you can try each program as you read through the book without having to reinstall. If you're short on space, you can choose only select archives. Refer to Appendix A for descriptions of each set of files.

4. After making a choice, the menu asks you to specify "Install_to_which_drive?" Type the drive letter of your hard drive followed by : (for example, C:), and press Enter.

5. The software will decompress and be installed to your hard drive. When you're finished installing from this disk, choose "Exit" to return to the DOS prompt.

   This installs all the files to a directory called \TGG on your hard drive.

6. Be sure to read the README.TXT file for more information on the programs you've installed. (Enter TYPE README.TXT to read the file, or use your favorite text editor.)

Compile Instructions

Executable files for all the programs are provided and installed automatically along with the C source code.

Most programs in this book use the TransGraphics system presented in Chapter 2. You can compile these programs without change under the Microsoft or Borland compilers, using the standard graphics libraries that came with your compiler, the Genus GX Graphics toolkit (an abbreviated version of which comes with the Sams book, *Graphics Programming Powerpack*, by Michael Jones), or Spyro Gumas' VSA256 library (a shareware version of which accompanies this book). You can also easily add support for other compilers or graphics libraries, as explained in the TG.TXT file and Appendix B.

To compile a TransGraphics-compatible program with your particular compiler and graphics library, simply use one of the following batch files:

Compiler/graphics library	Batch file to use
Microsoft/Microsoft Graphics	TGMS.BAT or TGMS2.BAT (see following note)
Borland or Turbo C/BGI	TCMS.BAT
Microsoft/GX Graphics	TGMSGX.BAT
Borland or Turbo C/GX Graphics	TCMSGX.BAT
Microsoft/VSA256	TGMSVSA.BAT
Borland or Turbo C/VSA256	TGTCVSA.BAT

Microsoft users: If you combined GRAPHICS.LIB into your main libraries when you installed the Microsoft C compiler, use TGMS2.BAT instead of TGMS.BAT because TGMS.BAT assumes you have a separate GRAPHICS.LIB. If you're not sure what all that means, look in the LIB compiler subdirectory for GRAPHICS.LIB. If it's there, use TGMS.BAT. If not, use TGMS2.BAT.

Borland users: When you run a program compiled to use the Borland Graphics Interface (BGI, the graphics library included with your compiler), you must make sure that EGAVGA.BGI, or another valid BGI driver file, is in the subdirectory where the program resides, on your PATH.

For example, to compile changes made in the MOIRE.C program in Chapter 1 with Microsoft C and the native graphics library that came with Microsoft C, you would enter:

```
TGMS MOIRE.C
```

In some cases, you must link in additional source code modules or .OBJ files as well. For example, to compile the TGAREAD.C program in Chapter 3, which requires the source code in TGA.C, you would enter:

```
TGMS TGAREAD.C TGA.C
```

As another example, to compile the FRAN.C program in Chapter 6, which requires you to link in the MUDI.OBJ file, you would enter:

```
TGMS FRAN.C MUDI.OBJ
```

The .EXE files supplied on the disk have been compiled with GX Graphics, which supports faster operations and smoother color animation than the Microsoft and Borland native libraries. Therefore, you should copy the originals to another directory for safekeeping before you recompile any of them.

The FPLAY program in Chapter 5 and the SCENE program in Chapter 6 require Microsoft C and do not use the TransGraphics system. All the Windows programs in Chapters 10, 11, and 12 require Borland/Turbo C version 3.0 or later. The IMAGEPRO program in Chapter 13 uses advanced features of the VSA256 and TIFF256 libraries directly, without TransGraphics. You can compile it with either the Microsoft or Borland compilers. See Appendix C and Appendix D for more details on using (and registering) the shareware VSA256 and TIFF256 libraries. Makefiles are provided for all compiler-specific programs.

Organization of This Book

This book is divided into five major parts, containing three chapters each. Though each chapter stands on its own, I recommend that you read through all the chapters of a major part in order.

Part I: More Than Just Pretty Pictures

Part I brings you up to speed on the latest techniques for creating and displaying graphics images. You also discover how to make graphics programs and files compatible with a wide variety of systems and software.

In Chapter 1, you learn how to display and manipulate visual information on your computer, from photographs to fantasies.

Chapter 2 introduces the TransGraphics system included with this book. With TransGraphics, you can use one set of drawing primitives, bit manipulation commands, and raster operations with any major C or C++ compiler and graphics library.

Chapter 3 reveals the inner structure of .TGA, .PCX, .TIF, .GIF, and .DXF files, along with several other standard formats.

Part II: Setting Things in Motion

Part II shows you how sophisticated real-world modeling and animation can bring your images to life.

Chapter 4 explains zooming, rotating, squashing, skewing, and other transformations that you can apply to any object. You also learn to automatically compute gradual transformations between any two objects. (A man metamorphoses into a werewolf.)

In Chapter 5, lightning-fast shaded spheres and textured objects go to work in a realistic planet generator, complete with craters. Along the way, you learn some otherwordly tricks such as anti-aliasing and using a super-fast ellipse drawing algorithm.

Chapter 6 gives you a new set of graphics tools called fractals, which enable you to draw realistic models of plants, clouds, galaxies, and mountains. Transform a fern into a tree, or collapse a spiralling galaxy into a black hole vortex. Welcome to infinity.

Part III: The Third Dimension

Both the real world and most of the unreal worlds you'd like to visit have three dimensions. In Part III, you learn to lift your graphics out of the flat screen into 3-D space.

In Chapter 7, you modify the animation tricks from Chapter 4 to work in 3-D. By extending two-dimensional geometry into the third dimension, you can place 3-D objects in a 3-D universe within your computer. The magic of anaglyphic stereoscopy (it's easier than it sounds) makes 3-D images literally leap out of your monitor. Put your red/blue glasses on and hold on to your seat!

Chapter 8 uses 3-D iterated functions to interactively rotate and move 3-D fractal plants and other wild stuff beyond description. You can also morph between any two 3-D fractals you design or between several prefabricated trees, ferns, and recursive spirals.

To make photo-realistic ray-traced images, you'll need to simulate the interaction of your 3-D models with light. In Chapter 9, the math gets deeper and the drawing gets slower, but the spectacular results are worth both the wading and the waiting.

Part IV: Graphics Within Microsoft Windows

Can you adapt all the snazzy graphics techniques you use in DOS to Windows? You bet! Part IV teaches you Windows' own bag of graphics magic tricks.

Chapter 10 introduces you to Windows and reviews the basics of Windows programming. With the Windows *Graphics Device Interface*, all your graphics are instantly compatible with any display or printer.

In Chapter 11, you learn how to draw basic shapes within Windows and how to access more advanced tools like pens, brushes, and fonts.

With the Windows bitmap functions introduced in Chapter 12, you can create fast and flashy "splash" graphics, animations, and custom fonts.

Part V: The Graphics of Tomorrow

Part V takes you beyond ordinary drawing and painting into a new world of interactive adventure. Explore the latest advances in PC graphics and learn hands-on techniques for manipulating visual information.

Enter the undercover world of the digital darkroom in Chapter 13. Learn to enhance and retouch any scanned photo or bitmapped image and to produce amazing effects you could never do without a computer.

In Chapter 14, you turn raw numerical data into visual images that you can understand and work with easily and intuitively. Watch chaos rear its head in a scientific simulation of the famous Lorenz water wheel.

Chapter 15 is an inside tour of the amazing graphics technologies and techniques we are exploring now—and you'll soon find on your desktop.

Appendices

The appendices supply you with more detailed information on the software included with this book and direct you toward further exploration.

Appendix A is a general reference to all the software.

Appendix B contains details on using graphics libraries with the TransGraphics system.

Appendices C and D are user's manuals for the VSA256 and TIFF256 libraries.

Appendix E points you toward further graphics adventures with an annotated listing of books, software, and other useful resources.

The glossary defines technical terms used in the book.

Conventions Used in This Book

The first few occurrences of a new term appear in italics. These terms appear in the glossary and index. Italics is also used *occasionally* for emphasis.

C source code appears in a monospaced font:

```
void main(void)
{    draw_fun_graphics();
}
```

Commands to type at the DOS prompt appear in monospaced capital letters. Filenames appear in capital letters.

Acknowledgements

No guru is an island, and much of the wisdom in this book resides in numerous quotes from industry experts and sages of old. We would like to thank the many publishers who gave permission to reprint this copyrighted material and the many authors whose words are quoted. You'll find specific references after each quote and in Appendix E, the annotated bibliography.

We would also like to thank our families for their patience, inspiration, and support over the many months that led to the creation of this book. Bob Zigon would especially like to thank his parents, Frank and Helen Zigon.

More Than Just
Pretty Pictures

Bitmapped Graphics

I magine a frontier without limits, a continent without shores, a universe of endless exploration. Your computer monitor can become a window into just such a universe, and this book will lead you to the edges of uncharted territory. Though you'll follow in the footsteps of many bold explorers, you will soon discover new treasures and fantastic vistas never seen before. Human beings have barely begun to intrude on this strange new wilderness, and your journey will be more of an adventure than a guided tour.

Like the pioneers of an earlier time, you may build your own craft to carry you into the unknown. Unlike those pioneers, you will often even create the territory itself. But don't think for a moment that you won't encounter any surprises. The computer graphics techniques that you master will help you visualize information, but information has structures and landscapes of its own. We "graphics gurus" are only beginning to perceive those structures and view the alien landscapes. We are just beginning to understand how fantastic worlds of our own creation are intimately connected to the concrete physical world.

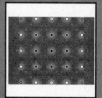

Ultimately, the goal of this book—and perhaps, this era of history—is to rediscover the world we thought we already knew. Through the window of your computer screen, you will advance through nether regions of artificial universes. The skills you gain in creating your own intangible worlds will give you insight into the tangible world as well. That same computer screen will also become a window into the real universe—a window that reveals real structures and real landscapes that you could never see without it.

Before you can see much through that window, however, you need to examine the window itself—your computer's display. This chapter teaches you the basics of how to display visual information on your computer, from fantasies to photographs.

If you are already quite familiar with PC graphics, this chapter provides a quick refresher and an update on the latest advances in video technology. If you're new to graphics, this chapter swiftly brings you up to speed on the basic architecture of your computer's display.

Computer Graphics Displays

From the earliest days, of course, computers were designed mainly to deal with numbers or letters. But in recent years even the least expensive and least sophisticated machines have come to be able to deal with graphics, in one form or another, with almost equal facility. With the coming of real graphic capabilities—whether interface or application, basic or advanced—an important cultural change is surely taking place. Few may have yet appreciated this shift, in part because few have been trained or accustomed to use effectively this fundamentally different and powerful visual medium.

—William J. Caffery, *The Visual Revolution*,
Gartner Group's Managing Advanced Technology Transfer Evaluation Review
(MATTER), Fall 1992

Your computer displays images as a two-dimensional collection of dots, called *pixels*. Once upon a time, the word *pixel* was an abbreviation for "picture element," but it has since made it into the dictionary as a word in its own right. (IBM employees, who generally aren't much for verbosity, sometimes call them *pels* instead of pixels. Nobody else knows what they're talking about most of the time.)

Within your computer, visual information is stored as a large array of *bits*. Each bit corresponds to one microscopic electronic *gate* that can be "open" or "closed," on or off. (Actually, the two states of a semiconductor gate correspond to high and low voltage, not an on/off switch. All that matters from the software side of things is that two states exist, usually referred to as 1 and 0.) Each dot in a picture is mapped to one or more bits in the computer's *memory*. Images stored and displayed this way are called *bitmapped images*, or simply *bitmaps*.

You can control what appears on the display by changing the state of the bits in your computer's *video memory*. The *video hardware* interprets the contents of the video memory to create a physical image on the monitor screen. In Chapter 2, "Graphics for Everyone," you learn how to use the C programming language to control a wide variety of video display hardware, and the rest of the book teaches you sophisticated techniques for creating spectacular graphics images. But first, this chapter introduces the basic concepts you'll need to wield that power.

Bitmaps Versus Vectors

You will often hear the term *bitmapped graphics* contrasted with the term *vector graphics*. When contrasted this way, these terms refer to the way that visual information is stored by software applications. *Bitmapped programs*, also known as *paint programs*, store images just as they are displayed on the bitmapped screen—as an array of small, square dots. When you edit pictures with a paint program, you control the coloring of each pixel directly. This type of image storage and manipulation is also called *raster graphics*. (A *raster* is the group of lines traced out by the cathode ray tube in your monitor.)

Vector-based programs, store mathematical descriptions of each element in an image separately. These include *draw programs* and software to do CAD (which stands for either computer-aided drafting or computer-aided design, depending on whether it's being used by a draftsman or a designer). For example, a draw program might store a line as a collection of colored pixel dots, whereas a painting program would store it as a collection of colored pixels. When you edit the line with a vector-based program, you change the mathematical description of the starting and ending points, and the program computes the necessary changes in pixel colors indirectly. CAD and draw programs must regenerate the actual bitmapped image each time it is displayed, whereas paint programs simply transfer the image data to the video memory to display it.

With vector graphics, you can re-create an image at a higher or lower resolution without significant loss of quality. Bitmaps, on the other hand, have a fixed resolution. If you try to enlarge a bitmap significantly, the individual dots look like big squares of color. If you try to shrink a bitmap, you will lose some dots, and the image may look fuzzy or choppy. Therefore, vector image storage is generally preferred for images

5

eventually printed or viewed at a different resolution than the screen of the computer on which they were originally created. Bitmapped storage is better when you want to create complex patterns that can't easily be described as mathematical lines and curves. Figure 1.1 shows a detailed bitmapped graphic, whereas Figure 1.2 is a smooth vector drawing.

Figure 1.1. *When you need complex detail or photographic realism, you should store images the same way the computer displays them: as bitmaps.*

In this book, you'll learn to create and store both bitmapped and vector image data. Your computer's display itself is always a bitmap, though, and you must always convert vector data to a bitmapped image to see it on-screen. (Once upon a time, a long time ago, vector-based displays thrashed CRT guns around to etch individual vectors directly on-screen rather than scanning through raster lines of pixels. Those days, and those displays, however, are far behind us now.) Therefore, you should start with a solid understanding of bitmapped graphics before you try to work with vector graphics.

Resolution and Video Modes

Each pixel on your screen corresponds to a numerical value in your computer's memory, which is interpreted by the video hardware to produce a physical colored dot. The number of pixels and color values on your screen determines the *resolution* of the display. The number of pixels in each row of dots on your screen is the *horizontal resolution*, the number of pixels in each column is the *vertical resolution*, and the total number of colors that can appear on-screen at any given time is the *color resolution*. Though the term *resolution* technically refers to both the size and color capability of your screen, it often refers to just the horizontal and vertical resolution. (For example, lackadaisical authors might pen inaccurate phrases such as, "Each type of video adapter has a maximum resolution and number of colors…" even though the number of colors is technically part of the resolution.)

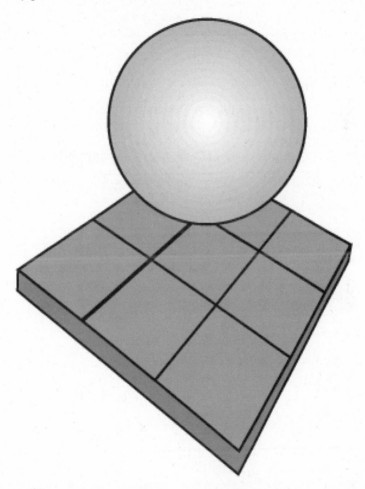

Figure 1.2. *When you want smooth curves to print clearly at any size, or you need to edit the elements of an image independently, you should use a vector storage format.*

Each type of video adapter has a maximum resolution and number of colors, from the 720×348, 2-color mode supported by the original Hercules graphics adapter to the 1024×768, 256-color or higher resolutions of today's Super VGA adapters. Most graphics hardware supports several *video modes* that enable you to choose the best balance of speed, resolution, and number of colors for any particular application.

With the increasing variety of graphics hardware available today, remembering the resolution and color capabilities of various video cards and video modes can be challenging. Table 1.1 summarizes the video modes supported by the major graphics cards available today for PC-compatible computers.

Table 1.1. Standard video modes for PC-compatibles.

	2 colors (1 bit)	4 colors (2 bits)	16 colors (4 bits)	256 colors (8 bits)
320×200		CGA	EGA lo-res	VGA/MCGA
640×350	EGA mono	Older EGAs	EGA hi-res	
720×348	Hercules			
640×480	VGA mono		VGA hi-res	VESA 101h
800×600	SVGA mono		VESA 102h	VESA 103h
1024×768	SVGA+ mono		VESA 104h	VESA 105h
1280×1024	SVGA+ mono		VESA 106h	VESA 107h

Resolutions higher than VGA are usually lumped under the vague classification of Super VGA (SVGA, or SVG for short). Some authorities, most notably PC Magazine, insist on using the term Super VGA to designate the 800×600 resolution in particular, and Super VGA+, SVGA+, or "beyond Super VGA" in reference to 1024×768 or higher resolution. (Few people pay much attention to this distinction, but a casual mention of it over coffee will convince your computer-jock friends that you really read all the fine print in those PC Mag articles.)

Because Super VGA is such a broad and nebulous category, many users have had a hard time finding software that supports their particular SVGA. And programmers have an even harder time writing software to support the multitude of SVGA boards. Fortunately, the Video Electronics Standards Association (VESA) was formed in the late 1980s to devise some desperately needed standardization for Super VGA. This consortium of video hardware and graphics software manufacturers published a preliminary 800×600 standard in 1989, which many industry leaders criticized as outdated even before it hit the streets. VESA quickly responded by issuing a more comprehensive standard in 1990, covering modes up to 1280×1024 with 256 colors. The VESA standard includes a software interface for programming Super VGA cards, which manufacturers of existing cards can support through special driver programs without changing their hardware. As a result, you will now find nearly universal software support for your Super VGA display, whether it is four years old or brand new. Table 1.1 includes the VESA standard mode numbers for Super VGA resolutions.

Notice that almost all modern Super VGA video cards are also capable of emulating the lower resolution modes of the classic *Computer Graphics Adapter* (CGA), *Enhanced Graphics Adapter* (EGA), and *Video Graphics Array* (VGA). Some also emulate the *Hercules Graphics Adapter* (also called the HGA, HGC, or just "Monochrome graphics"). The low-end Hercules standard is still common on ultra-cheapo PCs.

Nonstandard Video Modes

In addition to the "normal" modes that most people know about, most graphics adapters have undocumented "secret" modes, which usually require special programming to access. In fact, IBM's original VGA can theoretically be programmed to display up to 800×600 with 16 colors, or 360×480 with 256 colors. These modes are not included in Table 1.1, and you'll probably never encounter them, but some software just might use them to achieve a higher resolution or faster display speed than you thought your hardware could. The sneakiest programmers at least know these modes exist, and you should too.

You should also know that they often don't work reliably (perhaps that's why they were undocumented in the first place). Sometimes, programs that access the secret modes perform just fine on a brand-name graphics card, but crash and die a miserable death on "100% compatible" clones. If you are using a graphics program that doesn't seem to do what it should on your card, check the documentation to see if it's using a nonstandard video mode, and see if you can make it use a normal video mode instead. None of the programs in this book will use secret modes, so you shouldn't experience any compatibility problems.

Image Quality

The horizontal and vertical resolution of your screen can have a profound effect on the quality of any image you display. Figure 1.3 shows the same image in each of the standard resolutions. In theory, the striped tendrils of this fractal continue all the way down to the white regions, becoming infinitely skinny in the process. In practice, limited resolution makes the tendrils appear to vanish in a random sea of gray fuzz. The higher the resolution, the skinnier the tendrils become before they seem to dissolve.

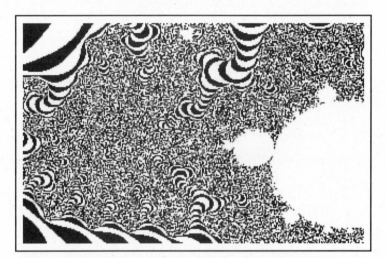

a

b

c

d

Figure 1.3. *A computer-generated image at (a) 320x200 resolution, (b) 640x480 resolution, (c) 800x600 resolution, and (d) 1024x768 resolution.*

The color resolution of your video hardware can also make a huge difference in image quality (even if you are dealing with monochrome images that employ 2, 4, 16, or 256 shades of gray instead of the full color spectrum). Each rendition of the scanned photograph in Figure 1.4 has the same horizontal and vertical resolution, but the image with 256 shades of gray (Figure 1.4d) appears dramatically more realistic than the black-and-white image (Figure 1.4a).

a

b

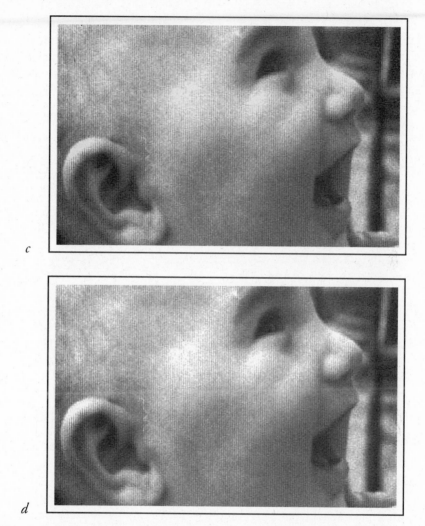

c

d

Figure 1.4. *A scanned photograph displayed at 320x200 resolution in (a) black and white only, (b) four shades of gray, (c) sixteen shades of gray, and (d) 256 shades of gray.*

Types of Color

Time was, the words computer graphics *implied line graphs and bar charts. Now, graphics and photography seem to have merged—at least, that's what you'd think looking at the results. Today, advanced computer graphics can create and manipulate color images in three dimensions with photographics precision and photorealism…*

Color in advanced graphics is another area where significant progress is being made. Putting great colors and a great many colors on the screen has been viable for some time now. In fact, some companies offer more colors than I can even imagine trying to choose from…

All this wonderful color talk may seem like a moot point if you use a PC-compatible machine. Workstation-quality graphics have moved to the Macintosh, but until recently, they hadn't made the trek into DOS land. Well, times have changed… when you're speaking of the graphics world, one line says it all: You've come a long way, baby.

—Jane Morrill Tazelaar,
"State of the Art: Advanced Graphics,"
BYTE, December 1990

When you want to display an image in color on your PC, you have two basic choices for representing colors: direct color and palette-based color. Direct color is the simplest choice. You simply specify the color of each pixel on-screen, and that's that. Yet, this simple scheme is used only for the wimpiest two-color systems and the most powerful photorealistic displays. In between, a limited palette of colors must be used, and specifying colors becomes more complex.

Palettes

What, exactly, does "256 colors" mean? Which 256? And which color goes where? You'll learn the ins and outs of writing color graphics programs in the next two chapters, but you can master the basic principles behind palette-based video modes right now.

When you use the video modes listed in Table 1.1, your software places a *color number* in the part of the computer's memory that corresponds to each pixel. In two-color modes, the color number can only have one of two possible values: 0 or 1. Usually, a color number of 0 means black, and a color number of 1 means white (or amber or green, if you have a monochrome monitor with tinted phosphors). Because the color of each pixel depends only on a single bit of information, this is called "1-bit" color.

For more complex coloring, each pixel on-screen obtains its physical color through a two-step process. First, the software places a color number in the part of the computer's memory that corresponds to each pixel. In a 16-color mode, the color number can have any value from 0 to 15. Because it takes 4 bits of information to store 16 distinct numbers, 16-color modes are also called "4-bit" modes. Likewise, pixels in a 256-color mode can have color numbers up to 255, and require 8 bits of information storage per pixel.

The Math Behind the Magic: Binary Numbers

Is this bit business new to you? Here's the scoop: each *bit*, or *binary digit*, can have two possible values: 0 or 1. So two bits can store four different values: 00, 01, 10, or 11. Four bits can store sixteen different values: 0000, 0001, 0010, 0011, 0100, 0101, 0110, 0111, 1000, 1001, 1010, 1011, 1100, 1101, 1110, and 1111.

If you treat each of those values as a *binary number*, you can store any number with a simple on/off (1/0) signal. The binary number 1 corresponds to the ordinary decimal number 1, binary 10 means decimal 2, binary 11 means 3, binary 100 means 4, and so on. In computer graphics, of course, these "numbers" often don't represent numerical values, but graphical information such as colors and patterns. Still, old habits die hard and just as graphics workstations are still called "computers," bits of visual information are still called "numbers," even by those who ought to know better.

In general, n bits can store 2 raised to the n power, or $2n$, different values. So, a single byte, which is eight bits, can store any number between 0 and 255. Using the same formula, 15 bits can store 32,768 values, 18 bits can store any number up to 262,144, 24 bits can count to 16,777,216, and so forth.

If you've never done it, go ahead and write down the 256 possible binary numbers that you can make with eight bits—and while you're at it, please go to the front of the class and write "I will never forget how to count in binary" on the blackboard 128 times....

To determine the actual physical color that corresponds to each color number, the video hardware refers to a palette of *color values*. The *palette* is a separate part of the video memory from the array which holds the color numbers for each pixel. Each palette color value indicates the mixture of red, green, and blue light (the primary colors) for every pixel on-screen that has a particular color number. Figure 1.5 depicts the relationship between the pixel color numbers and the palette color values.

The exact number of bits used to store each color value in the palette depends on the video hardware. Each color value in an EGA palette has 6 bits: 2 bits for red, 2 bits for green, and 2 bits for blue. Because 6 bits can store numbers from 0 to 63, you can choose each palette color value from 64 distinct colors on an EGA display. VGA and Super VGA adapters use 18 bits to store each palette color: 6 bits each for red, green, and blue. Therefore, you can choose each VGA palette color value from 262,144 distinct colors.

For example, to draw a yellow dot on your screen, your software might write the number 14 (that's 1110 in binary) to the portion of the video memory that corresponds to that pixel. In the standard EGA and VGA palettes, which are created automatically when you begin using a 16-color or 256-color video mode, the number 14 corresponds to the color yellow. (Table 1.2 lists the standard default EGA/VGA color values.) The color number doesn't actually stand for any one physical color—you can change the color value of color number 14 in the palette to any color you want.

Table 1.2. These color values are automatically placed in the EGA and VGA palette when you start a 16-color or 256-color video mode.

Color Number	Color Value
0	Black
1	Blue
2	Green
3	Cyan
4	Red
5	Violet
6	Brown
7	Light gray
8	Dark gray
9	Light Blue

Color Number	Color Value
10	Light Green
11	Light Cyan
12	Light Red
13	Light Violet
14	Yellow
15	White
256-color modes only	
16-31	Gray scale
32-103	Shades of high intensity blue, red, and green
104-175	Shades of moderate intensity blue, red, and green
176-247	Shades of low intensity blue, red, and green
248-255	Black

High Color

When it comes to representing photographic-quality images, even a carefully selected set of 256 colors, chosen from the 262,144 possible colors that the VGA can reproduce, can fall short of the kind of color variety you are used to getting from your 35mm camera. Your ordinary color slides or 4×5 snapshots also have a considerably higher resolution than a VGA display. Only in the last few years have truly *photorealistic* computer graphics become common on low-cost PCs.

Part of the quest for photorealism has involved upping the vertical and horizontal resolution of run-of-the-mill graphics cards to Super VGA levels. Color resolution is far more important to your eye, which can distinguish millions of subtle color gradations. Near photographic quality has arrived on the desktop with the recent advent of extremely inexpensive *Random Access Memory Digital Analog Converter* (RAMDAC) chips, which enable Super VGA cards to display upwards of 32,000 colors at a time.

These "high color" chips have appeared on almost every brand of Super VGA card, and software that supports them is becoming increasingly common. Celebration is obviously in order for users who enjoy the long-sought capability to see realistic color on their computer screens. And programmers might want to break out the champagne, too—high color video modes are much simpler to program because the added complexity of a limited palette is not needed. Instead of a pixel color number referencing a palette color value, high color programmers can simply specify a 15-bit color value for each pixel directly (5 bits each for the red, green, and blue channels). This type of color specification is called *direct color*, as opposed to *palette-based color*.

True Color

Even before the cheers for high color die down, a new graphics star strolls onto the stage. The ultimate in color resolution would provide more colors than the eye can perceive, and a few extra bits per pixel is all it takes. By specifying a 24-bit value for each pixel, (8 bits each for red, 8 bits for blue, 8 bits for green) *true color* cards can display precisely the right color in precisely the right place, every time. You just can't ask for more than that.

True color hardware, such as Truevision, Inc.'s popular Targa boards, has been available on PCs for a long time—for a price. A low end 24-bit Targa costs upwards of $2,000 for the video card alone. Add the cost of a fast 386 computer with 8M of memory and a 200M hard disk (a bare minimum configuration for handling large graphics files) at 1980's prices, and you were talking $10,000 just to get started with true color. Goodbye, average Joe.

Now, you can buy a fully loaded fast 486 for under $2,000, and you can pick up a 24-bit video card, such as the Diamond SpeedSTAR 24, for under $200. By the time you read this, those street prices should be even lower. Hello, Joe—welcome to true color.

Pleasantly enough, inexpensive true color cards can be at least as easy to work with as high color or palette-based graphics. Because true color cards usually use a *direct color* addressing scheme, you simply place the colors at the pixel locations you want. You'll also often find that color calculations are simpler when working with true color because each of the red, blue, and green color values is 8-bits (one byte), and PCs are optimized to handle 8-bit bytes more easily than the 5-bit data chunks that high color employs.

Some implementations of true color use 32 bits per pixel to take advantage of the 32-bit data paths within most contemporary microprocessors. (Apple, for example, has standardized 32-bit color on its high end video hardware and software for the Macintosh computers.) Don't let 'em fool ya, though. 32-bit color does *not* look any better than 24-bit color because 24-bit color already exceeds the color resolution of your eye by a considerable margin. The extra 8 bits, called the *alpha channel*, are used only for special effects such as transparency and the addition of black ink or a *spot color* in printing applications.

The first six color plates, located in the middle of this book, show off the capabilities of various color resolutions, from two-color to true-color. Figures 1.5 and 1.6 approximate these color images in monochrome. Figure 1.5 (and Plates 1 through 3) are a best-fit approximation of a scanned photograph. Figure 1.6 (Plates 4 through 6) are computer renderings of 3-D models. In both cases, 256 colors are the bare minimum for realistic representation, and true color is the graphics Holy Grail.

After all this acclaim for true color, you probably have the phone and checkbook in hand, ready to call PC Connection and order a 24-bit card shipped overnight. Before you dial, let me remind you that the silver lining of high color and true color still surrounds a giant cloud—a cloud filled with massive hard-disk gobbling graphics files. Remember that 24-bit color occupies three times as much storage space as 8-bit color—and takes three times as long to save or display.

For images that fit on your screen, this penalty isn't too severe—a 640×480, 24-bit image saved in the standard TGA file format will generally use around half a megabyte of disk space. (For comparison, a standard VGA 320x200 256-color image compresses neatly into 32K, or 1/30th of a megabyte.) If, however, you want to buy a 24-bit scanner (available for under $300 these days) and start scanning photos at a decent resolution, the situation gets out of hand fast. A 4×5 snapshot scanned at 400 dots per inch (dpi) weighs in at about 8M, compressed. Manipulating a bitmap this hefty with a graphics editing program can be a painfully slow process, even on a top-of-the-line 486. So go ahead and buy that true color card, but don't forget that photorealistic graphics is still on the technological cutting edge, and making it practical to buy is only the first step in making it practical to use.

Back on the sunny side of the street, this book shows you the latest techniques for generating spectacular true-color images of your own 3-D universes, *and* I'll teach you hot tricks for squeezing great graphics out of your standard VGA or Super VGA card.

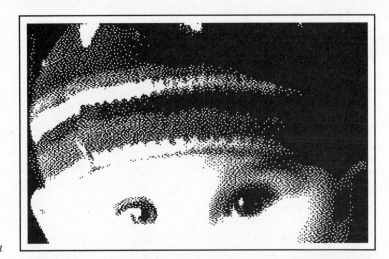

a

b

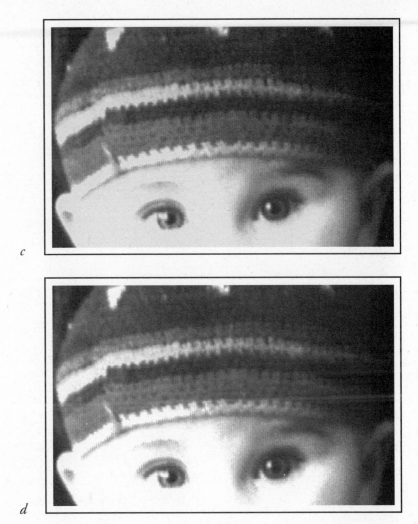

c

d

Figure 1.5. *A photograph scanned at 320x200 resolution and approximated in black and white (a), 16 colors (b), 256 colors (c), and true color (d). (See color Plates 1 through 3 in the center of this book for the color versions of these images.)*

a

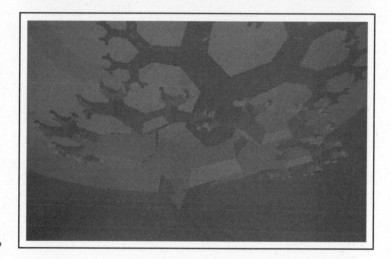

b

c

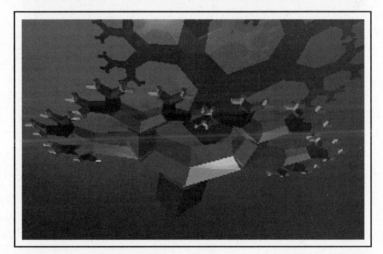

d

Figure 1.6. *A computer generated 3-D model rendered at 320x200 resolution in black and white (a), 16 colors (b), 256 colors (c), and true color (d). (See color plates 4 through 6 in the center of this book for color number comparisons of another ray-traced picture.)*

Because high color and true color are so new to the mass market, no universal standards for programming them have arisen yet. (VESA has issued a true color extension, but the pace of industry support has been leisurely at best.) Therefore, the graphics programs in this book will only use palette-based video modes for direct display. When you need or desire 24-bit color for enhanced realism, I'll show you how to create standard true color TGA files. The manufacturer of your high color or true color video card should be able to provide you with a utility to display TGA files on your specific hardware.

Graphics Programming

The subspecialty of computer graphics programming is a craft, an art, a science, and (for some) a bit of a religious avocation as well. It's hard to think of any other niche in our industry that can appeal to practitioners with such a wide range of backgrounds, levels of training, or native talent. Computer scientists and mathematicians develop ever-bigger-and-better algorithms for transformations, ray-tracing, and solid-modeling; the Silicon Valley engineers design ever-faster graphics coprocessors,; the Far-Eastern manufacturers crank out ever-cheaper color CRTs with ever-higher resolutions; the systems software people develop graphical user interfaces to soak up the pixels and CPU cycles as fast as they appear; and self-taught teenagers can write video games that make some of them wealthy before the are old enough to drive.

—Ray Duncan, "Programmer's Bookshelf,"
Dr. Dobb's Journal, August 1991

In the olden days (back in the 1980s), writing a program to display even the simplest graphics on an EGA or VGA was a complex task. Creating reasonably fast, visually interesting displays was a monumental undertaking. You would begin by committing a month or two to studying the hardware manuals, then you would experiment with strange and cryptic procedures to control the various video registers. Because PCs transfer data 8, 16, or 32 bits at a time and because you must manipulate several *latch bits*, *mask bits*, and *controller registers* every time you access the video memory, writing a single dot to the screen typically involves up to 15 lines of assembly language code (and assembly language it must be). Easy-to-learn languages such as BASIC and C were generally too slow and cumbersome to access all those registers and memory regions directly. So, pile four months of assembly language training onto the learning curve.

Luckily, those elite programmers who conquered that mountainous learning curve in the 1980s have installed a software gondola to the top for the rest of us in the 1990s. Well-crafted libraries of graphics functions now come with all the major C compilers, and even more powerful add-on graphics libraries are available for cheap. Even if you have a burning desire to wade through a hundred pages of obtuse technical specifications for each video card in existence, you will probably still see faster, more efficient graphics operations by using a library that has survived years of hand-tuning by a team of graphics programming experts.

For true masochists and die-hard do-it-yourselfers who want to try building a better graphics mousetrap, I recommend Richard Wilton's *Programmer's Guide to PC & PS/2 Video Systems* or Roger Stevens' *Graphics Programming in C.* You'll find enough technical poop in these books to re-create almost every function in your compiler's graphics library—as long as you don't want to support the latest Super VGA cards. For those who are more confident driving a sportscar than trying to build their own Ferrari, this book starts where those books leave off. Here, you skip over the nuts and bolts of taming the jungle of Bit Mask registers and timing controller logic in a VGA chip; instead, you focus on how to create sophisticated graphics with easy-to-use high level functions.

Chapter 2, "Graphics for Everyone," introduces a set of simple graphics operations to make your graphics programs work with every major compiler and graphics library. Before you dive into the technical details, though, take a look at a simple graphics program to see just how easy creating complex images can be.

A Simple Graphics Program

Throughout this book, **Working Code** sections list complete graphics programs to produce a wide variety of images using the C programming language. When you need to know some math to understand how the programs work, sections entitled **The Math Behind the Magic** succinctly present and explain the relevant equations. When you aren't in the mood for wrestling with equations and C code, you can easily skip these special sections and still glean the general workings of the program at hand from the regular text and the **You Can Do It** sections, which step you through using the ready-to-run program files supplied on the disk.

The short program listed in the following **Working Code** section doesn't appear to do much at first glance. In fact, it simply draws concentric colored circles on your screen by computing which circle the center of each pixel would intersect, and choosing a color accordingly.

The Math Behind the Magic: Nothing Up My Sleeve...

There isn't math going on here. A circle is defined as a set of points having equal distance from a center point. To draw equally spaced colored circles, you would determine each pixel's color by it's distance from the origin:

```
color = square root of( x * x + y * y )
```

(Programmer's generally use x * x instead of x ^ 2 to mean "x squared" because computers multiply faster than they raise to a power. Actually, if you slip up and say x ^ 2 in a program, your optimizing compiler will probably change it to x * x in the compiled program anyway.)

Because you have a limited number of colors available, you need to scale down the large distance. In the following program, it is divided by 1,024 by bit-shifting ten binary places. (If you want to divide by a power of two, such as 2, 4, 8, 16, 32, 64, and so forth, using the >> bit-shift operator is much faster than using the / division operator. A rule to live by: Multiply if you must, but never divide if you can possibly help it.)

To speed up the display even more, you could remove the most time consuming operation—the square root. You would still see concentric circles, but they would become more and more tightly spaced as they travelled further out from the center.

So the equation used is

```
c = (((long) x * x + (long) y * y) >> 10) % ncolors;
```

That % ncolors part ensures that c is never larger than ncolors, the total number of colors in the palette. You also need the (long) castes because two integers, each of which could have a value up to 32,767, are multiplied. The result could be as much as 32,767 * 32,767, or about a billion. Regular integer variables can't hold a value that big, so you need to remind the compiler to store the result in a long 32-bit integer variable instead.

Working Code: Surprising Circles

Before you run the program (and see the surprise patterns in color), glance over the following source code. The `setvidmode()` function sets the video mode after `detectmode()`, and `pickmode()` detects the best mode available on the your computer. The actual graphics display appears as a result of the `putpixel` macro, defined in the header file `tg.h`. Just before the end of the program, `closedown()` returns to text mode and shuts down the graphics system. You'll learn the picky details of using these functions and macros in the next chapter, but it really isn't any harder than it looks. You don't need to slog around among the video chip registers just to choose and start a graphics mode and put a few dots on-screen.

The `colorcyle()` function is a special treat that I'll discuss in depth in the next chapter. The following **You Can Do It** section will give you a sneak preview of the fun.

See the introduction to this book for instructions on compiling programs with your specific compiler and graphics library.

```
/* MOIRE.C
 *
 * This program creates animated color moire patterns
 * using TransGraphics variables, macros and functions
 */

#include <stdio.h>        /* Standard input/output libraries */
#include <stdlib.h>

#include "tg.h"      /* See TG.TXT for compile instructions */

void main(void)
{   int a, i, j, x, y,  /* counters for looping */
        c,              /* color to make each circle */
        key,            /* user's keypress */
        cx, cy,         /* x,y center of the screen */
        size;           /* size of square area to fill */
    char str[16];
    printf("MOIRE — from Tricks of the Graphics Gurus\n\n");
    printf("This program simply draws radial lines and "
           "concentric circles.\n"
           "Where do all the patterns come from?\n"
           "Try pressing the number keys when drawing...\n");
    tg_pickmode();          /* confirm video mode */
```

27

```
/* Draw some radial lines first,
   just to set the stage and show off the palette */

for (x = 0, i = tg_scrnx - 1; x < tg_scrnx; x++, i--)
{   tg_setcolor(x % tg_ncolors);
    tg_drawline(x, 0, i, tg_scrny);
}
for (y = 0, j = tg_scrny - 1; y < tg_scrny; y++, j--)
{   tg_setcolor(y % tg_ncolors);
    tg_drawline(0, y, tg_scrnx - 1, j);
}
cx = tg_scrnx / 2;
cy = tg_scrny / 2;                  /* find screen center */
size = cy;                          /* fill half the screen */
for (a = 1; a < 32765; a++)             /* main loop */
{   if (kbhit())            /* pause if user hits a key */
    {   if ((key = getch()) == 27)
            break;                      /* quit if Esc */

        /* If users hits a number key, cycle the palette
           colors at the corresponding speed */

        while ((key >= '1') && (key <= '9'))
        {   tg_colorcycle(key - '0');
            key = getch();
        }
    }
    for (x = a, i = 0;      /* scan a triangular slice of */
        i <= size;         /* the screen, pixel by pixel */
        x += a, i++)
    {   if (kbhit()) break;       /* let user escape */

/* Try changing x in the next line
   to (x << 4) or (x >> 4) for more patterns */

        for (y = x, j = i; j <= size; y += a, j++)
        {                           /* draw circles! */
            c = (((long) x * x +
                (long) y * y) >> 10) % tg_ncolors;
/* Draw eight pie slices to fill a square region.
 * We can get away with this speed-up trick,
 * since circles and squares have eight-way symmetry */
```

```
        {   tg_putpixel(cx + i, cy + j, c);
            tg_putpixel(cx + j, cy + i, c);
            tg_putpixel(cx + j, cy - i, c);
            tg_putpixel(cx + i, cy - j, c);
            tg_putpixel(cx - i, cy - j, c);
            tg_putpixel(cx - j, cy - i, c);
            tg_putpixel(cx - j, cy + i, c);
            tg_putpixel(cx - i, cy + j, c);
        }
      }
    }
  }
  tg_closedown();                    /* close down graphics */
}
```

So, the MOIRE program draws radial lines and concentric, increasingly tightly spaced circles, pixel by pixel. Nothing more.

Figures 1.7 and 1.8 show the surprising results of drawing these simple shapes on a 640x480 black-and-white screen.

Figure 1.7. *Alternating black and white lines somehow don't look like lines. Why? Because your screen really is a screen....*

a

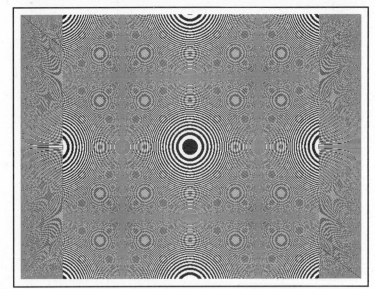

b

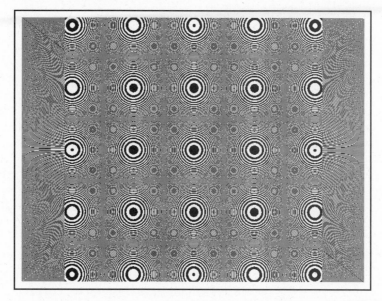

c

Figure 1.8. *Drawing successively smaller sets of concentric circles creates even more bizarre patterns—in fact, these "side effect" circles quickly overwhelm the "real" circles.*

You Can Do It: Mysterious Moiré

Whether you're a programmer or not, you can learn some graphics tricks—and pitfalls—from the MOIRE program listed previously. As with all the programs in this book, a ready-to-run EXE file is included on the disk. Try it:

1. From the DOS prompt, type MOIRE to start the program.

   A brief description of the program appears at the top of the screen, followed by a list of video modes. The TRY THIS ONE --> message appears in front of the best video mode which your hardware appears to support. Most programs in this book start by asking you to choose a video mode from this list.

2. Pick one of the video modes by pressing a letter or number. If you have a VGA or Super VGA card, press V for VGA 640×480, 16-color mode this time. If you have a CGA, EGA, or Hercules card, select the best mode for your hardware.

31

First, a set of radial lines going through the center of the screen appear. Next, the program draws a set of concentric circles, sweeping out from the center of the screen to the four corners but leaving a band of color along the left and right edges.

Next, a slightly smaller set of concentric circles replaces the first set. This time, you'll notice strange patterns along the horizontal, vertical, and diagonal axes. As the program draws more and more tightly spaced circles, these strange patterns will become more pronounced than the circles themselves.

What produces these patterns? They are *moiré patterns*, named after the French "water" fabrics that create a similar effect. Moiré patterns are actually an interference pattern between the pattern being drawn (the circles) and the grid pattern of the computer screen itself. You would see a similar effect if you held up a window screen—the old fashioned nonelectric wire kind of window screen—in front of a pattern of concentric circles.

If you were paying attention, you probably noticed a similar moiré effect toward the center of the radial lines when they were drawn. Though they produce fascinating effects, moiré patterns can often become your enemy when you try to produce high-quality computer graphics. Whenever you draw tightly spaced lines or shapes, you may see moiré patterns that detract from your intended image.

In two-color modes, moiré effects are even more pronounced. Here, have a look:

3. Press Esc to exit the program.

4. Enter MOIRE to start it again, and select a 2-color video mode this time. Try pressing M for VGA mono 640×480 2-color mode, for example.

   This time, the radial lines produce a very pronounced moiré effect, and the interference patterns quickly obscure any sign of the original circles that the program is actually computing and drawing.

   In this case, of course, moiré patterns are not your enemies, but your allies. By using the moiré effect intentionally, you can add fantastic special effects to your graphics displays.

However, you'd also like to know how to avoid that "through a screen" look when you want. The answer: resolution. Increasing the vertical and horizontal resolution will help a little:

5. Press Esc to exit, and start the MOIRE program again. Don't pick a video mode until you read this....

IMPORTANT NOTE: If the TRY THIS ONE --> message points to the VESA 101h mode, you probably have a Super VGA adapter. The automatic mode detector won't recommend any higher resolution than 640x480 because **you can physically damage your monitor** if you try to display a higher resolution than it can handle. Consult the documentation for your monitor to find out how high a resolution it can display, and choose the best 16-color mode you can. Remember that your video card is probably capable of 800x600 in 16-colors, but your monitor may not be!

6. If you know your hardware can do it, press 2 to select VESA mode 102h, 800×600 with 16-colors. Otherwise, press 0 for the 320×200 16-color mode, and you'll see the effect of a lower resolution instead of the effect of a higher resolution.

   Even though the lines and circles appear smoother at higher horizontal and vertical resolutions, the moiré effect is still quite pronounced.

7. Press the Spacebar a couple of times to skip to smaller circles without drawing the entire screen each time.

   Increasing the horizontal and vertical resolution doesn't do much to lessen the moiré effect, but increasing the color resolution is another story....

8. Press Esc to exit, and enter MOIRE once more.

9. Select a 256-color mode—press 1 for 640×480×256 if you have Super VGA, or press A for 320×200×256 if you don't. (EGA, CGA, and Hercules users can sit this one out.)

   This time, no moiré effect is visible in the radial lines, and the first few screens full of circles show only very subtle moiré patterns, even at the low 320×200 resolution. Because the default VGA 256-color palette consists mostly of gradual transitions between colors, the interference pattern between lines is dramatically reduced.

There's still fun to be had here, though. When the circles become small and cramped enough, spectacular multicolored moiré patterns do appear.

10. Let the program run for a while if you want to see moiré patterns gradually develop. (Those of you who chose the 320×200 mode won't have to wait long at all, but filling the 640×480 screen can take a while.) If you're impatient, press the Spacebar a few times to skip ahead.

    Moiré patterns are a neat trick, but you deserve at least a couple of good oohs and aahs from the first chapter of a book that struts around calling itself "Tricks of the Graphics Gurus," after all. Try this:

11. Press the number 1. Ooh!

12. Press 2. Press 4. Press 8. Aah!

13. Press the Spacebar to put on the brakes, and play around with this a bit. Each moiré is different, and you'll find that some of them contain spectacular waves of moving color when animated, whereas others just seem to sit there and jiggle.

14. If your monitor and video card will let you, press Esc, start MOIRE once more, and try the 1024×768 or 800×600 256-color modes. Remember that you can use the Spacebar to skip over the first few screens (but try animating them first).

    By the way, the color animation works in 16-color modes, too. It may be frighteningly fast in those modes, though, even at speed "1."

15. When you've seen enough, press Esc to escape from this madness.

How'd He Do That?

As Figures 1.10 and 1.11 demonstrate, when you draw with 256 colors, you have the option of eliminating unwanted moiré patterns or creating particularly spectacular moirés on purpose. When the lines or circles you draw are at least several pixels across (Figure 1.9), a gradual blend of palette colors dampens most interference with the bitmap screen grid. When you want to create moiré patterns, simply draw extremely tiny graphics elements (Figure 1.10) and the many colors will add to the effect. When you animate these colorful patterns with the `colorcyle()` function, the impress-your-friends quotient climbs quickly.

a

b

Figure 1.9. *Using a gradation of 256 colors virtually eliminates moiré patterns when the lines and circles are reasonably large relative to the size of the pixels.*

a

b

Figure 1.10. *When you draw very tiny circles with 256 colors, the resulting moiré patterns can be spectacular.*

The next chapter will reveal how color palette animation—and a complete set of other graphics operations—are done, and Chapter 13 will present more sophisticated palette-handling techniques. For now, suffice it to say that we have more than a few magic tricks in store....

Graphics for Everyone

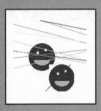

When you use a graphics program, you probably don't think at all about the library of functions that were available to its author. Well-crafted graphics functions, though, can make the difference between a slow, boring presentation and a snappy, snazzy performance. When you set out to create your own graphics programs, you'll want to carefully consider which graphics compiler and library you use. The right choice can make users of your programs feel like they're driving a new Lamborghini instead of an old Ford pickup.

But even a top-notch mechanic doesn't need to reinvent the wheel—and you don't need to create your own graphics library. A full range of speedy, professionally crafted graphics functions come packaged with all the major C and C++ compilers, and even faster and more robust libraries are readily available from third-party vendors.

Which brings up another problem— which library do you choose? You probably already have a specific compiler's native graphics library and may not be eager to invest in another one that duplicates its functions, but you would also like to be free to move to a more sophisticated graphics library later without rewriting every program you create. Also, when the next killer compiler comes out, you'll want to be able to take advantage of it—even if it's not the same brand you're using now.

Is this too much to ask? Until now, it was. But this chapter presents a system called TransGraphics, which gives you the freedom to switch compilers and graphics libraries—or distribute your source code to people who use a different compiler— without rewriting a single line of graphics code. TransGraphics is not a new graphics library, but a system of header files and functions that enable you to use the exact same graphics calls with every major compiler and graphics library. You can write a program for the Borland Graphics Interface that comes with Turbo C++ and Borland C++ then recompile the same program without any changes for the Microsoft Graphics library. Later, when you want the fastest possible graphics, you can compile the program with an add-on graphics library such as Genus Microprogramming's GX Graphics. When a new library or compiler comes out, you can simply create a header file for it, and all your programs will instantly take advantage of any improved speed or higher resolution video modes it may offer.

You might think that all this automated alchemy is impossibly complex, but creating and expanding TransGraphics files is actually quite simple. Most graphics libraries support the same basic functions—drawing points, lines, and other simple shapes, manipulating the palette, and so on. By defining a few C macros, you can easily translate your compiler's native graphics language into a common core of graphics operations. When a specific compiler doesn't support one of the functions you need, I'll pull a trick or two out of the hat to show you how to implement that function yourself.

Even if you're not a programmer, the following tour of the TransGraphics system introduces you to all the basic graphics operations used throughout this book. The test program is provided on the disk as a ready-to-run EXE file as well as C source code, so you don't need any compiler or graphics library to see how each of the graphics operations works.

Welcome to TransGraphics

Graphics programming is enthralling because it gives immediate feedback, translating your ideas into vivid visual images. It's also challenging—in many ways, it's one of the most demanding forms of programming—and overcoming its complexities enhances the satisfaction of it. End users have come to expect more and better graphics, which makes the discipline increasingly important. For all these reasons and more, we embark...on a voyage into the enchanted world of graphics programming.

—Kent Porter, *Graphics Programming*, DDJ, February 1989

Before I lead you below decks for a tour of TransGraphics' engine room, I'll welcome you aboard by highlighting the features and activities you will enjoy as a passenger. TransGraphics provides compiler-independent variables, macros, and functions for use in your programs. This common core of graphics functionality includes:

- Graphics overhead and screen control, such as choosing a video mode, setting up the graphics system, and clearing the screen

- Basic drawing operations, such as lines, points, text, rectangles, and other simple shapes

- Bitmap and vector animation, with XOR mode for quick and easy motion control

- Color palette control, including the capability to mix your own custom colors and interactively animate the palette

- Complete Microsoft-compatible mouse, trackball, and digitizer pad support

The next few sections introduce all these, and the TGDEMO program presented in the **You Can Do It** and **Working Code** boxes demonstrates each of the graphics operations in action.

You Can Do It: TransGraphics Demos

For a sampling of the basic graphics operations used throughout this book, run the TGDEMO program:

1. Enter TGDEMO at the DOS prompt.

2. A list of video modes appears. Choose the mode with "TRY THIS ONE -->" in front of it.

    (The TGDEMO.EXE program included on the disk was compiled with the GX Graphics library, so you may see a different list of video modes

---

when you compile and run the TGDEMO.C program listed in the **Working Code** boxes.)

A menu of six brief graphics demos appears. As you read through the rest of this chapter, you can choose the corresponding demonstration from the menu to see the graphics operations work. After each demo screen, the program waits for you to press a key before returning to the menu. You might like to take a sneak peak at each demo now.

3. Press 1 to see some "Dots and clipped lines."

4. Press a key to return to the menu and try the other choices.

These images aren't going to win many awards at the next National Computer Graphics Association conference, but they do manage to get the point across—and the line, rectangle, and ellipse across, too, for that matter (yuk yuk).

I'll use snapshots of the TGDEMO screens to illustrate the next few sections, which discuss each set of graphics operations in detail.

Graphics Screen Control

As you can see, in graphics programming on the PC and PS/2 we have to deal with quite a few combinations of adapters and monitors. So any help in the form of library routines that can be called from C is greatly appreciated.

—Nabajyoti Barkakati, *The Waite Group's Microsoft C Bible*, 1988

Every graphics program needs to start by selecting and setting a graphics video mode. You may also have to perform a certain amount of housekeeping before a program can get under way—some variables may need to be initialized, and memory may need to be allocated for remembering palette colors, for instance.

TransGraphics makes all this bothersome preparation as easy as possible for both the programmer and the user. When you write a graphics program you can just insert a single `tg_pickmode()` function call at the beginning, and TransGraphics will automatically handle all the picayune details of choosing and initializing a graphics mode.

When you run a program written with TransGraphics, you'll be asked to choose from a list of possible video modes. The apparent highest resolution video mode your hardware can handle will display a "TRY THIS ONE -->" message in front of it, but you may want to choose a different mode, depending on the nature of the program. (You might want lower resolution, but more colors, for example. Also, certain Super VGA video cards don't like to reveal which modes they can operate under, and you'll need to specify the correct mode yourself.) Figure 2.1 shows the list that tg_pickmode() displays when used with the GX Graphics library. Exactly which modes are listed depends on your compiler and graphics library.

```
TransGraphics Demo Program

from Tricks of the Graphics Gurus

Please choose a video mode, or press Q to quit.

                       C     CGA mono    640x200    2-color
                       H     Hercules    720x348    2-color
                       L     CGA lo-res  320x200    4-color
                       O     EGA lo-res  320x200    16-color
                       A     VGA lo-res  320x200    256-color
                       E     EGA hi-res  640x350    16-color
                       M     VGA mono    640x480    2-color
                       V     VGA hi-res  640x480    16-color
     TRY THIS ONE -->  1     VESA 101h   640x480    256-color
                       2     VESA 102h   800x600    16-color
                       3     VESA 103h   800x600    256-color
                       5     VESA 105h   1024x768   256-color

     Your choice:
```

Figure 2.1. *TransGraphics automatically lists the video modes that your graphics library supports and asks you to choose one.*

Once tg_pickmode() receives a video mode choice from the user, it adjusts the display to that mode, clears the screen, and performs whatever housekeeping chores are needed before drawing can begin. It also sets up several variables for you to use throughout the program, including the screen and color resolution and text character size. Table 2.1 lists the TransGraphics variables set up by tg_pickmode(). All these variables are integers of the int type. (The only initialization task that tg_pickmode() doesn't do is detecting and initializing the mouse—you'll learn how to do that shortly.)

Table 2.1. You can use the following variables in your graphics programs. The *tg_pickmode()* function sets their values automatically.

Name	Meaning
tg_scrnx	Horizontal resolution of the screen in pixels
tg_scrny	Vertical resolution of the screen in pixels

Table 2.1. continued

Name	Meaning
tg_viewx	Horizontal size of the current viewport
tg_viewy	Vertical size of the current viewport
tg_charx	Width of one text character in pixels
tg_chary	Height of one text character in pixels
tg_ncolors	Number of colors in the palette

As you've probably surmised, all TransGraphics function and variable names start with tg_ so that you can distinguish them from other C functions and variables.

Setting Up and Closing Down

At times, you may want to write a graphics program that doesn't ask the user to confirm a video mode. For those times, TransGraphics enables you to directly access the two functions that tg_pickmode() uses to do its thing: tg_detectmode(), which suggests the highest resolution video mode that it's sure the current hardware can do, and tg_setvideomode(), which actually sets the video mode and initializes the variables in Table 2.1.

You can use these two functions together to detect and set the best-guess video mode without asking the user anything. Here's the code that does this:

```
tg_setvideomode(tg_detectmode());
```

The tg_detectmode() function will pass a mode number to the tg_setvideomode() function, and away you go.

You can also give tg_setvideomode() the number of a particular video mode you want. Mode 1 will be the first video mode listed by tg_pickmode(), mode 2 will be the second mode on the list, and so forth. (The actual modes that correspond to these numbers vary from graphics library to graphics library, so you should only use this technique for quick-and-dirty programs that won't ever be compiled with a different library or a different version of the same library.) For example, to start in CGA 640×200 black-and-white mode with most compilers and graphics libraries, you could insert the following command in your program:

```
tg_setvideomode(1);
```

You can also access the text descriptions and key codes for each video mode with the `tg_modecode` and `tg_modedesc` arrays, in case you have the urge to write programs that enable the user to choose and switch video modes on the fly or do some other kind of fancy video mode shuffling. If you're at that level of expertise, you'll find that the definitions of these variables in the source code files are more than enough to go on.

You've seen how easy it is to begin a TransGraphics program. It's even easier to end one. Just call the `tg_closedown()` function before you exit the program. It takes care of any final housekeeping and sets the video display back to text mode. You can also use the `tg_settextmode()` macro to return to text mode without closing down the graphics system. You can then use `tg_setvideomode(0)` to return to the same graphics mode you were in before you called `tg_settextmode()`.

You may have noticed that I called `tg_closedown()` a *function*, but I called `tg_settextmode()` a *macro*. Most TransGraphics operations are not actually implemented as *functions*, but as *macros*. Created with the C #define directive, macros simply replace certain text with different text before the program is compiled. The following explanation of `tg_clearscreen()` more fully explains how macros work.

The Screen and the Viewport

You can use the `tg_clearscreen()` command to clear the graphics display screen, no such `tg_clearscreen()` function exists. Instead of being a full-fledged function, it's just a macro. When you look in the TransGraphics header file for Microsoft C (named TGMS.H), you'll find the following macro:

```
#define tg_clearscreen() _clearscreen(_GCLEARSCREEN)
```

When you compile the program under Microsoft C or C++, all occurrences of the TransGraphics `tg_clearscreen()` command are replaced with the Microsoft `_clearscreen(_GCLEARSCREEN)` library call before anything else happens. If you were to compile under Borland Turbo C++ instead, the corresponding TransGraphics header file would automatically drop in code for the Borland screen clear function. You wouldn't need to change the `tg_clearscreen()` command in your program at all.

When you start TransGraphics, any graphics operation can draw on any part of the screen. When you specify pixel locations, the top left corner of the screen is 0,0 and the bottom right corner is `tg_scrnx` - 1, `tg_scrny` - 1. (The actual values of `tg_scrnx` and `tg_scrny` depend on the resolution of your video mode.)

For some graphics programs, you may want to restrict output to a rectangular region of the screen, called a "window" or *viewport*. When you define the top left and bottom right corners of a viewport with the `tg_setviewport()` macro, TransGraphics won't allow anything to be drawn outside that area. Also, the coordinates for all drawing operations are automatically shifted so that the top left corner of the viewport is pixel location 0,0. For example, if you issued the following commands, the first line would appear as a diagonal from the top left corner of the screen to the location 100,100—down and to the right a little ways. The second line, however, would actually start at the screen location 200, 200 (the viewport's 0,0) and stop at 250, 250 (because it can't cross the edges of the viewport). I'll explain the `tg_drawline()` macro in the next section, but its meaning should be obvious in this context.

```
tg_drawline(0,0, 100,100);
tg_setviewport(200,200, 250,250);
tg_drawline(0,0, 100,100);
```

Because `tg_scrnx` and `tg_scnry` don't matter much when you're drawing within a viewport, TransGraphics gives you two variables named `tg_viewx` and `tg_viewy`, which always hold the horizontal and vertical size of the current viewport. If you never define a viewport, `tg_viewx` and `tg_viewy` are equal to `tg_scrnx` and `tg_scrny`. When you want to find out where the corners of the viewport are relative to the whole screen, `tg_getviewport()` returns the viewport corners set with the last call to `tg_setviewport()`.

To summarize, Table 2.2 lists the four functions and two macros which you use to set up and close down the graphics screen and viewport. Often, you will only need to use `tg_pickmode()` and `tg_closedown()` because these call all the other necessary functions that automatically set up and clear the screen and viewport for you.

Table 2.2. The `tg_pickmode()` **and** `tg_closedown()` **functions do all your housekeeping for you. A few other housekeeping functions and macros will come in handy for custom-tailored programs.**

Function	What it does
`void tg_pickmode(void)`	Asks the user to select a video mode, then sets it
`int tg_detectmode(void)`	Detects a default video mode automatically
`int tg_setvidmode(int vmode)`	Sets a video mode indexed in the `modecode` and `modedesc` arrays by `vmode`
`void tg_closedown(void)`	Closes down all graphics stuff

Macro	What it does
`tg_settextmode()`	Returns to text mode temporarily
`tg_clearscreen()`	Clears the graphics screen
`tg_setviewport()`	Restricts all graphics output to a rectangular viewport
`tg_getviewport()`	Reports the corners of the current viewport
`tg_clearviewport()`	Clears the current viewport

Working Code: Getting in the Right Mode

The TGDEMO program actually provides you with two ways to select a video mode:

■ You can specify a video mode on the DOS command line when you enter the name of the program.

■ You can choose a mode from a list after the program starts.

To choose the VGA 640×480 16-color mode from the command line, you would enter:

```
TGDEMO /V
```

If you don't specify a mode on the command line, the list of modes comes up automatically.

By mimicking the beginning of the `main()` function in the TGDEMO.C program that follows, you can imitate this fancy mode-selection footwork in all your graphics programs.

After settling on a video mode one way or another, the `main()` function displays and processes the main menu. By copying the basic format of the text descriptions and pointers to functions I used to implement the menu, you can gain a big head start in your own simple graphics program menus.

The `tg_setcolor()`, `tg_moveto()`, and `tg_outtext()` macros actually put the colored menu text on-screen. I'll give you details in the next section about how to use these operations. The next section also gives you some **Working Code** from TGDEMO.C that demonstrates the use of viewports.

Notice that this listing doesn't include the actual functions that display the various demo screens. Those are listed individually in the following sections, as I discuss the macros and functions they use.

You'll find instructions for compiling TransGraphics programs with your compiler and graphics library in the Introduction to this book.

```c
/* TGDEMO.C
 *
 * This program uses all the graphics operations supported by
 * the TransGraphics system from Tricks of the Graphics Gurus.
 *
 * It serves no noble purpose other than testing graphics header
 * files and demonstrating how the graphics operations work.
 */

#include <stdio.h>        /* Standard input/output libraries */
#include <stdlib.h>

#include "tg.h"       /* See TG.TXT for compile instructions */

#define NMENUITEMS 6                 /* Number of menu items */

/* Function prototypes for all the upcoming fun */

int main(int nargs, char **arg);
void dotsandlines(void);
void shapes(void);
void palettecolors(void);
void animate(void);
void mousearound(void);
void goaway(void);

/* Accept and process command line arguments from the user:
   nargs will be the number of command line arguments,
   arg will be an array containing the arguments themselves */

int main(int nargs, char **arg)
{
    /* text for the menu choices */

    char menutext[NMENUITEMS][40] =
```

```
                    {"Dots and lines in viewports",
                     "Rectangles, ellipses, and polygons",
                     "Custom color palette animation",
                     "Bitmap and vector animation",
                     "Just a little mousing around",
                     "No more. Exit. Go away. Vamoose."},
        menuline[50],          /* for displaying each line */
        a;                    /* to store what the users says */

    /* array of pointers to the menu functions */

    typedef void (*voidfunction)(void);
    voidfunction menufun[NMENUITEMS];

    int thismode,         /* the video mode to use this time */
        i, j,             /* just some counters for whatever */
        menucolor,         /* colors for the menu and title */
        titlecolor,
        menux, menuy;          /* where to put the menu text */

    thismode = 0;
    for (i = 1; i < nargs; i++)    /* step through the args */
    {   if (*(arg[i]) == '/')       /* starts with a slash? */
        {    a = arg[i][1];      /* just look at 1st letter */
             a = toupper(a);      /* make sure it's uppercase */

             /* If use specified mode /D, use auto-detect */

             if (a == 'D') thismode = tg_detectmode();

             /* Otherwise, thumb through the tg_modecode to
                find out which mode it's supposed to be */

             else
                for (i = 1; i <= tg_NMODES; i++)
                    if (a == tg_modecode[i]) thismode = i;
        }
    }

     /* User didn't specify a video mode, so introduce
        yourself and ask 'em what mode they'd like */
```

```
if (thismode == 0)
{   printf("\n\nTransGraphics Demo Program\n\n");
    printf("from Tricks of the Graphics Gurus\n");
    tg_pickmode();
}

/* User did specify a video mode, so set it.
   Don't bother them with a greeting because they seem
   to know what they're getting themselves into. */

else
{   if (tg_setvideomode(thismode) == 0)
    {   printf("\nUnable to set graphics mode: %s.\n",
            tg_modedesc[thismode]);
        exit(0);
    }
}

/* initialize everything */

menufun[0] = dotsandlines;
menufun[1] = shapes;
menufun[2] = palettecolors;
menufun[3] = animate;
menufun[4] = mousearound;
menufun[5] = goaway;
menux = tg_scrnx / 2 - 20 * tg_charx;
menuy = tg_chary * 4;
menucolor = 15 % tg_ncolors;
titlecolor = 11 % tg_ncolors;

/* do it 'til you just can't do it no more */

while(1)
{
    /* display the menu */

    tg_moveto(menux, menuy - tg_chary * 3);
    tg_setcolor(titlecolor);
    tg_outtext("TransGraphics Demo Menu");
    tg_moveto(menux, menuy - tg_chary * 2);
    tg_outtext("--------------------------------");
    tg_setcolor(menucolor);
```

```
        for (i = 0; i < NMENUITEMS; i++)
        {   tg_moveto(menux, menuy + tg_chary * i);
            sprintf(menuline, "%d: %s", i + 1, menutext[i]);
            tg_outtext(menuline);
        }
        tg_setcolor(titlecolor);
        i++;
        tg_moveto(menux, menuy + i * tg_chary);
        tg_outtext("Press the number of your choice.");

        /* do what the user says */

        a = getch() - '1';
        if ((a >= 0) && (a < NMENUITEMS))
        {   int red, blue, green;
            tg_clearscreen();
            menufun[a]();
            getch();
            tg_clearscreen();
        }
    }
}

/* close down the graphics and get the heck outta Dodge */

void goaway(void)
{   tg_closedown();
    printf("\n\nThanks for visiting TransGraphics.\n");
    printf("Welcome back to text mode.\n");
    exit(0);
}
```

Drawing with TransGraphics

While almost any model can be reproduced with a sufficiently dense matrix of dots (pointillism), most human operators generally think in terms of more complex graphic objects such as points, lines, circles, and ellipses. Since the inception of computer graphics, many algorithms have been developed to provide human users with fast, memory-efficient routines that generate higher-level objects of this kind.

—Roy A. Plastock, *Theory and Problems of Computer Graphics*, 1986

TransGraphics provides a complete set of commands for drawing text, dots, lines, rectangles, ellipses, polygons, and other shapes. Because they are streamlined and consistent, TransGraphics drawing commands are actually easier to use than direct graphics library calls. The next few sections will quickly get you up to speed with TransGraphics by demonstrating each of the drawing operations.

Displaying Text

The first TransGraphics drawing operation you'll probably use doesn't really *draw* at all. The tg_outtext() macro writes text on the graphics screen. To use it, use tg_setcolor() to set the color of the text and tg_moveto() to move to the bottom left corner of where you want the text to appear. (The tg_setcolor() and tg_moveto() functions also affect the color and location of other graphics operations, which I'll discuss momentarily.) Now call tg_outtext() with the text string you want to display, like this:

```
tg_outtext("Seeyalater, Larry Docker.");
```

In Figure 2.2, the tg_outtext() macro is used to report which functions the TGDEMO program is demonstrating.

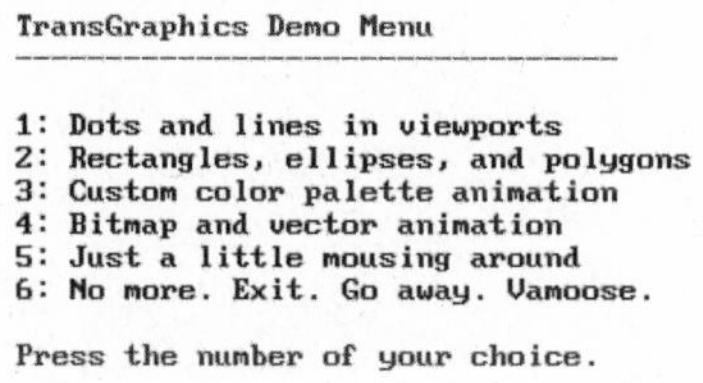

```
TransGraphics Demo Menu
-----------------------------------------

1: Dots and lines in viewports
2: Rectangles, ellipses, and polygons
3: Custom color palette animation
4: Bitmap and vector animation
5: Just a little mousing around
6: No more. Exit. Go away. Vamoose.

Press the number of your choice.
```

Figure 2.2. *You can display text messages at any location on the graphics screen, in any color.*

Notice that tg_outtext() doesn't do any formatting—the text you give it must be ready to go on-screen. If you want to format and display numbers or more complex assemblages of text data, use the standard C sprintf() function to prepare a string before you hand it to tg_outtext(). For example, to display the integer number x and the name stored in the myname string, you would say

```
sprintf(str, "Person number %d is named %s.", x, myname);
tg_outtext(str);
```

(If you're not familiar with sprintf(), read up on it in your favorite C book—you'll find my recommendations for other books in Appendix E. Don't worry too much about it now because you can create all the graphics in this book without knowing diddly-squat about sprintf().)

The tg_outtext() macro always displays text in the *system font*—the one that you would see if you were in text mode. Some graphics libraries offer extra bells and whistles like scalable fonts and text rotation, but no two libraries handle fonts the same way or even use the same kinds of font files. Therefore, any font finagling you do will be completely unportable between libraries. Because font technology is changing rapidly, font functions are often not even portable between two subsequent versions of the same compiler graphics library. As with the more obscure drawing functions, you can use your library's font functions and the TransGraphics graphics macros together without conflict. You'll still enjoy far greater freedom and portability with TransGraphics than you would without it.

In theory, you can place text at any location on your screen and control the line spacing as precisely as you like. If you are using Microsoft C, however, the text always appears at even multiples of the text character width and height, as if the graphics screen were divided into text-mode rows and columns. If you try to space several lines of text one and a half characters apart vertically, Microsoft C forces the lines to the closest "row," and you get single-spaced lines with frequent skipped lines between them. With Turbo C or GX Graphics, on the other hand, you'll see the evenly spaced lines you expect. If you want your programs to be portable to Microsoft Graphics, be careful to place lines of text exact multiples of tg_chary (the height of a text character) apart.

For a simple but useful implementation of tg_outtext(), peruse the **Working Code** for the TGDEMO main() function listed earlier in this chapter.

Drawing Points and Lines

To draw a point, line, rectangle, polygon, or ellipse with TransGraphics, you simply choose a palette color with tg_setcolor() and then use one of the graphics operations in Table 2.3 to draw the shape you want.

Table 2.3. TransGraphics defines a full set of drawing operation macros.

Macro	What it does
`tg_setcolor(c)`	Sets the current text and drawing color
`tg_getcolor()`	Gets the current text and drawing color
`tg_outtext(str)`	Outputs one line of text at current position
`tg_putpixel(x1, y1, c)`	Sets the screen pixel at x1, y1 to color c
`tg_getpixel(x1, y1)`	Gets the color of the screen pixel at x1, y1
`tg_moveto(x, y)`	Sets the current text and drawing position
`tg_lineto(x, y)`	Draws a line from the current position to x,y
`tg_drawline(x1, y1, x2, y2)`	Draws a line
`tg_drawrect(x1, y1, x2, y2)`	Draws the outline of a rectangle
`tg_fillrect(x1, y1, x2, y2)`	Fills a rectangle with the current color
`tg_drawpoly(poly, n)`	Draws a polygon array with n vertices
`tg_fillpoly(poly, n)`	Fills a polygon with the current color
`tg_drawellipse(x1, y1, x2, y2)`	Draws an outline of an ellipse
`tg_fillellipse(x1, y1, x2, y2)`	Fills an ellipse with the current color
`tg_floodfill(x, y, c)`	Fills a region of any shape, starting at x,y and expanding out until a boundary of color c is encountered

You can use `tg_putpixel()` to color an individual pixel and `tg_getpixel()` to read the current color of a single pixel on-screen. When you use these macros, specify the pixel's horizontal and vertical position as measured from the top left corner of the screen. In other words, the command to give the top left corner pixel palette color number 15 (which usually means white) would be

```
tg_putpixel(0, 0, 15);
```

To color the pixel in the bottom right corner, you could use the `tg_scrnx` and `tg_scrny` variables mentioned earlier, like so:

```
tg_putpixel(tg_scrnx - 1, tg_scrny - 1, 15);
```

You can draw a line in two different ways. You can use `tg_drawline()` to draw the line all at once, or you can use `tg_moveto()` to move to one end of the line and then use `tg_lineto()` to draw a line to the other end.

Unlike `tg_putpixel()`, the line drawing macros don't take a color number as part of the command. Instead, they use the last color selected with `tg_setcolor()`. In fact, `tg_putpixel()` is the only drawing command that doesn't use the color set with `tg_setcolor()`. (`tg_putpixel()` is different only because the functions to color a pixel in most graphics libraries work fastest when the color is specified as part of the command.)

Because you will usually want your programs to run in any video mode the user selects, you should make sure that the color you set with `tg_setcolor()` is smaller than the maximum color number in the current graphics mode. So, to draw a white line from the top left corner of the screen to the bottom right corner of the screen, you could say

```
tg_setcolor(15 % tg_ncolors);
tg_drawline(0, 0, tg_scrnx - 1, tg_scrny - 1);
```

In 16- or 256-color modes, `15 % tg_ncolors` just comes out to color number 15. In 2-color modes, it comes out to color number 1. In 4-color CGA mode, it comes out to color number 3. To make sure your graphics will look good in 2-color modes, just use even color numbers for anything that can safely disappear into black and odd color numbers for anything that must appear white. Also, keep in mind that the first 16 colors are identical in the default 16-color and 256-color palettes (see Table 1.2).

Figure 2.3 shows some pixels and lines drawn by the TGDEMO program. It also illustrates the use of viewports, discussed in the previous section. The images in each of the four rectangular areas were drawn with the exact same C code. (You can see that code in the following **Working Code** box.)

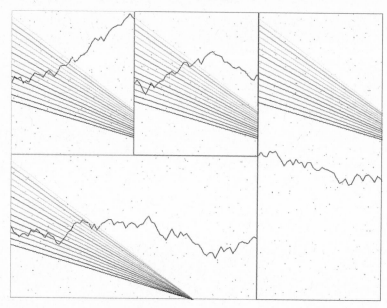

Figure 2.3. *Coloring individual pixels and drawing lines are the simplest possible graphics operations. The lines were automatically clipped to four rectangular viewports.*

Working Code: Dots and Clipped Lines

The dotsandlines() function from TGDEMO.C creates a computer doodle out of randomly placed dots and a pattern of lines. It uses the tg_putpixel(), tg_setcolor(), tg_setviewport(), tg_moveto(), tg_lineto(), and tg_drawline() macros to draw the doodle and verifies that the tg_getpixel(), tg_getcolor(), and tg_getviewport() macros correctly return the pixel values, colors, and clipping region.

```
/* draw some dots and lines in a clipping region and
   check to make sure everything is working as it should */

void dotsandlines(void)
{   int i, j, vp, c, x, y,  /* need a bunch of counters */
        vpx1[4], vpy1[4],
        vpx2[4], vpy2[4];    /* make four viewports */

    vpx1[0] = 0;
    vpy1[0] = 0;
    vpx2[0] = tg_scrnx / 3;
```

```
        vpy2[0] = tg_scrny / 2;

        vpx1[1] = tg_scrnx / 3;
        vpy1[1] = 0;
        vpx2[1] = 2 * tg_scrnx / 3;
        vpy2[1] = tg_scrny / 2;

        vpx1[2] = 0;
        vpy1[2] = tg_scrny / 2;
        vpx2[2] = 2 * tg_scrnx / 3;
        vpy2[2] = tg_scrny - 1;

        vpx1[3] = 2 * tg_scrnx / 3;
        vpy1[3] = 0;
        vpx2[3] = tg_scrnx - 1;
        vpy2[3] = tg_scrny - 1;

        /* fill up the screen so we can erase it */

        for (i = 0; i < tg_scrnx; i++)
        {   tg_setcolor(rand() % tg_ncolors);
            tg_drawline(i, 0, tg_scrnx - 1 - i, tg_scrny - 1);

            /* test to make sure it's working
               (you don't need to do this in your programs!) */

            if (tg_getpixel(i, 0) != tg_getcolor())
            {   tg_moveto(0, 0);
                tg_setcolor(15 % tg_ncolors);
                tg_outtext("either tg_getpixel or tg_getcolor "
                           "didn't work!");
                getch();
            }
        }

        /* Select each viewport one by one */

        for (vp = 0; vp < 4; vp++)
        {   tg_setviewport(vpx1[vp], vpy1[vp],
                           vpx2[vp], vpy2[vp]);

            /* check to make sure tg_getviewport() works
               (again, you normally don't need to bother!) */
```

55

```
tg_getviewport(i, j, x, y);
if ((i != vpx1[vp]) ¦¦ (j != vpy1[vp]) ¦¦
    (x != vpx2[vp]) ¦¦ (y != vpy2[vp]))
{   tg_moveto(60, 60);
    tg_outtext("tg_getclipregion didn't get "
            "what tg_setclipregion set!");
    getch();
}

/* clear and outline the viewport */

tg_clearviewport();
tg_setcolor(rand() % tg_ncolors);
tg_drawline(0, 0, 0, tg_viewy - 1);
tg_drawline(0, 0, tg_viewx - 1, 0);
tg_drawline(tg_viewx - 1, tg_viewy - 1,
            0, tg_viewy - 1);
tg_drawline(tg_viewx - 1, tg_viewy - 1,
            tg_viewx - 1, 0);

/* draw random dots all over the place
(to a region larger than the viewport) */

for (i = 0; i < tg_scrnx; i++)
{   x = rand() % tg_scrnx;
    y = rand() % tg_scrny;
    c = rand() % tg_ncolors;
    tg_putpixel(x, y, c);
}

/* now some some lines wandering across the screen */

tg_setcolor(15 % tg_ncolors);
j = tg_viewy / 2;
tg_moveto(0, j);
for (i = 0; i < tg_scrnx; i += 5, j += rand() % 21 - 10)
    tg_lineto(i, j);

/* more lines, but this time use tg_drawline */

for (i = 0; i < 16; i++)
```

```
    {   tg_setcolor(i % tg_ncolors);
        tg_drawline(0, i * 10,
                    tg_scrnx - 1, tg_scrny - i * 10);
    }
}

/* set the viewport back to the whole screen */

tg_setviewport(0, 0, tg_scrnx - 1, tg_scrny - 1);
}
```

Drawing and Filling Shapes

Besides dots and lines, TransGraphics offers three other drawing *primitives*: rectangles, polygons, and ellipses.

Rectangles are exactly what you think they are, and you draw them by specifying the top left corner point and bottom right corner point. tg_drawrect() draws an outlined rectangle, while tg_fillrect() fills in the rectangle with the current color.

Polygons are sequences of connected lines, with the corner points stored in an array variable. The last point is automatically connected to the first point to create a closed figure. Triangles, parallelograms, hexagons, and skewed rectangles are all examples of polygons. You can draw outlined and filled polygons with the TransGraphics tg_drawpoly() and tg_fillpoly() macros.

Filling polygons isn't as easy as you might think—when the shapes get complex, the logic becomes pretty nutty. All the graphics libraries I've used tend to make mistakes when filling complex polygons, especially when they need to be clipped to fit within the screen or the clipping region. Watch out for the Microsoft Graphics library in particular, which can actually crash your system if you try to fill a polygon which wholly falls on one horizontal line.

Ellipses are elongated circles, and you can draw them with the TransGraphics tg_drawellipse() and tg_fillellipse() commands. To describe what the ellipse will look like, you specify the top left and bottom right corner points of a *bounding box*—the rectangle that would just touch the top, bottom, and sides of the ellipse. If the bounding box is a square, your ellipse is a perfect circle.

When rectangles, polygons, and ellipses aren't enough, you can use the tg_floodfill() macro to color any weird-shaped region you want. Just draw the outline with any combination of points, lines, and shapes. Then you tell tg_floodfill() where to start pouring paint and at what color boundary to stop.

In Figure 2.4, some rectangles, ellipses, and polygons are lined up on the screen, with a weird looking flood-filled shape thrown into the bargain.

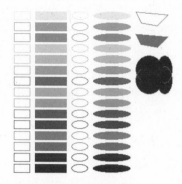

Figure 2.4. *Drawing and filling rectangles, ellipses, polygons, and colorful gobs with TransGraphics is pretty much a no-brainer.*

Most graphics libraries include more options for drawing and filling graphics primitives than you can access through TransGraphics. For example, you can usually fill shapes with hatch patterns, and some libraries let you draw arc segments and "pie slices." Unfortunately, the techniques and data structures involved vary wildly from one graphics library to the next. Therefore, TransGraphics focuses only on the most common and most useful drawing operations. If you find you need a function that your graphics library offers but that TransGraphics doesn't, use the native graphics library command or (for cleaner, more portable code) add a macro for that command to a header file. Because TransGraphics isn't a separate graphics library, you can mix and match TransGraphics macros and other graphics functions as you like. Keep in mind, however, that programs written with direct graphics function calls aren't portable to other compilers and graphics libraries the way "pure" TransGraphics programs are. (Of course, you can go in and change a few arc-drawing commands more easily than you can rewrite the entire program when you move up to a new graphics library.)

Working Code: All Shapes and Sizes

Using TransGraphics' shape-drawing functions is so simple your dog could do it (if he could type—or you could understand his dictation better). The only tricky thing you need to know is the structure of the polygon array that `tg_drawpoly()` and `tg_fillpoly()` expect. This should be a two-dimensional array of integers, with the point coordinates arranged like this:

```
{{x1, y1}, {x2, y2}, {x3, y3}... etc. }
```

Other than that, the only mental work you need to do is figuring out where on-screen you want to put stuff. Here, I lined up a few columns of rectangles and ellipses and slapped up a couple polygons and a flood-filled whatchamacallit beside them.

Because the columns of rectangles and ellipses use all the colors in order, this demo function also gives you an easy way to view the default palette.

```c
/* toss a few shapes on the screen,
   just to prove we can do it */

void shapes(void)
{   int i, poly[4][2] = {{250, 20},
                  {310, 25},
                  {290, 45},
                  {260, 40}}; /* Just your average polygon */

    /* Draw outlined and filled rectangles and ellipses */

    for (i = 1;
         (i < tg_ncolors) && ((i + 1) * 20 < tg_scrny);
         i++)
    {   tg_setcolor(i);
        tg_drawrect(20, i * 20, 50, (i + 1) * 20 - 5);
        tg_fillrect(60, i * 20, 120, (i + 1) * 20 - 5);
        tg_drawellipse(130, i * 20, 160, (i + 1) * 20 - 5);
        tg_fillellipse(170, i * 20, 240, (i + 1) * 20 - 5);
    }

    /* While we're at it, some outlined and filled polygons */

    tg_setcolor(13 % tg_ncolors);
    tg_drawpoly(poly, 4);
    for (i = 0; i < 4; i++) poly[i][1] += 40;
    tg_fillpoly(poly, 4);

    /* now draw a weird looking thing and fill it */

    tg_drawellipse(250, 100, 300, 150);
    tg_drawellipse(250, 120, 300, 170);
    tg_drawellipse(290, 100, 319, 150);
    tg_drawellipse(290, 120, 319, 170);
    tg_setcolor(0);
```

```
    tg_fillrect(260, 110, 300, 160);
    tg_setcolor(15 % tg_ncolors);
    tg_floodfill(270, 120, 13 % tg_ncolors);
}
```

Bitmap and Vector Animation

No graphics system would be complete without the capability to pick up an image from an area of the screen and put it down at a different location. Serious graphics programmers also expect to use an old trick called *XOR mode*, which makes animation fast, smooth, and easy. (XOR, pronounced "ex-orr," is a mnemonic for "exclusive or.") With TransGraphics, you can achieve all this by using the macros listed in Table 2.4.

Table 2.4. These macros enable you to grab and display bitmap images and turn on a graphics trick called XOR mode.

Macro	What it does
tg_makeimagebuffer(img, x, y)	Allocates an image buffer x by y pixels
tg_getimage(img, x1,y1, x2,y2)	Reads a portion of the screen into a buffer
tg_putimage(img, x ,y)	Displays an image buffer on-screen
tg_freeimagebuffer(img)	Frees up the memory used for an image buffer
tg_startxor()	Turns XOR mode on (When XOR is on, all graphics operations will invert the currently displayed image rather than overwrite it.)
tg_endxor()	Turns XOR mode off

To copy or move a portion of the screen bitmap, you need a place to put it outside of the video memory. To make an *image buffer* for that purpose, use the tg_makeimagebuffer() macro. You must tell it the name of a variable that you have created of type IMAGEBUFFER (a type defined in the TransGraphics header files) and the horizontal and vertical size of the portion of the image you want to grab. For example, to create an image buffer for a 100x100 pixel square region of the screen, say

```
IMAGEBUFFER imgbuf;
tg_makeimagebuffer(imgbuf, 100, 100);
```

Once you've made a buffer, you can store the image with tg_getimage(). To grab a square region in the top left corner of the screen, use

```
tg_getimage(imgbuf, 0, 0, 99, 99);
```

(Don't forget that 0 to 99 is 100 pixels—if you tried to store the region from 0,0 to 100,100, it would exceed the capacity of the buffer you just made and might crash the program by overwriting other important memory.)

To transfer the image from the buffer back onto the screen, use tg_putimage(). You need only specify the buffer name and the top left corner of where you want the image to go. For example, to place the image stored with the preceding commands back on-screen starting 150 pixels across and 100 pixels down from the top left corner, say

```
tg_putimage(imgbuf, 150, 100);
```

Because the image is stored in the buffer, you can put it back on-screen with tg_putimage() as many times as you want without having to use tg_getimage() again. This makes for easy animation, as Figures 2.5 through 2.7 illustrate.

Figure 2.5. *Will bitmap animation make you happy or drive you crazy? Mr. Almost-Happy-Face will show you how it works.*

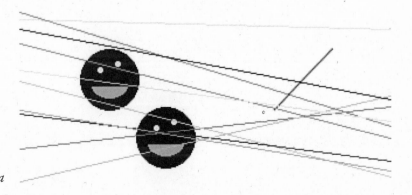

a

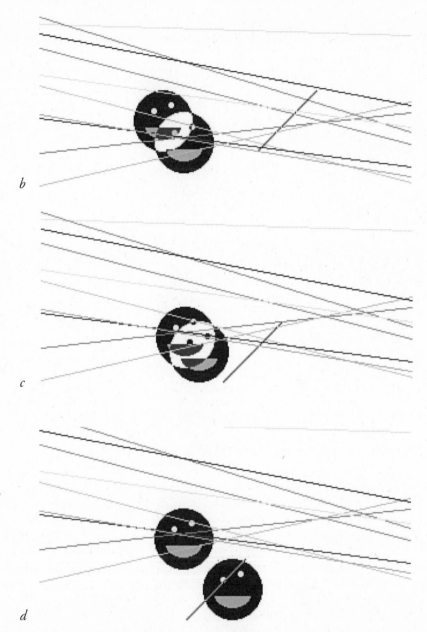

Figure 2.6. *If you use the XOR mode, Mr. A.H.F. can cruise around nice and easy without hurting the background or his brother—kind of like drinking decaf.*

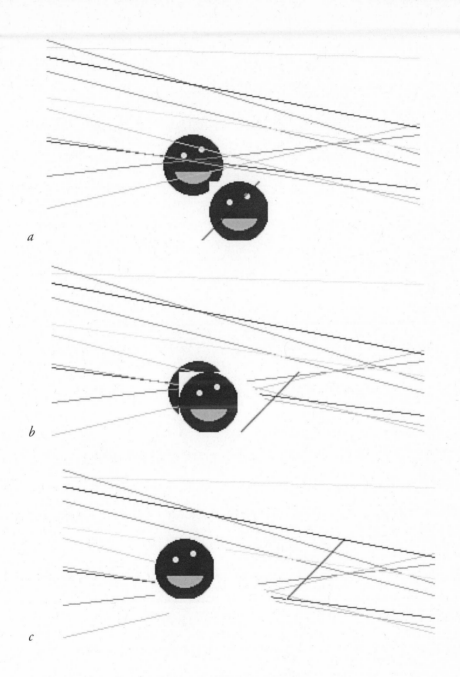

d

Figure 2.7. *Without XOR mode, Mr. A.H.F. moves faster but destroys everything in his path—more like Jolt Cola.*

Working Code: Smile as You Go By

This function from TGDEMO.C allocates an image buffer, draws a portrait of Mr. Almost-Happy-Face, picks him up, and tosses him around with and without XOR.

In case you're wondering, *XOR* stands for "exclusive-or," meaning that each bit of Mr. A.H.F.'s face will light up a bit on-screen if the existing screen bit "or" the bit of Mr. A.H.F.—but not both—are lit up. Some folks are surprised to find out that doing this twice over the same region always restores the region to it's initial appearance. If you're not much on logic tables, just say that XOR "negates" the screen area and XORing again makes it "positive." Either way, this is a heck of a lot easier and faster than saving each piece of the background in an off-screen buffer and putting it back each time Mr. A.H.F. moves along.

```
void animate(void)
{   IMAGEBUFFER imgbuf;         /* pointer to an image buffer */
    int i, j;

    /* draw a silly face */

    tg_setcolor(14 % tg_ncolors);
    tg_fillellipse(100, 100, 150, 150);
    tg_setcolor(15 % tg_ncolors);
    tg_drawellipse(100, 100, 150, 150);
    tg_setcolor(1);
```

```
tg_fillellipse(115, 115, 120, 120);
tg_fillellipse(130, 110, 135, 115);
tg_setcolor(5 % tg_ncolors);
tg_fillellipse(110, 120, 140, 140);
tg_setcolor(14 % tg_ncolors);
tg_fillrect(110, 120, 140, 130);

/* now grab the silly face and store it in a buffer */

tg_makeimagebuffer(imgbuf, 51, 51);
tg_getimage(imgbuf, 100, 100, 150, 150);

/* put some junk on the screen for background */

for (i = 0; i < 10; i++)
{   tg_setcolor(rand() % tg_ncolors);
    tg_drawline(0, rand() % tg_scrny,
                tg_scrnx - 1, rand() % tg_scrny);
}

/* turn on XOR mode, so one face can appear to move in
   front of everything */

tg_startxor();

/* put the face back in a different place,
   and draw a line to be a flying "arrow" */

tg_putimage(imgbuf, 20, 20);
tg_setcolor(15 % tg_ncolors);
tg_drawline(tg_scrnx - 20, 20, tg_scrnx - 70, 70);

/* now move the face and arrow down the screen */

for (i = 20; i < tg_scrny - 50;)
{
    /* first, erase the old face by XORing it again */
    tg_putimage(imgbuf, i, i);

    /* now move down a bit and draw the new face */

    i++;
```

```
            tg_putimage(imgbuf, i, i);

            /*  erase the old line, and draw a new one */

            tg_drawline(tg_scrnx - (i - 1), i - 1,
                        tg_scrnx - (i + 49), i + 49);
            tg_drawline(tg_scrnx - i, i,
                        tg_scrnx - (i + 50), i + 50);

            /* wait a little while between movements */

            for (j = 0; j < 4000; j = rand());
    }

    /* let's see what it looks like without the XOR */

    tg_endxor();

    /* this time, move back up the screen */

    for (i = tg_scrny - 50; i > 20; i--)
    {
            /* put the image and line on the screen */
            tg_putimage(imgbuf, i, i);
            tg_setcolor(15 % tg_ncolors);
            tg_drawline(tg_scrnx - i, i,
                        tg_scrnx - (i + 50), i + 50);

            /* take a quickie break */

            for (j = 0; j < 4000; j = rand());

            /* erase the trailing edges */

            tg_setcolor(0);
            tg_drawline(i + 50, i,
                        i + 50, i + 50);
            tg_drawline(i, i + 50,
                        i + 50, i + 50);
            tg_putpixel(tg_scrnx - (i + 50), i + 50, 0);
    }

    /* one last hello */
```

```
    tg_putimage(imgbuf, i, i);

    /* free up the memory used to store the face */

    tg_freeimagebuffer(imgbuf);
}
```

Color Palette Control

...These three colors of light—red, green, and blue—are known as the primary colors *(or the additive colors). They are the colors that are used in video, and appear on a desktop color monitor. When combined, they produce white light; when mixed in varying intensities, they can form every other color.*

We do not print with the primary colors. Rather, we print with the subtractive colors *(or secondary colors). These are the colors that are created when two wavelengths of light combine in the absence of the third. The subtractive colors are yellow, magenta, and cyan. When combined, they produce black.*

—Helene Eckstein, *Color in the 21st Century*, 1992

For many graphics programs, you will never need to change the standard palette of colors available when you set a color graphics mode. As Table 1.2 showed, the default 16-color EGA/VGA palette contains a crayon box full of basic colors in both dim and bright intensities. The default 256-color palette contains all the same colors, plus 240 more arranged according to brightness, saturation, and hue.

Sometimes, however, a particular color must perfectly match a color that meets your eye—or one that meets your mind's eye. Because precise color control is essential to most of the advanced techniques presented in this book, TransGraphics offers a complete set of palette color controls, listed in Table 2.5.

Table 2.5. These color controls will please even the most discriminating computer artists.

Macro	What it does
tg_makepalcolor(iclr, r,g,b)	Makes a color from red, green, and blue values

continues

Table 2.5. continued

Macro	What it does
tg_splitpalcolor(iclr, r,g,b)	Splits a color into red, green, and blue values
tg_getpalcolor(iclr)	Reads one color value in the palette (does not work on some EGA systems!)
tg_setpalcolor(iclr)	Sets one color value in the palette
tg_getallpalcolors()	Reads the whole palette all at once
tg_setallpalcolors()	Sets the whole palette all at once
Function	**What it does**
void tg_colorcycle(int step)	Rotates the palette for animation until you press a key

Your computer monitor creates colors by varying the intensity of red, green, and blue light from three separate electron guns. (That's obviously an inaccurate oversimplification of how the hardware works—especially if you're using one of the new color LCD laptop displays—but you get the idea.) Therefore, you define colors by specifying the intensity of the red, green, and blue *components*. This method of describing color is called the *RGB color model*.

If you're used to working with physical paint or printing ink, you are probably more accustomed to working with blue, red, and yellow (or, more accurately, cyan, magenta, and yellow) as your *primary colors*. This method of describing color is called the *CMYK model*, for cyan, magenta, yellow, and black. (Printers use K to stand for black ink, which is often added as a fourth color for better clarity and definition.) The RGB model is exactly the opposite of the CMYK model because it is based on *illumination* rather than *reflection*. In other words, the color that reaches your eye from your monitor depends on the illuminating light it emits, but the color of ink depends on the light it reflects. You may sometimes hear the RBG color model referred to as an *additive model* because the intensities of each color channel add up to provide the overall brightness of the color. The CMYK model, on the other hand, is *subtractive* because the brightness of the colors depends on how much light the pigments absorb.

Some artists and optical specialists use a more abstract way of defining colors, called the *HSV model*, based on hue, saturation, and value. *Hue* is the place where the color falls on the rainbow spectrum—red, orange, yellow, blue, and so forth.

Saturation is how dense the color is, and *value* is how light the color is. Art professors will rap me on the knuckles for that rather abbreviated summary, but the point here is that you really don't need to know how to use any color model besides RGB. All these models are mathematically equivalent, and you can define any color with any of them. If you think of all the possible colors you can see as a three-dimensional region of *color space*, where each unique color is a point in the region, these color models are simply different coordinate systems for locating a point in color space. Because your computer uses RGB, we'll stick with that model from now on.

Because your computer's RGB colors work differently than CMYK pigments, it may not be obvious at first how you can build the colors you want from red, green, and blue light. To help you get the hang of it, Table 2.5 tells you how to mix some common colors from red, green, and blue components. The numbers are scaled from 0 to 63 because VGA and Super VGA palettes use 6-bit numbers for each color channel.

Table 2.6. You can create all the colors of the rainbow—and quite a few that weren't in any rainbow I've seen—by combining red, green, and blue light.

Color	Red	Green	Blue
Red	63	0	0
Orange	63	31	0
Yellow	63	63	0
Green	0	63	0
Blue	0	0	63
Violet	31	0	63
Brown	31	15	0
Purple	60	0	60
Pink	60	24	24
Aqua	0	40	60
Pine	6	31	0
Gray	Equal amounts of each		
Black	0	0	0
White	63	63	63

The TransGraphics macro that you'll use most often for color custom control creation is `tg_makepalcolor()`. This assembles red, green, and blue components into a color and assigns that color to a palette color number. For example, the following command makes color number 3 a deep pine green:

```
tg_makepalcolor(3, 6, 31, 0);
```

To find out the current composition of a particular palette color, use `tg_splitpalcolor()` like this:

```
tg_splitpalcolor(3, red, green, blue);
```

After the previous command, the variables `red`, `green`, and `blue` (which you must define in your program) would contain the components of palette color number 3.

TransGraphics keeps a copy of the hardware palette color values in the `tg_palette` array. You should generally not access this array directly because its internal structure varies depending on the video mode and graphics library you're using. If you know what you're doing and want to shuffle the palette around for some reason, you can use `tg_setpalcolor()` to set a single hardware palette color to the value in the corresponding part of the `tg_palette` array or `tg_getpalcolor()` to read a hardware palette color into the `tg_palette` array. Similarly, `tg_setallpalcolors()` replaces the entire hardware palette with the values in `tg_palette`, and `tg_getallpalcolors()` reads the entire palette into `tg_palette` at once.

For most purposes, `tg_makepalcolor()` and `tg_splitpalcolor()` provide all the palette control you'll ever need while maximizing the simplicity and portability of your graphics programs.

Though you can't see the colors on this grey-scale illustration, Figure 2.8 (and Plate 9 in the color insert) is the TGDEMO screen that shows gradually blended shades of red, green, and blue made with `tg_makepalcolor()`.

The MOIRE program presented in the first chapter gave you a sneak preview of the most sophisticated TransGraphics function, `tg_colorcycle()`. This function employs a technique called *color cycling* to fill the entire graphics screen with dynamic animation by rotating the color values in the palette until the user presses a key.

When you use `tg_colorcycle()`, you control the speed of the animation by specifying how many steps the palette should jump each time it rotates. For example, the `tg_colorcycle(2)` command causes each palette color to rotate two positions during each cycle—color number 3 becomes color number 1, color 4 becomes color 2, color 5 becomes color 3, and so on.

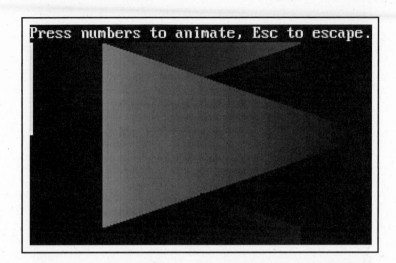

Figure 2.8. *The TGDEMO program demonstrates custom mixed palette colors. (Don't just sit there and look at this black-and-white picture—crank up the computer and try it!)*

I could have written the tg_colorcycle() function using only tg_splitpalcolor() and tg_makepalcolor() so that one version of the function would work with all graphics libraries and compilers. However, crafting a special version of the function for each library significantly speeds up performance. Unfortunately, most of the libraries cycle colors either painfully slowly or with a certain amount of jittery on-screen snow in the 256-color modes. The GX Graphics library is a delightful exception to this rule, as you can see from the speedy color cycling performed by the MOIRE.EXE and TGDEMO.EXE programs that accompanied this book.

Working Code: Custom Colors

You can have a lot of fun without writing much code when you use tg_makepalcolor() and tg_colorcycle(). Just remember that the red, green, and blue values you give tg_makepalcolor() should each be between 0 and 63.

```
void palettecolors(void)
{   int i, y1, y2, x, xinc, red, green, blue, intensity;

    /* don't bother if there aren't at least 16 colors */

    if (tg_ncolors < 16)
```

71

```
{   tg_moveto(0, 0);
    tg_outtext("Sorry, not enough colors to do "
                "palette animation in this video mode.");
    return;
}

/* Mix up some custom palette colors */

xinc = tg_scrnx / (tg_ncolors / 3);
y1 = tg_scrny / 3;
y2 = y1 = tg_scrny / 2;
for (i = 1, x = 0; i < tg_ncolors / 3; i++, x += xinc)
{   intensity = i * 192 / tg_ncolors;
    tg_makepalcolor(i, intensity, 0, 0);
    tg_setcolor(i);
    tg_fillrect(x, 0, x + xinc, y1);
    tg_makepalcolor(i + tg_ncolors / 3, 0, intensity, 0);
    tg_setcolor(i + tg_ncolors / 3);
    tg_fillrect(tg_scrnx - x, y1,
                tg_scrnx - (x + xinc), y2);
    tg_makepalcolor(i + 2 * tg_ncolors / 3,
                    0, 0, intensity);
    tg_setcolor(i + 2 * tg_ncolors / 3);
    tg_fillrect(x, y2, x + xinc, tg_scrny - 1);
    y1--, y2++;
}

/* Now for the fancy stuff -- color animation! */

tg_makepalcolor(1, 60, 60, 60);
tg_setcolor(1);
tg_moveto(0, 0);
tg_outtext("Press numbers to animate, Esc to escape.");

while(1)
{   if (kbhit())
    {   if (((i = getch()) >= '1') && (i <= '9'))
        {   tg_colorcycle(i - '0');
        }
        else
        {   if (i == 27) break;
        }
    }
```

```
}
    tg_makepalcolor(15, 60, 60, 60);
    tg_makepalcolor(11, 0, 60, 60);
}
```

Mouse Support

From humble beginnings as an odd-looking, one-button, wooden prototype, the mouse has evolved into a sleek, sophisticated tool that is nearly as familiar to today's computer user as the keyboard.

—*The Microsoft Mouse Programmer's Reference*, 1989

In this day and age, nobody would even think of producing a major graphics application without mouse support. That's both bad and good news for a budding graphics maven such as yourself. The bad news is that, even though almost every computer now comes with a mouse, almost none of the major compilers come with mouse support. (Okay, I admit that they support mouse input within Microsoft Windows, and I'll tell you how to work with that in Chapters 10 through 12, but neither Microsoft nor Borland give you mouse functions for their DOS-based graphics libraries.) The good news is that TransGraphics will save the day by giving you complete mouse support that works with any compiler. Table 2.7 summarizes the TransGraphics mouse macros.

Table 2.7. Whether your graphics library includes mouse functions, you can use all these macros to support Microsoft-mouse compatible input devices.

Function	What it does
tg_findmouse()	Checks if the user has a mouse and sets tg_mouson to -1 (true) or 0 (false) accordingly
tg_showmouse()	Makes the mouse cursor visible
tg_hidemouse()	Makes the mouse cursor invisible
tg_getmousebuttons(lb, rb)	Puts the left button status (1 or 0) into lb, and the right button status into rb
tg_getmousepos(mx, my)	Gets the current mouse cursor position
tg_setmousepos(mx, my)	Sets the current mouse cursor position

continues

Table 2.7. continued

Function	What it does
tg_mousewait()	Waits for a keypress or mouse click
tg_getmouse()	Waits for a mouse click (ignoring the keyboard)

The first TransGraphics mouse command you'll need is tg_findmouse(), which checks to see if the user has a Microsoft-compatible mouse, trackball, or digitizer tablet. If a mousey sort of device exists, tg_findmouse() sets the variable named tg_mouseon to –1. Otherwise, it sets tg_mouseon to 0. Whenever you go to access the mouse in your programs, you should always check to make sure tg_mouseon isn't 0 before you try to use any of the other mouse functions. (I'm not saying anything's going to *happen* to you if you try to access the mouse functions without checking tg_mouseon first. But, as Huckleberry Finn said when he accidentally turned over the salt-cellar at breakfast, "There is ways to keep off some kinds of bad luck, but this wasn't one of them kind...")

Once you know that a mouse is really out there, you need to make the *mouse cursor* (you know, that little arrow thingy) visible so the user can see where he or she is pointing. A quick call to the tg_showmouse() macro does the trick nicely. When you need to update the screen, you should always hide the mouse cursor with tg_hidemouse() until the action has died down. (Otherwise, well, as Huck Finn says, "I've always reckoned that looking at the new moon over your left shoulder is one of the carelessest and foolishest things a body can do." He never heard tell, though, of what might happen if you don't hide your mouse cursor before you draw on-screen...)

To get much use out of that mouse, you need to know where the cursor is pointing and whether the mouse buttons are being pressed. The tg_getmousepos() macro puts the mouse cursor position into two variables (one for horizontal position, one for vertical position), and tg_getmousebuttons() puts the left and right button status into two variables. When a mouse button is up, tg_mousebuttons() puts the value of 0 in the corresponding variable; when a button is down, it puts a value of 1 in the variable instead. As an example of how you might use these macros, the following lines would wait until the left mouse button is pressed and put the mouse cursor position into variables named mx and my.

```
do
{    tg_mousebuttons(leftb, rightb);
} while(leftb == 0);
tg_getmousepos(mx, my);
```

Usually, the user uses the mouse to tell the program what to do. As a user, you'll enjoy that arrangement, but there are times when a program must stand up for itself and put the mouse cursor where it should go, no matter what the user tries to say about the matter. When those occasions arise, the `tg_setmousepos()` macro will give your program the clout it needs. For example, to put the mouse cursor in the center of the screen, you can write

```
tg_setmousepos(tg_scrnx / 2, tg_scrny / 2);
```

Though this may seem a bit pushy at first, it can actually help the user constrain mouse movement. In the following TGDEMO mouse demo function, for example, I use `tg_setmousepos()` to help the user make perfectly square boxes on-screen—a difficult task to accomplish by hand and eye alone.

Even though using the mouse macros is quite a straightforward process, the business of waiting for a button to go down then monitoring it until it comes up consumes few lines of code. Combine this with the need to keep an ear out for the keyboard, and it can take a bit of typing just to write the code to wait for the user to "press any key or mouse button to continue." You will wish a one-line macro existed that simply waited for a keypress or mouse click—and so there is. It's called `tg_mousewait()`, and you'll probably end up using it quite often. When you want to ignore the keyboard and wait for a mouse click, you can use `tg_getmouse()` instead. (Think of it as a rodent rendition of the familiar C `getch()` function.)

To start you in the promising career of mouse manipulation, the TGDEMO program includes a quickie square-drawing demonstration. What follows is Figure 2.9, which shows the mouse at work, and the **Working Code** that uses the mouse handling function.

Figure 2.9. *Here you see an ordinary user suddenly endowed with the extraordinary hand-eye coordination to draw perfectly square rectangles with the help of his trusty seeing-eye mouse.*

75

Working Code: Mousing Around

```
void mousearound(void)
{   int lb, rb, mx, my, oldmx, oldmy, x1, y1;
    tg_moveto(0, 0);
    tg_setcolor(15 % tg_ncolors);

    /* If there's a mouse, try using it */

    tg_findmouse();
    if (tg_mouseon)
    {   tg_outtext("Drag with the left mouse button "
                   "to draw squares.");
        tg_moveto(0, tg_chary);
        tg_outtext("Click the right button to escape.");
        tg_showmouse();
        while(1)
        {
            /* find out the button status, and get outta here
               if user clicks the right button */

            tg_getmousebuttons(lb, rb);
            if (rb)
            {
                /* wait for button release, then skiddadle */

                while(rb)
                {   tg_getmousebuttons(lb, rb);
                }
                break;
            }

            /* If the left button goes down, start making
               "rubber-band" squares */

            else if (lb)
            {   tg_getmousepos(x1, y1);
                tg_setcolor(rand() % tg_ncolors);
                tg_startxor();

                /* the first rectangle is just a dot */
```

```
           mx = oldmx = x1, oldmy = my = y1;
           tg_drawrect(x1, y1, mx, my);

           while(lb)
           {
               /* don't draw again until the mouse moves
                  along the horizontal axis */

               tg_getmousepos(mx, my);
               if (mx != oldmx)
               {
                   /* hide the mouse cursor and
                      erase the last square */

                   tg_hidemouse();
                   tg_drawrect(x1, y1, oldmx, oldmy);

                   /* force a perfect square
                      and put it on the screen */

                   my = y1 + mx - x1;
                   tg_setmousepos(mx, my);
                   tg_drawrect(x1, y1, mx, my);
                   oldmx = mx, oldmy = my;
                   tg_showmouse();
               }
               tg_getmousebuttons(lb, rb);
           }

           /* user has let go of the right button,
              so fill in the square */

           tg_endxor();
           tg_hidemouse();
           tg_fillrect(x1, y1, mx, my);
           tg_showmouse();
       }
   }
   tg_hidemouse();

   /* make sure tg_getmouse() and tg_mousewait() work */
```

```
        tg_moveto(0, 120);
        tg_setcolor(15 % tg_ncolors);
        tg_outtext("Press a mouse button to continue.");
        tg_getmouse();
        tg_clearscreen();
        tg_moveto(0, 0);
        tg_outtext("Now press a key or mouse button.");
        tg_mousewait();
    }
    else
    {   tg_outtext("No mouse detected.");
    }
}
```

How Does It Work?

Burn the libraries, for their value is in this one book.

> —Caliph Omar, Brandishing the Koran
> at the capture of Alexandria

In this chapter, I've given you the drawing tools you need to build sophisticated graphics software with any major C or C++ compiler or graphics library. Most of the programs throughout the book use these TransGraphics macros and functions for maximum portability.

If you would like to find out how TransGraphics manages to reconcile the differences between diverse graphics libraries, Appendix B presents and explains the actual TransGraphics source code, including mouse routines that will work with or without the rest of TransGraphics.

In the next chapter, I introduce you to a variety of techniques for storing and recalling the graphics you create. You also discover how to exchange images with almost any graphics software through several standard file formats.

Standard Graphics File Formats

E veryone knows the going rate for a good picture these days is at least a kiloword. But the snazziest photo-realistic masterpiece ever created isn't worth half an ASCII character if nobody but the creator can look at it. So, before my coauthors and I show you how to make a world of impressive images, I'll show you how to make your images portable enough to impress the world.

What that world needs is a standard graphics file format for exchanging images. Unfortunately, the world already has about a hundred standard graphics file formats. And we aren't likely to attain the ideal of a single universal format any time in the imaginable future—mostly because nobody actually wants such a thing. The way you store images neces-sarily depends on what you plan to do with them. If you plan to post a picture by modem

to an electronic bulleten board system (BBS), you want maximum data compression and compatibility with other types of computers. If you want to present computer animation or slide shows, speed of playback is more important than data compression or cross-platform compatibility. If you want to edit the image with a particular piece of software, you must first get it into a format that the software can read.

There are many other factors that come into play when you decide which format to use for storing an image. One thing is always certain: you don't want to be locked into one single graphics format. This chapter presents several of the most common file formats for PC graphics, each of which is the current standard for a particular type of graphics application:

■ The Targa (or TGA) format was designed by the industry leader in high-end graphics hardware, TrueVision, Inc., for storing true color images. TGA files, which can store palette-based images as well as true color and high color, are very easy to read, write, and manipulate, but offer little or no data compression. Almost all programs that edit or create true color images, such as electronic photo retouch software or ray tracers, support the TGA format.

■ The Graphics Interchange Format (GIF) was designed by Compuserve Information Service (CIS, the world's largest online information service) for exchanging bitmapped images between a wide variety of computers. GIF files offer maximum data compression to keep your phone bills low, but storing and displaying GIFs is relatively slow. Any graphics software which creates or reads images that may need to be uploaded or downloaded to a BBS should support the GIF format.

■ The PCX format, which originated as the native file format for ZSoft's popular PC Paintbrush program, is probably the most widely used PC graphics file format for 16-color and monochrome pictures, though extensions of the format can also store 256-color and true color images. Because PCX files store image data in the same order as in the PC's video memory, they offer maximum display speed on PCs. Decoding and creating them on other types of computers is cumbersome, however. Most paint programs and scanners for PCs support the PCX format.

■ The tagged image file format (TIFF) was born out of a joint effort by Aldus and Microsoft to achieve worldwide peace and/or worldwide market dominance in desktop publishing software. The same power and flexibility that have made TIFF a widespread success have also produced a confusing variety of semi-incompatible TIFF "flavors." Most serious desktop publishing tools offer

TIFF as the preferred choice of several supported file formats. You'll find a shareware Super VGA TIFF programming library included on the disk with this book, and documented in Appendix Y.

Almost every PC graphics application you use will accept one or more of these standard file formats. This chapter gives you working C code to load and save each of them. You'll undoubtedly encounter others, and this chapter gives you the low-down on DXF, IGES, NAPLPS, PIC, WPG, WMF, BMP, DIB, CGM, EPS, PICT, IFF, JPEG, MPEG, and FIF files, too.

TGA Files

The success of the TGA File Format for storing color images can be attributed to its ease of use, the small amount of program memory needed to parse the file, and the fact that it was the first true-color file format widely available. Truevision defined the TGA file format in 1984 for use with its first videographics products. Since then, it has been estimated that today over 80 percent of the color images stored on hard drives employ some variation of the TGA file format.

—Truevision TGA File Format Specification Technical Manual,
January 1991

Once upon a time, Targa files were used only by the computer graphics elite in their institutional castles on high. TrueVision's Targa boards were the first commercially successful true color video adapters for the PC, and they commanded too regal a price for the masses to show much interest. True color applications, such as full-color publishing and photorealistic rendering, required super-fast PCs which themselves brandished price tags fit for a king. Only recently has the price of true-color-capable hardware decended to the level of the PC peasantry. TrueVision's TGA file format has come along to meet the populace.

Using Your Header

If you're a graphics programmer, you'll love TGA files. They are ultra-simple to read and write, yet they also handle program-specific extensions with ease. Most Targa files are just a big uncompressed list of red, green, and blue color values for each pixel in the picture. This image data is preceeded by a short header that indicates the size of the picture and may also give the picture an identifying name. By adding other fields to the header, you can also create more complex TGA files that incorporate color palettes, data compression, and additional information about the image. Table 3.1 lists the meaning of each byte in the 18-byte TGA file header.

Table 3.1. A TGA file always starts with an 18-byte header that tells the size and type of the image.

Byte #	(Size)	Meaning	Possible values
1	(1 byte)	ID Length	Length of text identification string (0 if no id)
2	(1 byte)	Color Map Type	0 = no color map (palette) included 1 = color map (palette) included
3	(1 byte)	Image Type	0 = no image data 1 = uncompressed, color-mapped image 2 = uncompressed, true color image (most common) 3 = uncompressed, black-and-white image 9 = compressed, color-mapped image 10 = compressed, true color image 11 = compressed, black-and-white image
4	(2 bytes)	First Color Entry	which palette color to start with (almost always 0)
6	(2 bytes)	Color Map Length	Number of colors in the palette (usually 256, should be 0 if Color Map Type is 0)
8	(1 byte)	Color Map Bits	Number of bits per color map entry (usually 24—one byte each for red, green, and blue)

Byte #	(Size)	Meaning	Possible values
9	(2 bytes)	X Origin	Horizontal pixel position to begin image (usually 0)
11	(2 bytes)	Y Origin	Vertical pixel position to begin image (usually 0)
13	(2 bytes)	Width	Horizontal size of the image in pixels
15	(2 bytes)	Height	Vertical size of the image in pixels
17	(1 byte)	Pixel Bits	Number of bits per pixel, usually 24. (would be 8 for a 256-color palette based image)
18	(1 byte)	Descriptor	Bits 4 and 5 tell the orientation of the picture (almost always 32, meaning start in top left corner. 0 means start at bottom left, 16 means start at bottom right, 48 means start at top right)

Trimming the Fat

The official specification for TGA files includes the option of compressing the size of the file with a technique called *run length encoding* (RLE). When a long string of the pixels all have the same color, you can save space by counting the number of times the color is repeated and putting a special code followed by that *run length* into the file instead of repeating the actual color value that many times. RLE can cut the space needed to store an image dramatically for some types of images, especially those produced by paint programs, which often have large uniform-colored shapes (see Figure 3.1).

Those aren't the kind of images that one normally stores in a Targa file, however. Scanned photos (Figure 3.2) and complex realistic renderings (Figure 3.3) are far more common TGA fare. These types of images don't usually have many long strings of identical colors, and RLE compression doesn't reduce storage requirements significantly. Consequently, most TGA files are stored uncompressed, and many TGA-handling programs—including the **Working Code: Reading and Writing Targa Files** section later in this chapter—don't bother dealing with RLE data compression at all. (You'll find more details on run-length encoding and decoding in the upcoming section on PCX files.)

Figure 3.1. *Simple hand-drawn pictures can easily be compressed when they are stored because they contain large regions of unchanging color.*

If you find yourself storing a lot of images with large regions of unchanging color, I recommend you use a sophisticated compression program such as Stac Electronics' Stacker or the built-in data compression utility that comes with MS-DOS 6.0. These programs automatically compress TGA files much more efficiently than the simple RLE encoding scheme that some TGA implementations use. Because there is a limit to the amount you can compress any data without destroying part of it, an RLE-compressed image usually won't take up any less space on a Stacker or DOS 6.0 hard drive than the same image stored in the normal, non-RLE Targa format.

Anyone who sends giant Targa files over the phone lines—where data compression means nickels in your pocket—should first compress the files with an LZW compression utility such as LHA.EXE (which comes on the disk with this book). Again, the file won't end up any smaller if it was first compressed with some half-hearted scheme like RLE.

Figure 3.2. *Scanned photos seldom have large regions without any color variation, so trying to compress them with run-length encoding would be silly.*

Super VGA Viewing

Almost all the graphics programs you'll work with in this book use the TGA file format. In some cases, the TGA files you create will have 256-color palettes that your VGA adapter can display. When you want to make photorealistic renderings, however, you need true color TGA files. Does that mean you can't see your pictures with an ordinary 256-color VGA or Super VGA adapter?

Now, would I do a sneaky thing like that to you? Of course not. You can use the Super VGA image viewer that came on the disk with this book to look at any of the TGA files you create with almost any VGA or Super VGA graphics card. The SVGA.EXE program will automatically approximate true color images with the closest 256-color palette it can create (or, if you have a high color card, 15-bit approximations of the 24-bit colors).

Figure 3.3. *Photorealistic renderings tend to have the same complex color variations that real photos do. Therefore, runlength encoding would be silly.*

The next **You Can Do It** box shows you how to set up and use the SVGA program. Please note that SVGA is shareware, which means that the copy included with this book is for your evaluation only. If you find it useful (which I'm sure you will, unless you happen to be hooked on another file viewer that came with your video card or favorite image editor), please register by sending the $15 directly to the program's author:

John P. Silva
3429 Maywood Drive
Richmond, CA 94803

I think you'll agree that fifteen smackers is a small price to pay for the most robust Super VGA image viewer I've found anywhere. Owners of high color cards will be especially grateful to John for letting them take full advantage of their fancy hardware. If you toss in an extra $10 to the registration fee, he'll send you a printed manual and a disk with the latest program enhancements.

You Can Do It: Create and View a Color Triangle

You probably don't have a true color video board. Therefore, when you create a complex computer-generated true color image—the kind that usually goes into a TGA file—you will need to write each pixel straight to the file rather than displaying it on the screen. You can then use a TGA file viewer such as John Silva's SVGA program to view the best approximation of your image that your hardware can reproduce.

The COLORTRI program (the first file listed in the **Working Code: Reading and Writing Targa Files** section) creates a "color triangle" containing every possible color that can be made by combining fully saturated red, green, and blue light. (See color plate number 85 in the middle of the book.) The COLORTRI program doesn't even set a graphics mode—it just computes a different color for each pixel and dumps them in the correct order to a TGA file.

To create a color triangle of your very own:

1. Type COLORTRI at the DOS prompt and press Enter.

   You won't see anything except a brief text message notifying you when the program begins and ends. Depending on the speed of your computer, it may take the program a few seconds to write the COLORTRI.TGA file to your hard disk.

2. Type SVGA to start the Super VGA picture viewer.

3. You will see a list of files. Use the arrow keys to choose COLORTRI.TGA and press Enter.

   A rounded triangular shape full of colors appears. The top corner of the triangle is blue, the bottom left is red, and the bottom right is green. In between, the primary colors blend with gradually varying intensity. How gradually they blend, and the size of the whole triangle, depends on the capabilities of your particular video card. SVGA normally displays images at the highest resolution your card can display. You can easily adjust the resolution and control how SVGA approximates the image, however.

4. Press Esc to return to the file list, then press the F1 function key.

A summary of the program control keys appears on the left, and information about your specific video hardware and memory configuration appears on the right. You don't need to memorize these controls because you can always just hit F1 when you want to see the list again.

5. Press any key to return to the file list, and I'll take you on a quick tour of the SVGA controls.

   Usually, the only controls you'll need are the F9 and F10 function keys, which decrease and increase the resolution of the screen.

6. Try it now: Press F9 to decrease the resolution, making the image look bigger. (The current resolution is highlighted in yellow at the top of the file list screen.)

7. Press Enter to see the picture at the new resolution.

8. You don't need to return to the file list every time you want to adjust the resolution. Press F9 again now, to zoom in on the image again.

If you have a graphics adapter that supports one or more high color video modes (such as one of the many video adapters based on the Tseng ET4000 and Sierra HiColor chips), you will quickly notice that the colors pattern you see in 640x480 resolution differs dramatically from the colors at higher or lower resolutions. Instead of a few wide bands of color, you get many ever-so-gradually changing hues. If you were seeing true 24-bit color, there would be no bands at all—just perfectly smooth gradations. Until you get one of those new 24-bit cards and the software drivers to go with it, you'll have to forgo 24-bit smoothness and settle for the 15-bit "Don Johnson" look. Still, you sure can tell when that HiColor chip kicks in.

Lest ye owners of olde fashioned VGA and Super VGA cards sink too deeply into woe at the rough 256-color approximations on your screen, let me show you a nifty trick that only works if you *aren't* in a high color video mode. (High color users should use the F10 key to increase the resolution and idle their graphics engines back down to 256 colors before preceeding.)

When you are looking at an image in a palette-based mode, SVGA lets you adjust the color balance by pressing the first eight function keys.

9. Press F1 a few times. Red! Now try F2. No more red. Likewise, F3 and F4 increase and decrease the amount of green. F5 and F6 increase and decrease the amount of blue. You can also adjust the overall brightness of the image with the F7 and F8 keys.

You'll often find the brightness controls especially handy for fine tuning SVGA's automatic 256-color approximations of true color images.

You did remember to send John Silva his much-deserved $15 registration fee so that you can legally continue to use SVGA, didn't you? I thought so. Thanks.

Working Code: Reading and Writing Targa Files

Three files are listed in this section. The first two (COLORTRI.C and TGAREAD.C) demonstrate how easy it is to use the Targa file handling functions in the third (TGA.C).

The COLORTRI program simply creates a "color triangle" by computing and writing each pixel to a true color Targa file. First, you use the `starttga()` function to open the file for writing and put in the header. Then you call `writetgapixel()` for each pixel in the image. You must always write the pixels in left-to-right, top-to-bottom order (the same order you write English letters on a page).

Though its use isn't demonstrated in COLORTRI.C, you also have the option of writing a 256-color or 16-color Targa file directly from the screen with the `writetgascreen()` function in TGA.C.

Reading a Targa file is also easy, as the short TGAREAD.C program shows. It opens a Targa file for reading with `opentga()` and then displays the image with `readtga()`. If it's a palette-based image, `opentga()` and `readtga()` will display it in color. If it's a true color image, a grey-scale approximation of it will appear on the screen.

As I mentioned earlier, none of the routines in TGA.C attempt to deal with image compression. If they did, writing or reading the files would be considerably more complex, since you couldn't just toss read and write each individual pixel without reading and processing larger chunks of the image.

Listing 3.1. COLORTRI.C computes a color triangle and writes it to a true color Targa file.

```c
/* COLORTRI.C
 *
 * This file tests the Targa file input/output from TGA.C
 * by creating a color triangle on the screen
 * from Tricks of the Graphics Gurus
 */

#include "tg.h"                  /* See TG.TXT for more info. */
#include <stdio.h>               /* for standard input/output */
#include <math.h>                  /* for sqrt() function */

#define MAX 255     /* maximum value for each color channel */

/* To make a bigger image, increase all the following
   constants by the same ratio. For example, to make a
   512x512 image, define XX and YY as 512, then
   define DIV as 2.0 and YUP as 68 */

#define XX 256                    /* horizontal size of image */
#define YY 256                    /* vertical size of image */
#define DIV 1.0                    /* speed of color change */
#define YUP 34        /* vertical offset for bottom corners */
#define radius 40
#define shiner 10

/* macro to compute distance between two points */

#define dist(j, i, x, y) \
    ((int) sqrt((double) \
        ((double) (x - j) * (double) (x - j) \
        + (double) (y - i) * (double) (y - i))))

/* just do it */

void main(void)
{   int i, j, red, green, blue, incircle,
        rx, ry, gx, gy, bx, by;
    rx = XX / 2, ry = 0;         /* corners of the triangle */
    gx = 0, gy = YY - YUP;
```

```
bx = XX - 1, by = YY - YUP;
printf("\n\nCOLORTRI.C\n"
        "from Tricks of the Graphics Gurus\n\n"
        "Hang on a sec while I create COLORTRI.TGA...\n");

/* create a 24-bit Targa file */

setuptga("colortri.tga", XX, YY, 24);

/* compute the exact color of each pixel,
   based on its distance from each corner of a triangle */

for (i = 0; i < YY; i++)
    for (j = 0; j < XX; j++)
    {   red = dist(j, i, rx, ry) / DIV;
        green = dist(j, i, gx, gy) / DIV;
        blue = dist(j, i, bx, by) / DIV;
        if ((red > MAX) || (green > MAX) || (blue > MAX))
            red = green = blue = 0;
        else
            red = MAX - red,
            green = MAX - green,
            blue = MAX - blue;
            /*
        incircle = dist(j, i, (rx + radius), (by + radius));
        if (incircle < radius)
        {   red = dist(j, i, (rx + shiner), (by + shiner));
            green = red;
            blue = red;
        }    */
        pixel2tga(red, green, blue);
    }

/* That's all there is to it!
   Notice that we didn't even set a graphics mode */

closetga();
printf("COLORTRI.TGA created. So there you are.");
}
```

Listing 3.2. TGAREAD.C reads a Targa files and displays them in the video mode of your choice.

```c
/* TGAREAD.C
 *
 * from Tricks of the Graphics Gurus
 * This program reads and displays a Targa file.
 * (It must be linked with TGA.C to work!)
 */

#include <stdio.h>        /* Standard input/output libraries */
#include <stdlib.h>

#include "tg.h"       /* See TG.TXT for compile instructions */

void main(void)
{   char str[16];
    printf("TGAREAD  from Tricks of the Graphics Gurus\n\n");
    printf("Enter a filename (include the .TGA extension)\n");
    scanf("%s", str);
    tg_pickmode();                      /* confirm video mode */
    opentga(str);
    readtga();                  /* read and display the file */
    getch();            /* hang out til they tell you to go */
    tg_closedown();                 /* close down graphics */
}
```

Listing 3.3. The functions in TGA.C make creating and reading Targa files easy.

```c
/* TGA.C
 *
 * Targa file input and output
 * from Tricks of the Graphics Gurus
 */

#include <stdio.h>
#include "tg.h"

FILE *tgafile;

typedef struct
```

```
{   char idlength;             /* length of image ID string */
    char colormaptype;         /* 1 if a color-map is included */
    char imagetype;            /* Image type: 0 => no image
                                              1 => color-mapped
                                              2 => true color
                                              3 => monochrome */
    unsigned int colormapstart;    /* index to start of map */
    unsigned int colormaplength;   /* number of map entries */
    char colormapbits;             /* number of bits per entry */
    unsigned int xstart;           /* top left corner of image */
    unsigned int ystart;
    unsigned int width;             /* size of image in pixels */
    unsigned int depth;
    char bits;                      /* number of bits per pixel */
    char descriptor;           /* 0x20 means start at top left
                                  0x21 means top right
                                  0x00 means bottom left
                                  0x01 means bottom right
                                  (generally, always use 0x20) */
} TGAHEADER;

TGAHEADER tga;

/* compute a grey level from and rgb color value */

#define approximate(r,g,b) ((((r * 30) / 100) \
                + ((g * 59) / 100) \
                + ((b * 11) / 100)) / (256 / tg_ncolors))

/* this would give a VERY rough color approximation */

/* #define approximate(r, g, b) (((r / 50) * 36) + \
                    ((g / 50) * 6) + \
                    (b / 50) + 16)
*/

/* Create a TGA file and put a head on it */

int setuptga(char *filename, int width, int depth, int bits)
{   int i, j, c, r, g, b;
```

continues

Listing 3.3. continued

```
/* open the file */

if ((tgafile = fopen(filename, "wb")) == NULL) return(0);

/* create a TGA file header */

memset((char *)&tga, 0, sizeof(TGAHEADER));
tga.descriptor = 0x20;
tga.width = width;
tga.depth = depth;
tga.idlength = 0;
if(bits == 1)                              /* monochrome */
{   tga.imagetype = 3;
    tga.bits = 1;
}
else if(bits > 1 && bits <= 8)          /* 256-color */
{   tga.colormaptype = 1;
    tga.imagetype = 1;
    tga.colormaplength = 256;
    tga.colormapbits = 24;
    tga.bits = 8;
}
else
{   tga.imagetype = 2;                     /* True color */
    tga.bits = 24;
}
putc(tga.idlength, tgafile);
putc(tga.colormaptype, tgafile);
putc(tga.imagetype, tgafile);
putw(tga.colormapstart, tgafile);
putw(tga.colormaplength, tgafile);
putc(tga.colormapbits, tgafile);
putw(tga.xstart, tgafile);
putw(tga.ystart, tgafile);
putw(tga.width, tgafile);
putw(tga.depth, tgafile);
putc(tga.bits, tgafile);
putc(tga.descriptor, tgafile);

/* write the color map if there is one */
```

```
        if(tga.bits == 8)
        {   for(i = 0; i < 256; ++i)
            {   tg_splitpalcolor(i, r, g, b);
                putc(r << 2, tgafile);
                putc(g << 2, tgafile);
                putc(b << 2, tgafile);
            }
    }

    /* don't write the bitmap yet --
        pixel2tga() does that, one pixel at a time
        or you can use screen2tga() to write the whole screen */

    if(ferror(tgafile)) return(0);
    else return(1);
}

/* write the whole screen to the TGA file
    previously started with setuptga(), then close the file
    (no need to call closetga() afterwards) */

int screen2tga(void)
{   int i, j, c, r, g, b;
    for(i = 0; i < tga.depth; i++)
    {   if (kbhit()) if (getch() == 27) break;
        for (j = 0; j < tga.width; j++)
        {   c = tg_getpixel(j, i);
            if (tga.bits == 1)
            {   c = c << 7;
                c &= tg_getpixel((++j), i) << 6;
                c &= tg_getpixel((++j), i) << 5;
                c &= tg_getpixel((++j), i) << 4;
                c &= tg_getpixel((++j), i) << 3;
                c &= tg_getpixel((++j), i) << 2;
                c &= tg_getpixel((++j), i) << 1;
                c &= tg_getpixel(j + 1, i);
                putc(c, tgafile);
            }
            if (tga.bits == 8) putc(c, tgafile);
            else if(tga.bits == 24)
```

continues

95

Listing 3.3. continued

```
                { tg_splitpalcolor(c, r, g, b);
                    putc(r << 2, tgafile);
                    putc(b << 2, tgafile);
                    putc(g << 2, tgafile);
                    }
            }
    }
    fclose(tgafile);
    if(ferror(tgafile)) return(0);
    else return(1);
}

/* close the TGA file previously opened with opentga() and
   written with pixel2tga() */

int closetga(void)
{   fclose(tgafile);
    if(ferror(tgafile)) return(0);
    else return(1);
}

/* write a single 24-bit pixel to the TGA file
   previously opened with setuptga().

   IMPORTANT: All pixels MUST be written in left-to-right,
   top-to-bottom order, just like you write English text.

   And don't forget to call closetga() when all pixels
   have been written. */

int pixel2tga(int r, int g, int b)
{   if (tga.bits == 24)
    {   putc(r, tgafile);
        putc(b, tgafile);
        putc(g, tgafile);
    }
    else return(0);
    if (ferror(tgafile)) return(0);
    else return(1);
}
```

```
/* open a Targe file and read the header */

int opentga(char *filename)
{   int i, j, c, r, g, b;

    /* open the file */

    if ((tgafile = fopen(filename, "rb")) == NULL) return(0);

    /* read the file header */

    memset((char *)&tga, 0, sizeof(TGAHEADER));
    tga.idlength = getc(tgafile);
    tga.colormaptype = getc(tgafile);
    tga.imagetype = getc(tgafile);
    tga.colormapstart = getw(tgafile);
    tga.colormaplength = getw(tgafile);
    tga.colormapbits = getc(tgafile);
    tga.xstart = getw(tgafile);
    tga.ystart = getw(tgafile);
    tga.width = getw(tgafile);
    tga.depth = getw(tgafile);
    tga.bits = getc(tgafile);
    tga.descriptor = getc(tgafile);

    /* read the image id if there is one */

    if (tga.idlength)
        fseek(tgafile, (long) tga.idlength, SEEK_CUR);

    /* read the color map if there is one */

    if ((tga.colormaptype) && (tga.bits == 8))
    {   for(i = 0; i < tga.colormaplength; ++i)
        {   r = getc(tgafile);
            g = getc(tgafile);
            switch(tga.colormapbits)
            {   case 15:              /* five bits per color */
                case 16:
                    b = g << 3;
```

continues

97

Listing 3.3. continued

```
                        g = ((g >> 5) & ((r & 3) << 3)) << 2;
                        r = r & 252;
                        break;
                    case 24:   /* eight bits per color -- easy! */
                        b = getc(tgafile);
                        break;
                    case 32:            /* skip the alpha channel */
                        r = g;
                        g = getc(tgafile);
                        b = getc(tgafile);
                        break;
                }
                tg_makepalcolor(i, (b >> 2), (g >> 2), (r >> 2));
            }
    }
    else    /* no color map, so set up a grey scale palette */
    {   for (i = 0; i < tg_ncolors; i++)
        {   r = i * (256 / tg_ncolors);
            tg_makepalcolor(i, (r >> 2), (r >> 2), (r >> 2));
        }
    }
    /* this would VERY roughly approximate colors
    {   i = 16;
        for (r = 0; r < 6; r++)
            for(g = 0; g < 6; g++)
                for(b = 0; b < 6; b++)
                {   tg_makepalcolor(i, r * 50, g * 50, b * 50);
                    i++;
                }
    } */

    /* don't read the bitmap yet --
       readtga() does that */

    if(ferror(tgafile)) return(0);
    else return(1);
}

int readtga(void)
{   int x, y, c, r, g, b, i,
```

```
        xinc, yinc, xstart, ystart, xend, yend;

        /* don't try to read compressed files */

        if (tga.imagetype > 3) return(0);

        /* which corner do we start in? */

        if (tga.descriptor & 0x20)        /* from the top down */
            yinc = 1,
            ystart = tga.ystart,
            yend = tga.ystart + tga.depth;
        else                              /* from the bottom up */
            yinc = -1,
            ystart = tga.ystart + tga.depth,
            yend = tga.ystart;
        if (tga.descriptor & 0x10)        /* right to left */
            xinc = -1,
            xstart = tga.xstart + tga.width,
            xend = tga.xstart;
        else                              /* left to right */
            xinc = 1,
            xstart = tga.xstart,
            xend = tga.xstart + tga.width;
        for (y = ystart; y != yend; y += yinc)
        {   if (kbhit()) if (getch() == 27) break;
            for (x = xstart; x !=xend; x += xinc)
            {   if (tga.colormaptype)   /* color map -- easy! */
                {   c = getc(tgafile);
                    tg_putpixel(x, y, c);
                }
                else
                {   if (tga.bits == 1)  /* monochrome */
                    {   c = getc(tgafile);
                        for (i = 0; i < 8; i++)
                        {   tg_putpixel(x, y, c & 1);
                            c = c >> 1;
                            x += xinc;
                        }
                    }
                    else
```

continues

99

Listing 3.3. continued

```
        {   r = getc(tgafile);
            g = getc(tgafile);
            switch(tga.bits)
            {   case 15:
                case 16:
                    b = g << 3;
                    g = ((g >> 5) &
                        ((r & 3) << 3)) << 2;
                    r = r & 252;
                    break;
                case 24:
                    b = getc(tgafile);
                    break;
                case 32:
                    r = g;
                    g = getc(tgafile);
                    b = getc(tgafile);
                    break;
            }
            c = approximate(b, g, r);
            tg_putpixel(x, y, c);
        }
    }
  }
}
fclose(tgafile);
if(ferror(tgafile)) return(0);
else return(1);
}
```

PCX Files

Through its numerous incarnations, rewrites, ports, and bug fixes, ZSoft's PC Paintbrush program remains as one of the most popular PC drawing tools short of yellow highlighters that draw on a monitor... The PCX standard, although still evolving, has been around for a long time, as is the case with the software that was originally designed to work with PCX files. Actually, "evolving" might not be the best word to describe it. It's been having things bolted onto it for quite some time, with 24-bit PCX files being one of the more elegant additions.

—Steven Rimmer, *Supercharged Bitmapped Graphics*, 1992

The PCX file format was never voted "most likely to succeed", but it has somehow managed to become the most popular file format on the PC. Its success has arisen partly out of its simple-minded approach to image storage. If the hoards of PCX files could speak, their motto would be "Keep it Short and Simple." (Yes, you can also apply whatever variations on the "K.I.S.S." theme you've heard at the company water cooler.)

An Accidental Standard

Back when the programmers at ZSoft, Inc. decided how their new PC Paintbrush program should store pictures, 16-color palettes were the "high end" of PC display technology. They probably didn't imagine that PC Paintbrush would sell half a zillion copies, let alone that anyone would be interested in viewing PC Paintbrush files on any computer besides a PC. Therefore, they chose to store image data in a PCX file exactly as it appears in EGA and VGA video memory in 16-color modes. This means you can display PCX files quickly and easily on your VGA-equipped PC, but decoding PCXes on a Macintosh is like trying to order grilled cheese in China.

Much to the surprise (and financial benefit) of those ZSoft programmers, the PCX standard has endured and made its way into environments that don't deal with video memory at all like the original PC Paintbrush program did. Though the latest incarnations of PC Paintbrush (Figure 3.4) can still toss images in and out of video memory at will, some PCX-compatible applications, such as Windows Paintbrush (Figure 3.5), use entirely different memory-access schemes and must do elaborate translations to get the image data into a format they can use.

In this day and age, several computer-industry centuries after the advent of the PCX format (one computer-industry century being equivalent to five auto-industry years), the PCX file format is largely obsolete from a technical perspective. Though the PCX standard has been expanded to handle 256-color, high color and true color images, you'll find the Targa, GIF, and TIFF formats more versatile and portable for today's image files.

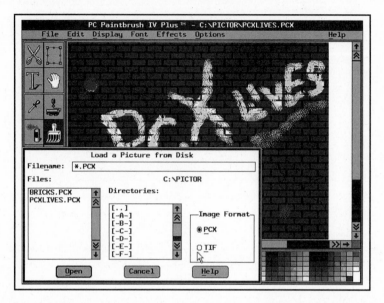

Figure 3.4. *Even PC Paintbrush, the original PCX program, now supports multiple image file formats.*

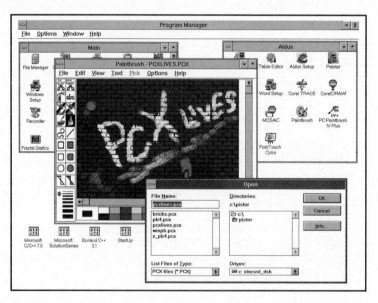

Figure 3.5. *Almost every PC graphics program will read and write PCX files, including Windows Paintbrush.*

Still, PCX files do retain one major advantage over other formats: display speed. PCXes are great when you want an image to pop up fast on your PC, and don't care much about anything else. You can also expect more PC applications to accept PCX files than any other format. Though the nerd in me protests, when it comes to exchanging images, popularity often matters more than intelligence.

The next **Working Code** section gives you quick-and-dirty routines for reading and writing PCX files. If you're primarily interested in the speed advantage of PCXes, these routines will zap images in and out of your EGA/VGA video memory quicker than you can say "Pernitious Cacophany of Xylophones."

If you're serious about reading PCX files created by a wide variety of other software, however, you may want to consider using a complete PCX library such as the Genus PCX Toolkit (available from Genus Microprogramming, 1155 Dairy Ashford, Ste 200, Houston, TX 77079-3012, phone: 800-227-0918) or MetaGraphics PCX-Lab (from MetaGraphics, Inc., PO Box 66779, Scotts Valley, CA 95067, phone: 408-438-1550). There are no less than 20 variations, or *flavors*, of the PCX standard in widespread use, and homebrewing a PCX reader that is robust enough to interpret them all correctly is no small undertaking. For casual image hacking, use the routines in the next section. For building real-world applications, blow a C-note or two on a bullet-proof professional PCX library. If your identity wavers between dabbler and die-hard, I recommend Michael Jones' *Graphics Programming PowerPack* book and disk (SAMS Publishing, 1992), which includes the basic PCX functions from Genus Microprogramming's PCX Toolkit for about 1/8th the price.

Header Bytes and Bit-Planes

If you do use an add-on PCX library, you won't need to know anything about the innards of the PCX files you work with. But I bet you're still just a wee bit curious, aren't you? Because PCX files are a straightforward combination of the inner structure of your video memory and the oft-used data compression technique called RLE, there's more to be learned here than just a file format.

Before you get to frolick in the image data, however, you'll need to finish your homework and learn about the 128-byte header that starts every PCX file. Table 3.2 summarizes the meaning of each field in the header.

Table 3.2. Every PCX file starts with a 128-byte header.

Byte	Size	Name	Meaning
0	1	Manufacturer	This is always 10
1	1	Version	0 = Version 2.5 of PC Paintbrush 2 = Version 2.8 with palette stored in file 3 = Version 2.8 without palette (use standard palette) 5 = Version 3.0 (high color or true color)
2	1	Encoding	Always 1
3	1	Bits/Pixel	Number of bits per pixel *in each plane*
4	2	Xmin	Smallest X value; Location of left edge
6	2	Ymin	Smallest Y value; Location of top edge
8	2	Xmax	Largest X value; Location of right edge
10	2	Ymax	Largest Y value; Bottom right Y value
12	2	Hres	Horizontal resolution in dots-per-inch (for printing scanned images)
14	2	Vres	Vertical resolution in dots-per-inch
16	48	Colormap	EGA or VGA 16-color palette
64	1	Reserved	When reading, ignore this byte. When writing make it 0
65	1	NPlanes	Number of color planes
66	2	Bytes/Line	Number of bytes per scanline *in each plane* (always even)
68	2	Palette Type	1 = Color or black and white 2 = grayscale
70	58	Unused	58 Bytes of wasted space. Ignore it.

The following **Working Code**, which I adapted from the ZSoft Technical Reference manual, looks simpler than it is. At first glance, the readpcx() function seems to take a quick peek at the PCX header, then grab pixel color data from the file and toss it into memory. The hidden trick here is that neither your video memory nor the PCX files store data pixel-by-pixel. Instead, each *color plane* is stored by itself. That means that when readpcx() reads a 4-bit (16-color) file, it actually reads four separate lines of data for each line of pixels. First, it reads a line of "first bits," then a line of "second bits," and so on until all the bits are read.

For 16-color images, the palette is stored in the header as indicated in Table 3.2. Each red, green, and blue value in the palette is scaled so that the maximum value is 255, rather than the maximum value of 63 that EGA and VGA hardware uses. When ZSoft added support for 256-color palettes, there was no room in the header for them. Therefore, 256-color palettes are tacked onto the end of the image data as the final 768 bytes in the file, with the decimal number 12 in front so that you can verify you found the right place before you read the palette.

24-bit true color PCX files were an even later addition to the standard. To make a 24-bit PCX, you store the pixels as if the hardware had 3 color planes with 8 bits in each plane. The first plane is red, the second green, and the third blue.

To thicken the plot, PCX files also use *run-length encoding* (RLE) to compress image data. This simply means that a PCX file writer looks for long strings of identical bytes in each color plane. When more than two identical consecutive bytes are found, you write a special code byte equal to the number of identical bytes (the *run-length*) plus 192. This code byte is then followed by the actual value to repeat during the run. Runs never continue from one *scanline* to the next, even if the first byte of the next line is the same as the last byte of the current line. Runs can, however, continue from one color plane to the next within a scanline.

Reading run-length encoded data is easier than writing it. Just read a byte, see if it's bigger than 192. If not, put it into memory as a byte of image data. If it is larger than 192, subtract 192 from it to get the run-length and put that many copies of the next byte you read into memory.

Flavorless Files

When you start reading and writing odd-sized images, some ambiguities arise. For example, the official standard states that an arbitrary amount of extra blank data may appear at the end of each scanline. When reading a file, you should subtract Xmin from Xmax (both of which are in the header) to see how long the lines really are, and skip the difference between this and the bytes-per-line value after each scanline. Many

PCX-compatible programs don't really pay attention to this (because it's rather inefficient, not to mention downright silly). Some PCX readers also don't obey the rule that run-length packets can continue from one color plane to the next within a scanline. Thus arise some of the many flavor variations in the format. Your best bet for compatibility is to remember the PCX motto ("K.I.S.S.") and try to keep the scanline length and the image size the same whenever possible while never creating a run-length that goes past the end of a scanline.

Working Code: Reading and Writing PCX Files

To read and write image data with these functions, you must allocate a block of memory big enough to hold all the image data. Then, pass this pointer to the readpcx() and writepcx() functions.

Listing 3.4. These quick-and-dirty functions will read and write plain vanilla PCX files.

```
/* PCX.C
 *
 * PCX file reader and writer
 * from Tricks of the Graphics Gurus
 * (adapted from the ZSoft Technical Reference Manual)
 */


/**** Please note that this listing is incomplete.
It is included for general copyediting reference only! ****/


#include <stdio.h>

typedef struct
{   char manufacturer;
    char version;
    char encoding;
    char bitsperpixel;
    int xmin;
    int ymin;
    int xmax;
    int ymax;
    int hres;
    int vres;
    char colormap[48];
```

```
     char reserved;
    char nplanes;
    int bytesperline;
    int palettetype;
     char filler[58];
} PCXHEADER;

PCXHEADER pcxhdr;

/* Read an entire file and store it in a (large) buffer,
   pointed to by the variable bufr
   filename is the name of the file,
   including the .pcx extension */

int readpcx(char *bufr, char *filename)
{   int i;
    long l, linesize;
    unsigned char block, count;
    FILE *pcxfile;
    if ((pcxfile = fopen(filename, "rb")) == NULL) return(0);
    pcxhdr.manufacturer = getc(pcxfile);
    if (pcxhdr.manufacturer != 10)
    {   fclose(pcxfile);
        return(0);
    }
    pcxhdr.version = getc(pcxfile);
    pcxhdr.encoding = getc(pcxfile);
    pcxhdr.bitsperpixel = fgetc(pcxfile);
    pcxhdr.xmin = getw(pcxfile);
    pcxhdr.ymin = getw(pcxfile);
    pcxhdr.xmax = getw(pcxfile);
    pcxhdr.ymax = getw(pcxfile);
    pcxhdr.hres = getw(pcxfile);
    pcxhdr.vres = getw(pcxfile);
    fread(pcxhdr.colormap, 48, sizeof(char), pcxfile);
    pcxhdr.reserved = getc(pcxfile);
    pcxhdr.nplanes = getc(pcxfile);
    pcxhdr.bytesperline = getw(pcxfile);
    pcxhdr.palettetype = getw(pcxfile);
    fread(pcxhdr.filler, 58, sizeof(char), pcxfile);
    linesize = (long) pcxhdr.bytesperline * pcxhdr.nplanes *
                    (1 + pcxhdr.ymax - pcxhdr.ymin);
```

continues

107

Listing 3.4. continued

```
    for (l = 0; l < linesize; )                /* increment by count below */
    {   if (readpcxblock(&block, &count, pcxfile) == EOF) break;
        for (i = 0; i < count; i++)
            *bufr++ = block;
        l += count;
    }
}


/* Read one encoded block from the pcx
   file and store a count and data byte.
   If the code is greater than 0xc0 (192), go for a run.
   Otherwise, just grab a byte.
   Result: 0 = valid data stored
           EOF = out of data in file

    int *pblock;        where to place data
    int *pcount;        where to place count
    FILE *pcxfile;          image file handle
*/

int readpcxblock(int *pblock, int *pcount, FILE *pcxfile)
{   int i;
    *pcount = 1;
    if ((i = getc(pcxfile)) == EOF) return(EOF);
    if (0xc0 == (0xc0 & i))         /* is it greater than 192? */
    {   *pcount = 0x3f&i;           /* subtract 192 to get count */
        if((i = getc(pcxfile)) == EOF) return(EOF);
    }
    *pblock = i;
    return(0);
}


/* This subroutine encodes one scanline
   and writes it to a pcx file, given:
   unsigned char *inBuff;   pointer to scanline data
   int inLen;               length of raw scanline in bytes
   FILE *pcxfile;               file to be written to

   returns number of bytes written into outBuff,
   or 0 if failed
*/
```

```c
int writepcxline(unsigned char *inBuff, int inLen, FILE *pcxfile)
{   unsigned char this, last;
    int srcIndex, i;
    register int total;
    register unsigned char runCount;
    total = 0;
    last = *(inBuff);
    runCount = 1;
    for (srcIndex = 1; srcIndex < inLen; srcIndex++)
    {   this = *(++inBuff);
        if (this == last)
        {   runCount++;
            if (runCount == 63)      /* max single run is 63 */
            {   if (!(i=writebyte(last, runCount, pcxfile)))
                    return(0);
                total += i;
                runCount = 0;
            }
        }
        else
        {   if (runCount)
            {   if (!(i=writebyte(last, runCount, pcxfile)))
                    return(0);
                total += i;
            }
            last = this;
            runCount = 1;
        }
    }
    if (runCount)                /* finish up */
    {   if (!(i=writebyte(last, runCount, pcxfile)))
            return(0);
        return(total + i);
    }
    return(total);
}

/*  Write an encoded byte pair (or single byte if it
    doesn't encode) to a pcx file
    (returns count of bytes written, 0 if err)
*/
```

continues

Listing 3.4. continued

```
int writebyte(unsigned char byt, unsigned char cnt, FILE *pcxfile)
{   if(cnt)
    {   if( (cnt==1) && (0xc0 != (0xc0&byt)) )
        {   if(EOF == putc((int)byt, pcxfile))
                return(0); /* disk write error (probably full) */
            return(1);
        }
        else
        {   if(EOF == putc((int)0xC0 ¦ cnt, pcxfile))
                return(0);      /* disk write error */
          if(EOF == putc((int)byt, pcxfile))
                return(0);      /* disk write error */
          return(2);
        }
    }
    return(0);
}
```

GIF Files

Most hardware-specific formats make use of a positional structure. In such a scheme, the location of data in the file determines what the data means... While this structure is very efficient, it is also resistant to change. And while this may not necessarily be bad, changes are inevitable in a long-lived program... One approach to alleviating this problem is to place a tag at the beginning of each data field. This tag tells the reading software what the following data is. You can then easily add new fields or even delete old ones. Old software can simply ignore the fields it does not understand. While this does not eliminate all problems, it helps considerably by creating a flexible format that can readily be expanded to incorporate new features.

The Graphics Interchange Format was developed by CompuServe in 1987 to fill a need for a color-image transfer protocol. GIF was designed to support image dimensions of up to 64,000 pixels, 256 colors our of a 16-million-color palette, multiple images in a single file, rapid decoding for on-line viewing, efficient compression, and hardware independence. The format itself makes some use of tag fields. Although most of the file information is stored in a positional header, the format switches to a tag structure thereafter.

—Gerald L. Graef, "Graphics Formats," *BYTE* September 89

CompuServe's graphics interchange format (GIF) is one of the most stable and clearly defined image file standards around. You've gotta give the folks at CIS some brownie points for creating a standard that could survive essentially unchanged for nearly a decade and still be a long way from obsolescence. (Of course, they weren't going for brownie points—they were after megabucks, which they neatly capture from all the users who upload and download GIF files at upwards of $12 an hour.) About the only inconsistency you'll encounter when dealing with GIFs is how the acronym is pronounced: The CIS gods on high proclaim that, "choosy users choose GIF," whereas a marginal majority of choosy users accept the standard as a "GIFT" without the final T.

To achieve such consistent standardization, CompuServe is rather uptight about legal ownership of the name "GIF" and the file format specification itself. They demand that any GIF-compatible application prominently display the message: "The Graphics Interchange Format © is the Copyright property of CompuServe Incorporated. GIF ™ is a Service Mark property of CompuServe Incorporated." They do, however, generously grant a "limited, non-exclusive, royalty-free license for the use of the Graphics Interchange Format™ in computer software" to anybody and everybody, including you and me.

After all these years of faithful service, however, the GIF standard is beginning to show its age. For one thing, the GIF specs don't whisper a word about high color or true color. Because GIF files can only handle images with 256 colors or less, most high-powered graphics applications don't support the GIF format for output— though they usually will read a GIF file and translate it into a more flexible format.

LZW Compression

To minimize your online transfer time for downloading an image by modem (and thus entice you into downloading even more images), CompuServe uses one of the most efficient data compression algorithms known to humankind. This technique, called Limpel-Ziv & Welch (LZW) compression after the folks who originally hacked it out in the early 1980s, is essentially the same algorithm used by all major data compression programs, including Stacker, DOS 6.0, PKZIP, and LHA. Other advanced data compression algorithms can pack data more tightly, and simple algorithms such as RLE are faster than LZW. But LZW provides a good middle-of-the-road approach—it's the most space-efficient compression algorithm that can pack up a good-sized image file in a few seconds or less on today's PCs.

To compress an image using LZW, you create a *string table* that holds each pixel pattern found in the file. As you scan through the image, you compare each string of pixels on the screen with each pattern in the string table. If you find a match, you can store the string number instead of the whole string itself. If you don't find a match, you write the whole string itself to the file and add the pattern to the string table. As you continue through the rest of the pixels, you are essentially building a custom lookup table of every recognizable pattern in the image.

The magical part of LZW is that you don't need to store the string table with the image. Because each new string was stored in the file as it was recognized, you can reconstruct the whole table as you decompress the image.

When Terry Welch revealed the secrets of LZW compression to the world in 1984, he left some room for variations in the algorithm. For example, you could theoretically use strings of any length for the pattern matching. You could even vary the length of the strings as you proceed through the file, building a few simple, short patterns first and then looking for longer patterns once the simple ones were pretty much exhausted. The GIF standard implements a simple version of variable-length strings: when storing 8-bit pixels, the first few strings will be 9-bit codes. When you add the 512th entry to the string table, you start using 10-bit codes. At the 1024th entry, you switch to 11-bit codes and, at the 2048th entry, to 12-bit codes. (When encoding small images, you will reach the end of the image before you make it to 12 bits.)

GIF files also use another extension to the LZW algorithm: *clear codes.* Saving all those string patterns takes up more and more memory as you go along. In some cases, an encoder program may not have enough memory available to store every pattern it finds in the table. It must then clear the string table and start building it all over again. When this happens, the encoder can write a special code called a clear code to the file. The clear code tells any decoder that reads the file to clear its string table at the same point.

Remember that GIF's fancy compression algorithm won't save you two bits of disk space or telephone time if you already use an LZW compression program on your files. If you've got DOS 6.0 on your hard drive and habitually "zip up" your modem transmissions with PKZIP or LHA, a cold-molasses GIF encoder will just waste your time. Consider using a faster, more flexible image format such as TGA or PCX for image storage and use GIFs only when you have to (that is, when exchanging images via CompuServe). If you are not accustomed to compressing everything you store or send, GIF painlessly ensures that at least your image files are using as little disk space and modem time as possible.

Jumping into the Data Stream

The structure of a GIF file is much more complex than the image formats I discussed earlier in this chapter. Instead of a simple header followed by a big gob of image data, GIF files can contain several different types of *data blocks*. There are three basic types of data blocks: *control blocks* contain identifying information about the hardware configuration and how to process the other types of blocks, *graphic-rendering blocks* contain the actual image data, and *special purpose blocks* contain application-specific information and comments. The assemblage of all these blocks is called the *data stream*. (Can you tell that the guys at CompuServe get a kick out of making up new techie-sounding phrases? Part of the fun of owning a standard, you know.)

Table 3.3 lists each of the data blocks you'll find in the GIF data stream, as defined in the original GIF specification. The more recent specification, called GIF89a, is identical to the original, called GIF87a, except for the addition of several application-specific extension blocks not listed in Table 3.3. If you need to add special secret information to your GIF files, download the GIF89A.DOC file mentioned earlier for all the nitty-gritty on the new block types. Otherwise, always put the header "GIF87a" on your GIF files for maximum compatibility with all GIF readers.

Table 3.3. To construct a GIF file, toss a few of these data blocks into the data stream.

Block Name	Size	Format and Description
Header	6 bytes	The ASCII text "GIF87a" or "GIF89a" (must be the first block in the data stream)
Logical Screen Descriptor	7 bytes	Size of the screen or screen window (must be the second block in the data stream)
		Bytes 0-1 = logical screen width
		Bytes 2-3 = logical screen height

continues

Table 3.3. continued

Block Name	Size	Format and Description
		Bits 0-2 of byte 4 = Size of global color table - 1 (7 means 8-bit color, 3 means 4-bit color)
		Bit 3 of byte 4 = Color table sort flag (0 means the color table is not sorted, 1 means sorted with most frequently used color first)
		Bits 4-6 of byte 4 = Color resolution - 1 (e.g. for 8-bit color, use 7)
		Bit 7 of byte 4 = Global color table flag (0 means no global color table, 1 means a global color table follows)
		Byte 5 = Global background color (color number to use for blank areas)
		Byte 6 = Pixel aspect ratio (height/width * 64 - 15)
Global Color Table	768 or 16	Color values for palette to apply to all images (Three bytes per color in red, green, blue order)
Image Descriptor	10	Description of the next image
		Byte 0 = Image separator (always = 48 decimal)
		Byte 1-2 = Image left edge relative to logical screen
		Bytes 3-4 = Image top edge relative to logical screen
		Bytes 5-6 = Image width
		Bytes 7-8 = Image height
		Bits 0-2 of byte 9 = Size of local color table - 1 (7 means 8-bit color, 3 means 4-bit color)

Block Name	Size	Format and Description
		Bits 3-4 of byte 9 = Meaningless (reserved for future use)
		Bit 5 of byte 9 = Sort flag
		(0 means unsorted color local table,
		1 means sorted with more frequently used color first)
		Bit 6 of byte 9 = Interlace flag
		(0 means image is not interlaced,
		1 means image is interlaced)
		Bit 7 of byte 9 = Local color table flag
		(0 means use global color table,
		1 means local color table follows)
Local Color Table	768 or 16	Palette color values for the next image only
Image Data	(size varies)	One byte containing the minimum (starting) LZW code size, followed by the actual LZW-compressed image data
Data Sub-block	(size varies)	One byte specifying the size of the block, followed by whatever data type was previously specified in a control block
Block Terminator Sub-block	1	Just the number 0. Used to terminate a series of Data Sub-blocks

To Saturn and Back in a GIF

Whether you add GIF support to your own graphics programs, or simply use the SVGA shareware file viewer included with this book to check out the images you download from graphics bulletin board systems, you will discover a universe of GIFs out there to explore. Almost all online services (CompuServe, GEnie, America Online, and so on) have libraries of fascinating computer-generated scenes, NASA space photos, and other hard-to-find images. If your hormones are hyped and you can't pry yourself away from the computer long enough to go buy a copy of Playboy, you may want to join some of the BBSs that specialize in racy shots, too. Figures 3.6 and 3.7 are a couple of GIFs that I found on my favorite BBS, The Graphics Alternative (510-524-2780, the first 90 days access are free). If you have a modem and are eager to snag some stunning GIFs of your own, try dialing a few of the other graphics BBS numbers listed in the bibliography of this book.

Figure 3.6. *256-color Voyager digital photos such as this flyby of Saturn and its moons are among the most popular GIF files on many BBSs.*

Figure 3.8 demonstrates why the GIF standard now includes specifications for application-specific data blocks. In addition to the actual pixel data for the image, this GIF contains information about the fractal type and mathematical parameters used to generate the image in the first place. If you loaded this GIF into FRACTINT, the freeware fractal generator used to create it, the application-specific blocks would give the program enough information to recompute the image at a higher resolution, or to zoom in and magnify a region of the image far beyond the level of detail you see here. When another graphics application (such as the SVGA viewer) loads this GIF, it will simply ignore the FRACTINT-specific extension blocks and read the image itself.

Figure 3.7. *Most graphics Bulletim Board Systems, such as the Trinity BBS, are operated by dedicated graphics gurus and have oodles of computer-generated GIFs online.*

Figure 3.8. *Some places you just can't go without a computer. This GIF image of a mathematical formula was produced with the famous freeware fractal program, FRACTINT.*

117

Where to Find GIF Code

Though GIF routines are not included with this book, you'll find plenty of source code for encoding and decoding GIFs in the Graphics Support Forum (GO GRAPHSUP) Developer's Den (Library 13) on CompuServe Information Service. If you drop by the Developer's Den, you'll find many other GIF readers and encoders for a variety of computer systems, as well as a 30-page text file (GIF89A.DOC) describing the GIF format in painstaking detail. Many other graphics BBSes also have GIF code and copies of the GIF89A.DOC file, as well.

TIFF Files

TIFF (or Tagged Image File Format) is one of the most versatile—and frustrating—formats on the market today. It's versatile because the latest version (6.0) supports many different imaging technologies. That same versatility, though, creates the frustration: Given all the possible variations and combinations, conflicts are bound to arise. A vendor might support only a subset of the TIFF specification. If another program doesn't provide the same or overlapping functions, it will exhibit compatibility problems. It is particularly annoying that applications tend to be great at telling you they can't import a particular file, but universally terrible about telling you why *they can't.*

—Frank J. Derfler, Jr., "Solutions: Graphics,"
PC Magazine, March 16, 1993

Neither TGA nor PCX nor GIF alone can serve all your graphics needs. If you juggle a lot of graphics files, you have no doubt fantasized about a universal file format. Desktop publishers, who often need to deal with images from diverse sources, are especially prone to the frustrations of time-consuming file conversions. In the mid 1980s, graphics software giants Aldus and Microsoft put their corporate heads together to formulate a universal file format for scanner vendors and desktop publishing software.

Their brainchild, which they christened *tagged image file format* (TIFF), has grown far beyond the expectations of its designers. Almost all desktop publishing and advanced graphics editing software now support some form of TIFF. Aye, but there's the rub: there are so many varieties of TIFF files that one man's TIFF is often another man's trash. As mentioned earlier, multiple flavors can make reading PCX files like taking a kid to the ice cream shop—try a little of each, and see which one tastes right. But if reading a PCX is like buying Ben & Jerry's, choosing the right flavor of TIFF is more like visiting a Baskin-Robbins. This confusion of flavors means that TIFF is indeed universal enough for almost any kind of file. It also means that dealing with incompatible TIFF variations is distasteful enough so that many graphics connoisseurs turn up their noses at TIFFs whenever any other format is available.

A True TIFF Story

Because TIFFs are so flexible, they are ideal when you use a set of graphics applications that you know enjoy the same flavor of TIFF. For example, Figures 3.9 through 3.12 tell the tale of a desktop publishing project I actually created for an art reception scheduled for a year from today. The true color and 8-bit grayscale TIFF files meandered through the maze of Windows graphics software without a hitch, from the rough sketch and scan to the final PageMaker document.

Figure 3.9. *I sketched this portrait with a WACOM digitizing pen and tablet using Fractal Design Corporation's Painter software and saved it as a true color TIFF file.*

Tag—You're It

Like a GIF file, a TIFF file consists of a very short header, followed by a series of data blocks. Each block (called a *field* in TIFF-lingo) has a coded *tag* identifying the type of data contained in the block.

Figure 3.10. *I scanned this hand-marbled rice paper within Logitech FotoTouch Color software and also saved it as a true color TIFF.*

Figure 3.11. *In Aldus Photostyler, I loaded the TIFFs shown in Figures 3.09 and 3.10, adjusted the contrast, and converted them to grayscale. Then I pasted the cartoon over the marbled design and saved the result as another TIFF.*

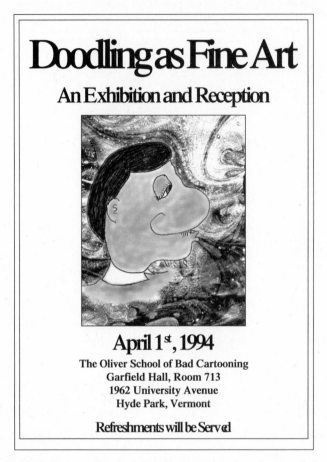

Figure 3.12. *To produce this finished document, I placed and cropped the TIFF in Aldus PageMaker, added the text, and printed the result on my laser printer.*

Unlike a GIF, however, a TIFF file also contains an *image file directory* (IFD) which lists the type and location of every data block in the file. Each entry in the directory contains a *pointer* to the location of the associated data in the file. Because these directory entries can point to any part of the file, you can actually write *strips* of image data to the file in any order you like when creating a TIFF. Table 3.4 lists the parts of a TIFF file in the normal order that they occur.

Table 3.4. A TIFF file starts with a small header, followed by the image file directory. The actual data comes last, at the locations specified in the directory.

Header	(Always the first 8 bytes in the file)	
Byte order	(2 bytes)	LL means least to most significant (Motorola order)
		MM means most to least significant (Intel order)
Version	(2 bytes)	Use the number 42
Location of directory	(4 bytes)	Offset of image file directory from start of file
Image File Directory		
Number of Entries	(2 bytes)	Always at the start of the directory
Directory Entries	(Each entry contains the following 12 bytes)	
Tag	(2 bytes)	Coded value indicating the nature of the data
Data type	(2 bytes)	Coded value indicating the exact type of data
Length of data	(4 bytes)	Size of data in terms of type
Locatation of data	(4 bytes)	Offset of data from start of file
Location of next directory	(4 bytes)	Offset of next image file directory from beginning of file
Data values	(Actual data referenced in the directory)	

In order to read and write TIFF files yourself, you obviously need to know the actual code values for the Tags and data types, along with a slew of other technical details. You need to trust me on this one—you don't want to venture into the labyrinth of TIFF by yourself. TIFF files can support several types of image compression, several different color models, and several obscure parameters, such as *planar configurations, transparency masks, gamma correction,* and even a bunch of Group 3 and 4 FAX options. If you have the time and ambition to wade through this quagmire, by all means call up Microsoft, ask for a copy of the complete TIFF standard, and jump in. But if you can think of more interesting things to do with your computer (which I bet you can), you might prefer to try a TIFF toolkit.

A TIFF Toolkit

Spyro Gumas, the graphics guru who will guide you to image processing enlightenment in Chapter 13, has built a road through the swamplands of TIFF. His TIFF256 Library Extension for C Programmers is included on the disk with this book. So, if you want TIFF input and output for your programs, take off your hip waders and stroll down TIFF256 Boulevard instead.

To use the TIFF256 library, you'll also need to take advantage of the VSA256 library, which is also included on the disk. VSA256 is a Super VGA graphics library that supports many advanced rendering tools not found in any other graphics programming system. These souped-up Super VGA tools include color-shaded lines and triangles as well as super-fast functions to read and write raster lines—the kind of stuff that advanced TIFF-oriented applications need, but the other graphics libraries supported by TransGraphics just don't offer.

Spyro ordinarily distributes reduced-performance versions of VSA256 and TIFF256 as shareware, and then offers the full package only to registered users. To help you make the most of Super VGA and TIFF without waiting for the upgrade, the complete *registered* versions of both libraries are included on the disk with complete text documentation manuals (see Appendix C and Appendix D). Please note that, even though the most advanced versions of the libraries are included on the disk, you must still pay Spyro the shareware registration fee of $25 if you wish to continue using the software after you evaluate it. (This special $25 offer covers use of both the VSA256 library and TIFF256 library, which normally cost $20 each.)

In addition to peace of mind and an infinite pile of chocolate chip cookies in the afterlife, you will get some immediate tangible benefits from registering. Spyro is constantly improving the libraries, and by the time you read this, he will be able to send you a new version of the libraries supporting more TIFF file types and options. Please send your registration fee (which includes an update to the absolute latest and greatest) directly to:

Spyro Gumas
1668 Shady Brook Drive
Fullerton, CA 92631

Important: Because the libraries included with this book are *not* normally distributed as shareware, you may not copy or distribute them without written permission of their author.

If you want to learn more about the VSA256 and TIFF256 libraries now, refer to Appendix C and Appendix D.

Vector File Formats

One of the simplest and most versatile graphics formats is the shape-defined format. This format defines as image as a series of geometric shapes and patterns. CAD programs store images in this manner because it is usually not necessary for them to define color values for every pixel.

       —Gerald L. Graef, "Graphics Formats," *BYTE*, September 1989

Some image file formats don't actually store images at all—they store mathematical descriptions of points, lines, rectangles, and other two- or three-dimensional shapes. These shapes are recreated from the mathematical descriptions (called *vector data*) each time you display a file. Vector-based formats are ideal when you want to be able to rearrange and alter individual elements in a picture, or redraw the picture at different sizes without loss of image quality.

DXF Files

Autodesk, Inc., originally designed the *Drawing eXchange Format* (DXF) as a means of getting information in and out of its AutoCAD application from almost any source. Due to the commercial success of AutoCAD and the ease with which developers can add DXF support to their programs, DXF has become the most popular vector file format on PCs. Any Computer Aided Drafting or Computer Aided Design (CAD) program worth its salt will import and export DXF files.

DXF files are made up of normal ASCII text. This means that, unlike bitmapped image files, you can actually open up a DXF file with a word processor or test editor and read or modify it by hand if you understand the basic format. Table 3.5 presents a general overview of a DXF file.

Table 3.5. Drawing eXchage Format (DXF) files can contain all these sections, but they often contain just the ENTITIES and END OF FILE sections.

Section	Contents
HEADER	General information about the drawing, in the form of variable names and their associated values.
TABLES	Definitions of line types, layers, text style, coordinate systems, and other technical stuff.
BLOCKS	Definitions of entities which should be associated with one another to form "blocks" in the drawing.
ENTITIES	The meat and potatoes. All the actual shape definitions go here.
END OF FILE	Just what you think it is.

You could spend a long time learning the official names and uses of all th HEADER variables, TABLES definitions and ENTITIES types that can go into a DXF file. But one of the beauties of DXF is that you only need to know the codes for the specific entities you want to deal with. If you only needed to draw outlined polygons, for example, you could create a DXF file with a number of 3DLINE entities without learning anything about the many other types of entities that might occur in other DXF files. Likewise, you could easily create a DXF reader that ignored anything other than 3DLINE entities.

Listing 3.7 shows you what the DXF file pictured in Figure 3.13 would look like if you read it with a text editor or word processor. (The comments, preceded by < - - are not part of the file.)

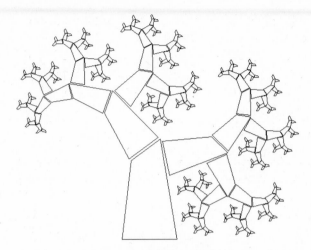

Figure 3.13. *The DXF file in Listing 3.7 looks like this when the geometry is interpreted by a DXF-compatible CAD or graphics program.*

Listing 3.5. This DXF file was created by the 3DLINES program in Chapter 7. It draws a number of lines in 3-D space, called 3DLINES in DXF-talk.

```
0      <-- 0 means we're starting something
SECTION   <-- What are we starting? A section.
2      <-- What section? The ENTITIES section --
ENTITIES  <-- (The only section you really need.)
0      <-- Starting something else
3DLINE  <-- A line segment in 3-D space.
10   <-- First X coordinate coming up
218.998734     <-- The x coordinate
20   <-- First Y coordinate coming up
-454.996979     <-- The y coordinate
30 <-- First Z coordinate coming up
111.345833        <-- The z coordinate
11 <-- Second X coordinate coming up
235.077179        <-- Second x
21 <-- Second Y coordinate coming up
-311.133514        <-- Second y
31 <-- Second Z coordinate coming up
132.345688        <-- Second z
```

continues

127

Listing 3.5. continued

```
0
3DLINE  <-- next polyline

...more coordinates and 3-D lines...

0
ENDSEC    <-- End of ENTITIES section
0
EOF  <-- End of file
```

Because DXF files contain complex geometry, C functions to read and write DXFs must be tailored to the specific application at hand. The two-dimensional and three-dimensional animation programs presented in Chapters 7 and 8 contain working code to create DXF files. If you want to know more about the DXF standard, complete specifications are available from Autodesk, Inc. (2320 Marinship Way, Sausalito, CA 94965).

An NAPLPS a Day...

DXF is by no means the only player in the vector storage field. Before the advent of DXF, the most popular geometry-description file format was the *North American Presentation-Level Protocol Syntax* (NAPLPS) defined by the American National Standards Institute (ANSI). (For those of you who like to know these things, the actual standard number implemented in most NAPLPS files is X3.110-1983.) NAPLPS is actually a bit more nimble than DXF when it comes to fancy footwork like scaled, rotated text and mosaic graphics. DXF has endured longer on the dance floor, however, due to the fact that it is much easier to implement and it handles composite "mesh" shapes, solid geometry, and surfaces more elegantly than NAPLPS.

IGES Told You...

Though DXF is currently the star of the vector-geometry show and NAPLPS is the old-time favorite, another ANSI standard history may record IGES as the most enduring and talented file-transfer standard of our time. IGES stands for *Initial*

Graphics Exchange Specification. Like DXF, it is a plain-text format designed primarily for transferring drawings from one CAD program to another. You won't find any software that actually uses IGES for day-to-day drawing storage (each program has its own proprietary file format), but all major CAD systems support IGES import and export.

IGES files consist almost entirely of cryptic numerical codes, so you will find it much easier to read and write DXF files. If you do have a need to support IGES in your own programs, the complete specification is available from the American National Standards Institute. You'll find their address in the bibliography.

And All the Rest

Behold, they are one people, and they have all one language; and this is only the beginning of what they will do; and nothing that they propose to do will now be impossible for them. Come, let us go down, and there confuse their language, that they may not understand one another's speech.

—The Lord speaks of the city Babel, Genesis 11:6-7

Back at the dawn of time (about 1945), there was a single universal file format for everything. This was largely due to the fact that there was only one digital computer in existence. Shortly thereafter, the Lord pulled that "confuse their language" trick again and the rest is history.

These days, a 486 tower is about as far from the Tower of Babel as you can get, especially when it comes to graphics file formats. In addition to the major players covered earlier in this chapter, there are literally dozens of languages and dialects in common use for storing images. I can't describe all of them for you (this book only has a thousand pages or so, and I want to save most of them for much more exciting material). I can, however, tell you enough about all but the most obscure formats so that you'll at least know what you've got if you find some WPG or PIC files laying around on your hard drive. Table 3.6 is your quick-reference to the PC graphics polyglot.

Table 3.6. The three-letter file extension attached to a graphics file will usually give away where it came from and what software you need to read it.

Extension	What is it?
AI	Adobe Illustrator Postscript (vector) drawing (a valid EPS file in disguise)
BMP	Microsoft Windows bitmap (can be used for Windows wallpaper)
CDR	CorelDRAW vector drawing file
CGM	Computer Graphics Metafile (another "universal standard" that never caught on)
DCX	A bunch of PCX images all crammed into one file (thank Intel for it)
DIB	Microsoft Windows Device Independant Bitmap
DRW	Micrografx Designer vector drawing file
DXF	AutoCAD vector Drawing eXchange File
EPS	Encapsulated Postscript file (can be printed or read by most Postscript-compatible programs)
FIF	Fractal Image Format file (highly compressed bitmapped image stored as fractals)
FLC	Autodesk Animator Pro high-resolution bitmapped animation file
FLI	Autodesk Animator low-resolution (320x200 256-color) animation file
GIF	CompuServe Graphics Interchange Format compressed bitmap
HPG	Hewlett-Packard Plotter Graphics Language (used by vector printing devices)
IFF	A graphics file that snuck onto your machine from an Amiga (also called HAM)
JPG	Highly compressed format design by the Joint Photographic Experts Group (JPEG)

Extension	What is it?
MAC	MacPaint format from the Apple Macintosh computer
MPG	Bitmapped animation using JPEG compression
PCL	Hewlett Packard Printer Control Language (for LaserJet-compatible printers)
PCT	Apple MacIntosh PICT format bitmap (also sometimes given the PIC extension)
PCX	ZSoft's PC Paintbrush bitmap format
PIC	Could be a picture from Pictor/PC Paint or from Lotus 1-2-3 charting (several other programs also use this extension for incompatible file formats!)
PUB	Used by a number of desktop publishing programs, including Microsoft Publisher and PFS:First Publisher
RLE	Either an old CompuServe bitmap (from before GIF was invented)...
RLE	...or a Microsoft Windows run-length encoded bitmap
TGA	Bitmap format originally created for Truevision Targa boards
TIF	Tagged Image File Format used by many graphics programs
WMF	Microsoft Windows MetaFile (either a DIB image or just a link to the drawing application)
WPG	WordPerfect vector drawing or bitmap image

Converting Between Formats

If you find yourself encountering several of these formats during the course of your graphics pursuits, consider buying a dedicated graphics file conversion program. Three commercial programs that do a passable job with most of the formats listed in Table 3.6 are Conversion Artist ($149 from North Coast Software, 18A Shipley Rd, PO Box

459, Barrington, NH 03825), HiJaak for Windows ($249 from Inset Systems, 71 Commerce Dr, Brookfield, CT 06804) and Image Pals ($249 from U-Lead Systems, 970 West 190th St, Suite 520, Torrance, CA 90502). All of these run under Microsoft Windows, though Inset Systems also offers a version of HiJaack for DOS.

I personally use Graphic Workshop ($40 from Alchemy Mindworks, PO Box 500, Beeton, Ontario, Canada, L0G 1A0) for almost all my file conversion, printing, and image shuffling. Graphic Workshop is also available as shareware, and you can get a full working copy to evaluate for $5 (see the order form in the back of this book). If you have an image editing program that supports multiple file formats (such as the shareware Paintshop Pro, also on the order form in the back), you can convert between them by simply loading an image from one type of file and saving it to another.

Onward and Upward

All in all, selecting and implementing a storage format for your graphics files is a crazy and complicated business. For the rest of the book, we'll use the ready-to-call functions provided in this chapter to save and load files and you won't have to mess around with the kind of picky details we've covered here again.

Instead, you can mess around with real-time animation, 3-D rendering, inter-active modeling, and high-powered functions to make high-impact images. Away we go...

Setting Things in Motion

II

Tweening and Morphing

Morphing, the magical transformation of one shape, animal, or person into another, is one of today's most coveted graphics special effects. It's also the key to all serious computerized animation. To explain these sacred secrets of graphics alchemy, I call upon the powers of graphics guru Scott Anderson, the author of FantaVision animation software (Wild Duck Software, 1991) and the hot new book, *Morphing Magic* (SAMS Publishing, 1993). In this chapter and the next, Scott will teach you how to perform a repertoire of transformation tricks, and some surprising graphics sleight of hand as well.

In Chapter 7, I (Dick Oliver) will return to show you how Scott's morphing magic can be applied to infinitely detailed, natural-looking shapes called fractals. See you then.

Computer Animation

In traditional animation, images are painted on clear acetate sheets called "cels." Every gesture of the characters must be reduced to tiny advancements of movement from cel to cel. So much drawing is required that animation studios are organized so that the work can be divided efficiently. There is usually a principal animator who draws the key-frames, the definitive moments in the sequence, while intermediate frames are drawn by others, the so-called "in-betweeners."

—Richard Mark Friedhoff, *Visualization*,
1989, Harry N. Abrams, Inc.: New York

Tweening and *morphing* are funny words for two powerful animation techniques. At root, these concepts are virtually identical, yet one yields simple prosaic animation, whereas the other produces mesmerizing transformations. In this chapter, I touch upon these methods as they apply to polygon-based animation. Several programs and animations illustrate these concepts. I also discuss bit-mapped image morphing, made popular by *Terminator II* and the Michael Jackson video, "Black or White."

Although these techniques may seem relatively limited, you'll be surprised at the wide range of problems they address. Modern movie-making would not be the same without them. As the previous quote suggests, animation is not for the faint of heart. Tweening and morphing immediately find favor with those artists who have toiled over the cels and appreciate the difficulty involved.

As you will discover, this is a perfect niche for a computer: performing a tedious exercise over and over. Rather than putting people out of work, this technology liberates them to pursue their most creative ideas without the hindrance and expense of traditional animation.

Tweening

Photography is truth. The cinema is truth twenty-four times per second.

—Jean-Luc Godard

Animation is a trick. Flash a few pictures fast enough, and you can be fooled into seeing motion. Hundreds of years before pictures were projected on a beam of light, they were printed on flip books. Then came the *phenakistiscope* (1832), the *zoetrope* (1834), the *phantasmatrope* (1870), the *praxinoscope* (1892) and the *cinematographe* (1895). Mercifully, if perhaps unpoetically, we can now just go to the movies.

The illusion occurs because of a phenomena called the *persistence of vision*. Peter Mark Roget first sketched out this theory in 1824—when he wasn't too busy writing the Thesaurus (really). The theory goes like this: while one image fades, the next one is received. The brain registers the slight changes between the two images as continuous motion. The faster the images are presented, the smoother the effect.

Rapidity requires two conditions:

- The images must be fast enough so they don't fade from the "mind's eye."

- They must be fast enough for only a slight change in position. If the position changes too much, motion will either be misperceived or not perceived at all.

An example of misperception is the backward-moving wagon wheel in western movies. As the chase heats up, you suddenly notice that the spoked wheels on the stagecoach are lazily spinning backward. The camera has captured the wheel at a rate too slow to follow its spokes. The eye makes a match with the closest spoke, but it's not the same spoke (and it's in the wrong direction). Seeing is believing, and in this case perception overrides logic. Against all the other evidence, your eye convinces you that the wheels are slowly rolling backward.

At first glance, persistence of vision seems a rather strange and relatively useless visual capacity, but you can easily see how it might come in handy. It is persistence of vision that enables you to see someone moving behind a picket fence or a bamboo thicket. These confounding foregrounds act as the shutter blades of a camera, permitting you to see only a slice of the picture at a time. Without persistence of vision, you couldn't tell the difference between a loaf of bread and a stalking lion behind the trees in the jungle. That could make the difference between *having* lunch and *being* lunch.

A TV screen flashes images at 30 frames per second. A feature at the movie theater runs 24 frames per second. Any slower than that, and the illusion breaks up. The first movies were shot at about 15 frames per second. This is right at the edge of working, and you can recognize an old movie from their flickering. Sometimes these movies are played back at 20 frames per second to reduce flicker, but then everyone runs around at high speed, looking slightly silly and out of breath.

For a typical cartoon, all frames are hand-drawn. This makes traditional animation a Herculean effort. Dozens of artists are required for the simplest animation.

When the coyote straps on Acme springs and hops off in pursuit of the roadrunner, that 10 seconds of action can require 200 or more drawings! No wonder the credits are so long. A lot of people work very hard to produce the smooth motion that makes a good cartoon.

In most major animation studios, a few artists with seniority draw the key frames of the cartoon, such as the coyote eyeing the Acme box, or pulling out the springs, or strapping them on. Depending on the scene, the key frames may be one to ten seconds apart. They then send these pictures to the dozens of artists who draw the frames in-between those key frames. These folks are called *in-betweeners* or "*tweeners,*" and they draw the "tweens." These drawings change very little from frame to frame, so the tweener's job is exacting and tedious, not to mention underpaid.

How does a tweener do the job? One way is to look at the two key frames and draw a picture midway between them. That's a good start, but usually more than one frame stands between two key frames. So a tweener could draw another frame between the first and the middle frame, and yet another between the middle and the last. Now three equally spaced frames lie between the first and last. The first tween frame stands one quarter of the way between the key frames. The second is half way, and the third is three-quarters of the way.

If you continue this process of drawing a frame between two others, you finally achieve smooth motion. This leads us to a method for simple computerized tweening: divide the difference between the first and second key frames into the desired number of steps. For instance, if you wanted ten frames from the coyote looking left to the coyote looking right, the first tween would go one tenth of the way there.

But what does it mean to a computer to go one-tenth of the way from looking left to looking right? What does the "difference between key frames" mean? And how do you divide that up?

To answer these nagging questions, you need to review geometry a bit—but don't worry. This is easy. I'll do it with pictures. Figure 4.1 shows the two key frames. Frame 1 is a horizontal line on the left, and Frame 2 is a vertical line on the right. To animate smoothly from one line to the other, you've probably guessed that you'll need a diagonal line somewhere. Here's how you could calculate this.

Figure 4.2 shows both lines with dashes connecting their ends. I've marked the middles of the dashed lines.

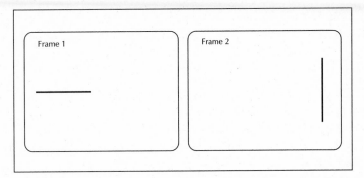

Figure 4.1. *Two key frames, with a line to be tweened. The starting line is in Frame 1 and the target line is in Frame 2.*

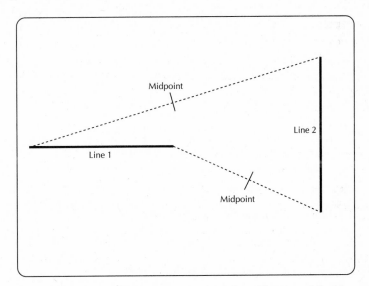

Figure 4.2. *To calculate the middle tween, connect the endpoints of the lines and find their midpoints.*

In Figure 4.3, you connect these midpoints to create the middle tween. Just as you suspected, it's a diagonal line.

Subdividing the dashed lines again in Figure 4.4 produces two more tweens. They look exactly as expected. You just did your first tweening, and it wasn't hard at all. Was it?

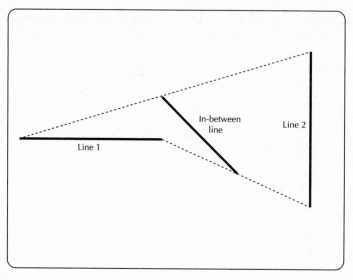

Figure 4.3. *Connect the midpoints to create a new line that lies halfway between the starting and ending lines.*

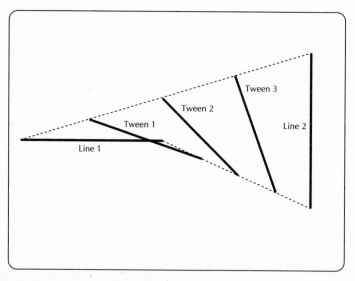

Figure 4.4. *Following the same procedure, the lines connecting the endpoints are further subdivided, producing two more tweened lines.*

If you grab a ruler and measure these lines, you'll quickly see that this algorithm does not preserve the length of the segments as it tweens. This is sometimes a problem. As you might suspect, dozens of interesting solutions exist. The most common methods involve tweening along an arc. Even this may not preserve length, so the artist must still intervene on occasion.

"But this is just a line," you might protest. "Does the same trick work with pictures?" Figure 4.5 shows a cartoon parrot drawn with straight line segments. Using enough segments, you can simulate a curved line, so you can use this trick all over the place. Later on you'll see how to tween curved lines.

Figure 4.5. *Many short, straight lines can suggest curves if they are properly placed.*

You Can Do It: The Tweening Samples

On the disk, you'll find several programs that illustrate the concepts I've just covered. One program lets you enter your own data; the others run through a random set of point values.

TWEEN1   This program lets you enter the endpoint coordinates of two line segments. Then, it tweens one line into the other, leaving a trail behind for you to examine.

Enter TWEEN1 to run the program, and select a video mode. The program prompts you for the four endpoints. Try tweening lines that span the screen, like 0,0 to 640,350 and 0,300 to 640,10. Remember that 0,0 is the top left corner of the screen, and the bottom right corner depends on the video resolution of your graphics card. If you enter points that are outside the range of your video screen, they will be clipped, so feel free to experiment. When you've entered the data, the program tweens the first line segment to the second line segment, displaying all the tweened lines in magenta. When you are through admiring your handiwork, press Esc.

Notice that you often see patterns that appear curved. If you examine the screen closely though, you'll see that all lines are straight and that the spacing between endpoints is always regular. The curves are an artifact of the rotating line.

TWEEN2   This program is similar to TWEEN1, except that it saves you the trouble of entering points. Instead, it generates random endpoints for both lines, then tweens them, again leaving a colored trail. As in TWEEN1, these trails create curved paths, suggesting an interesting use for tweens as a design element, not only for animation. Enter TWEEN2 to run the program, and select a video mode. To quit, press the Esc key.

TWEEN3   This program is a variation on TWEEN2, but without the trails. Now you see tweening in action as an animation tool. Enter TWEEN3 to run the program, and select a video mode. Again, the program generates random line segments and tweens them, but the program erases the previous image when it draws the new one, so the eye sees a moving line. Notice that the line rotates often, as it tweens from line to line. These rotations correspond to the pseudo-curved lines you saw in TWEEN2. Here, you can see that really only straight lines exist in the animation, and the curves are just an effect of the trails left behind. To quit, press the Esc key.

TWEEN4   This program extends the concept of tweening to two-dimensional polygons. Enter TWEEN4 to run the program, and select a video mode. The program generates random triangles and tweens them into each other. A trail is left behind so you can follow the algorithm. To quit, press the Esc key.

The Math Behind the Magic: 2-D Interpolation

Given two points A and B, how can you find the point midway between them? Point A is specified by the coordinates (A_x, A_y) and point B by (B_x, B_y). The midpoint M is halfway between the X values and halfway between the Y values. To go half of the way between the X values, take half the distance separating them and add it to the smaller value:

$$M_x = A_x + (B_x - A_x)/2$$

which simplifies to

$$M_x = (A_x + B_x)/2$$

This is also how you compute the average of two numbers. So you see that you can think of the midpoint as the average of the two endpoints. Computers do most things fast, but one thing they do *really* fast is divide by two. That makes this a good algorithm to keep hanging around.

The same analysis applies to Y, so you get the coordinates for M:

$$M = \{(A_x + B_x)/2, (A_y + B_y)/2\}$$

What if you want to calculate two points in between? You call these tweening points *T1* and *T2*. You can modify the first equation to go one-third of the way:

$$T1_x = A_x + (B_x - A_x)/3$$

and

$$T2_x = A_x + 2 * (B_x - A_x)/3$$

for the X coordinates and the same for Y.

In general, for the ith tween of N total tweens, you can write:

$$Ti = \{A_x + i * (B_x - A_x)/N, A_y + i * (B_y - A_y)/N\}$$

where i goes from 1 to N. Notice that when i = 0, the tweening point is just the starting point, and when i = N, it becomes the endpoint. If you precalculate the interpolation increment D (corresponding to the Delta array), you avoid the multiplication and just add D. Addition is always faster than multiplication on a PC, so do it when you can. In a loop through the tweens from 1 to N, you can repeatedly add to point A the X and Y differences given by D:

$$D_x = (B_x - A_x)/N$$
$$D_y = (B_y - A_y)/N$$

After adding this quantity N times, point A moves to point B. Although faster, any time you substitute repeated addition for multiplication, you must watch out for round-off errors.

Working Code: Sample Tweening

The two key routines of the tweening programs, calcTweens and tweenObject, are in TWEEN.C. The structures and constants needed by TWEEN.C are defined in the TWEEN.H header file. These routines use fixed-point arithmetic to represent the X and Y coordinates of the polygons to be tweened. To compile the tweening programs on the disk, use a command such as:

```
tgms tween2.c tween.c
```

This command should compile and link the modules necessary to make TWEEN2.EXE. See the introduction for more details on compiling programs with your favorite C compiler and graphics library.

The first routine is called `calcTweens`, and it creates an array named `Delta` that stores the tweening increment. This array is equal to the difference between the target and source points, divided by the number of tweens. It also initializes the array named `Tween` with the values of the starting polygon. This routine is called once every time you want to tween.

Both these arrays are in a fixed-point format, with a two byte integer and a two byte fraction. This enables faster multiplication and division on a PC, albeit without the precision of floating-point. However, because the PC graphics screen has small dimensions, this is all the precision you need. Someday all computers will have fast floating-point processors, and all programmers will be happy and have time to spare. Until then, we have fixed-point arithmetic.

This program implements fixed-point numbers in a structure called `FIXED`, which is the union of a 32-bit long word and two 16-bit integers. The long value is used in calculations. The bottom 16 bits are the fractional part, and the higher 16 bits are the actual screen coordinates. This enables you to interpolate with an accuracy of one part in 65,536—certainly good enough for most purposes.

The high words of the `Delta` array are calculated by rotating left sixteen bits before dividing by the number of tweens. This initializes the fractional part of the array. Later on, you'll see another implementation of fixed-point arithmetic.

tweenObject

The second routine is called `tweenObject`, and it adds the `Delta` array to the `Tween` array. This provides a small incremental motion to the original polygon for the given number of increments. After all that tweening, the source polygon is transformed into the target polygon.

TWEEN.H

```
/* TWEEN.H
 *
 * This header creates structures, variables and defines
 * for the tweening routines. It includes fixed-point
 * structures and unions for faster calculation of points.
 *
 * by Scott Anderson, 1/23/1993
 */


/***** Define some general constants *****/
```

145

```
#define YES             1
#define NO              0

#define BLACK       0           /* Some color defines */
#define    MAGENTA       13
#define WHITE       15          /* The top color */

#define FACTOR      16          /* bitshift factor for integer math */
#define MAX_POINTS  8           /* max dimension of point arrays */

/***** Define some structures for the point arrays *****/

typedef struct
{    /* for the screen coordinates */
     int x, y;
} POINT;

typedef struct
{    /* The difference array gets added to Tween */
     long x, y;
} DELTA;

typedef struct
{    /* The high & low words in a long word */
     int lo, hi;
} LO_HI;

typedef union
{    /* A Fixed-point union:
*a long word broken up into low & high words */
     long lword;                /* The long word portion */
     LO_HI word;                /* The high and low words of this long word */
} FIXED;

typedef struct
{    /* A fixed-point coordinate pair */
     FIXED x, y;
} TWEEN;
```

TWEEN2.C

As an example of how to call these routines, here's the code for TWEEN2. This program generates random line pairs and tweens one into another without erasing, so you can examine the process.

```c
/* TWEEN2.C
 *
 * This program tweens random lines, leaving a trail behind.
 *
 * by Scott Anderson, 1/23/1993
 */


/***** Includes *****/

#include <stdio.h>        /* Standard i/o libraries */
#include <stdlib.h>

#include "TG.H" /* See TG.TXT for more info. */
#include "TWEEN.H"
/* structures and defines */


/***** Defines *****/

#define NPOINTS 2 /* Two points for a line segment */
#define NTWEENS 20 /* The number of in-betweens */
/***** Globals *****/

int Quit = NO;

/* These arrays are declared in tween.c */
extern POINT     Source[MAX_POINTS];
extern POINT     Target[MAX_POINTS];
extern DELTA     Delta [MAX_POINTS];
extern TWEEN     Tween [MAX_POINTS];


/***** Prototypes*****/

int getXY(POINT *point);
extern int calcTweens (int npoints, int ntweens)
;
extern int tweenObject(int npoints, int ntweens);
```

```
/***************************************************************
*
* main()
*
* Get random coordinates for the first and last lines, then
* tween them leaving a trail behind.
*/
     main()
     {
     tg_pickmode();
while (!Quit)
{
getLines(); /* get random source & target lines */
          tg_setcolor(random(0, WHITE));
                                   / * Set random color *
                                   / calcTweens(NPOINTS, NTWEENS);
          tweenObject(NPOINTS, NTWEENS);
          checkForKey();
     }
tg_closedown(); /* back to text before quitting */
}


getLines ()
{ /* get random endpoints
     for the line segments */
     getXY (&Source[0]); /* first point */
          getXY (&Source[1]); /* second point */
          getXY (&Target[0]); /* first point */
 getXY (&Target[1]); /* second point */
          }
          getXY(POINT *point)
{ /* get clipped x,y coordinates for the endpoints */
point->x = random (0, tg_scrnx-1);
point->y = random (0, tg_scrny-1);
     }
drawObject()
{
tg_drawline (Tween[0].x.word.hi, Tween[0].y.word.hi,
Tween[1].x.word.hi, Tween[1].y.word.hi);
}
```

```
checkForKey()
{    /* Check to see if a key was hit. If so, ESC sets Quit */
     if (kbhit() && (getch() == 27))
          Quit = YES;
}
```

Morphing

As Gregor Samsa awoke one morning from uneasy dreams, he found himself transformed in his bed into a gigantic insect.

—Franz Kafka, *The Metamorphosis*, 1915

So far, I have only discussed tweening as an aid for animation, but you can effectively employ this same technique to metamorphose dissimilar shapes, like a man and a werewolf, a bat and a vampire, or even an orchid and a butterfly as in Figure 4.6. Around Hollywood and Silicon Valley, this process is called *morphing*.

Figure 4.6. *An orchid metamorphoses into a butterfly in fifteen steps.*

For the best effect, you must ensure that the points describing the features correspond to each other. You want the teeth of the man to change into the fangs of the werewolf, and his nose to become a snout. The animator must take care to properly correlate these points, or the motion will be unnatural. This is one of the hardest problems of two-dimensional tweening and still requires the careful attention of the animator.

You Can Do It: The Werewolf

Enter PLAY WEREWOLF. This is a simple line drawing made with Fantavision to illustrate the concept of morphing. Although the image appears to have curves, straight line segments actually compose it. To create the animation, the man was first drawn and copied to a new frame. There, it was stretched and pulled into a werewolf. The polygons have the same number of vertices. Only their positions differ. Therefore, the points correspond in a one-to-one ratio. The images have dozens of tweens separating them.

To run the movie faster, press a number from 6 to 9 (fastest). To slow it down, press a number from 1 (slowest) to 4. Press 5 to restore the original speed. The new speed does not take effect until the next key frame is reached, so you may need to be patient. These number commands increase or decrease the number of tweens between key frames. This is useful when compensating for computers that run slower or faster than the original machine on which the movie was composed. Press Esc to quit.

What if the points don't match up? If you relax the rules a bit, you can transform any shape into any other shape. A hexagon can metamorphose into a triangle. The simplest method distributes the point mismatch around the polygon. First, determine which polygon of the transforming pair is smaller. Then, add enough points to it to match the bigger one. Add the points on top of the existing points. Distribute them around the polygon, so each vertex, or corner, has approximately the same number of duplicate points. This is the method used in the program Fantavision, and it is particularly well-suited for novices and students, who can easily put things in motion without sweating the details.

For instance, to metamorphose a square into an octagon, double up each point in the square. Now you have a square with eight points, each corner having two points on top of each other. When you tween the shapes, each corner of the square spreads apart to become the octagon, and the movement is simple and smooth. Of course, you can metamorphose these shapes in many ways, and the artist will often want to retain control by putting the extra points exactly where desired.

You Can Do It: Square to Octagon

Enter PLAY SQUARE to view the Fantavision sequence of a square turning into an octagon. Notice how each corner of the square splits off and slides over to form the eight corners of the octagon. Press Esc to quit.

As another method, indicate certain points as *control* or *anchor points*. The program forces these points to correspond, whereas the points around them are free to roam. For instance, you might anchor the top and bottom of Pinocchio's nose, and add new points to stretch out the end of that profound proboscis.

Transformations

He thought he saw an Albatross That fluttered round the lamp: He looked again, and found it was A Penny-Postage Stamp. 'You'd best be getting home,' he said: 'The nights are very damp!'

He thought he saw a Garden-Door That opened with a key: He looked again, and found it was A Double Rule of Three: 'And all its mystery,' he said, 'Is clear as day to me!'

—Lewis Carroll, *Through the Looking Glass*

Another great virtue of polygon animation is that a few points can represent thousands of pixels. In 640×480 mode, just four corner points can describe a rectangle that includes 307,200 pixels! You can manipulate these four polygon points much faster than the pixels they represent. The equations that massage the polygon data are called *transformation equations*.

Of course, you can process pixel-based images with transformation equations too. It just takes a long time to transform every pixel in the image—but that's how Hollywood produces many of its special effects. Their high-powered graphics workstations make quick work of the transformations presented here.

You have seen how to create animation by drawing each key frame by hand. The beauty of a transformation is that you can let mathematics create the key frames for you. When a ball hits the ground, it squashes. You can draw the squashed ball, or you can have an equation squash it for you. Unless you are pursuing art as therapy, you'll let the computer help you out.

When you combine transformations with tweening and morphing, you leverage a little work into a lot of animation. In a program like Fantavision, you can accomplish transformations with a single mouse click. Let me show you a movie created by Fantavision to illustrate these effects.

You Can Do It: Goodies

From the DOS prompt, type >PLAY GOODIES.

This movie illustrates zooming, squashing, flipping, leaning, and turning. It also has sound effects. If they irritate you or your friends, press the S key. As with all the Fantavision movies, S toggles the sound on and off.

The Math Behind the Magic: Transforming Equations

The following are some standard transformations that take care of practically any situation. By combining different transformations, you can create even more remarkable effects.

Zoom

This function shrinks or enlarges a polygon. As with all the following transformations, the equation is applied to every point in the polygon. The primed variables (X', Y') are the new values of the coordinates (X, Y) after the transformation.

If the object is centered at the origin (0,0), most transformations are obvious. For instance, zoom is just a multiplication:

$$X' = X * Xscale$$

$$Y' = Y * Yscale$$

where *Xscale* and *Yscale* are the zoom factors, usually equal to each other. To double the size, you would simply multiply all the points by two.

This is simple and it even makes sense—that's why I showed it to you—but it's useless. If the object is not conveniently centered at zero or if you want the zoom to have a different center, you must compensate. Here are the somewhat homelier general-purpose equations:

$$X' = X_c + (X - X_c) * Xscale$$

$$Y' = Y_c + (Y - Y_c) * Yscale$$

where (X_c, Y_c) are the coordinates of the transformation's center, which can be the middle of the object, the middle of the screen, a user supplied location, or any place you want. Every point transforms radially from that center.

This equation directs the computer to subtract the center from the coordinate: to *normalize* the value. This is similar to sliding the object back over to the center of the coordinate system. Then, a simple multiplication performs the actual zoom. If the scale is greater than one, it magnifies the polygon; if it's less than one, it shrinks it. To finish up, you need to return the object to its starting position by adding back the center coordinate that you subtracted out.

That's it. Pretty simple, huh? The remaining transformations are similar: they slide (or translate, in math-speak) to the center, do the calculations, and slide back.

Squash

This function is simply a type of zoom. Squashing is a zoom in the Y direction only; X stays the same. This is equivalent to letting *Xscale* = 1 in the zoom equations:

$$X' = X$$

$$Y' = Y_c + (Y - Y_c) * Yscale$$

You could also squash in the X direction by letting *Yscale* = 1 and changing *Xscale*. In fact, whenever *Xscale* and *Yscale* are different, some sort of squashing occurs.

Flip

With the left-right version of this transformation, you want to mirror the X values. With the mythical centered polygon, you would simply have

$$X' = -X$$

Everything on the positive side becomes negative and vice versa, doing a perfect flip. This is simple, intuitive and, of course, useless. Most polygons aren't centered at zero. To flip the X values around a vertical line at some other location, such as X_c, you want

$$X' = X_c - (X - X_c)$$

which simplifies to:

$$X' = 2 * X_c - X$$

and in this flip, nothing is happening to the Y values:

$$Y' = Y$$

Around a horizontal line at Y_c, the X and Y roles are swapped to give you a top-bottom flip:

$$X' = X$$

$$Y' = 2 * Y_c - Y$$

Lean

This function is slightly different, in that the X values depend on Y:

$$X' = X + (Y - Y_c) * Xscale$$

$$Y' = Y$$

The farther away the Y values are from the center of the lean, the greater the impact on X. Here, the scale can be negative as well as zero. When it is negative, the lean is to the left instead of the right. When $Xscale$ is zero, no change occurs.

By swapping the roles of X and Y, you get a lean that goes up-down instead of left-right:

$$X' = X$$

$$Y' = Y + (X - X_c) * Yscale$$

Turn

This transformation is the most complicated. This is where you wish you had paid more attention in trigonometry class. I'm not even going to derive it for you:

$$X' = X_c + (X - X_c) * \cos(A) - (Y - Y_c) * \sin(A)$$

$$Y' = Y_c + (X - X_c) * \sin(A) + (Y - Y_c) * \cos(A)$$

Notice the new variable A: the angle to rotate the polygon. In addition to the traditional polygon sliding, this transformation performs the trig necessary for rotation. Notice that when the angle is 0, the cosine = 1 and the sine = 0, and nothing changes—just as you would hope.

You Can Do It: Trans

TRANS.C is a program to explore the transformation equations. To run it from the DOS prompt, type >TRANS.

A polygon appears on-screen. A set of keys triggers the desired transformation. Then, the program tweens the polygon to its new, transformed state. A trace is left behind, so you can examine the transformation.

All the transformations described previously are represented. Their keyboard commands are as follows:

Key	Function
t	Turn clockwise
T	Turn counter-clockwise
z	Zoom in
Z	Zoom out
l	Lean right
L	Lean left
s	Squash down
S	Stretch up
f	Flip left-right
F	Flop up-down
Arrows	Move left, right, up and down
C, c	Clear the screen
N, n	New polygon
Esc	Quit

Play with the transformation commands. Lean, turn, and move the polygon. If you make a big mess, press C to clear the screen. To start with a new polygon, press N.

To keep things simple, I'm only keeping the integer part of the transformation. This is sufficient to illustrate the idea, but it causes some round-off error. Successive applications of the transformation compound the error. Turn is very susceptible to this particular problem; it produces numbers that are consistently rounded down. This causes a spiraling-in effect that is too nice to pass up—so I didn't fix it.

If you shrink a polygon to 0, that polygon is finished. All its points are equal to the center point, and no amount of zooming or stretching can rejuvenate it. Just press N for another polygon, and keep on playing.

Kind of fun, isn't it? Well, there's more to do, so press Esc to quit, and I'll show you the source code.

Working Code: Trans

This program shares some code and uses the same header files as the tween programs you looked at before. The program named main waits for the user to press a transformation key; it transforms the target polygon and tweens to it.

The transformation is applied to each point of the polygon in the transformPoint subroutine. The equations you see here should remind you of the mathematics section (previously). As well as the *transformations*, there are the *translations*. These are the sliding commands: left, right, up, and down. The arrow keys supply the direction.

The checkForKey input routine sets the transformation type and the appropriate scaling factor. It also checks for Esc, the quit key.

A normal scale factor is the do-nothing state. For a zoom, the normal scale factor is 1. When you put scale = 1 into the zoom or squash equations, you get your original point back. Zoom-out is greater than one, zoom-in is a value less than one.

For lean, the normal scale factor is 0. Negative and positive determine the direction of the lean. Flip doesn't have any scale factors; it just mirrors the data back and forth (by changing the sign), so it also avoids round-off errors.

Without further ado, here is the transformation program:

Listing 4.1. TRANS.C. The transformation program.

```c
/* TRANS.C
 *
 * This program transforms a random polyon.
 *
 * by Scott Anderson,  4/11/1993
 */

/***** Includes *****/

#include <stdio.h>          /* Standard input/output libraries */
#include <stdlib.h>
#include <math.h>

#include "TG.H"             /* instructions and header info. */
#include "TWEEN.H"          /* structures and defines */

/***** Defines *****/

#define YES         1
#define NO          0

#define MAXPOINTS   8       /* number of points in the polygon */
#define NTWEENS     10      /* The number of in-betweens */

#define ESC_KEY     27      /* Some keyboard values */
#define LEFT_KEY    75      /* Arrow key ASCII values */
#define RIGHT_KEY   77
#define UP_KEY      72
#define DOWN_KEY    80

#define MOVE_DIST   40      /* How far to move with arrow keys */

#define ZOOM        1       /* The transformation types */
#define SQUASH      2
#define FLIP        3
#define FLOP        4
```

continues

Listing 4.1. continued

```
#define LEAN        5
#define TURN        6
#define LEFT        7
#define RIGHT       8
#define UP          9
#define DOWN        10

/***** Globals *****/

int     Npoints;                /* number of points in the polygon */

int     Direction = 1;          /* direction of the transformations */
int     Transform = 0;          /* Transformation type */

float   Xscale, Yscale;         /* scaling factors for transforms */
int     Xc, Yc;                 /* center of the transformations */
float   A;                      /* angle for rotations */

int     FillColor, LineColor;
int     Quit = NO;

/* These arrays are declared in tween.c */
extern  POINT   Source[MAX_POINTS];
extern  POINT   Target[MAX_POINTS];
extern  TWEEN   Tween [MAX_POINTS];

/***** Prototypes *****/

int         getXY(POINT *point);
int         getPoly(POINT poly[]);
int         copyArray(POINT source[], POINT target[]);

extern int  calcTweens (int npoints, int ntweens);
extern int  tweenObject(int npoints, int ntweens);

/***************************************************************
 * main()
 *
 * Get random coordinates for the source and target polygons,
 * then tween them, leaving a trail.
 */
```

```
main()
{
    tg_pickmode();
    tg_clearscreen();
    Xc = tg_scrnx / 2;              /* Set the center of the screen */
    Yc = tg_scrny / 2;
    newPoly ();                      /* Get a new polygon to start off */

    while (!Quit)
    {
        transformPoly (Target);         /* Apply transformation */
        calcTweens(Npoints, NTWEENS);   /* calculate tweens */
        tweenObject(Npoints, NTWEENS);  /* add the tweens */
        copyArray(Target, Source);      /* make new source */
        checkForKey();                  /* get transformation from user */
    }
    tg_closedown();
}


getPoly(POINT array[])
{   /* Generate a random set of points for a polygon */
    int point;
    for (point = 0; point < Npoints; point++)
        getXY (&array[point]);
}


transformPoly(POINT array[])
{   /* Apply transformation to each point of the polygon */
    int point;
    if (Transform)
        for (point = 0; point < Npoints; point++)
            transformPoint(&array[point]);
}


transformPoint(POINT *point)
{   /* Based on Transform, apply proper transformation */
    switch(Transform)
    {
        case ZOOM:
            point->x = Xc + (point->x - Xc) * Xscale;
```

continues

159

Listing 4.1. continued

```
                point->y = Yc + (point->y - Yc) * Yscale;
                break;
        case SQUASH:
                point->y = Yc + (point->y - Yc) * Yscale;
                break;
        case FLIP:
                point->x = 2 * Xc - point->x;
                break;
        case FLOP:
                point->y = 2 * Yc - point->y;
                break;
        case TURN:
                point->x = Xc   + (point->x - Xc) * cos(A)
                                - (point->y - Yc) * sin(A)
                + rand() % 1;
point->y = Yc   + (point->x - Xc) * sin(A)
                                + (point->y - Yc) * cos(A)
                + rand() % 1;
break;
        case LEAN:
                point->x += (point->y - Yc) * Yscale;
                break;
        case LEFT:
                point->x -= MOVE_DIST;
                break;
        case RIGHT:
                point->x += MOVE_DIST;
                break;
        case UP:
                point->y -= MOVE_DIST;
                break;
        case DOWN:
                point->y += MOVE_DIST;
                break;
    }
}

copyArray(POINT source[], POINT target[])
{   /* Copy the source array to the target array */
    int point;
```

```
        for (point = 0; point < Npoints; point++)
            target[point] = source[point];
}

getXY (POINT *point)
{   /* Set random x,y coordinates for this point */
    point->x = random (20, tg_scrnx -20);
    point->y = random (20, tg_scrny -20);
}

newPoly ()
{   /* Create a new source poly and copy to the target */
    Npoints = random (3, MAX_POINTS);
    FillColor = random(0, WHITE);   /* random fill color */
    LineColor = random(0, WHITE);   /* random outline color */
    getPoly (Source);
    copyArray(Source, Target);
}

drawObject()
{   /* Put the coordinates into array & draw the poly */
    int poly[MAX_POINTS][2];
    int point;

    int fillOK = NO;
    int oldY = Tween[0].y.word.hi;

    for (point = 0; point < Npoints; point++)
    {   /* get the coordinates from the Tween array */
        poly[point][0] = Tween[point].x.word.hi;
        poly[point][1] = Tween[point].y.word.hi;

        /* The following code is to fix a fatal bug in the Microsoft
         * polygon fill routine that occurs when all of the Y-values
         * are the same (a horizontal line). There is also a bug when
         * the bottom line of the poly is horizontal, but at least
         * that bug doesn't crash the machine...*/

        if (poly[point][1] != oldY)
            fillOK = YES;        /* if y is different, fill poly */
    }
```

continues

Listing 4.1. continued

```c
    tg_setcolor(FillColor);
    if (fillOK)                    /* don't crash the system! */
        tg_fillpoly(poly, Npoints);
    tg_setcolor(LineColor);
    tg_drawpoly(poly, Npoints);
}

checkForKey()
{   /* Check for a key was hit & set Transform accordingly */
    int key;
    Transform = 0;

    if (!kbhit())
        return 0;

    key = getch();
    if (key == ESC_KEY)
        Quit = YES;
    else if (key == 'c' || key == 'C')
        tg_clearscreen();
    else if (key == 'n' || key == 'N')
        newPoly();

    else if (key == 't') {
        Transform = TURN;
        A = 3.14159/18; /* The angle for rotations */
    }
    else if (key == 'T') {
        Transform = TURN;
        A = -3.14159/18;
    }
    else if (key == 'z') {
        Transform = ZOOM;
        Xscale = Yscale = .75;
    }
    else if (key == 'Z') {
        Transform = ZOOM;
        Xscale = Yscale = 1.25;
    }
    else if (key == 'l') {
```

```
        Transform = LEAN;
        Yscale = -.5;
    }
    else if (key == 'L') {
        Transform = LEAN;
        Yscale = .5;
    }
    else if (key == 's') {
        Transform = SQUASH;
        Xscale = Yscale = .75;
    }
    else if (key == 'S') {
        Transform = SQUASH;
        Xscale = Yscale = 1.25;
    }
    else if (key == 'f')
        Transform = FLIP;
    else if (key == 'F')
        Transform = FLOP;

    else if (key == LEFT_KEY)
        Transform = LEFT;
    else if (key == RIGHT_KEY)
        Transform = RIGHT;
    else if (key == UP_KEY)
        Transform = UP;
    else if (key == DOWN_KEY)
        Transform = DOWN;

    return 1;
}
```

Fantavision

There is only one thing that can kill the Movies, and that is education.

—Will Rogers, *Autobiography of Will Rogers*, 1949

Several years ago (I'd rather not be too specific), I set out to make some educational animations on the computer. I was inspired by the wonderful Disney movies I'd seen in grade school that explained everything from atoms to the stars. They involved some tough concepts, but animation proved to be the perfect medium for clarifying the issues.

For some reason, Disney has stopped producing these gems. A whole generation of children has missed the valuable contribution these animations added to our education. It's a great shame.

At the time of my musing, the only computer with color graphics was the Apple II. As a recent college graduate, I was thrilled to have a computer that was all mine. No time-sharing, no logon passwords, and no system managers to get in the way. If you are too young to know what that stuff is, count your blessings.

I quickly found out that Apple had no animation tool. I wasn't particularly surprised—few animation tools were on *any* computer at that time. So, I figured I'd write a little animation program.

I wanted to design a tool that I could use professionally, but one that was simple enough for kids to use, if possible. I was going to produce animation, but I also wanted kids to be animators. Making cartoons could be fun and could also interest kids in computers.

I took my first attempt to Brøderbund Software and showed it to Gary Carlston, one of the founders. He was immediately captivated and agreed to further fund the development of what was to become Fantavision.

This wasn't a simple project. At first, the program was keyboard-based. Laugh if you must, but this was in the dark days before introduction of the mouse. No other good way existed to input data into the computer. Actually, I sometimes used the joystick, but it left a lot to be desired as a drawing tool.

The literature on computer graphics was harder to find than a spotted owl. In fact, it was just being written. I ended up inventing my own graphics primitives such as dots, lines, and polygons. Years would pass before I would see a polygon routine in the literature—too late to do me any good. Now these functions are regularly included in compilers, and you may never need to know how to fill a polygon. Lucky you.

Then came the mouse. Suddenly, the project changed course—it had to. The mouse (and the windows, menus and icons that came along with it) made the perfect environment for Fantavision. Unfortunately, Apple's windowing environment was text-based only. For Fantavision, I needed to write a graphics version of the entire windowing system.

Fantavision was all machine language, so it was fast and lean, but not necessarily fun to work on. When you program in machine language, you are continuously reminded just how stupid a computer really is. The 6502 chip, the brains of the Apple, could add, subtract, rotate bits, and jump. That's about it. If you wanted to multiply, you had to write a subroutine to do it.

The program, along with space for a movie, was being crammed into a 48K Apple. Despite the problems, after many long months, I finished the program.

Except for a few bugs I told Gary that I had fixed an error that caused the objects to flash on-screen.

"But that's my favorite effect," he complained, "don't *fix* it!"

It wasn't the first time (and it won't be the last) that a bug was relabeled a feature. I called it lightning mode and added it to the other special effects.

When it finally came out, Fantavision was a hit with students and teachers. Nevertheless, it was only 1984, and not everyone was ready for a draw program that could tween and morph. Today, Fantavision is a little easier to explain. But *just* a little.

Since then, Fantavision has been converted to run on the Amiga, the Apple IIGS, and the IBM PC and its clones. It has been translated into Spanish, German, French, and Japanese.

In 1991, I formed a company with my wife Candyce, called Wild Duck, to pick up where Brøderbund left off. I obtained the marketing rights from Brøderbund and started aiming at schools. So far, our small company is doing well, despite the shocking money shortage in our school system.

In the meantime, I had almost forgotten what I set out to do in the first place. I just wanted to make some animations. Many keystrokes later, I finally had my tool.

Now I'm animating and having a great time. I recently finished a project for the Dana-Farber Cancer Institute and Harvard Medical School. It illustrates some of the latest discoveries in human embryology and receives a great response when played at biology conventions. Viewers comment that they get a better feel when a subject is animated than when still pictures are used.

I'm not surprised. That's just what I thought when I saw those Disney films as a kid.

A Fantavision Player

Now that you've seen the essential pieces of an animation program, let's put them all together. The program listed here, FPLAY.C, runs most Fantavision movies—using only C commands.

In color Plates 18 through 26, you can see a few stills from one of the many Fantavision movies on the disk. In this particular blockbuster, a fish evolves into a reptile, which evolves into a bird. Other movies illustrate cell reproduction, jazz dancing, cute chicks, and lots of other racy Hollywood-type stuff.

You Can Do It: Let's Go to the Movies!

The FPLAY program takes a movie filename, loads the movie, and plays it. The file must be an .MVE file created by Fantavision. If it isn't, you'll receive an error. You don't need to type in the .MVE extension: it will automatically be appended to the name. For instance, to run the CHICK.MVE movie, go to the DOS prompt and enter

FPLAY EVOLUT

There are many more MVE files included on the disk. Type DIR *.MVE to get a list of them, grab some popcorn, and try them all!

FPLAY is a subset of the Fantavision player. Although it doesn't do everything the commercial version of Fantavision can do, it's written in C, so you can examine and compile it. Where the commercial version has machine-language routines, this version uses the graphics primitives provided by your compiler.

One thing missing in FPLAY is the background mode. Fantavision enables the user to load in a .PCX background screen and animate on top of that. Because this useful drawing mode isn't supported by makers of compilers, FPLAY skips the background mode. Also missing is sound because machine language handles that. These simplifications make FPLAY run faster than it otherwise would.

A shortcoming of most compilers is that they don't let you read a file into "far" memory. If you don't know what that means, don't worry. The upshot is that some long movies do not load with FPLAY, and you'll get an out of memory error. You can deal with this in several ways (read a little bit at a time, then move it to far memory, and so on), but rather than bog you down with routines to skirt the deficiencies of your compiler, I've kept it simple—and small.

With these caveats, I think you'll find this program very revealing. Before discussing the routines in FPLAY, I need to cover a few important concepts such as screen flipping, the movie structure, erasing, fixed-point arithmetic, polygon filling and flood filling.

Screen Flipping

Even though the computer does things very fast, it still does them one thing at a time. To draw a face, you might draw a flesh colored circle with two white circles for eyes and a red polygon for the lips. The computer draws the face, then the eyes, then the lips. If you wait until all these parts are drawn, you see the face, just as expected. But if you display the drawing too soon, you might see a one-eyed, lipless monster. The problem is the raster scan.

The *raster scan* is the magic of television. It converts a TV signal into an image on-screen. The signal (in our case, the information stored in the computer screen buffer), controls an electron beam that hits the screen, lighting up phosphorescent chemical dots printed on the inside of the tube.

As its name implies, the raster scans across the screen. It starts at the top left corner and sweeps to the right, leaving a trail of glowing dots in its wake. Then, it quickly moves back to the left of the screen, just below the last line.

Even though the electron beam is on the second line, the top line is still lit up because the phosphors are persistent: they continue to glow for about a 30th of a second. As the raster continues to scan, it builds a two-dimensional phosphorescent picture on your monitor.

This is the miracle of television and the bane of computer animators. The raster scan is unrelenting and out of the programmer's control. Depending on the monitor, the screen is *refreshed*, or redrawn, up to 70 times per second. If the raster is displaying your picture while you are still drawing it, you'll see things you don't want to see.

The way to deal with this is called screen swapping, page flipping, or some variation on that theme. You set up another area of graphics memory for a second screen. While you draw on one screen, you are looking at the other one. When you're done, you flip the screen to display the finished picture. While you display this picture, you are busy constructing the next image in the other screen area.

Sound complicated? Well it is, a little, but it provides a way to produce flicker-free animation.

Not every graphics mode has two screens to flip. For instance, 320x200 VGA mode with 256 colors has only one screen. This is really unforgivable: this otherwise great screen format can only produce clunky animation. Actually, there are ways of making VGA mode do screen flipping, but the BIOS or the compiler makers don't support them. To avoid machine language routines, I'll stick with EGA mode, which does have screen swapping.

Erasing and Animation

Just how do you display animation on a computer? Like film animation, you need to display a series of slightly changed images in rapid succession (at least 20 frames each second). Here's a plan:

1. Clear the screen to the background color

2. Draw the objects from the first frame

3. Flip the screen

4. Clear the screen

5. Draw the next frame, and so on

This will certainly do the job, and it's pretty straightforward, but it clears the entire screen for every frame. This is time-consuming and makes it hard to hit the 20 frames-per-second goal. To speed things up a bit, you can erase the objects themselves. Unless the objects are huge, this method requires less work than erasing the whole screen. So the new plan is

1. Erase the previous objects

2. Draw the new ones

3. Flip the screen

4. Erase the previous objects, and so forth

This is the time-honored method of computer animation: page flipping and erasing. Now you know the secret.

Fixed-Point Arithmetic

I promised earlier in this chapter that I would show you another implementation of fixed-point arithmetic. Here it is.

As you remember, tweening uses many fractional numbers. The most obvious thing is to use floating-point numbers. That is what C provides to deal with fractional numbers, but floating-point arithmetic is notoriously slow, unless you have the floating-point chip—and not everyone does. What's the perplexed programmer to do?

The answer is fixed-point arithmetic. As you recall, the decimal point is fixed in these numbers. Again, you use four bytes, where the top two are the integer part and the bottom two are the fractional part. This time, however, there are no structures. Instead, you rotate the given integer into the high word of the long value. You can do all your calculations in long arithmetic and when you want the integer part, you rotate it back out. That's what FPLAY does.

First, the coordinate values are rotated left by sixteen bits to create the fixed-point number. Then, thirty-two bit calculations are performed assuming the lower sixteen bits are the fractional part. At the conclusion of the calculations, the fixed-point number is rotated right by sixteen bits. This yields the desired integer part.

It seems a bit clumsy, but it works. It would be nice if compilers understood fixed-point arithmetic and included it. Until they become so enlightened or until floating point processors are ubiquitous, this is the kludge we must live with.

The Movie Structure

A Fantavision movie has a header and a series of frames. The *header* contains such things as the background color and the number of frames in the movie.

Each following frame has a header and a list of objects. The frame header describes the tweening speed and contains sound and color palette information. The objects are dots, lines, or polygons, and they are drawn on-screen in order, from the first object to the last.

Each object in the frame has its own header and a list of points. The *object header* contains the number of points to follow, their color, dimension (dot, line, or polygon), and animation mode (lightning, animation, background, or trace). The points themselves follow the object header.

The frames and objects are a type of linked list structure. The frame header contains the offset to the next frame, and the object header contains the offset to the next object. When the movie is loaded, the program uses these offsets to locate the frames. It creates a global array that points to each frame, so they can be randomly accessed.

Polygon Filling

The act of coloring in a triangle or a square is called polygon filling, and it is the crux of Fantavision animation. Although lines and dots are supported, the polygons are the workhorses. If they aren't fast enough, you don't have animation. You have a slide show.

A polygon is filled by looking through its points, or vertices, as you scan down the screen. For every horizontal line on-screen, you check the polygon. If you find a new vertex on that line, you start the left and right edges of the filled-in area. As you scan, you fill in the polygon between these edges until you come to another vertex. Each new vertex can add, change, or delete edges.

Because you're working with a compact data set, these calculations are relatively fast. Most compilers today have built-in polygon fills. That's what FPLAY uses.

Flood Filling

Flood fill is a good, descriptive name. You draw an outline on-screen and pick any spot within it. From that point out to the perimeter, the selected color floods the area.

This algorithm was originally developed for paint programs and is usually represented by a bucket of paint or a paint roller. This is a great way to fill an area with color, but unfortunately it is somewhat slow for large or complicated objects. It uses a boundary on-screen—not a set of data—to control the action. So it must read from the screen all around the starting point to see if it has hit the boundary yet. This is fine for a draw program, but it's murder on animation.

Fantavision doesn't use flood fills for that reason. Instead, it uses polygon fills to achieve a similar effect in a fraction of the time. However, FPLAY uses a flood fill to draw dots. In FPLAY, the dots are actually filled ellipses. This process is a bit slow, but otherwise just fine—until the dots overlap something else on-screen. The ellipse is drawn, and the center is chosen as the starting point for the flood fill. But if the flood of color runs into an interfering border, it stops right there. The ellipse doesn't totally fill. So when you see your solid dots turn into improperly filled outlines, you'll know why.

Fantasies of a Graphics Programmer

I have this fantasy. I am a VIP, and hardware manufacturers come to me for advice. Ok, quit laughing, I said it was a fantasy. Anyway, representatives of Big Computer Company, wearing impressive suits, come visit me. They want to know what I would like to see in the New Graphics Adapter, and I tell them:

- Thirty-two bits per pixel, with 24 of those bits for color and the rest for overlays and special effects. I'm tired of hassling with color look-up tables.

- A resolution of at least 800×600 with *square* pixels. All graphics programmers *hate* nonsquare pixels. Rectangular pixels should be *illegal*. An HDTV standard would be nice to have too, whenever they figure out what that is.

- Fast, fast memory, and lots of it, for multiple screen swapping. Memory is cheap and I can never get enough. And as long as we're page flipping, let's do it right: during vertical blanking when it won't mess up the screen. Or, short of that, let me know where the scan-line is, so I can figure out when to flip.

- Built-in graphics primitives that are debugged and blindingly fast. I want 2-D and 3-D object support. Not just wireframes, but filled, shaded, anti-aliased polygons. And it would be very nice if I could erase these objects to a background screen.

- If you can't provide built-in graphics, at least give me a reasonable screen map, and I'll write my own.

At the end of my masterful presentation, the representatives of the Big Computer Company laugh in my face and leave. Even fantasy has a limit, you know.

But my daydream doesn't stop there. In the end, my adoring fans chip in to buy me a Silicon Graphics Workstation, and we all live happily ever after.

A Tour of the Program

The `loadMovie` routine loads the movie header that contains the length of the rest of the movie, among other things. Space is allocated for the movie header and the movie frames. When everything has been loaded, an initialization routine is called, and `loadMovie` returns with the address of the movie.

The movie initialization routine, `movieInit` sets up the background color and creates an array of pointers to the individual frames. Using this array, you can access any frame you desire. As previously discussed, this is faster and more flexible than a linked list.

Given a pointer to the movie, the `runMovie` routine goes through the frames, adds tweening to them, and plays the resulting movie. This routine extracts the desired frame and puts it into a special display buffer. The next frame is also extracted, and `calcTweens` creates the tweening array. After displaying the frame, these tweens are added to the frame values.

To display the frame, use `drawAndFlip`, which sets the active screen as the one not being viewed—so it can work in secret. It erases the animated objects previously drawn on this screen, draws the frame, and saves a copy of it to erase later.

The routine that extracts a frame is called `unpackFrame`. It copies the frame to the display buffer, shifting the X and Y coordinates into long values for fixed-point arithmetic (see **Fixed-Point Arithmetic**, previously).

The `calcTweens` routine, given two frames, calculates the tweening array. This array contains the differences (plus and minus) that must be added to the frame to smoothly tween it. These values are also fixed-point numbers. The point loop at the end of this routine does the deed:

```
for (pt = 0; pt < srcPoints; pt++, srcPt++, dstPt++, deltaPt++) {
    deltaPt->x = (dstPt->x - srcPt->x) / tweens;
    deltaPt->y = (dstPt->y - srcPt->y) / tweens;
}
```

The tweening differences, pointed to by `deltaPt`, are calculated as the difference between the point values, divided by the number of tweens. This is the first half of the interpolation algorithm.

With the `expandObject` function, you can tween polygons with a different number of vertices. If the starting (source) image is smaller that the ending (destination) image, expand it. To do that, double up some of the points in the smaller polygon. For instance, to tween a square into an octagon, you would double up the points at each corner of the square. It would still look like a square, but it would have eight points, not four. This makes it easy to tween to the octagon. Similarly, if the source has more points than the destination, expand the destination polygon.

When the tweening array has been calculated, you're ready to use it. After the frame is drawn, add the tweening "deltas" (the small changes) to each point of each polygon.

This is what addTweens does. The key code is again in the point loop at the end of the function:

```
for (pt = 0; pt < points; pt++, srcPt++, deltaPt++) {
    srcPt->x += deltaPt->x;
    srcPt->y += deltaPt->y;
}
```

These routines are the heart of Fantavision. This is what gives the animation fluidity and rescues the animator from the tedium of hand-tweening.

The eraseFrame routine clears the screen for the new frame. It erases all the animated objects previously drawn on this screen.

To create the frame from its polygonal objects, you need to draw them, one at a time. That is the job of drawFrame. You also need to draw any objects from the other screen that are in trace or background mode. This program doesn't really do a background mode; it converts it to trace mode. In that mode, an object leaves a trail, or trace, as it moves across the screen. This is useful for special effects or to create ornate, layered images. These objects are also rendered by drawFrame.

Each object in the frame goes through the drawObject routine, which sets the object or background color, depending on whether it is drawing or erasing the object. It then farms out the actual drawing, depending on the dimension (dot, line, or polygon).

The drawDot, drawLine, and drawPoly routines use the built-in commands of the compiler to draw these graphics primitives. Each primitive has an option that is interpreted differently, depending on the dimension. The option for a dot dictates the size of the dot. There are ten sizes. The option is an index into a radius table that determines the actual screen size of the dot.

The option for a line indicates gaps in the line. You can have open or closed lines (where the last point connects to the first point) or you can have gaps that occur after one to nine segments. Option 2, for instance, would instruct drawLine to draw two line segments, skip the next, then draw two again, and so on.

For a polygon, the option specifies an outline, or border style. The default is no border, but black or white borders are available, and they can be open or closed, just like lines.

That pretty much covers the relevant tweening and morphing code. Though the full C source for FPLAY.C is too lengthy to print here in the book, it is on the disk. Look it over. All the parts you need to make your own animation and special-effects tools are here. Enjoy!

Morphing Hollywood-Style

Animation, at best, is a costly procedure, in both time and money, and anything that eases its birth process should not be ignored. If audiences only knew all that is involved in any animated production... A typical team for the production of a large-scale animated film includes a lot of people: a director, a producer, a number of animators and assistant animators, a team of in-betweeners, and special-effects artists... Considering all the personalities involved, it is often a miracle that any animation films get made at all.

—Tony White, *The Animator's Workbook*, 1986, Watson-Guptill Publications: New York

Although this chapter has concerned *polygon* tweening, it is worth noting that similar methods are used to tween photographic images such as those in *Terminator II* or the Michael Jackson video "Black or White." In these cases, the polygons represent control points or lines that define the areas you want to morph. A polygon is defined for the source image and a corresponding polygon is defined for the target image. Then, a simple linear interpolation is applied to warp the source into the target. As the images are warped, they are simultaneously *faded*, or blended. Thus, both the contours and the colors are metamorphosed with this hypnotic special effect.

In just a few short years, tweening and morphing have made enormous inroads into the Hollywood establishment. These techniques have added new vigor to cartoons and an amazing new realism to feature films.

The most profound impact, however, may be on the small studios and independent filmmakers. Without the manpower and gigantic budgets of the large studios, these groups have been denied the advantages of animation. As the entry prices for these tools fall, the medium becomes more democratic, and we can expect completely new ideas to surface.

Today's desktop computers can perform some limited manipulation of polygons, as you have seen with the examples on this disk. But it will take more powerful machines to handle the thousands of polygons and bit-mapped images needed for cinematic quality. Computers become faster every day, so it won't take long. With the tools introduced here, you'll be ready to participate in this fascinating field.

Pseudo-3-D: Voyage to Distant Planets

If we shadows have offended,
Think but this, and all is mended,
That you have but slumber'd here
While these visions did appear.

—William Shakespeare, *A Midsummer Night's Dream*

This chapter introduces the Scene Generator. It is a fun and fairly simple program that simulates the vistas you might see on a faraway planet. The Scene Generator appears to be 3-D, but it is all a trick. The program allows you to generate the images quickly, without worrying about strict realism.

This project stems from a multiplayer space game I was writing with an excellent programmer named Robert Leyland in 1989. The game required views from the hundreds of planets you could colonize. At first, I was drawing the planetary landscapes by hand.

Each one was taking at least a day to complete. At that rate, it would have taken several years to create enough images to avoid repeats. But as I painted them, I started to analyze them. I realized I was manually executing graphics algorithms as I drew.

So I wrote a few routines to automate the drawing process. It worked—the computer drew the pictures for me! It was also a lot faster than I was. It took less than 10 seconds to create an image. My days as a landscape artist were over.

The scenes in this program are not quite as interesting as the ones I did by hand, but in some respects they are very similar. Robert programmed texture routines for the Scene Generator that added a lot of charm; however, in this limited space I have to exclude that fairly convoluted enhancement. In its place I have a devised a much cruder but shorter random "texture" algorithm.

The Scene Generator is an amazing exercise in random number generation. Everything is random: the sky, planets, moons, mountains and clouds. Even the color ranges are random (and kind of lousy at times—the computer has no color sense), and almost every pixel is randomized by dithering.

As a result, you can just watch while the computer does all the work. But random number generation is about the closest a computer gets to creativity, and it leaves a lot to be desired. Only a computer would take the time to draw a comet, cover it up with a planet, and then wipe them both out with a mountain range.

(A better approach is probably to have certain values tied down or submitted to the Scene Generator and have just the *details* randomly generated. That would give you more control over the paintings. But I'll leave that as an exercise for the energetic reader.)

Adventures in Not-Quite-3-D Graphics

But the Devil whoops, as he whooped of old: 'It's clever, but is it art?'

—Rudyard Kipling, *The Conundrum of the Workshops*

It would be great if you could do all your graphics in three dimensions. Reality is three-dimensional, so to put reality on the screen, we need 3-D graphics. Elsewhere in this book, you will find programs to do just that. But this chapter is concerned with mimicking reality simply and quickly. 3-D graphics are neither simple nor fast.

This chapter could be called "Cheap Tricks of the Graphics Gurus." Here I'll discuss something called 2 ½-D graphics, which are better than flat 2-D, but not quite real 3-D.

2 ½-D is a bad name. The fractional dimension is just someone's idea of cuteness (not mine). Don't confuse this with the fractional dimensions in fractals. There is absolutely no connection, OK?

The Inspiration: A Sphere from a Filled Ellipse

The first thing I tried was to modify an ellipse program. Ellipse programs are a dime a dozen and I had about a quarter's worth of them hanging around. These routines are all based on the Bresenham ellipse function, which is named in honor of J.E. Bresenham, who invented it in 1965 for an IBM plotting machine. It manages to draw an ellipse without multiplying or dividing inside a loop. It's fast.

Why an ellipse and not just a circle? Well, it's because the engineers who designed the IBM graphics displays blew it and didn't make square pixels.

This is bad news to all graphics programmers. Without square pixels, *everything* you draw must be scaled. If you try to draw a circle without scaling, it comes out as a tall ellipse, because the pixels you draw it with are tall rectangles. So, to compensate, you draw a squashed oval and it comes out circular. It's nuts, but that's why you use an ellipse algorithm instead of the much simpler circle algorithm.

The algorithm takes advantage of the four-fold symmetry in an ellipse—an ellipse looks the same flipped around its horizontal or vertical axis, as you can see in Figure 5.3. So you only need to calculate one quadrant and mirror that around the two axes.

For instance, you calculate the upper right quadrant and flip it around the vertical axis to get the upper left quadrant. Now the top half is done. Flip that half around the horizontal axis to get the lower half, and you're done.

To fill this ellipse, draw a horizontal line from the left edge to the right edge. This draws a solid oval on the screen.

But what if the horizontal line isn't solid? What if it is a shaded line that goes from black to white?

As you may have guessed, this might make a more or less spherical-looking shape. Let's look at a demonstration.

You Can Do It: The BALL Program

At the DOS prompt, type:

```
>BALL
```

This program draws a circular ellipse on the screen, filled with colors that are shaded from black to white. It's not perfect, but it's fast—and it *does* appear spherical.

You will notice something that looks like longitude lines (see Figure 5.1). This unplanned and unwanted effect is known as banding. Banding is a result of the limited colors available on the IBM graphics cards. The colors are just not close enough to blend together.

Figure 5.1. *Banding results when the colors aren't close enough to smoothly blend.*

There is a way to fix banding. It's called *dithering*, which means nervous and jittery. By dithering you let the pixels jump around a little bit.

To explore this, exit from the program by hitting any key. Then type:

```
>BALL 1
```

Figure 5.2. *Dithering (randomizing the colors) eliminates the banding on the ball.*

This allows the pixels to jump a maximum of one color away from their exact color. The result jumbles the edges, thereby blending the colors. (See Figure 5.2.) You can also try larger values of dithering. Type:

```
>BALL 6
```

This makes a granite-like surface on the ball. The smoothing is great, but the texture may be a bit distracting. A value from 1 to 6 achieves a good, smooth dither without too much added texture. That's what the Scene Generator uses.

MATH
+ - =

The Math Behind the Magic: Ellipses

The equation for an ellipse centered at the origin is:

$$\frac{x^2}{a^2} + \frac{y^2}{b^2} = 1$$

or

$$b^2 x^2 + a^2 y^2 - a^2 b^2 = 0$$

where *b* is the minor axis and *a* is the major axis of the ellipse, as shown in Figure 5.3.

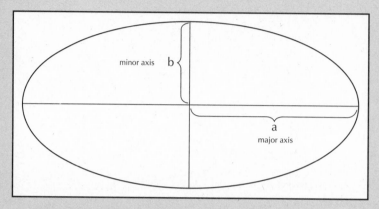

Figure 5.3. *An ellipse is like a squashed circle with two different radii. The short radius is called the minor axis and the long radius is the major axis.*

To get accurate answers for this equation you could use floating-point numbers and do the requisite multiplying and squaring. Or you could do it Bresenham's way and just add and subtract integers.

Bresenham figured there must be a way to get to the next point on an ellipse from the last point with a minimum of fuss. This is called an incremental algorithm—you increment, or step, through the curve from one point to the next. You are dealing with differences each step of the way.

Differences can eliminate the worst parts of an equation, simply by subtracting them out. This is a very nice and widely applied trick of the graphics trade, so pay attention. The following algorithm is a variation on the Bresenham theme, called the midpoint algorithm. It calculates the upper right quadrant and reflects it around the origin.

At the top of the ellipse, the slope is "slow." That is, the rise (*dy*) is less than the run (*dx*), so the slope (*dy*/*dx*) is less than 1. It follows that from a given point at the top of an ellipse, the next point is always to the right. It can be directly to the right or down one and to the right. That's it. There is only one decision to make. But how do we decide?

A cunningly simple method uses the midpoint between the two choices. (See Figure 5.4.) If you plug the value of the midpoint (x^m, y^m) into the preceding ellipse equation, it comes out negative if it's inside the ellipse and positive if it's outside. If it is directly on the ellipse, the equation is zero, as you might expect. This is our switch variable, *s:*

$$s = b^2 x_m^2 + a^2 y_m^2 - a^2 b^2$$

where

$s < 0$ (inside the ellipse)

$s > 0$ (outside the ellipse)

$s = 0$ (right on the ellipse)

and the midpoint is

(xm, ym) = (x, y - 1/2)

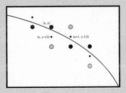

Figure 5.4. *For slow slopes, the curve always goes to the right. If it passes above the midpoint (small black dot), the top dot is chosen. Below the midpoint, the lower dot is chosen.*

If the midpoint is *inside* the ellipse, it means the ellipse passes above it, and you choose the *top* point to the right. If the midpoint is *outside* of the ellipse, you want the *bottom* point to the right.

The magic of an incremental algorithm is that by subtracting two complicated equations, you can get a simpler equation. In this case we subtract the switch variable at the second point from the switch variable at the first point. This difference is just what you need to add to get to the third point, and so on.

At the top of the ellipse, you start out going to the right, as discussed above. The second midpoint has the same y-value, but x has increased by one:

$(x, y - 1/2)$ (first midpoint)

$(x + 1, y - 1/2)$ (second midpoint)

So the difference between the switch values is:

$dx = s2 - s1$

$= b^2(x + 1)^2 + a^2(y - 1/2)^2 - a^2 b^2$

$- \{b^2 x^2 + a^2(y - 1/2)^2 - a^2 b^2\}$

$= 2b^2 x + b^2$

As you can see, a bunch of terms canceled out. Notably, there are no x^2 terms, and y is gone completely. Not only that, but you can replace the multiplication (x times $2b^2$) with a repeated addition (of $2b^2$). You just need to adjust the starting value.

In this and the following equations, I am using the terms x and y to indicate the incrementing coordinate. The different terms are added to either the x- or y-value to compute the next point.

So far, so good. We can just keep adding this difference to get to the next value. As long as we keep going to the right.

But what happens when the ellipse goes to the lower pixel? Then you need to adjust the y-value as well as the x-value. To adjust for moving the midpoint down, do the following:

$(x, y + 1/2)$ Last midpoint (1)

$(x, y - 1/2)$ Current midpoint (2)

The difference between the switch values is:

$dy = s2 - s1$

$= b^2 x^2 + a^2(y - 1/2)^2 - a^2 b^2$

$- \{b^2 x^2 + a^2(y + 1/2)^2 - a^2 b^2\}$

$= -2a^2 y$

Again, so far so good. But remember I said the slope starts out slow. To complete the ellipse, it must get steeper—to infinity. At the point where the slope changes from slow to fast, we need a new plan.

For these values, the two possible successor points are below and below right. (See Figure 5.5.) For the point below, *x* stays the same, and *y* goes down one:

$(x + 1/2, y)$ (last midpoint—1)

$(x + 1/2, y - 1)$ (current midpoint—2)

The *y* difference is:

$$dy = s2 - s1$$
$$= b^2(x + 1/2)^2 + a^2(y - 1)^2 - a^2 b^2$$
$$- \{b^2(x + 1/2)^2 + a^2 y^2 - a^2 b^2\}$$
$$= -2a^2 y + a^2$$

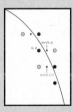

Figure 5.5. *For fast sloping curves, the next point is always down. If the curve passes to the left of the midpoint, the left coordinate is chosen, otherwise the right coordinate is chosen.*

For the move to the right, y stays the same while x moves over one, as follows:

$(x - 1/2, y)$ (last midpoint—1)

$(x + 1/2, y)$ (current midpoint—2)

The x difference is

$$dx = s2 - s1$$

$$= b^2(x + 1/2)^2 + a^2y^2 - a^2b^2$$

$$- \{b^2(x - 1/2)^2 + a^2y^2 - a^2b^2\}$$

$$= 2b^2x$$

These are the four differences we need to increment around the first quadrant of an ellipse:

$$dx = 2b^2x + b^2 \qquad \text{(for slow slopes)}$$

$$dy = -2a^2y$$

and

$$dx = 2b^2x \qquad \text{(for fast slopes)}$$

$$dy = -2a^2y + a^2$$

But when does the slope change from slow to fast? That occurs when the slope is unity. Actually, because we are going down the right side of the ellipse, the dividing slope is *minus* 1. Now you get to use some of that calculus they beat into you at school. You remember that the slope of a curve is just the derivative of the equation. In this case, we want the derivative of Equation 1:

$$\frac{d}{dx}\left(b^2x^2 + a^2y^2 = a^2b^2\right)$$

$$2b^2x + 2a^2y\frac{dy}{dx} = 0$$

$$\frac{dy}{dx} = \frac{-2b^2x}{2a^2y} = -1$$

So

$$2b^2x = 2a^2y$$

when the slope changes. These quantities should look familiar. They are already being calculated for the incremental drawing. This fortuitous circumstance is exploited by the algorithm, which only needs to compare these two pre-existing terms.

When the slope change is detected, you need to fix one last detail. The algorithm puts the midpoint to the right—and that's wrong. The point should go down instead. So when the slope changes, we need a one-time correction:

$(x + 1, y - 1/2)$ (the last—wrong—midpoint)

$(x + 1/2, y - 1)$ (the correct midpoint)

$d = s2 - s1$

$\quad = b^2(x + 1/2)^2 + a^2(y - 1)^2 - a^2 b^2$

$\quad - \{b^2(x + 1)^2 + a^2(y - 1/2)^2 - a^2 b^2\}$

$\quad = 3(a^2 - b^2)/4 - (b^2 x + a^2 y)$

That's the midpoint version of the Bresenham ellipse. Next we'll look at some code that implements this nifty algorithm.

Working Code: The BALL Program

The main routine parses the command line value as the dither, initializes the graphics mode to 256 colors, and sets up a color range before it calls the ball routine.

The routine setSpread creates the color range. It starts with a dark and a light color and calculates a smooth ramp of colors in between. The number of colors used here is 32. There are actually 64 shades of gray on a VGA card, but this range will do the job nicely.

Next comes the ball routine. It initializes the variables, then starts the loop. There are two while loops. The first one is for the slow slope portion of the ellipse, and the second one is for the fast part. The multipliers twoAsquared and twoBsquared are summed up with each iteration, to simulate a multiplication.

You will notice a bit of fudging in the color department. It turns out that if you simply go from the darkest to lightest on every line, you get something more like a football than a sphere. And there is a big gap between colors on the short lines at the top and bottom of the ellipse. They are just too short to fit the entire range of colors.

To correct for this unhappy situation, I initialize the dark and light values to the middle of the range, and increase the range as I go down the ellipse. The top starts out gray and gradually gains contrast as the dark gets darker and the light gets lighter. This improves the 3-D effect considerably.

After the x and y values and the color range are determined, the ball routine calls twoLines. In this routine, two lines are drawn. Each line goes from ($-x$, y) to (x, y). One is in the top half of the ellipse, and the other in the bottom half, reflected around the horizontal axis.

The lines are drawn with a call to shadedLine. This is the routine that does the actual drawing. It divides the color range by the length of the line to get the color delta. This is the amount of color to add for each increment of x. Notice the use of fixed-point arithmetic, where an integer is used to carry a fraction in its lower bits. To get the integer part of a fixed-point number, you rotate it right, popping the fraction off the bottom.

This is where the dithering is done, with the following code:

```
for (x = x1, rotColor = rotColor1;
            x <= x2; x++, rotColor += rotColorDelta) {
    color = (rotColor + (rand() % (rotDither + 1)))
                                                        >>
fractionBits;
    setpixel(x, y, color);
}
```

Here rotColor is the rotated, fixed-point number that gets incremented by rotColorDelta. To form the actual color, you add the dithering, which is a random number between zero and the dither value. Notice that one is added to the dither before doing the modulo. If you try to do a modulo of 0, you will get a divide-by-0 error, and the program will die. Don't do it.

It is important to add the dithering to the fixed-point number *before* you rotate out the fractional part. Otherwise, you will still have banding. It will be speckled banding, but banding nonetheless. Throughout the Scene Generator, this is the simple way dithering is accomplished.

Please note that the following BALL.C program does not use the TransGraphics system, and requires Microsoft C to compile.

```c
/*BALL.C
*
* Draw a shaded sphere in the center of the screen
*
*   Created  2/27/1993
*
*   Copyright (c) 1993, Scott Anderson
*/

/* INCLUDES */

#include <graph.h>

/* DEFINES */

#define COLORS              256
#define COLOR_RANGE         32

/* TYPEDEFS */

/* the RGB components of the color palette */
typedef struct {
    unsigned char red;
    unsigned char green;
    unsigned char blue;
}
Component;

/* PROTOTYPES */

void ball(int x0, int y0, int radius,
int color1, int color2, int dither);
void twoLines(int x1Rel, int x2Rel, int yRel, int x0, int y0,
                            int color1, int color2, int dither);
void shadedLine(int x1, int x2, int y,
int color1, int color2, int dither);
void setGraphicsMode();
```

```
void setTextMode();
void setpixel(int x, int y, int color);
void setpalcolor(int index, int red, int green, int blue);

/* GLOBAL DATA */

int AspectX;
int AspectY;

int Xmin, Xmax;
int Ymin, Ymax;

Component   Colors[COLORS];

/* CODE */

void
main(int argc, char *argv[])
{
    int dither, radius;
    int dark, lite;
    Component colorA, colorB;

    if (argc > 1)   /* User specified random seed */
        dither = atoi(argv[1]);
    else            /* use time as a unique seed */
        dither = 0;

    setGraphicsMode();

    dark = 32;
    lite = dark + COLOR_RANGE-1;
    colorA.red = colorA.green = colorA.blue = 5;
    colorB.red = colorB.green = colorB.blue = 60;
    setSpread (dark, lite, &colorA, &colorB);

    radius = Ymax/2 - 10;
    ball(Xmax/2, Ymax/2, radius,
                dark, lite, dither);
```

```
    _getch();
    setTextMode ();
}

/* Create a color spread in the palette
*between the dark and lite pointers,
*       with a smooth transition between the start and end colors.
*/

#define SHIFT_BITS 8

setSpread(int dark, int lite,
Component *colorA, Component *colorB)
{
    int index, dIndex;
    int rotRed, rotGreen, rotBlue;
    int dRed,   dGreen,   dBlue;

    rotRed   = (int) colorA->red   << SHIFT_BITS;
    rotGreen = (int) colorA->green << SHIFT_BITS;
    rotBlue  = (int) colorA->blue  << SHIFT_BITS;

    dIndex  = lite - dark;
    dRed    = ((int)(colorB->red   - colorA->red)
<< SHIFT_BITS) / dIndex;
    dGreen  = ((int)(colorB->green - colorA->green)
<< SHIFT_BITS) / dIndex;
    dBlue   = ((int)(colorB->blue  - colorA->blue)
<< SHIFT_BITS) / dIndex;

    for (index = dark; index <= lite; index++) {
        Colors [index].red   = (char) (rotRed   >> SHIFT_BITS);
        Colors [index].green = (char) (rotGreen >> SHIFT_BITS);
        Colors [index].blue  = (char) (rotBlue  >> SHIFT_BITS);

        setpalcolor(index,  rotRed   >> SHIFT_BITS,
                            rotGreen >> SHIFT_BITS,
                            rotBlue  >> SHIFT_BITS);
```

```
        rotRed      += dRed;
        rotGreen    += dGreen;
        rotBlue     += dBlue;
    }
}


/*Draw a shaded ball at x0,y0 with the given radius
* and color range. This is a Bresenham incremental
* ellipse algorithm. Use the equation of an ellipse:
*                             2      2        2
*                    (b x)  + (a y)  - (a b)  =  0
*
*        As you plot integer values of the function,
*this equation will not
        be exactly zero.
*This excess is the distance from the actual ellipse
*        to the integer approximation.  Whether this point is
*inside or outside
        of the actual ellipse determines
*the position of the next point.

void
ball(int x0, int y0, int radius,
int color1, int color2, int dither)
{
    int c1, c2, colorDelta;
    int x, y;
    long a, aSquared, twoAsquared;
    long b, bSquared, twoBsquared;
    long d, dx, dy;

    x = 0;
    y = radius;
    a = radius * AspectY / AspectX;
    aSquared = a * a;
    twoAsquared = 2 * aSquared;
    b = radius;
    bSquared = b * b;
    twoBsquared = 2 * bSquared;
```

```
/* this is the initial excess distance */
   d = bSquared - aSquared * b + aSquared / 4L;

   dx = 0; /* these 2 guys are used to calculate d */
   dy = twoAsquared * b;

   c1 = c2 = (color2 + color1) / 2;    /* middle color */
   colorDelta = COLOR_RANGE / 5;
   while (dx < dy) {   /* slow slope > -1 */
      if (d > 0) {     /* midpoint is outside, go down */
          --y;
          dy -= twoAsquared;
          d -= dy;

          /* when you go down a line, fix the colors & draw the line */
          if (c1 > color1) c1 -= colorDelta;
          if (c2 < color2) c2 += colorDelta;
          if (colorDelta > 1) colorDelta >>= 1;
          twoLines (-x, x, y, x0, y0, c1, c2, dither);

          ++x;
          dx += twoBsquared;
          d += bSquared + dx;
      }
      else {
          ++x;    /* midpoint is inside */
          dx += twoBsquared;
          d += bSquared + dx;
      }
   }
   /* reset d for the fast slope section */
   d += (3L * (aSquared - bSquared) / 2L - (dx + dy)) / 2L;

   while (y > 0) { /* fast slope < -1 */
      if (d < 0) {          /* midpoint is outside */
          ++x;
          dx += twoBsquared;
          d += dx;
      }
```

193

```
            --y;    /* midpoint is inside */
        if (c1 > color1) c1 --; /* continue to increase */
        if (c2 < color2) c2 ++; /* the color range       */

        twoLines (-x, x, y, x0, y0, c1, c2, dither);
        dy -= twoAsquared;
        d += aSquared - dy;
    }
}

/* Draw two shaded, horizontal lines above and below the center
*          (x0, y0) of an ellipse.*/

void
twoLines(int x1Rel, int x2Rel, int yRel,
int x0, int y0, int color1, int color2, int dither)
{
    int y;
    int x1 = x0 + x1Rel;    /* form the plotting coordinates */
    int x2 = x0 + x2Rel;    /* from the Relative values */
    if (x2 >= Xmin && x1 <= Xmax && x1 <= x2) {
        /* first, the top line */
        y = y0 - yRel;
        shadedLine (x1, x2, y, color1, color2, dither);
        if (yRel) {
            /* then the bottom line, if not redundant (yRel = 0) */
            y = y0 + yRel;
            shadedLine (x1, x2, y, color1, color2, dither);
        }
    }
}

/* Draw a horizontal line shaded from left to right color. */

void
shadedLine(int x1, int x2, int y,
int color1, int color2, int dither)
{
    int     x, color;
    int     fractionBits;
```

```c
    long    rotColor, rotColorDelta;
    long    rotColor1, rotColor2;
    long    rotDither;

    fractionBits = 12;
    rotDither = (long) dither << fractionBits;
    rotColor1 = (long) color1 << fractionBits;
    rotColor2 = (long) color2 << fractionBits;
    rotColorDelta = (rotColor2 - rotColor1) / (x2 - x1);
    for (x = x1, rotColor = rotColor1; x <= x2;
            x++, rotColor += rotColorDelta) {
        /* do horizontal line */
        color = (rotColor + (rand() % (rotDither+1)))
                    >> fractionBits;
        if (color > color2) color = color2;

        setpixel (x, y, color);
    }
}


/* Initialize the graphics display
/* adapter to VGA 256 color mode*/

void
setGraphicsMode()
{
    struct _videoconfig vid;

    _setvideomode(_MRES256COLOR);
    _getvideoconfig(&vid);

    Xmin = Ymin = 0;
    Xmax = vid.numxpixels - 1;
    Ymax = vid.numypixels - 1;

    /* The aspect ratio of this graphics mode */
    AspectX = vid.numypixels / 3;
    AspectY = vid.numxpixels / 4;
}
```

```
/* set the palette register to the color components*/

void
setpalcolor(int index, int red, int green, int blue)
{
    _outp (0x3c7, index-1);
    _outp (0x3c9, red);
    _outp (0x3c9, green);
    _outp (0x3c9, blue);
}
```

The Scene Generator

Ever charming, ever new,
When will the landscape tire the view?

—John Dyer, *Grongar Hill*

That brings us to the end of your first exercise with spheres. They are the basis of the moons and planets in the Scene Generator. Now we will move on to some further refinements to increase the realism of the planets. But first, let's look at the Scene Generator so you'll know what I'm talking about.

You Can Do It: Voyage to Distant Planets

To activate the Scene Generator from the DOS prompt, type:

>SCENE

The screen will clear and the program will start to paint the scene. It will throw up a planet or a moon or two, perhaps a double sun or maybe a comet. Then it will draw a foreground of foggy mountains or a rocky plain. (See color Plates 16 and 17 in the middle of the book.) That's it. It's pretty simple, yet occasionally quite effective. Of course, some of the scenes are duds and some of the color combinations are almost painful to look at. But in a few seconds it can make another scene from scratch, so I tend to forgive its failures.

The program lets you admire its latest masterpiece for about ten seconds. Then it starts a new one. If you hate the current landscape, press the Enter key. It will skip to the next one. If you find one that you want to examine, press the space bar. That will put the computer on hold until you press another key.

If you really love a scene, you can save it as a 256-color PCX file on your disk. Just type S and the current screen is saved as VIEW1.PCX. If you type S for another picture, it will be saved as VIEW2.PCX, and so on. Be forewarned: The next time you run the program, it will start numbering from 1 again, and it will overwrite your previous pictures. To keep that from happening, copy the pictures somewhere else, or rename them before running the program again.

When you are done gazing at these alien vistas, press the ESC key to return back to earth—and DOS.

Color and the Computer

The eye perceives color with specialized cells in the retina called cone cells. There are three types of cone cells and they are each receptive to a different color. It turns out that the three colors are close to red, green and blue. When light strikes the cones, they compile their different inputs to produce the sensation of color.

As strange as it seems, a combination of red and green light looks yellow. Yellow light has its own frequency, as do red and green. But there are no yellow frequencies in a mix of red and green. Nevertheless, the eye can be fooled by this trick because of our tricolored cones.

When it came time to add color to television, the engineers wisely chose red, green, and blue as fundamental. By combining different amounts of the three primary colors, they could make almost any color of the rainbow—or at least those that the human eye can see. This is called the RGB color system.

On the PC, you can mix 64 shades of red, green and blue to produce more than a quarter million different colors. That sounds like a lot, but the human eye can distinguish over *sixteen million* colors! A computer that can display all of those is called a true-color system. It will have 256 shades of each primary color and is the ultimate in color graphics. However, you don't get that capability on most PCs (yet!).

A further restriction on the PC graphics cards is that you can only display 256 colors at a time. Given these formidable limitations, it's a wonder you can do any kind of graphics at all on a PC. But there are tricks we can use to beat the system.

197

Color Spreads for Skies and Foregrounds

While hand-painting the landscapes for the space game, I often followed certain procedures over and again. For instance, the first thing I did when drawing a planet was to create a range of continuously changing colors. Most paint programs will create a spread of colors that smoothly blend between two given colors. So I would pick the darkest planet color and the lightest planet color and create a spread between them. That would be the planet color range.

For the surface, I would pick two more colors and create the surface color range.

With the ranges defined, I could then make color blends in any given area. Naturally, when I handed my paintbrush over to the computer, I included this color scheme. It turns out that color ranges were a lucky choice for several reasons.

First, I got my color spreads. That is what creates the skies and the foregrounds in the Scene Generator. It also makes possible the smoothly shaded spheres used for planets and moons.

Second, I got a new plotting algorithm. Because the colors are sorted from dark to light, to lighten a pixel I can just look up the current color index and increase it by one or two. I don't have to analyze the color and create a new one. Similarly, a pixel can be darkened by subtracting from the index. Furthermore, if the color is out of the range, this plot function ignores it. This allows you to selectively "lock" parts of the screen.

Third, dithering became simpler. As with the plotting function, I can now refer to a color by its index. To dither, I can just pick a color above or below the current index. There is no need to calculate an appropriate dither color—they are all in the range. And if a dithered color goes out of range, it is easy to detect and to clip the value.

Fourth, I was able to significantly speed up anti-aliasing—but now I am getting ahead of myself.

Needless to say, creating a set of color ranges has a number of benefits. The downside is that color spreads tend to be somewhat monochromatic, which is boring. Perhaps you can devise a better spread algorithm that includes more variety.

Let's continue this colorful saga with an explanation of anti-aliasing.

Anti-Aliasing

There is an annoying problem with pixel graphics. Especially in the low-resolution 320 ×200 mode, the pixels are large rectangles. When you draw an ellipse, the edge is blocky and jagged (see Figure 5.6). With the linguistic abandon typical of engineers, this was dubbed *aliasing*.

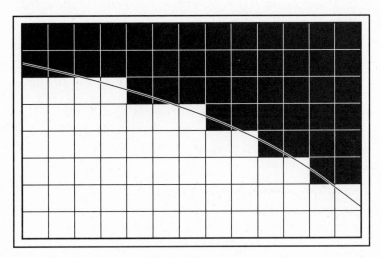

Figure 5.6. *Ugly, jagged edges result when rectangular pixels are used to draw curves.*

To an engineer, an alias is a spurious signal that results when high frequency data is sampled too slowly. This is analogous to what happens when our smooth curve is forced onto integer pixels. A better term for this phenomenon—and one that is picking up momentum—is *the jaggies*, which is nicely descriptive. Whatever its name, there is a cure, of sorts. For aliasing, the cure is called anti-aliasing (although I call it smoothing). Here's what it's all about:

If you put a gray outline around a white circle on a black background, it will soften the edge. This is a primitive form of anti-aliasing. A better idea is to use several shades of gray to soften it even more. But how do you decide what shades to use where?

Because you are drawing an ellipse using rectangles, you can't be very accurate. For every point you plot, there is a fraction of the next pixel that should be plotted too. But you can't plot a piece of a pixel. Or can you? Therein lies the secret to anti-aliasing.

Let's say you are drawing an ellipse and you want to plot just one-tenth of a pixel. What if we try to fake it by plotting the whole pixel, but with just one-tenth of the color?

It turns out that this idea works. For every partial pixel you want to plot, select a color that is between the foreground and background color. If you want to plot one-fourth of a pixel, mix 25 percent of your foreground color with 75 percent of the background color.

This is what is done in Figure 5.7. If a pixel is cut in half by the curve, it is 50 percent gray. If more of the pixel is outside the curve, it is darker (and vice versa).

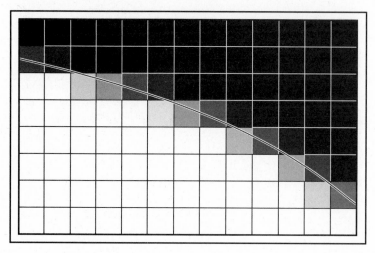

Figure 5.7. *A smoother edge results by shading the pixels according to how much of the pixel is inside or outside of the curve.*

In our ellipse routine, that fractional pixel is proportional to *d,* the difference value that determines the next position. Because it is already calculated, adding anti-aliasing poses no real problem.

In the preceding discussion, I used the gray scale as an example. If the world were all gray, that would be the end of the story. And presumably, color-blind people can skip this section. But for the rest of us, there are some problems when it comes to anti-aliasing colored pixels.

Let's say we have a planet with dozens of shades of orange against a sky with many hues of green. (Yuck.) Around the planet, we want to mix orange and green for an intermediate color. Unfortunately, the color between green and orange is not in the green range or the orange range. It is a completely new color that you need to calculate and then add to the color table.

Did I mention that there are only 256 colors? As you go merrily anti-aliasing along, you are going to generate a *lot* of new colors. Most of the colors have already been taken before you even start. The situation is grim.

The answer is to introduce a little slop into the equations. Like fuzzy logic, this means that you accept a *range* of answers instead of the one optimal answer. That way you don't create as many new colors.

So the anti-aliasing algorithm is: Find out what fraction of a pixel you want to plot, then calculate the appropriate contribution of the foreground and background to the anti-alias color. With that color as a guide, look through the currently assigned colors for a close fit. If nothing is remotely suitable, then create a new entry in the color table. If there is no room in the color table, then use the closest color you found.

One last word on anti-aliasing. If you do a lot of anti-aliased pixels, or worse yet, you anti-alias the same pixel more than once (as I often do), you look through the color table a lot. That hurts. A sequential search like that takes too much time.

Fortunately, I have organized most of the color table into sorted color ranges. Knowing the first and last colors for the range, you can quickly determine if the desired color is in that range or not. If it is, you can calculate which index has the color, so you never have to search the sorted color ranges. This little shortcut makes the smoothing routine about ten times faster.

Selected Effects

Cratered Moons

A trip to the moon on gossamer wings.
—Cole Porter, *Just One of Those Things*, 1935

One of the more compelling effects in the Scene Generator is also the easiest. The craters on the moon and on the surface of the planet are just two ellipses.

The method is simple. First, determine the direction of the sun. In these examples, the sun is always to the right. Now draw an ellipse in a light color, then a dark one immediately to the left of it, as shown on the left of Figure 5.8. This fools the eye into seeing the raised rim of a crater. To make the crater darker, just draw a dark, filled ellipse (do that first, so you don't erase the rim) as shown on the right of Figure 5.8. This will look as if a meteor hit the surface and blasted the light-colored topsoil away to reveal the dark bedrock beneath.

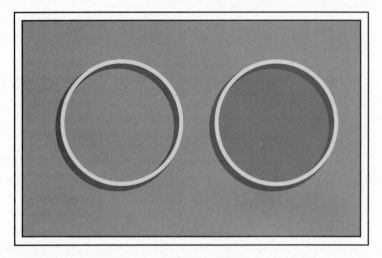

Figure 5.8. *Two offset circles give a raised 3-D effect that forms the basis for a crater. The circle on the right is filled in with a slightly darker color, like many of the craters on the moon.*

Of course Figure 5.8 doesn't look even mildly like a crater, but once it is randomized and dithered, it looks like the craters in Figure 5.9. Not bad for such a cheap trick.

Figure 5.9. *Each shaded crater on the large planet is made up of two ellipses.*

Suns

Second to the right, and straight on till morning.
—Sir James M. Barrie, *Peter Pan*, 1904

The first color range is the sun's. Most of the color ranges are 32 colors apiece. Traditionally, the first 16 colors in the VGA color table are set to mimic the 16 default EGA colors. I leave them alone. The sun doesn't need that much of a color range; it's mostly just bright. So I only use the second 16 colors for it.

Before drawing the sun, the program creates a glow in the sky by drawing concentric circles using the lighten-up plot routine. A highly dithered glow is subtle, as in Figure 5.10. Without the dither, the glow takes on a sparkle, with horizontal and vertical rays spiking out, as in Figure 5.9 (above). This is just an accident that occurs when you try to draw circles with little rectangular pixels. It looks like the flare of a camera lens or halos in the fog, but it's an interesting effect, so I've kept it.

Figure 5.10. *A sparkly sun adds a romantic twilight effect.*

Then the sun is drawn as two circles on top of each other—first with the dark color, then smaller with the light color. This makes a nice corona around the sun.

Banded Planets

What a delightful thing this perspective is!
                                  —Paolo Uccello, Italian painter, 1397-1475

To simulate banded gas-giant planets (as in Figure 5.11), I use yet another ellipse routine. It draws lighter or darker bands on the planetary sphere with pseudo-perspective, as seen in Plates 1 and 2. The ellipses are larger than the planets, but they are clipped to the planet color range. The greater the eccentricity of the ellipses, the greater the perspective effect.

Figure 5.11. *Banded clouds make this moon into a Jovian giant. (See Plate 16 for a color rendition.)*

Don't confuse this purposeful effect with color banding, the problem we mentioned (and solved) earlier.

The effect could use some tweaking. It seems a little too regular. You could say that about a lot of the features of the Scene Generator, but I think the banding is the worst.

Foggy Mountains

But I'm not so think as you drunk I am.
                                  —John Collings Squire, *Ballade of Soporific Absorption*

One of the more simple yet dramatic effects in the Scene Generator is the mountain scene. This was inspired by watching the foggy Sonoma mountains as they fan out to the ocean. I painted these by "cutting" mountains out of color spreads and pasting them on top of other mountains. The algorithm mimics this procedure.

It uses brownian motion, a poor man's fractal, to create the profile of the mountain. Brownian motion is random, but not entirely so. Each point is related to the previous point. It is sometimes called correlated noise, but I avoid that term because it seems to make people nervous; I stick to brownian.

The name honors Robert Brown, an English botanist who saw ink particles moving around in his microscope in the early 1800s. He thought they were caused by unseen microorganisms, and he may have been right. The contending theory is that he was watching a large-scale manifestation of thermodynamics. The proponent of that outrageous point of view was the young Albert Einstein in 1905. Oddly enough, the facts are still in contention. Whatever caused Robert Brown's ink to jitter, the motion itself became a subject of study.

Another name for this phenomenon is the drunken walk. This is a term with great visual appeal. The drunk staggers from point to point, randomly. But he can only fall so far with each lurch. That is how each point is related to the previous point. And that is the profile of the mountain—a drunken walk.

You select how rough you want the mountains to be with the size of the maximum lurch. With a large whiskey lurch, you get the craggy, rugged Rockies. With a small wino lurch, you get the rolling, sinuous hills of Sonoma.

From the selected profile, the mountain fades down to the fog bank below (Figure 5.12).

For perspective, I make the next mountain range twice as tall and start it lower on the screen.

Clouds

The clouds are really just misty streaks. They are produced with a random shifting of sine functions. This gives them some of the features of the banded cirrus clouds that provided my model (see Figures 5.9, 5.10, and 5.12 in this chapter and color Plate 17). This routine could use some more variety. Maybe you could make some cumulus clouds if you put your mind to it. You might be able to convert the rock routines to make puffy clouds.

Figure 5.12. *Spaceship pilots hate landing on craggy mountains in the fog, but the view on the way down sure is pretty. (See Plate 17 for a color snapshot.)*

Rocks

The rocks are pretty dumb. Starting with a basic bun-shape, I add some random elements. Certain key aspects, like the size and the relative height and width, are modified by random multipliers. Then the outline of the bun is randomized. That's a rock.

Take a bunch of rocks, group them around the same approximate *y*-value, and you have a rock group. Maybe not the Rolling Stones, but a rock group nonetheless.

If you throw down a dark ellipse at the right angle, you can make the rock cast a shadow. (See color plate 16.) This is a cheap trick, and I know it, but it's fast and convincing. Feel free to play with this code. You can get some pretty strange-looking objects by altering the height and width parameters.

Comets

Comets start with a small version of the glow that I used for the sun(s). Then a tail is added. The tail of a comet has to point away from the sun, so the angle from the sun is computed by the arc tangent function. From there, the tail is drawn by successively narrower cones radiating out from the comet's head.

For the final touch, the head of the comet is drawn in a bright sun color. (See Figure 5.10, presented earlier.)

Crescents

Crescents are the usual occurrence in space, where there is little in the interplanetary medium to diffuse the light.

The Scene Generator draws crescents by setting a cut-off color in the color spread. This is passed to the horizontal line routines that distribute the colors. If the color is less than the cut-off value, then a dark color is plotted. Otherwise, the lighter colors in the spread are plotted as usual. (See Figure 5.9 through 5.12 and color Plates 16 and 17.)

Because the cut-off value follows the curve of the planet, the resulting shape is a crescent. This is another really cheap trick.

Working Code: Setting the Scene

The rather lengthy SCENE program is not listed here in the book, but you'll find complete source code for it on the disk in the files SCENE.C, FEATURES.C, GRAPHICS.C, MATH.C, and MATH.H (which replaces, and should not be confused with, the math.h file that came with your compiler).

Note that the SCENE program does not use the TransGraphics system, and requires Microsoft C to compile.

The following notes on each source file will help you jump into the code and add your own creative scene enhancements.

SCENE.C

The main program is in SCENE.C. It initializes the global color range parameters and the areas to which they correspond. There is a color range and an area limit for the sun, sky, planet, moon, and surface. The area limits provide a simple mechanism for confining color searches and "locking out" parts of the screen.

The color table is declared with room for 256 colors. It will later be filled with the color spreads. Each spread has 32 colors, except the sun, which has 16. The colors are a component type—a structure with the three RGB components: red, green and blue.

A group of global variables that define the scene are declared. These variables indicate how many suns are visible, whether there is an atmosphere, how big the crescent is on the moon, etc. A more sophisticated approach would be to make these variables members of a structure and pass them as arguments to any interested subroutines. As nice as that is, it makes a short program wordier. To keep things simple, I have left them as globals, and any function that cares to can get easy access to them.

The main program parses the command line to get a random "seed" for the first scene. This number is all you need to specify a scene. While running the Scene Generator, you may see a scene you want to examine. Press the N key to print the number of the scene. That number is the random seed, and can be used to re-create the same scene, even while running a debugger. For instance, to repeat scene #24558, you would type:

```
>SCENE 24558
```

That number will start the "random" number generator at the same point, and it will create the same scene as before. If you don't specify a number, the program will create a random seed from the current clock reading. This ensures that you will see a different scene every time you run the program.

Next the graphics mode is turned on, and the program starts to loop through random scenes. It initializes the major aspects of the scene, placing the results in the appropriate global variables. Then each feature of the scene is drawn, layer upon layer.

First the sky is drawn, then comets, suns, planets and moons. The farther away something is, the earlier it gets displayed.

The surface is painted, and craters, rocks, or mountains are added. Finally, the clouds are drawn on top of both the sky and the foreground.

That's the basic setup. After the drawing is complete, the program waits about ten seconds for you to view the scene or press a key. Then it gets a new random seed and starts another scene.

The routine initScene uses random numbers to generate the important features of the scene. You can play with this routine to add more or less variety to the pictures. This routine also creates the color spreads for each area. It calls one of the three spread functions, normSpread, monoSpread, or rainbowSpread.

The spread functions attempt to produce spreads with certain characteristics. normSpread doesn't do anything fancy; it just makes a dark color and a light color within the specified range and then does the spread.

monoSpread tries to ensure that one component of the RGB triplet is enhanced over the others, so that a monochromatic spread is produced.

rainbowSpread does just the opposite, trying to get a *different* color for the dark and light shades. These spreads not only get lighter through their range, but the color changes as well. These colorful ranges are used for the sky.

The next few routines in SCENE.C draw the various layers of the landscape. They check certain global variables and, based on them, call various graphics primitives to accomplish their task. These routines, such as drawMoon, drawPlanet and drawSurface, make random decisions about the size, locations, and other aspects of the scene. This is a good place to experiment, because it is fairly straightforward, and pretty resilient. Just be sure to back up everything before you make any big changes.

At the end of SCENE.C are some miscellaneous routines. OrbCoordinates calculates the positions of the planets and moons on a straight line, with a little fluctuation. (See the moons in Plate 17.) Most stable planetary systems evolve to have a planar form, and that is what I am trying to mimic here.

SaveScreen writes a numbered PCX file to your disk.

CheckKey is called after every picture is drawn. It checks the keyboard for the space-bar (pause), Esc (quit), Enter (continue), S (save), or N (number) keys. If Esc is pressed, the program resets the text mode and exits through quit.

The header file, SCENE.H contains the constants used by SCENE.C and other files. It defines the color ranges by name. This is where the structures are defined, such as the Component, Layer and Range structure.

Component is a structure defining the red, green and blue components of a color.

Layer and Range are structures that describe some aspects of a feature like a planet, moon or surface. Layers can be either above or below the horizon, with an associated color spread. The Range structures define the color spreads themselves.

Right now, the Ranges and Layers are linked, but that doesn't have to be the case; there could be several layers sharing a color range.

FEATURES.C

This file contains the basic parts of the layers. The various skies, surfaces, and planetary features are all here.

The first routine, blackSky, creates a sky full of stars. It clears the sky to a dark color, then calls starryField. That routine draws stars that are just random points plotted with light colors. Sometimes the stars have a light sky color, and sometimes they are a sun color. (See Plate 16.)

Then comes skySpread, which draws a sky with vertically blended colors. The sky is darkest at the top and gets lighter toward the horizon. Some skies have an additional horizontal spread, with the sky getting lighter toward the right, where the sun is assumed to be. (See Plate 17.)

SurfaceSpread is similar to skySpread. It has an added feature, though. It increases the dithering from the horizon down. This makes the "closer" parts of the surface more textured, heightening the perspective effect (Plate 16).

Comet is the next routine. It calculates the angle to the sun to determine the direction of its tail. It puts a small glow in the sky where the head of the comet is, then draws the tail as a series of randomized cones. It tops this off with a dot of sun color at the head. (See Figure 5.10.)

Sun puts a glow on the screen, then draws two circles—a dark sun and a smaller, lighter sun on top of it. The solid circles are painted by calling ball with the same value for both the dark and light colors, so it can't do a spread. A sun is a big emitter of light, so it doesn't have any shadows to make it look spherical; it is just a bright disk in the sky. Sometimes there are two suns. (See Plate 17.)

SkyGlow is called by both sun and comet. It draws concentric circles in a lighter color. Depending on whether it is dithered or not, the glow will be subtle (Figure 5.10) or flared (Figure 5.9). As discussed previously, this is a consequence of pixel round-off errors. But if it works, I keep it.

The dither is based on global scene variables, so if there are multiple suns or comets, they will all have the same dither. I think it makes things a bit more realistic, but you can change it to a random number if you like. The line is:

```
int dither = SkyDither % 3;
```

To make each glowing object have its own random glow, you might try:

```
int dither = RAND(3);
```

Craters figures out how many craters to put on a moon and where. The number of craters is based on the radius of the moon, so bigger moons have more craters. Craters calls the routine crater, which does one crater at a time.

Crater just draws a light and a dark ellipse offset by 1 in both x and y from each other (see Figure 5.8). Some of the large craters are filled in with a darker color to create mares or "seas." The ellipses are drawn at an angle appropriate to their position on the moon. Ellipses close to the moon's edge are warped, with a smaller curvature toward the edge. This makes them look as if they are wrapping around the sphere.

That is another cheap trick, and I hope you like it.

Bands is the routine that puts the stripes on the planets. It just draws a series of half-ellipses, mirrored around the equator of the planet. Some of the bands are lighter than the planet surface, some are darker. This routine could use some jazzing up. It needs more randomness or something like turbulence to look more realistic.

CrateredPlain scatters a bunch of craters over the surface spread. Again, the craters are just offset ellipses. To fake perspective, the craters are added in layers that get taller as they move down the screen. Thus the foreground has larger craters than the distant horizon, as you would expect.

SurfaceCrater does the actual drawing of the craters.

SmoothHorizon draws an anti-aliasing line or two between the sky and the surface. This eases an otherwise abrupt transition. Because the horizon is supposed to look far away, it shouldn't have sharp features.

FogScene is the routine that puts up layers of mountains. The first layers are small, but as more layers are drawn, they get larger and move down the screen. The part of the code that does this is as follows:

```
layers = 2 + RAND(3);
yLen = (Ymax - Horizon) / (layers * layers);
for (layer = 1; layer <= layers;
                        layer++, ylen += ylen) {
...
}
```

You start off by defining a random number of layers, then you create the height of the layer (yLen) by dividing the total height (Ymax - Horizon) by the number of layers squared. The loop draws the layers, doubling the height of each layer as it goes. This gives you perspective without having to multiply or divide inside the loop. A similar procedure is used to space the craters and rocks on the surface.

The fogScene routine then calculates a random mountain profile as it goes from left to right. From the top pixel of the range down, the mountain is lightened up until it is equal to the light fog color of the surface.

211

The next five routines are for the overly complicated rocky plains. The first routine, rockyPlains, sets up the perspective layers and scans across x to deposit groups of rocks by calling rockGroup. RockGroup in turn makes a little batch of rocks of different sizes, all nestled around the same *y*-value. For each stone, the routine calls rock. This is the routine that actually does the drawing. If the rock is less than a certain size, the program calls pebble. The final routine in this suite is called smoothRock and it anti-aliases the edges of the rocks.

You are encouraged to play with these rock routines. They could use a lot of streamlining. There must be a better way to do a dumb rock. Let me know if you figure it out.

Clouds are drawn on top of both surfaces and skies—low and high. The low clouds are clipped to be beneath the horizon and they are limited to the surface color range. The high clouds are above the horizon and use the sky color range.

The clouds are drawn with multiple horizontal line segments. Each line lightens or darkens the pixels underneath. The intensity of the shading is determined by a randomized sine function. There is a lot of room for experimentation in this routine. Tweak the variables and see what happens. I bet you can improve on these ratty clouds.

GRAPHICS.C

This file contains all of the graphics primitives used by the features. It starts out with setGraphicsMode which clears the screen to graphics and sets up the window clipping variables Xmin, Ymin, Xmax, and Ymax. After that comes setTextMode, which resets the original text screen when you quit the program.

There are three text routines that are used for printing out the random number seed. (Type N while the program is running.) They are setTextPosition, setTextColor and gprintf.

There are the standard utility routines to get a pixel and set a pixel.

To set a palette color, I use output ports (setpalcolor). There is a way to do this in most C compilers, but the Microsoft version takes about a hundred times longer, so I use this method instead.

SetSpread is the routine that forms a smooth blend of colors between the selected endpoints. Following that is smooth, the anti-aliasing routine, which is well described earlier in this chapter.

Next are three plot routines. ShadePlot draws a pixel that is either darker or lighter that the current pixel. SmoothPlot draws a pixel that has a percentage mix of the given color with the screen color. Smooth2plot is similar, except that it draws a color a percentage of the way between the two given colors.

Ellipse is the routine that gets so much use making craters and banded planets. Unlike ball, which is a Bresenham ellipse, these ellipses need to be rotated. For this we need to call out the big guns and use some trig functions. If the ellipse is just an outline, ellipse calls arcEllipse. Otherwise, it fills an ellipse by creating an array of left and right edges, then filling between them.

The last routines should be familiar. They are the Bresenham ball routines. A few things have been added to the ball routine we saw in the first part of the chapter. This version of ball has anti-aliasing built in.

And it has an extra feature in the crescent routine. Ball calls twoLines, which calls shadedLine, which calls shadeColor. When a crescent planet is displayed on an atmospheric spread, shadeColor is used to fill in the dark side of the planet. Instead of just using the dark planet or moon color, shadeColor returns a sky value. These sky values are another spread, but darker than the sky. This gives a good simulation of a shaded moon in an overcast sky.

MATH.C and MATH.H

MATH.C contains the random number and trig functions. For maximum speed, these routines are implemented as table look-ups.

ISin and iCos are the integer sine and cosine functions. They return a value from a predefined table of sines. The first quadrant of values is all that is needed, because every other value can be derived from them:

$$\theta > \frac{\pi}{2}: \qquad \sin(\theta) = \sin(\pi - \theta)$$

$$\theta > \pi: \qquad \sin(\theta) = -\sin(\theta - \pi)$$

Similarly, the cosine is related to the sine:

$$\cos(\theta) = \sin\left(\theta - \frac{\pi}{2}\right)$$

You might be wondering how you can have an integer version of sine or cosine. Don't those functions produce fractional values between 1 and -1? Well, yes. But this is a tricks book, and here is another trick.

The integer returned by these functions is just the numerator of the actual fraction. To produce the true sine or cosine, you must divide by 32,768, the scale factor (SCALE). To use these values, you multiply by another number (usually a radius of some sort) and *after* that, you divide by SCALE. We economize two ways: first by looking up the value, and second by using integer arithmetic instead of floating point.

MATH.H has some constants and macros to make the trig functions a little more understandable. It defines the full, half and quarter-circle constants. A FULL_CIRCLE is defined to be 1,080, which gives the routines a resolution of one-third of a degree. The macro TRIG_MULT does the required long multiplication and division, then recasts it as an integer.

In addition to the trig functions, MATH.C has the random number routines. The Scene Generator calls for a random number thousands of times to generate a planetary landscape. Unfortunately, the standard random number routine is quite slow.

I have implemented a very fast solution to the problem. I generate a random number table at the beginning of the scene and then just increment my way through it. In places where the repeating pattern might be noticed, I scramble the table index (FAST_INDEX) occasionally to start in another spot. Believe it or not, this actually works.

InitFastRandom sets up the table. FastRandom returns the table value and increments FAST_INDEX. ReseedFastRandom generates a new random index.

MATH.H has some useful macros for these functions. FASTRAND(n) looks up a table value and returns the modulo(n) of it. This is the most popular version of the random calls. Modulo(n) returns a number between 0 and n-1. So a call to FASTRAND(n) returns a random number up to n-1, making it easy to dither and set random ranges. Notice that the fastRandom function is not called. Instead, a direct reference to the random table is inserted into the code. This avoids the considerable overhead of a function call and makes getting a random number pretty simple.

However, the modulo function itself is not so fast, so I have included the most super-fast random number macro I have ever seen. It's pretty silly, but it works in *some* situations. It is called AND_FASTRAND(n), and it produces a random number between 0 and n.

This is just great, but there is a restriction, and it is a pretty severe one. The limit number (n) must be a power of two, minus one. This includes the numbers 1, 3, 7, 15, 31, 63, 127, 255, 1023 and so on. But if these numbers will work for you, AND_FASTRAND should be your choice over FASTRAND. It works by ANDing the bits from the random table, effectively masking off the desired number of high bits. ANDing is one of the things a computer does really well—and fast. Again, AND_FASTRAND does not call a function; it is a direct access of the random table.

If time is not critical, you can also use the RAND or AND_RAND macros. These do the same as their FAST counterparts, but they call the compiler's built-in random function. It is slower but "more random."

That wraps up our discussion of the Scene Generator. There are tricks galore for you to play with, and with a few changes, I think you could make the computer a much better artist. Along the way, you will pick up techniques for dithering and anti-aliasing that will be helpful in any graphics environment, not just "2 ½-D."

One warning: This program is a lot of fun to play with, and it might interfere with your legitimate work. I am not liable for your lost hours, so show some restraint.

With that minor caveat, I wish you a bon voyage on your journey to the stars. Send me a postcard, OK?

Fractals and Fractal Animation

You have probably heard about the new science of *chaos* and its companion geometry, *fractals*. Scientists in diverse disciplines from astrophysics to zoology are using chaos and fractals to model and understand complex phenomena that previously eluded investigation. The infinitely intricate shapes called fractals are being discovered in every corner of the natural world.

Fractals, however, were discovered first in the unnatural world—the world behind the computer screen. It is the graphics gurus, not the mathematicians and scientists, who have mesmerized the masses with convincing fractal models of plants, galaxies, clouds, mountains, and a million other-worldly images beyond description. Almost any image that can be represented with traditional geometry can be represented more compactly with fractals.

In this chapter, you'll learn how to interactively design your own fractals and master some cutting-edge graphics tricks for producing dramatic fractal animation sequences. Along the way, you'll also learn how IFS fractal image compression—one of the hottest graphics techniques to hit the streets in years—can store pictures in a fraction of the space needed by any other image storage technology.

What's a Fractal?

If you wish to advance into the infinite, explore the finite in all directions.

> —Johann Wolfgang von Goethe, *Epigrams*, early nineteenth century

Fractals are infinitely detailed shapes. No matter how closely you examine a fractal— even under a billion-zillion power microscope—you find complex detail. Traditional linear shapes, on the other hand, always appear smooth when you look at them closely (See Figure 6.1).

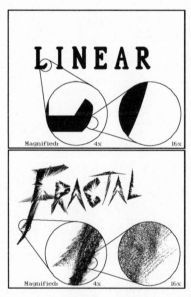

Figure 6.1. *Smooth curves look like lines when magnified enough, but fractals don't.*

On The Way to Infinity

How can finite creatures such as us describe infinitely detailed shapes? Start with an ordinary finite shape, such as the triangle in Figure 6.2a. You then *transform* it in some way—for example, you might shrink it, spin it, and move it over and up a bit, as in Figure 6.2b. Repeating that transformation over and over eventually gets you nowhere (Figure 6.2c).

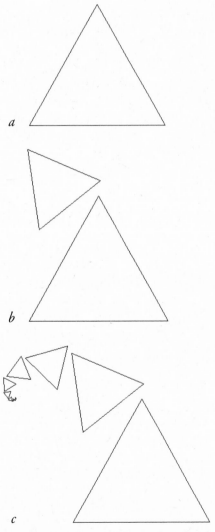

Figure 6.2. *Take a simple shape and transform it over and over. If you use just one transformation, you won't get far.*

Add another transformation, however, and things start to get interesting. Figure 6.3a shows the original triangle transformed in two different ways. To produce Figure 6.3b, each of the resulting triangles was run through the same two transformations repeatedly. This yields a complex—though still not infinite—shape. Only if you could do an infinite number of repetitions would you get the fractal shape in Figure 6.3c. Figure 6.4 shows a similar sequence applied to four transformations of a simple shape.

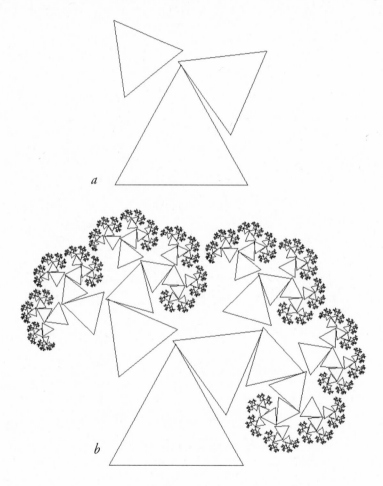

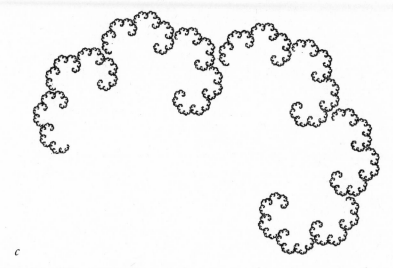

c

Figure 6.3. *When you repeat more than one transformation at a time, however, you can approximate an infinitely detailed fractal.*

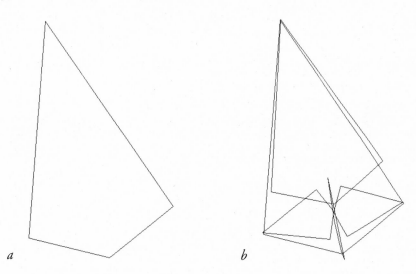

a

b

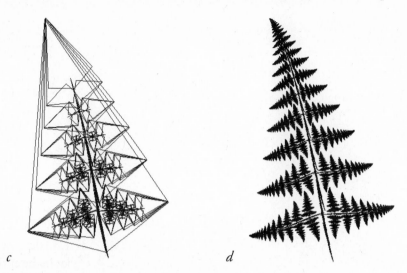

c   d

Figure 6.4. *The same transform-and-repeat approach can approximate complex natural shapes when you use several transformations.*

Thus, one way to draw a fractal is to repeatedly transform a simple shape to draw successive approximations of an infinitely detailed shape. Benoit Mandelbrot (the "father of fractals" himself) used this approach—aptly referred to as the *successive approximation algorithm*—to construct the earliest computer-generated fractal images.

The Chaos Game

Wouldn't it be nice if you could skip all those repetitions and jump right to the infinitely detailed fractal? Thanks to a mathematical magic trick invented by Dr. Micheal Barnsley and his fellow mathematicians at Georgia Tech, you can do just that.

The fractal in Figure 6.3c was actually generated by playing a "chaos game" with the following rules:

1. Imagine the large triangle and the two smaller triangles in Figure 6.3a—don't draw them, but write down a "recipe" that tells you how to transform the big triangle into each of the small ones. For example, the recipe for the first transformation might be "shrink to half-size, turn counter-clockwise 30 degrees, and move up and to the left." (Your recipe would say exactly how far up and to the left relative to the size of the triangle.)

2. Draw a point anywhere on the screen.

3. Choose one of the two transformation "recipes" at random. (Flip a coin—heads we go up and left, tails we go up and right.)

4. Apply your recipe to the point you just drew to locate and draw a new point.

5. Repeat steps 3 and 4 until you've drawn 5,000 points.

That's it. Yes, it's magic. And yes, it works. Honest.

Self-Similarity

Why does the recipe work? Because fractals made this way are always *self-similar*, meaning that each part resembles the whole. Notice that the shape in Figure 6.3c consists of two miniature copies of itself. If you took every dot in the entire big shape and moved it according to your transformation recipe, you would get one of those two miniatures. When you apply your transformation recipe to jump from one point to another, you are leaping from a point on the whole big shape to the corresponding point on a smaller copy of it. Leap around this way on the shape for a long time, and you end up landing on almost all the dots in both copies.

When you use more than three transformations (as in Figure 6.4), you get shapes made up of more than three copies of themselves.

(If you find this self-similarity business mind-boggling, don't worry. Working with fractals involves an entirely new way of seeing shapes and images. After exploring this new geometry for a while, your intuition will start to shift and you may experience an "Aha!" or two as the principles and procedures become suddenly "instinctual.")

Interactive Fractal Design

Fractals know some of Nature's algorithms... The advantages are compelling:

■ *Greater naturalness. The controlled randomness of fractal techniques gives a more natural image than does building from conventional geometric forms.*

■ *Deep naturalness. Fractal geometry apparently accurately models the process of growth and the underlying grammar of the natural forms it simulates.*

■ *Greater efficiency. Fractal images have absurdly modest storage requirements, if stored in the form of the generator function and generated at need.*

■ *Greater power. Fractal techniques use recursive image generation to allow any level of detail to be produced from a single stored generator function.*

—Michael Swaine, *Dr. Dobb's Journal*, 1990

To make fractals on your computer, you need an easy way to describe a wide variety of transformation recipes. As discussed in Chapter 4, the possible geometric transformations include rotational *spin*, straight-line *translation*, resizing *zoom*, *skew* (similar to *lean* or *shear*), and *squashing*. The next **Math Behind the Magic** section explains how you can mix and match all these transformation types with a simple set of numbers, called *iterated function system* (IFS) codes.

By interactively adjusting these transformations while displaying the resulting fractal on your screen, you can design and animate your own custom fractal shapes. In the following **You Can Do It** and **Working Code** sections, you can explore the fractal universe with an interactive fractal animator program called FRAN.

Figure 6.5 shows a sample FRAN session. I started with the maple leaf fractal included on the disk (LEAF.IFS), and interactively altered the transformations to make a fractal plant.

 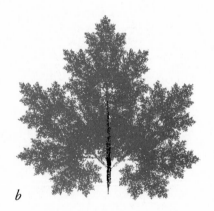

a   *b*

c

d

e

f

g

h

Figure 6.5. *The FRAN program lets you design your own fractals by altering an existing fractal. Here, I change a leaf into a plant by editing each of four transformations.*

225

You Can Do It: Interactive Fractal Animation

Meet FRAN. She may seem a little strange at first, but she's really a lot of fun once you get used to her. Here, she and I will help you turn a maple leaf into a fractal shrub...

1. To ask FRAN to let you modify the fractal named LEAF.IFS and save a new fractal called NEWLEAF.IFS, enter the following command at the DOS prompt:

```
FRAN LEAF.IFS NEWLEAF.IFS
```

When the leaf appears, part of it is highlighted in white, and a menu of controls appears at the bottom of the screen. These controls are:

Next	(Tab key)	Highlights a different part of the fractal
Size	(* or /)	Enlarge or shrink the highlighted part
Spin	(+ or -)	Rotate the highlighted part
Skew	(; or ')	Rotate only the x-axis of the part
Squash	([or])	Squish or stretch only the x-axis of the part
Color	(Enter key)	Change the color of the whole fractal
Save/Quit	(Esc key)	Save the modified fractal and quit

You can also use the arrow keys to move the highlighted part up, down, left, and right.

2. Press ; (the semicolon key, meaning Skew) three or four times to make the central part of the leaf into more of a skinny stem shape.

3. Press the Tab key to highlight the next part of the fractal. (Notice that each part is a transformed copy of the whole.)

4. Press / (the forward-slash key) two or three times to shrink the highlighted part.

Remember that fractal *parts* are intimately connected with the *whole*, and you are really changing one of the transformations that defines the entire shape. Therefore, your changes are reflected throughout all areas of the fractal, rather than being restricted to the white highlighted region.

5. Use the arrow keys to move the highlighted part until its "mini-stem" connects to the side of the main stem.

6. Press the Tab key again to select the next part.

7. Press the / key a couple of times to shrink that part.

8. Use the arrow keys to move the part over until its stem connects with the main stem.

9. Finally, press Tab again and then press * to enlarge the upper part of the plant a bit.

At this point, you might like to press Esc to save the plant fractal as NEWLEAF.IFS, which you can then use as a starting point for future designs.

There are several fractals on the disk, including some named TWO.IFS, THREE.IFS, FOUR.IFS and so forth. The numerical names refer to the number of transformations (parts) that each fractal has, so you can experiment with simpler or more complex fractal designs.

As you play with the various transformations, you'll develop an intuition for fractal symmetry and design. As you get used to thinking about *parts* as transformations and working with self-reflective patterns, you will learn to predict how a particular change will affect the whole fractal.

If you find fractal design and animation addictive, you can upgrade to a full-blown fractal design and modeling system called Fractal Grafics with the registration/order form in the back of this book. You'll also get a free copy of my 500-page illustrated book, *FractalVision*, which explains the real-world applications and implications of fractals and chaos theory in depth.

The Math Behind the Magic: Iterated Function Systems

You can express all the transformations mentioned in the last You Can Do It section with six variables:

```
movex = translation along the x axis
movey = translation along the y axis
```

```
sizex = size along the x axis
sizey = size along the y axis
spinx = rotation of the x axis
spiny = rotation of the y axis
```

As you might surmise, `movex` and `movey` just specify an x,y distance to move. When `sizex` and `sizey` are the same, they specify a relative size. When `sizex` is less than `sizey`, an object becomes skinnier, and when `sizex` is larger than `sizey`, the object becomes fatter. Similarly, when `spinx` and `spiny` are equal, a normal rotation occurs; when they differ, objects appear to be skewed.

The FRAN program listed in the **Working Code** section below changes the values of the above six variables based on keypresses from a simple menu. You could repeatedly apply the formulas given in Chapter 4 for each of the transformations to create a fractal. However, all those calculations—especially the sine and cosine calculations needed to spin—are very time-consuming, and the 5,000 iterations needed to fill in a fractal would take quite some time, even on a fast 486.

Fortunately, matrix algebra provides a mathematical shortcut for calculating all of the above transformations in one fell swoop. The formula to transform an x,y point is quick and simple:

```
newx = x * a + y * b + movex
newy = x * c + y * d + movey
```

You must iterate these formulas thousands of times, but you can do the most time-consuming portions of the calculations just once by precomputing a, b, c, and d with these formulas:

```
a = sizex * cos(spinx)
b = - sizey * sin(spiny)
c = sizex * sin(spinx)
d = sizex * sin(spiny)
```

Notice that a, b, c, and d don't have any intuitively obvious geometric meaning—it would be hard to predict what kind of change in the transformation you'd see by just changing the value of b, for example. Therefore, the FRAN program lets the user modify the size, spin, and move variables and calculates a, b, c, and d from those in the `computef()` function.

To save a fractal design for future use, you can simply write the values of a, b, c, d, movex, and movey to a disk file. FRAN writes these *IFS Codes* to an ASCII text file in a format that can be read by two of the most popular fractal programs, the famous freeware FRACTINT and my own interactive fractal design system, Fractal Grafics. There is no need to store sizex, sizey, spinx, and spiny because they can be reconstructed with the following formulas:

```
spinx = atan(c/a)
spiny = atan(-b/d)
sizex = a / cos(spinx)
sizey = d / cos(spiny)
if (a = 0) sizex = abs(c)
if (d = 0) sizey = abs(b)
```

Where atan(c/a) means the arctangent of the ratio of c to a, and abs(c) means the absolute value of c.

If you examine one of the IFS code files on the disk, you'll find seven values on each line. The first six numbers are the values of a, b, c, d, movex, and movey. The final number is a measure of the *relative area*, usually referred to as a *probability* (*p*) of visiting the portion of the fractal defined by the other six numbers. This is needed by some programs so that they can put more dots in large regions of the fractal than in small regions. Otherwise, the larger regions would appear noticeably more faint. The FRAN program ignores this seventh number when it reads the file, but recomputes the relative area of each part of the fractal every time a change is made to a transformation.

The relative area of a transformation is simply:

```
a * d - b * c
```

The paint() function, which displays the fractal, sums up the total areas of all the transformations, then sets up an array p[] with the cumulative relative area of each transformation. It then uses p[] as the probability of selecting each transformation.

When you create an IFS file, the values of *p* should be between 0.0 and 1.0, with the sum total of all the *p*s always adding up to 1.0. For example, a set of IFS codes defining four transformations, all covering the same relative area, should have four lines of numbers and the last number on each line should be 0.25.

You can edit IFS files with any text editor if you want to fool around with the numbers and see what happens.

Working Code: Do It Yourself Fractals

Because they involve thousands of calculations, fractals can take a long time to display. Because those calculations are *iterative*—feeding the results of a formula back into the same formula over and over—they also require a lot of precision. To put the pedal to the metal without sacrificing accuracy, FRAN uses 64-bit *fixed-point* integer variables and custom assembly language routines to optimize multiplication and division for 8086, 286, and 386 processors. This allows FRAN to display a fractal up to ten times as fast as an ordinary program using the floating-point math routines that came with your compiler.

Fixed-point math is a technique for storing and doing calculations with nonintegers (numbers with some digits after the decimal point) as though they were integers. This speeds up everything because your computer takes much longer to multiply or divide two noninteger *floating-point* numbers than it does to multiply or divide two integers. The trick is simple: Simply move the decimal point to the right a few places before you store a number, and *then* chop off the noninteger part. When you retrieve the number, move the decimal point back to the left again.

In a computer, of course, the decimal point isn't *decimal*, it's binary. You need to scale by a power of two instead of a power of ten. FRAN uses a scaling factor of 65536 (referred to as M1 or MF in the code).

The assembly language `multiply()` and `divide()` routines are precompiled into an object file named MUDI.OBJ. You don't need an assembler to link them with FRAN or any of your own programs—just put an `#include "mudi.h"` statement in the beginning, and add MUDI.OBJ to the compile line like this:

```
TGMS FRAN.C MUDI.OBJ
```

(If you are using a different compiler or graphics library, use the appropriate command instead of TGMS. See the introduction to this book for complete compilation instructions.)

Notice that the key functions in this program are very short and sweet—`paint()` calculates the relative areas and then displays the fractal with a simple loop, while `loadifs()` and `saveifs()` are simpler still. You should find it very easy to read and write IFS codes from your own programs, and to fool around with different coloring schemes or transformation formulas.

Listing 6.1. Include this header file with any program that links in MUDI.OBJ to use fast 32-bit fixed-point math.

```c
/* MUDI.H
 *
 * Header File to be used with MUDI.ASM
 * for fast 32-bit fixed-point "integer" math functions
 *
 * Note that you must also link MUDI.OBJ with your program!
 *
 * from Tricks of the Graphics Gurus
 * Copyright 1993 by Dick Oliver
 */

#include <stdio.h>
#include <stdlib.h>
#include <math.h>
#include <ctype.h>
#include <process.h>

/* M1 and MF are the scaling factors for 32-bit integer arithmetic
 * BITSH is the corresponding bit shift factor
 * MAXINT is the maximum signed short integer
 */

#define M1 65536L
#define MF 65536.0
#define BITSH 16

/* macros to use the long int arithmetic routines in MUDI.ASM */

#define mu(a, b) MULTIPLY(a, b, BITSH)
#define di(a, b) DIVIDE(a, b, BITSH)
#define cputype() CPUTYPE()

/* Routines from MUDI.ASM */

extern int CPUTYPE(void);
extern long MULTIPLY(long x, long y, int bitsh);
extern long DIVIDE(long x, long y, int bitsh);
```

Listing 6.2. FRAN is a fast and easy-to-use FRactal ANimation and interactive design system.

```
/* FRAN -- A Fractal Animator
 *
 * Header File
 * from Tricks of the Graphics Gurus
 * Copyright 1993 by Dick Oliver
 */

#include <stdio.h>
#include <stdlib.h>
#include <math.h>
#include "mudi.h"    /* for fast 32-bit integer math */

/* PI and friends are just what you think they are
 * MAXSIZE could be called "almost one", scaled up by M1
 * MAXINT is the maximum value of a short int */

#define PI (3.1415927 * M1) /* 205887L */
#define TWOPI (PI * 2L) /* 411774L */
#define ALMOST0 16L
#define MAXSIZE 65532L
#define MAXINT 32767

/* These are the values of key bindings */

#define ENTER 13
#define ESC 27
#define TAB 9
#define UNTAB -15
#define UP -'H'
#define DN -'P'
#define LT -'K'
#define RT -'M'

/* macro getch() replacement */

#define geta if ((a = getch()) == 0) a = -getch();\
            else if (a > 0) a = toupper(a)
```

```
#define NTRANS 19    /* maximum number of parts */
#define INISIZEINC 10486L /* initial ratio of re-size for each step */
#define INIMOVEINC 655360L    /* initial amount of movement for each step
*/
#define INISPININC PI / 16 /* initial amount of spin for each step */

#define NAMELEN 40   /* maximum length of filenames, including path */


/* FRAN.C -- An Interactive Fractal Animator
 *
 * from Tricks of the Graphics Gurus
 * Copyright 1993 by Dick Oliver
 *
 * Load an IFS fractal and interactively change it,
 * then save the resulting new fractal to another IFS file
 */

#include "tg.h"                /* See TG.TXT for more info. */
#include "fran.h"         /* definitions specific to FRAN.C */

FILE *diskfile;            /* used for all disk file access */
char savename[NAMELEN];    /* filename for modified fractal */

long spininc = INISPININC,      /* amount to spin each time */
     sizeinc = INISIZEINC,       /* size change each time */
     moveinc = INIMOVEINC;       /* movement step each time */

long fa[NTRANS], fb[NTRANS],     /* Iterated Function System */
     fc[NTRANS], fd[NTRANS],
     sizex[NTRANS], sizey[NTRANS],  /* fa,fb,fc,fd from the */
     spinx[NTRANS], spiny[NTRANS],  /* user's point of view */
     movex[NTRANS], movey[NTRANS];

/* NOTE: All of the above variables are 32-bit integers,
 * scaled by the amount defined as M1 (equal to 65536).
 * The mu() and di() macros call assembly language routines
 * to multiply and divide these numbers without screwing up
 * the scaling factor. Storing these as integers instead of
```

continues

233

Listing 6.2. continued

```c
 * floating point values speeds processing by a factor of 3
 * on 8086-based machines, a factor of 5 on 80286 machines,
 * and a factor of 10 on 80386 machines.  It also makes this
 * source code harder to read, but the speed is worth it!   */

int tofile = 0,                          /* used to save DXF files */
    white,              /* color to make menu and current part */
    thiscolor = 3,      /* color to make rest of the fractal */
    i, j,                          /* miscellaneous counters */
    thistran = 0,                  /* current transformation */
    ntrans,                        /* number of transformations */
    cpu;              /* used by mudi.obj to identify cpu type */

/* function prototypes */

int main(int nargs, char **arg);
void computef(int i);
void paint(void);
extern int loadifs(char *name);
extern int saveifs(char *name);

int main(int nargs, char **arg)
{   char a;                          /* current keypress */
    cpu = cputype();          /* find out what cpu we have */
    printf("\n\n FRAN -- An Interactive FRactal ANimator");
    printf("\n\n from Tricks of the Graphics Gurus\n\n");
    if (nargs < 3)          /* make sure files were specified */
    {   printf("To use this program:\n\n");
        printf("FRAN FILE.IFS FILE2.IFS\n\n");
        printf("Where FILE1.IFS is an existing 2D ifs file\n");
        printf("and FILE2.IFS is a name for the new file.\n");
        exit(0);
    }
    if (loadifs(arg[1]) == 0)  /* load the starting fractal */
    {   printf("Could not load the file named %s\n\n", arg[1]);
        exit(0);
    }
```

```
strcpy(savename, arg[2]);   /* remember the name to save */
   tg_pickmode();               /* ask user for a video mode */
   white = 15 % tg_ncolors;     /* define the color white */
   for (i = 0; i < ntrans; i++)
       computef(i);             /* compute the IFS codes */
   tg_moveto(0, tg_scrny - tg_chary);     /* show a menu */
   tg_outtext("Next=Tab   Size=*/  Spin=+-  Skew=;\' "
           " Squash=[]  Color=Enter  Save/Quit=Esc");
   tg_setviewport(0, 0, tg_scrnx - 1, tg_scrny - tg_chary);
   while(1)                              /* main menu loop */
   {   tg_clearviewport();       /* clear all but the menu */
       paint();                  /* display the fractal */
       geta;                     /* then get the next keypress */
       switch(a)                 /* what shall we do now? */
       {   case LT:                          /* move left */
               movex[thistran] -= moveinc;
               break;
           case RT:                          /* move right */
               movex[thistran] += moveinc;
               break;
           case UP:                          /* move up */
               movey[thistran] -= moveinc;
               break;
           case DN:                          /* move down */
               movey[thistran] += moveinc;
               break;
           case TAB:               /* select the next part */
               if (++thistran >= ntrans) thistran = 0;
               break;
           case ENTER:                     /* change color */
               thiscolor++;
               if ((thiscolor >= tg_ncolors) ||
                   (thiscolor >= 15)) thiscolor = 1;
               break;
           case '*':                  /* grow (increase size) */
               if ((sizex[thistran] =
                   mu(sizex[thistran], sizeinc + M1))
                   > MAXSIZE)
                       sizex[thistran] = MAXSIZE;
```

continues

235

Listing 6.2. continued

```
                  if ((sizey[thistran] =
                      mu(sizey[thistran], sizeinc + M1))
                      > MAXSIZE)
                          sizey[thistran] = MAXSIZE;
                  break;
              case '/':              /* shrink (decrease size) */
                  if ((sizex[thistran] =
                      di(sizex[thistran], sizeinc + M1))
                      < ALMOST0)
                          sizex[thistran] = ALMOST0;
                  if ((sizey[thistran] =
                      di(sizey[thistran], sizeinc + M1))
                      < ALMOST0)
                          sizey[thistran] = ALMOST0;
                  break;
              case '-':                     /* spin clockwise */
                  if ((spinx[thistran] -= spininc) < 0L)
                      spinx[thistran] += TWOPI;
                  if ((spiny[thistran] -= spininc) < 0L)
                      spiny[thistran] += TWOPI;
                  break;
              case '+':          /* spin counter-clockwise */
                  if ((spinx[thistran] += spininc) >= TWOPI)
                      spinx[thistran] -= TWOPI;
                  if ((spiny[thistran] += spininc) >= TWOPI)
                      spiny[thistran] -= TWOPI;
                  break;
              case '\'':              /* skew x-axis clockwise */
                  if ((spinx[thistran] += spininc) >= TWOPI)
                      spinx[thistran] -= TWOPI;
                  break;
              case ';':    /* skew x-axis counter-clockwise */
                  if ((spinx[thistran] -= spininc) < 0L)
                      spinx[thistran] += TWOPI;
                  break;
              case '[':                      /* squish x-axis */
                  if ((sizex[thistran] =
                      di(sizex[thistran], (sizeinc + M1)))
```

```
                    < ALMOST0)
                        sizex[thistran] = ALMOST0;
                break;
            case ']':            /* de-squish (stretch) x-axis */
                if ((sizex[thistran] =
                    mu(sizex[thistran], (sizeinc + M1)))
                    > MAXSIZE)
                        sizex[thistran] = MAXSIZE;
                break;
            case ESC:               /* save new IFS and quit */
                tg_closedown();
                saveifs(savename);
                printf("\n\nSeeyalater!\n");
                exit(0);
        }
        computef(thistran);          /* recompute IFS codes */
    }
}

/* Compute the IFS codes given size and spin */

void computef(int i)
{   fa[i] = sizex[i] * cos((double) spinx[i] / M1);
    fb[i] = -sizey[i] * sin((double) spiny[i] / M1);
    fc[i] = sizex[i] * sin((double) spinx[i] / M1);
    fd[i] = sizey[i] * cos((double) spiny[i] / M1);
}

/* Display the fractal using "random iteration" */

void paint(void)
{   int i, j, k, xx, yy,           /* miscellaneous counters */
        p[NTRANS],         /* probability (area) of each part */
        tc;                       /* color to give a pixel */
    long x1 = 0L, y1 = 0L, x2, y2;       /* current pixel */
    unsigned long ct = 0L;      /* how many pixels to paint */
    long f1 = 0L, f2, ff[NTRANS];    /* used to compute p[] */
```

continues

Listing 6.2. continued

```
/* first, find the relative area of each transformation */

    for (i = 0; i < ntrans; i++)
        f1 += (ff[i] = labs(mu(fa[i], fd[i]) - mu(fb[i], fc[i])));
    if (f1 == 0L) f1 = 1L;
    f2 = di((long) MAXINT, f1);

    /* now make a cumulative probability of visiting each */

     j = 0;
    for (i = 0; i < ntrans - 1; i++)
    {   if ((k = (int) mu(ff[i], f2)) == 0) k = 1;
        p[i] = (j += k);
    }

    /* skip around for a little while to find the fractal */

    for (j = 0; j < 8; j++)
    {   i = rand() % ntrans;
        x2 = mu(x1, fa[i]) + mu(y1, fb[i]) + movex[i];
        y2 = mu(x1, fc[i]) + mu(y1, fd[i]) + movey[i];
          x1 = x2, y1 = y2;
    }

    /* now show it on the screen by hopping around on it */

    while(—ct > 0)
    {   if (kbhit()) return;      /* go home if a key is hit */
        j = rand();        /* pick a tranformation at random */
        for (i = 0; i < ntrans - 1; i++) if (j < p[i]) break;
        x2 = mu(x1, fa[i]) + mu(y1, fb[i]) + movex[i];
        y2 = mu(x1, fc[i]) + mu(y1, fd[i]) + movey[i];
        x1 = x2, y1 = y2;
        if (i == thistran) tc = white;    /* one part white */
        else tc = thiscolor;
        xx = (int) (x2 >> BITSH) + (tg_scrnx >> 1);
        yy = (int) (y2 >> BITSH) + (tg_scrny >> 1);
        tg_putpixel(xx, yy, tc);       /* display on screen */
    }
}
```

```
/* The following two routines load and save
 * Fractal Grafics and FRACTINT compatible
 * two-dimensional Iterated Function System codes
 * Note that loadifs() only reads the very first set
 * of IFS codes in the file and ignores the name label
 * in the file entirely. Likewise, saveifs() only writes
 * one set of codes per file and gives them
 * the same name as the file itself. */

int loadifs(char *name)
{   float aa, bb, cc, dd, ee, ff, pp;
    char a;
    int n = 999, ret = 1;
    double d1, d2;
    if ((diskfile = fopen(name, "r")) == NULL) return(0);
    while(((a = fgetc(diskfile)) != '{') &&
          (a != '(') && (a != EOF));
    if ((a != '{'))
    {   fclose(diskfile);
        return(0);
    }
    for (n = 0; n < NTRANS; n++)
    {   if (fscanf(diskfile,
                 " %f %f %f %f %f %f %f\n",
                   &aa, &bb, &cc, &dd, &ee, &ff, &pp) != 7)
            break;
        else
        {   movex[n] = (long) (ee * -50.0 * MF);
            movey[n] = (long) (ff * -50.0 * MF);
            d1 = atan2(cc, aa);
            d2 = atan2(-bb, dd);
            spinx[n] = (long) (d1 * MF);
            spiny[n] = (long) (d2 * MF);
            sizex[n] = (long) (aa * MF / cos(d1));
            sizey[n] = (long) (dd * MF / cos(d2));
            if (aa == 0) sizex[n] = (long) fabs(cc * MF);
```

continues

239

Listing 6.2. continued

```
            if (dd == 0) sizey[n] = (long) fabs(bb * MF);
             computef(n);
          }
      }
      if (n > 0) ntrans = n;
      if (((n < 2) ¦¦ (ferror(diskfile) != 0))) ret = 0;
      fclose(diskfile);
      return(ret);
}

int saveifs(char *name)
{   int i, ret = 1;
    long f1 = 0L, ff[NTRANS];
    float xx;
    if ((diskfile = fopen(name, "w")) == NULL) return(0);
    fprintf(diskfile, "\n %s {\n", name);
    for (i = 0; i < ntrans; i++)
        f1 += (ff[i - 1] =
             labs(mu(fa[i], fd[i]) - mu(fb[i], fc[i])));
    if (f1 == 0L) f1 = 1L;
    for (i = 0; i < ntrans; i++)
    {   if ((xx = (float) di(ff[i - 1], f1) / MF) < 0.01)
           xx = 0.01;
        fprintf(diskfile,
               " %.2f %.2f %.2f %.2f %.2f %.2f %.2f\n",
               (float) fa[i] / MF,
               (float) fb[i] / MF,
               (float) fc[i] / MF,
               (float) fd[i] / MF,
               (float) movex[i] / (MF * -50.0),
               (float) movey[i] / (MF * -50.0), xx);
    }
    if (ferror(diskfile) != 0) ret = 0;
    fprintf(diskfile, " }");
     fclose(diskfile);
    return(ret);
}
```

Fractal Tweening

It seems that nobody is indifferent to fractals. In fact, many view their first encounter with fractal geometry as a totally new experience from the viewpoints of aesthetics as well as science.

—Benoit Mandelbrot, *The Beauty of Fractals*, 1986

In Chapter 4, Scott Anderson unraveled the mysteries of smooth animation by exposing the algorithms for automatic *tweening*. With a few additional clues, you will discover how to apply those techniques to fractals. Before the case is closed, you will see an innocent fractal plant metamorphose into a mathematical monster and watch Chaos itself coalesce to form a perfect leaf.

Because the fractals painted by FRAN are made up of individual dots, the most obvious way to gradually change one fractal into another would be to compute the in-between locations for every point that gets drawn on the screen. Although this would work, the time and memory involved in tweening several thousand points might prove prohibitive on a humble personal computer.

There is a better way. Because the shape of each fractal is defined by just a few transformations, you can compute the in-betweens for those transformations only. You then can reconstruct the image for each frame with a `paint()` function similar to the one that FRAN uses.

The Math Behind the Magic: Tweening IFS Codes

Computing the IFS transformation that falls exactly in-between two given IFS transformations is no more difficult than tweening the endpoints of a line. You simply average the values of a, b, c, d, x, and y.

To compute a set of n tweens, just divide the difference between the final IFS and the initial IFS by n. You then add that delta to the IFS each time you produce a new tween frame. For example, to find 10 tweens between two IFS transformations, you first compute the change in each variable for each frame. In classic engineering style, I shall call these incrementcal changes the deltas:

```
da = (a2 - a1) / 10
db = (b2 - b1) / 10
dc = (c2 - c1) / 10
dd = (d2 - d1) / 10
dx = (x2 - x1) / 10
dy = (y2 - y1) / 10
```

You then add the deltas to the IFS to make successive tweens by repeating the following ten times:

```
(display the fractal defined by a, b, c, d, x, and y)
a = a + da
b = b + db
c = c + dc
d = d + dd
x = x + dx
y = y + dy
```

The **Working Code** for the FREEN program below uses this elementary algorithm to produce all of its intricate gyrations.

Figure 6.6 depicts a fractal fern gradually changing into a famous fractal called *Heighway's Dragon.* The triangles on the left represent the transformations (relative to the large grey triangle) that define the fractal at each tween, while the fractal itself metamorphoses on the right.

This sequence depicts the history of fractal geometry in reverse, by the way. Koch invented his "coastline" curve back in the 1800's as an example of mathematical "pathology" just to prove that there could exist a continuous curve that had no derivatives or tangent lines, and which therefore could not be analyzed with modern calculus. Curves like this were considered "unnatural" and basically useless for real-world problems. The fern fractal, on the other hand, was popularized by Michael Barnsley in the 1980's as a symbol of fractal geometry's ability to model real-world natural form and function. History has transmuted a "mathematical monster" into "the geometry of nature," and my little animation sequence whimsically changes it back again.

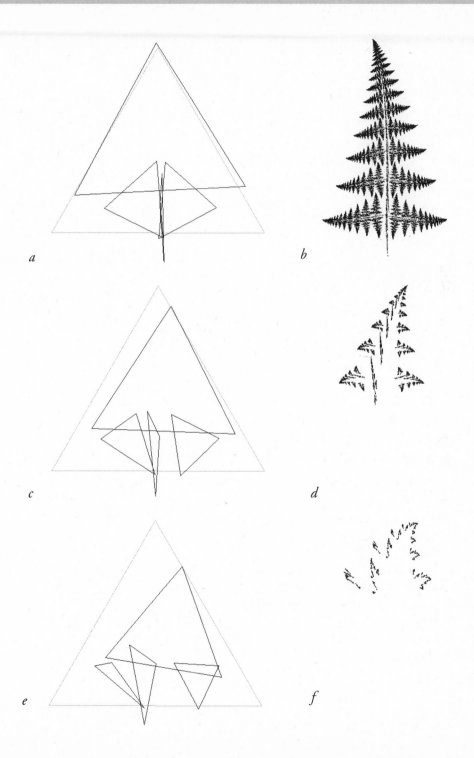

a

b

c

d

e

f

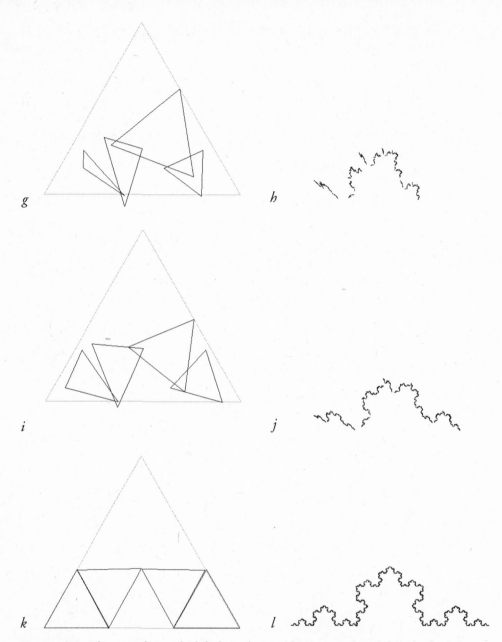

Figure 6.6. *The triangles on the left show the transformations that define the fractals on the right. Both sequences were generated with automatic tweening.*

Both the starting and ending fractals in Figure 6.6 were defined by the same number of transformations—the four small triangles on the left define four "copies of the whole" in the fractals on the right. If you want to tween two fractals that have a different number of transformations, you can add "dummy" transformations to one of them first. For example, the fractal maple leaf in Figure 6.7 is defined by just four transformations, whereas the word CHAOS has no less than 19 transformations. To transform Chaos into the leaf, you must map each of the 19 transformations onto one of the four leaf transformations. That way, the many pieces of Chaos will appear to coalesce into the simple shape of the leaf.

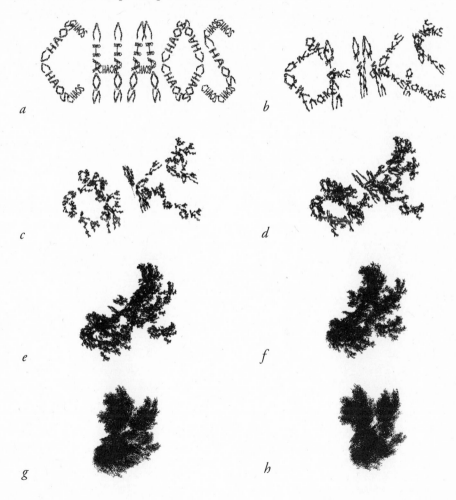

i　　　　　　　　　　*j*

Figure 6.7. *"What else, when chaos draws all forces inward to shape a single leaf?"*
—*Conrad Aiken*

If you wanted to turn the leaf into Chaos, you would first need to create several duplicates of the transformations that define the leaf and hide them exactly behind the original four. The would look the same, but could then split up into 19 pieces to become CHAOS.

In the **You Can Do It** and **Working Code** sections below, you will meet FRAN's companion named FREEN. FREEN is a FRactal twEENer that automatically metamorphoses any IFS fractal into any other.

You Can Do It: Between Infinities

Thanks to FREEN, all your favorite fractals can magically metamorphose into one another at will.

1. To watch FREEN do its stuff, enter a command like the following at the DOS prompt:

```
FREEN FERN.IFS KOCH.IFS 20
```

where FERN.IFS and KOCH.IFS could be any two-dimensional IFS files and the number at the end indicates how many tween frames to display in the metamorphosis. (If you don't specify the number on the command line, it will default to 10.)

2. When each frame appears, you can press any key to proceed to the next frame.

3. If you want to quit before the sequence is complete, hit the Esc key. Otherwise, FREEN will return you to the DOS prompt after the specified number of frames.

The IFS files specified in the first step are the ones used to make Figure 6.6. To reproduce Figure 6.7, enter FREEN CHAOS.IFS LEAF.IFS instead. You can use TWEEN with any of the IFS files, except those whose names start with "3D" (Chapter 9 presents FRAN3D and FREEN3D to work with those three-dimensional fractals).

Working Code: A Fractal Tweener

The paint() and loadifs() routines in FREEN are almost—but not quite—identical to the ones in the FRAN program presented earlier in this chapter. This version of the paint() function colors each part of the template a different color so that you can see the tweening more clearly. Because there is no user interaction, the loadifs() function doesn't need to figure out values for the spinx, spiny, sizex, and sizey used in FRAN.

Listing 6.3. The FREEN program automatically computes and displays a given number of "tween" frames between any two infinitely detailed fractals.

```
/* FREEN.C -- A Fractal Tweener
 *
 * from Tricks of the Graphics Gurus
 * Copyright 1993 by Dick Oliver
 *
 * Load two IFS fractals and gradually change one into
 * the other and back again in a specified number of steps
 */

#include "tg.h"                  /* See TG.TXT for more info. */
#include "mudi.h"                /* for fast 32-bit integer math */


FILE *diskfile;                  /* used for all disk file access */
```

continues

Listing 6.3. continued

```
long fa[NTRANS], fb[NTRANS],                    /* First IFS */
     fc[NTRANS], fd[NTRANS],
     movex[NTRANS], movey[NTRANS],
     fa2[NTRANS], fb2[NTRANS],                  /* Second IFS */
     fc2[NTRANS], fd2[NTRANS],
     movex2[NTRANS], movey2[NTRANS],
     fad[NTRANS], fbd[NTRANS],          /* Delta between 1 & 2 */
     fcd[NTRANS], fdd[NTRANS],
     movexd[NTRANS], moveyd[NTRANS];

/* NOTE: All of the above variables are 32-bit integers,
 * scaled by a factor of 65536. The mu() and di() macros
 * call assembly language routines to multiply and divide
 * these numbers without screwing up the scaling factor. */

int ntrans, ntrans2,           /* number of transformations */
    cpu;             /* used by mudi.asm to identify cpu type */

/* function prototypes */

int main(int nargs, char **arg);
void tween(int nsteps);
void paint(void);
int loadifs(char *name);

int main(int nargs, char **arg)
{   int nsteps, i;
    cpu = cputype();             /* find out what cpu we have */
    printf("\n\n FREEN -- A Fractal Tweener");
    printf("\n\n from Tricks of the Graphics Gurus\n\n");
    if (nargs < 3)        /* make sure files were specified */
    {  printf("To use this program:\n\n");
       printf("FREEN FILE.IFS FILE2.IFS N\n\n");
       printf("Where FILE1.IFS and FILE2.IFS are existing\n");
       printf("2D IFS files and N is the number of tweens\n");
       printf("to create between the two shapes.\n");
       exit(0);
    }
    if (loadifs(arg[2]) == 0)     /* load the second fractal */
```

```
      {  printf("Could not load the file named %s\n\n", arg[2]);
         exit(0);
      }
   }
   ntrans2 = ntrans;
   for (i = 0; i < ntrans2; i++)    /* copy into second IFS */
   {   fa2[i] = fa[i];
       fb2[i] = fb[i];
       fc2[i] = fc[i];
       fd2[i] = fd[i];
       movex2[i] = movex[i];
       movey2[i] = movey[i];
   }
   if (loadifs(arg[1]) == 0)     /* load the first fractal */
   {  printf("Could not load the file named %s\n\n", arg[1]);
      exit(0);
   }
   if (nargs < 3) nsteps = 10;
   else sscanf(arg[3], "%d", &nsteps);
   tg_pickmode();                /* ask user for a video mode */
   tween(nsteps);           /* compute and display the tweens */
   tg_closedown();               /* close down the graphics */
   printf("That's all, folks!");
}

/* Compute and display a given number of fractal tweens */

void tween(int nsteps)
{   int i, j, k;
    char a;

    /* if there are a different number of transformations,
       double-up as necessary to make the same number */

    if (ntrans2 < ntrans)
    {   for (i = ntrans2; i < ntrans; i++)
        {   fa2[i] = fa2[i % ntrans2];
            fb2[i] = fb2[i % ntrans2];
            fc2[i] = fc2[i % ntrans2];
            fd2[i] = fd2[i % ntrans2];
            movex2[i] = movex2[i % ntrans2];
            movey2[i] = movey2[i % ntrans2];
        }
```

continues

Listing 6.3. continued

```
      ntrans2 = ntrans;
 }
else
{   if (ntrans < ntrans2)
    {   for (i = ntrans; i < ntrans2; i++)
        {   fa[i] = fa[i % ntrans];
            fb[i] = fb[i % ntrans];
            fc[i] = fc[i % ntrans];
            fd[i] = fd[i % ntrans];
            movex[i] = movex[i % ntrans];
            movey[i] = movey[i % ntrans];
        }
        ntrans = ntrans2;
    }
}

/* compute the deltas */

for (j = 0; j <= ntrans; j++)
{   fad[j] = (fa2[j] - fa[j]) / nsteps;
    fbd[j] = (fb2[j] - fb[j]) / nsteps;
    fcd[j] = (fc2[j] - fc[j]) / nsteps;
    fdd[j] = (fd2[j] - fd[j]) / nsteps;
    movexd[j] = (movex2[j] - movex[j]) / nsteps;
    moveyd[j] = (movey2[j] - movey[j]) / nsteps;
}

/* display the tween by repeatedly adding the deltas */

for (k = 0; k <= nsteps; k++)
{   tg_clearscreen();
    paint();
    if (k == nsteps) break;
    if (kbhit())
    {   a = getch();
        if (a == 27) break;
    }
    for (j = 0; j <= ntrans; j++)
    {   fa[j] += fad[j];
        fb[j] += fbd[j];
```

```
                fc[j] += fcd[j];
                fd[j] += fdd[j];
                    movex[j] += movexd[j];
                    movey[j] += moveyd[j];
            }
        }
}


/* Display the fractal using "random iteration"
   (See FRAN.C for more detailed comments) */


void paint(void)
{   int i, j, k, xx, yy,          /* miscellaneous counters */
        p[NTRANS],        /* probability (area) of each part */
        tc;                      /* color to give a pixel */
    long x1 = 0L, y1 = 0L, x2, y2;        /* current pixel */
    unsigned long ct = 0L;      /* how many pixels to paint */
    long f1 = 0L, f2, ff[NTRANS];    /* used to compute p[] */
    for (i = 0; i < ntrans; i++)   /* compute relative area */
        f1 += (ff[i] = labs(mu(fa[i], fd[i]) -
                            mu(fb[i], fc[i])));
    if (f1 == 0L) f1 = 1L;
    f2 = di((long) MAXINT, f1);
    j = 0;                 /* compute cumulative probability */
    for (i = 0; i < ntrans - 1; i++)
    {   if ((k = (int) mu(ff[i], f2)) == 0) k = 1;
        p[i] = (j += k);
    }
    for (j = 0; j < 8; j++)          /* skip the first few */
    {   i = rand() % ntrans;
        x2 = mu(x1, fa[i]) + mu(y1, fb[i]) + movex[i];
        y2 = mu(x1, fc[i]) + mu(y1, fd[i]) + movey[i];
          x1 = x2, y1 = y2;
    }
    while(--ct > 0)
    {   if (kbhit()) return;      /* go home if a key is hit */
        j = rand();        /* pick a tranformation at random */
        for (i = 0; i < ntrans - 1; i++) if (j < p[i]) break;
        x2 = mu(x1, fa[i]) + mu(y1, fb[i]) + movex[i];
        y2 = mu(x1, fc[i]) + mu(y1, fd[i]) + movey[i];
        x1 = x2, y1 = y2;
        xx = (int) (x2 >> BITSH) + (tg_scrnx >> 1);
        yy = (int) (y2 >> BITSH) + (tg_scrny >> 1);
```

continues   **251**

Listing 6.3. continued

```
            if (tg_ncolors == 2)
            {   tg_putpixel(xx, yy, 1);


            }
            else
            {   tg_putpixel(xx, yy, i + 1);            /* display */
            }
        }
}

/* The following routine loads Fractal Grafics and FRACTINT
 * compatible two-dimensional Iterated Function System codes.
 * Note that it only reads the very first set of IFS codes
 * in the file and ignores the name label entirely. */

int loadifs(char *name)
{   float aa, bb, cc, dd, ee, ff, pp;
    int n = 999, ret = 1;
    char a;
    double d1, d2;
    if ((diskfile = fopen(name, "r")) == NULL) return(0);
    while(((a = fgetc(diskfile)) != '{') &&
          (a != '(') && (a != EOF));
    if ((a != '{'))
    {   fclose(diskfile);
        return(0);
    }
    for (n = 0; n < NTRANS; n++)
    {   if (fscanf(diskfile,
                   " %f %f %f %f %f %f %f\n",
                   &aa, &bb, &cc, &dd, &ee, &ff, &pp) != 7)
            break;
        else
        {   fa[n] = (long) (aa * MF);
            fb[n] = (long) (bb * MF);
            fc[n] = (long) (cc * MF);
            fd[n] = (long) (dd * MF);
            movex[n] = (long) (ee * -50.0 * MF);
            movey[n] = (long) (ff * -50.0 * MF);
```

```
        }
    }
    if (n > 0) ntrans = n;
    if (((n < 2) ¦¦ (ferror(diskfile) != 0))) ret = 0;
    fclose(diskfile);
    return(ret);
}
```

Mandelbrot and Julia Set Animation

The Mandelbrot set broods in silent complexity at the center of a vast two-dimensional sheet of numbers called the complex plane. When a certain operation is applied repeatedly to the numbers, the ones outside the set flee to infinity. The numbers inside remain to drift or dance about. Close to the boundary minutely choreographed wanderings mark the onset of instability. Here is an infinite regress of detail that astonishes us with its variety, its complexity and its strange beauty.

—A.K. Dewdney, "Computer Recreations," *Scientific American*, August 1985

You have seen how to make your own fractals using Iterated Function Systems. But some of the most famous and spectacular fractals were not designed intentionally— they were discovered by mathematicians who never suspected that such visual splendor lay behind simple, time-worn formulas. Many believe that the mathematical fractal called the *Mandelbrot set* will go down in history as one of the most important discoveries of our century.

While the mathematicians scratch their heads, wondering how a tiny formula like $z^2 + c$ could weave so tangled a thread between order and disorder, you can use the results of their experiments to produce breathtaking animated graphics.

To paint the Mandelbrot set (Figure 6.8), each point on a computer display is multiplied by itself repeatedly, adding the original point each time. The next **Math Behind the Magic** section explains how to "multiply a point by itself." Once you know the formula, creating a Mandelbrot set picture is quite straightforward.

Figure 6.8 depicts the Mandelbrot set in its entirety, while Figure 6.9 shows a few interesting regions visited with the MANIMATE program presented below. (See Table 6.1 below for the exact coordinates of the regions in Figure 6.9.)

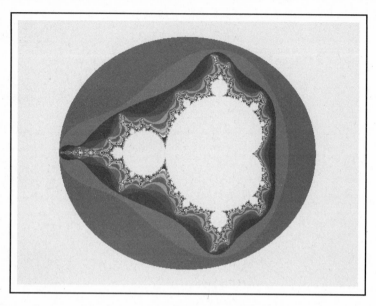

Figure 6.8. *The Mandelbrot set has been variously called, "the granddaddy of all fractals," "Amygdala, the great almond," and "the most complicated object in mathematics."*

a

b

c

d

Figure 6.9. *Some close-ups of the Mandelbrot set.*

The Math Behind the Magic: Iteration on the Complex Plane

You've seen spectacular pictures of the Mandelbrot set (the "great granddaddy of all fractals") in countless magazine articles, advertisements, and book covers. The chaotic convolutions of this set and its children, the Julia sets, arise out of the simplest possible iteration of x,y coordinates.

The basic formula used to compute the Mandelbrot set is:

```
z <= z * z + c
```

which reads "the new z becomes the old z squared plus a constant c".

To get the pretty pictures, the results of this equation are fed back into the same equation over and over again. Eventually, z either gets bigger and bigger until it wanders off to infinity or it settles down into some sort of cycle. Which behavior you observe depends on what value you use for c.

The Mandelbrot set proper is simply the set of all values of c which settle down instead of rushing away to infinity.

The hidden trick to all this is that z and c are not your run-of-the-mill numbers. They are actually *complex numbers* of the form

```
z = x + i * y
```

where i is the square root of negative one. (Yes, I know that negative one doesn't have a square root. That's why the second half of a complex number is called *imaginary*.) Because z is made up of two *components* (x and y), you can visualize all possible values of z as a two-dimensional plane where the value of x is a horizontal coordinate and the value of y is a vertical coordinate. When you think of it this way, the *complex plane* can easily be depicted on a two-dimensional computer screen using ordinary x,y coordinates.

Any book on algebra will tell you more about the ins and outs of working with complex numbers, but all you need to know to make fractals is how to multiply and add them. To compute z squared, you simply multiply x + iy times itself (remembering that i squared is −1) to get

```
x <= x * x - y * y
```

```
y <= 2 * x * y
```

To add a complex number c, you simply add the x coordinate cx to x and the y coordinate cy to y, yielding:

```
x <= x * x - y * y + cx
```

```
y <= 2 * x * y + cy
```

The MANIMATE.C program presented later in this chapter iterates these preceding equations and checks to see if they zoom off to infinity in some user-specified number of iterations. How does it know if they go to infinity? Fortunately, a mathematical theorem proves that any point that strays further than 2 units from the point 0,0 will eventually go to infinity. The distance from any point from 0,0 is:

```
square root of (x * x + y * y)
```

To eliminate the time-hogging square root function, MANIMATE just checks to see if the square of the distance (equal to x * x + y * y) is greater than 4. If it is, MANIMATE stops iterating x and y and gives the point c a color according to how many iterations it took to "escape." This method of constructing a colored picture of the region surrounding the Mandelbrot set is known as the *escape-time algorithm*.

The closer you look at the Mandelbrot set, the more intricate and visually magnificent detail you'll see (the following **You Can Do It** section will take you into this fantastic landscape momentarily). Just in case infinite detail isn't enough for you, however, each and every point in the Mandelbrot set actually contains a complete, infinitely detailed landscape of its own, called a *Julia set*.

Julia sets are drawn the same way the Mandelbrot set is drawn, but with the assumption that you are taking an infinitely close close-up of a particular point. Therefore, each point is infinitely close to that particular point. I won't work through the infinitely sticky math to formally prove that this assumption results in the equations you'll find in the next **Working Code** section. You'll just have to take my word for it that the Julia set images in Figure 6.10 are what you'd see if you zoom infinitely far into the Mandelbrot set—and then zoomed in some more. Considering the wildness and weirdness of the images, it may be easy to believe that they come from the land beyond infinity—especially when you see them animated in color.

How do you animate them in color? Glad you asked! Mathematical fractals are the best possible candidates for the *color cycling* techniques introduced in Chapters 1 and 2. Because palette colors are assigned in gradual succession based on how close points are to the complex boundaries of the fractal sets, simply rotating the palette produces the illusion of mesmerizing intricate motion all over the screen.

So many hours have been spent staring at these hypnotic, zooming color fields that they have actually become a widely recognized symbol of computer art. Fortunately, no amount of enthusiastic image-mining is likely to exhaust the supply of visual gems buried within infinitely many infinite landscapes. If you explore for a while, you are certain to come upon breathtaking patterns that have never been seen by human eyes.

Figure 6.10 shows each of the Julia sets associated with the points in Table 6.1. On the left, you see birds-eye views overlooking the entire Julia sets. On the right are bugs-eye views from deeper within.

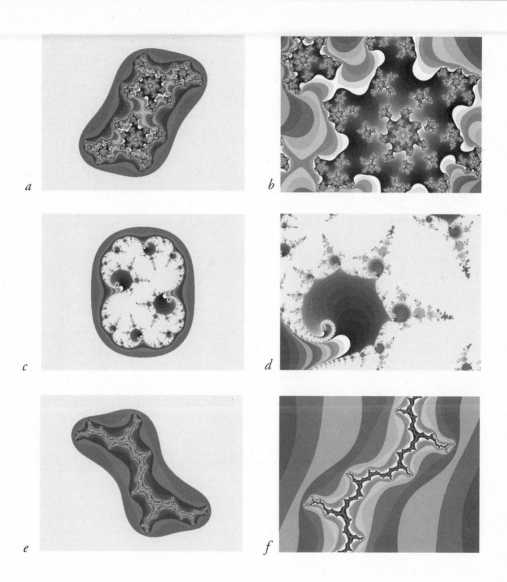

a

b

c

d

e

f

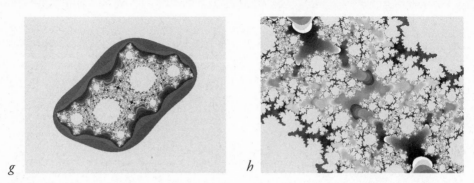

g   *h*

Figure 6.10. *A sampling of Julia sets (left), with a close-up of each (right).*

Table 6.1. Coordinates for generating the Mandelbrot and Julia set images in Figures 6.9 and 6.10 with the MANIMATE program.

Mandelbrot Set

Figure	From	x =	y =	To x =	y=
6.9a		−0.95	−0.32	−0.85	−0.22
6.9b		−0.2	1.02	−0.13	1.07
6.9c		−0.607	0.617	−0.523	0.672
6.9d		−1.78	0	−1.76	0.013

Julia Set

Figure	x =	y =
6.10a & b	0.11031	−0.67037
6.10c & d	0.27334	0.00742
6.10e & f	0	1
6.10g & h	−0.39054	−0.59

You Can Do It: Mandelbrot Animation

The MANIMATE.C program included on this disk may be the best place to start exploring the Mandelbrot and Julia sets. The code (listed in the **Working Code** section below) is simple enough to mess about with, yet fast enough to produce complex fractal images without leaving the computer running overnight for each picture.

1. Type MANIMATE at the DOS prompt, and select a 256-color video mode. I recommend starting your explorations in mode A, the 320×200 resolution. This will give you maximum speed and still result in eye-popping 256-color animation.

2. You will be asked whether you would like to see part of the Mandelbrot set or part of a Julia set. For now, enter 0 for Mandelbrot.

3. Next, you will be asked which part of the Mandelbrot set you want to see. To reproduce Figure 6.8, the Mandelbrot set in its entirety, enter -2.25 for the left x coordinate, -1.0 for the top y coordinate, 1.0 for the right x coordinate and 1.0 for the bottom y coordinate.

   (Table 6.1 below summarizes a few coordinate sets for close-up views of interesting regions of the Mandelbrot set that you might like to try when you run the program again.)

4. The program reminds you of the screen resolution you selected and asks how big you want the actual fractal image to be. If you have a slow computer, enter small numbers (less than 100). If you have a 386 or 486, go ahead and enter 320 for x and 200 for y to take advantage of the full screen.

5. Enter 256 for the maximum number of iterations. When you draw extremely close-up views of a set, you should use more iterations to capture all the details.

6. Enter 256 for the number of colors to use. If you enter fewer colors, you'll get interesting striped pictures—try 2 colors sometime, too!

7. When you are asked if you want to change any of the above entries, glance over the numbers you entered to make sure you didn't enter a screen resolution of 32 by 20,000 or something silly like that, and press N to continue.

   The fractal will take a while to appear. (If you don't have a 386, it may take a *loooong* while to appear. Take heart in the fact that this code is five or ten times faster than it would be if it used the math routines that most C compilers provide!)

8. When the image is complete, a beep will sound. At that point, you can press a number key (try 1 first) to start the animation. Weee!

When you're ready to try another one, press the Esc key and go back to step 1.

To see a Julia set instead of the Mandelbrot set, just enter 1 at the first question. Because each point has its own Julia set, you'll get an extra question that didn't appear for the Mandelbrot set. The bottom part of Table 6.1 below lists some interesting Julia set points to look at. (Note that every Julia set spans from x = -1.5, y = -1.5 to x = 1.5, y = 1.5. As with the Mandelbrot set, you can zoom in closer by using number in between for the view coordinates. From x = -0.1, y = -0.1 to x = 0.1, y = 0.1 will zoom in on the very center of the Julia set, for instance.

When you get a glimpse of these fractals in motion, you'll want to see more—but you'll quickly tire of entering all those numbers. I recommend the freeware program FRACTINT, which includes every bell and whistle imaginable for viewing mathematical fractals, including massive speed-up tricks, an interactive zoom-box for sniffing out interesting regions to view, over 60 different fractal types, superb palette color control and animation, the ability to define your own fractal formulas without compiling any source code, and a slew of other features. You can even map your fractals onto 3-D landscapes with perspective projection and/or sphere mapping for fractal planets. Best of all, FRACTINT is available for about $5 to cover postage and the disk almost anywhere—including the Cedar Software registration/order form in the back of this book.

The complete C and assembler source code for FRACTINT is also freely available, though be warned that it is several orders of magnitude more complex than the **Working Code** below, and may overwhelm all but the most C-worthy hackers. So start by playing with MANIMATE to get off the ground, then get FRACTINT to blast off into the vast universe of fractal abstraction.

Working Code: Mandelbrot in Motion

Like the FRAN and FREEN programs, MANIMATE uses the fast 32-bit integer math routines in MUDI.OBJ to speed things up a bit. If you look closely, you'll also notice another subtle but important speed-up trick. Instead of calculating x * x and y * y in the main iteration formula and then calculating the same squares again in the if statement that tests to see if a point has "escaped," I store the values in variables named xsquared and ysquared. This eliminates two multiplications per cycle. As you'll see if you wait for the program to generate a 640 × 480 or larger image, any speed gain you can get is well worth the trouble!

As mentioned at the end of the **You Can Do It** section above, ultra-slick fractal programs such as the famous freeware FRACTINT employ many additional speed-up tricks. Generally, you can expect FRACTINT to be several times faster. MANIMATE's value lies in its simplicity—you can fool around with different fractal formulas and coloring schemes without wading through thousands of lines of code. (Try any little modification that pops into your head, and you'll probably discover a new fractal of your very own!)

Listing 6.4. Don't let the simplicity of this little program fool you—an infinite universe of mind-boggling beauty awaits within.

```
/* MANIMATE.C
 *
 * A program to display and animate
 * the Mandelbrot and Julia sets.
 */

#include <stdio.h>       /* standard input/output */
#include <conio.h>

#include "tg.h"          /* TransGraphics header file */
#include "mudi.h"        /* for fast 32-bit math */

#define drawclr 15        /* color for outline box */

int niter,               /* maximum number of iterations */
    px, py,              /* current pixel */
    nx, ny,              /* number of pixels */
```

continues

Listing 6.4. continued

```
    nc,               /* number of colors to use */
    i, j,             /* counters for miscellaneous use */
    keepon,           /* 1 = keep going, 0 = abort */
    jul;              /* 1 = Julia Set,  0 = Mandelbrot */

long x, y,            /* last point on orbit */
    xx, yy,           /* next point on orbit */
    xsquared, ysquared, /* used to speed up computations */
    dx, dy,           /* theoretical size of pixels */
    cx, cy,           /* number to add each iteration */
    x0, y0,           /* starting x,y */
    xI, yI;           /* ending x,y */

void getparms(void);

void main(void)
{   char key;
    tg_pickmode();              /* get and set video mode */
    tg_settextmode();   /* go back to text mode momentarily */
    getparms();     /* ask the user what they'd like to see */
    dx = (xI - x0) / nx;        /* compute size of pixels */
    dy = (yI - y0) / ny;
    tg_setvideomode(0);    /* then set graphics mode again */
    keepon = 1;                /* keepon tells when to abort */
    tg_setcolor(drawclr); /* rectagle around drawing region */
    tg_drawrect(0, 0, nx - 1, ny - 1);
    for (px = 0; (px < nx) && (keepon); px++)  /* main loop */
        for (py = 0; (py < ny) && (keepon); py++)
        {   x = x0 + px * dx,    /* start julia on pixel */
            y = y0 + py * dy;
            if (jul == 0)     /* start mandelbrot set on 0,0 */
                cx = x, cy = y,
                x = 0L, y = 0L;        /* and use pixel for c */
/* main iteration loop; go until the distance to the origin is
 * greater than 2 (i.e. square of the distance > 4), or we hit
 * the maximum number of iterations */
                xsquared = 0L, ysquared = 0L;
                for (i = 0; (i < niter) &&
```

```
                      (xsquared + ysquared < (M1 * 4)); i++)
            {   xsquared = mu(x, x);
                ysquared = mu(y, y);
                xx = xsquared - ysquared + cx;
                yy = (mu(x, y) << 1) + cy;
                x = xx, y = yy;
            }
            if (i == niter) i = 0;      /* hit limit, color 0 */
            else i = (i % nc);       /* color determined by i */
            tg_putpixel(px, py, i);      /* lite up the pixel */
            if (kbhit() && (getch() == 27))
                keepon = 0;            /* stop if user hit Esc */
        }
    printf("\7");                       /* beep when done */
    key = getch();
    while ((key >= '1') && (key <= '9'))      /* animate it */
    {   tg_colorcycle(key - '0');
        key = getch();
    }
    tg_closedown();
}

/* Ask the user which set and region they want to display */

void getparms(void)
{   double inx, iny;
    printf("\n\n");
    printf("This program displays pictures of "
            "the Julia and Mandelbrot Sets.\n");
    printf("You will be asked for information "
            "needed to create a picture.\n");
    printf("To quit the program, press ctrl+C during "
            "input or Esc during display.");
     while(1)
    {   printf("\n\n");
        printf("Enter 0 now for the Mandelbrot Set, "
                "or 1 for a Julia Set: ");
        scanf("%d", &jul);
        if (jul)
```

continues

Listing 6.4. continued

```
{   printf("\n");
    printf("Each point between -2,-2 and 2,2 "
            "has its own Julia Set.\n");
    printf("Compute a Julia Set for the point: x = ");
    scanf("%lf", &inx);
    printf("                                y = ");
    scanf("%lf", &iny);
    cx = (long) (inx * MF);
    cy = (long) (iny * MF);
    printf("\nThe Julia Set spans "
            "from -1.5, -1.5 to 1.5, 1.5.");
}
else
{   printf("\nThe Mandelbrot Set spans "
            "from -2.25, -1.5 to 0.75, 1.5.");
  }
printf("\nThe minimum (top left) point to view: x = ");
scanf("%lf", &inx);
printf("                                y = ");
scanf("%lf", &iny);
x0 = (long) (inx * MF);
y0 = (long) (iny * MF);
printf("\nMaximum (bottom right) point to view: x = ");
scanf("%lf", &inx);
printf("                                y = ");
scanf("%lf", &iny);
xI = (long) (inx * MF);
yI = (long) (iny * MF);
printf("\nThe whole screen is %d by %d pixels.",
        tg_scrnx, tg_scrny);
printf("\nThe size of the image in pixels: x = ");
scanf("%d", &nx);
if (nx > tg_scrnx) nx = tg_scrnx;
printf("                                y = ");
scanf("%d", &ny);
if (ny > tg_scrny) ny = tg_scrny;
printf("\nMore iterations show more detail, "
        "but take longer.");
printf("\nThe number of iterations = ");
```

```
            scanf("%d", &niter);
            if (tg_ncolors > 2)
            {   printf("\nYou can use any number "
                        "of colors from 2 to %d", tg_ncolors);
                printf("\nThe number of colors to use = ");
                scanf("%d", &nc);
            }
            else nc = 2;
            if (nc > tg_ncolors) nc = tg_ncolors;
            printf("\n\nWould you like to change "
                    "any of the above? (Y or N)");
            switch(getch())
            {   case 'n':
                case 'N': return;
            }
    }
}
```

Fractal Image Compression

Using fractals to simulate landscapes and other natural effects is not new; it has been a primary application... What is new is the ability to start with an actual image and find the fractals that will imitate it to any desired degree of accuracy. Because our method includes a compact way of representing these fractals, we end up with a highly compressed data set for reconstructing the original image.

—Michael Barnsley and Alan Sloan,
"A Better Way to Compress Images," *BYTE,* 1988

Michael Barnsley and Alan Sloan, who developed the IFS fractals that you learned about earlier in this chapter, have developed a technique for storing literally any image as fractals. By storing only the IFS codes and throwing away the original pixel-by-pixel data, they can achieve image compression ratios up to 1,000 to 1 or more.

As of yet, their company (Iterated Systems, Inc. 5550-A Peachtree Parkway, Norcross, GA 30092) is the only player in this exciting new field, but they market developer's kits that let you add fractal image compression technology to your own DOS or Windows graphics programs. Unfortunately, they have taken what may be a suicidal policy of limiting purchasers of their Software Development Kit to distributing only 20 copies of any application that supports fractal compression. If you want to distribute your applications to a wider market, you'll need to pay them lots and lots of royalties. This, coupled with the $500+ price tag of their SDK and the success of competing compression techniques such as JPEG and MPEG, has prevented widespread adoption of their Fractal Image Format as an industry standard. When other companies jump on the fractal compression bandwagon (as they are sure to do, given the awesome potential of the technology), you should see prices and distribution policies come down to earth.

How does fractal image compression work? You can actually do it by hand with a program like FRAN—though the time and effort involved make manual compression impractical for any purpose other than learning how the technique works. Put the original image on the screen (with any of the image display tools from Chapter 3), and then use an interactive IFS editor like FRAN to match a fractal up as closely as possible to the shape of a particular colored region in the picture. Mathematician John Elton has rigorously proven that IFS fractals can conform to any such shape whatsoever, given enough transformations.

The more transformations you use, the easier it will be to match a given shape. Therefore, fractal image compression gives you a choice between compression efficiency (lowest number of transformations) and reproduction accuracy. To achieve the highest possible compression ratios, some image data will be lost and the reconstructed image may be noticeably different than the original.

Figure 6.11 is a sample PCX file—just Joe Average image. Figure 6.12 shows the transformations that might be used to compress a multi-colored part of the image, and Figure 6.13 shows the resulting fractal. By repeating this process for each colored region in the image, I could construct a fractal approximation of the entire picture.

Automatic fractal compression programs maintain an indexed mathematical "library" of IFS fractals, and use edge recognition algorithms and other advanced image processing techniques to recognize regions of the image and find fractals to fit them. This is a complex and time-consuming process, and compressing a single image can take several minutes without special hardware to assist the process. Decompression is faster, and low-resolution images can be decompressed at animation speeds of up to 30 frames per second.

Figure 6.11. *To turn this scanned image into fractals, first select a colored region to mimic...*

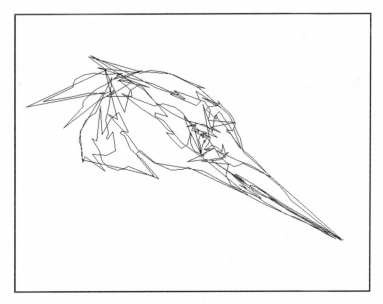

Figure 6.12. *...then find transformations that will tile the region with copies of itself...*

Figure 6.13. ...*the resulting fractal will mimic part of the picture. Repeat the process for each colored region in the image, and you can store the entire picture as IFS codes.*

This impressive decompression speed, coupled with the dramatic compression ratios, opens up a world of possibilities including real-time video transmission over normal telephone lines. Other benefits of fractal image compression include the ability to reconstruct an image smaller or even larger than its original size without apparent loss of image quality.

With the explosion in graphics applications and the resulting storage crunch as everyone tries to cram all those multimedia files on their hard drives, fractal image compression is too big an advance to be held back for long by one company's paranoid distribution policies. When a public domain fractal decompression program appears (as it eventually must) and personal computers get just a wee bit speedier, expect fractal compression to make a big splash in the graphics pool.

Don't Stop Here

If the properties we assign to the natural world are partly expressions of the way we think and our capacity for understanding, then the introduction of new tools such as the computer will change those properties. The computer, like the microscope, expands our senses. The world made visible by the computer seems limitless.

—Clifford Pickover, *Computers, Pattern, Chaos, and Beauty*, 1990

Whether you build them yourself with the help of FRAN or explore the nether regions of mathematics' own Nature with MANIMATE, the fractals you find may be some of the most stunning graphics you'll ever see. Add the animation secrets unveiled in this chapter, and you'll be pushing red-line on the Wow meter.

But don't stop here. Get ready to jump into the world of 3-D modeling, 3-D animation—and, yes—3-D fractals, too.

The Third Dimension

Graphics in Space

All the graphics tricks covered in previous chapters use two-dimensional geometry to draw and animate two-dimensional images on your two-dimensional screen. In this chapter, your computer screen will become a window into a three-dimensional universe of your own creation. With a treasure chest of 3-D mathematical magic and some slight of hand called *anaglyphic stereoscopy*, three-dimensional shapes will almost literally leap out of your monitor before your very eyes.

So get out those 3-D glasses that came with the book, fasten your seat belt, and prepare for lift-off. After the initial training, where you'll learn to move and spin in space, you will launch on a mission to build the first manned Tibetan space station from geometric points, lines and faces.

Stereoscopic Animation

Although the common PC has come a long way in display technology, it stall lacks the characteristic most responsible for making the actual visual world around us realistic—depth....

You are able to see depth because each eye 'sees' your world from a slightly different viewpoint and calculates the distance of objects using mental triangulation, a process more commonly known as depth perception. While these actions could be simulated with a computer in several different ways, ...the old 'red and blue glasses' or anaglyphic technique. ...produces beautiful images of strikingly realistic depth, and all you need are a couple pieces of inexpensive, colored plastic and your VGA.

—Dale Nassar, "Three-Dimensional Graphics by Computer: Computer-Generated Anaglyphs," *Circuit Cellar Ink*, Dec. 1991.

Your brain is smart—so smart that it's easy to fool. 3-D computer graphics take advantage of your subconscious intelligence to trick you into thinking that two-dimensional dots and lines on your computer screen are really three-dimensional. In some cases, simply calculating a 2-D *projection* of a 3-D shape and drawing that projection on the screen will be enough to fool the average brain into seeing the intended spatial relationships. Mathematically, that's as easy as discarding the third dimension (the *z coordinate*) and just plotting the x and y coordinates as if the shape data didn't have a third dimension at all.

Unfortunately, most brains aren't quite *that* smart—or that easily fooled. Only a few simple shapes—such as the wireframe cubes that most people doodle while talking on the phone—are familiar enough to be recognized easily from a straightforward two-dimensional projection. Even then, optical illusions and ambiguities arise from throwing away a dimension. When you want to represent more complex 3-D objects, you need to give the brain some additional *depth cues*.

In real life, your brain navigates through space with the help of four types of depth cues. In this chapter and Chapter 9, I'll show you how to mimic all four types:

1. *Motion cues.* Even when you're standing still, your eyes are always in motion. By calculating 3-D movement and rotation, you can "look around" your own computer-generated objects.

2. *Perspective.* A far away object makes a smaller image on your retina than the same object up close. To get this effect on a computer monitor, you need to scale everything you draw according to its location along the z axis.

3. *Stereo vision.* You have two eyes. Use them! The red/blue glasses and a simple algorithm allow you to send a separate image to each eye. For those with normal stereoscopic perception ability, the results can be dramatic.

4. *Interaction of light.* Hidden surfaces, shadows, highlights, and reflections can all be calculated at once by simulating the interaction of light rays with your 3-D models. Chapter 9 will show you how to use *ray tracing* to achieve all these effects and more.

Tracing light rays is a sophisticated and time consuming procedure, but 3-D motion, perspective, and stereo vision are easier than you think. What's more, they're *fast* enough to be truly interactive. I'll show you what I mean.

Spinning in Stereo

The sequence in Figure 7.1 is a simple 2-D projection of a cube as it tumbles in space. As most of us figured out by the age of 12, your brain can interpret each of these images at least two ways with equal facility. Budding graphics gurus can waste entire elementary school math periods drawing such projections and trying to get them to flip inside out by blinking and bobbing their heads.

By animating these images in true perspective and adding stereoscopic depth perception, the 3DCUBE program presented below eliminates the ambiguity. Figure 7.2 shows a perspective view of a cube, where the distant end appears smaller than the near end. Until we figure out how to print motion pictures on the pages of a book, you'll have to go through the **You Can Do It** section below with your computer to see the stereoscopic animation.

You Can Do It: A Tumbling Cube

For a quick demonstration of 3-D stereo motion:

1. Enter 3DCUBE at the DOS prompt.

2. Select a 16-color video mode. (EGA 640×350 mode is the fastest, but VGA 640×480 mode looks nicer and isn't all that much slower on most systems.)

   A cyan-colored cube appears, tumbling head over heels in the middle of the screen, and a brief menu appears across the bottom of the screen.

3. Press the * key (shift-8 or the times key on the numeric keypad) to spin faster. Then try the / key to spin slower.

   Notice that "front" and "back" are ambiguous in this simple 2-D projection—you may find that the cube seems to turn inside out and start spinning the other way once in a while. Some people even see the cube squish and expand like a bellows instead of spinning.

4. Now for the fun part. Put on the red/blue 3-D glasses that came with the book (red lens over the left eye), and press G to turn on the stereo glasses display.

   Many people find that it takes a few seconds for the stereo effect to "kick in." After that, the cube appears to be floating half inside and half outside the monitor, and there is no ambiguity at all about which side is front and which is back.

   You may also notice another optical illusion: The front face of the cube seems to get slightly smaller than the back face. This effect (which not everyone sees) is due to the fact that your brain expects distant objects to appear smaller. Since the program isn't computing *perspective* yet, the front and back faces are actually the same size. But some people's brains can't turn off their automatic compensation, so they interpret the back face to be larger than the front.

5. To turn on perspective viewing, press P.

6. Try pressing the N and F keys to move yourself nearer and farther from the cube, and notice how it changes the perspective effect.

   To calculate the red and blue images, the 3DCUBE program must make an assumption about the distance between your eyes relative to the size of your monitor and the distance of your face from the screen. If the cube appears elongated, you can adjust the angular separation between the left and right eye images:

7. Press I to enhance the stereo effect. This is equivalent to enlarging your head, or moving your eyes further apart. (Goliath had great depth perception, even though his peripheral vision was a little shaky.)

8. Press O to move your eyes closer together. If you press O enough times, the eye positions will reverse and the cube will appear to spin in the opposite direction.

The **Math Behind the Magic** and **Working Code** sections of this chapter will reveal how all this spinning stereoscopy works.

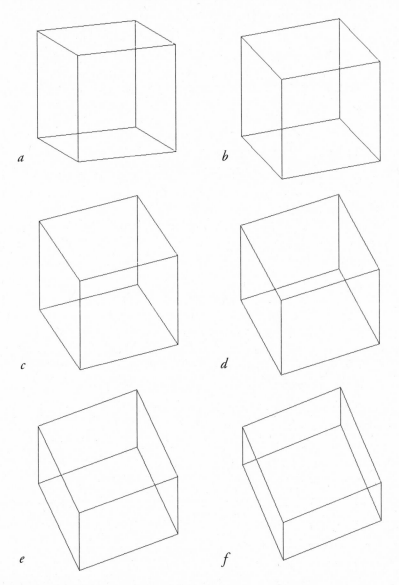

Figure 7.1. *These 2-D projections of a 3-D spinning cube are not quite enough to fool your brain into seeing 3-D.*

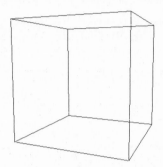

Figure 7.2. *In this perspective view, distant parts of the cube appear smaller. The 3DCUBE program adds stereo vision to complete the illusion of three dimensions.*

Points, Lines, and Rotations

You'd think that defining three-dimensional shapes would be only slightly more complex than defining two-dimensional ones. That's true for 3-D points; there you simply use three coordinates (x, y and z) instead of two (x and y).

Although the three dimensions themselves are almost always designated x, y, and z, there is some variation on how these axes are oriented relative to a computer screen. Some 3-D software packages call the vertical axis z and the axis that runs perpendicular to the screen y. Most people find it more natural to call the up/down axis y (just as we do when dealing with 2-D graphics) and the in/out axis z. I'll use the latter convention throughout this book.

But the more you try to do in space, the harder it gets. Think about polygons, for example. Given a few two-dimensional points, you can usually find one obvious way to "connect the dots" to make a closed polygon, such as a rectangle, a pentagon, or a "stop-sign" octagon. When you have a bunch of 3-D points, however, the possibilities are much less cut-and-dried. Beyond the five "platonic solids" (tetrahedron, cube, octahedron, icosahedron, and dodecahedron), there is no particularly obvious way to connect a given set of 3-D points. Therefore, any 3-D shape editor (like the one I present later in this chapter) must enable you to attach any point to any other to make 3-D lines.

Furthermore, 3-D surfaces (often called "faces" for short) can theoretically have any number of points arranged to form all manner of strange convoluted forms. Creating and working with them is considerably more challenging than filling in a region of a single 2-D plane.

The final—and most severe—leap in complexity occurs when you start rotating in 3-D space. Instead of the two directions of rotation that are possible in 2-D (clockwise and counter-clockwise), you must choose between no less than six different directions of rotation in 3-D (clockwise and counter-clockwise around each of the three axes). The 3DCUBE program listed below demonstrates two of the six directions of spin—after an initial one-time spin around the y-axis, the cube continually spins around the x-axis.

Whether you call these spins clockwise or counter-clockwise depends on how you're oriented in 3-D space when you look at the rotation. The *right hand rule* is a common convention for naming rotations: You curve your right hand so the fingertips point in the direction of rotation, and then view the rotation from the end of your thumb. By this convention, the continual rotation you see in the 3DCUBE program would be called counter-clockwise around the x-axis. (Unless you happened to put your 3-D glasses on backwards, in which case the rotation appears clockwise!) Another application of the right hand rule will poke its head up again later when you start putting faces on your 3-D shapes.

Note that 3-D rotations cannot be combined in an arbitrary order. For example, spinning 3 units around the x axis, then 2 units around the y axis, then 5 units around the z axis will *not* end up with the same orientation as spinning 5 units around the z axis, then 2 units around the y axis, then 3 units around the x axis.

Furthermore, if you spin a bit around x, then a bit around y and then try to get back to your original orientation by reversing the x spin and then reversing the y spin, it won't work! Instead, you would have to reverse the y spin first and then reverse the x spin. In other words, to reverse a series of 3-D spins, you must retrace your steps in exact backwards sequence.

If all this sounds rather confusing, it is. In fact, I thought there was a bug in my first 3-D graphics program because the command sequence x-spin, y-spin, reverse-x-spin, reverse-y-spin didn't get me back where I started. A beta-tester called and reported the same "bug." Much to our chagrin, we both eventually concluded that the "bug" was a fundamental property of 3-D space, and no amount of clever coding was going to change it.

You'll get a chance to play with 3-D rotations in the 3DLINES and 3DFACES programs coming up, but you may want to turn a real live physical object around in your hands for a while to confirm that the same 3-D rotations applied in a different order will end up at different orientations. I still have to flip-flop a floppy disk on my desk once in a while to get this straight in my mind when I'm working with advanced 3-D software.

Anaglyphic Stereoscopy

To create red/blue stereoscopic images, you simply draw a shape in red, then rotate the shape slightly around the y axis and draw it again in blue. This simulates the angular offset of your eyes. Stereo pictures made to be viewed with red/blue 3-D glasses are called *anaglyphs*, and the practice of creating and viewing them is called *anaglyphic stereoscopy*. (The word "anaglyph" originally referred to embossed reliefs or cameos made by etching precious metals. It was later adopted to refer to any type of "simulated 3-D," and has eventually come to connote the red/blue glasses thing specifically.)

Figure 7.3 shows two slightly different angles on a 3-D cube. If these were red and blue instead of grey and black, you could don your 3-D spectacles and watch it jump out of the page.

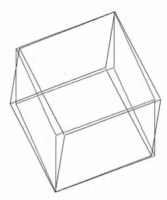

Figure 7.3. *On your computer screen, stereo shapes like this will be colored red and blue so you can view them with the 3-D glasses included with this book.*

Another sneaky way to print 3-D pictures is to use *stereo pairs*. Figure 7.4 shows the same two cubes pictured above, but instead of being superimposed over one another, they are separated by about the same distance your eyes are. To view them in stereo, stand a folded sheet of paper up between them and rest your nose on its edge. Make sure the light level on each side of the paper is about the same, without any shadows. Then try to refocus your eyes by looking *past* the book, through the images. The two separate images should move together and eventually fuse into one stereoscopic image. Some folks find it easy to view stereo pairs, others find it impossible. Most get the hang of it after a few minutes of trying. If you're having trouble fusing the images, sometimes it helps to look at a distant object and then quickly look down at the page before your eyes have a chance to change their focus.

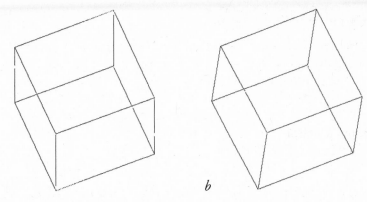

a b

Figure 7.4. *To view this stereo pair, stand a piece of paper up between them and try to focus your eyes so that the two shapes fuse into one stereoscopic image.*

You'll have many more opportunities to view stereo images. But right now, I'm sure the techies among you are itching for some algorithms and source code.

The Math Behind the Magic: 3-D Geometry

If a point in 3-D space is designated by the variables x, y, and z, moving that point is as easy as adding some offset to one or more of those variables. To move 4 units to the right, 1 unit up 5 units "into the screen," you would say:

$x = x + 4$

$y = y + 1$

$z = z + 5$

Scaling, or resizing a shape made up of 3-D points is equally straightforward—you just multiply by a scaling factor. To double the size of a set of points centered at 0,0,0, just multiply each coordinate of each point by 2:

$x = x * 2$

$y = y * 2$

$z = z * 2$

Rotation, however, is trickier. As you recall from chapter 4, spinning a point by an angle A in two dimensions looks like this:

$$x = x * cos(A) + y * sin(A)$$

$$y = y * cos(a) - x * sin(A)$$

In three dimensions, you can use the same formula, but you have the choice of spinning around the x, y, or z axes. These three choices look like:

[1] Spin around the z axis (looks like ordinary 2-D spinning)

$$x = x * cos(A) + y * sin(A)$$

$$y = y * cos(A) - x * sin(A)$$

[2] Spin around the y axis (horizontal rotation)

$$x = x * cos(A) - z * sin(A)$$

$$z = x * sin(A) + z * cos(A)$$

[3] Spin around the x axis (vertical tumbling)

$$y = y * cos(A) + z * sin(A)$$

$$z = z * cos(a) - y * sin(A)$$

By combining these rotations, you can get to any orientation in space. The 3DCUBE program described in this chapter uses formula #2 to offset the cube a bit horizontally at the beginning of the program, and then applies formula #3 to tumble the cube continuously. Formula #2 is applied again to offset the red/blue images for 3-D glasses display.

The final step in tossing 3-D lines on the screen is to add perspective, so that far away objects are drawn smaller than close objects. Though the effect can be dramatic, the math is trivial. Just determine the distance in pixels from your eye to the screen, called the *perspective distance* (half the height of the screen is a good starting value). Then scale the x and y coordinates by the perspective distance times the z coordinate, which of course represents the distance of the point from the observer. Using d to represent the perspective distance, this transformation is just:

$$x <= (x / (z + d)) * d$$

$$y <= (y / (z + d)) * d$$

Why divide by z + d instead of just z? This simply moves your eye from the middle of the shape to the distance d away from it. Otherwise, the shape would actually wrap around the back of your head, which makes the perspective effect rather surreal to say the least. (Programmers might want to try changing the code below to check out this bizarre effect, by the way.)

Working Code: Animating 3-D Lines

To animate a spinning cube, 3DCUBE.C uses several arrays. First the 3D.H header defines a point3D data type, which simply consist of an x, y, and z coordinate set. The points[] array contains the 8 corner points of the cube. The linefrom[] and lineto[] arrays then define the 12 edges of the cube by referring to positions in the points[] array. Each time the cube is drawn on the screen, the endpoints of the lines are copied into integer arrays called drawpt1[] and drawpt2[] for the fastest possible erasing of the lines just before each new line is drawn. This keeps the time between the erasing of a line and the drawing of the same line in its new, rotated position to an absolute minimum to reduce "flicker."

Some of the definitions in the 3D.H header file listed below are not used in 3DCUBE.C. (The same header file is included in the 3DLINES.C and 3DFACES.C programs, presented later in this chapter.) The most important #defines used by 3DCUBE.C are SINOCULAR, COSOCULAR, OCULARDIST, and OCULARINC. These set up the angular distance between your eyes and precompute the cosine and sine of that angle for quick display.

Like the programs in Chapter 6, all the programs in this chapter use fixed-point long-integer routines from MUDI.H and MUDI.OBJ. This eliminates the roundoff errors you saw when using short integers in Chapter 4 while providing a dramatic speed increase over floating point operations.

Note that all the programs in this chapter use the TransGraphics system, and must be linked with the MUDI.OBJ file. For example. to compile the 3DCUBE program under Microsoft C, you would enter:

TGMS 3DCUBE.C MUDI.OBJ

For Borland, use TGTC instead of TGMS. See the general compile instructions in the introduction for more details on using TransGraphics with your compiler and graphics library of choice.

Listing 7.1. The 3D.H header file defines the basic operations used for 3-D geometry and stereoscopic viewing.

```c
/* 3D
 *
 * Header File for 3DLINES.C and 3DFACES.C
 * from Tricks of the Graphics Gurus
 */

#include <stdio.h>
#include <stdlib.h>
#include <math.h>
#include <ctype.h>
#include <process.h>
#include "mudi.h"
#include "tg.h"

/* These are the values of key bindings */

#define ENTER 13
#define ESC 27
#define INSERT -'R'
#define DELETE -'S'
#define TAB 9
#define UP -'H'
#define DN -'P'
#define LT -'K'
#define RT -'M'

/* macro getch() replacement */

#define geta if ((a = getch()) == 0) a = -getch();\
          else if (a > 0) a = toupper(a)

#define HAND 16              /* size of handle in pixels */
#define NPTS 64              /* maximum number of points */
#define NLINES 64            /* maximum number of lines */
#define NFACES 64            /* maximum number of faces */
#define SIZEINC 10486L    /* ratio of re-size for each step */
```

```
#define MOVEINC (16L << BITSH)     /* movement for each step */
#define PI 205887L                     /* (3.1415927 * M1) */
#define SPININC (PI >> 4)    /* amount of spin for each step */

#define NAMELEN 40                       /* length of name */
#define EOFILE 0xff                /* end of file character */

#define COSOCULAR (long) (0.995004 * MF)
#define SINOCULAR (long) (0.099833 * MF)
#define OCULARDIST 0.1
#define OCULARINC 0.05
#define RIGHTCLR 1
#define LEFTCLR 4

/* add two 3D points p1 and p2, putting the result into p3.
 * (p3 can be the same variable as p1 or p2 without problems)
 */

#define addpt(p1, p2, p3) \
        { p3.x = p1.x + p2.x; \
          p3.y = p1.y + p2.y; \
          p3.z = p1.z + p2.z; }

/* cosf and sinf return the cosine or sine
 * of a scaled long int as a double */

#define cosf(x) (cos((double) x / M1))
#define sinf(x) (sin((double) x / M1))

/* perspective transformation */

#define perx(p) \
    (perspective ? mu(di(p.x, p.z + pdist), pdist) : p.x)
#define pery(p) \
    (perspective ? mu(di(p.y, p.z + pdist), pdist) : p.y)

typedef struct { long x, y, z; } point3d;
```

Listing 7.2. 3DCUBE.C displays a tumbling three-dimensional wireframe cube, with or without 3-D glasses stereo display and perspective.

```c
/* 3DCUBE.C
 *
 * A spinning 3D cube to demonstrate anaglyphic stereo
 *
 * from Tricks of the Graphics Gurus
 */

#include "3d.h"

#define I (M1 * 100)

point3d point[NPTS] =                /* corner vertex points */
        {-I, -I,  I,  I, -I,  I,  I,  I,  I, -I,  I,  I,
         -I, -I, -I,  I, -I, -I,  I,  I, -I, -I,  I, -I},
     drawpt1[NPTS], drawpt2[NPTS];  /* for quick erasing */

long cosocular = COSOCULAR,        /* precomputed cos and sin */
     sinocular = SINOCULAR,
     spininc = SPININC >> 2,
     pdist;                        /* perspective distance */
double oculardist = OCULARDIST;    /* distance between eyes */

/* NOTE: All of the above variables are 32-bit integers,
 * scaled by the amount defined as M1. The mu() and di()
 * macros call assembly language routines to multiply and
 * divide these numbers, maintaining the scaling factor. */

int drawclr,                       /* color to give the shape */
    white,                         /* color to give menus and cursor */
    glasses = 0,        /* 1 = red/blue 3D glasses, 0 = normal */
    i, j,                          /* general purpose counters */
    perspective = 0,               /* perspective 1=on, 0=off */
    npts = 8,                      /* total number of points */
    linefrom[NLINES] = {0, 1, 2, 3, 0, 4, 7, 1, 5, 6, 6, 5},
    lineto[NLINES] =   {1, 2, 3, 0, 4, 7, 3, 5, 6, 2, 7, 4},
    nlines = 12,                       /* number of lines */
    cpu;                    /* used by cputype() in mudi.asm */

unsigned int pause = 8092;         /* pause between movements */
```

```
/* function prototypes */

int main(int nargs, char **arg);
void draw3dline(point3d p1, point3d p2, int color);

int main(int nargs, char **arg)
{   char a;                                /* current keypress */
    point3d pointi;
    cpu = cputype();            /* find out what cpu we have */
    printf("\n 3DCUBE -- A Spinning 3D Cube in Stereo");
    printf("\n\n from Tricks of the Graphics Gurus\n\n");
    tg_pickmode();              /* ask user for a video mode */
    white = 15 % tg_ncolors;       /* define the color white */
    drawclr = 11 % tg_ncolors;    /* define color for shape */
    pdist = (long) tg_scrny << BITSH;  /* perspective dist. */
    tg_moveto(0, tg_scrny - tg_chary);       /* show a menu */
    tg_outtext(" Faster=*  Slower=/  Glasses=G"
    " EyeDistance=IO  Perspec=P Near=N Far=F  Quit=Esc");
    tg_setviewport(0, 0, tg_scrnx - 1, tg_scrny - tg_chary);
    for (i = 0; i < npts; i++)   /* spin a bit horizontally */
    {   pointi = point[i];
        point[i].x = pointi.x * cosf((SPININC << 1)) -
                     pointi.z * sinf((SPININC << 1));
        point[i].z = pointi.x * sinf((SPININC << 1)) +
                     pointi.z * cosf((SPININC << 1));
    }
    for(i = 0; i < nlines; i++)    /* set up for quick erase */
    {   drawpt1[i] = point[linefrom[i]];
        drawpt2[i] = point[lineto[i]];
    }
    while(1)                         /* main menu loop */
    {   for (i = 0; i < npts; i++)         /* spin a little */
        {   pointi = point[i];
            point[i].y = pointi.y * cosf(spininc) +
                         pointi.z * sinf(spininc);
            point[i].z = pointi.y * -sinf(spininc) +
                         pointi.z * cosf(spininc);
        }
        for(i = 0; i < nlines; i++)         /* draw the cube */
        {   draw3dline(drawpt1[i], drawpt2[i], 0);
```

continues

289

Listing 7.2. continued

```
              draw3dline(drawpt1[i] = point[linefrom[i]],
                      drawpt2[i] = point[lineto[i]], drawclr);
      }
      if (kbhit())
      {   geta;                    /* get the next keypress */
          switch(a)                /* what shall we do now? */
          {   case '*':                          /* faster */
                  spininc *= 2;
                  if (spininc > 32768) spininc = 32768;
                  break;
              case '/':                          /* slower */
                  spininc /= 2;
                  if (spininc < 2L) spininc = 2L;
                  break;
              case 'G':     /* red/blue 3D glasses on/off */
                  if (glasses) glasses = 0;
                  else glasses = 1;
                  tg_clearviewport();
                  break;
              case 'I':           /* adjust eye separation */
                  oculardist += OCULARINC;
              case 'O':
                  if (a == 'O') oculardist -= OCULARINC;
                  cosocular = (long) (cos(oculardist) * MF);
                  sinocular = (long) (sin(oculardist) * MF);
                  glasses = 1;
                  tg_clearviewport();
                  break;
              case 'P':
                  if (perspective) perspective = 0;
                  else perspective = 1;
                  tg_clearviewport();
                  break;
              case 'F':
                  pdist *= 2;
                  tg_clearviewport();
                  break;
              case 'N':
                  pdist /= 2;
                  if (pdist < 4L) pdist = 4L;
```

```
                              tg_clearviewport();
                              break;
                      case ESC:                        /* quit */
                              tg_closedown();
                              printf("\n\nAu revoir!\n");
                              exit(0);
                }
            }
        }
}


/* draw a 3D line from p1 to p2 */

void draw3dline(point3d p1, point3d p2, int color)
{   int x1, y1, x2, y2;
    x1 = (int) (perx(p1) >> BITSH) + (tg_scrnx >> 1);
    y1 = (int) (pery(p1) >> BITSH) + (tg_scrny >> 1);
    x2 = (int) (perx(p2) >> BITSH) + (tg_scrnx >> 1);
    y2 = (int) (pery(p2) >> BITSH) + (tg_scrny >> 1);
    tg_setcolor(color);
    if (glasses)
    {   if (color != 0)
        {   tg_setcolor(LEFTCLR);
        }
        tg_drawline(x1, y1, x2, y2);
        if (color != 0)
        {   tg_setcolor(RIGHTCLR);
        }
        tg_drawline((int) ((mu(perx(p1), cosocular) +
                        mu(p1.z, sinocular)) >> BITSH) +
                        (tg_scrnx >> 1), y1,
                   (int) ((mu(perx(p2), cosocular) +
                        mu(p2.z, sinocular)) >> BITSH) +
                        (tg_scrnx >> 1), y2);
    }
    else
    {   tg_drawline(x1, y1, x2, y2);
    }
}
```

Interactive 3-D Modeling

Computer graphics is finally as fundamental to computers as vision is to humans, and soon, 3-D graphics will be in the home and available in portable and desktop computers. Of course, 2-D will also be around because it's a subset of 3-D.

Even though real-time 3-D graphics emerged almost 30 years ago, its greatest growth has occurred in the last five years, when it became more affordable. This growth rate will accelerate as the world begins to appreciate the applications for 3-D graphics.

As recently as 1984, there were people who couldn't understand this passion for real-time interaction. I once demonstrated an intelligent real-time information system to a reporter who said, 'I can't visualize why you need all those graphics.' Today, the needs are obvious, and the applications are all around us.

> —Jim Clark, "Roots and Branches of 3-D," *BYTE*, May 1992

You've learned how to display and manipulate objects in three dimensional space. In order to put that knowledge to work, you need to know how to create and reshape those objects in the first place. You also need a convenient way to store objects—preferably in a format that can be read by almost any 3-D graphics program in existence. The 3DLINES program I'm about to present will meet all those needs, with the added fun of interactive anaglyphic stereo display.

When I introduced the DXF file format in Chapter 3, I promised that you'd get some working code to read and write DXF files later in the book. Well, now it's later. The 3DLINES program will read three-dimensional lines from a DXF file, allow you to interactively edit, rotate, and resize the wireframe shape, and save your modified model to another DXF file. Since DXF is a text-based file format, you can also examine and hand-edit the files with any text editor or word processor if you wish. Every major 3-D graphics software package (and almost every minor 3-D graphics software package) on the market can read and write DXF files, so you'll be able to take the 3-D models you create with 3DLINES into any CAD, modeling, and rendering software.

Editing a 3-D Shape

Working in three-dimensional space while looking at a two-dimensional screen isn't always easy, even with stereoscopic rendering. By learning to use interactive motion during the modeling process, you can dramatically enhance your ability to visualize what you're doing. When you can instantly rotate your model in any direction, the resulting visual feedback can resolve a weird-looking tangle of lines into a clearly discernible 3-D shape.

Figures 7.5 through 7.8 show the steps in editing a hexagonal tube to become a space-age yurt. (What's a yurt? It's a round yak-hair house where Mongolians joyfully carve beautiful symbols in rocks while they warm themselves by burning yak dung at 10 below zero. Yurts were also a popular form of affordable housing among aging flower children in the '70s. Who ever said that computer graphics books don't give you any good material for winning at Trivial Pursuit?) The **You Can Do It** section that follows will give you step-by-step instructions for building a yurt of your very own. Later, your architectural creation will make the move from ancient to ultramodern as I put it into orbit on a 3-D space station.

You Can Do It: Framing a Tubular House

The 3DLINES program lets you interactively edit wireframe shapes. By following the steps below, you can explore 3-D design and transform the hexagonal TUBE provided as a DXF file into the yurt model picture in Figure 7.8 earlier.

Before your course in Himalayan Housebuilding, I'll take you on a brief tour of the 3DLINES program controls.

1. To start the 3DLINES program and tell it which file to load and which file to save when you're done, enter the following command at the DOS prompt:

```
3DLINES TUBE.DXF PLAY.DXF
```

2. Press V to choose the VGA 16-color video mode.

3. If you found that the red/blue 3-D glasses worked well for you with the 3DCUBE discussed earlier in this chapter, press G now and put the glasses on.

   The shape that appears on your screen doesn't look like much of anything when viewed head-on. To spin the shape around, you must choose the axis of rotation by pressing X, Y, or Z and then use the + or - key to spin.

4. Press Y to choose the y axis, then press + a couple times to spin around the y axis.

5. Press X and then hold down the + key to spin for a little while.

(If you are using the 3-D glasses, you might want to use the I and O keys to adjust the angular distance between the right and left eye images now. Most people don't need to bother, since the default distance should be about right. You can also turn perspective viewing on with the P key, and adjust the perspective distance with the N and F keys. All these options work just like they did in the 3DCUBE program, even though they don't appear on the menu on the bottom of the screen in this program.)

6. Try the Size controls a couple times each just to see what they do: Press * * / /

7. Try the Squash controls by pressing the [key and then the] key. Notice that the shape only squishes and stretches along the axis you last selected with the X, Y or Z key.

8. Try the Skew controls by pressing the ; key and then the ' key. This time, the selected axis rotates while the other two axes remain unchanged.

   You may want to fool around with some more of the controls listed at the bottom of the screen to see if you can tell what they do. (Don't worry if you don't figure them all out immediately—I'm about to show you how to use them.)

9. Once you're done playing, press the Esc key to save your modifications to a file named PLAY.DXF and exit the program.

Now I'll help you modify the tube shape you just saw to become a hut. First, start over from the original TUBE.DXF file.

1. Type 3DLINES TUBE.DXF YURT.DXF and press Enter.

2. Choose 16-color mode V again.

   I recommend that you leave the 3-D glasses off for this one, so that you can distinguish the white crosshair cursor from the rest of the lines more easily.

3. First, you need to squish the shape vertically. Press the Y key and then press the] key five times.

   The white plus-shaped crosshair shows you which corner point you are currently "holding." In a moment, you'll see how to use the arrow keys to move a point, and how to make and break connecting lines between points. But first, make a new point to serve as the peak of a conical roof.

4. Insert a new corner point and line by pressing the Insert key. The crosshair cursor moves to the new point, slightly below the existing point.

5. Press the up arrow key four times to move the point you just made up above the others.

   That new point will become the tip of a cone-shaped roof. To center it, you need to rotate the whole shape around the x axis to get a "top view."

6. Press X and then press the - key eight times. (This spins exactly 90 degrees.)

7. Use the arrow keys to move the point to the approximate center of the shape.

   When you inserted the point, one line was created automatically. To complete the roof, you need to connect that same point to each of the other "support beams" at the top corners of the walls.

8. Press the + key four times. This lets you view the model at an angle so you can distinguish the points more easily.

9. To choose a second point for a new connecting line, press , (the comma key). A white line comes out of the cursor to one of the other corner points.

10. Press , again. The white connecting line goes to one of the top corners of a wall.

11. To make a new line, press . (the period key).

12. Repeat steps 10 and 11 four times, until you've made lines connecting every top corner of the walls to the peak of the roof.

   Your little hut isn't much of a domicile without a doorway. You'd better take out part of a wall and erect a door frame in its place.

13. Two corner points are lower than the rest. Press the Tab key until the crosshair cursor is on the leftmost of these.

You will make the doorway between the current point and the one to its right. To do that, you need to knock out the bottom line that connects them.

14. Press , (comma) once. The white connecting line reaches from the current point to the one to the right.

15. Press . (period) to destroy the line between the two selected points. (Notice that the same control that makes a connecting line also breaks an existing connection.)

    You want to construct your doorway on the same plane as the wall. Therefore, you should spin the model so that the wall is parallel to the computer screen. Then you'll be able to use the up, down, left, and right arrow keys to place the corners of the door.

16. Press the + key four times to spin the model until it's parallel to the screen.

17. Press the Insert key to make a new point and line.

18. Press the up arrow key once and the right arrow key once to place the lower left corner of the door.

19. Press Insert to make another new point and line.

20. Press the up arrow six times to place the top left corner of the door.

    In order to make sure the door is centered, construct the other side of it starting at the other side of the wall:

21. Press the Tab key three times to move the cursor to the lower right corner of the wall.

22. Press Insert.

23. Press the up arrow key once and then the left arrow key once.

24. Press Insert again.

25. Press the up arrow key six times.

    Finally, you need to connect the top left and top right corners of the door.

26. Press , (comma) fourteen times to put the connecting cursor line on the top left corner of the door.

27. Press . (period) to lay that final beam across the doorway.

28. Press the Esc key to save your finished yurt.

You can examine your masterpiece and spin it with the 3-D glasses on by running the 3DLINES program again and typing YURT.DXF as the first filename. (Enter anything you like for the second filename, as long as you don't duplicate the name of an existing DXF file in the same directory. Just use YURT2.DXF if you can't think of anything offhand.)

Actually, the hut is just a framework of sticks right now. Later in this chapter, you'll get a chance to nail the walls—3-D faces, that is—onto the frame you created here.

If you didn't make it all the way through the construction process, you can have a look at my humble hut, named MYYURT.DXF. There are also several other DXF shapes included with the 3DLINES program that you might like to explore. To see a listing, just enter DIR *.DXF and then use any of the files you see as the first filename on the command line when you run the 3DLINES program.

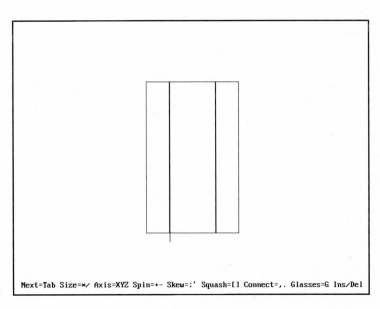

a

Next=Tab Size=*/ Axis=XYZ Spin=+- Skew=;' Squash=[] Connect=,. Glasses=G Ins/Del

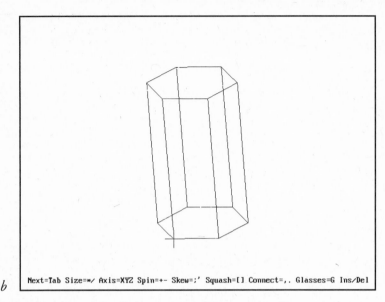

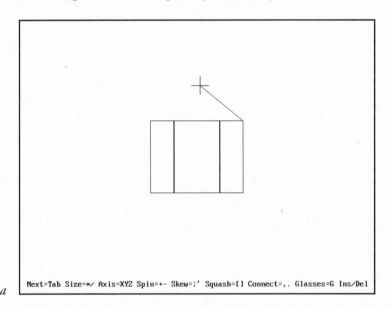

Figure 7.5. *This hexagonal tube was imported from a DXF file.*

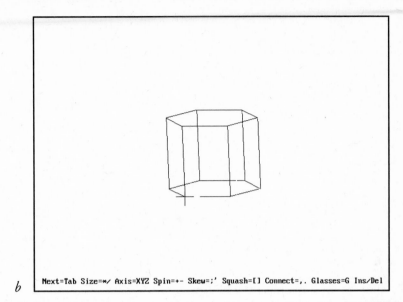

Next=Tab Size=*/ Axis=XYZ Spin=+- Skew=;' Squash=[] Connect=,. Glasses=G Ins/Del

b

Figure 7.6. *By squishing along the y axis, the tube becomes the frame for a six-walled house.*

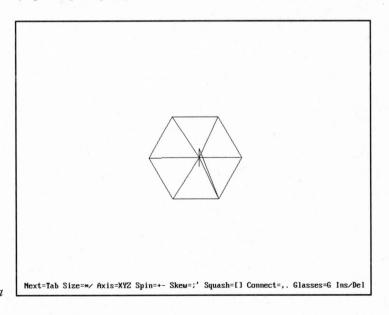

Next=Tab Size=*/ Axis=XYZ Spin=+- Skew=;' Squash=[] Connect=,. Glasses=G Ins/Del

a

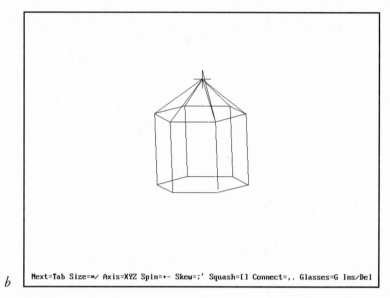

Next=Tab Size=*/ Axis=XYZ Spin=+- Skew=;' Squash=[] Connect=,. Glasses=G Ins/Del

b

Figure 7.7. *Add a roof and you have a building which resembles a Himalayan yurt.*

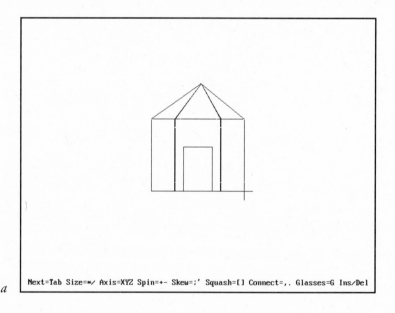

Next=Tab Size=*/ Axis=XYZ Spin=+- Skew=;' Squash=[] Connect=,. Glasses=G Ins/Del

a

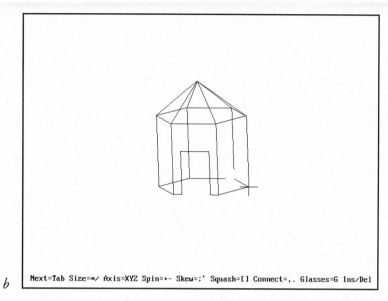

b `Next=Tab Size=*/ Axis=XYZ Spin=+- Skew=;' Squash=[] Connect=,. Glasses=G Ins/Del`

Figure 7.8. *Add a doorway to the front and you're ready to move in.*

Reading and Writing DXF Files

Before you examine the **Working Code** for the 3DLINES program, you might like to know a little more about the DXF files it reads and writes. A DXF file can describe just about anything that lurks in the far reaches of 3-D space, but the 3DLINES program ignores everything except 3DLINE entities when it reads a DXF. As you might expect, the DXF files it creates also contain only 3DLINE entities. (Toward the end of this chapter, you'll learn how to read and write 3DFACE entities as well.)

Because you only need to deal with 3-D lines for now, the DXF you write can be quite simple. Each DXF will begin with the following text.

```
0
SECTION
2
ENTITIES
```

This signals the beginning of the ENTITIES section of the DXF, which is the only section you need for the task at hand. (Other sections for more complex DXFs might include coordinate system definitions, color and layer setup information, and so forth.)

301

At the end of the DXF, you always put the following text to signal the end of the ENTITIES section and the end of the file.

```
0
ENDSECT
0
EOF
```

In between, all you need are the endpoints of the 3DLINEs, in the following format. (The <— characters and the comments following them are not part of the DXF file.)

```
0
3DLINE
10              <— 1 means X, 0 means first point
-159.953613     <— Coordinate values are in decimal format
20              <— 2 means Y, 0 means first point
-62.174316
30              <— 3 means Z, 0 means first point
15.486816
11              <— 1 means X, 1 means second point
41.85499
21              <— 2 means Y, 1 means second point
-92.881348
31              <— 3 means Z, 1 means second point
-138.962418
```

That's all there is to writing a valid DXF file. It's actually easier in some cases to create a DXF than to display the geometry on the screen. To read a DXF, you just ignore everything that doesn't match the preceding format, and process everything that does. In the following **Working Code** section, the DXF reader functions are a bit more complex because they check each point as it comes in to see if it's identical to a previous point. If it is, the program simply sets up a line using the previous point instead of duplicating it. This is not technically necessary, but it makes storing and editing the points much more efficient.

Working Code: Editing 3-D Lines

The 3DLINES.C program listed here uses the 3D.H header file, listed earlier along with the 3DCUBE.C program. It also uses the same geometric formulas for spinning and sizing, with the added capability of sizing or spinning only one axis at a time. This makes for nifty "squash" and "skew" effects.

Note that you must link in MUDI.OBJ if you compile this program. For example, the Microsoft C compile command would be:

```
TGMS 3DLINES.C MUDI.OBJ
```

To compile with Borland C, use TGTC instead of TGMS. See the introduction for more detailed compile instructions.

Listing 7.3. 3DLINES.C reads the 3DLINE entities from a DXF file, lets you edit them, and saves them to another DXF.

```c
/* 3DLINES.C
 *
 * Load the 3DLINE entities from a DXF file,
 * allow the user to interactively view and edit the shape,
 * then save the modified shape into another DXF file.
 *
 * from Tricks of the Graphics Gurus
 */

#include "3d.h"

FILE *diskfile;                 /* used for all disk access */
char savename[NAMELEN];     /* filename for modified shape */

point3d point[NPTS],               /* corner vertex points */
        drawpt1[NPTS], drawpt2[NPTS],  /* for quick erasing */
        handbtm, handtop,       /* ends of crosshair handle */
        handlft, handrgt, handbak,
        tempt,      /* for miscellaneous temporary storage */
        mid;                     /* midpoint of the shape */

long delta,                 /* amount or direction to change */
     pdist,                       /* perspective distance */
     cosocular = COSOCULAR,     /* precomputed cos and sin */
     sinocular = SINOCULAR;
double oculardist = OCULARDIST;    /* distance between eyes */

/* NOTE: All of the above variables are 32-bit integers,
 * scaled by the amount defined as M1. The mu() and di()
```

continues

303

Listing 7.3. continued

```
 * macros call assembly language routines to multiply and
 * divide these numbers, maintaining the scaling factor. */

int drawclr,                        /* color to give the shape */
    white,                    /* color to give menus and cursor */
    glasses = 0,      /* 1 = red/blue 3D glasses, 0 = normal */
    i, j, k, xx, yy, zz,          /* general purpose counters */
    thispt = 0,                       /* current corner point */
    connectpt = 0,       /* second point of connecting line */
    npts,                        /* total number of points */
    perspective = 0,           /* perspective 1=on, 0=off */
    linefrom[NLINES], lineto[NLINES], /* start/end of lines */
    nlines,                           /* number of lines */
    cpu;                 /* used by cputype() in mudi.asm */

enum {X, Y, Z} thisaxis = X;        /* for spin, size, etc. */


/* function prototypes */

int main(int nargs, char **arg);
void midpoint(void);
void warpz(long sizex, long sizey);
void warpy(long sizex, long sizez);
void warpx(long sizey, long sizez);
void sizepts(point3d resize);
void draw(void);
void draw3dline(point3d p1, point3d p2, int color);
void connect(void);
void insert(void);
void delete(void);

int main(int nargs, char **arg)
{   char a;                              /* current keypress */
    cpu = cputype();          /* find out what cpu we have */
    printf("\n 3DLINES -- An Interactive 3D Shape Editor");
    printf("\n\n from Tricks of the Graphics Gurus\n\n");
    if (nargs < 3)         /* make sure files were specified */
    {   printf("To use this program:\n\n");
        printf("3DLINES FILE1.DXF FILE2.DXF\n\n");
        printf("Where FILE1.DXF is an existing DXF file\n");
```

```
      printf("containing some 3DLINE entities to edit,\n");
      printf("and FILE2.DXF is a name for the new file.\n");
      exit(0);
}
tg_pickmode();            /* ask user for a video mode */
if (loaddxf(arg[1]) == 0)        /* load starting shape */
{  tg_closedown();
   printf("Could not load the file named %s\n\n", arg[1]);
   exit(0);
}
strcpy(savename, arg[2]);  /* remember the name to save */
white = 15 % tg_ncolors;      /* define the color white */
drawclr = 9 % tg_ncolors;     /* define color for shape */
pdist = (long) tg_scrny << BITSH;  /* perspective dist. */
tg_moveto(0, tg_scrny - tg_chary);      /* show a menu */
tg_outtext("Next=Tab Size=*/ Axis=XYZ Spin=+- Skew=;\' "
           "Squash=[] Connect=,. Glasses=G Ins/Del");
tg_setviewport(0, 0, tg_scrnx - 1, tg_scrny - tg_chary);
midpoint();        /* move the shape to center of screen */
for(i = 0; i < nlines; i++)  /* prepare for quick erase */
{   drawpt1[i] = point[linefrom[i]];
    drawpt2[i] = point[lineto[i]];
}
handbtm = handtop = handlft = handrgt = point[thispt];
while(1)                            /* main menu loop */
{   draw();                    /* display current shape */
    geta;                      /* get the next keypress */
    switch(a)                  /* what shall we do now? */
    {   case LT:                          /* move left */
            point[thispt].x -= MOVEINC;
            break;
        case RT:                         /* move right */
            point[thispt].x += MOVEINC;
            break;
        case UP:                            /* move up */
            point[thispt].y -= MOVEINC;
            break;
        case DN:                          /* move down */
            point[thispt].y += MOVEINC;
            break;
```

continues

Listing 7.3. continued

```
case TAB:                    /* select the next part */
    if (++thispt >= npts) thispt = 0;
    connectpt = thispt;
    break;
case 'C':                        /* change color */
    drawclr++;
    if ((drawclr >= tg_ncolors) ¦¦
        (drawclr >= 15)) drawclr = 1;
    break;
case 'X':    /* choose axis for spin and sizing */
    thisaxis = X;
    break;
case 'Y':
    thisaxis = Y;
    break;
case 'Z':
    thisaxis = Z;
    break;
case '*':              /* grow (increase size) */
    tempt.x = tempt.y = tempt.z = M1 + SIZEINC;
    sizepts(tempt);
    break;
case '/':              /* shrink (decrease size) */
    tempt.x = tempt.y = tempt.z =
        di(M1, (M1 + SIZEINC));
    sizepts(tempt);
    break;
case '-':                            /* spin */
    delta = -1;
case '+':
    if (a == '+') delta = 1;
    switch(thisaxis)
    {   case X:
            warpx(SPININC * delta,
                SPININC * delta);
            break;
        case Y:
            warpy(SPININC * delta,
                SPININC * delta);
            break;
```

```
            case Z:
                warpz(SPININC * delta,
                    SPININC * delta);
        }
        break;
    case '\'':            /* skew (spin x-axis only) */
        delta = -1;
    case ';':
        if (a == ';') delta = 1;
        switch(thisaxis)
        {   case X:
                warpz(SPININC * delta, 0L);
                break;
            case Y:
                warpx(-SPININC, 0L);
                break;
            case Z:
                warpy(0L, SPININC * delta);
        }
        break;
    case '[':            /* squash or stretch x-axis */
    case ']':
        delta = M1 + SIZEINC;
        if (a == ']') delta = di(M1, delta);
        tempt.x = tempt.y = tempt.z = M1;
        switch(thisaxis)
        {   case X:
                tempt.x = delta;
                break;
            case Y:
                tempt.y = delta;
                break;
            case Z:
                tempt.z = delta;
        }
        sizepts(tempt);
        break;
    case ',':            /* select a connecting point */
        if (++connectpt >= npts) connectpt = 0;
        break;
```

continues

Listing 7.3. continued

```
        case '.':    /* make or break a connecting line */
            connect();
            tg_clearviewport();
            break;
        case INSERT:    /* insert a new point and line */
            insert();
            tg_clearviewport();
            break;
        case DELETE:    /* delete a point and its lines */
            delete();
            tg_clearviewport();
            break;
        case 'G':    /* turn red/blue 3D glasses on/off */
            if (glasses) glasses = 0;
            else glasses = 1;
            tg_clearviewport();
            break;
        case 'I':                /* adjust eye separation */
            oculardist += OCULARINC;
        case 'O':
            if (a == 'O') oculardist -= OCULARINC;
            cosocular = (long) (cos(oculardist) * MF);
            sinocular = (long) (sin(oculardist) * MF);
            glasses = 1;
            tg_clearviewport();
            break;
        case 'P':
            if (perspective) perspective = 0;
            else perspective = 1;
            tg_clearviewport();
            break;
        case 'F':
            pdist *= 2;
            tg_clearviewport();
            break;
        case 'N':
            pdist /= 2;
            if (pdist < 4L) pdist = 4L;
            tg_clearviewport();
```

```
                    break;
              case ESC:              /* save new shape and quit */
                  tg_closedown();
                  savedxf(savename);
                  printf("\n\nHappy trails...\n");
                  exit(0);
          }
      }
}

/* compute the midpoint, or "center of gravity"
   and move the shape so that it centers on 0,0,0 */

void midpoint(void)
{   mid.x = 0L, mid.y = 0L, mid.z = 0L;
    for (i = 0; i < npts; i++) addpt(mid, point[i], mid);
    mid.x /= -npts, mid.y /= -npts, mid.z /= -npts;
    for (i = 0; i < npts; i++)
    {   point[i].x += mid.x;
        point[i].y += mid.y;
        /* addpt(point[i], mid, point[i]); */
    }
}

/* draw the shape and a "handle" on the current point */

void draw(void)
{   int i;
    for(i = 0; i < nlines; i++)
    {   draw3dline(drawpt1[i], drawpt2[i], 0);
        draw3dline(drawpt1[i] = point[linefrom[i]],
                   drawpt2[i] = point[lineto[i]], drawclr);
    }
    draw3dline(handtop, handbtm, 0);
    draw3dline(handlft, handrgt, 0);
    draw3dline(handbtm, handbak, 0);
    handbtm = handtop = handlft = handrgt = point[thispt];
    handtop.y += ((long) HAND << BITSH);
    handlft.x -= ((long) HAND << BITSH);
    handrgt.x += ((long) HAND << BITSH);
```

continues

309

Listing 7.3. continued

```
        handbtm.y -= ((long) HAND << BITSH);
        if (connectpt == thispt) handbak = handbtm;
        else handbak = point[connectpt];
        draw3dline(handtop, handbtm, white);
        draw3dline(handlft, handrgt, white);
        draw3dline(handbtm, handbak, white);
}

/* draw a 3D line from p1 to p2 */

void draw3dline(point3d p1, point3d p2, int color)
{   int x1, y1, x2, y2;
    x1 = (int) (perx(p1) >> BITSH) + (tg_scrnx >> 1);
    y1 = (int) (pery(p1) >> BITSH) + (tg_scrny >> 1);
    x2 = (int) (perx(p2) >> BITSH) + (tg_scrnx >> 1);
    y2 = (int) (pery(p2) >> BITSH) + (tg_scrny >> 1);
    tg_setcolor(color);
    if (glasses)
    {   if (color != 0)
        {   tg_setcolor(LEFTCLR);
        }
        tg_drawline(x1, y1, x2, y2);
        if (color != 0)
        {   tg_setcolor(RIGHTCLR);
        }
        tg_drawline((int) ((mu(perx(p1), cosocular) +
                            mu(p1.z, sinocular)) >> BITSH) +
                            (tg_scrnx >> 1), y1,
                 (int) ((mu(perx(p2), cosocular) +
                            mu(p2.z, sinocular)) >> BITSH) +
                            (tg_scrnx >> 1), y2);
    }
    else
    {   tg_drawline(x1, y1, x2, y2);
    }
}

/* resize the shape */

void sizepts(point3d resize)
```

```
{   int i;
    for(i = 0; i < npts; i++)
    {   point[i].x = mu(point[i].x, resize.x);
        point[i].y = mu(point[i].y, resize.y);
        point[i].z = mu(point[i].z, resize.z);
    }
}


/* spin around the z axis */

void warpz(long spinx, long spiny)
{   point3d pointi;
    int i;
    for (i = 0; i < npts; i++)
    {   pointi = point[i];
        point[i].x = pointi.x *  cosf(spinx) +
                     pointi.y *  sinf(spiny);
        point[i].y = pointi.x * -sinf(spinx) +
                     pointi.y *  cosf(spiny);
    }
}


/* spin around the y axis */

void warpy(long spinx, long spinz)
{   point3d pointi;
    int i;
    for (i = 0; i < npts; i++)
    {   pointi = point[i];
        point[i].x = pointi.x * cosf(spinx) -
                     pointi.z * sinf(spinz);
        point[i].z = pointi.x * sinf(spinx) +
                     pointi.z * cosf(spinz);
    }
}


/* spin around the x axis */

void warpx(long spiny, long spinz)
{   point3d pointi;
```

continues

Listing 7.3. continued

```
    int i;
    for (i = 0; i < npts; i++)
    {   pointi = point[i];
        point[i].y = pointi.y * cosf(spiny) +
                     pointi.z * sinf(spinz);
        point[i].z = pointi.y * -sinf(spiny) +
                     pointi.z * cosf(spinz);
    }
}

/* If a line exists between thispt and connectpt, kill it.
   Otherwise, make one. */

void connect(void)
{   int connected = 0;
    for (i = 0; i < nlines; i++)
    {   if (((linefrom[i] == connectpt) &&
             (lineto[i] == thispt)) ||
            ((linefrom[i] == thispt) &&
             (lineto[i] == connectpt)))
        {   connected = 1;
            --nlines;
            for (j = i; j < nlines; j++)
                linefrom[j] = linefrom[j + 1],
                lineto[j] = lineto[j + 1];
        }
    }
    if (!connected)
    {   linefrom[nlines] = connectpt;
        lineto[nlines] = thispt;
        ++nlines;
    }
}

/* insert a new point, offset it slightly in the y direction,
   and make a new line connecting to the current point */

void insert(void)
{   point3d tempt;
    if ((npts < NPTS) && (nlines < NLINES))
```

```
    {   for (i = npts; i > thispt; i—) point[i] = point[i - 1];
        point[thispt].y += MOVEINC;
        for (i = 0; i < nlines; i++)
        {   if (linefrom[i] >= thispt) ++(linefrom[i]);
            if (lineto[i] >= thispt) ++(lineto[i]);
        }
        linefrom[nlines] = thispt;
        lineto[nlines] = thispt + 1;
        ++nlines;
        ++npts;
    }
}

/* delete the current point and all lines connected to it */

void delete(void)
{   if (npts > 1)
    {   for (i = 0; i < nlines; i++)
        {   if ((linefrom[i] == thispt) || (lineto[i] == thispt))
            {   --nlines;
                for (j = i; j < nlines; j++)
                {   linefrom[j] = linefrom[j + 1];
                    lineto[j] = lineto[j + 1];
                }
                --i;
            }
            else
            {   if (linefrom[i] > thispt) --(linefrom[i]);
                if (lineto[i] > thispt) --(lineto[i]);
            }
        }
        if (thispt == --npts) --thispt;
        else
            for (i = thispt; i < npts; i++)
                point[i] = point[i + 1];
        connectpt = thispt;
    }
}

/* Save the lines to a DXF file */
```

continues

Listing 7.3. continued

```c
int savedxf(char *name)
{   int i;
    if ((diskfile = fopen(name, "wb")) == NULL) return(0);
    fprintf(diskfile, "0\r\nSECTION\r\n2\r\nENTITIES\r\n");
    for (i = 0; i < nlines; i++)
        fprintf(diskfile,
                "0\r\n3DLINE\r\n"
                "10\r\n%lf\r\n20\r\n%lf\r\n30\r\n%lf\r\n"
                "11\r\n%lf\r\n21\r\n%lf\r\n31\r\n%lf\r\n",
                (double) point[linefrom[i]].x / MF,
                (double) -point[linefrom[i]].y / MF,
                (double) point[linefrom[i]].z /MF,
                (double) point[lineto[i]].x / MF,
                (double) -point[lineto[i]].y / MF,
                (double) point[lineto[i]].z / MF);
    fprintf(diskfile, "0\r\nENDSEC\r\n0\r\nEOF\r\n");
    fprintf(diskfile, "%c", EOFILE);
    fclose(diskfile);
    return(1);
}

/* macro to call readdxfgroup() from within loaddxf() */

#define readgroup() \
    if (readdxfgroup(&groupcode, groupname, &value) == 0) \
        return(0)

/* load the 3DLINE entities from a DXF file */

int loaddxf(char *name)
{   int i, groupcode;
    char groupname[80];
    point3d p1, p2;
    long value;
    npts = nlines = 0;
    if ((diskfile = fopen(name, "rb")) == NULL) return(0);
    do
    {   readgroup();
    } while((groupcode != 0) ||
            (strcmp(groupname, "SECTION") != 0));
```

```
do
{   readgroup();
} while((groupcode != 2) ||
        strcmp(groupname, "ENTITIES") != 0);
do
{   readgroup();
} while(groupcode != 0);
while(1)
{   if (strcmp(groupname, "ENDSEC") == 0) break;
    if (strcmp(groupname, "3DLINE") == 0)
    {   p1.x = p1.y = p1.z = 0L;
        p2.x = p2.y = p2.z = 0L;
        do
        {   readgroup();
            switch(groupcode)
            {   case 10: p1.x = value; break;
                case 11: p2.x = value; break;
                case 20: p1.y = -value; break;
                case 21: p2.y = -value; break;
                case 30: p1.z = value; break;
                case 31: p2.z = value;
            }
            if (groupcode == 0)
            {   for (i = 0; i < npts; i++)
                {   if ((point[i].x == p1.x) &&
                        (point[i].y == p1.y) &&
                        (point[i].z == p1.z))
                    {   linefrom[nlines] = i;
                        break;
                    }
                }
                if (i >= npts)
                {   point[npts] = p1;
                    linefrom[nlines] = npts;
                    npts++;
                }
                for (i = 0; i < npts; i++)
                {   if ((point[i].x == p2.x) &&
                        (point[i].y == p2.y) &&
                        (point[i].z == p2.z))
```

continues

315

Listing 7.3. continued

```
                            {   lineto[nlines] = i;
                                break;
                            }
                    }
                    if (i >= npts)
                    {   point[npts] = p2;
                        lineto[nlines] = npts;
                        npts++;
                    }
                    nlines++;
                }
            } while(groupcode != 0);
        }
        else
        {   do
            {   readgroup();
            } while(groupcode != 0);
        }
    }
    fclose(diskfile);
    return(1);
}

/* read two lines of the DXF file, expecting the first
 * line to be a groupcode number and the second line to
 * be either a groupname string or a numerical value */

int readdxfgroup(int *groupcode,
                 char *groupname,
                 long *value)
{   char linein[255];
    fscanf(diskfile, "%s", linein);
    if ((*linein <= '9') && (*linein >= '0'))
        *groupcode = atoi(linein);
    else return(0);
    fscanf(diskfile, "%s", groupname);
    *value = (long) (atof(groupname) * MF);
    return(1);
}
```

Modeling 3-D Surfaces

One of the major concepts in computer graphics is modeling *of objects and pictures. By this we mean description of the objects and pictures to the computer so as to produce a visual display that simulates the real thing.*

One way to do this is to use a set of primitives or geometric forms that are simple enough to be easily implemented on the computer but flexible enough to represent or model a variety of objects. We can build a model of our object by assembling these primitives either through the use of a prepared display file or by interactively constructing the model.

—Roy A. Plastock and Gordon Kalley,
Theory and Problems of Computer Graphics, 1986

Dots and lines are the stuff a geometer's dreams are made of. To bring 3-D graphics out of the realm of abstraction and into the real world, you need to work with surfaces, called *3DFACE entities* or just *3-D faces* in the lingo of the day.

In Chapter 9, you'll learn how to model the interaction of light with your 3-D faces to produce photorealistic renderings. But first, you need to know how to define the faces themselves.

Putting a Face On It

In theory, 3-D surfaces can wind and twist in all manner of strange topologies. For practical purposes, however, you can approximate any 3-D surface with a set of triangles or rectangles. The math for rendering a triangle or rectangle is relatively simple, while the math for rendering more complex polygons and contours gets outrageously complex. Therefore, most 3-D software requires all surfaces to be defined as a collection of individual 3-point or 4-point faces. In some cases, a lattice of many adjacent triangles or rectangles can be defined as a single *mesh* entity. Although the mesh data can be stored in a more compact form, the geometry and algorithms for dealing with mesh entities are essentially the same as if the faces were defined one at a time.

With the 3DFACES program presented in the **You Can Do It** and **Working Code** sections that follow, you can add 3-D faces to the wireframe models made with 3DLINES or any other DXF-compatible program.

If you plan to render your 3-D faces with some 3-D software (such as the ray tracer presented in Chapter 9), you can speed the lengthy calculations involved by employing a little design trick from the outset. By paying careful attention to the order in which you assign corner points to a face, you can whisper a secret in the ear of your rendering software. Most 3-D programs will use the point order to determine which side of the face is the "out side" and which is the "in side." By skipping the math to check for interactions with the "in side," some programs can cut the rendering time almost in half.

So which side is "in" and which side is "out?" The same *right hand rule* that you employed to name 3-D rotations can also tell you which side of your face you are looking out of. Curve the fingers of your right hand so that your palm is on the first point and your finger tips are on the last point, with your knuckles representing the one or two points in between. The direction your thumb points is "out." That side of the face will be rendered, and the "in" side will be ignored. By the way, the imaginary line which sticks out of the face in the direction of your thumb is called the *normal*.

Of course, almost all 3-D renderers will let you turn on a "two sided" feature for those times when you goofed up on (or had no control over) the order of the points in the face. Some programs also have advanced algorithms to *unify the normals*, meaning that they can guess which side is out and rearrange the point order for you.

When you use the 3DFACES program, the order in which you assign points to a face will be preserved in the resulting DXF file. Figures 7.9 and 7.10 illustrate the process of "walling-in" the hut you created earlier in this chapter. Note that I carefully assigned the points in counter-clockwise order in Figure 7.9 so that the normal of the wall would be on the outside of the building.

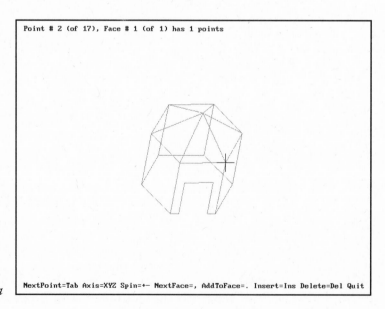

a

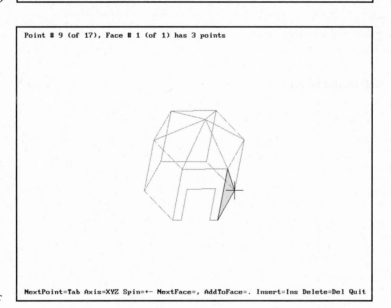

b

c

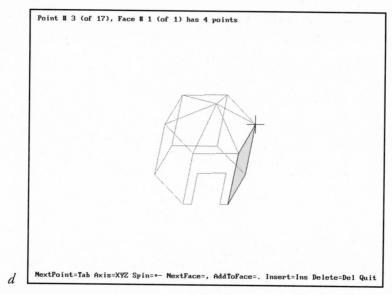

d

Figure 7.9. *To erect a wall with the 3DFACE program, you simply select each corner point one by one.*

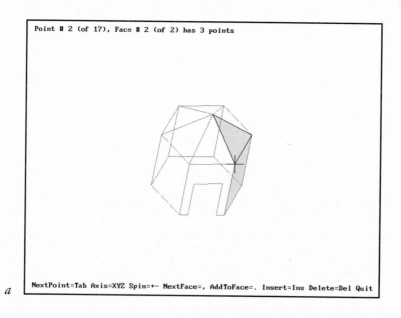

a

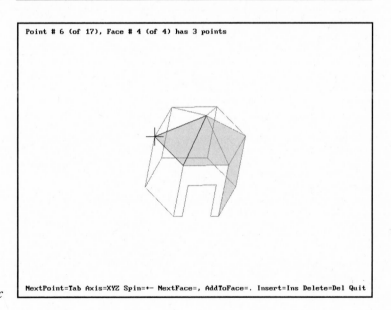

```
Point # 1 (of 17), Face # 3 (of 3) has 3 points
```

```
NextPoint=Tab Axis=XYZ Spin=+- NextFace=, AddToFace=. Insert=Ins Delete=Del Quit
```

b

```
Point # 6 (of 17), Face # 4 (of 4) has 3 points
```

```
NextPoint=Tab Axis=XYZ Spin=+- NextFace=, AddToFace=. Insert=Ins Delete=Del Quit
```

c

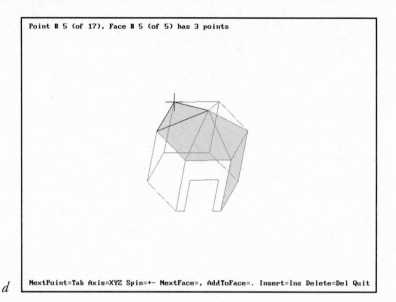

Point # 5 (of 17), Face # 5 (of 5) has 3 points

NextPoint=Tab Axis=XYZ Spin=+- NextFace=, AddToFace=. Insert=Ins Delete=Del Quit

d

Point # 4 (of 17), Face # 6 (of 6) has 3 points

NextPoint=Tab Axis=XYZ Spin=+- NextFace=, AddToFace=. Insert=Ins Delete=Del Quit

e

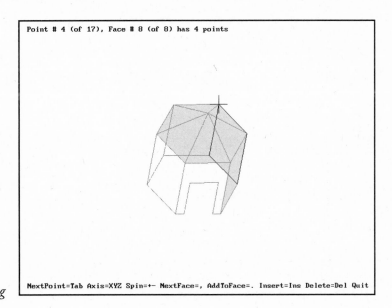

f

g

Point # 5 (of 17), Face # 9 (of 9) has 4 points

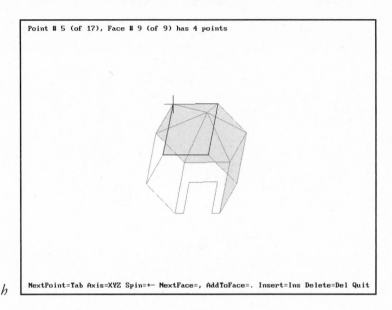

NextPoint=Tab Axis=XYZ Spin=+- NextFace=, AddToFace=. Insert=Ins Delete=Del Quit

h

Point # 6 (of 17), Face # 10 (of 10) has 4 points

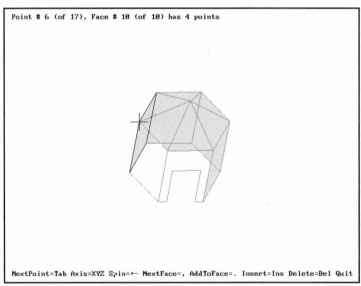

NextPoint=Tab Axis=XYZ Spin=+- NextFace=, AddToFace=. Insert=Ins Delete=Del Quit

i

Point # 1 (of 17), Face # 11 (of 11) has 4 points

NextPoint=Tab Axis=XYZ Spin=+- NextFace=, AddToFace=. Insert=Ins Delete=Del Quit

j

Point # 2 (of 17), Face # 12 (of 12) has 4 points

NextPoint=Tab Axis=XYZ Spin=+- NextFace=, AddToFace=. Insert=Ins Delete=Del Quit

k

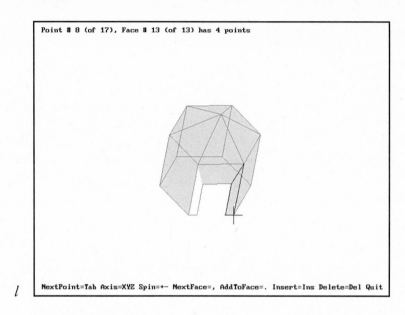

l

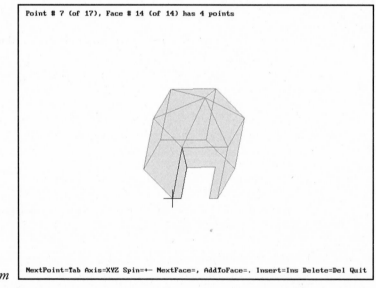

m

Figure 7.10. *Repeat the process for each 3-D face you want to define. Note that a single face can have no more than four corners, so the wall around the door must be defined as three separate faces.*

You Can Do It: Face It.

At 30 or 40 degrees below zero, the Himalayan wind blowing through your hovel can put quite a chill on your bones. That's why the rosy-cheeked folks who live at the top of the world seldom live in wireframe houses. Since you probably don't have any yak-hair felt handy, I'll show you how to wall-in your yurt with mathematically defined faces. And since you probably don't have much yak dung to burn for your fire either, we won't worry about putting a smoke hole in the roof.

1. To start the 3DFACES program, load the YURT.DXF file you created earlier, and specify WALLS.DXF as the name for your finished work, enter the following command at the DOS prompt.

    ```
    3DFACES YURT.DXF WALLS.DXF
    ```

    (If your YURT.DXF turned out as lop-sided as your last cub-scout birdhouse project, just subsitute MYYURT.DXF on the command line instead.)

2. Select VGA 16-color mode V.

    You won't be using the arrow keys to line up points, so it doesn't matter if the model is aligned to the plane of your computer screen. In fact, you'll be able to see what you're doing better if you turn the model to view it at an angle.

3. Press X - - - - to spin four steps around the x axis, then press Y + to spin a bit around the y axis. All the points should now be visible without any point or line hiding behind any other.

    In the top left corner of the screen, a status message reports that the crosshair cursor is on "Point #1 (of 17)," and that "Face #1 (of 1) has 0 points." This status message will help you navigate as you add faces and assign points to each face.

    Start by constructing a wall:

4. Press the Tab key once to move to point #2.

5. Press the . (period) key to assign point #2 as the first point in face #1.

6. Press the Tab key repeatedly until you get to point #8, the one right below the point you just assigned. (If you go past point #8 by accident, just keep pressing Tab until you come around to it again.)

7. Press . to assign point #8 as the second point in face #1. Notice that a white line appears, indicating the two assigned corners of the current face.

8. Press the Tab key once to go to point #9.

9. Press . to assign the third point to face #1. A white triangle filled with transparent blue shows the current face.

10. Press Tab repeatedly until you get to point #3, the final corner of the wall.

11. Press . to assign the point to complete face #1. The triangle turns to a four-cornered 3-D face.

    Your wall is complete. Before you finish the other walls, you'd better put on the roof. (In the high country you never know when it's going to snow.)

12. Press the Insert key to start a new face. Notice that the blue face you just made remains in place, but the white outline disappears. (That white outline always highlights just the current face.) The status message also changes, telling you that "Face #2 (of 2) has 0 points."

13. Press . to assign point #3 to face #2.

14. Use the Tab key to go to point #13, and press . to assign it to the face.

15. Use Tab to go to point #2, and press . to assign it to the face. This triangular roof patch will only have three corner points.

16. Complete the rest of the roof and walls, using the table below as a guide. For each face listed, press Insert to start the face, then press . to assign the first point (which, in this model, will always be the same as the final point of the previous face). Then use Tab and . to go to each subsequent point listed and assign it to the face.

Face number	First point	Second point	Third point	Fourth point (if any)
3	3	13	2	
4	2	13	1	

Face number	First point	Second point	Third point	Fourth point (if any)
5	1	13	6	
6	6	13	5	
7	5	13	4	
8	4	13	3	
9	3	9	10	4
10	4	10	11	5
11	5	11	12	6
12	6	12	7	1

All that remains is the wall around the doorway. Since each face can only have 4 points, you must use three separate panels to fill in around the door.

17. Use the following table as a guide, just as you did above. Be sure to notice that the first point in face 15 is not the same as the last point in face 14. You'll need to break your "rhythm" and use the Tab key after you press Insert but before you press the period key for that one.

Face number	First point	Second point	Third point	Fourth point
13	1	15	17	2
14	2	17	16	8
15	14	15	1	7

You're done. But before you save your hard-won habitation, it's a good idea to line it up with the screen. That way, the walls and edges will be oriented along the y axis when you import it into a rendering program.

18. Press Y - and then press X + + + + to reverse the spins you did at the beginning. The walls should all be vertical.

19. Press Esc to save the shape and exit the program.

Any of the DXF files on the disk can be loaded into the 3DFACES program. Some are just wireframes, which you can add faces to. Others have faces already defined. When you load these into 3DFACES, you can use the , (comma) key to thumb through the faces, and the Delete key to delete a face. Of course, you can also use Insert and the period key to construct new faces as in the steps above.

Though the 3DFACES program doesn't support all the shape editing features of the 3DLINES program or red/blue 3-D glasses display, you can interactively rotate around any axis to see your models. The faces appear transparent, so you can easily see all of your model from any orientation.

Reading and Writing DXF Faces

3DFACES reads and writes two types of DXF entities: 3DLINE entities and 3DFACE entities. Since each of these data types is handled separately, the functions to read and write DXF files in the 3DFACES.C program listed below are about twice as long as the corresponding DXF-handling functions in 3DLINES.C. Like the 3DLINES program, 3DFACES does some extra work when reading a DXF to avoid storing identical points more than once.

Storing 3DFACE entities in a DXF file is pretty much a no-brainer. They go in the ENTITIES section along with the 3DLINE entities, and look like this (less the comments starting with "<—"):

```
0
3DFACE
10                 <— First X value preceeded by "10"
43.072281
20                 <— First Y value preceeded by "20"
64.931549
30                 <— First Z value preceeded by "30"
-57.441315
```

```
11                      <— Second X value preceeded by "11"
43.176743
21                      <— Second Y value, etc.
-66.333939
31
-56.809677
12
85.792694
22
-66.095505
32
18.075653
13
85.686905
23
65.169113
33
17.443878
```

Something to keep in mind is that all 3DFACE entities must have exactly four points in order to get the official Autodesk stamp of approval. If your face only has three points, you should duplicate the last point to make a fourth. Many (perhaps even most) DXF readers and writers actually ignore this and allow you to create triangular faces without wasting disk space storing a fake fourth vertex. But far be it from me to condone such unabashed dissension from Autodesk's holy word. So I push you toward unwavering conformity: The 3DFACES program always inserts that fourth point in there and sacrifices a few bytes of disk space for the greater good of CAD and country.

Working Code: How to Edit Your Face

Everything in 3DFACES.C is reminiscent of 3DLINES.C, with the addition of some variables to store the face data. While nfaces holds the total number of faces, nfacepts[] keeps track of the number of points in each face. The facepts[][] array references a position in the points[] array for each point in each face. For the fastest possible erase and redraw, the actual x,y screen positions of the faces are stored as an array TransGraphics polygons named drawface[][][].

I left 3-D glasses support and perspective view out of the 3DFACES program to save space in the program listing. You can easily cut and paste these features from 3DLINES.C if you like.

Like the other programs in this chapter, 3DFACES uses the fast integer math routines in MUDI.OBJ. When you compile, be sure to include MUDI.OBJ on the command line, like this:

TGMS 3DFACES.C MUDI.OBJ

Borland users should say TGTC instead of TGMS. See the introduction for more detailed compile instructions.

Listing 7.4. With 3DFACES.C, you can edit 3-D face data from any DXF file that contains 3DLINE and/or 3DFACE entities.

```
/* 3DFACES.C
 *
 * Load 3DLINE and/or 3DFACE entities from a DXF file,
 * let the user edit the faces, then save to a new DXF
 *
 * from Tricks of the Graphics Gurus
 */

#include "3d.h"

FILE *diskfile;                 /* used for all disk access */
char savename[NAMELEN];    /* filename for modified shape */


point3d point[NPTS];              /* corner vertex points */


char msg[80];                /* status line message string */


int lineclr, faceclr,          /* colors to give the shape */
    white,                /* color to give menus and cursor */
    i, j, k, xx, yy, zz,        /* general purpose counters */
    thispt = 0,                  /* current corner point */
    thisface,                 /* currently selected face */
    lastpt = 99, lastface = 99,  /* previous point and face */
    delta,                        /* direction to spin */
    npts,                      /* total number of points */
    linefrom[NLINES], lineto[NLINES], /* start/end of lines */
    drawx[NPTS], drawy[NPTS],       /* for quick draw/erase */
    handlex, handley,         /* center of crosshair handle */
    nlines,                        /* number of lines */
    ndrawfacepts,           /* number of face points to draw */
```

```
    drawface[NFACES][NPTS][2], /* polygons for face display */
    cpu,                  /* used by cputype() in mudi.asm */
    facept[NFACES][4],        /* corner points of each face */
    nfacepts[NFACES],      /* number of points on each face */
    nfaces;                        /* number of faces */

enum {X, Y, Z} thisaxis = X;                  /* for spinning */

/* function prototypes */

int main(int nargs, char **arg);
void midpoint(void);
void draw(void);
void erase(void);
void warpz(long spinx, long spiny);
void warpy(long spinx, long spinz);
void warpx(long spiny, long spinz);
int savedxf(char *name);
int loaddxf(char *name);
int readdxfgroup(int *groupcode, char *groupname,
             long *value);

int main(int nargs, char **arg)
{   char a;                          /* current keypress */
    cpu = cputype();          /* find out what cpu we have */
    printf("\n 3DFACES -- An Interactive 3D Face Editor");
    printf("\n\n from Tricks of the Graphics Gurus\n\n");
    if (nargs < 3)         /* make sure files were specified */
    {   printf("To use this program:\n\n");
        printf("3DFACES FILE1.DXF FILE2.DXF\n\n");
        printf(
          "Where FILE1.DXF is an existing 3D DXF file\n");
        printf(
          "and FILE2.DXF is a name for the new file.\n");
        exit(0);
    }
    tg_pickmode();              /* ask user for a video mode */
    if (loaddxf(arg[1]) == 0)        /* load starting shape */
    {   tg_closedown();
        printf("Could not load the file named %s\n\n", arg[1]);
```

continues

Listing 7.4. continued

```
    exit(0);
}
strcpy(savename, arg[2]);   /* remember the name to save */
white = 15 % tg_ncolors;      /* define the color white */
lineclr = 9 % tg_ncolors;     /* define color for lines */
faceclr = 1 % tg_ncolors;     /* define color for faces */
tg_moveto(0, tg_scrny - tg_chary);        /* show a menu */
tg_outtext("NextPoint=Tab Axis=XYZ Spin=+- NextFace=, "
           "AddToFace=. Insert=Ins Delete=Del Quit=Esc");
tg_setviewport(0, tg_chary + 1,
               tg_scrnx - 1, tg_scrny - tg_chary);
midpoint();
draw();
while(1)                                 /* main menu loop */
{   erase();                           /* erase last shape */
    draw();                        /* display current shape */
    geta;                        /* then get the next keypress */
    switch(a)                      /* what shall we do now? */
    {   case TAB:                    /* select the next part */
            if (++thispt >= npts) thispt = 0;
            break;
        case ',':                  /* select the next face */
            if (++thisface >= nfaces) thisface = 0;
            if (nfaces == 0)
            {   nfaces = 1;
                nfacepts[0] = 0;
                thisface = 0;
            }
            break;
        case '.':                      /* add or delete point */
            lastface = 0;  /* is point already in face? */
            for (i = 0; i < nfacepts[thisface]; i++)
            {   if (facept[thisface][i] == thispt)
                {   lastface = 1;              /* found it */
                    for (j = i;            /* so delete it */
                        j < nfacepts[thisface] - 1; j++)
                    {   facept[thisface][j] =
                            facept[thisface][j + 1];
                    }
                    --(nfacepts[thisface]);
```

```
            }
        }
        if ((lastface == 0) &&      /* didn't find it */
            (nfacepts[thisface] < 4))  /* so add it */
        {   facept[thisface][nfacepts[thisface]] =
                thispt;
            ++(nfacepts[thisface]);
        }
        tg_clearviewport();
        lastface = 99;          /* redraw the screen */
        break;
    case INSERT:                    /* insert new face */
        if (nfaces < NFACES)
        {   nfaces++;
            thisface = nfaces - 1;
            nfacepts[thisface] = 0;
        }
        tg_clearviewport();
        lastface = 99;          /* redraw the screen */
        break;
    case DELETE:                        /* delete a face */
        if (nfaces > 0)
        {   for (i = thisface; i < nfaces - 1; i++)
            {   nfacepts[i] = nfacepts[i + 1];
                for (j = 0; j < nfacepts[i]; j++)
                    facept[i][j] = facept[i + 1][j];
            }
            if (nfaces > 1) nfaces--;
            else nfacepts[0] = 0;
            if (thisface >= nfaces) thisface--;
        }
        tg_clearviewport();
        lastface = 99;          /* redraw the screen */
        break;
    case 'X':           /* choose axis for spinning */
        thisaxis = X;
        break;
    case 'Y':
        thisaxis = Y;
        break;
```

continues

335

Listing 7.4. continued

```
            case 'Z':
                thisaxis = Z;
                break;
            case '-':                        /* spin */
                delta = -1;
            case '+':
                if (a == '+') delta = 1;
                switch(thisaxis)
                {   case X:
                        warpx(SPININC * delta,
                              SPININC * delta);
                        break;
                    case Y:
                        warpy(SPININC * delta,
                              SPININC * delta);
                        break;
                    case Z:
                        warpz(SPININC * delta,
                              SPININC * delta);
                }
                break;
            case ESC:             /* save new DXF and quit */
                tg_closedown();
                savedxf(savename);
                printf("\n\nHappy trails...\n");
                exit(0);
        }
    }
}

/* compute the midpoint, or "center of gravity" */

void midpoint(void)
{   point3d mid;
    mid.x = 0L, mid.y = 0L, mid.z = 0L;
    for (i = 0; i < npts; i++) addpt(mid, point[i], mid);
    mid.x /= -npts, mid.y /= -npts, mid.z /= -npts;
    for (i = 0; i < npts; i++) addpt(point[i], mid, point[i]);
}
```

```
/* draw the shape and a "handle" on the current point */

void draw(void)
{   int f, i;
    handlex = (int) (point[thispt].x >> BITSH) + (tg_scrnx >> 1);
    handley = (int) (point[thispt].y >> BITSH) + (tg_scrny >> 1);
    for (i = 0; i < npts; i++)
    {   drawx[i] = (int) (point[i].x >> BITSH) +
                   (tg_scrnx >> 1);
        drawy[i] = (int) (point[i].y >> BITSH) +
                   (tg_scrny >> 1);
    }
    tg_setcolor(faceclr);
    for (f = 0; f < nfaces; f++)              /* draw the faces */
        if (nfacepts[f] > 2)
        {   for (i = 0; i < nfacepts[f]; i++)
            {   drawface[f][i][0] = drawx[facept[f][i]];
                drawface[f][i][1] = drawy[facept[f][i]];
            }
            tg_fillpoly((drawface[f]), (nfacepts[f]));
        }
    tg_setcolor(lineclr);                     /* draw the lines */
    for(i = 0; i < nlines; i++)
        tg_drawline(drawx[linefrom[i]], drawy[linefrom[i]],
                drawx[lineto[i]], drawy[lineto[i]]);
    tg_setcolor(white);      /* put the handle on the screen */
    tg_drawline(handlex, handley - HAND,
            handlex, handley + HAND);
    tg_drawline(handlex - HAND, handley,
            handlex + HAND, handley);
    if (nfacepts[thisface] > 2)
    {   tg_drawpoly((drawface[thisface]),
                (nfacepts[thisface]));
    }
    else if (nfacepts[thisface] == 2)
    {   tg_drawline((drawx[facept[thisface][0]]),
                (drawy[facept[thisface][0]]),
                (drawx[facept[thisface][1]]),
                (drawy[facept[thisface][1]]));
    }
```

continues

Listing 7.4. continued

```
        if ((lastpt != thispt) || (lastface != thisface))
        {   tg_setviewport(0, 0, tg_scrnx - 1, tg_chary);
            sprintf(msg, "Point # %d (of %d), "
                         "Face # %d (of %d) has %d points ",
                     thispt + 1, npts,
                     thisface + 1, nfaces, nfacepts[thisface]);
            tg_moveto(0, 0);
            tg_outtext(msg);
            tg_outtext("                            ");
            tg_setviewport(0, tg_chary + 1,
                           tg_scrnx - 1, tg_scrny - tg_chary);
            lastpt = thispt;
            lastface = thisface;
        }
}

void erase(void)
{   int i;
    tg_setcolor(0);
    for (i = 0; i < nfaces; i++)           /* draw the faces */
        if (nfacepts[i] > 2)
        {   tg_fillpoly((drawface[i]), (nfacepts[i]));
        }
    for(i = 0; i < nlines; i++)
        tg_drawline(drawx[linefrom[i]], drawy[linefrom[i]],
                    drawx[lineto[i]], drawy[lineto[i]]);
    tg_drawline(handlex, handley - HAND,
                handlex, handley + HAND);
    tg_drawline(handlex - HAND, handley,
                handlex + HAND, handley);
}

/* spin around z axis */

void warpz(long spinx, long spiny)
{   point3d pointi;
    int i;
    for (i = 0; i < npts; i++)
    {   pointi = point[i];
        point[i].x = pointi.x *  cosf(spinx) +
```

```
                            pointi.y *  sinf(spiny);
            point[i].y = pointi.x * -sinf(spinx) +
                            pointi.y *  cosf(spiny);
    }
}


/* spin around y axis */

void warpy(long spinx, long spinz)
{   point3d pointi;
    int i;
    for (i = 0; i < npts; i++)
    {   pointi = point[i];
        point[i].x = pointi.x * cosf(spinx) -
                        pointi.z * sinf(spinz);
        point[i].z = pointi.x * sinf(spinx) +
                        pointi.z * cosf(spinz);
    }
}


/* spin around x axis */

void warpx(long spiny, long spinz)
{   point3d pointi;
    int i;
    for (i = 0; i < npts; i++)
    {   pointi = point[i];
        point[i].y = pointi.y * cosf(spiny) +
                        pointi.z * sinf(spinz);
        point[i].z = pointi.y * -sinf(spiny) +
                        pointi.z * cosf(spinz);
    }
}


/* Save lines and faces to a DXF file
 * (Note that all faces are saved with exactly 4 vertices,
 * as per the official Autodesk DXF specifications.) */

int savedxf(char *name)
{   int i;
```

continues

339

Listing 7.4. continued

```c
    if ((diskfile = fopen(name, "wb")) == NULL) return(0);
    fprintf(diskfile, "0\r\nSECTION\r\n2\r\nENTITIES\r\n");
    for (i = 0; i < nlines; i++)
        fprintf(diskfile,
                "0\r\n3DLINE\r\n"
                "10\r\n%lf\r\n20\r\n%lf\r\n30\r\n%lf\r\n"
                "11\r\n%lf\r\n21\r\n%lf\r\n31\r\n%lf\r\n",
                (double) point[linefrom[i]].x / MF,
                (double) -point[linefrom[i]].y / MF,
                (double) point[linefrom[i]].z /MF,
                (double) point[lineto[i]].x / MF,
                (double) -point[lineto[i]].y / MF,
                (double) point[lineto[i]].z / MF);
    if (nfaces)
    {   for (i = 0; i < nfaces; i++)
        {   fprintf(diskfile, "0\r\n3DFACE\r\n");
            for (j = 0; j < 4; j++)
            {   if (j >= nfacepts[i])
                    facept[i][j] = facept[i][j - 1];
                fprintf(diskfile,
                "1%d\r\n%lf\r\n2%d\r\n%lf\r\n3%d\r\n%lf\r\n",
                j, (double) point[facept[i][j]].x / MF,
                j, (double) -point[facept[i][j]].y / MF,
                j, (double) point[facept[i][j]].z / MF);
            }
        }
    }
    fprintf(diskfile, "0\r\nENDSEC\r\n0\r\nEOF\r\n");
    fprintf(diskfile, "%c", EOFILE);
    fclose(diskfile);
    return(1);
}

/* macro to call readdxfgroup() from within loaddxf() */

#define readgroup() \
    if (readdxfgroup(&groupcode, groupname, &value) == 0) \
        return(0)

/* load the 3DLINE and 3DFACE entities from a DXF file */
```

```c
int loaddxf(char *name)
{   int i, n, groupcode;
    char groupname[80];
    point3d p[4];
    long value;
    npts = nlines = nfaces = 0;
    if ((diskfile = fopen(name, "rb")) == NULL) return(0);
    do
    {   readgroup();
    } while((groupcode != 0) ||
            (strcmp(groupname, "SECTION") != 0));
    do
    {   readgroup();
    } while((groupcode != 2) ||
            strcmp(groupname, "ENTITIES") != 0);
    do
    {   readgroup();
    } while(groupcode != 0);
    while(1)
    {   if (strcmp(groupname, "ENDSEC") == 0) break;
        else if (strcmp(groupname, "3DLINE") == 0)
        {   p[0].x = p[0].y = p[0].z = 0L;
            p[1].x = p[1].y = p[1].z = 0L;
            do
            {   readgroup();
                switch(groupcode)
                {   case 10: p[0].x = value; break;
                    case 11: p[1].x = value; break;
                    case 20: p[0].y = -value; break;
                    case 21: p[1].y = -value; break;
                    case 30: p[0].z = value; break;
                    case 31: p[1].z = value;
                }
                if (groupcode == 0)
                {   for (n = 0; n < 2; n++)
                    {   for (i = 0; i < npts; i++)
                        {   if ((point[i].x == p[n].x) &&
                                (point[i].y == p[n].y) &&
                                (point[i].z == p[n].z))
                            {   if (n) lineto[nlines] = i;
                                else linefrom[nlines] = i;
```

continues

341

Listing 7.4. continued

```
                              break;
                    }
                }
                if (i >= npts)
                {   point[npts] = p[n];
                    if (n) lineto[nlines] = npts;
                    else linefrom[nlines] = npts;
                    npts++;
                }
            }
            nlines++;
        }
    } while(groupcode != 0);
}
else if (strcmp(groupname, "3DFACE") == 0)
{   for (n = 0; n < 4; n++)
        p[n].x = p[n].y = p[n].z = 0L;
    do
    {   readgroup();
        if ((groupcode >= 10) && (groupcode <= 33))
        {   i = groupcode - (int) (groupcode / 10) * 10;
            if (i > 3) i == 3;
            switch((int) (groupcode / 10))
            {   case 1: p[i].x = value; break;
                case 2: p[i].y = -value; break;
                case 3: p[i].z = value; break;
            }
        }
        if (groupcode == 0)
        {   for (n = 0; n < 4; n++)
            {   for (i = 0; i < npts; i++)
                {   if ((point[i].x == p[n].x) &&
                        (point[i].y == p[n].y) &&
                        (point[i].z == p[n].z))
                    {   facept[nfaces][n] = i;
                        break;
                    }
                }
                if (i >= npts)
```

```
                          {   point[npts] = p[n];
                              facept[nfaces][n] = npts;
                              npts++;
                          }
                          if (n >= nfacepts[nfaces])
                              nfacepts[nfaces] = n + 1;
                      }
                      nfaces++;
                  }
              } while(groupcode != 0);
          }
          else
          {   do
              {   readgroup();
              } while(groupcode != 0);
          }
      }
      fclose(diskfile);
      if (nfaces == 0)
      {   nfaces = 1;
          nfacepts[0] = 0;
          thisface = 0;
      }
      return(1);
}


/* read two lines of the DXF file, expecting the first
 * line to be a groupcode number and the second line to
 * be either a groupname string or a numerical value */

int readdxfgroup(int *groupcode, char *groupname, long *value)
{   char linein[255];
    fscanf(diskfile, "%s", linein);
    if ((*linein <= '9') && (*linein >= '0'))
        *groupcode = atoi(linein);
    else return(0);
    fscanf(diskfile, "%s", groupname);
    *value = (long) (atof(groupname) * MF);
    return(1);
}
```

A Sampling of Rendering Techniques

There are few things so mysterious as how a computer program can create a lifelike three-dimensional picture—not just any picture, but one that can fool the human eye. Sometimes the only clue that a computer-generated image is not real is the fact that it exceeds reality as people normally perceive it. A computer, or more correctly, a computer artist, can create a picture of the dark side of the moon, and only our knowledge that it can't be real prevents us from accepting it as such....

With the breadth of rendering algorithms available, the best pictures come from a combination of techniques. This is evidenced by images created with high-end products from companies such as Alias, Wavefront, Pixar, and TDI.

With enough creativity, it's also possible to get stunning results with modest tools available for Amigas, Macs, and PCs. For example, Autodesk's 3D Studio software for 386 and 486 PCs is based on a simple Phong shader, with texture, bump, and limited transparency and reflection capabilities. Images from 3D Studio have shown up everywhere from network TV to computer games. Other programs are capable of the same level of realism. The truth is, low-cost tools can create images every bit as impressive as more expensive systems. And, with a fast 486 computer, there isn't that much difference in speed.

—Evan Yares, "Photo-realism: Computing Images that
Look Like Real Objects and Scenes," *BYTE*, May 1992

In Chapter 9, you'll learn to use state-of-the-art rendering techniques and ray tracing to take computerized snapshots of your 3-D models. First, however, you should be familiar with the variety of 3-D rendering options you have at your disposal. In the rest of this chapter, your humble yurt will evolve from a wireframe shape into an almost-photorealistic Tibetan spaceship.

Hidden Faces

The first step towards realism is to add *perspective*, wherein distant objects and lines appear smaller than close ones. You've already got that one under your belt. Figure 7.11 shows the wireframe yurt rendered with perspective.

Next on the wish list is hidden line and face removal. It wouldn't hurt to color each face according to its relationship to a light source, either. Figure 7.12 employs both of these enhancements to bring the realism quotient up a few notches.

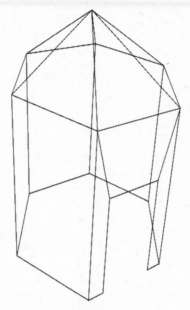

Figure 7.11. *Perspective rendering makes distant parts of the model look smaller.*

Figure 7.12. *Hide the back faces and color the rest according to their proximity to a light source, and your model starts to look like a 3-D object.*

345

By the way, I created Figures 7.12 through 7.17 by importing the DXF file from my 3DFACES into Autodesk 3D Studio, the leading 3-D rendering and animation package for the PC. Although 3D Studio is a bit pricey (like four digits kind of pricey) it has no peer on the market to date. A few "inexpensive" (under $2000) packages—such as CrystalGraphics' Desktop Animator and Presidio's 3D Workshop—come close to 3D Studio in ease of use and advertisable features, but none of them achieves quite the same level of spit and polish. My advice: If you're going to go out and blow a thousand bucks or more on a 3-D rendering package, go whole hog and get the best. But wait for 3D Studio release 3, which, as of this writing, is slated to appear Real Soon Now. See the bibliography for contact information for Autodesk, CrystalGraphics, Presidio, and other 3-D software vendors.

Better yet, put the thousand dollar bills back in your pocket and stick to the rendering and ray tracing techniques presented later in this book. (The DXF2PI program in Chapter 9 will let you import any of the models you design with the 3DFACES program into the POLYRAY ray-tracer.) Believe it or not, a shareware ray tracer will give you even more realistic pictures than any of those rendering Big Boys, and leave your wallet intact. The catch? Time. A package like 3D Studio is relatively fast, is relatively easy to learn, and contains all the features you may need packed into a tightly integrated, interactive environment. If you're a graphics professional rendering on a schedule, blow the two or three grand. If not, save the dough and just wait an hour or two (overnight if you have a slow computer) for your spectacular ultra-realistic images.

You'll see the promised land of ray-tracing soon. Now, we continue the tour of what the quickie professional 3-D techniques can do.

Lighting and Shading

To bring your 3-D models up to par with the cardboard models old-fashioned architects used to make, you can add spotlights and shadows. Figure 7.13 simulates the interaction of a directional light source with the 3-D faces and an added floor.

Texture Maps and Bump Maps

What if you don't want to live in a hut made out of cardboard? Most rendering software allows you to map images onto the surface of your objects and fine tune their reflective properties, giving them the appearance of any surface material you can capture with a scanner. In Figure 7.15, I mapped the simulated wood shingles and polished marble of Figure 7.14 onto the yurt and floor.

Figure 7.13. *By assigning light values according to the distance from the center of a spotlight beam and calculating a shadow, you can start to approach photorealism.*

With the most advanced software, you can fake the appearance of bumpy textures, as I did to carve pits and machine-like ridges of Figure 7.16 into the space station in Figure 7.17. The color of each point in the texture map controls not only the color of the surface at that point, but also the angle at which light is considered to hit the surface.

Some Final Reflections

In Chapter 9, you'll learn how to achieve most of the preceding effects the easy way. What's more, several other visually stunning effects—such as mirror reflections, transparency, and metalic sheen—will pop out of the same algorithmic box.

But before Chapter 9 opens the ray-tracing treasure chest, Chapter 8 explores the enchanted forest of three-dimensional fractals. However eager you may be for photorealism, the fantastic fun of fractals in space will be well worth donning those 3-D glasses again for a while.

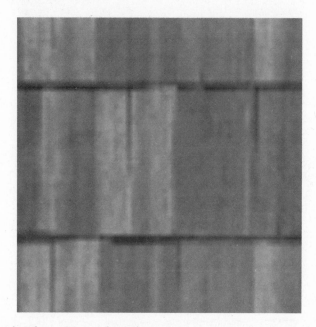

Figure 7.14. *These textures, from the image library that comes with Autodesk 3D Studio, were mapped onto the 3-D models to create Figure 7.15.*

Figure 7.15. *Surface texture maps make a dramatic difference in the quality and visual complexity of your renderings.*

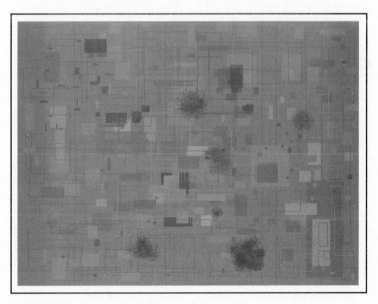

Figure 7.16. *This image was bump-mapped onto the space station in Figure 7.17 below.*

Figure 7.17. *Bump maps, a NASA backdrop, and a truly enlightened Tibetan monk complete the journey to photorealism and beyond.*

3-D Fractal Animation

In Chapter 6, you saw how to design intricate, organic shapes called fractals. In Chapter 7, you discovered how to create and render three-dimensional objects. This chapter combines all those tricks and shows you how to interactively create and manipulate 3-D fractals.

This chapter is relatively short, but the graphics goodies you'll receive are sweet. First, you extend the FRAN and FREEN fractal animation programs from Chapter 6 into the third dimension. Then, I set you up with a way to hand your 3-D fractals to the POLYRAY ray-trace renderer (introduced in the next chapter) or any DXF-compatible software for some ultra-cool surrealistic realism.

3-D Transformations

A fractal set generally contains infinitely many points whose organization is so complicated that it is not possible to describe the set by specifying

directly where each point in it lies. Instead, the set may be defined by "the relation between the pieces." It is rather like describing the solar system by quoting the law of gravitation and stating the initial conditions. Everything follows from that. It appears always to be better to describe in terms of relationships.

—Michael Barnsley, *Fractals Everywhere*, 1988

To create fractals, you need to define several *transformations*. (Review Chapter 6 if this doesn't ring a bell.) Just as in two dimensions, transformations in three-dimensional space consist of three basic operations: rotation, scaling, and translation. I usually call these *spin*, *size*, and *move* because I like short words.

When working in two dimensions, you move in four distinct directions—back and forth along each of the two axes. Likewise, you can resize four ways—larger or smaller along each axis. You can also spin four ways by skewing each axis clockwise or counterclockwise. By spinning both axes equal amounts, you can achieve an ordinary rotation instead of a skew effect.

Jumping to three dimensions is pretty straightforward for the move and size operations. In each case, moving back and forth along three axes instead of two means that you have six directions from which to choose instead of four. However, as mentioned in Chapter 7, three-dimensional spinning is considerably more complex. You can skew *each axis* four ways—making a total of 12 distinct directions of spin. For example, you can skew the x-axis clockwise around the z-axis, counterclockwise around the z-axis, clockwise around the y-axis, or counterclockwise around the y-axis. To perform an ordinary rotation instead of a skew effect, you can combine equal amounts of any two axis spins. This means you can rotate any two axes clockwise or counterclockwise around the remaining axis—a total of six 3-D rotational directions, where only two rotational directions were possible in 2-D.

Whew! If all that sounds like a lot to keep straight, just remember that you *live* in 3-D space all the time. You mix and match 3-D rotations and movements all day without paying much attention to the complexities of spacial geometry. You'll find, though, that 3-D transformations are easier to work with than to discuss.

Okay, all this spin and size stuff is old news if you've read Chapter 7, but in order to utilize it for making 3-D fractals, you need a quick way to do the spinning and sizing over and over again… like *fast*. The following **Math Behind the Magic** section introduces some matrix math to repeat, or *iterate*, 3-D transformations while performing the most time-consuming part of the calculations only once at the outset.

The Math Behind the Magic: 3-D Affine Transformations

Subtitle: Matrix algebra swoops to the rescue once again. To combine a set of 3-D spins, resizes, and movements all at once, do this:

$x <= x * a + y * b + z * c + movex$
$y <= x * d + y * e + z * f + movey$
$z <= x * g + y * h + z * i + movez$

If you're familiar with matrix operations, you'll notice that this is just a matrix multiplication where *a, b, c, d, e, f, g, h,* and *i* are the elements of a 3×3 matrix (called the transformation matrix):

a b c	x	movex
d e f	y	movey
g h i	z	movez

x, y, and *z* are the elements of a 1×3 matrix (that defines a 3-D point) and *movex, movey,* and *movez* are the elements of another 1×3 matrix (which defines the displacement part of the transformation) to be added after the multiplication:

(If you're not up on matrices, you'll need to trust me a little on this one. It works whether you understand the algebra or not.)

So where do you get *a, b, c* and friends? You can compute them from spin, size, and move variables like this:

$a = sizex * \cos(spinz) * \cos(spiny)$
$b = sizey * (\cos(spinz) * \sin(spiny) * \sin(spinx) + \sin(spinz) * \cos(spinx))$
$c = sizez * (\sin(spinz) * \sin(spinx) - \sin(spiny) * \cos(spinz) * \cos(spinx))$
$d = -sizex * \cos(spiny) * \sin(spinz)$
$e = sizey * (\cos(spiny) * \cos(spinz) - \sin(spinz) * \sin(spiny) * \sin(spinx))$
$f = sizez * (\cos(spinz) * \sin(spinz) + \cos(spinx) * \sin(spiny) * \sin(spinz))$
$g = sizex * \sin(spinz)$
$h = -sizey * \cos(spinz) * \sin(spinx)$
$i = sizez * \cos(spiny) * \cos(spinx)$

where:

spinz is the rotation of the X- and y-axes around the z-axis
spiny is the rotation of the X- and z-axes around the y-axis

spinx is the rotation of the Y- and z-axes around the x-axis

sizex is the amount to resize along the x-axis

sizey is the amount to resize along the y-axis

sizez is the amount to resize along the z-axis

If you want to skew, you'll need six spin variables instead of three (you might call them *spinxy*, *spinxz*, *spinyx*, *spinyz*, *spinzx*, and *spinzy*) and the formula becomes a little more complex.

It's more than complex enough already. Furthermore, it assumes that you do the rotation around the z-axis first, then around the y-axis, then around the x-axis. To do them in a different order, you need a different (equally involved) set of formulas.

Fortunately, there is a better way. If you just want to change an existing transformation matrix, rather than define one from scratch, you can transform the matrix itself, using only the spin or size variables needed for the specific type of transformation you want to do right now.

To apply a rotation around the z-axis only, use this formula:

$a <= a * \cos(spinzx) - b * \sin(spinzx)$

$b <= a * \sin(spinzy) + b * \cos(spinzy)$

$c <= c$

$d <= d * \cos(spinzx) - e * \sin(spinzx)$

$e <= d * \sin(spinzy) + e * \cos(spinzy)$

$f <= f$

$g <= g * \cos(spinzx) - h * \sin(spinzx)$

$h <= g * \sin(spinzy) + h * \cos(spinzy)$

To apply a rotation around the y-axis only, here's the recipe:

$a <= a$

$b <= b * \cos(spinyx) - c * \sin(spinyx)$

$c <= b * \sin(spinyz) + c * \cos(spinyz)$

$d <= d$

$e <= e * \cos(spinyx) - f * \sin(spinyx)$

$f <= e * \sin(spinyz) + f * \cos(spinyz)$

$g <= g$

$h <= h * \cos(spinyx) - i * \sin(spinyx)$

$i <= h * \sin(spinyz) + i * \cos(spinyz)$

And here's how to do a rotation around the x-axis only:

$a <= a * \cos(spinxy) + c * \sin(spinxy)$
$b <= b$
$c <= -a * \sin(spinxz) + c * \cos(spinxz)$
$d <= d * \cos(spinxy) + f * \sin(spinxy)$
$e <= e$
$f <= -d * \sin(spinxz) + f * \cos(spinxz)$
$g <= g * \cos(spinxy) + i * \sin(spinxy)$
$h <= h$
$i <= -g * \sin(spinxz) + i * \cos(spinxz)$

Notice that all these rotation formulas allow for skew by using two separate spin variables. If both spin variables are the same, a normal rotation occurs. If they are different, a skew effect happens.

To resize along one or more axes, do this:

$a <= sizex * a$
$b <= sizey * b$
$c <= sizez * c$
$d <= sizex * d$
$e <= sizey * e$
$f <= sizez * f$
$g <= sizex * g$
$h <= sizey * h$
$i <= sizez * i$

If *sizex*, *sizey*, and *sizez* are all equal, the entire object grows or shrinks. Otherwise, it appears to stretch or squish along one or more axes.

The 3DLINES program in Chapter 7 carried out these same operations but without the intermediate step of computing the a, b, c, d, e, f, g, h, and i coefficients. Because you were transforming a simple shape just once every time a key was pressed, rather than repeatedly iterating transformations to produce complex fractals, you did not need to precompute the coefficients. When you repeat these transformations thousands of times in the course of making a fractal, precomputing the coefficients with the previous formulas becomes a crucial time saver.

Enough obtuse algebra. It's time to add the additional complication of fractal geometry to the fray. Here we go…

Interactive 3-D Fractals

Geometry is concerned with making our spatial intuitions objective.… Fractal geometry is an extension of classical geometry. It can be used to make precise models of physical structures from ferns to galaxies.

—Michael Barnsley, *Fractals Everywhere*, 1988

You remember good old FRAN. Back in Chapter 6, she taught you how to interactively design fractals. FRAN's sister, FRAN3D, is a lot like FRAN—though she's a bit more spacey. By applying 3-D transformations instead of 2-D transformations, FRAN3D lets you manipulate three-dimensional Iterated Function System (IFS) codes as you watch the resulting fractal change before your eyes.

FRAN3D also uses the stereoscopic tricks from Chapter 7 to help you visualize intricate 3-D fractals on your 2-D screen and adds the capability to grab the entire fractal at once and spin or resize it in 3-D space.

The FRAN3D program loads an IFS file, enables you to interactively edit the fractal, and saves the result into another IFS file. FRAN3D can load the same two-dimensional IFS files that FRAN used (see Chapter 6 for details on the file format), or it can load true three-dimensional IFS files. The IFS files that FRAN3D saves are always three-dimensional.

The three-dimensional IFS files on the disk have the same .IFS file extension as the two-dimensional IFS files, but their names begin with 3D. For example, 3DFERN1.IFS and 3DSIERP.IFS are three-dimensional IFS files, whereas FERN.IFS and LEAF.IFS are two-dimensional.

To see a list of all the IFS files on the disk, enter DIR *.IFS at the DOS prompt. To list only the 3-D IFS files, enter DIR 3D*.IFS instead. You can use any name you like for the IFS files you create with FRAN3D, but I recommend using the .IFS file extension and starting each file name with 3D to avoid confusion with other types of files.

To turn the IFS transformation codes into a picture, use the *random iteration algorithm* presented in Chapter 6. The program hops around in space, randomly selecting a transformation to send it from dot to dot on the fractal. As it hops, it illuminates the points on-screen that correspond to your eye's view of each point in space as viewed through the plane of the computer screen.

In the following **You Can Do It** section, FRAN3D takes you on a tour of her workshop as you twist and tumble a three-dimensional fern and a curvaceous triangular fractal. Figures 8.1 through 8.6 depict some highlights of the excursion.

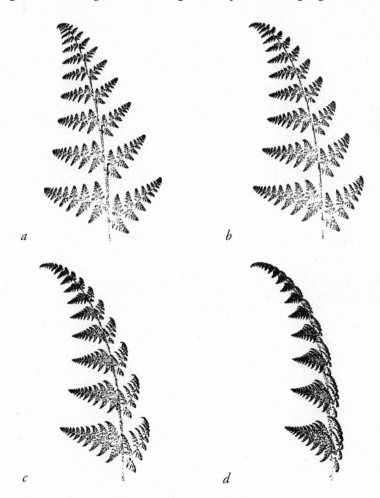

Figure 8.1. *With the FRAN3D program, you can spin entire fractals at once in 3-D space. Here, a fern spins around the y-axis.*

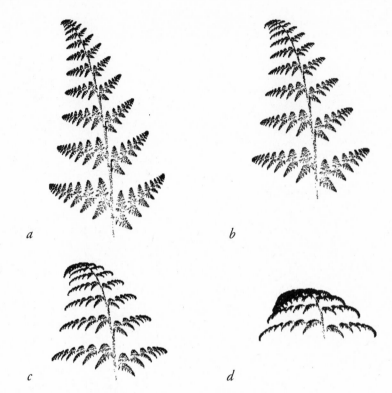

a   *b*

c   *d*

Figure 8.2. *The same fern, spinning around the x-axis.*

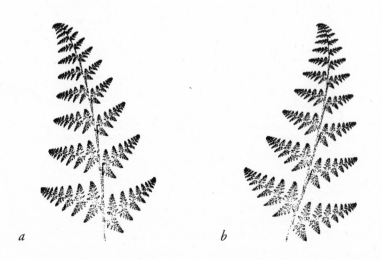

a   *b*

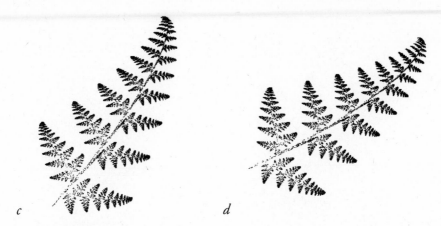

Figure 8.3. *Spinning around the z-axis is just like a normal two-dimensional rotation.*

In Figures 8.1 through 8.3, you can see an entire fractal spinning along each of the three axes. Of course, the party begins when you grab just one part of the fractal and spin it. Figures 8.4 through 8.6 depict the bottom left frond of the fern spinning around each of the three axes. As it spins, every left frond and sub-frond and sub-sub-frond spins simultaneously.

c

d

Figure 8.4. *As you spin the bottom left frond, each reflection of it throughout the whole also spins. Notice that the frond spins around its own y-axis, not the y-axis of the screen.*

a

b

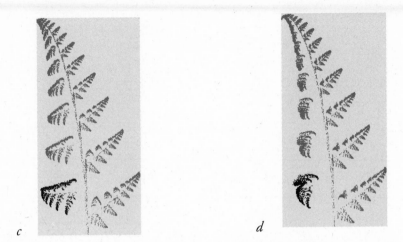

c   *d*

Figure 8.5. *Here, the bottom left frond spins around its x-axis.*

a

b

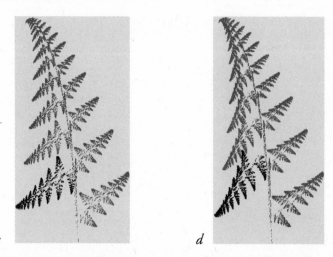

c   *d*

Figure 8.6. *The same frond spinning around its z-axis creates a different surreal effect.*

Ferns are the most famous fractals of all, but realistic plant forms tell just one side of the fractal story. You can also easily create mind-boggling abstract shapes that curl and twist in 3-D space. In Figures 8.7 through 8.11, a well-known two-dimensional fractal called *Sierpi´nski's Triangle* curls in the third dimension to become a dramatic fractal "parachute" pattern.

a

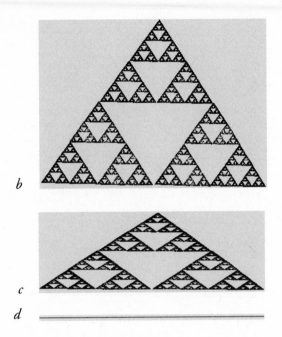

b

c

d

Figure 8.7. *This two-dimensional fractal appears to squish down to a line as it spins around the x-axis to give you an edge-on view.*

a

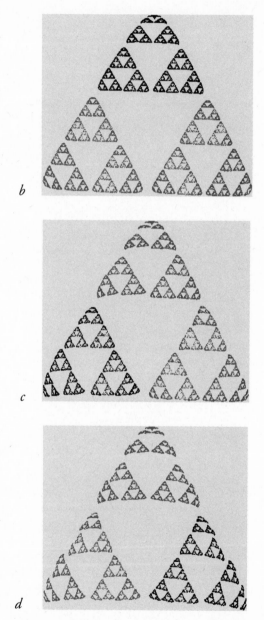

b

c

d

Figure 8.8. *By spinning each of the "triangle's" three parts, you can give it a 3-D look.*

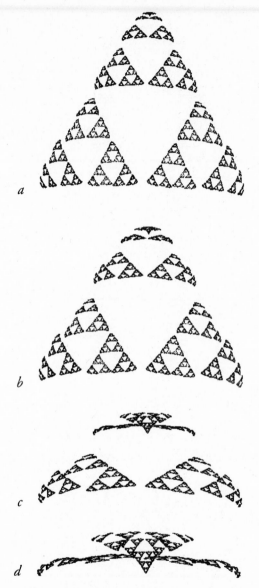

a

b

c

d

Figure 8.9. *When the modified fractal spins around the x-axis, it no longer resembles a line.*

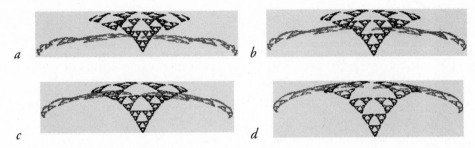

Figure 8.10. *To smooth the curve a bit, you might move the middle part down to meet the edge of the other two parts.*

Figure 8.11. *Some spinning around all three axes shows the gently swooping form of your 3-D fractal creation.*

You Can Do It: Fractals in Space

In the quick tour that follows, you'll edit a three-dimensional IFS file named 3DFERN1.IFS and save your changes as 3DFERN2.IFS. Then you'll load a two-dimensional IFS file named TRI.IFS and curve it in the third dimension to make a new 3-D fractal called 3DTRI.IFS.

1. Enter the following command at the DOS prompt:

   ```
   FRAN3D 3DFERN1.IFS 3DFERN2.IFS
   ```

2. Press V to select the VGA 640x480 16-color video mode.

3. A white fern appears in the center of the screen with a menu of control keys along the bottom of the screen.

   Unlike the FRAN program in Chapter 6, with FRAN3D you can spin, size, and move the entire fractal at once. To perform any of these transformations, you must first select an axis by pressing X, Y, or Z.

4. Press Y to choose the y-axis.

5. Press the + key to spin around the y-axis.

   Depending on the speed of your computer, the fern may take a while to fill in after each change.

6. Press + a few more times, waiting between each keypress for the fern to fill in enough so that you can see the rotation.

7. Try spinning around the other axes. Press Z and then press + a few times. Press X and then press + a few times.

8. To enlarge the entire template in all directions at once, press the * key.

9. To shrink in all directions at once, press the / key.

10. To stretch one axis only, press that axis letter (try Y now) and then press the [(left bracket) key.

11. To squish one axis only, use the] (right bracket) key.

12. To move along the selected axis, use the left and right arrow keys. (Try it now.)

Up until this point, you've been transforming the entire fern. You can also change the individual transformations that define the fern fractal.

13. Press the Tab key to select the next part of the fractal.

    Most of the fern is now colored with only one frond highlighted in white. Now, when you spin, resize, or move, only the highlighted transformation changes. Of course, because this is a self-reflective fractal you're dealing with, the rest of the fractal is also affected by the change in that one part. Here, try it and you'll see...

14. Press Y and then press + to spin around the y-axis.

    The highlighted part spins a bit, and so does every left frond of every left frond of every left frond everywhere. Notice that the part spins around its own y-axis, not the y-axis of the screen or the whole fractal.

15. Press + a few more times to twirl the frond some more.

16. Try X + + and Z + + to see what spinning around the other axes looks like.

17. Press Tab again to select another part.

18. Press / to shrink that part.

    The best way to get used to 3-D spinning is to play for a while. Use the Tab, X, Y, Z, +, and - keys to twirl various parts, and the entire fractal. (When you thumb through all four parts with Tab, you'll return to editing the entire thing at once the next time you press Tab.)

    Once you start to get the hang of it—or even if you're still a bit mystified—you might try turning on the 3-D glasses by pressing G. Notice that the currently selected part is highlighted in a brighter red and blue than the rest.

19. Press Esc to save your playful permutation of the fractal fern.

Next, you get the chance to bring a 2-D fractal into the third dimension.

1. Type the following command at the DOS prompt:

```
FRAN3D TRI.IFS 3DTRI.IFS
```

2. Press V to choose the VGA mode.

   A famous fractal called *Sierpin' ski's Triangle* appears.

3. Press X, and then press + ten times to verify that the triangle is a flat, 2-D shape spinning in 3-D space. (After eight presses of the + key, you should be looking at the triangle edge-on, and it will look like a line. A couple more + presses tilts the fractal a bit so that you're looking at it from a slight elevation.)

4. Press the Tab key to select the first small triangle of the three that define the fractal pattern.

5. Press the - key twice to tilt that part of the fractal. Notice that the corresponding parts throughout the whole also tilt.

6. Press the Tab key again to select the next part.

7. Press Y and then press - twice to tilt that part sideways.

8. Press Tab again to select the last of the three parts.

9. Press the + key twice to tilt that part in the opposite direction that you just tilted the last one.

   You have now turned the 2-D *Sierpin' ski's Triangle* into a curving 3-D fractal. By spinning the whole thing, you can get a good look at your geometric creation.

10. Press Tab once more. The entire fractal is highlighted indicating that you can now manipulate it as a whole.

11. Use the X, Y, Z, +, and - keys to spin in whatever direction tickles your fancy.

12. While you're at it, why not press G and put on the stereoscopic shades for a while? Once your eyes adjust, the 3-D effect will kick in, and you'll see the recursive curves that much more clearly.

    You'll notice that two of the fractal's main parts are now offset from the other one. As a final touch, you might like to move them up to make a more continuous parachute-like shape.

13. Press Tab twice.

14. Press Z and then press the left arrow twice.

15. Press Tab, then the left arrow twice again.

    Pressing Tab one more time highlights the entire shape again for further spinning and viewing. This is a great time to twiddle and fiddle with the shape to see what you can do.

16. When you'd like to save your shape and quit the program, press the Esc key.

Working Code: 3-D Fractal Animation

As you know if you went through the previous **You Can Do It** section, 3-D fractal animation is spectacular—if a bit on the slow side. If the display speed seems too leisurely for your taste, take solace in the fact that this program runs at least ten times faster than it would without the fast integer math and matrix algebra algorithms. Also, remember that you are among the first human beings on the planet to work with interactive 3-D fractal animation at *any* speed.

The "overall transformation" used to interactively spin, size, and move the entire fractal is stored in the first (zero) position of the trans[] array, and the transformations that actually define the fractal itself are in positions 1 onward. When you see (*trans), that means the same thing as trans[0]—a reference to that overall transformation. If you look closely, you'll notice that (*trans) gives each point one final transform before it gets booted out the screen door in paint().

For maximum speed, FRAN3D doesn't include support for perspective viewing. You could easily add perspective calculation to the draw3dpoint() function with the simple algorithm explained in Chapter 7 and included in the 3DLINES and 3DFACES programs.

Note that you must link FRAN3D.C with MUDI.OBJ when you compile it with the appropriate TransGraphics batch file. For example, to compile under Microsoft C, type:

TGMS FRAN3D.C MUDI.OBJ

For Borland, use TGTC instead of TGMS. See the introduction for more details on compiling TransGraphics programs.

Listing 8.1. The FRAN3D.H header file is #*included* in both the FRAN3D.C program listed below and FREEN3D.C, introduced later in this chapter.

```
/* FRAN3D.C
 *
 * An Interactive Three-dimensional Fractal Animator
 * Header File
 *
 * from Tricks of the Graphics Gurus
 */

#include <stdio.h>
#include <stdlib.h>
#include <math.h>
#include <ctype.h>
#include <process.h>
#include "tg.h"              /* for TransGraphics macros */
#include "mudi.h"            /* for fast 32-bit integer math */

/* PI and friends are just what you think they are
 * The two slightly different values for HALFPI and ALMOST0
 * are necessary to prevent round-off errors in some routines
 * MAXSIZE could be called "almost one", scaled up by M1
 * MAXINT is the maximum value of a short int
 */

#define PI 205887L /* (3.1415927 * M1) */
#define TWOPI (PI * 2L) /* 411774L */
#define HALFPI (PI / 2L) /* 102944L */
#define HALFPI2 (PI / 2L) /* 108135L */
#define ALMOSTZERO 4L
#define ALMOST0 16L
#define MAXSIZE 65532L
#define MAXINT 32767
```

continues

371

Listing 8.1. continued

```
/* These are the values of key bindings */

#define ENTER 13
#define ESC 27
#define TAB 9
#define UP -'H'
#define DN -'P'
#define LT -'K'
#define RT -'M'

/* macro getch() replacement */

#define geta if ((a = getch()) == 0) a = -getch();\
            else if (a > 0) a = toupper(a)

#define NTRANS 64                /* maximum number of parts */
#define INISIZEINC 10486L /* ratio of re-size for each step */
#define INIMOVEINC 655360L        /* movement for each step */
#define INISPININC PI / 16   /* amount of spin for each step */

#define EOFILE 0xff /* end of file character */

#define COSOCULAR (long) (0.995004 * MF)
#define SINOCULAR (long) (0.099833 * MF)
#define OCULARDIST 0.1
#define OCULARINC 0.05
#define RIGHTCLR 1
#define LEFTCLR 4
#define RIGHTBRITE 9
#define LEFTBRITE 12

#define NAMELEN 40              /* maximum length of filenames */

/* add two 3D points p1 and p2, putting the result into p3.
 * (p3 can be the same variable as p1 or p2 without problems)
 */

#define addpt(p1, p2, p3) \
        { p3.x = p1.x + p2.x; \
```

```
                p3.y = p1.y + p2.y; \
                p3.z = p1.z + p2.z; }

/* multiply a 3D point p1 by a 3x3 transformation matrix m1,
 * putting the result into the 3D point p2.
 * p1 and p2 should NOT be the same variable! */

#define mupt(p1, m1, p2) \
  { p2.x = mu(p1.x, m1.a) + mu(p1.y, m1.b) + mu(p1.z, m1.c); \
    p2.y = mu(p1.x, m1.d) + mu(p1.y, m1.e) + mu(p1.z, m1.f); \
    p2.z = mu(p1.x, m1.g) + mu(p1.y, m1.h) + mu(p1.z, m1.i); }


/* find the cosine or sine of a scaled long int as a double */

#define cosf(x) (cos((double) x / M1))
#define sinf(x) (sin((double) x / M1))

/* find the determinant of a 3x3 matrix */

#define determ(m1) \
    (mu(m1.a, mu(m1.e, m1.i) - mu(m1.h, m1.f)) - \
    mu(m1.b, mu(m1.d, m1.i) - mu(m1.g, m1.f)) + \
    mu(m1.c, mu(m1.d, m1.h) - mu(m1.g, m1.e)))

/* type definitions for 3D transformations and points */

typedef struct { long a, b, c, d, e, f, g, h, i; } matrix3x3;
typedef struct { long x, y, z; } point3d;
```

Listing 8.2. FRAN3D.C brings interactive fractal design into the third dimension.

```
/* FRAN3D.C
 *
 * An Interactive Three-dimensional Fractal Animator
 *
 * from Tricks of the Graphics Gurus
 */
```

continues

Listing 8.2. continued

```c
#include "fran3d.h"

FILE *diskfile;      /* file handle used for all disk access */
char savename[NAMELEN];    /* filename for modified fractal */

matrix3x3 trans[NTRANS + 1], /* size & spin transformations */
         temat;             /* for temporary calculations */
point3d move[NTRANS + 1],   /* displacement transformations */
        tempt;              /* for temporary calculations */

long spininc = INISPININC,   /* amount (in radians) to spin */
     sizeinc = INISIZEINC,    /* ratio to resize each time */
     moveinc = INIMOVEINC,    /* number of pixels to move */
     cosocular = COSOCULAR,   /* pre-computed sin and cos */
     sinocular = SINOCULAR;    /* for 3D glasses support */

double oculardist = OCULARDIST;   /* distance between eyes */

char a;                   /* for storing current keypress */

int white,           /* color to make menu and current part */
    thiscolor = 3,     /* color to make rest of the fractal */
    i, j, k,             /* miscellaneous loop counters */
    thistran = 0,            /* current transformation */
    ntrans,            /* total number of transformations */
    glasses = 0,     /* red/blue 3D Glasses: 1 = on, 0 = off */
    cpu;              /* used by cputype() in mudi.asm */

enum {X, Y, Z} thisaxis = X;   /* axis for spin, size, etc. */

/* function prototypes */

int main(int nargs, char **arg);
void paint(void);
void spinz(matrix3x3 *mat, long spinx, long spiny);
void spiny(matrix3x3 *mat, long spinx, long spinz);
void spinx(matrix3x3 *mat, long spiny, long spinz);
void sizeit(matrix3x3 *mat, point3d resize);
```

```
void draw3dpoint(point3d pt, int clr);
void axismove(int direction);
void sizeall(int direction);
void axissize(int direction);
void axisspin(int direction);
void axisskew(int direction);

int main(int nargs, char **arg)
{   char a;                             /* current keypress */
    cpu = cputype();            /* find out what cpu we have */
    printf("\n FRAN3D -- An Interactive 3D FRactal ANimator");
    printf("\n\n from Tricks of the Graphics Gurus\n\n");
    if (nargs < 3)          /* make sure files were specified */
    {   printf("To use this program:\n\n");
        printf("FRAN3D 3DFILE.IFS 3DFILE2.IFS\n\n");
        printf(
           "Where 3DFILE1.IFS is an existing 3D IFS file\n");
        printf(
           "and 3DFILE2.IFS is a name for the new file.\n");
        exit(0);
    }
    tg_pickmode();              /* ask user for a video mode */
    if (load3difs(arg[1]) == 0)     /* load starting fractal */
    {   tg_closedown();
        printf("Could not load the file named %s\n\n", arg[1]);
        exit(0);
    }
    strcpy(savename, arg[2]);  /* remember the name to save */
    white = 15 % tg_ncolors;        /* define the color white */
    tg_moveto(0, tg_scrny - tg_chary);       /* show a menu */
    tg_outtext("Next=Tab Size=*/ Axis=XYZ Spin=+- Skew=;\' "
               "Squash=[] Color=C Glasses=G Quit=Esc");
    tg_setviewport(0, 0, tg_scrnx - 1, tg_scrny - tg_chary);
    while(1)                            /* main menu loop */
    {   tg_clearviewport();         /* clear all but the menu */
        paint();                     /* display the fractal */
        geta;                    /* then get the next keypress */
        switch(a)                   /* what shall we do now? */
        {   case LT:                         /* move left */
                axismove(-1);
                break;
```

continues

Listing 8.2. continued

```
case RT:                              /* move right */
    axismove(1);
    break;
case TAB:                /* select the next part */
    if (++thistran > ntrans) thistran = 0;
    break;
case 'C':                             /* change color */
    thiscolor++;
    if ((thiscolor >= tg_ncolors) ¦¦
        (thiscolor >= 15)) thiscolor = 1;
    break;
case 'X':     /* choose axis for spin and sizing */
    thisaxis = X;
    break;
case 'Y':
    thisaxis = Y;
    break;
case 'Z':
    thisaxis = Z;
    break;
case '*':                /* grow (increase size) */
    sizeall(1);
    break;
case '/':                /* shrink (decrease size) */
    sizeall(-1);
    break;
case '-':                         /* spin clockwise */
    axisspin(-1);
    break;
case '+':                /* spin counter-clockwise */
    axisspin(1);
    break;
case '\\':               /* skew x-axis clockwise */
    axisskew(-1);
    break;
case ';':      /* skew x-axis counter-clockwise */
    axisskew(1);
    break;
```

```
                case '[':                        /* squish x-axis */
                    axissize(-1);
                    break;
                case ']':            /* de-squish (stretch) x-axis */
                    axissize(1);
                    break;
                case 'G':
                    if (glasses) glasses = 0;
                    else glasses = 1;
                    break;
                case ESC:                    /* save new IFS and quit */
                    tg_closedown();
                    save3difs(savename);
                    printf("\n\nSeeyalater!\n");
                    exit(0);
            }
        }
}

void sizeit(matrix3x3 *mat, point3d resize)
{   mat->a = mu(mat->a, resize.x);
    mat->d = mu(mat->d, resize.x);
    mat->g = mu(mat->g, resize.x);
    mat->b = mu(mat->b, resize.y);
    mat->e = mu(mat->e, resize.y);
    mat->h = mu(mat->h, resize.y);
    mat->c = mu(mat->c, resize.z);
    mat->f = mu(mat->f, resize.z);
    mat->i = mu(mat->i, resize.z);
}

void spinx(matrix3x3 *mat, long spinx, long spiny)
{   long cosspin, sinspin;
    temat = *mat;
    cosspin = (long) (cosf(spinx) * MF);
    sinspin = (long) (sinf(spinx) * MF);
    mat->b = mu(temat.b, cosspin) - mu(temat.c, sinspin);
    mat->e = mu(temat.e, cosspin) - mu(temat.f, sinspin);
```

continues

Listing 8.2. continued

```
        mat->h = mu(temat.h, cosspin) - mu(temat.i, sinspin);
        cosspin = (long) (cosf(spiny) * MF);
        sinspin = (long) (sinf(spiny) * MF);
        mat->c = mu(temat.b, sinspin) + mu(temat.c, cosspin);
        mat->f = mu(temat.e, sinspin) + mu(temat.f, cosspin);
        mat->i = mu(temat.h, sinspin) + mu(temat.i, cosspin);
}

void spiny(matrix3x3 *mat, long spinx, long spinz)
{   temat = *mat;
    mat->a = temat.a *  cosf(spinx) + temat.c * sinf(spinx);
    mat->d = temat.d *  cosf(spinx) + temat.f * sinf(spinx);
    mat->g = temat.g *  cosf(spinx) + temat.i * sinf(spinx);
    mat->c = temat.a * -sinf(spinz) + temat.c * cosf(spinz);
    mat->f = temat.d * -sinf(spinz) + temat.f * cosf(spinz);
    mat->i = temat.g * -sinf(spinz) + temat.i * cosf(spinz);
}

void spinz(matrix3x3 *mat, long spinx, long spiny)
{   temat = *mat;
    mat->a = temat.a * cosf(spinx) - temat.b * sinf(spinx);
    mat->d = temat.d * cosf(spinx) - temat.e * sinf(spinx);
    mat->g = temat.g * cosf(spinx) - temat.h * sinf(spinx);
    mat->b = temat.a * sinf(spiny) + temat.b * cosf(spiny);
    mat->e = temat.d * sinf(spiny) + temat.e * cosf(spiny);
    mat->h = temat.g * sinf(spiny) + temat.h * cosf(spiny);
}

void draw3dpoint(point3d pt, int clr)
{   int lc = LEFTCLR, rc = RIGHTCLR;
    if (glasses)
    {   if (clr == white) lc = LEFTBRITE, rc = RIGHTBRITE;
        tg_putpixel(((int) (pt.x >> BITSH)),
                    ((int) (pt.y >> BITSH)), lc);
        tg_putpixel(((int) ((mu(pt.x, cosocular) +
                    mu(pt.z, sinocular)) >> BITSH)),
                    ((int) (pt.y >> BITSH)), rc);
```

```
    }
    else
    {   tg_putpixel(((int) (pt.x >> BITSH)),
                    ((int) (pt.y >> BITSH)), clr);
    }
}

void axismove(int direction)
{   long xx = 0L, yy = 0L, zz = 0L;
    switch(thisaxis)
    {   case X:
            xx = moveinc * direction;
            break;
        case Y:
            yy = moveinc * direction;
            break;
        case Z:
            zz = moveinc * direction;
    }
    if (thistran == 0)   /* if on seed, change *movex,*movey */
        (*move).x += mu(xx, (*trans).a) +
                     mu(yy, (*trans).b) +
                     mu(zz, (*trans).c),
        (*move).y += mu(xx, (*trans).d) +
                     mu(yy, (*trans).e) +
                     mu(zz, (*trans).f),
        (*move).z += mu(xx, (*trans).g) +
                     mu(yy, (*trans).h) +
                     mu(zz, (*trans).i);
    else
    {   move[thistran].x += xx;
        move[thistran].y += yy;
        move[thistran].z += zz;
    }
}

void sizeall(int direction)
{   if (direction == -1)
    {   tempt.x = tempt.y = tempt.z = di(M1, (M1 + sizeinc));
        sizeit(trans + thistran, tempt);
    }
```

continues

379

Listing 8.2. continued

```
    else
    {   tempt.x = tempt.y = tempt.z = M1 + sizeinc;
        sizeit(trans + thistran, tempt);
    }
}

void axissize(int direction)
{   long delta;
    delta = M1 + sizeinc;
    if (direction == -1) delta = di(M1, delta);
    switch(thisaxis)
    {   case X:
            tempt.x = delta;
            tempt.y = tempt.z = M1;
            break;
        case Y:
            tempt.y = delta;
            tempt.x = tempt.z = M1;
            break;
        case Z:
            tempt.z = delta;
            tempt.y = tempt.x = M1;
    }
    sizeit(trans + thistran, tempt);
}

void axisspin(int direction)
{   switch(thisaxis)
    {   case X:
            spinx(trans + thistran, spininc * direction,
                                    spininc * direction);
            break;
        case Y:
            spiny(trans + thistran, spininc * direction,
                                    spininc * direction);
            break;
```

```
            case Z:
                spinz(trans + thistran, spininc * direction,
                                    spininc * direction);
        }
}

void axisskew(int direction)
{   switch(thisaxis)
    {   case X:
            spinz(trans + thistran, spininc * direction, 0L);
            break;
        case Y:
            spinx(trans + thistran, spininc * direction, 0L);
            break;
        case Z:
            spiny(trans + thistran, 0L, spininc * direction);
    }
}

/* display the fractal */

void paint(void)
{   int i, j, p[NTRANS - 1], tc;
    point3d p1, p2;
    long xx, f1 = 0L, f2, ff[NTRANS];
    unsigned long count = 0L;
    for (i = 1; i <= ntrans; i++)
        f1 += (ff[i - 1] = labs(determ(trans[i])));
    if (f1 == 0L) f1 = 1L;
    f2 = di((long) MAXINT, f1);
   j = 0;
    for (i = 0; i < ntrans - 1; i++)
    {   if ((xx = (int) mu(ff[i], f2)) == 0) xx = 1;
        p[i] = (j += xx);
    }
    p1 = *move;
  for (j = 0; j < 8; j++)
    {   i = rand() % ntrans + 1;
        mupt(p1, trans[i], p2);
```

continues

Listing 8.2. continued

```
            addpt(p2, move[i], p2);
            p1 = p2;
    }
    while(--count > 0)
    {   if (kbhit()) return;
        j = rand();
        for (i = 0; i < ntrans - 1; i++) if (j < p[i]) break;
        i++;
        mupt(p1, trans[i], p2);
        addpt(p2, move[i], p2);
        p1 = p2;
        if ((thistran == 0) ¦¦ (i == thistran))
            tc = white;                     /* one part white */
        else tc = thiscolor;
        if (tc > 0)
        {   mupt(p2, (*trans), tempt);
            addpt(tempt, (*move), tempt);
            draw3dpoint(tempt, tc);
        }
    }
}

int load3difs(char *name)
{   char str[NAMELEN + 15], scanstr[80], rc;
    float aa, bb, cc, dd, ee, ff, gg, hh, ii, xx, yy, zz, pp;
    int n = 999, ret = 1;
    if ((diskfile = fopen(name, "r")) == NULL) return(0);
    while(((rc = fgetc(diskfile)) != '(') &&
        (rc != EOF) && (rc != '{'));
    if (rc == '{')                          /* 2D ifs codes */
    {   for (n = 1; n <= NTRANS; n++)
        {   if (fscanf(diskfile, " %f %f %f %f %f %f %f\n",
                &aa, &bb, &cc, &dd, &ee, &ff, &pp) != 7) break;
            else
            {   move[n].x = (long) (ee * -50.0 * MF);
                move[n].y = (long) (ff * -50.0 * MF);
                move[n].z = 0L;
                trans[n].a = (long) (aa * MF);
                trans[n].b = (long) (bb * MF);
```

```
                    trans[n].c = 0L;
                    trans[n].d = (long) (cc * MF);
                    trans[n].e = (long) (dd * MF);
                    trans[n].f = 0L;
                    trans[n].g = 0L;
                    trans[n].h = 0L;
                    trans[n].i = labs(trans[n].a);
            }
        }
    }
    else
    {   if ((rc == EOF) ¦¦
            (fgetc(diskfile) != '3') ¦¦
            (fgetc(diskfile) != 'D') ¦¦
            (fgetc(diskfile) != ')') ¦¦
            (fgetc(diskfile) != ' ') ¦¦
            (fgetc(diskfile) != '{'))
        {   printf("\7Not a valid set of 3D codes.");
            geta;
            return(0);
        }
        for (n = 1; n <= NTRANS; n++)
        {   if (fscanf(diskfile,
                " %f %f %f %f %f %f %f %f %f %f %f %f %f\n",
                &aa, &bb, &cc, &dd, &ee, &ff, &gg, &hh, &ii,
                &xx, &yy, &zz, &pp) != 13) break;
            move[n].x = (long) (xx * -50.0 * MF);
            move[n].y = (long) (yy * -50.0 * MF);
            move[n].z = (long) (zz * -50.0 * MF);
            trans[n].a = (long) (aa * MF);
            trans[n].b = (long) (bb * MF);
            trans[n].c = (long) (cc * MF);
            trans[n].d = (long) (dd * MF);
            trans[n].e = (long) (ee * MF);
            trans[n].f = (long) (ff * MF);
            trans[n].g = (long) (gg * MF);
            trans[n].h = (long) (hh * MF);
            trans[n].i = (long) (ii * MF);
        }
    }
```

continues

Listing 8.2. continued

```
        if (n > 1) ntrans = n - 1;
        if ((n < 2) ¦¦ (ferror(diskfile) != 0)) ret = 0;
        (*move).x  = (long) tg_scrnx << (BITSH - 1);
        (*move).y  = (long) tg_scrny << (BITSH - 1);
        (*move).z  = 0L;
        (*trans).a = M1; (*trans).b = 0L; (*trans).c = 0L;
        (*trans).d = 0L; (*trans).e = M1; (*trans).f = 0L;
        (*trans).g = 0L; (*trans).h = 0L; (*trans).i = M1;
        fclose(diskfile);
        return(ret);
}

int save3difs(char *name)
{   int i, ret = 1;
    long f1 = 0L, ff[NTRANS];
    float xx;
    if ((diskfile = fopen(name, "w")) == NULL) return(0);
    fprintf(diskfile, "\n %s (3D) {\n", name);
    for (i = 1; i <= ntrans; i++)
        f1 += (ff[i - 1] = labs(determ(trans[i])));
    if (f1 == 0L) f1 = 1L;
    for (i = 1; i <= ntrans; i++)
    {   if ((xx = (float) di(ff[i - 1], f1) / MF)
            < 0.01) xx = 0.01;
        fprintf(diskfile,
                " %.2f %.2f %.2f %.2f %.2f %.2f"
                " %.2f %.2f %.2f %.2f %.2f %.2f %.2f\n",
                (float) trans[i].a / MF,
                (float) trans[i].b / MF,
                (float) trans[i].c / MF,
                (float) trans[i].d / MF,
                (float) trans[i].e / MF,
                (float) trans[i].f / MF,
                (float) trans[i].g / MF,
                (float) trans[i].h / MF,
                (float) trans[i].i / MF,
                (float) move[i].x / (MF * -50.0),
                (float) move[i].y / (MF * -50.0),
                (float) move[i].z / (MF * -50.0), xx);
```

```
    }
    fprintf(diskfile, "}");
    if (ferror(diskfile) != 0) ret = 0;
  fclose(diskfile);
    return(ret);
}
```

Automatic 3-D Fractal Tweening

In the mind's eye, a fractal is a way of seeing infinity.

—James Gleick, *Chaos,* 1986

You've seen a lot of tweening and morphing in this book. Scott Anderson showed you how to metamorphose lines and linear shapes in Chapter 4, and I applied the same techniques to fractals in Chapter 6. All those magical morphs were restricted to two dimensions, however. It's about time you learned to tween 3-D shapes, don't you think? I think so, too.

The FREEN3D program I'll introduce shortly below takes any two three-dimensional fractals and automatically creates in-between frames depicting the gradual transition from one to the other. Like FRAN3D, it reads definitions of the 3-D fractals from IFS files.

Before you put FREEN3D to the test, you might like to know a little bit more about those IFS files.

You may recall from Chapter 6 that a two-dimensional IFS file looks like this:

```
tri.ifs {
0.50 0.00 0.00 0.50 0.00 1.96 0.01
-0.25 0.43 -0.43 -0.25 1.82 -0.68 0.33
-0.25 -0.43 0.43 -0.25 -1.42 -0.88 0.33
}
```

Each line corresponds to one transformation that defines a part of the fractal. The first four numbers on each line are the elements of the 2×2 transformation matrix, the next two numbers are the *movex* and *movey* displacement, and the final number indicates the relative area of the transformation.

Three-dimensional IFS files use almost exactly the same format, except that the transformation matrix is 3×3 (containing nine elements), and you need values for *movex*, *movey*, and *movez*. Each line in a 3-D IFS file therefore has 13 numbers instead of 7. For example:

```
3dtri.ifs (3D) {
 0.50 0.00 0.00 0.00 0.46 -0.19 0.00 0.19 0.46 0.00 1.96 0.00 0.50
 -0.23 0.43 -0.10 -0.40 -0.25 -0.16 -0.10 0.00 0.23 1.82 -0.68 -1.00 0.25
 -0.23 -0.43 0.10 0.40 -0.25 -0.16 0.10 0.00 0.23 -1.42 -0.88 -1.00 0.25
}
```

When you want to tween two IFS fractals, simply compute the in-between values for each number in the IFS file (except the relative area values, which are recomputed for each display frame). Find the amount to change each number with the same formula you used for all other types of tweening:

$$delta_a = (a_1 - a_2) / (number\ of\ frames)$$

Apply this formula to find the delta for *b*, *c*, *d*, *e*, *f*, *g*, *h*, *movex*, *movey*, and *movez* as well as *a*. Then just add the deltas to each number after each frame. Couldn't be simpler. The following **Working Code** section gives you plain C to do it. Figures 8.12 and 8.13 and the **You Can Do It** section show you the results.

Figures 8.12 and 8.13 also demonstrate an easy trick for fine-tuning your tweens. The FREEN3D program matches the first transformation in one IFS file to the first transformation in the other file, the second line to the second line, and so forth. You can control which parts of the starting fractal get morphed into which parts of the ending fractal by rearranging the lines of the IFS file with your favorite text editor or word processing program. The starting and ending fractals in Figures 8.12 and 8.13 are identical. (They're called 3DFERN1.IFS and 3DSIERP.IFS, by the way.) The only difference between the two animation sequences is that I moved the first line of 3DSIERP.IFS down to the third line by cutting and pasting within a text editor. As you can see, the resulting tween came out quite different, even though the reordering made no difference in the appearance of the final fractal.

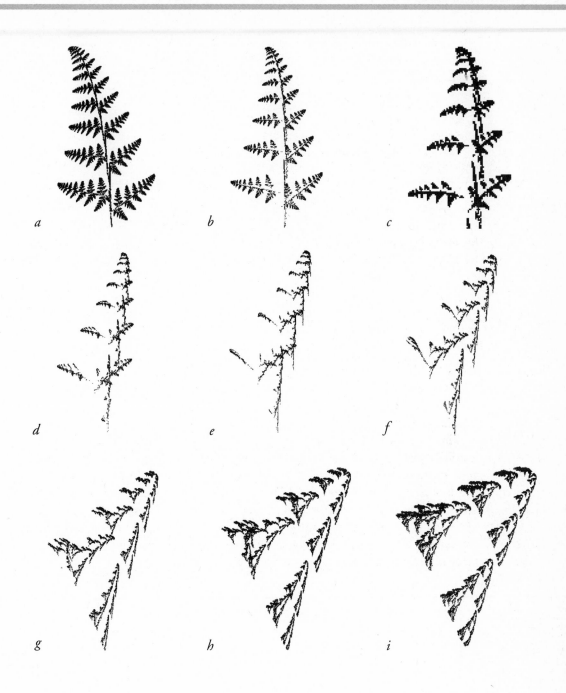

Figure 8.12. *Automatic tweening is almost as easy in three dimensions as it was in two.*

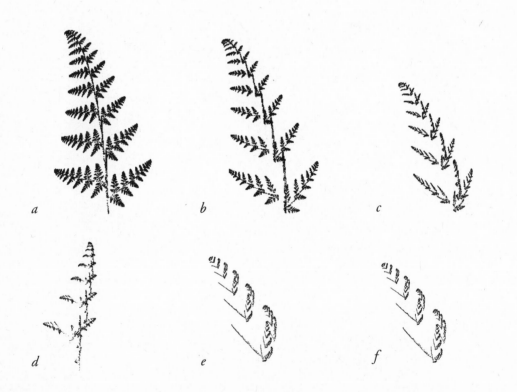

Figure 8.13. *By rearranging the lines in the second IFS file, you can make the same two fractals do a different dance.*

You Can Do It: Tweening in 3-D

To watch a 3-D fractal morph into another 3-D fractal, type FREEN3D, followed by both IFS file names and the number of frames you'd like to see. To advance from one frame to the next, press any key. This works with any of the IFS files with names that start with 3-D. Try the following commands for starters, and then try morphing some of your own fractals that you make with the FRAN3D program presented earlier.

```
FREEN3D 3DFERN1.IFS 3DSIERP.IFS 20

FREEN3D 3DPLANT.IFS 3DPLANT2.IFS 10

FREEN3D 3DCURL.IFS 3DGALAXY.IFS 15
```

Working Code: I Wish I Was a Three-Dimensional Tweener...

The paint() and load3difs() functions in the following listing are almost identical to the ones you saw in FRAN3D. One slight difference is that no overall transformation is used, so the entire trans[] array contains transformations that define the fractal itself. (In FRAN3D, the trans[0] element contained a transformation for orienting the whole shape on-screen, and trans[1] through trans[ntrans] defined the actual fractal.)

FREEN3D contains another small change to the load3difs() routine: unlike the version in FRAN3D, this one only loads true three-dimensional IFS codes. It won't accept 2-D codes the way FRAN3D did. Of course, if you want to tween 2-D fractals, just use the FREEN program from Chapter 6.

The serious business in FREEN3D all takes place in the tween3d() function, which bears a close resemblance to the tween() function from FREEN.C in Chapter 6. Just a few more variables—the basic algorithm is the same.

Remember to link MUDI.OBJ with this program if you compile it. For example, the Microsoft compile command would be:

TGMS FREEN3D.C MUDI.OBJ

Borland users say TGTC instead of TGMS. See the introduction for more specifics on compiling with TransGraphics.

Listing 8.3. FREEN3D transforms any 3-D fractal into any other.

```
/* FREEN3D.C
 *
 * A Three-dimensional Fractal Tweener
 *
 * from Tricks of the Graphics Gurus
 */

#include "fran3d.h"          /* same header used by FRAN3D.C */

FILE *diskfile;      /* file handle used for all disk access */

matrix3x3 trans[NTRANS],      /* size & spin transformations */
          trans2[NTRANS],
          dtrans[NTRANS];  /* "delta" change for each frame */
point3d move[NTRANS],         /* displacement transformations */
        move2[NTRANS],
        dmove[NTRANS];        /* "delta" change for each frame */

long cosocular = COSOCULAR,     /* pre-computed sin and cos */
     sinocular = SINOCULAR;        /* for 3D glasses support */

double oculardist = OCULARDIST;    /* distance between eyes */

char a;                     /* for storing current keypress */

int white,                      /* color to make menu */
    i, j, k,                 /* miscellaneous loop counters */
    ntrans, ntrans2,      /* total number of transformations */
    glasses = 0,    /* red/blue 3D Glasses: 1 = on, 0 = off */
    cpu;                   /* used by cputype() in mudi.asm */




/* function prototypes */
```

continues

Listing 8.3. continued

```c
int main(int nargs, char **arg);
void paint(void);
void draw3dpoint(point3d pt, int clr);
void tween3d(int nsteps);


int main(int nargs, char **arg)
{   int nsteps, i;
    cpu = cputype();            /* find out what cpu we have */
    printf("\n\n FREEN3D -- A 3D Fractal Tweener");
    printf("\n\n from Tricks of the Graphics Gurus\n\n");
    if (nargs < 3)        /* make sure files were specified */
    {   printf("To use this program:\n\n");
        printf("FREEN3D 3DFILE1.IFS 3DFILE2.IFS N\n\n");
        printf("Where 3DFILE1.IFS and 3DFILE2.IFS are\n");
        printf("3D IFS files and N is the number of tweens\n");
        printf("to create between the two shapes.\n");
        exit(0);
    }
    if (load3difs(arg[2]) == 0)  /* load the second fractal */
    {   printf("Could not load the file named %s\n\n", arg[2]);
        exit(0);
    }
    ntrans2 = ntrans;
    for (i = 0; i < ntrans2; i++)   /* copy into second IFS */
    {   trans2[i] = trans[i];
        move2[i] = move[i];
    }
    if (load3difs(arg[1]) == 0)   /* load the first fractal */
    {   printf("Could not load the file named %s\n\n", arg[1]);
        exit(0);
    }
    if(nargs<3)nsteps=10;
    else sscanf(arg[3], "%d", &nsteps);
    tg_pickmode();                /* ask user for a video mode */
    tween3d(nsteps);      /* compute and display the tweens */
    tg_closedown();               /* close down the graphics */
    printf("Good day, 'ey!");     /* Canadian for Seeyalater */
}
```

```
/* Compute and display a given number of fractal tweens */

void tween3d(int nsteps)
{   int i, j, k;
    char a;

    /* if there are a different number of transformations,
       double-up as necessary to make the same number */

    if (ntrans2 < ntrans)
    {   for (i = ntrans2; i < ntrans; i++)
        {   trans2[i] = trans2[i % ntrans2];
            move2[i] = move2[i % ntrans2];
        }
        ntrans2 = ntrans;
    }
    else
    {   if (ntrans < ntrans2)
        {   for (i = ntrans; i < ntrans2; i++)
            {   trans[i] = trans[i % ntrans];
                move[i] = move[i % ntrans];
            }
            ntrans = ntrans2;
        }
    }

    /* compute the deltas */

    for (j = 0; j < ntrans; j++)
    {   dtrans[j].a = (trans2[j].a - trans[j].a) / nsteps;
        dtrans[j].b = (trans2[j].b - trans[j].b) / nsteps;
        dtrans[j].c = (trans2[j].c - trans[j].c) / nsteps;
        dtrans[j].d = (trans2[j].d - trans[j].d) / nsteps;
        dtrans[j].e = (trans2[j].e - trans[j].e) / nsteps;
        dtrans[j].f = (trans2[j].f - trans[j].f) / nsteps;
        dtrans[j].g = (trans2[j].g - trans[j].g) / nsteps;
        dtrans[j].h = (trans2[j].h - trans[j].h) / nsteps;
        dtrans[j].i = (trans2[j].i - trans[j].i) / nsteps;
        dtrans[j].a = (trans2[j].a - trans[j].a) / nsteps;
        dmove[j].x = (move2[j].x - move[j].x) / nsteps;
```

continues

Listing 8.3. continued

```
        dmove[j].y = (move2[j].y - move[j].y) / nsteps;
        dmove[j].z = (move2[j].z - move[j].z) / nsteps;
    }

    /* display the tween by repeatedly adding the deltas */

    for (k = 0; k <= nsteps; k++)
    {   tg_clearscreen();
        paint();
        if (k == nsteps) break;
        if (kbhit())
        {   a = getch();
            if (a == 27) break;
        }
        for (j = 0; j < ntrans; j++)
        {   trans[j].a += dtrans[j].a;
            trans[j].b += dtrans[j].b;
            trans[j].c += dtrans[j].c;
            trans[j].d += dtrans[j].d;
            trans[j].e += dtrans[j].e;
            trans[j].f += dtrans[j].f;
            trans[j].g += dtrans[j].g;
            trans[j].h += dtrans[j].h;
            trans[j].i += dtrans[j].i;
            move[j].x += dmove[j].x;
            move[j].y += dmove[j].y;
            move[j].z += dmove[j].z;
        }
    }
}

void draw3dpoint(point3d pt, int clr)
{   int lc = LEFTCLR, rc = RIGHTCLR, px, py;
    px = (int) (pt.x >> BITSH) + (tg_scrnx >> 1);
    py = (int) (pt.y >> BITSH) + (tg_scrny >> 1);
    if (glasses)
    {   int px2;
        px2 = (int) ((mu(pt.x, cosocular) +

                    mu(pt.z, sinocular)) >> BITSH) +
                    (tg_scrnx >> 1);
```

```
            if (clr == white) lc = LEFTBRITE, rc = RIGHTBRITE;

            tg_putpixel(px, py, lc);
            tg_putpixel(px2, py, rc);
        }
        else
        {   tg_putpixel(px, py, clr);
        }
}

/* display the fractal */

void paint(void)
{   int i, j, p[NTRANS - 1], tc;
    point3d p1, p2;
    long xx, f1 = 0L, f2, ff[NTRANS];
    unsigned long count = 0L;
    for (i = 0; i < ntrans; i++)
        f1 += (ff[i] = labs(determ(trans[i])));
    if (f1 == 0L) f1 = 1L;
    f2 = di((long) MAXINT, f1);
  j = 0;
    for (i = 0; i < ntrans - 1; i++)
    {   if ((xx = (int) mu(ff[i], f2)) == 0) xx = 1;
        p[i] = (j += xx);
    }
    p1 = *move;
  for (j = 0; j < 8; j++)
    {   i = rand() % ntrans;
        mupt(p1, trans[i], p2);
        addpt(p2, move[i], p2);
        p1 = p2;
    }
    while(--count > 0)
    {   if (kbhit()) return;
        j = rand();
        for (i = 0; i < ntrans - 1; i++) if (j < p[i]) break;
        mupt(p1, trans[i], p2);
        addpt(p2, move[i], p2);
        p1 = p2;
        if (tg_ncolors == 2) tc = 1;
        else tc = i + 1;                    /* color each part */
```

continues

Listing 8.3. continued

```
            if (tc > 0) draw3dpoint(p2, tc);
        }
    }

/* load a set of FRACTINT and Fractal Grafics compatible
 * three-dimensional IFS codes. Unlike the load3difs()
 * function in FRAN3D.C, this one does not handle 2D IFS */

int load3difs(char *name)
{   char str[NAMELEN + 15], scanstr[80], rc;
    float aa, bb, cc, dd, ee, ff, gg, hh, ii, xx, yy, zz, pp;
    int n = 999, ret = 1;
    if ((diskfile = fopen(name, "r")) == NULL) return(0);
    while(((rc = fgetc(diskfile)) != '(') &&
          (rc != EOF) && (rc != '{'));
    if ((rc == '{') || (rc == EOF) ||
        (fgetc(diskfile) != '3') ||
        (fgetc(diskfile) != 'D') ||
        (fgetc(diskfile) != ')') ||
        (fgetc(diskfile) != ' ') ||
        (fgetc(diskfile) != '{'))
    {   printf("\7Not a valid set of 3D codes.");
        geta;
        return(0);
    }
    for (n = 0; n < NTRANS; n++)
    {   if (fscanf(diskfile,
            " %f %f %f %f %f %f %f %f %f %f %f %f %f\n",
            &aa, &bb, &cc, &dd, &ee, &ff, &gg, &hh, &ii,
            &xx, &yy, &zz, &pp) != 13) break;
        move[n].x = (long) (xx * -50.0 * MF);
        move[n].y = (long) (yy * -50.0 * MF);
        move[n].z = (long) (zz * -50.0 * MF);
        trans[n].a = (long) (aa * MF);
        trans[n].b = (long) (bb * MF);
        trans[n].c = (long) (cc * MF);
        trans[n].d = (long) (dd * MF);
        trans[n].e = (long) (ee * MF);
        trans[n].f = (long) (ff * MF);
        trans[n].g = (long) (gg * MF);
```

```
        trans[n].h = (long) (hh * MF);
        trans[n].i = (long) (ii * MF);
    }
    if (n > 0) ntrans = n;
    if ((n < 2) || (ferror(diskfile) != 0)) ret = 0;
    fclose(diskfile);
    return(ret);
}
```

Fractal DXF Files

In the popular mind, computer-generated images have a mechanistic quality, perhaps due to the fact that popular computer drawing and paint tools come equipped with a repertoire of regular shapes such as lines, circles, and squares. But if the computer artist can supplement those with tools that create fractal shapes, with roughness, texture, branching, and cloudiness, then the mechanistic feel will be replaced by the earthiness of the natural world.

—Timothy Wegner and Mark Peterson, *Fractal Creations*, 1991

Because you can paint IFS fractals as "point clouds," the simplest rendering techniques can produce very good 3-D effects, especially when viewed with the red/blue glasses. Sooner or later, however, you'll want to try bringing your fractals into more powerful rendering software such as the POLYRAY ray tracer presented in Chapter 9 or another 3-D rendering program such as Autodesk *3-D Studio*, Presidio's *3-D Workshop*, or CrystalGraphics *Desktop Animator*.

To make 3-D fractals accessible to almost every rendering program in existence, you can revisit the ubiquitous Drawing eXchange File format introduced in Chapter 3 and put it to work in Chapter 7.

Putting 3-D points into a DXF is extremely easy. Just start the file with:

```
0
SECTION
2
ENTITIES
```

Then toss in a few points which look like this (without the comments):

```
0
POINT
10              <-- 10 means X coordinate to follow
-159.953613     <-- Coordinate values are in decimal format
20              <-- 20 means Y coordinate to follow
-62.174316
30              <-- 30 means Z coordinate to follow
15.486816
8               <-- 8 means layer number to follow
1               <-- This point goes on layer number 1
```

Many 3-D programs use the layer number to group entities together. The following IFS2DXF program gives each major part of the fractal its own layer number. When you've dumped a few hundred points in there, close up shop by tacking the following on the end of the file.

```
0
ENDSECT
0
EOF
```

Some 3-D rendering software programs, such as the ray tracer presented in the next chapter, handle POINT entities quite nicely by pretending that they're tiny spheres. Many others, however, shrug their cybernetic shoulders and say, "Where's the faces?" To make your fractals visible to those programs, you need some sort of 3-D shape around each point. The following IFS2DXF program gives you the option of creating a cube—complete with six 3DFACE entities—into the DXF file for each point in the fractal. You can specify the size of the cube when you run the program, or tell it just to use POINT entities instead.

To make Figure 8.14, I used IFS2DXF to bring the curving 3-D *Sierpin' ski's Triangle* from FRAN3D into a DXF file with 5,000 cubes, each 5 pixel-widths in size. I then imported the DXF into Autodesk 3-D Studio, added a sandy earth and some spotlights, and assigned colored materials to the parts of the fractal according to the layer number given by IFS2DXF.

In Chapter 9, I present another program, called IFS2PI, which is nearly identical to the IFS2DXF program except that it creates tiny spheres for rendering with the POLYRAY ray-tracer instead of tiny cubes and dots. Because IFS2PI is so similar to IFS2DXF, the source code isn't listed here or in the next chapter. (Of course, the full source for both IFS2DXF.C and IFS2PI.C is on the disk.)

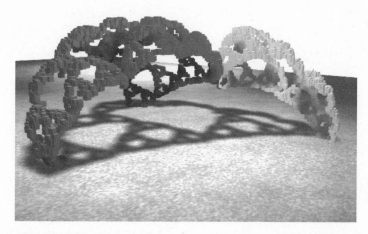

Figure 8.14. *With the IFS2DXF translator, you can save 3-D fractals into DXF files for use with ray-tracers or rendering programs like Autodesk 3-D Studio.*

You Can Do It: Flitting Fractals From File Format to File Format

To use the IFS2DXF program, specify the name of the IFS file to load, a name to give the DXF file, and a number of points to save. You can specify either two-dimensional or three-dimensional IFS files. For example, to save 500 points on the fractal defined by 3DSIERP.IFS to a DXF file named 3DSIERP.DXF, enter the following command.

```
IFS2DXF 3DSIERP.IFS 3DSIERP.DXF 500
```

While the DXF file is being created, you'll see the points appear on-screen. When the program ends, your fractal will be nicely packaged into a handy-dandy DXF. Any DXF-compatible software that accepts point clouds can then read and display the fractal.

To make a DXF full of cubes instead of points, add another number to the end of the command line to tell IFS2DXF what size you want each cube to be (measured in screen pixel widths). For instance, to build a DXF fern from tiny little boxes you could enter:

```
IFS2DXF 3DFERN1.IFS 3DFERN1.DXF 600 5
```

This makes the fractal visible to programs that need 3DFACE entities to do their stuff.

The IFS2PI program (for output to the POLYRAY ray-tracer) works exactly the same way as IFS2DXF, except the final number refers to the diameter of each tiny sphere instead of the width of tiny cubes. See the first **You Can Do It** section in Chapter 9 for an example of IFS2PI syntax.

Working Code: A Thousand Points of Light...

By now, all the routines in this program are, well, *routine* to an old graphics hand like you. The paintdxf() function is just the paint() function from FRAN3D and FREEN3D with a little DXF file output thrown in. I'm not even listing the load3difs() function because it's identical to the one in FRAN3D.

Another function has also been partially omitted from the following listing. The savecube() routine, which actually puts the little cubes into a DXF file, would have taken several pages of paper to print, even though it doesn't do anything you haven't already seen in Chapter 7. The Curious Georges among you will peek into the IFS2DXF.C source file and find a whole slew of extremely repetitive fprintf() statements that meticulously spell out every vertex of every face on a cube.

Listing 8.4. The IFS2DXF.C program converts a fractal IFS file to an ordinary DXF by saving many POINT or 3DFACE entities.

```
/* IFS2DXF.C
 *
 * Program to save IFS fractals as point-clouds in
 * Drawing eXchange File format for rendering
 *
 * from Tricks of the Graphics Gurus
 */
```

```
#include "fran3d.h"

#define POINT 1
#define CUBEFACES 2

FILE *diskfile;      /* file handle used for all disk access */
char savename[NAMELEN];                  /* filename for DXF */
matrix3x3 trans[NTRANS + 1]; /* size & spin transformations */
point3d move[NTRANS + 1];   /* displacement transformations */
int ntrans,              /* total number of transformations */
    cpu;                   /* used by cputype() in mudi.asm */
float cubesize;          /* size of cubes (0 means points) */

int main(int nargs, char **arg);
int paintdxf(unsigned long count, float cubesize);
void savecube(point3d p2, float cubesize, int layer);
int load3difs(char *name);

int main(int nargs, char **arg)
{   unsigned long count;  /* number of points/cubes to save */
    float cubesize;                 /* size of cubes to save */
    cpu = cputype();        /* find out what cpu we have */
    printf("\n IFS2DXF -- Fractal DXF Creator");
    printf("\n\n from Tricks of the Graphics Gurus\n\n");
    if (nargs < 4)        /* make sure files were specified */
    {   printf("To use this program:\n\n");
        printf("FRAN3D 3DFILE.IFS 3DFILE2.IFS N C\n\n");
        printf(
          "Where 3DFILE1.IFS is an existing 3D IFS file,\n");
        printf(
          "FILE2.DXF is a name for the DXF file, and\n");
        printf(
          "N is the number of cubes or points to save.\n");
        printf(
          "C is the size of the cubes to save. If C is 0 or\n");
        printf(
          "absent, points will be saved instead of cubes.\n");
        exit(0);
    }
    tg_pickmode();              /* ask user for a video mode */
```

continues

Listing 8.4. continued

```c
    if (load3difs(arg[1]) == 0)     /* load starting fractal */
    {  tg_closedown();
       printf("Could not load the file named %s\n\n", arg[1]);
       exit(0);
    }
    strcpy(savename, arg[2]);  /* remember the name to save */
    count = atol(arg[3]);         /* number of points to save */
    if (count < 100L) count = 100L;  /* minimum no. of pts. */
    cubesize = atof(arg[4]) / 2.0;
    if (cubesize <= 0.0) cubesize = 0.0;
    paintdxf(count, cubesize);   /* display and save points */
    tg_closedown();
    printf("\n\nA-river-ditchy!\n");  /*  Italian for seeya */
}

/* display and save the fractal */

int paintdxf(unsigned long count, float cubesize)
{   int i, j, p[NTRANS - 1], tc;
    point3d p1, p2;
    long xx, f1 = 0L, f2, ff[NTRANS];
    for (i = 1; i <= ntrans; i++)
        f1 += (ff[i - 1] = labs(determ(trans[i])));
    if (f1 == 0L) f1 = 1L;
    f2 = di((long) MAXINT, f1);
  j = 0;
    for (i = 0; i < ntrans - 1; i++)
    {   if ((xx = (int) mu(ff[i], f2)) == 0) xx = 1;
        p[i] = (j += xx);
    }
    p1 = *move;
  for (j = 0; j < 8; j++)
    {   i = rand() % ntrans + 1;
        mupt(p1, trans[i], p2);
        addpt(p2, move[i], p2);
        p1 = p2;
    }
    if ((diskfile = fopen(savename, "wb")) == NULL) return(0);
    fprintf(diskfile, "0\r\nSECTION\r\n2\r\nENTITIES\r\n");
    while(--count > 0)
```

```
    {   if (kbhit()) return(1);
        j = rand();
        for (i = 0; i < ntrans - 1; i++) if (j < p[i]) break;
        i++;
        mupt(p1, trans[i], p2);
        addpt(p2, move[i], p2);
        p1 = p2;
        tg_putpixel((int) (p2.x >> BITSH) + tg_scrnx >> 1,
                    (int) (p2.y >> BITSH) + tg_scrny >> 1,
                    i + 1);
        if (cubesize == 0.0)
            fprintf(diskfile,
                    "0\r\nPOINT\r\n"
                    "10\r\n%lf\r\n20\r\n%lf\r\n30\r\n"
                    "%lf\r\n8\r\n%d\r\n",
                    (double) p2.x / M1,
                    (double) -p2.y / M1,
                    (double) p2.z / M1, i + 1);
        else savecube(p2, cubesize, i + 1);
    }
    fprintf(diskfile, "0\r\nENDSEC\r\n0\r\nEOF\r\n");
    fprintf(diskfile, "%c", 0xFF);
    fclose(diskfile);
    return(1);
}

void savecube(point3d p2, float cubesize, int layer)
{       fprintf(diskfile,
            "0\r\n3DFACE\r\n"
            "10\r\n%lf\r\n20\r\n%lf\r\n30\r\n%lf\r\n"
            "11\r\n%lf\r\n21\r\n%lf\r\n31\r\n%lf\r\n"
            "12\r\n%lf\r\n22\r\n%lf\r\n32\r\n%lf\r\n"
            "13\r\n%lf\r\n23\r\n%lf\r\n33\r\n%lf\r\n"
            "8\r\n%d\r\n",
            (double) p2.x / M1 - cubesize,
            (double) -p2.y / M1 - cubesize,
            (double) p2.z / M1 - cubesize,
            (double) p2.x / M1 + cubesize,
            (double) -p2.y / M1 - cubesize,
            (double) p2.z / M1 - cubesize,
            (double) p2.x / M1 + cubesize,
```

continues

403

Listing 8.4. continued

```
                (double) -p2.y / M1 - cubesize,
                (double) p2.z / M1 + cubesize,
                (double) p2.x / M1 - cubesize,
                (double) -p2.y / M1 - cubesize,
                (double) p2.z / M1 + cubesize, layer);
        fprintf(diskfile,
            "0\r\n3DFACE\r\n"
            "10\r\n%lf\r\n20\r\n%lf\r\n30\r\n%lf\r\n"
            "11\r\n%lf\r\n21\r\n%lf\r\n31\r\n%lf\r\n"
            "12\r\n%lf\r\n22\r\n%lf\r\n32\r\n%lf\r\n"
            "13\r\n%lf\r\n23\r\n%lf\r\n33\r\n%lf\r\n"
            "8\r\n%d\r\n",
            (double) p2.x / M1 + cubesize,
            (double) -p2.y / M1 - cubesize,
```

... and so forth ... (It goes on like this for a while, and then there's
the load3difs() function, too.) We'll spare the trees and end the listing
here.)

Next Up: Bob and Ray

Now, Black Spleenwort Ferns have been around for a rather long time, and they sure
are pretty, but nobody ever accused them of being very bright. Could the exact same
process [used in computer simulation] be used by the real fern to teach itself how to
grow?

To me, the odds are overwhelming that does seem to be the case. We thus appear to
be tampering with some heavy-duty stuff here.

> —Don Lancaster, Hardware Hacker, *Radio Electronics*, 1990

This chapter, and Chapter 6, have focused on the graphical side of fractal geometry.
As you may have guessed—or read on the front page of your favorite science
magazine—you can use the same flexibility and complexity that produce outrageous
graphics images to produce real-world scientific models. If you'd like to learn more
about the applications of fractals and the related study of chaos that are revolutionizing
almost every branch of modern science, you might enjoy my book/software bundle,

FractalVision. It explains the serious side of fractals and chaos. Also, the *FractalVision Software* included with the book takes all the 2-D interactive fractal design tricks covered in this book several steps further. (The new *FractalVision for Windows* edition should be out by the time you read this.) For more fun with 3-D fractals, my company sells a complete 3-D fractal design system called *Fractal Grafics 3D*. See the Cedar Software order form in the back of this book for more details. (This shameless plug brought to you by your cheerful guru/host, Dick "Cedar Software" Oliver.)

Meanwhile, stay tuned as special guest guru Bob Zigon brings some of the innermost secrets of the graphics world to light—literally. Ray tracing takes all the shapes we've made in Chapters 7 and 8, shines some cyberspace sunbeams on them, and renders them realer than real.

Realistic Rendering with Ray Tracing

In this chapter, guest guru Bob Zigon and I expose the darkest secrets of light itself. By modeling the interaction of light rays with 3-D objects, you can create stunning, ultrarealistic renderings of anything imaginable.

Like many fun things in life, ray tracing is easier done than said. Thanks to the POLYRAY ray-tracer program (a complete, fully functional shareware copy that's included with this book), you can jump into the excitement of ray tracing without typing a single line of C code. Instead of worrying about the equations for illumination, you can focus on the actual creation of your 3-D objects and scenes. Frankly, the following **You Can Do It** section and a quick skim through the POLYRAY.DOC manual on the disk may be all you need to read of this chapter.

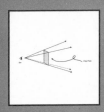

Please note that the copy of POLYRAY that comes with this book is for your evaluation only. If you continue to use the program, you are asked to send the shareware registration fee of $35 directly to the author at the following address:

Alexander Enzmann
20 Clinton St.
Woburn, MA 01801

Please include your name and mailing address.

The author of POLYRAY (who goes by "Xander," a guru-like name if ever there was one), adds

If you formally register this program, you will receive free the next release of Polyray, when it occurs. In addition, you will be contributing to my ability to purchase software tools to make POLYRAY a better program. If you don't register this program, don't feel bad—I'm poor too—but you also shouldn't expect as prompt a response to questions or bugs. Note that the Polyray executable files and the Polyray documents (including POLYRAY.DOC) are copyrighted. The data files are public domain, you may use them any way you please.

You Can Do It: Ray Tracing with POLYRAY

The POLYRAY program has one purpose in life: to transform a scene description text file (usually having the extension .PI) into a bitmapped image file (usually a standard .TGA file). Though you can specify many optional parameters on the command line, the simplest and most common command to ray trace an image looks like this:

```
polyray sample.pi -o sample.tga
```

If you don't specify an output file with the -o switch, POLYRAY will put the image in a file called OUT.TGA (destroying any previous OUT.TGA file that was in the current directory).

Refer to the POLYRAY.DOC manual on the disk for a complete summary of command-line options. We'll just mention a couple of the most handy ones here. To change the resolution of the finished image from that specified within the scene description file itself, use the -x and -y switches, like this:

```
polyray sample.pi -o sample.tga -x 800 -y 600
```

POLYRAY sometimes displays a 320×200 approximation of the image being ray traced on your monitor as it works. Don't worry if this image looks horrible—it's just a rough draft! Use the SVGA program introduced in Chapter 3 to view the TGA files once they're finished.

POLYRAY normally creates high color (15 bits per pixel) images because most people don't have true 24-bit color video cards and couldn't see the extra color resolution. If you do have a way of viewing or printing 24-bit color, you can instruct POLYRAY to create true color files with the -p switch, like this:

```
polyray sample.pi -o sample.tga -p 24
```

A truckload of spectacular public domain scene files are included for you to explore, with batch files to automate the ray tracing of all of them at once if you want. (Again, see POLYRAY.DOC for more details.)

You can also ray trace the 3-D models you created with software from Chapters 7 and 8 of this book. Two programs to translate into POLYRAY format scene files are included on the disk for this purpose: DXF2PI converts .DXF faces into POLYRAY faces and IFS2PI turns .IFS fractals into a collection of POLYRAY spheres. To use DXF2PI, simply go to a directory containing any .DXF file created with the 3DFACES program from Chapter 7, and type:

```
dxf2pi myyurt.dxf myyurt.pi
```

(You can use any names for the .dxf and .pi files, myyurt is just an example.) A complete scene, including a camera pointed at the object and a light source to illuminate it, will be created.

The IFS2PI program works similarly, but you must specify the number of spheres to create and the diameter of each sphere. For example:

```
ifs2pi 3dfern1.ifs fern.pi 5000 5
```

creates a .pi file with 5,000 spheres, each of diameter 5 (that is, a radius of 2.5). Color plates 48 and 50 show ray-traced fractals made with IFS2PI.

If you want to ray trace any scene file that isn't in the same directory as the POLYRAY program (like most of the examples, that are sorted into a number of subdirectories), you should copy the POLYRAY.EXE file to someplace on your hard disk that is on your PATH (defined when your computer starts, in the AUTOEXEC.BAT file). Most people have a directory on their hard disk where they keep utilities, with a name like UTIL or BIN or CMD or something like that. To copy POLYRAY into the UTIL directory, for example, you would enter:

```
copy c:\tgg\polyray.exe c:\util
```

at the DOS prompt. You need only do this once before you run POLYRAY for the first time. (Old-time DOS experts will immediately recognize half a dozen other ways to make POLYRAY.EXE accessible from anywhere on the hard disk. Go ahead and do it whichever way you prefer.) If you're not familiar with fundamental DOS concepts such as PATH and AUTOEXEC.BAT, consult your DOS manual or ask a computer wiz friend to help you copy the POLYRAY.EXE file to the appropriate place on your hard disk.

What is Ray Tracing?

Ray tracing is a method for the generation of [photorealistic] three-dimensional images using the principles of geometric optics. Ray tracing models, albeit simply, the interaction of light and objects within a scene, making possible many of the effects that increase the realism of images: perspective, shadowing, reflection, refraction, and texturing are a few examples. These effects provide the depth information to the viewer's brain that enhances the three-dimensional effects contained in a two-dimensional image.

—Craig A. Lindley, *Practical Ray Tracing in C*, 1992

Ray tracing is a technique for creating two-dimensional images of a three-dimensional world. Imagine your computer screen as a window into a 3-D scene. Now, place your eye (or the camera) at arm's length from the screen. You are now free to look anywhere you like in space, as long as you restrict your vision to the rectangular region defined by the screen. What you see is a world of complex objects. Keep in mind, you can't see the entire 3-D world at once. Something is always behind you. If you want to see it, you have to turn around.

The objects you see have color and texture. If a ball looks red, it's because red light is reaching your eye. Some surfaces look smooth and shiny, other surfaces have a matte look. The shiny surfaces reflect light; the matte surfaces don't reflect as much.

Some of the objects are lamps without shades that give off light in all directions. Yet another source of light is a spotlight, which radiates light in some particular direction. Some of the objects cast a shadow. The shadows move as you reposition the camera. The edges of the shadows are soft and diffuse or sharp and well-defined. You can see some objects in the surface of others. The light rays bounce all around in the scene. The rays that reach the camera lens supply you with the visual sensation of the scene.

Ray tracing has produced the most realistic images to date in computer graphics and is the most complete simulation of an illumination-reflection model in graphics. We've carefully chosen the impressive images of scenes to demonstrate the attributes of ray tracing; primarily the capability to deal with multiple reflections. The classical scenes abound with spheres because of the simple mathematical model required to represent them.

The basic philosophy of ray tracing is that you see a point on a surface as a result of the interaction of the surface at that point with light rays bouncing around elsewhere in the scene. You can achieve the creation of a photorealistic image with a computer via ray tracing after considering the following three elements.

First, you must devise a language to describe the scene. You need elements to describe the location of the camera. This language describes and locates spheres, planes, and quadrics in general within the scene. Each of these objects possess surface characteristics that supply the viewer with the visual sensation of texture. Finally, the language must describe how light illuminates the scene. The lighting component describes the location, intensity, and color of each light.

The next required component is illumination model support. The illumination models are responsible for expressing the factors that determine the color of a surface at a point. The simplest models include support for ambient, diffuse, and specular reflection. In the real world, though, light does not simply reflect. It can also refract (or bend) as it transmits through a surface. The classic example of refraction is viewing a pencil as you place it in a glass of water. The portion of the pencil underwater leads you to believe that it's bent underwater. The pencil is not bending, but the light entering your eye is!

Keep in mind, these lighting models are not always 100 percent physically correct. They are approximations to the underlying rules of optics. The simplifications of Mother Nature's equations that are traditionally implemented in a ray tracer are known as *hacks* and *kludges*. Though the hacks and kludges lack a firm grounding in theory, they work well in practice and deliver usually pleasing results.

The final component is the renderer itself. The renderer is responsible for generating the rays from your eye, through the image plane, and into the scene. Once in the scene, the renderer looks for the intersection of the rays of light with objects. If no intersection is found, the ray flies off into infinity (that is, the background). If the ray does intersect an object, the local color calculations determine the color that results from the direct and indirect illumination received by that point on the surface. If the surface characteristics are such that other objects in the scene influence the color by way of indirect illumination, the renderer fires off (or generates) new rays of light from that point in a direction that approximates nature.

The Language of the Ray Tracer

The ray-tracing approach attempts to simulate light rays within a three-dimensional scene. You begin creating an image by describing a scene as a collection of objects and light sources. The objects are 3-D shapes in space—for example, spheres, polygons, and boxes. A light source is often nothing more than a single point that radiates light uniformly in all directions… You view a scene from a point in space called the eye, through a rectangular window in space called the viewplane.

—Andrew S. Glassner, "Ray Tracing for Realism," *BYTE*, December 1990

The input to the ray tracer is a mathematical model of objects in a three-dimensional world. An ASCII text file describes the mathematics of the objects. The objects consist of cameras, spheres, planes, and light sources. Let's take a look at the attributes of these objects.

Describing the Camera

First, there's the camera. The simplest physical camera model available is the pinhole camera (Figure 9.1). Imagine placing a flat piece of film at the back of a light-proof box. You use a pin to pierce a single hole into the front of the box. Light enters the pinhole and strikes the film, causing a chemical change in the film. When you're done exposing the film, simply cover the pinhole.

You may be wondering why the pinhole is necessary. Well, if you simply exposed the entire sheet of film to the light emanating from the scene, light from all directions would strike all points on the film. Light would saturate the film. The pinhole eliminates this problem by permitting only a very small number of light rays to pass from the scene to the film. In fact, each point on the film can receive light only along the line joining that piece of film and the pinhole. As the pinhole gets bigger, each bit of the film receives more light rays from the scene. This causes the image to become brighter and more blurry.

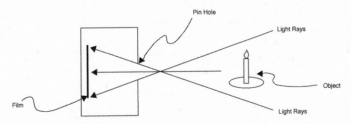

Figure 9.1. *Ray tracing works like a pinhole camera.*

The classic ray tracing version of the pinhole camera moves the plane of the film out in front of the pinhole and renames the pinhole as the eye (Figure 9.2). If you built a real camera this way, it wouldn't work, but our model is fine for computer simulation. In this model, the eye is the ultimate focal point. The film (or recording medium) is now analogous to the computer screen.

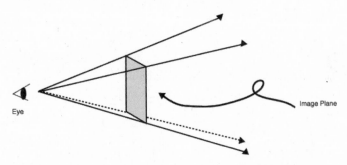

Figure 9.2. *The image, or "film," is a window into the viewing frustrum.*

Keep in mind that in our computer model, the film (or image plane) is a rectangular region. The only objects that the eye can directly see are those that lie within all four edges of the film. In addition, only objects in front of this plane can project an image onto it. If you want to see something behind you, you must turn around so that the film is always between your eye and the object you're seeing.

The three-dimensional volume visible to the eye and bounded by the edges of the film (your screen) is called the *viewing frustrum*. The walls of the frustrum are called *clipping planes.* The plane of the screen is called the *image plane,* and the location of your eye is the *eye position.*

In the POLYRAY scene description language, these collective objects are called a viewpoint. A viewpoint consists of a camera that looks from a convenient point in 3-D space. The three-dimensional coordinate system has the x-axis parallel to the bottom of your monitor, the y-axis parallel to the side of your monitor, and the z-axis comes out of your monitor (Figure 9.3). You need to point the camera in some viewing direction. You can derive that direction by telling the camera at which point in 3-D space to look. Telling the camera where it is and which way to point is not enough. You also have to tell it which way is up. I've included this for completeness of the camera model. Generally, you'll want to orient the camera so that up is always in the positive Y direction. As you become better at describing scenes, though, you may want to vary the resulting image by rotating the camera about the viewing axis. You do this by changing the location of the sky with the up keyword.

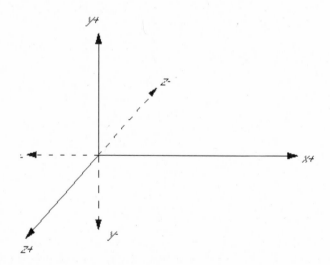

Figure 9.3. *The standard orientation of the x-, y-, and z-axes.*

Finally, you should describe the edges of the image plane in a way that defines the viewing frustrum. You can do this with the angle keyword, followed by a number that describes the field of view in terms of degrees. For example, if the angle is 90 degrees, the viewer can see objects that are 45 degrees to the right and left of the viewing direction.

To define the theoretical size ratio between the horizontal and vertical size of the image plane, use the aspect keyword. The resolution keyword specifies the actual horizontal and vertical resolution of the screen. Generally, you'll want the aspect ratio equal to the ratio between the horizontal and vertical resolution. For example, if the resolution is 640,480, the aspect should be 640,480, which equals 4/3.

If you recall, we previously said that one of the constraints of the pinhole camera was that you could only see objects in front of the image plane. Given this restriction, the maximum value for the angle is 180 degrees.

As you experiment with these values in your scene description, you'll see that you can use them to create visual effects similar to that of telephoto and zoom lenses.

Below, you see an example of the viewpoint component in a scene description file. The viewpoint { keyword begins the definition and the } terminates it. The arguments to from, at, and up are three-dimensional x,y,z coordinates, which you should always enclose in <> and separate by commas. Finally, use numbers to describe the angle, resolution, and aspect.

```
viewpoint {
    from <0, 0, -150>
    at <0, 0, 0>
    up <0, 1 0>
    angle 40
    resolution 640, 480
    aspect 4/3
    }
```

Describing Objects

In addition to the location of the camera, the scene description language governs the geometry and placement of the objects themselves. Look around you for a moment. What do you see? My stereo speakers are parallelpipeds (a type of elongated cube). The flourescent lights overhead are basically cylinders with a finite length. The nerf ball that my daughter is throwing at me is a sphere. The floor my chair rests on is a plane with a somewhat rectangular shape. You see, you can break down the scene that surrounds you into some pretty simple shapes. Ray tracers use a little bit of algebra to calculate the intersection between the light rays and these objects. The two simplest geometric primitives to consider are a sphere and a disc.

Geometric Attributes

An object possesses geometric attributes, positional attributes, and surface attributes. The geometric attributes govern the shape of the object.

The Sphere

Two of the simplest shapes to consider are a sphere and a disc. What we now need is a way to describe these two objects.

The simplest object that is typically supplied for modelling purposes is the sphere. The sphere keyword is followed by the x,y,z location of the center and radius of the sphere.

For example, the following definition tells POLYRAY to place a sphere of radius 4 centered at location 0,0,0:

```
object {
   sphere <0, 0, 0>, 4

   ... positional attributes
   ... surface attributes

}
```

Each object definition begins with the keyword object { and ends with a }. Notice that this is syntactically similar to the definition of a viewpoint.

If you've ever seen a ray-traced picture before, spheres were almost certainly present in the image. The reason behind the seemingly mandatory presence of a sphere is simple: spheres are relatively interesting objects (more so than a plane) that you can generate without incurring the high computational costs of more complex objects described by quartic polynomials. Examples of complex objects include a torus (doughnut) and a piriform (a Hershey's chocolate kiss).

Discs

Here's how you would define a disc of radius 4 centered at 0,0,0, with the flat surface of the disc oriented horizontally.

```
object {
   disc <0, 0, 0>, <0, 1, 0>, 4
```

```
... positional attributes
... surface attributes


}
```

The first set of `<x, y, z>` cordinates specifies the center of the disc, and the second set specifies the direction of the *normal vector*, which describes the direction of a line sticking straight out from the center of the disc, perpendicular to its flat surface. In this case, the *normal* is identical to the up vector defined earlier in the `viewpoint` section. Therefore, someone standing on the disc would be pointing their head up.

Let's investigate the mathematics of a sphere and disc by digressing for a moment into a bit of mental gymnastics.

The Math Behind the Magic: Distance and Plane Equations

To express the equation for a sphere, simply find all points that are a given distance (the radius) from the center. This equation does it:

$$\text{distance} = \sqrt{x^2 + y^2 + z^2}$$

The vector equation of a plane that passes through the point $P:(X_1, Y_1, Z_1)$ and is perpendicular to vector $N = [Nx\ \ Ny\ \ Nz]$ is

$$\vec{N} \cdot \vec{R} = 0$$

where $R = [X{-}X_1\ \ Y{-}Y_1\ \ Z{-}Z_1]$ is the vector represented by the line segment from P to an arbitrary point Q in the plane. You may not recall this definition of a plane from calculus. In fact, most people are more familiar with the equation

$Ax + By + Cz + D = 0$

As it turns out, you can derive Equation 9.3 from Equation 9.2 by performing the dot product indicated between N and R in Equation 2. This gives

$[Nx\ \ Ny\ \ Nz] \bullet [X{-}X_1\ \ Y{-}Y_1\ \ Z{-}Z_1] = 0$

$Nx(X{-}X_1) + Ny(Y{-}Y_1) + Nz(Z{-}Z_1) = 0$

$NxX + NyY + NzZ + (-NxX_1 - NyY_1 - NzZ_1) = 0$

> If you look carefully at Equations 9.3 and 9.4, you can now see that Nx is A, Ny is B, Nz is C, and D is $-NxX_1 - NyY_1 - NzZ_1$. Nx, Ny, and Nz describe the generic orientation of the plane in space, whereas D picks out one of the members of the family.
>
> To slice a disc out of the plane, simply use the distance formula in Equation 9.1 to find the intersection of the plane and a sphere.

Positional Attributes

The next attribute of an object is its positional attribute. As you recall, the three basic transformations you can perform on an object in 3-D space—or 2-D space, for that matter—are *rotating*, *scaling*, and *translating* (also called *spin*, *size*, and *move*). Each of these transformations are applied to the object in the top down order that they appear in the scene description file. You can apply any or all of these three tranformation types to any object, like this:

```
object {
   disc <0, 0, 0>, <0, 1, 0>, 4

   rotate    <10, 0, 0>
   translate <0, 10, 0>
   scale     <40, 40, 40>

   ... surface attributes

}
```

Rotating, Translating, and Scaling an Object

The rotate keyword is followed by the clockwise angular rotation in degrees of the object about a particular axis. When the rotate keyword appears as the previous example, the object first rotates about the x-axis, the y-axis, and finally the z-axis. However, because matrix multiplication is not commutative, you may be wondering how to rotate about the z-axis, y-axis, and then x-axis. That's simple. The scene description language permits multiple instances of the rotate, translate, and scale keywords to facilitate the positioning of an object. So, here's how you would describe a rotational transformation about the z-, y-, and x-axes.

```
object {
    disc <0, 0, 0>, <0, 1, 0>, 4

    rotate      <0, 0, 20>
    rotate      <0, 10, 0>
    rotate      <155, 0, 0>
    translate <0, 10, 0>
    scale       <40, 40, 40>

    ... surface attributes

}
```

The `translate` keyword precedes the displacement that is added to each point on the object. Recall that translation does not suffer from the commutative problems that rotation does. As such, you can reduce consecutive translations to one.

Finally, the `scale` keyword precedes values that represent the stretching of each point along a particular axis. Scaling values greater than one causes an object to grow in size. Values greater than zero and less than one cause the object to shrink. Values less than 0 cause the object to be mirrored across the scaling axis. Like translation, scaling does not suffer from the commutative problems that rotation does.

Surface Attributes

The final attribute of an object is its surface attribute. As you might imagine, this attribute is responsible for the level of photorealism in the ray traced image. To complete the description of your disc object, you can introduce the `color`, `ambient`, `diffuse`, and `specular` keywords.

```
object {
    disc <0, 0, 0>, <0, 1, 0>, 4

    rotate      <0, 0, 20>
    rotate      <0, 10, 0>
    rotate      <155, 0, 0>
    translate <0, 10, 0>
    scale       <40, 40, 40>

    texture {
        surface {
```

```
        color <1, 0, 0>
        ambient 0.2
        diffuse 0.8
        specular 1
        }
    }
}
```

The surface attributes of an object always start with `texture { surface {` and end with `} }`.

The `color` keyword describes the color of the object by assigning a fractional number from 0 to 1 to the red, green, and blue components.

Using this system, `<0, 0, 0>` is black, `<1, 1, 1>` is white, and `<0.5, 0.5, 0.5>` is medium gray. The reason behind using the RGB color system is purely arbitrary. Because most 24-bit frame buffers are implemented at the hardware level using red, green, and blue components, this may seem a natural choice. After all, when the color of a point on an object is calculated, each component of the resulting RGB value can be multiplied by 256 (the number of color levels per component) and then written into the frame buffer. However, be aware that other color models exist that facilitate a more intuitive "feel" of color. One such model is the HSV model. HSV stands for hue, saturation, and value. This user-oriented model is based on the intuitive appeal of the artist's tint, shade, and tone. The use of this color model can make the specification of an object's color easier to imagine (at the expense of learning how the system works). Many digital paint packages present the user with an HSV or RGB based model when asking the user to interactively specify a color from a palette.

The remaining surface attribute keywords are called `ambient`, `diffuse`, and `specular`. The `ambient` value describes the amount of ambient light that an object reflects. This coefficient is a material property. Think of it as characterizing the material that composes the object.

The `diffuse` keyword describes the amount of light reflected by an object as a function of the direction and distance to the light source.

Finally, the `specular` keyword describes the degree of shininess of an object. For example, imagine illuminating an apple with a bright white light. The highlight on the apple results from the apple's specular reflection properties, whereas the light reflected from the rest of the apple results from diffuse reflection. Like the `ambient` keyword, the value of `specular` is closely associated with the object's underlying material properties.

The section concerning illumination model support discusses the `ambient`, `diffuse`, and `specular` keywords in greater detail.

POLYRAY also enables you to create reflective surfaces with the `reflection` keyword and to define complex textures once at the beginning of a file rather than spelling out the entire definition for each object. For example, you could define a mirror texture like this:

```
define mirror
  texture {
    surface {
      color white
      ambient 0.1
      diffuse 0.1
      specular 0
      reflection 1
      }
    }
```

You could then give any object a mirrored surface by simply specifying the word `mirror` within its `object` definition. Notice that POLYRAY enables you to use color names like `white`, `red`, `blue`, and so forth without defining them yourself.

Composite Objects

Now that we've described the basics of an object, we'd like to introduce a useful extension to the POLYRAY scene description language that simplifies the building of complex models. At this point, the only two types of objects we can describe are discs and spheres. We might add a `cylinder` object that represents a cylinder with radius 2 and is parallel to the z-axis somewhere in the x-y plane with a radius of R. Let's then describe a dumbell by placing two `sphere` objects with a radius of 4 along the z-axis at z = 15 and z = -15.

If we decided to move the resulting dumbbell, we would have to add a `translate` keyword to each of the three object definitions.

What a nuisance!

Let's instead enclose the three `object` definitions within a single composite `object` definition, using the + symbol to add them together. Then, as shown below, we can simply add any combination of the positional and texture attributes to the composite object.

```
object {
  object {
```

```
    sphere <-7, 0, 0>, 4
    } +
object {
    sphere <7, 0, 0>, 4
    } +
object {
    cylinder <-5, 0, 0>, <5, 0, 0>, 2
    }
scale <0.5, 0.5, 0.5>
rotate <0, 60, 0>
translate <20, -2, 5>
mirror
}
```

The result is a model that is much simpler to maintain.

Light Sources

The last type of keywords in our scene description language describe the attributes of the light sources. Here again, look around you and observe how your environment is illuminated. The two shaded lamps in my office provide me with enough light to do my job, while adding a warm glow with some soft shadows in the background. However, my 4-year-old daughter has just walked in and decided to blast me with the light from her Mickey Mouse flashlight.

The light keyword enables us to model the light from the lamp shades, whereas the spot_light keyword describes the directional light source that Mickey emits. The light has a very basic syntax. It is light <Px Py Pz> where Px, Py, and Pz are the coordinates of the light source. This type of light source gives off light in all directions. It is useful for flooding a scene with light. For example, to set up a point light source at 30,–100,100, you would simply say:

```
light <30,-100,100>
```

The spot_light keyword is much more interesting. Imagine viewing the Mickey Mouse flashlight from the side. It is an excellent model of the spot_light light source. The light originates from some point in space and is directed to some point. Then, we face the issue of the light itself. The rays of light emanate from a point light source but are constrained by the boundaries of a cone (Figure 9.4). The *hotspot,* or *tightness* of the light, determines how quickly the brightness of the light changes from the center to the edges of the cone. To complicate matters further, the light does not suddenly stop at the edges of the spotlight cone, but gradually fades out. Therefore, you need to specify a minimum angle for the light cone and a maximum angle called the *falloff*. The overall syntax of the `spot_light` keyword is

```
spot_light <from>, <to>, tightness, angle, falloff
```

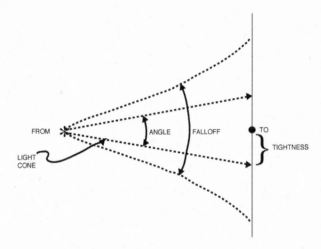

Figure 9.4. *The structure of a spotlight beam.*

For example, to create a spotlight at 0,100,10 pointing at 0,0,0 with a tightness of 3, a cone angle of 5, and a falloff angle of 20, you would say:

```
spot_light white, <0, -100, 10>, <0, 0, 0>, 3, 5, 20
```

Putting all the previous examples together, you would have

```
// Simple sample POLYRAY scene description
// from Tricks of the Graphics Gurus

viewpoint {                    //first, set up the camera
    from <0, 0, -40>           //location of the eye
    at <0, 0, 0>               //where the eye is looking
    up <0, -1, 0>              //which way is up
    angle 40                   //vertical view angle
    resolution 640, 480        //size of the image in pixels
    aspect 4/3                 //aspect ratio of image (x/y)
    }

background <0.5, 0.5, 1> //make the background light blue
```

```
light <30, -100, -100>      //a point light and a spotlight
spot_light white, <0, -100, 10>, <0, 0, 0>, 3, 5, 20

define shiny_red            //define the word shiny_red
  texture {                 //to mean a surface texture and color
    surface {
      color <1, 0, 0>       //you could also say "color red" here
      ambient 0.2           //a little red color everywhere
      diffuse 0.8           //a lot of red wherever light hits
      specular white, 0.9   //and a shiny white highlight
      }
    }

define mirror               //define a mirror texture
  texture {
    surface {
      color white           //eqivalent to "color <1, 1, 1>"
      ambient 0.1           //a little white all over
      diffuse 0.1           //a little more where light hits
      specular 0            //no shiny highlights at all
      reflection 1          //totally reflective
      }
    }

object {                    //first object is a sphere
  sphere <0, 0, 0>, 4       //centered at 0,0,0 with radius 4
  shiny_red                 //give it the texture defined above
    }

object {                    //next object is a disc
  disc <0, 0, 0>, <0, 1, 0>, 1   //center, normal, radius
  scale     <20, 1, 20>     //enlarge it 20 times along x and z
  rotate    <0, 45, 0>      //spin 45 degrees around the y-axis
  rotate    <15, 0, 0>      //then tilt 15 degrees around x
  translate <0, 6, 0>       //move it down 6
  texture {                 //red squares and mirrored squares
    checker shiny_red, mirror
    scale <0.3, 0.3, 0.3>   //textures can be scaled, too!
    }
  }
```

```
object {                    //a compound dumb bell object
   object {
      sphere <-7, 0, 0>, 4
      } +
   object {
      sphere <7, 0, 0>, 4
      } +
   object {
      cylinder <-5, 0, 0>, <5, 0, 0>, 2
      }
   scale <0.5, 0.5, 0.5>
   rotate <0, 60, 0>
   translate <20, -2, 5>
   mirror                    //give it the mirror texture
   }
```

This example is in the file called sample.pi on the disk, if you want to ray trace it yourself or make modifications.

Figure 9.5 shows the result of ray tracing the SAMPLE.PI file with POLYRAY.

Figure 9.5. *The SAMPLE.PI file listed previously looks like this when it becomes a ray-traced picture.*

Animation support

POLYRAY has built-in support for animation sequences, too. You can simply specify a start_frame, end_frame, and several total_frames, and then use the frame keyword as a number in any definition, position attribute, or any other number. For example, the following listing of the ANIMBALL.PI file shows how the sphere in SAMPLE.PI could be made to bounce.

```
// Simple sample POLYRAY animation
// from Tricks of the Graphics Gurus

start_frame   0          //first frame number of animation
end_frame     19         //final frame number
total_frames 20          //total number of frames
outfile anima            //first 5 letters of output files

define floor_height -6
define ball_radius 4
define max_deform 2
define ball_height (floor_height + max_deform) *
                cos(radians(360 / total_frames * frame))
define ball_def    (ball_height < (floor_height + ball_radius) ?
                (ball_height - floor_height) / ball_radius : 1)
define ball_deform ball_def * (1 + (1 - ball_def))

viewpoint {              //first, set up the camera
    from <0, 0, -40>     //location of the eye
    at <0, 0, 0>         //where the eye is looking
    up <0, 1, 0>         //which way is up
    angle 40             //vertical view angle
    resolution 320, 200  //size of the image in pixels
    aspect 4/3           //aspect ratio of image (x/y)
    }

background <0.5, 0.5, 1> //make the background light blue
light <30, 100, -100>    //set up one point light source

define shiny_red         //define the word shiny_red
  texture {              //to mean a surface texture and color
```

```
    surface {
      color <1, 0, 0>      //you could also say "color red" here
      ambient 0.2          //a little red color everywhere
      diffuse 0.8          //a lot of red wherever light hits
      specular white, 0.9  //and a shiny white highlight
      }
    }

define mirror              //define a mirror texture
  texture {
    surface {
      color white          //eqivalent to "color <1, 1, 1>"
      ambient 0.1          //a little white all over
      diffuse 0.1          //a little more where light hits
      specular 0           //no shiny highlights at all
      reflection 1         //totally reflective
      }
    }

object {                   //first object is a sphere
   sphere <0, ball_height, 0>, ball_radius
   scale <1, ball_deform, 1>
   shiny_red               //give it the texture defined above
     }

object {                   //next object is a disc
   disc <0, 0, 0>, <0, 1, 0>, 1   //center, normal, radius
   scale     <20, 1, 20>   //enlarge it 20 times along x and z
   rotate    <0, 45, 0>    //spin 45 degrees around the y-axis
   translate <0, floor_height, 0>    //move it down
   texture {               //red squares and mirrored squares
     checker shiny_red, mirror
     scale <0.3, 0.3, 0.3>  //textures can be scaled, too!
     }
   }
```

Figure 9.6 shows the ray-traced results of the previous scene description.

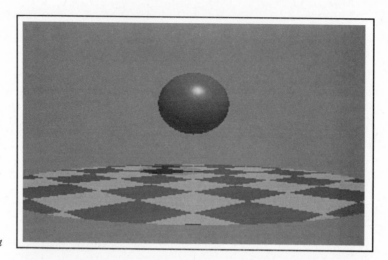

a

b

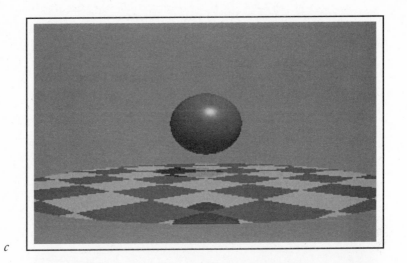

c

d

e

f

Figure 9.6. *The ANIMBALL.PI sequence described above. Notice that the ball even deforms as it bounces!*

A special sample file, called ANIM.PI, contains the camera and light setup to make any scene created by DXF2PI or IFS2PI rotate in 3-D space. Simply replace the viewpoint and light settings in the .PI file you want to animate with the contents of ANIM.PI, then trace away. Figure 9.7 shows some frames from a sequence created with IFS2PI.EXE and ANIM.PI.

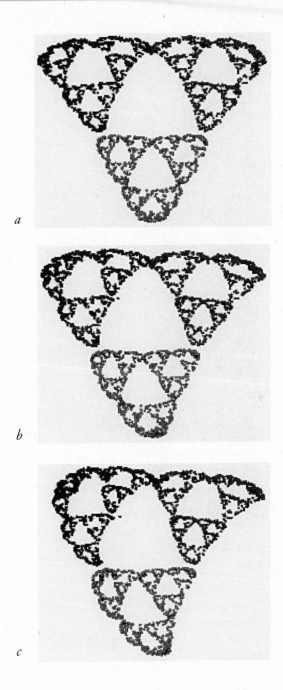

a

b

c

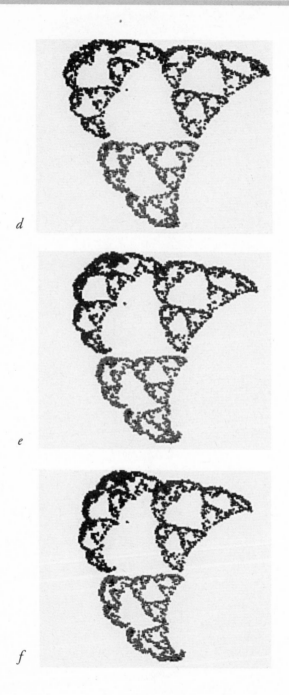

d

e

f

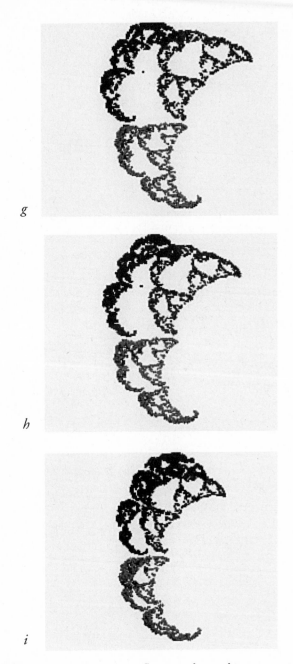

g

h

i

Figure 9.7. *The ANIM.PI file lets you fly around any object.*

To assemble multiple-frame sequences into a single .FLI format animation file, I recommend the freeware program DTA (Dave's Targa Animator), available for a $5 distribution fee using the Cedar Software order form in the back of this book or from on your favorite graphics Bulletin Board System.

The POLYRAY.DOC File

At this point, you may want to skim through the POLYRAY.DOC manual on the disk—especially the quick tutorial section—and ray trace some of the many sample scenes. (A few of the examples, including a sampler of all the POLYRAY shapes used in ALLPRIMS.PI, appear in the color plates in the middle of this book.)

In the rest of this chapter, we'll open up the hood and show you how a ray tracer really works. This is heady business, and the separate **Math Behind the Magic** sections will fall by the wayside as formulas and somewhat technical text mingle on the page. So, if you just want to create ray-traced pictures, crank up the computer and spend your time getting your feet wet rather than squinting at the next few pages.

Illumination Model Support

Photorealism is within your grasp. Follow the light.

—Andrew Glassner, "Ray Tracing for Realism," *BYTE*, December 1990

In the previous section, we introduced the language that you can use to describe a scene for POLYRAY to ray trace. The next step is to express the factors that determine a surface's color at a given point. Many of the illumination models traditionally used in raytracing include simplifications of the underlying optics that deviate significantly from theory but that work well in practice. These simplifications are usually implemented because modelling reality just takes too long to compute.

In order to generate realistics images, you need to understand how light behaves on the surfaces of objects. This is not an easy issue to discuss because many of the subtleties of light are still poorly understood. However, you can use some approximations to generate surprisingly good images. Before examining the intensity equation that you'll use to describe the color of a point, take a moment to look at the issues surrounding light.

When you look at an ordinary white light bulb, you see "white" light, but white light is not a pure spectral color. There is no single photon of light that can vibrate to give you the impression of white light. Instead, the impression of white arises when photons of many different colors strike your eye at the same time. Your eye blends each of the colors together to give you the impression of white. But what are these colors? Well, high school physics teachers have taught their classes about ROY G. BIV for years. ROY G. BIV is an acronym for red, orange, yellow, green, blue, indigo, and violet. These are the colors of light in the visible portion of the electromagnetic spectrum, that when blended together produce the sensation called white light.

For simplicity, all the light sources in our scene description language are white light. When you associate a color with an object, you are really saying that when an incident ray of white light hits your object, the object absorbs all the light except the color that you designate. For example, when you shine a white light upon a red ball, you describe the ball as being red because red is the color that reaches your eyes. All the other spectral components of the white light are absorbed by the material of the ball.

The Illumination Equation

Now that you understand the meaning of color, you need to create a mathematical model that you can use to implement in the ray tracer. The purpose of this model is to describe the intensity of a given ray of colored light that is bouncing off an object toward your eye. Here's Equation 9.5, the simplified illumination equation. Whatever you do, don't panic. After we're done explaining it, you'll see that it's really not that nasty looking.

$$I = I_a K_a + \sum_{i=1}^{M} Ip_i \left[K_d \left(\vec{N} \cdot \vec{L_i} \right) + K_s \left(\vec{R_i} \cdot \vec{V} \right)^n \right]$$

Ambient Reflection

You can express an illumination model by an illumination equation in variables associated with the point on the object being shaded. The illumination equation that expresses the simplest model is

$I = Ia\, Ka$

In this model, I is the resulting intensity of light, Ia is the intensity of the ambient light, and Ka, the *ambient reflection* coefficient, is the amount of ambient light reflected from an object's surface. This coefficient reflects the objects underlying material properties because it characterizes the material of which the object is made. What does this mean in the context of our scene description language? Well, each of our objects has a `color` associated with it. They may also have an `ambient` keyword. For simplicity, the intensity of the ambient light, Ia, is equivalent to the `color` of the object. The coefficient that follows the `ambient` keyword corresponds to Ka, the ambient reflection coefficient. Equation 9.6 is applied to each of the red, green, and blue components of the `color` to produce the intensity of the object (in terms of its ambience) at a given point. For example, assume you defined a sphere like this:

```
object {
    sphere <0, 0, 15>, 4
    texture {
        surface {
            color  <1, 0.5, 1>
            ambient 0.75
            }
        }
    }
```

The color of the ambient light reflected by all points on the sphere would equal `<0.75, 0.375, 0.75>`. You simply multiply 0.75 by each of the components in the `color` to produce the color of the reflected ambient light. Easy, huh.

Diffuse Reflection

Let's continue the dissection of Equation 9.5. Although objects illuminated by ambient light are more or less brightly lit in direct proportion to the ambient intensity, they are still uniformly illuminated across their surfaces. Now, consider illuminating the object from a point light source with rays emanating uniformly in all directions from a single point. Think about the results of this for a moment. The object's brightness now varies from one point on the surface to the next, depending on the direction of and the distance to the light source.

Dull, matte surfaces, such as chalk, exhibit *diffuse reflection*, also known as *Lambertian reflection*. These surfaces appear equally bright from all viewing angles because they reflect light with equal intensity in all directions. For a given surface, the brightness depends only on the angle θ between the direction L to the light source and the surface normal N (Figure 9.8).

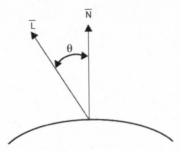

Figure 9.8. *The illumination of a surface depends on the angle at which a light ray strikes it.*

Again, take a moment to think about this. Stand behind a flashlight and shine it at some point on a dull surface. Observe the amount of light reflected back into your eye. Then, while pointing the light at the same point and staring at the point, move your head out from behind the flashlight to the left or right. Though you are no longer observing the point along the axis of the light, the amount that your eye receives does not change. In fact, the only way to change the amount of light that reaches your eye (independent of the position of your eye), is to change the angle between the ray of light and the surface normal at the point you are observing. Thus, for Lambertian surfaces, the amount of light seen by the viewer is independent of the viewer's direction and proportional only to cos θ. This results in a diffuse illumination equation of:

$I = Ip\ Kd \cos \theta$

In this equation, *Ip* is the intensity of the point light source, and *Kd* is the diffuse reflection coefficient, typically a value from 0 to 1. Given the vast number of computations that a ray tracer must perform, keeping them as simple as possible is always a good idea. The question is "How are we going to determine the cosine of θ if we don't know θ?" Recall that the dot product of two normalized vectors equals the cosine of the angle between them. So, when evaluating Equation 9.7, normalize *L* and *N* by dividing each by their length, and then dot the two normal vectors.

The result is ready to be multiplied by *Kd* to determine the intensity of the diffusely reflected light (Equation 9.8).

$$I = I_p K_d \left(\vec{N} \cdot \vec{L_i} \right)$$

Again, in the context of our ray tracer, *Ip* is equal to 1 because the light sources are white with each of the red, green, and blue components at full intensity. *Kd* of course corresponds to the coefficient that follows the `diffuse` keyword. By combining Equations 9.6 and 9.8, you're left with something looking more and more like Equation 9.5.

Specular Reflection

The final term in Equation 9.5 concerns specular reflection. This is a phenomenon that you can observe on any shiny surface such as that of an apple. When illuminated with white light, the highlight is caused by specular reflection, whereas the light reflected from the rest of the apple results from diffuse reflection. Also, note that the highlight appears to be white, the color of the light source. Now, move your head and notice how the highlight also moves. It does so because shiny surfaces reflect light unequally in different directions. In fact, on a mirror, light reflects only in the direction of reflection R, which is I mirrored about N. Thus, the viewer V can only see specularly reflected light from a mirror when the direction R corresponds to the direction from the point on the object to the viewer himself (Figure 9.9).

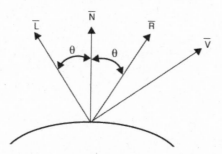

Figure 9.9. *Specular reflection scatters light slightly as it reflects.*

"Huh?" you say. Well, look at an example. Imagine you're on a basketball court, and you want to pass the ball to your teammate by bouncing it on the ground. You'd probably aim the ball to bounce about halfway between you and your teammate. If your teammate is located along the vector R, he receives the ball. Otherwise, he misses the pass. All this, of course, happens in a perfect world. Our model of specular reflection is a gross simplification of what happens. The fact is, no such thing as a perfectly specular surface exists. This leads back to one of my opening statements about lighting models being hacks or kludges. This may not be an absolute model of reality, but it comes close.

Phong Bui-Tuong developed a popular model for nonperfect reflectors like the apple. This model assumes that maximum specular reflectance occurs when Σ, the angle between R and V, is zero. The reflectance then falls off sharply as Σ increases. This rapid falloff is approximated in Phong's model by $\cos n\Sigma$, where n is the material's specular reflection exponent. A value of 1 provides a gentle falloff, whereas higher values simulate a sharp, focused highlight (Figure 9.10).

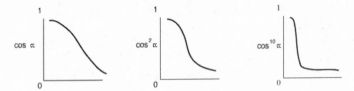

Figure 9.10. *Phong shading creates specular highlights.*

If the direction of reflection R, and the viewpoint direction V are normalized, then $\cos n\Sigma = R - V$. Phong's model can then be written as $\cos n\Sigma = (R - V)n$. In the context of POLYRAY, this corresponds to the coefficient that follows the `specular` keyword. This value and n are selected experimentally (like most of the coefficients) to produce aesthetically pleasing results. Note that the color of the specular component in Phong's model is not dependent on any material property. Because the properties of the surface itself affect specular reflection, it may have a different color than diffuse reflection when the surface is made of several materials.

After showing you Phong's model for the specular component, Equation 9.5 should finally make sense (with the possible exception of the summation (Σ) and the use of i as a subscript). You see, the derivation work is for finding the color of a point on a surface when illuminated by one light source. If multiple light sources exist in the scene description, you perform the similar calculation for each one and add them all together. The result is Equation 9.5, the illumination equation.

The problem with the summation in Equation 9.5 is that the resulting I can exceed the maximum displayable pixel value. You can use several aproaches to avoid the overflow. The simplest is to limit the normalized value of each component of I to 1. Yep, that's right. If the red component of I is greater than 1, set the red component equal to 1. The other possibility is to write each of the calculated values to the output file. When the ray tracing is done, a post processing program can rescale the values in the image after searching for the minimum and maximum values present. I personally prefer the simpler method mentioned.

Sweet Simplicity

Due to the computational overhead of ray tracing, ray trace-aholics are always looking for ways of writing complex equations more simply. Most vectors in Equation 9.5 will be given to you, except R, the reflection vector. Fortunately, you can calculate this without expensive trigonometric functions (Figure 9.11).

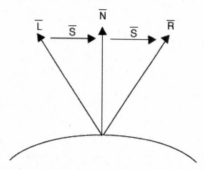

Figure 9.11. *You can calculate reflection vectors without using computationally expensive trigonometric functions.*

First, assume N and L are normalized (if they aren't, divide each component of N and L by the length of each of the respective vectors). You then have the projection of L onto N as $N \cos (\theta)$. Now, using a little vector arithmetic you can see that

$$R = N \cos (\theta) + S$$

By similar triangles, though, S is just $N \cos (\theta) - L$. If you substitute $N \cos (\theta) - L$ for S into the previous definition of R, you have

$$R = 2N \cos (\theta) - L$$

Because $N \cdot L$ equals $\cos (\theta)$, you're left with

$$R = 2N (N \cdot L) - L$$

The Renderer

Of all the methods to render solids, ray tracing is probably the easiest to understand. Basically, you take a straight line (ray), drawn from your eye through a pixel on the screen, and see what objects it hits in the computer universe. You then find whichever object is closest to the origin of that line (your eye), and color the pixel on the screen the color of the object. If that object reflects or refracts, you just need to compute the new direction of the line and repeat the process from the new origin. Pretty simple, really.

—Daniel Lyke, "Ray Tracing: Rendering Solid Objects is Easier than You Think," *Dr. Dobb's Journal,* September 1990

We've now described the language of the ray tracer and the equations governing the color of an object. The third and final component to address is the overall mechanics of ray tracing. Keep in mind what you are trying to accomplish. The purpose of ray tracing is to determine the visibility of a surface and establish its color by tracing imaginary rays of light from the viewer's eye to the objects in the scene.

Establishing the color of the surface is a simple matter of determining how much light falls upon the point from a light source. The trick here is that the light source may be the surface of another Object A. The light source for Object A may be Object B. Finally, a real live light source illuminates Object B (Figure 9.12). This self-defining statement leads to an obvious implementation choice: recursion. Therein lies the elegance of the solution.

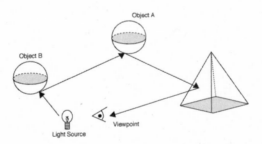

Figure 9.12. *A ray may reflect off multiple objects before it reaches your eye.*

Start by looking at the pseudocode for a simple recursive ray tracer. The Trace function in Listing 9.1 determines the closest intersection the ray makes with an object and calls Shade to determine the shade at that point. The Shade function proceeds to implement the illumination equation described earlier. If you aren't too deep in the tree of reflected rays, a recursive call is made to trace the reflected ray. The ultimate goal is to return a color that corresponds with a pixel on the projection plane. When all pixels in the projection plane have a color assigned, the synthesizing is complete. It really is that simple.

441

Listing 9.1. A recursive ray tracer.

```
Parse the scene description file and create an internal representation

Select the center of projection

FOR each scan line in the image DO

    FOR each pixel in the scan line DO
    BEGIN

        Ray = The ray from the center of projection through the pixel
thePixelColor = Trace(Ray, 1)
        Write thePixelColor

    END

END


COLOR Trace(Ray, Depth)
BEGIN

    Determine intersection of ray with all objects to find
        the closest object


    If an object is hit then
    BEGIN

        Compute surface normal at intersection point

        return Shade(closest object, ray, intersection, normal, depth)

    END
    else
        return theBackgroundColor

END


COLOR Shade(object, ray, point, normal, depth)
BEGIN
```

```
color = AmbientTerm

FOR each light DO
BEGIN

    color = color + DiffuseTerm + SpecularTerm
END

If depth < MaximumDepth
BEGIN
    reflectedRay   = ray in reflection direction from point
    reflectedColor = Trace(reflectedRay, depth+1)
    color          = color + reflectedColor
END

return color
END
```

Ray-Plane Intersection

Unfortunately, we have glossed over a veritable olympiad of mental gymnastics. These gymnastics involve the calculation of the intersection between a ray and object. In our original introduction to the POLYRAY scene description language, we allowed for the creation of two primitive objects. One object was a plane and the other a sphere. Begin by investigating the effort to compute the intersection between a ray and a plane.

The intersection calculations are easily computed using parametric representations of the ray and plane. First, define a ray as shown in Equation 9.9.

$Ro = [Xo \ Yo \ Zo]$ (the ray's origin)

$Rd = [Xd \ Yd \ Zd]$ (the ray's direction, assumes Rd is normalized)

$R(t) = Ro + tRd$ (parametric representation)

Next, you need to define the plane. Equation 9.3 has already done this for us. So, the distance from the ray's origin to the intersection with the plane is derived by substituting the parametric definition of the ray into Equation 9.3. This yields

$$A(Xo + tXd) + B(Yo + tYd) + C(Zo + tZd) + D = 0$$

and solving for *t* you get

$$t = \frac{-(AX_o + BY_o + CZ_o + D)}{AX_d + BY_d + CZ_d}$$

In vector notation, this equation is

$$t = \frac{-(P_n \cdot R_o + D)}{P_n \cdot P_d}$$

The goal now is to minimize unnecessary calculations in determining whether the ray and plane intersect. You do this by first calculating *Pn • Rd*. If the result is zero, the ray is parallel to the plane and no intersection occurs. Otherwise, compute the number and perform the required division to yield *t*. If *t* is less than zero, the line defined by the ray intersects the plane behind the ray's origin, so no intersection occurs. Otherwise, the intersection point is

= [*Xo+tXd Yo+tYd Zo+tZd*]

Ray-Sphere Intersection

The intersection calculations between a ray and plane are a good warm-up for our next event. To calculate the intersection between a ray and sphere, you will use a similar algebraic approach based upon parametric representations. The parametric form of the ray in Equation 9.9 will work fine, but, like the plane, you will use the implicit form of the sphere. The surface of the sphere is expressed in Equation 9.10. In this form, points on the surface cannot be directly generated. Instead, each point [*Xs Ys Zs*] can be tested by the implicit equation. If the point satisfies the equation, it is on the surface.

Sr   (the sphere's radius)

Sc = [*Xc Yc Zc*]   (the sphere's center)

The sphere's surface is the set of points [*Xs Ys Zs*] that satisfy

$$(Xs{-}Xc)^2 + (Ys{-}Yc)^2 + (Zs{-}Zc)^2 = Sr^2$$

To solve for the intersection between the ray and the sphere, the ray equation is substituted into the sphere equation. From this you obtain

$$(Xo{+}tXd{-}Xc)^2 + (Yo{+}tYd{-}Yc)^2 + (Zo{+}tZd{-}Zc)^2 = Sr^2$$

This can be simplified into a quadratic equation of the form

$At^2 + Bt^2 + C = 0$

where

$$A = X_d^2 + Y_d^2 + Z_d^2$$

$B = 2[Xd(Xo-Xc) + Yd(Yo-Yc) + Zd(Zo-Zc)]$

$C = (Xo-Xc)2 + (Yo-Yc)2 + (Zo-Zc)2 - Sr2$

however, $A = 1$ because it was assumed in Equation 9.9 that the direction of the ray was normalized. By substituting the values of A, B, and C into the quadratic equation, you find the two roots, t_0 and t_1, to be

$$t_0 = -B - \frac{\sqrt{B^2 - 4C}}{2}$$

$$t_1 = -B + \frac{\sqrt{B^2 - 4C}}{2}$$

When the discriminant (the expression under the radical) is negative, the ray misses the sphere. Otherwise, the smaller, positive real root is the closest intersection distance on the ray. Then, in fashion similar to the ray-plane intersection, the value of t is substituted into the following equation to determine the actual intersection point

$Ri = [Xo+tXd \ \ Yo+tYd \ \ Zo+tZd]$

Looking Forward

We've presented the basics of the POLYRAY scene description language, the beginnings of an illumination model, and a description of how a renderer actually operates. After you've toyed with what we have described, you may begin looking for the next level of complexity in ray tracing. POLYRAY is capable of much more than we've described in this chapter, including:

- Calculation of shadows
- Accounting for occluded light sources
- Mapping textures or patterns onto a surface
- Antialiasing the image by super sampling the scene
- Support for cones, ellipsoids, donuts, trigonometrics, and polynomials
- Depth-of-field support in the model of the camera
- Support for refraction of light rays as they pass through an object

This list is by no means complete. It's meant as a springboard for enhancements to the foundation that's been laid. The POLYRAY.DOC file and the numerous example files show you the syntax of all these advanced features and more. With them, we hope you enjoy the journey into the land of ray tracing as much as we do.

IV

Graphics Within
Microsoft Windows™

The Windows Graphics Device Interface

I f you like graphics programs that are easy to use, easy to learn, and easy to create (and don't mind jumping into a new, sometimes disorienting computing environment to obtain them) you'll love Microsoft Windows. Everyone knows that Windows includes a slew of hot features to make users' lives easier. The consistent *graphical user interface* (GUI) makes learning new Windows applications a snap, *multitasking* enables you to run several Windows programs at once, and *what-you-see-is-what-you-get* (WYSIWYG) text and graphics let you create and print snazzy documents with ease.

One of the biggest secrets to Windows' success, however, is hiding behind the Windows shades. Users couldn't reap all the benefits of Windows today if programmers had to slave for ten years to churn out a great Windows application. Fortunately, the Windows operating system offers at least as many advantages to graphics programmers as to the people who use their programs.

In this chapter, Windows guru James McCord will join me (Dick Oliver, your smiley *Tricks of the Graphics Gurus* host) to show you how you can make Windows do half the work for you. You'll create a simple Windows program from the ground up with just a few powerful function calls. Jim and I also introduce you to the *graphics device interface* (GDI), the keystone of Windows' powerful graphics system. When you learn to use the GDI, your graphics programs are instantly compatible with nearly every graphics card, display, and printer in existence.

Even if you aren't a programmer—and you don't plan on becoming one any time soon—you will benefit from a glance behind those Windows shades. You can skip the **Working Code** sections and still gain an understanding of how and why Windows works and of what to expect when using Windows graphics applications.

Welcome to Windows

We now have a standard hardware architecture, the PC. We desperately need a standard software platform, one that provides mainframe amenities like virtual memory management and preemptive multitasking. We must have one standard user interface, so that computing can become as common and transportable a skill in our society as driving a car.

If both technical capability and market presence are equally necessary (and they are), Windows, while far from perfect, is our best shot.

—Jeff Dunteman, "Windows Outlook," *PC Techniques*, Feb/March 1992, p. 48

The primary job of many graphics programmers is to develop an intuitive, attractive GUI for the applications they develop. During application development, programmers devote a great deal of time and energy to designing and developing the user interface. Of course, once you design the interface, you still must develop the actual *functionality*—the work that the program was meant to do in the first place.

For those of you who have attempted to create a GUI from the ground up (as most of us who developed serious DOS applications have), you know just how difficult designing and implementing an effective GUI can be. Even without adding functionality to the interface, you can easily spend months designing and debugging the interface itself.

Microsoft Windows is a *graphical user interface operating system*: a *GUI OS* (pronounced "Gooey Oh-Ess"). (Don't get caught calling it a "Gooey Os," which is something else entirely.) Windows provides a *multitasking environment*, enabling you to run several applications at a time. Because Windows uses a consistent windowing and menu structure for its applications, Windows applications are easier to learn and use than traditional DOS-based programs. Figure 10.1 shows the current version of Windows: Windows 3.1.

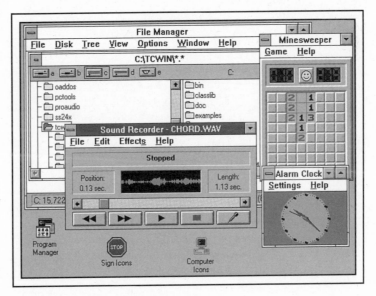

Figure 10.1. *The Windows environment.*

Windows offers relief from many of the tedious, painful tasks involved with developing applications that incorporate GUIs. This chapter shows you some advantages that Windows offers to users and programmers. In addition, you'll examine the structure of a typical Windows program and learn the main components of a Windows application. To wrap up, you will create a simple Windows program that illustrates the fundamental structure of any Windows application.

Why Windows?

Windows and applications designed for Windows offer many advantages over other GUIs to both the user and the programmer. Users enjoy the benefits of features such as point-and-click capabilities and multitasking. Programmers find the device-independent graphics and enhanced memory management helpful. The following sections describe some advantages of Windows for the user and the programmer.

Advantages of Windows to the User

When you use Windows and Windows applications, you'll appreciate the consistent user interface of this environment. Because most users work with several different software packages, each with its own interface, the consistency of the user interface's design is very important. Each window in the Windows environment contains the same basic features. Because these basic features are consistent among applications, you can adapt to new applications more easily.

Windows users also benefit from graphics-based images that represent applications and data. Because Windows is a GUI, graphics images represent physical data structures such as files, applications, windows, and directories. You can manipulate these physical structures with a mouse by selecting, double-clicking, dragging, and so forth. Double-clicking an *icon*—a small picture that represents an application—is easier and faster than typing cryptic commands to navigate directories and then typing the name of the file to launch the program.

WYSIWYG (pronounced "Whizzy-Wig" or "Whizzy-Wiggy") is a major advantage to Windows users (not to mention a great scrabble word). It stands for *what-you-see-is-what-you-get*: text and graphics appear the same on your printer as they appear on your screen.

Most non-Windows software packages use the read-only memory, basic input-output system (ROM BIOS) character sets for the screen display. Because the ROM BIOS character sets are not proportional and have no direct correlation to the font used by an application, the text displayed on-screen usually does not correspond to the resulting text output on the printer. With the WYSIWYG feature, however, Windows can treat text as a series of graphics images that are drawn onto the screen as they will appear when printed.

Color Gallery

Plate 1. *A true color (24 bits per pixel) scanned image from Chapter 1.*

Plate 2. *The same photo scanned with 256 colors (8 bits per pixel) is noticeably degraded.*

Plate 3. *With only 16 colors (4 bits per pixel), the photo can't be approximated very well at all.*

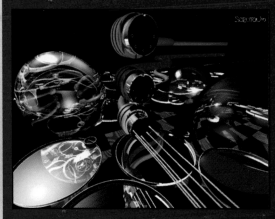

Plate 4. *A true color (24 bits per pixel) computer-generated image from Chapter 13.*

Plate 5. *The image above, converted to 8 bits per pixel using the best 256 colors available.*

Plate 6. *Although 256 colors are usually too few, 256 levels of gray are plenty.*

Plate 7. *On your screen, you'll see these moiré patterns shift and move as you "cycle" the colors.*

Plate 8. *With the TransGraphics system from Chapter 2, your graphics programs work with any compiler.*

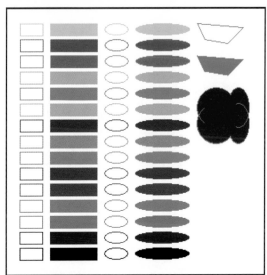

Plate 9. *TransGraphics supports a variety of shapes and graphics operations.*

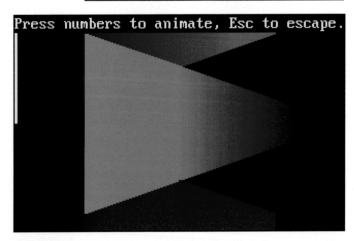

Plate 10. Different types of graphics programs use different file formats. Paint programs often use PC Paintbrush (.PCX) files.

Plate 11. Realistic computer-generated renderings usually use Targa (.TGA) files.

Plate 12. Left *Photo-retouch and image processing programs use TIFF (.TIF) files.*

Plate 13. Right *Vector drawing programs use Postscript (.EPS or .AI) files.*

Plate 14. Bottom Left *Shareware and freeware programs such as FRACTINT generally use graphics interchange format (.GIF) files.*

Plate 15. Bottom Right *Computer-aided drafting and design programs use the drawing exchange file (.DXF) format.*

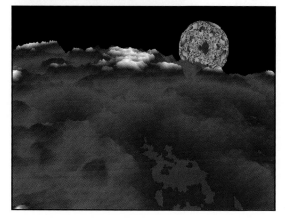

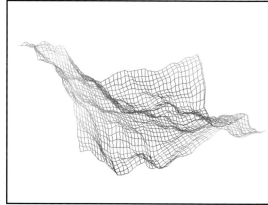

Plate 16.
With the scene generator program from Chapter 4, you can generate worlds of your own.

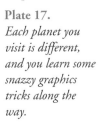

Plate 17.
Each planet you visit is different, and you learn some snazzy graphics tricks along the way.

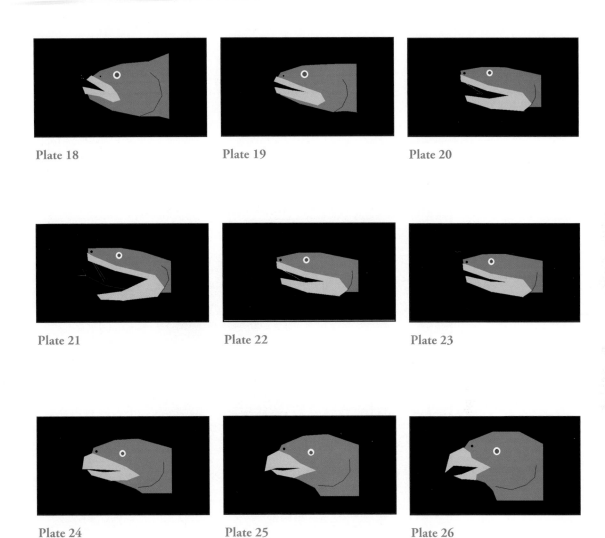

Plate 18

Plate 19

Plate 20

Plate 21

Plate 22

Plate 23

Plate 24

Plate 25

Plate 26

Plates 18 through 26. *With automatic "tweening" and "morphing," you can transform any shape into any other. Here, a fish evolves into a reptile and the reptile evolves into a bird. Several other color movies are included for you to explore.*

Plate 27

Plate 28

Plate 29

Plates 27 through 32. *"What else, when chaos draws all forces inward to shape a single leaf?"* —Conrad Aiken

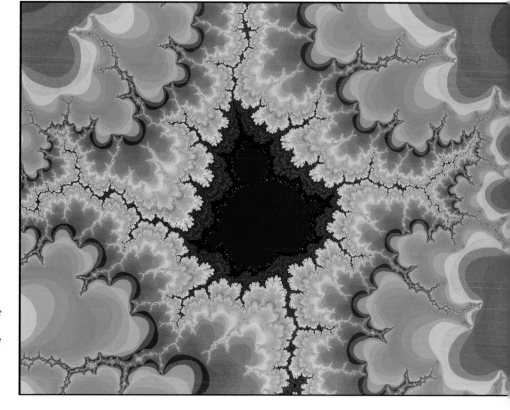

Plate 33. *If you think this close-up of the Mandelbrot set fractal looks wild now, wait 'til you see it animated in color!*

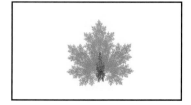

Plate 35

Plate 36

Plate 37

Plate 30

Plate 31

Plate 32

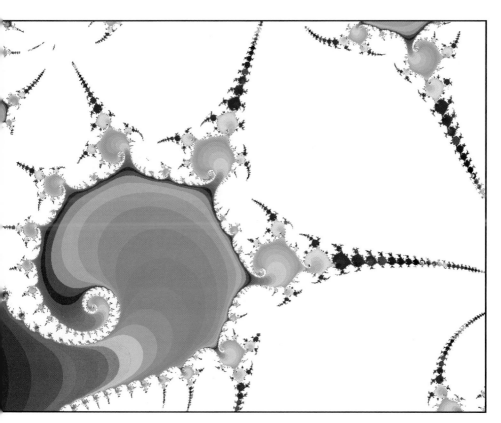

Plates 35 through 40. *Tweening works with fractals, too. Here, a maple leaf morphs into a fern.*

Plate 34. *You can explore an infinite number of infinitely intricate fractals called Julia sets.*

Plate 38

Plate 39

Plate 40

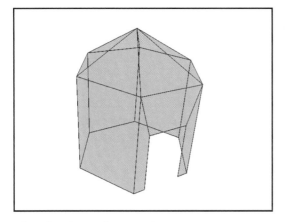

Plate 41. *A wire-frame rendering.*

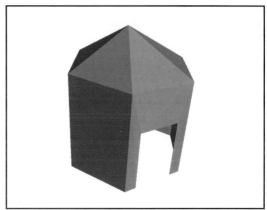

Plate 42. *Hidden surfaces and light-source shading.*

Plate 43. *Shadows and spot-lighting.*

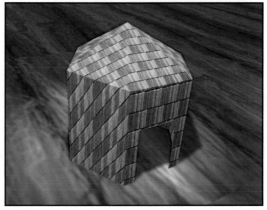

Plate 44. *Texture maps.*

Plate 45. *To make this image (and Plates 41 through 44), I designed a 3-D yurt with the programs in Chapter 7, then imported the DXF file into Autodesk 3D Studio for photorealistic rendering.*

Next=Tab Size= / Axis=XYZ Spin=+- Skew=;' Squash=[] Color=C Glasses=G Quit=Esc

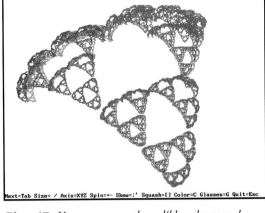

Next=Tab Size= / Axis=XYZ Spin=+- Skew=;' Squash=[] Color=C Glasses=G Quit=Esc

Plate 46. *Design your own 3-D fractals with the software from Chapter 8.*

Plate 47. *You can put on the red/blue glasses and view any of your 3-D models in stereo.*

Plate 48. *A fern rendered with the POLYRAY ray tracer included with this book.*

Plate 49. *A fractal saved as a DXF file for rendering with Autodesk 3D Studio.*

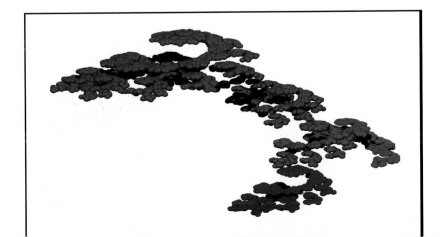

Plate 50. *This fractal spiral, designed and rendered in true color at 2,000x1,500 resolution with software from Chapters 8 and 9, contains 10,000 individual spheres. It took under an hour to render on a 50Mhz 486 computer.*

Plate 51. *A complete, fully functional shareware evaluation copy of the POLYRAY ray tracer is included on the disk with this book. It supports a wide variety of shape types (above), automatic multiframe animations like the one pictured in Plates 52 through 59, and many advanced lighting and mapping effects such as those shown in Plates 60 through 65.*

Plates 52 through 59. *A robot arm animation.*

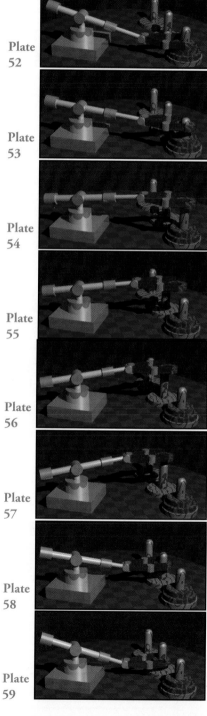

Plate
52

Plate
53

Plate
54

Plate
55

Plate
56

Plate
57

Plate
58

Plate
59

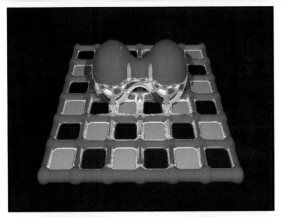

Plate 60. *With blob shapes, you can weld spheres and cylinders smoothly.*

Plate 61. *Advanced mapping simplifies the creation of complex scenes.*

Plate 62. *You can ray trace almost any mathematical function.*

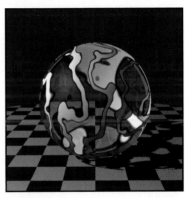

Plate 63. *Transparency, reflections, and texture mapping combined.*

Plate 64. *Can you find the fractal in this fountain?*

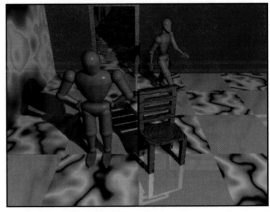

Plate 65. *POLYRAY man and his clone at home.*

Plate 66. *The subject is cute, but this scanned photo needs image processing work.*

Plate 68. *Then, enhance the contrast. Now the portrait does her justice!*

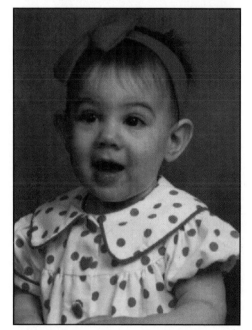

Plate 67. *First, increase the brightness by adjusting the color look up table.*

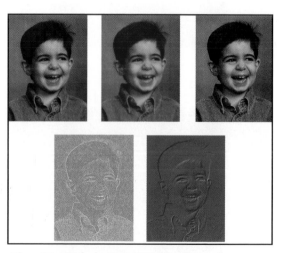

Plate 69. *With the IMAGEPRO software from Chapter 13, you can also blur, sharpen, enhance edges, create "emboss" effects, and more.*

Plate 70. *Some pretty red flowers…*

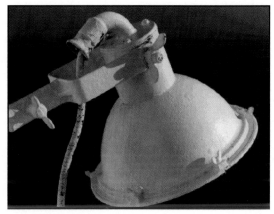

Plate 72. *An ordinary sea ship's lamp.*

Plate 71. *…or were they blue? With digital image processing, it's up to you to decide.*

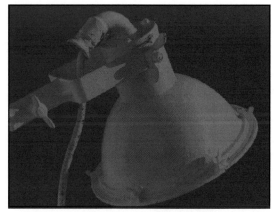

Plate 73. *A not-so-ordinary sea ship's lamp.*

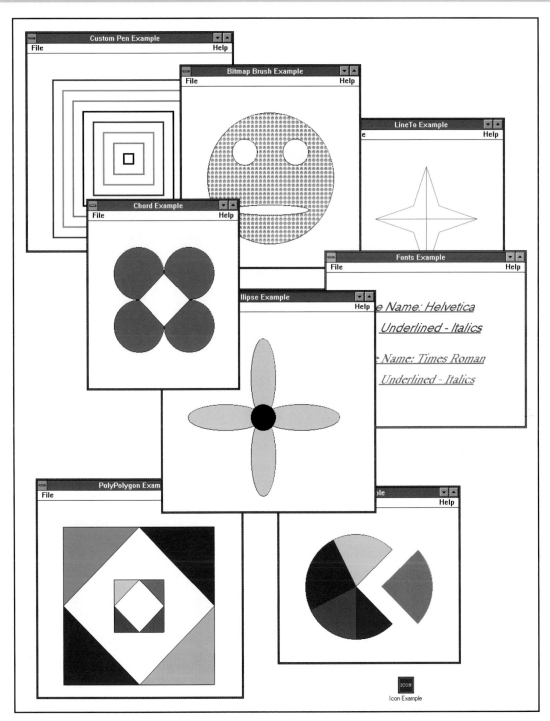

Plate 74. *A sampling of the Windows example programs from Chapters 10, 11, and 12.*

Plate 75. Top Left *This book gives you a programmer's primer on the Microsoft Windows Graphics Device Interface (opposite page). It also shows you the graphics magic you can do with the latest generation of Windows software, such as Fractal Design Painter (Plates 75 and 76), and Aldus Photostyler (Plates 77 through 79).*

Plate 76. *An automatic "chalk clone" of the photo above.*

Plate 77. *This scanned photo has too much shadow and no color.*

Plate 78. *Photo editing software lets you do good…*

Plate 79. *…or evil!*

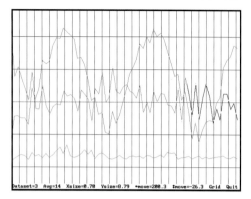

Plate 80. *This page is just a small sampling of the 30 graphics programs that come with this book. With DATAVIEW, you can interactively visualize numbers.*

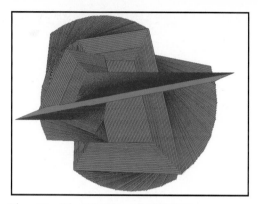

Plate 81. *The TRANS and TWEEN programs demonstrate a variety of geometric transformations and morphs.*

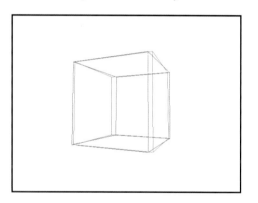

Plate 82. *Learn to do stereoscopic 3-D animation with 3DCUBE, 3DLINES, and 3DFACES.*

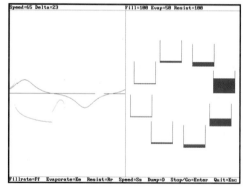

Plate 83. *WHEEL is a real-time visual simulation of a chaotic dynamical system.*

Plate 84. *FRAN, FREEN, FRAN3D, FREEN3D, and MANIMATE let you explore fractal animation.*

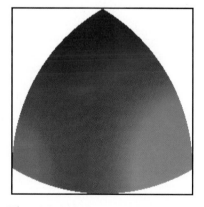

Plate 85. *TGAREAD, COLORTRI, and SVGA read and write Targa files and other graphics formats. The disks include full C source code for 52 programs.*

Windows also provides the very important capability of *multitasking*. Because several applications can run simultaneously, you don't need to save the file you're working on and exit the application to enter another application; you can simply keep several programs running side-by-side and switch among them at will. Windows' memory management capabilities enhance multitasking. Windows provides access to all available memory resources, so you can optimize the system more easily.

Advantages of Windows to the Programmer

When you write Windows programs, you'll utilize many of the same advantages that you enjoy as a Windows user. The consistent user interface, for example, benefits programmers because the basic interface design and tools are already established. Because the interface is basically the same for every application, you can spend more time on the application's functionality and less time on the interface design.

The basic design of the GUI is another reason for Windows' popularity. With Windows, you can design graphical representations of physical structures, such as files and directories. Windows provides convenient features such as pop-up menus and dialog boxes and supports direct mouse and keyboard input, which significantly decreases application development time.

As a programmer, you'll especially appreciate Windows' memory management features that enable you to access more memory than you can with traditional MS-DOS applications. Consequently, you can make the most of the system memory resources while maintaining flexibility in system design.

Windows also provides the capability to develop *device-independent* graphics. Because well-designed Windows applications do not access the graphics hardware (the screen and printer) directly, Windows applications operate with any video subsystem or printer that has a Windows device driver. For programmers, device-independent graphics means that your programs don't depend on a certain system configuration. Windows spares you the torturous task of reinventing device drivers for every possible video display, adapter, and printer each time you create an application.

Now that you know why Windows is so popular with both users and programmers, I'll show you the standard components of a typical Windows application.

The Standard Components of a Window

The discipline of the Windows 3.0 interface is slowly but surely spawning a generation of more computer-literate users. Make no mistake, understanding the nuances of the Windows 3.0 interface isn't as easy as Microsoft's big bucks marketing juggernaut would have us believe. The learning curve is relatively steep, but it is a single learning curve. The elegance of the Windows 3.0 interface is that once you've learned it, you can pick up nearly any off-the-shelf retail Windows application and begin to use the package immediately.

—Stan Miastkowski, "Windowing: Not by DOS Alone," *BYTE*, Outlook '92 Special Edition, p. 172

A Windows application uses an *application window* for output and input to and from the screen. The Windows application creates the application window and has primary access to the window. However, the application shares the responsibility of managing the application window with the Windows operating system itself. Windows is responsible for managing the size, position, and components of the window, whereas the application is responsible for managing what happens within the working area of the window.

Every application window contains some, and often all, of the following components:

- window border
- client area
- control menu box
- control menu
- horizontal scroll bar
- maximize box
- menu bar
- minimize box
- title bar
- vertical scroll bar

The Notepad application window (Figure 10.2) contains each of the components in the previous list. Before you try your hand at creating an application window yourself, take a closer look at each component of a typical application window.

As you read the following paragraphs, you might want to start Windows, open the Notepad application, and try using each component to refresh your memory of how they work. Because these standard components surround every window you create, you should familiarize yourself with their operation before you start designing Windows applications.

The Border

The *window border* surrounds the outside edge of the application window and consists of three basic elements:

■ the four corners

■ the vertical sides

■ the horizontal sides

By grabbing and dragging any of the four window corners with the mouse, you can size the window vertically and horizontally at the same time. To size the window border in the horizontal direction, grab and drag the vertical sides. Finally, you can size the window vertically by using the horizontal sides of the window border.

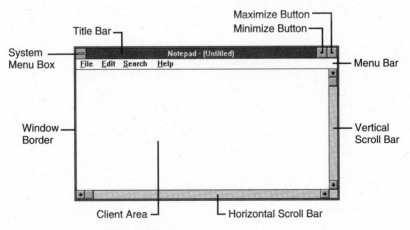

Figure 10.2. *The Windows components.*

The Client Area

No, it's not where impatient patients read magazines while the doctor flirts with the receptionist. The *client area* is the physical part of the window that is not occupied by the menu bar, scroll bars, borders, or other components. The application uses the client area as its workspace.

The application maintains the client area, and Windows maintains the position, size, and components of the application window. In other words, Windows is the humble *server* that keeps house for its *client*, your application. (This makes for great coffee table conversation: "Oh, little Billy Gates does most of my housekeeping for me. He says I'm one of his best clients....")

The System Menu

You'll find the *System menu box* in the top left corner of every application window. Not surprisingly, the System menu box provides access to the *System menu*.

Through the menu options of the System menu, you can restore, move, size, minimize, maximize, and close the application window. The System menu (Figure 10.3) provides the primary access to the various components in the application window if you aren't using a mouse.

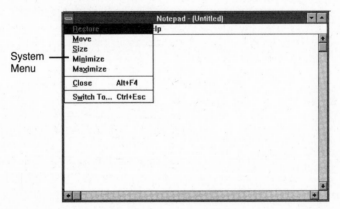

Figure 10.3. *The System menu.*

The Horizontal Scroll Bar

With the *horizontal scroll bar*, you can move through documents and images that are too large for the current size of the client area. The horizontal scroll bar contains three elements:

- The *left arrow* is positioned at the left end of the scroll bar. Clicking this arrow displays a part of the document or image located to the left of the left window border.

- The *right arrow* is positioned at the right end of the scroll bar. Clicking this arrow displays a part of the document or image located to the right of the right window border.

- The *scroll thumb* enables you to thumb through the contents of the window. The solid square appears at the *thumb position* in the scroll bar, indicating the current view position relative to the far left and far right sides of the document or image. By moving the thumb position with the mouse, you can quickly jump to the beginning, middle, or end of the view area.

The Maximize Button

Clicking the *Maximize button* enlarges the application window to fill the screen. After you click the Maximize button, the Restore button replaces it. You can click the Restore button to restore the window to its previous size. When the window is restored to its previous size, the Maximize button replaces the Restore button.

The Menu Bar

The *menu bar* lists the menus that the application provides for the user. The File, Edit, and Help menus are common to most applications. As a Windows programmer, however, you can customize the number and type of menus available to the user.

The Minimize Button

The *Minimize button* shrinks the application window to an icon. Double-clicking the minimized window (the icon) restores the window to its previous size.

The Title Bar

The *title bar* lists the application name and often the active filename for the application window. The title bar of the active window often displays a different color and/or intensity than the title bars of inactive windows.

The Vertical Scroll Bar

You can use the *vertical scroll bar* to move through documents and images that are too large for the current size of the client area. Like the horizontal scroll bar, the vertical scroll bar contains three components.

- The Up arrow is positioned at the top of the scroll bar. Clicking this arrow displays a part of the document or image located above the top window border.

- The Down arrow is positioned at the bottom of the scroll bar. Clicking this arrow displays a part of the document or image located below the bottom window border.

- The scroll thumb indicates the thumb position of the current view area. The solid square in the scroll bar indicates the current view position relative to the top and bottom of the document or image.

Now that you've seen the basic components of an application window, here's how you can create Windows applications.

Windows Programming Basics

This is the crux of event-driven programming: You write the code that determines how events are processed, but it is the user who initiates the events... In responding to various Windows messages, the most important thing to remember is that almost all actions are initiated by the user's triggering Windows messages... Once you've begun visualizing your program as a series of responses to events, you'll really have gotten the message.

—Zack Urlocker, "Polymorphism Unbound,"
Windows Tech Journal, March 1992

Windows programming has a bad reputation. Programmers who are familiar with the traditional, *sequential* programming style used with DOS often find the *event-driven* structure of Windows programming difficult to grasp.

If you're willing to open your mind to new concepts, you'll find that learning to program Windows is no more difficult than learning the ins and outs of any structured language—you just have to learn the basic code structure and programming style. For most programmers, the biggest hurdle to learning Windows programming is an unwillingness to discard traditional programming methodologies. If you willingly adopt the Windows programming methodologies and approach Windows with an open mind, you will quickly adapt to Windows' event-driven programming concepts.

Event-Driven Programming

What is *event-driven programming*, and how does it differ from sequential, *procedure-driven programming*?

The majority of MS-DOS programs are written using sequential, procedure-driven programming, where procedures have a distinct beginning and a distinct end. The program directly controls the sequence of program events.

Windows programs, by contrast, are *event driven*—they are controlled by the occurrence of events, rather than by the order in which the program code was written. The following example quickly demonstrates the primary difference between sequential, procedure-driven programs and event-driven programs.

Suppose you had to write a program that averages the grades of a class that had taken three tests during the semester. The procedure for generating the averages is

1. Enter the names of the students.

2. Enter the grades for test one.

3. Enter the grades for test two.

4. Enter the grades for test three.

5. Calculate and display the averages.

In a sequential, procedure-driven program, the flow of events and decisions looks something like that shown in Figure 10.4. The program displays a screen that prompts you for the names of the students. After you enter the names of the students, the next screen prompts you for the grades for test one. Again, another screen prompts you for the grades for test two. After completing the grades for test two, a screen displays that enables you to enter grades for test three. After you enter the test three grades, the final screen containing the calculated averages displays. This approach is very logical and follows a structured sequence of events. To use the program as intended, however, you must follow the procedure as designed. You can't change a grade in step 3 once you are in step 5, for example.

All programs must be able to handle problems or *exceptions*—going back to fix a mistake in an earlier test grade or the occurrence of a hard-disk error during data entry, for example). Sequential, procedure-driven programs need to constantly check for problems at every point in the program; this can be rather cumbersome. Once an exception is detected, correcting it and returning to the right place in the program can be rather tricky. Event-driven programs are designed to avoid these limitations.

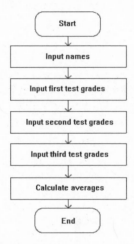

Figure 10.4. *Procedural programming.*

Event-driven programming revolves around the generation and processing of *messages* about events that have occurred. For example, whenever a user presses a key or a mouse button, a message is sent. Another message is sent when the key or mouse button is released. Your job as a Windows programmer involves, to a large extent, sorting and managing Windows messages sent to and from your program. Because Windows messages are event-driven, messages do not appear in any predefined order.

You can easily implement the previous example of a student grading program using the event-driven approach (see Figure 10.5). The full functionality of the sequential, procedure-driven program is still there; however, the user does not have to go through each step, in sequence, to calculate the grades. The user may skip around the various items while adding or modifying data. For example, with the event-driven application, you can enter grades for the third test without previously having entered the test scores for tests one and two. With the procedure-driven approach, this would be much more difficult.

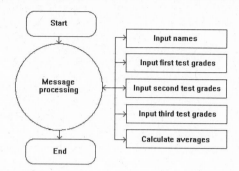

Figure 10.5. *Event-driven programming.*

If an exception such as a hard disk error occurs during the event-driven program, it simply generates an appropriate message to your application. Your exception-handling procedures automatically jump to the rescue when they hear the message without your having to check over and over again in every procedure to see if an exception has occurred.

Event-driven programming methodologies provide many benefits and are very useful for applications that require extensive user interaction.

The WinMain Function

Now that you've seen the differences between event-driven and sequential program-ming, you're ready to look at a few common segments of a typical Windows application—the WinMain function, the message loop, window procedures, Windows functions, and Windows messages.

The WinMain function is the entry point for all Windows programs. The WinMain function contains three basic parts: *procedure declaration, program initialization*, and the *message loop*.

Working Code: Introducing the WinMain Function

The procedure declaration for the WinMain function looks like this:

```
int PASCAL WinMain (HANDLE hInstance, HANDLE hPrevInstance,
                    LPSTR lpszCmdLine, int cmdShow);
```

hInstance is a *handle* identifying the program. hPrevInstance specifies the program to which hInstance is related, if any. Programs are considered related if they share the same *module name*. `lpszCmdLine` specifies the *command-line arguments* for the program. `cmdShow` specifies the state of the main window when the window is first opened.

Program initialization forms the bulk of the `WinMain` function. You use the program initialization portion of the `WinMain` function to create a window. In the process of creating a window, you must define the window class. The first part of the initialization portion of the `WinMain` function defines the various members of a `WndClass` data structure. In this part of the code, you define

■ the cursor used for the window

■ the brush used to fill the window background

■ the name of the window procedure

■ the window class style, the main menu of the window

■ the class name

The program initialization portion of the example presented later in Listing 10.1 follows:

```
if (!hPrevInstance)
    {
    WndClass.cbClsExtra = 0;
    WndClass.cbWndExtra = 0;
    WndClass.hbrBackground = GetStockObject(WHITE_BRUSH);
    WndClass.hCursor =  LoadCursor(NULL, IDC_ARROW);
    WndClass.hIcon = LoadIcon (NULL, "END");
    WndClass.hInstance = hInstance;
    WndClass.lpfnWndProc = WndProc;
    WndClass.lpszClassName = "FUNDWIN";
    WndClass.lpszMenuName = "MENU";
    WndClass.style = CS_HREDRAW | CS_VREDRAW;

    RegisterClass (&WndClass);
    }

hWnd = CreateWindow ("FUNDWIN", /* class name */
        "Fundamental Window", /* Caption */
        WS_OVERLAPPEDWINDOW,  /* Style */
        CW_USEDEFAULT,        /* x position */
        0,                    /* y position */
        CW_USEDEFAULT,        /* cx - size */
        0,                    /* cy - size */
        NULL,                 /* Parent window */
```

```
NULL,                    /* Menu */
hInstance,               /* Program Instance */
NULL);                   /* Parameters */
```

Once the program window is initialized, all the WinMain function needs to do is retrieve messages from the application queue and send each message to the appropriate window function. In the next section, you'll see just how simple this message loop can be.

The Message Loop

Windows applications receive input in the form of messages. These messages contain information about the device that generated the input, the current state of the keyboard, the position of the cursor, the state of the mouse, and the system time. Windows monitors all the input devices and places input messages into the *system queue*. Windows then copies the input messages from the system queue into the appropriate *application queue*. The application's *message loop* retrieves the messages from the application queue and sends each message to the appropriate window function. Figure 10.6 diagrams this message-handling process.

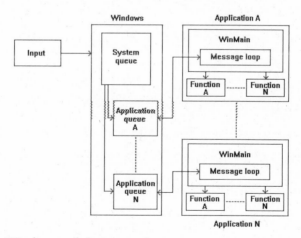

Figure 10.6. *Windows and the message loop.*

Working Code: Getting the Message

Writing a message loop for your WinMain function is easy:

```
while (GetMessage (&Message, NULL, 0, 0))
```

```
    {
    TranslateMessage (&Message);
    DispatchMessage (&Message);
    }
return Message.wParam;
```

In this message loop, `Message` refers to a data structure of type `MSG`. That's all you need for the main loop of a Windows program!

Window Procedures

The terms *procedure* and *function* take on new meanings in Windows programming. *Window procedures* are functions that receive and process messages. *Windows functions*, on the other hand, are the actual routines you use to put graphics on-screen and carry out other tasks.

The message loop is responsible for retrieving messages from the application queue and sending the message to the appropriate *window procedures*. The window procedure determines the action taken when a certain message is received.

Working Code: A Window Procedure

Window procedures are generally structured using one or more `switch` statements with a `case` for each message. Each `case` reflects the action taken when the corresponding message is received. The following code, taken from the example (Listing 10.1), presented later in this chapter, is a simple window procedure:

```
long FAR PASCAL WndProc (HWND hWnd, WORD iMessage,
                         WORD wParam, LONG lParam)
{
switch (iMessage)
    {
    case WM_COMMAND:
        switch(wParam)
        {
        case 101:
            SendMessage(hWnd, WM_CLOSE, 0, 0L);
            return 0;
```

```
        case 102:
            MessageBox(hWnd,
              "Sample Application",
              "Windows Graphics",
              MB_ICONINFORMATION¦MB_OK);
            return 0;
        }
      return 0;

  case WM_DESTROY:
      PostQuitMessage(0);
      return 0;

  default:
      return(DefWindowProc(hWnd, iMessage, wParam,
          lParam));
   }
}
```

In this window procedure, only two conditions are checked, the receipt of the
WM_COMMAND and the WM_DESTROY messages. Although this window procedure is simple,
the same structure is used and expanded for more complex window procedures.

Windows Functions

Windows functions are the heart of a Windows application. When you worked with
DOS-based programs in the previous chapters, you used C functions to draw graphics
on-screen and to interface with MS-DOS. When you develop Windows applications,
you use the Windows functions to take advantage of the capabilities of Windows and
of its device independence.

Hundreds of Windows functions exist in dozens of categories. You'll get to see
and use many of the Windows functions throughout the next two chapters.

Using Projects to Develop Windows Applications

Depending on the compiler and development system you have, you can build
Windows applications using an integrated development environment (IDE) and

Project Manager, using a command-line compiler, or using a makefile. Whatever compiler or development system you use, the basic process for building Windows applications is the same.

The process for creating a Windows application includes the basic steps shown in Figure 10.7. C or C++ source files are compiled into object code using your compiler. The resulting object code is linked with definition and library files to form executable code. The resource compiler then binds the resource files with the executable code to create a Windows application.

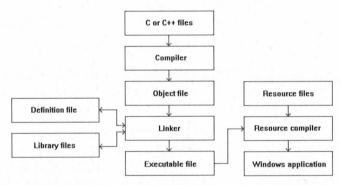

Figure 10.7. *Building a Windows application.*

The Windows programs in this book were developed with Turbo C++ for Windows, Version 3.0. If you are familiar with Turbo C++ for Windows or Borland C++, you have probably used projects to develop your applications. If you have never used Turbo C++, however, or have never developed an application using the Project Manager features of the Borland Integrated Development Environment, you should quickly review the process used to develop the examples in this book.

Note: If you are using Borland C++ 3.1 or later, be sure to set the compiler for Windows 3.0 compatibility before compiling the examples in this book. Otherwise, you will get several warnings and errors. (We've made the code compatible with Windows 3.0 and Borland Turbo C++ 3.0 so that those of you who have these older versions can still compile it.) All the code will still compile and run fine under Windows 3.1 and Borland C++ 3.1, as long as you remember to select the Version 3.0 compatibility option. Typically, this can be found under the environment settings in the Borland Integrated Development Environment. Check your compiler manual for details on setting the environment string for 3.0 compatibility if you aren't sure how to do this.

You Can Do It: Building a Windows Program

When using the Borland Project Manager and the Borland Integrated Development Environment for creating Windows applications, you must follow seven basic steps:

Note: The following steps describe how to build a project with Turbo C++ for Windows or with Borland C++. If you are using another compiler to build these applications, you should refer to your compiler's documentation for the proper procedure to build the application.

1. Start the IDE by double-clicking the Turbo C++ for Windows icon.

2. Create all appropriate C or C++ source files, module definition files, and resource files. The following paragraphs contain more information on these files.

3. Select Project | Open. Type the filename, using a .PRJ extension, in the Project Name dialog box. Click the OK button, or press Enter to continue.

4. Select Project | Add item. Add the appropriate C or C++ source files, module definition files, and resource files. Figure 10.8 shows the Integrated Development Environment and the project for building the fundamental window example in Listing 10.1. Close the Project dialog box when you are done.

5. Select Options | Application. The Set Application Options dialog box will appear. Select Windows App to indicate that you are developing a Windows application.

6. Select Run | Run. This selection builds the project into a Windows application and displays your application window if the project compiles successfully.

7. If any errors occur, modify the appropriate file or files and repeat step 6.

This process is relatively simple and provides you with access to the powerful features of the Borland Integrated Development Environment and Project Manager. Again, this process is used for all the examples in this book. Each example contains a listing of the files used in the application project.

Your windows applications projects will generally contain three types of files:

■ the *C or C++ source code file(s)*

■ the *module definition file*

■ the *resource file(s)*

The following sections discuss each of these file types.

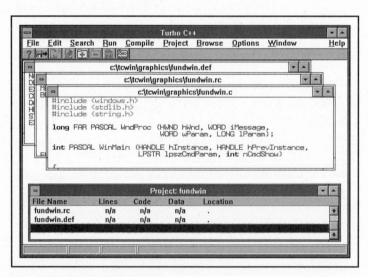

Figure 10.8. *Application development with Turbo C++ for Windows.*

C or C++ Source Code Files

Quiz time: *What's in a C or C++ source code file?* If you guessed the C or C++ source code for your Windows application, score yourself six bonus points. (If you thought it was a trick question and guessed "source code written by the guy buried in Grant's Tomb" or "18 minutes of digitized tape recordings of Richard Nixon," subtract 3 points from your score and give up on winning any big game show money in this lifetime.)

As with traditional C or C++ projects, more than one C or C++ file may be included in a project. Each C or C++ source code file contains a combination of C and/or C++ keywords and functions, Windows functions, Windows messages, and references to *include files* such as windows.h.

The Module Definition File

The module definition file provides the linker with specific information about the application's code and data segments, the size of the application's local heap, and the size of the application's program stack.

Does all this sound cryptic to you? Well, it should unless you're already a certified programming guru yourself. Not to worry, though—you can sneak by this file without having to take a graduate level course in microcomputer memory management architectures. Just use the examples from this book, and you'll probably never need to modify a module definition file again.

If you are one of those people who stay up at night fretting about whether your local heap could submit 4K to your stack, or if you should preload your data segment, here's a brief explanation of each line in the module definition file to fuel your insomnia:

```
NAME
DESCRIPTION
EXETYPE
CODE
DATA
HEAPSIZE
STACKSIZE
EXPORTS
```

in which

NAME defines a module as an executable file.

DESCRIPTION adds the specified text to the executable file.

EXETYPE indicates the type of program the linker should create. WINDOWS is used for Windows applications.

CODE provides information on the application's code segments. Possible values include PRELOAD, FIXED, MOVEABLE, and DISCARDABLE.

DATA provides information on the application's data segments. Possible values include PRELOAD, MOVEABLE, and MULTIPLE.

HEAPSIZE defines the initial size of the application's local heap.

STACKSIZE defines the size of the application's stack.

EXPORTS enables you to specify the window and dialog procedures for your application.

See your compiler and linker documentation for more details.

Resource Files

Most Windows applications use *resources* such as icons, cursors, bitmaps, and dialog boxes. You can use *resource editors* such as the Borland Resource Workshop to create these resources. After you create a resource, it is stored in a resource file. Resource files created by the Resource Workshop are source files, and you must compile them with the Resource Compiler and bind them to the executable file so that they are available at runtime.

The Resource Compiler compiles the resource source file, binds the compiled file with the compiled .EXE or .DLL module, and generates a Windows-compatible application. You'll learn more about creating and using resources in the next two chapters.

The Fundamental Window Example

Now that I've introduced you to the files, code segments, and procedures used to build a typical Windows application, you're ready for a real live Windows program. Your program will create a window with all the standard window components, including a menu bar.

The sample program in the following **Working Code** box brings together the code segments presented earlier to create a *fundamental window*, which you can size, move, close, minimize, or maximize. This window also contains a menu bar with two popup menus, File and Help. The File menu contains one option, Exit. The Help menu also contains one option, About. (The next great desktop publishing application it ain't, but with an aggressive marketing budget this just might sell. It's got an easy learning curve, snappy user-interface, no calories, caffeine free...)

Figure 10.9 shows the exciting fundamental window application in action.

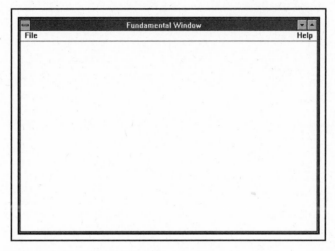

Figure 10.9. *The fundamental window example.*

Working Code: Fundamentally Windows

Using the Turbo C++ Integrated Development Environment Version 3.0 and the Project Manager, I followed the process outlined so far in this chapter to create and build the project. The project used to build this example is called fundwin.prj and contains the files fundwin.c, fundwin.rc, and fundwin.def. The following project description summarizes the project. A similar summary is used for every example in this book.

Listing 10.1. The fundamental window example.

```
Project Name:    fundwin.prj
Project Files:   fundwin.c
                 fundwin.rc
                 fundwin.def
```

Filename: fundwin.c

```c
#include <windows.h>
#include <stdlib.h>
#include <string.h>

long FAR PASCAL WndProc (HWND hWnd, WORD iMessage,
                WORD wParam, LONG lParam);

int PASCAL WinMain (HANDLE hInstance, HANDLE hPrevInstance,
            LPSTR lpszCmdParam, int nCmdShow)

{
HWND hWnd;
MSG Message;
WNDCLASS WndClass;

if (!hPrevInstance)
    {
    WndClass.cbClsExtra = 0;
    WndClass.cbWndExtra = 0;
    WndClass.hbrBackground = GetStockObject(WHITE_BRUSH);
    WndClass.hCursor =  LoadCursor(NULL, IDC_ARROW);
    WndClass.hIcon = LoadIcon (NULL, "END");
    WndClass.hInstance = hInstance;
    WndClass.lpfnWndProc = WndProc;
    WndClass.lpszClassName = "FUNDWIN";
    WndClass.lpszMenuName = "MENU";
    WndClass.style = CS_HREDRAW | CS_VREDRAW;

    RegisterClass (&WndClass);
    }
```

```
hWnd = CreateWindow ("FUNDWIN", /* class name */
        "Fundamental Window", /* Caption */
        WS_OVERLAPPEDWINDOW,  /* Style */
        CW_USEDEFAULT,        /* x position */
        0,                    /* y position */
        CW_USEDEFAULT,        /* cx - size */
        0,                    /* cy - size */
        NULL,                 /* Parent window */
        NULL,                 /* Menu */
        hInstance,            /* Program Instance */
        NULL);                /* Parameters */

ShowWindow (hWnd, nCmdShow);
while (GetMessage (&Message, 0, 0, 0))
    {
    TranslateMessage(&Message);
    DispatchMessage(&Message);
    }
return Message.wParam;
}


/***********************************************************/
/*            Window Procedure: WndProc            */
/***********************************************************/

long FAR PASCAL WndProc (HWND hWnd, WORD iMessage,
                    WORD wParam, LONG lParam)
{
switch (iMessage)
    {
    case WM_COMMAND:
        switch(wParam)
         {
        case 101:
            SendMessage(hWnd, WM_CLOSE, 0, 0L);
            return 0;

        case 102:
            MessageBox(hWnd,
              "Sample Application",
```

continues

473

Listing 10.1. continued

```
                "Windows Graphics",
                MB_ICONINFORMATION¦MB_OK);
            return 0;
        }
        return 0;

    case WM_DESTROY:
        PostQuitMessage(0);
        return 0;

    default:
        return(DefWindowProc(hWnd, iMessage, wParam,
            lParam));
    }
}
```

Filename: fundwin.rc

```
MENU MENU LOADONCALL MOVEABLE PURE DISCARDABLE
BEGIN
  POPUP "File"
  BEGIN
    MenuItem "Exit", 101
  END
  POPUP "Help", HELP
  BEGIN
    MenuItem "About", 102
  END
END
```

Filename: fundwin.def

```
NAME           FUNDWIN
DESCRIPTION    'Fundamental Window'
EXETYPE        WINDOWS
CODE           PRELOAD MOVEABLE
DATA           PRELOAD MOVEABLE MULTIPLE
HEAPSIZE       1024
STACKSIZE      5120
EXPORTS        WndProc
```

As you can see from the size of the listing, quite a few source code lines are required to generate even a fundamental window. The C source code file contains the WinMain and the WndProc functions. WinMain, explained earlier in this chapter, is the entry point for the application. WndProc is the window procedure for the window generated by the application. WndProc is responsible for processing the messages for the resulting window. A typical window procedure contains a switch statement. The actions of the window procedure are triggered by the receipt of certain messages. For the fundamental window example, WndProc monitors and provides actions for only two messages, WM_DESTROY and WM_COMMAND. Most window procedures, however, define actions for dozens of messages.

When WndProc detects the WM_DESTROY message, the PostQuitMessage function is called and the window is terminated. When the WM_COMMAND message is received, the application determines the source of the message by checking the wParam paramater of the WM_COMMAND message. The wParam parameter tells the application the source of the message. If the WM_COMMAND message is sent when the user selects the Exit option of the File menu, a message is sent to terminate the application. If the WM_COMMAND message is sent when the user selects the About option of the Help menu, a message dialog box displays. The default window procedure, DefWndProc handles all other messages sent to WndProc. When working with window procedures, remember that only Windows calls WndProc; WinMain references WndProc but never calls WndProc directly.

The application's resource script file, fundwin.rc, defines the resources used for this example. Resources include dialog boxes, icons, menus, bitmaps, and so forth. The only resource used for this example was the menu.

The fundamental window serves as a starting point for your Windows graphics programs. Though the previous listing might seem rather lengthy for a program that doesn't actually do anything, think how much longer it would be if you had to write all the code to draw and manage fancy menus and scroll bars yourself!

But what good is a beautiful, precision-crafted window if it looks out at a brick wall? To give your windows a magnificent view, you need to employ the Windows *graphics device interface* (GDI) and learn the concepts used for graphics output in the Windows environment.

The Graphics Device Interface (GDI)

The Windows Graphics Device Interface (GDI) gives you *device-independent graphics*. Because a computer system can contain many combinations of output and display devices, device-independent graphics enable you to program without worrying about specific hardware configurations.

Windows applications use the GDI and Windows device drivers to support device-independent graphics. A *device driver* converts a general drawing command into the precise actions needed to implement the command on the specified output device. As long as the device driver for the output device is available to Windows, the programmer does not need to be overly concerned with the hardware configuration of the system.

As a Windows graphics programmer, you may rest assured that every manufacturer of video cards, printers, and graphics accessories such as film recorders and giant-screen displays will produce a device driver that supports your software. No MS-DOS based graphics library can offer the universal device support that Microsoft has drummed up for Windows. (The downside is that you have no control over the quality of the device drivers supplied by manufacturers. A few software developers still prefer to write their own custom drivers for the most popular displays and printers. Generally, however, you can trust the driver gurus to do their part and concentrate on making flashy graphics.)

The rest of this chapter introduces some features and terminology of the GDI.

The Device Context

You can control how Windows displays graphics, colors, and fonts through the *device context*, a set of attributes determining the location and appearance of GDI output for any device.

You access the device context and its attributes by using a *handle*. When your program requests the handle for a device context, Windows creates a device context containing the default values listed in Table 10.1 for all its attributes. You can then modify any of the attributes to meet the requirements of your application by using the functions listed.

Table 10.1. The device context attributes.

Attribute	Default	Related function(s)
Background color	White	GetBkColor, SetBkColor
Background mode	OPAQUE	GetBkMode, SetBkMode

Attribute	Default	Related function(s)
Bitmap	None	CreateBitmap, CreateBitmapIndirect, CreateCompatibleBitmap, SelectObject
Brush	WHITE_BRUSH	CreateBrushIndirect, CreateDIBPatternBrush, CreateHatchBrush, CreatePatternBrush, CreateSolidBrush, SelectObject
Brush origin	(0,0)	GetBrushOrg, SetBrushOrg, UnrealizeObject
Clipping region	Display surface	ExcludeClipRect, IntersectClipRect, OffsetClipRgn, SelectClipRgn
Color palette	DEFAULT_PALETTE	CreatePalette, RealizePalette, SelectPalette
Current pen position	(0,0)	GetCurrentPosition, LineTo, MoveTo
Drawing mode	R2_COPYPEN	GetROP2, SetROP2
Font	SYSTEM_FONT	CreateFont, CreateFontIndirect, SelectObject
Intercharacter spacing	0	GetTextCharacterExtra, SetTextCharacterExtra
Mapping mode	MM_TEXT	GetMapMode, SetMapMode
Pen	BLACK_PEN	CreatePen, CreatePenIndirect, SelectObject
Polygon filling mode	ALTERNATE	GetPolyFillMode, SetPolyFillMode
Stretching mode	BLACKONWHITE	SetStretchBltMode
Text color	Black	GetTextColor, SetTextColor

continues

477

Table 10.1. continued

Attribute	Default	Related function(s)
Viewport extent	(1,1)	GetViewportExt, SetMapMode, SetViewportExt
Viewport origin	(0,0)	GetViewportOrg, OffsetViewportOrg, SetViewportOrg
Window extents	(1,1)	GetWindowExt, SetMapMode, SetWindowExt
Window origin	(0,0)	GetWindowOrg, OffsetWindowOrg, SetWindowOrg

At this point, you may not know exactly what each of these attributes does or how to use the functions listed. For now, just browse Table 10.1 to get an intuitive feeling for some of the possibilities—you'll find working code for dealing with most of these functions and attributes in the next two chapters.

Figure 10.10 shows the relationship of the device context and the application software and system hardware.

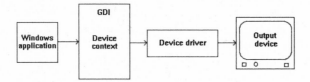

Figure 10.10. *The device context.*

The Mapping Mode

Throughout this book, you draw graphics images on-screen using *pixel coordinates*. For example, when you want a line from the top left corner to the bottom right corner of a 640×480 pixel screen, you would give the drawline function the coordinates 0,0 and

639,479. Windows enables you to choose between several coordinate measurement systems besides the traditional pixels. For example, you can measure all your graphics in inches. Then Windows will automatically make sure that a line from 0,0 to 0,1 is always one inch long, whether it is displayed on a 640×480, 72 dpi screen or a 300 dpi laser printer.

The *mapping mode* affects the appearance of output on the display device and defines the unit of measure used to transform logical units into device units. The mapping mode also defines the orientation of the device's x- and y-axes. Table 10.2 lists the mapping modes defined by Windows.

Table 10.2. Windows mapping modes.

Mapping mode	Logical unit
MM_ANISOTROPIC	x and y are arbitrary units where x and y can be scaled independently
MM_HIENGLISH	.001 inch
MM_HIMETRIC	.01 mm
MM_ISOTROPIC	x and y are arbitrary units where x and y are scaled uniformly
MM_LOENGLISH	.01 inch
MM_LOMETRIC	.1 mm
MM_TEXT	Pixel
MM_TWIPS	1/1440 inch

The mapping mode that you choose for your application is important. The MM_TEXT mapping mode—equivalent to the pixel-based mapping you're accustomed to—is most commonly used and is quite sufficient for most purposes. By using the MM_TEXT mode, however, you may get surprising results. For example, a 100×100 pixel image on a VGA screen does not have the same size or appearance as a 100×100 pixel image on a CGA screen. The results, therefore, may not be what you desire. The various mapping modes offer unique advantages and disadvantages, such as direct mapping to pixels, arbitrary scaling, and scaling by inches or millimeters. The requirements of your application dictate the best mapping mode to choose.

Figures 10.11 and 10.12 illustrate the relationships between the logical and physical coordinate systems for the MM_TEXT and MM_LOGENGLISH mapping modes, respectively.

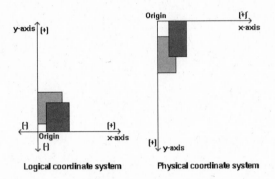

Figure 10.11. *The* MM_TEXT *mapping mode.*

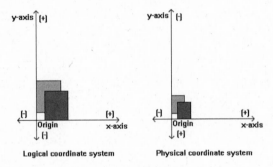

Figure 10.12. *The* MM_LOENGLISH *mapping mode.*

The Drawing Coordinates

Windows uses several coordinate systems that are generally grouped under two classifications, device and logical.

There are three distinct device coordinate systems:

- the screen coordinate system
- the whole-window coordinate system
- the client area coordinate system

These device coordinate systems express units of measurement in terms of pixels. Remember that pixels only change relative to video mode; units of measurement change relative to the device context and mapping mode.

The screen coordinate system uses the entire screen. The top left corner of the screen is the origin of the coordinate system. The x-axis increases from left to right; the y-axis increases from top to bottom. Screen coordinates are generally used with functions that move objects relative to a physical location on-screen.

The whole-window coordinate system uses the entire physical size of a window including the window border. The top left corner of the window border is the origin of the coordinate system. The x-axis increases from left to right; the y-axis increases from top to bottom. Programmers might use the whole window system when they want to access the entire window to do something unusual such as creating icons on the window's border—in other words, not very often.

The client area coordinate system is the most commonly used coordinate system. The *client area* is the working area of the window and excludes the window borders, the Menu bar, and the scroll bars. Because your program generally manipulates only the client area, the client area coordinate system is appropriate for most applications. The top left corner of the client area is the origin of the coordinate system. The x-axis increases from left to right; the y-axis increases from top to bottom.

Now here's the catch: When you use a Windows graphics function, you won't actually specify the coordinates in any of the device coordinate systems mentioned previously. You will use a *logical coordinate system* instead. The mapping mode specifies how the logical units specified in GDI functions are converted to device coordinates. Logical units are associated with a window, and device coordinates are associated with a viewport, which usually is the same as the client area. The logical units of a window are expressed in units specified by the mapping mode. Before you can draw an object, Windows must translate these logical units to one of the device coordinate systems.

Fortunately, it's much easier to use all these coordinate systems than it is to describe them. When using the MM_TEXT mapping mode, you can usually think of the logical coordinate system and the client area coordinate system as equivalent to one another. In practice, drawing to the client area in a Windows application isn't much more complex than drawing to the screen in a DOS graphics program. The next chapter gives you oodles of working code demonstrating the use of logical coordinates with most of the Windows GDI functions.

Summary: Don't Leave the Driving to Us...

Fenestracryptophobia: *The fear of Windows programming. Symptoms range from mild headaches to outright disorientation and confusion. In worst cases, suffering programmers find it difficult to manage even simple events such as opening a window... Windows 3.1 promises relief for some of these programmer phobias while, at the same time, introducing significant enhancements... This is good news to new and seasoned fenestracryptographers...*

—Michael Floyd, "What? Me Worry About Windows Programming?"
Doctor Dobb's Journal, December 1991, p. 4

This chapter has provided a fast and furious excursion into Microsoft Windows and Windows programming. From the standard components of an application window, through event-driven programming, to a fundamental window example and the graphics device interface, you've glimpsed all the landmarks from a "Windows seat" on the graphics programmers' tour bus. In Chapter 11, you get to jump into the driver's seat and explore the world of Windows graphics. I'll help you navigate through several working programs to display text and graphics in the client area of the application window.

Windows Graphics Functions

I n this chapter and the next, you'll find more **Working Code** sections and less explanatory material than in other chapters. The Working Code sections refer you to files included on the disks. The mission of these chapters is to get you up to speed quickly in Windows graphics programming by cruising through all the major graphics functions available in the Windows *application programming interface* (API).

Most graphics libraries provide you with basic drawing capabilities, and the Windows API is no exception. This chapter introduces the Windows drawing functions and presents concepts and principles behind Windows points, drawing modes, lines, pens, brushes, rectangles, polygons, ellipses, text, and fonts.

You may be tempted to simply substitute Windows graphics calls for the general-purpose graphics functions used in the rest of the book, but the power of Windows demands that you take a slightly different approach, even with the simplest graphics operations such as drawing a line or point. Because Windows graphics are *device independent,* you don't know how many colors or even what resolution the user's screen will have when you write a Windows graphics program. Therefore, you won't usually deal with the color palette and screen coordinates directly, as you did with MS-DOS based graphics. These changes, coupled with the unique event-driven architecture of Windows, mean that you should jump into Windows graphics afresh and leave your old conceptions (and program structures) behind.

We'll begin by showing you the Windows way to draw the simplest of all graphics entities, the point.

Points

Under Windows 3.0 [and Windows 3.1], colors in the palettes kept by applications and by the system are defined as 24-bit values (8 each for red, green, and blue). When these values are output to a device that can't display 24 bits, the display driver converts them to a value the display can produce.

—Adam Bellin and Pier Del Frate, "True Color for Windows,"
BYTE, December 1990, p. 284

Like almost every graphics package, the Windows GDI provides the capability to draw a point on-screen. Drawing a point in the client area of the application window is easy with the Windows SetPixel function.

In the following **Working Code** box, you'll draw a series of dots on-screen using four different colors: red, green, blue, and black. You specify the colors using red-green-blue (RGB) triplet values. You specify red with the RGB triplet value RGB(255,0,0), which indicates that only the red color is used. Similarly, the RGB triplet values RGB(0,255,0) and RGB(0,0,255) specify green and blue respectively. The RGB triplet value RGB(0,0,0) indicates black, and RGB(255,255,255) means you used too much Clorox.

Now, if you can set each of the three (red, green, or blue) values up to 255, that's eight bits worth of information per color channel or 24 bits of color data for each pixel. Does that mean that every Windows user has an expensive 24-bit True-color video adapter? No. It means that some users have 24-bit color and that Windows automatically converts the color values to the best approximation it can create for everyone else. As a Windows programmer, you never need to concern yourself with confusing strategies for approximating true color with 256-color or 16-color palettes.

The point example in the following **Working Code** section, like all the examples I present in this chapter, follows the basic format of the fundamental window example presented in Chapter 10, "The Windows Graphics Device Interface." The application window for each example in this chapter is a standard, sizeable window and contains the same menu bar presented in the fundamental window example from Chapter 10. The examples in this chapter, however, do monitor one additional Windows message, the WM_PAINT message.

The WM_PAINT message is sent to an application when the application window is created or sized and indicates that the application should repaint the client area of the screen. In the examples presented in this chapter, the code associated with the WM_PAINT message performs that action. For the point example, the code associated with WM_PAINT draws the points in the client area of the application window whenever it receives the WM_PAINT message. Figure 11.1 shows the application window for the point example.

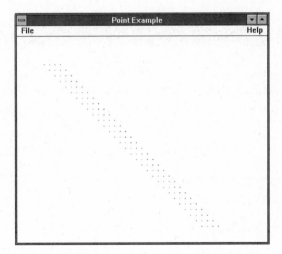

Figure 11.1. *The point example.*

Look closely at the following portion of code that begins with `case WM_PAINT:` and ends with `EndPaint(hWnd, &PtStr);`. In this code segment, which redraws the client area of the application window, the `SetPixel` function is used to draw four distinct points, each in a different color, for each iteration of the `for` loop. The four points are drawn horizontally from left to right in red, green, blue, and black. Notice that the `BeginPaint` and `EndPaint` functions are used with the `WM_PAINT` code segment. These functions perform the actions necessary to start and end painting in the client area. The `BeginPaint` function also returns the device context you need for calling graphics functions such as `SetPixel`. The first parameter of the Windows graphics functions is usually the device context that can be obtained from the `BeginPaint` function.

Working Code: Making a Point

The point example in Listing 11.1 requires three files:

- The pointex.c file is the C source code file containing the source code that draws the points in the client area of the screen.

- The pointex.rc file defines the menu resource for the application window.

- The pointex.def file is the module definition file for the application.

BUILD If you have Turbo C++ for Windows or Borland C++, you can open pointex.prj from the IDE and select the Run option from the IDE's Run Menu to build the application. Otherwise, create the appropriate make file or project file for your compiler to build the application using the pointex.c, pointex.rc, and pointex.def files.

For this example, I list all three files in the book. In future examples in this and the next chapter, you can find the code on the accompanying disks. (I didn't want to overwhelm you with code, so I left it in a safe spot on the disk—don't worry, it's still there!)

Listing 11.1. The Point example.

```
Project Name:    pointex.prj
Project Files:   pointex.c
                 pointex.rc
                 pointex.def
```

Filename: pointex.c

```
#include <windows.h>
```

```
#include <stdlib.h>
#include <string.h>

long FAR PASCAL WndProc (HWND hWnd, WORD iMessage,
             WORD wParam, LONG lParam);

int PASCAL WinMain (HANDLE hInstance, HANDLE hPrevInstance,
            LPSTR lpszCmdParam, int nCmdShow)

{
HWND hWnd;
MSG Message;
WNDCLASS WndClass;

if (!hPrevInstance)
     {
     WndClass.cbClsExtra = 0;
     WndClass.cbWndExtra = 0;
     WndClass.hbrBackground = GetStockObject(WHITE_BRUSH);
     WndClass.hCursor =  LoadCursor(NULL, IDC_ARROW);
     WndClass.hIcon = LoadIcon (NULL, "END");
     WndClass.hInstance = hInstance;
     WndClass.lpfnWndProc = WndProc;
     WndClass.lpszClassName = "POINTWIN";
     WndClass.lpszMenuName = "MENU";
     WndClass.style = CS_HREDRAW | CS_VREDRAW;

     RegisterClass (&WndClass);
     }

hWnd = CreateWindow ("POINTWIN", /* class name */
        "Point Example",      /* Caption */
        WS_OVERLAPPEDWINDOW,  /* Style */
        CW_USEDEFAULT,        /* x position */
        0,                    /* y position */
        CW_USEDEFAULT,        /* cx - size */
        0,                    /* cy - size */
        NULL,                 /* Parent window */
        NULL,                 /* Menu */
        hInstance,            /* Program Instance */
        NULL);                /* Parameters */
```

continues

Listing 11.1. continued

```
ShowWindow (hWnd, nCmdShow);
while (GetMessage (&Message, 0, 0, 0))
     {
     TranslateMessage(&Message);
     DispatchMessage(&Message);
     }
return Message.wParam;
}


/**********************************************************/
/*              Window Procedure: WndProc                 */
/**********************************************************/

long FAR PASCAL WndProc (HWND hWnd, WORD iMessage,
                         WORD wParam, LONG lParam)
{
HDC hDC;
PAINTSTRUCT PtStr;
int x, y;

switch (iMessage)
     {
     case WM_COMMAND:
         switch(wParam)
          {
          case 101:
               SendMessage(hWnd, WM_CLOSE, 0, 0L);
               return 0;

          case 102:
               MessageBox(hWnd,
                 "Sample Application",
                 "Windows Graphics",
                 MB_ICONINFORMATION¦MB_OK);
               return 0;
          }
         return 0;

     case WM_PAINT:
```

```
        hDC = BeginPaint(hWnd, &PtStr);

        y = 50;
        for (x=50; x<350; x=x+10)
            {
            SetPixel(hDC,x,y,RGB(255,0,0));
            SetPixel(hDC,x+10,y,RGB(0,255,0));
            SetPixel(hDC,x+20,y,RGB(0,0,255));
            SetPixel(hDC,x+30,y,RGB(0,0,0));
            y=y+10;
            }

        EndPaint(hWnd, &PtStr);
        return 0;

    case WM_DESTROY:
        PostQuitMessage(0);
        return 0;

    default:
        return(DefWindowProc(hWnd, iMessage, wParam,
            lParam));
    }
}
```

Filename: pointex.rc

```
MENU MENU LOADONCALL MOVEABLE PURE DISCARDABLE
BEGIN
  POPUP "File"
  BEGIN
    MenuItem "Exit", 101
  END
  POPUP "Help", HELP
  BEGIN
    MenuItem "About", 102
  END
END
```

Filename: pointex.def

```
NAME            POINTWIN
```

continues

489

Listing 11.1. continued

```
DESCRIPTION      'Point Example'
EXETYPE          WINDOWS
CODE             PRELOAD MOVEABLE
DATA             PRELOAD MOVEABLE MULTIPLE
HEAPSIZE         1024
STACKSIZE        5120
EXPORTS          WndProc
```

As the next step, you'll draw lines and other complex figures inside the client area of an application window. You typically draw lines and figures using two Windows objects, pens and brushes. You draw lines and the outlines of figures with a Windows object called the *pen*. You fill the inside of a figure with a Windows object called the *brush*. Before you begin drawing lines and figures, however, look more closely at pens and brushes.

Pens

Pens are most dangerous tools, more sharp by odds
Than swords, and cut more keen than whips or rods.

—John Taylor, *News from Hell, Hull, and Halifax*

Windows uses an object called the pen to draw lines and figure borders. The pen has several attributes that specify the color, width, and style of the resulting line or figure border. Windows provides three predefined pens: the black pen, the null pen, and the white pen. You can use the `GetStockObject` function to select one of these predefined pens. With Windows, you can also create your own custom pens by using the `CreatePen` or `CreatePenIndirect` functions.

Pen Styles

The pen style affects the way lines appear as you draw them. Windows provides seven predefined pen styles as listed in Table 11.1.

Table 11.1. Pen styles.

Constant	Meaning
PS_SOLID	Solid pen
PS_DASH	Dashed pen
PS_DOT	Dotted pen
PS_DASHDOT	Dash-dotted pen
PS_DASHDOTDOT	Dash-dot-dotted pen
PS_NULL	Null pen
PS_INSIDEFRAME	Pen that draws a line inside the frame of ellipses and rectangles when using the Chord, Ellipse, Pie, Rectangle, and RoundRect functions

I'll show you an example that demonstrates how these pen styles vary. In the next **Working Code** section, you'll discover how to use the pen styles that Windows provides. For each of the seven pen styles, you'll draw a line using the pen style and label each line with text to indicate the pen style you're using. Figure 11.2 shows the application window for the pen style example.

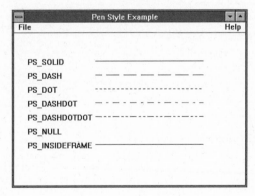

Figure 11.2. *The pen style example.*

As with all the examples in this chapter, the only part of the **Working Code** you need to examine closely is the WM_PAINT code segment. In this code segment, the

TextOut function is used to draw the text labelling each line. The CreatePen function creates the pens using the various line styles. The pens are created with a pen width of one pixel and are black. The SelectObject function makes the newly created pen the current pen. The lines are then drawn using the MoveTo and LineTo functions.

Working Code: Using Pens with Style

The pen style example on the disk requires three files:

- The penstyex.c file is the C source code file containing the source code that draws the lines using the current pen and the various line styles.

- The penstyex.rc file defines the menu resource for the application window.

- The penstyex.def file is the module definition file for the application.

BUILD If you have Turbo C++ for Windows or Borland C++, you can open penstyex.prj from the IDE and select the Run option from the IDE's Run Menu to build the application. Otherwise, create the appropriate make file or project file for your compiler to build the application using the penstyex.c, penstyex.rc, and penstyex.def files.

Listing 11.2. The pen style example.

```
Project Name:   penstyex.prj
Project Files:  penstyex.c
                penstyex.rc
                penstyex.def
```

Custom Pens

You have seen how to use the standard pen styles provided by Windows. You can also create custom pens with a width, color, and style of your own choosing.

In this example, you create four custom pens: one red pen, one blue pen, one green pen, and one black pen. (Think of them as fish and consider yourself the Dr. Suess of computer graphics.) You'll use the PS_SOLID pen style for your custom pens and define each pen with a pen width of 3 pixels. In the last example, you used the

CreatePen function to create pens. This time, you'll use the CreatePenIndirect function to create the four custom pens. Once you've created the pens, you'll use them to draw some rectangles.

The first step you must take when you create a custom pen with the CreatePenIndirect function is to define the pen structures used by the function. You must define one LOGPEN structure for each pen you create. The lines starting with LOGPEN in the following code define four LOGPEN data structures for your four custom pens. The line starting with HPEN defines variables for the pen handles that are returned when you call the CreatePenIndirect function to create your pens.

Once you've defined the LOGPEN structures and the pen handle variables, you can create your pens. For this example, you'll create your pens and perform your drawing when the application's window procedure receives the WM_PAINT message. The code segment beginning with case WM_PAINT: creates the pens, draws the rectangles, and deletes the pens. In this code segment, the CreatePenIndirect function creates the four pens. The SelectObject function selects each pen, in turn, and the Rectangle function draws rectangles using the currently selected pen. Finally, the DeleteObject function deletes the pens. Figure 11.3 shows the application window for the custom pen example.

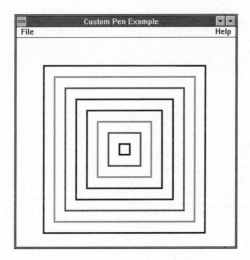

Figure 11.3. *The custom pen example.*

Working Code: A Pen of Your Very Own

The custom pen example in Listing 11.3 requires three files:

■ The cstpenex.c file is the C source code file containing the source code that creates and uses the custom pen.

■ The cstpenex.rc file defines the menu resource for the application window.

■ The cstpenex.def file is the module definition file for the application.

BUILD If you have Turbo C++ for Windows or Borland C++, you can open cstpenex.prj from the IDE and select the Run option from the IDE's Run Menu to build the application. Otherwise, create the appropriate make file or project file for your compiler to build the application using the cstpenex.c, cstpenex.rc, and cstpenex.def files.

Listing 11.3. The custom pen example.

```
Project Name:    cstpenex.prj
Project Files:   cstpenex.c
                 cstpenex.rc
                 cstpenex.def
```

Now that you're handy with pens, try your hand at drawing with brushes.

Brushes

A brush is normally an [8x8] pixel pattern used to paint the screen. Windows or an application can request that the display driver create a brush that has a foreground and/or a background color. If the display device cannot output the colors requested in the brush, the driver generates an [8x8] pixel dithered pattern that most closely represents the colors requested.

—Adam Bellin and Pier Del Frate, "True Color for Windows," *BYTE*, December 1990, p. 284

Windows uses an object called the brush to fill the inside of figures. Windows provides six predefined brushes that you can select with the GetStockObject function.

Value	Meaning
BLACK_BRUSH	Black brush
DKGRAY_BRUSH	Dark-gray brush
GRAY_BRUSH	Gray brush
HOLLOW_BRUSH	Hollow brush
LTGRAY_BRUSH	Light-gray brush
NULL_BRUSH	Null brush
WHITE_BRUSH	White brush

In addition to using the stock objects, you can create a brush by using the CreateSolidBrush, CreateHatchBrush, CreatePatternBrush, or CreateBrushIndirect functions. The CreatePatternBrush enables you to define a custom brush that uses a custom bitmap. The CreateSolidBrush and CreateBrushIndirect functions also enable you to create custom brushes.

Stock Brushes

In this example, you draw filled rectangles using the seven stock Windows brushes. You'll use the SelectObject and GetStockObject functions to select the appropriate stock Windows brush and draw a filled rectangle with the Rectangle function. As usual, you should focus on the part of the code that handles the WM_PAINT message (the rest of the program is identical to the previous examples). Figure 11.4 shows the application window for the stock brush example.

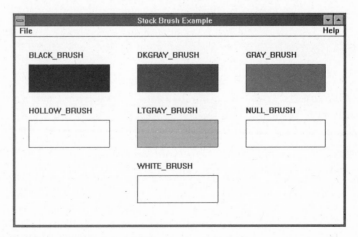

Figure 11.4. *The stock brush example.*

Working Code: Brushing Up on Brushes

The stock brush example in Listing 11.4 requires three files:

- The stckbrex.c file is the C source code file containing the source code that displays figures filled using the various stock brushes.

- The stckbrex.rc file defines the menu resource for the application window.

- The stckbrex.def file is the module definition file for the application.

BUILD If you have Turbo C++ for Windows or Borland C++, you can open stckbrex.prj from the IDE and select the Run option from the IDE's Run Menu to build the application. Otherwise, create the appropriate make file or project file for your compiler to build the application using the stckbrex.c, stckbrex.rc, and stckbrex.def files.

Listing 11.4. The stock brush example.

```
Project Name:     stckbrex.prj
Project Files:    stckbrex.c
                  stckbrex.rc
                  stckbrex.def
```

Now that I've shown you stock brushes, here's a look at the Windows hatch brushes.

Hatch Brushes

In addition to the stock brushes, Windows gives you hatch brushes. A hatch brush creates a pattern when filling an area. Hatch brushes are useful for differentiating figures when only a few colors are available. Just by using the six hatch brush patterns, you can fill six figures—each which looks unique—while only using one foreground color.

Windows provides six predefined hatch brushes that you can use (see Table 11.2). The following hatch brush example shows how you can use the CreateHatchBrush function to create hatch brushes. Although this example creates black hatch brushes, you can easily create colored hatch brushes by adjusting the RGB triplet value specified in the CreateHatchBrush function. In this example, you'll simply create some hatch brushes and draw a rectangle using each of them.

Table 11.2. Hatched brush patterns.

Value	Meaning
HS_BDIAGONAL	45-degree upward hatch
HS_CROSS	Crosshatch with vertical/horizontal lines
HS_DIAGCROSS	45-degree crosshatch
HS_FDIAGONAL	45-degree downward hatch
HS_HORIZONTAL	Horizontal hatch
HS_VERTICAL	Vertical hatch

To create the brushes, you first need to establish a variable for holding the handle to your created hatch brush. The code to do this is simply:

```
HBRUSH hBrush;
```

The remaining code that creates the brushes and draws the filled rectangles is associated with the WM_PAINT message. Whenever the application's window procedure receives the WM_PAINT message, the TextOut function labels the rectangles, the CreateHatchBrush function creates a hatch brush, the SelectObject function selects the newly created hatch brush, the Rectangle function draws a filled rectangle using the new hatch brush, and the DeleteObject function deletes the brush object you created. Figure 11.5 shows the application window for the hatch brush example.

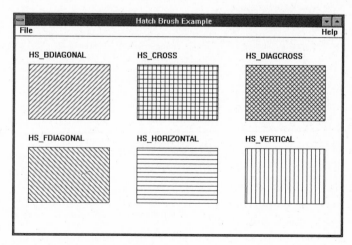

Figure 11.5. *The hatch brush example.*

Working Code: Down the Hatch with Some Brushes

The hatch brush example in Listing 11.5 requires three files:

- The htchbrex.c file is the C source code file containing the source code that loads and uses the standard Windows hatch brushes.

- The htchbrex.rc file defines the menu resource for the application window.

- The htchbrex.def file is the module definition file for the application.

BUILD If you have Turbo C++ for Windows or Borland C++, you can open htchbrex.prj from the IDE and select the Run option from the IDE's Run Menu to build the application. Otherwise, create the appropriate make file or project file for your compiler to build the application using the htchbrex.c, htchbrex.rc, and htchbrex.def files.

Listing 11.5. The hatch brush example.

```
Project Name:   htchbrex.prj
Project Files:  htchbrex.c
                htchbrex.rc
                htchbrex.def
```

Now that you've reviewed how Windows handles pens and brushes when drawing lines and objects, here are some ways you can create straight and curved lines in the Windows environment.

Lines

True genius walks along a line, and, perhaps, our greatest pleasure is in seeing it so often near falling, without being ever actually down.

—Oliver Goldsmith, "The Characteristics of Greatness," *The Bee*, 1759

Windows provides several functions for drawing lines. You can draw straight lines with the LineTo and Polyline functions, whereas you can draw elliptical arcs with the Windows Arc function.

The LineTo function is the most basic line drawing function. LineTo draws a line from the current pen position to the specified point. The MoveTo function is often used to move the current pen position before the LineTo function is called.

The Polyline function enables you to connect an array of points with lines. Because it enables you to store all the points you want to draw in a single array, you'll often find the Polyline function more convenient to use than the MoveTo and LineTo functions.

With the Arc function, you can draw an elliptical arc. The elliptical arc drawn by the Arc function is actually part of an underlying ellipse with points that are calculated but not actually drawn. The underlying ellipse is specified by the first two coordinate pairs that are passed as parameters to the Arc function. These coordinate pairs specify the corners of a rectangle that bind the underlying ellipse. The third coordinate pair passed to the function specifies the starting point of the ellipse. The arc begins at the point where the line—beginning at the center of the underlying ellipse and extending to the point specified in the third coordinate pair—intersects the ellipse. The arc is then drawn in a counterclockwise direction until it reaches the point where the line—drawn between the center of the underlying ellipse and the fourth coordinate pair passed to the Arc function—intersects the ellipse.

Windows uses the current pen and the drawing mode when drawing lines. The current pen defines the color, width, and style of the resulting line, whereas the drawing mode defines the way that the line interacts with existing objects and colors on-screen. Windows provides the drawing modes specified in Table 11.3.

Table 11.3. Drawing modes.

Value	Meaning
R2_BLACK	Pixel is black
R2_COPYPEN	Pixel is the pen color
R2_MASKNOTPEN	Pixel is the combination of the common colors of the display and the inverse of the pen
R2_MASKPEN	Pixel is the combination of the common colors of the pen and the display

continues

Table 11.3. continued

Value	Meaning
R2_MASKPENNOT	Pixel is the combination of the common colors of the pen and the inverse of the display color
R2_MERGENOTPEN	Pixel is the combination of the display color and the inverse of the pen color
R2_MERGEPEN	Pixel is the combination of the pen and display colors
R2_MERGEPENNOT	Pixel is the combination of pen color and inverse of display color
R2_NOP	Pixel is not changed
R2_NOT	Pixel is the inverse of display color
R2_NOTCOPYPEN	Pixel is the inverse of pen color
R2_NOTMASKPEN	Pixel is the inverse of R2_MASKPEN
R2_NOTMERGEPEN	Pixel is the inverse of R2_MERGEPEN
R2_NOTXORPEN	Pixel is the inverse of the R2_XORPEN color
R2_WHITE	Pixel is white
R2_XORPEN	Pixel is the combination of the colors in the pen and in the display, but not both

You've already used pens to draw lines. Now see how the drawing mode affects the way that lines are drawn on-screen.

Drawing Modes

The drawing mode affects the way lines are drawn. In the next **Working Code**, you'll see the effects of the various drawing modes. You'll use each of the drawing modes to draw two lines. You'll draw the first line with the black pen. The line begins in the white background of the application windows client area, and you'll draw it through a black rectangle. You'll draw the second line with the white pen. This line will also begin in the white background of the client area and will be drawn through a black rectangle. The resulting application window demonstrates the effects of the various line modes.

As with the other examples in this chapter, the WM_PAINT code segment performs the graphic actions you want. In the WM_PAINT code segment, the SetROP2 function selects the current drawing mode. The SelectObject function selects the appropriate stock pen, and the LineTo function draws a line using the current pen and drawing mode. You repeat these steps for each drawing mode.

Figure 11.6 shows the application window for the drawing mode example. As you can see from this figure, the drawing mode definitely affects the way lines are drawn across objects and on the application window background.

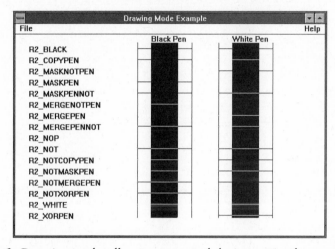

Figure 11.6. *Drawing modes allow you to control the interaction between the lines you draw and the background.*

Working Code: A Demonstration of Drawing Modes

The drawing mode example in Listing 11.6 requires three files:

■ The drawmdex.c file is the C source code file containing the source code that draws a line using both the black and the white pen in each of the various drawing modes.

■ The drawmdex.rc file defines the menu resource for the application window.

■ The drawmdex.def file is the module definition file for the application.

> **BUILD** If you have Turbo C++ for Windows or Borland C++, you can open drawmdex.prj from the IDE and select the Run option from the IDE's Run Menu to build the application. Otherwise, create the appropriate make file or project file for your compiler to build the application using the drawmdex.c, drawmdex.rc, and drawmdex.def files.

Listing 11.6. The drawing mode example.

```
Project Name:    drawmdex.prj
Project Files:   drawmdex.c
                 drawmdex.rc
                 drawmdex.def
```

Now that you've seen the effects of the drawing mode, here's how you can use the LineTo function to create lines and figures.

Straight Lines

Although Windows lets you draw several types of lines, the LineTo function is the easiest way to draw straight lines. In the next **Working Code** section, you use the LineTo and the MoveTo functions to draw a four-pointed star with a series of straight lines.

Again, the code segment that does the drawing is associated with the WM_PAINT message, and you need only pay attention to the part of the program after the case WM_PAINT: statement. When the application's window procedure receives the WM_PAINT message, the MoveTo function is used to move the current drawing position without drawing. The LineTo function then draws a line from the current drawing position to the specified position. Figure 11.7 shows the application window for the LineTo example.

Working Code: Drawing Lines the Easy Way

The LineTo example in Listing 11.7 requires three files:

■ The linetoex.c file is the C source code file containing the source code that demonstrates how you can use the MoveTo and LineTo functions to draw figures.

■ The linetoex.rc file defines the menu resource for the application window.

■ The linetoex.def file is the module definition file for the application.

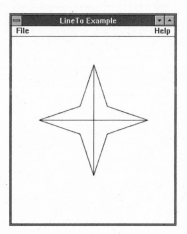 **BUILD** If you have Turbo C++ for Windows or Borland C++, you can open linetoex.prj from the IDE and select the Run option from the IDE's Run Menu to build the application. Otherwise, create the appropriate make file or project file for your compiler to build the application using the linetoex.c, linetoex.rc, and linetoex.def files.

Listing 11.7. The *LineTo* example.

```
Project Name:    linetoex.prj
Project Files:   linetoex.c
                 linetoex.rc
                 linetoex.def
```

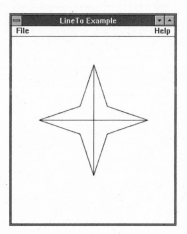

Figure 11.7. *The* LineTo *example shows you how to draw a continous sequence of connected lines.*

Now look at how you can use the Polyline function to draw a series of straight lines.

Multiple Lines

With the Polyline function, you can draw a series of straight lines by calling the function only once. In the following Polyline example, you'll draw a figure that

503

contains 21 points. You define these points in an array of POINT structures. You'll use this array with the Polyline function so you can draw lines between each two consecutive points with only one call to the Polyline function.

The first step you must take in drawing your figure with the Polyline function is to define your points. You'll define the points as a series of POINT structures, with the last point being equal to the first, like this:

```
POINT pt[] = {50,50,100,100,50,150,100,200,50,250,
         100,200,150,250,200,200,250,250,300,200,350,250,
         300,200,350,150,300,100,350,50,
         300,100,250,50,200,100,150,50,100,100,50,50};
```

The code that actually draws the figure is associated with the WM_PAINT message. When the application's window procedure receives the WM_PAINT message, the Polyline function is called to draw the figure. The figure is drawn using the stock black pen, which was selected with the SelectObject function. Notice that the case WM_PAINT: segment in the following **Working Code** section is quite short. It would be much longer if you had to use a separate LineTo function call for every one of the 21 lines. Figure 11.8 shows the application window for the Polyline example.

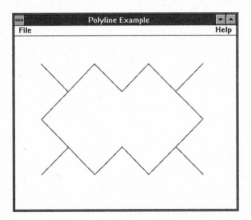

Figure 11.8. *With the* Polyline *example, you can make outlined polygons.*

Working Code: Using Polyline

The `Polyline` example in Listing 11.8 requires three files:

- The polylnex.c file is the C source code file containing the source code that demonstrates how you can use the `Polyline` function to draw figures.

BUILD

- The polylnex.rc file defines the menu resource for the application window.

- The polylnex.def file is the module definition file for the application.

If you have Turbo C++ for Windows or Borland C++, you can open polylnex.prj from the IDE and select the Run option from the IDE's Run Menu to build the application. Otherwise, create the appropriate make file or project file for your compiler to build the application using the polylnex.c, polylnex.rc, and polylnex.def files.

Listing 11.8. The *Polyline* example.

```
Project Name:    polylnex.prj
Project Files:   polylnex.c
                 polylnex.rc
                 polylnex.def
```

You've seen two ways to draw straight lines. Now here's one way you can draw curved lines.

The Arc Example

With the Arc function, you can draw circular and elliptical arcs. As you may recall from high school geometry class, an arc is part of a circle or ellipse.

Once again, the WM_PAINT code segment is used for the series of arcs. In the WM_PAINT portion of the **Working Code** that follows, the Arc function is used to draw a series of concentric circular arcs centered at 0, 90, 180, and 270 degrees. The arcs are drawn using the stock black pen selected with the SelectObject function. Figure 11.9 shows the application window for the Arc example.

Working Code: Building the Arc

The Arc example in Listing 11.9 requires three files:

- The arcex.c file is the C source code file containing the source code that draws a series of arcs on-screen.

- The arcex.rc file defines the menu resource for the application window.

- The arcex.def file is the module definition file for the application.

BUILD If you have Turbo C++ for Windows or Borland C++, you can open arcex.prj from the IDE and select the Run option from the IDE's Run Menu to build the application. Otherwise, create the appropriate make file or project file for your compiler to build the application using the arcex.c, arcex.rc, and arcex.def files.

Listing 11.9. The *Arc* example.

```
Project Name:    arcex.prj
Project Files:   arcex.c
                 arcex.rc
                 arcex.def
```

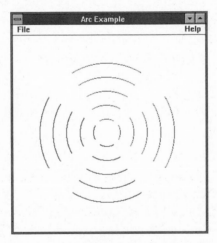

Figure 11.9. *Arcs are one of the fancier Windows graphics primitives.*

Now I'll show you more complex figures, rectangles and polygons.

Rectangles and Polygons

I do not know much of the feminine tribe, But I've watched one or two in the Tube,
And I've seen very few you could fairly describe As a couple of squares and a cube.

—A.P. Herbert, "Triangular Legs"
(a poetical treatise on modern art)

Windows provides several functions for drawing rectangles and polygons. Windows uses the current pen to draw the borders of rectangles and polygons. The current brush is used to fill the interior of the rectangles and polygons.

With the Windows `Rectangle` and `RoundRect` functions, you can draw rectangles. The `Rectangle` function draws a standard rectangle. When you call the `Rectangle` function, you must pass two coordinate pairs. The first coordinate pair specifies the top left corner of the rectangle. The second coordinate pair specifies the bottom right corner of the rectangle.

The `RoundRect` function is similar to the `Rectangle` function but draws a rectangle with rounded corners. Like the `Rectangle` function, you must pass two coordinate pairs when calling it. The first coordinate pair specifies the top left corner of the rectangle. The second coordinate pair specifies the bottom right corner of the rectangle. The `RoundRect` function also requires you to pass two additional parameters. These parameters specify the width and height, respectively, of the rectangle's rounded corners.

In addition to drawing rectangles, Windows enables you to draw polygons. Windows provides the `Polygon` and `PolyPolygon` functions for drawing polygons. The `Polygon` function creates a polygon from the specified array of `POINT` data structures. The `Polygon` is closed automatically and is drawn with the current pen and filled with the current brush.

The `PolyPolygon` function draws a series of polygons. With the `PolyPolygon` function, you can draw several polygons with only one call to the function. The points for all the polygons are specified in an array of `POINT` data structures. An additional integer array indicates the number of points that each polygon contains. Each polygon is filled using the current polygon-filling mode and is not closed automatically. You can specify the current polygon-filling mode with the `SetPolyFillMode` function.

A few examples will demonstrate how you can draw rectangles and polygons. You'll start with a demonstration of the `Rectangle` and `RoundRect` functions.

Rectangles

The Rectangle function draws a rectangle using the current pen to draw the borders and the current brush to fill the rectangle. In the Rectangle example, you'll use the Rectangle and RoundRect functions to draw a series of filled rectangles. The RoundRect function is similar to the rectangle function but draws a rectangle with rounded corners.

The following **Working Code** uses stock pens and brushes to draw a few rectangles. As in the previous examples presented in this chapter, the code associated with the WM_PAINT message performs the drawing actions for the example. The WM_PAINT message code segment uses the Rectangle and RoundRect functions to draw five cascading rectangles: three regular rectangles and two rounded rectangles. The SelectObject function is used to specify the stock pen and brush used to draw each rectangle. Figure 11.10 shows the application window for the Rectangle example.

Figure 11.10. *What would a Graphics Device Interface be without the venerable rectangle?*

Working Code: Rectangles and Rounded Rectangles

The `Rectangle` example in Listing 11.10 requires three files:

■ The rectex.c file is the C source code file containing the source code that demonstrates how you can use the `Rectangle` and `RoundRect` functions to draw rectangles.

■ The rectex.rc file defines the menu resource for the application window.

■ The rectex.def file is the module definition file for the application.

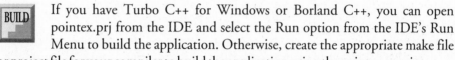 If you have Turbo C++ for Windows or Borland C++, you can open pointex.prj from the IDE and select the Run option from the IDE's Run Menu to build the application. Otherwise, create the appropriate make file or project file for your compiler to build the application using the pointex.c, pointex.rc, and pointex.def files.

Listing 11.10. The rectangle example.

```
Project Name:    rectex.prj
Project Files:   rectex.c
                 rectex.rc
                 rectex.def
```

Now here's a look at the Windows Polygon function, which enables you to draw complex, multisided figures.

Polygons

The `Polygon` function creates a closed polygon. The `Polygon` function draws straight lines between points that are defined in an array of `POINT` structures. The `Polygon` example draws an eight-sided, irregular figure using the `Polygon` function. The stock black brush is used to draw the border of the figure. The stock light gray brush is used to fill the figure.

As before, this example performs its drawing when the application's window procedure receives the `WM_PAINT` message. In this example, the code segment associated with the `WM_PAINT` message draws the multisided figure using the points defined in an array of `POINT` data structures. The array of `POINT` structures is initialized as follows.

```
POINT pts[8];
```

The WM_PAINT message code segment defines the values for each of the members of the POINT structures in the array of point values. Once these values have been defined, the figure is drawn by calling the Polygon function. The SelectObject function is used to select the stock pen and the light gray brush for drawing the figure. Figure 11.11 shows the application window for the Polygon example.

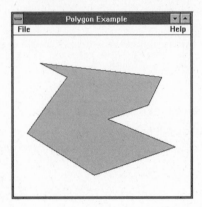

Figure 11.11. *Filled polygons aren't easy to draw, but Windows manages it with aplomb.*

Working Code: A Filled Polygon

The polygon example in Listing 11.11 requires three files:

- The polygnex.c file is the C source code file containing the source code that demonstrates how you can use the Polygon function to draw irregular shapes on-screen.

- The polygnex.rc file defines the menu resource for the application window.

- The polygnex.def file is the module definition file for the application.

BUILD If you have Turbo C++ for Windows or Borland C++, you can open polygnex.prj from the IDE and select the Run option from the IDE's Run Menu to build the application. Otherwise, create the appropriate make file or project file for your compiler to build the application using the polygnex.c, polygnex.rc, and polygnex.def files.

Listing 11.11. The polygon example.

```
Project Name:    polygnex.prj
Project Files:   polygnex.c
                 polygnex.rc
                 polygnex.def
```

Windows also provides a way to draw a series of closed polygons with the `PolyPolygon` function.

Multiple Polygons

In the next example, you use the `PolyPolygon` function to draw four closed polygons: two squares and two diamond shapes. As with the `Polygon` function, the `PolyPolygon` function uses an array of `POINT` data structures to define all the points for the polygons. The `PolyPolygon` also uses an array of integers to define the number of points in each polygon drawn with the `PolyPolygon` function. In this example, you use five points to define each of the four-sided polygons you want to draw. The first point and the last point of the points that define each four-sided polygon are the same to ensure a closed polygon because the `PolyPolygon` function does not close each polygon automatically.

The following code segment establishes the arrays required by the `PolyPolygon` function:

```
POINT pts[20];
int pcount[4];
```

As with previous examples, the `WM_PAINT` code segment in the following **Working Code** section performs the drawing actions. In the `WM_PAINT` message code segment, the array values are defined just prior to calling the `PolyPolygon` function.

Working Code: Where Has `PolyPolygon` Gone?

The `PolyPolygon` example in Listing 11.12 requires three files:

■ The plyplyex.c file is the C source code file containing the source code that demonstrates how you can draw a series of polygons with only one call to the `PolyPolygon` function.

- The plyplyex.rc file defines the menu resource for the application window.

- The plyplyex.def file is the module definition file for the application.

BUILD If you have Turbo C++ for Windows or Borland C++, you can open plyplyex.prj from the IDE and select the Run option from the IDE's Run Menu to build the application. Otherwise, create the appropriate make file or project file for your compiler to build the application using the plyplyex.c, plyplyex.rc, and plyplyex.def files.

Listing 11.12. The `PolyPolygon` **example.**

```
Project Name:   plyplyex.prj
Project Files:  plyplyex.c
                plyplyex.rc
                plyplyex.def
```

Figure 11.12 shows the application window for the `PolyPolygon` example.

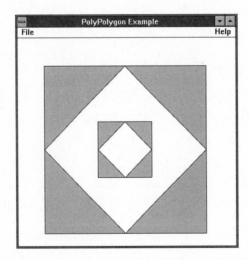

Figure 11.12. *Multiple polygons from a single function call? No problem with the handy-dandy* `PolyPolygon` *function.*

Now I'll present a few ways you can draw circles and ellipses in the Windows environment.

Circles and Ellipses

Was Sheba the Queen, who made Solomon gape, A collection of parallel lines?
Was Juliet just an elliptical shape With a few geometrical signs?

—A.P. Herbert, "Triangular Legs"

Windows provides several functions for drawing circles and ellipses. These functions include the `Ellipse`, `Chord`, and `Pie` functions. With the `Ellipse` function, you can draw circles and ellipses. The `Ellipse` function draws the circle or ellipse inside a bounding rectangle specified by two coordinate pairs passed to the function. The first coordinate pair specifies the top left corner of the bounding rectangle; the second coordinate pair specifies the bottom right corner of the bounding rectangle. The ellipse is drawn using the current pen and filled with the current brush.

The `Chord` function creates a chorded ellipse. A *chord* is an ellipse cut at the intersection of a line segment. The chorded ellipse is drawn inside the bounding rectangle specified by the first two coordinate pairs passed to the function. Two additional coordinate pairs specify the line segment that intersects and cuts the ellipse. The chorded ellipse is drawn using the current pen and filled with the current brush.

The `Pie` function draws a pie-shaped wedge using the current pen and brush. Four coordinate pairs specify the pie-shaped wedge. The first two coordinate pairs respectively specify the top left and bottom right corners of the bounding rectangle used to create the ellipse portion of the wedge. The third coordinate pair specifies the point used to determine where the arc for the pie-shaped wedge begins. A line projects from the center of the ellipse to the point specified in the third coordinate pair. The arc for the wedge begins where this projected line intercepts the ellipse. The arc extends in a counterclockwise direction and ends at the point where the line projects between the center of the ellipse and the fourth coordinate pair intercepts the ellipse.

Now look at three examples that demonstrate how you can use these functions. I'll start with the `Ellipse` function.

Ellipses

The `Ellipse` function provides an easy way to draw filled circles and ellipses. In this example, you use the `Ellipse` function to draw a flower with four petals. The elliptical petals are oriented at 0, 90, 180, and 270 degrees. A circle is drawn in the center of the flower.

513

In the WM_PAINT code segment, where the drawing action occurs, you select the stock black pen and the stock gray brush with the SelectObject function. The Ellipse function uses these objects to draw the elliptical petals at 0, 90, 270, and 360 degrees. The Ellipse function then selects the stock black brush and uses it to draw the center of the flower. Figure 11.13 shows the application window for the Ellipse example.

Figure 11.13. *An* Ellipse *by any other name would still draw as sweetly.*

Working Code: Elliptical Flower Petals

The Ellipse example in Listing 11.13 requires three files:

■ The ellipsex.c file is the C source code file containing the source code that demonstrates how to use the Ellipse function.

■ The ellipsex.rc file defines the menu resource for the application window.

■ The ellipsex.def file is the module definition file for the application.

BUILD If you have Turbo C++ for Windows or Borland C++, you can open ellipsex.prj from the IDE and select the Run option from the IDE's Run Menu to build the application. Otherwise, create the appropriate make file or project file for your compiler to build the application using the ellipsex.c, ellipsex.rc, and ellipsex.def files.

Listing 11.13. The *Ellipse* example.

```
Project Name:   ellipsex.prj
Project Files:  ellipsex.c
                ellipsex.rc
                ellipsex.def
```

Now I'll show you a way to draw chorded ellipses with the Chord Windows function.

Chorded Ellipses

The Chord function enables you to draw a chorded ellipse. A *chorded ellipse* is an ellipse cut at the intersections of a specified line segment. In this example, you draw four chorded ellipses. The line segments cutting the ellipses are situated so that the resulting chorded sections are shaped like a diamond.

The chorded ellipses are drawn whenever the application's window procedure receives the WM_PAINT message. Once the SelectObject function selects the stock black pen and gray brush, the Chord function draws four chorded ellipses. Figure 11.14 shows the application window for the Chord example.

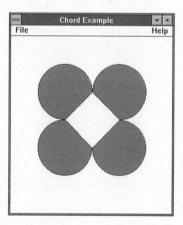

Figure 11.14. *The* Chord *example demonstrates a nifty function to draw pieces of ellipses chopped off by lines.*

515

Working Code: Playing Those Chords

The Chord example in Listing 11.14 requires three files:

- The chordex.c file is the C source code file containing the source code that demonstrates how you can use the Chord function to draw a chorded ellipse.

- The chordex.rc file defines the menu resource for the application window.

- The chordex.def file is the module definition file for the application.

If you have Turbo C++ for Windows or Borland C++, you can open chordex.prj from the IDE and select the Run option from the IDE's Run Menu to build the application. Otherwise, create the appropriate make file or project file for your compiler to build the application using the chordex.c, chordex.rc, and chordex.def files.

Listing 11.14. The Chord example.

```
Project Name:    chordex.prj
Project Files:   chordex.c
                 chordex.rc
                 chordex.def
```

Here's a way to draw elliptical pie-shaped wedges in Windows.

Pie Pieces

Windows provides the Pie function for drawing filled, pie-shaped, elliptical wedges. In the Pie example, you use the Pie function to create an exploded pie chart. The pie chart will contain five pieces with one of the five pieces exploded from the pie chart.

As with the previous examples, all drawing occurs when the application's window procedure receives the WM_PAINT message. The first four pieces of the Pie chart are drawn using the same bounding rectangle. The fifth, exploded piece of the pie chart uses a bounding rectangle that is offset from the previous bounding rectangle. The offset bounding rectangle gives the fifth piece its exploded appearance. Figure 11.15 shows the application window for the Pie example.

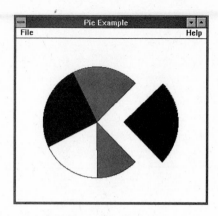

Figure 11.15. *Drawing these wedges was as easy as...*

Working Code: Making a Pie

The Pie example in Listing 11.15 requires three files:

- The pieex.c file is the C source code file containing the source code that draws an exploded pie chart using the Pie function.

- The pieex.rc file defines the menu resource for the application window.

- The pieex.def file is the module definition file for the application.

> **BUILD** If you have Turbo C++ for Windows or Borland C++, you can open pieex.prj from the IDE and select the Run option from the IDE's Run Menu to build the application. Otherwise, create the appropriate make file or project file for your compiler to build the application using the pieex.c, pieex.rc, and pieex.def files.

Listing 11.15. The *Pie* example.

```
Project Name:    pieex.prj
Project Files:   pieex.c
                 pieex.rc
                 pieex.def
```

Now that you've seen how Windows handles basic drawing, you'll see how Windows handles text.

Text and Fonts

The use of fonts in a variety of styles and sizes is an increasingly common practice in graphics applications. This is no doubt due in part to the rapid growth of desktop publishing and in part to the development of the printer technologies needed to fully exploit the software. Together, these have raised awareness of typography and expectations regarding text quality. Indeed, the average user now rolls off phrases such as "12 point condensed italic" or "ITC Avant Garde Gothic Book" with the ease of a professional typesetter.

—Marv Luse, "Resizing Bitmapped Fonts,"
The C Gazette, Summer 1989, p. 11

Talking about text output may seem a little strange in a graphics book, but Windows uses the GDI for text output. Although Windows provides extensive text and font support, you'll simply take a quick look at the basics of Windows text and fonts.

In the Windows environment, text characters are drawn according to the currently selected font. The font contains specific information on the shape and appearance of each character, number, and punctuation mark in the character set. By using defined device-independent font sets, Windows maintains its device independence while providing the benefits of WYSIWYG.

Windows provides several device context attributes for text. These attributes define the way that text is drawn; they can be modified but are set to the default values specified in Table 11.4.

Table 11.4. Device context attributes for text.

Attribute	Default Value
Background color	White
Background mode	OPAQUE
Font	SYSTEM_FONT

Attribute	Default Value
Intercharacter spacing	0
Text color	Black

The background color attribute specifies the color used to fill the areas around, inside, and between characters. This attribute is also used to fill both the areas between hatches in a hatched brush pattern and the spaces in a styled line pattern.

The background mode attribute is set to either OPAQUE or TRANSPARENT. The default setting, OPAQUE, turns the background color on; the TRANSPARENT setting turns the background color off.

The font attribute specifies the current font. The current font contains the patterns that specify the shape, size, and appearance of the text characters. The intercharacter spacing attribute specifies the number of logical units to insert between characters. The text color attribute specifies the color used to draw the text. This attribute must be a pure color with no color shades created using hatched or dithered patterns.

I'll present three quick examples to introduce you to the basic Windows text capabilities. In the TextOut example, you'll learn the most common way to display text. In the TabbedTextOut example, you'll see how you can easily display columns of text. In the fonts example, you'll discover how to display text using different fonts and text sizes.

Displaying Text

The TextOut function offers an easy way to display text in your application window. In the TextOut example, you use the TextOut function to display a column of text containing a column heading, a line divider, and ten lines of text.

The text in the TextOut example displays each time the application's window procedure receives the WM_PAINT message. The TextOut function occurs repeatedly in the following **Working Code** section to display each line of text in the column. Figure 11.16 shows the application window for the TextOut example.

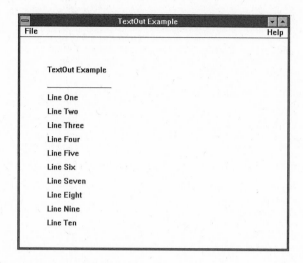

Figure 11.16. *The extensive support for text formatting is well known. The* TextOut *function is your key to unlock this treasure.*

Working Code: Text the Easy Way

The TextOut example in Listing 11.16 requires three files:

- The txtoutex.c file is the C source code file containing the source code that demonstrates how you can use the TextOut function to draw text.

- The txtoutex.rc file defines the menu resource for the application window.

- The txtoutex.def file is the module definition file for the application.

BUILD If you have Turbo C++ for Windows or Borland C++, you can open txtoutex.prj from the IDE and select the Run option from the IDE's Run Menu to build the application. Otherwise, create the appropriate make file or project file for your compiler to build the application using the txtoutex.c, txtoutex.rc, and txtoutex.def files.

Listing 11.16. The *TextOut* example.

```
Project Name:    txtoutex.prj
Project Files:   txtoutex.c
                 txtoutex.rc
                 txtoutex.def
```

Although the TextOut function is easy to use, it provides no way to display formatted text. Next you'll see the TabbedTextOut function, which enables you to display multiple columns of tabbed text.

Formatted Text

The TabbedTextOut function is similar to the TextOut function but enables you to display text containing tabs; this makes it easy to display formatted columns of text. In the TabbedTextOut example, you display two columns of text using the TabbedTextOut function. Each column of text contains a column header, a line divider, and ten lines of text.

The text for the TabbedTextOut example displays whenever the application's window procedure receives the WM_PAINT message. The TabbedTextOut function is used to display each line of text. You should notice that \t is used in the text string to indicate a tab position. Text to the right of \t is tabbed to the next column.

Figure 11.17 shows the application window for the TabbedTextOut example.

Working Code: Put That Text on My Tab

The TabbedTextOut example in Listing 11.17 requires three files:

■ The tabtxtex.c file is the C source code file containing the source code that draws the tabbed text.

■ The tabtxtex.rc file defines the menu resource for the application window.

■ The tabtxtex.def file is the module definition file for the application.

521

If you have Turbo C++ for Windows or Borland C++, you can open tabtxtex.prj from the IDE and select the Run option from the IDE's Run Menu to build the application. Otherwise, create the appropriate make file or project file for your compiler to build the application using the tabtxtex.c, tabtxtex.rc, and tabtxtex.def files.

Listing 11.17. The *TabbedTextOut* example.

```
Project Name:    tabtxtex.prj
Project Files:   tabtxtex.c
                 tabtxtex.rc
                 tabtxtex.def
```

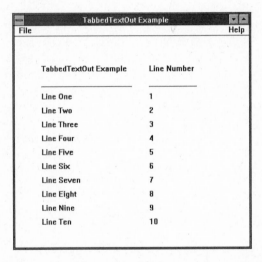

Figure 11.17. *For creating tables and highly formatted text, the* TabbedTextOut *function is your one-stop solution.*

Now take a quick look at one last text-related issue: the use of fonts for displaying text.

Using Fonts

In Windows, any font available to the system is available to your application. In the fonts example, you use the CreateFontIndirect function to create fonts from the standard Windows Helvetica and Times Roman fonts. You'll then use the fonts you've created to display some sample text.

When creating and using the fonts, you follow three basic steps.

1. Establish the variables you need. The following code segment establishes variables for the font handles and a LOGFONT data structure for specifying font parameters.

```
static HANDLE hTmsRmn;
static HANDLE hHelv;
LOGFONT LogFont;
```

2. Create the fonts you want to use. In the following **Working Code** section, you create fonts when the window is created. By creating your fonts when the window procedure receives the WM_CREATE message (which the window procedure receives when the window is created), you can assure that your fonts are ready when needed. The case WM_CREATE: code segment uses the CreateFontIndirect function to create fonts in the next **Working Code** section.

3. The application's text output is drawn when the application's window receives the WM_PAINT message. When the WM_PAINT message is received, the SelectObject function selects the appropriate font and the TextOut function displays text using the currently selected font. You don't actually have to do anything in this step — the wheel is in motion and you can sit back and read the pretty words that appear on your screen.

Figure 11.18 shows the application window for the fonts example.

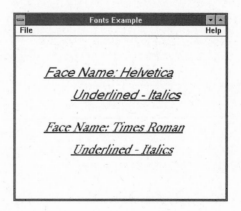

Figure 11.18. *Once the exclusive concern of typographers, fancy fonts are becoming standard graphics fare.*

523

Working Code: Sneaky Font Tricks

The fonts example in Listing 11.18 requires three files:

- The fontsex.c file is the C source code file containing the source code that loads and uses two standard fonts.

- The fontsex.rc file defines the menu resource for the application window.

- The fontsex.def file is the module definition file for the application.

BUILD If you have Turbo C++ for Windows or Borland C++, you can open fontsex.prj from the IDE and select the Run option from the IDE's Run Menu to build the application. Otherwise, create the appropriate make file or project file for your compiler to build the application using the fontsex.c, fontsex.rc, and fontsex.def files.

Listing 11.18. The fonts example.

```
Project Name:   fontsex.prj
Project Files:  fontsex.c
                fontsex.rc
                fontsex.def
```

Summary

This chapter has introduced many of the Windows functions that provide the backbone for Windows graphics output. Numerous examples demonstrating these graphics functions were presented. This chapter provided the following examples:

- The point example—Demonstrates how you can draw individual points on-screen.

- The pen style example—Shows the standard pen styles provided by Windows.

- The custom pen example—Creates several custom pens and uses these pens to draw a series of rectangles.

■ The stock brush example—Shows the patterns created by the various Windows stock brushes.

■ The hatch brush example—Shows the hatch patterns created by the standard Windows hatch brushes.

■ The drawing mode example—Demonstrates the effect that the current drawing mode has when drawing lines.

■ The `LineTo` example—Creates a complex figure using the `MoveTo` and `LineTo` functions.

■ The `Polyline` example—Demonstrates how you can create a complex figure with the `Polyline` function.

■ The `Arc` example—Creates a series of circular arcs using the `Arc` function.

■ The `Rectangle` example—Demonstrates how you can use the `Rectangle` and `RoundRect` functions to draw rectangles.

■ The `Polygon` example—Creates a complex, multisided figure using the `Polygon` function.

■ The `PolyPolygon` example—Demonstrates how you can draw a series of closed polygons using one call to the `PolyPolygon` function.

■ The `Ellipse` example—Shows how you can use the `Ellipse` function to draw both circles and ellipses.

■ The `Chord` example—Demonstrates how you can draw chorded ellipses using the `Chord` function.

■ The `Pie` example—Creates an exploded pie chart using the `Pie` function.

■ The `TextOut` example—Demonstrates how you can use the `TextOut` function to draw text.

■ The `TabbedTextOut` example—Creates two columns of aligned text using the `TabbedTextOut` function.

■ The fonts example—Demonstrates how you can use more than one font.

In the next chapter, several more **Working Code** examples will introduce you to Windows bitmaps. You'll learn to employ Windows' powerful resource-handling functions to do simple animation, and create your own custom cursors and icons.

Bitmapped Graphics, Windows Style

M ost graphics programmers are familiar with bitmapped graphics. In the first few chapters of this book, you learned how to use a variety of graphics libraries to display and animate bitmapped images.

Windows provides an easy way to deal with bitmapped graphics. Windows uses *resources* that represent many of the application's data and characteristics including dialog boxes, menus, accelerator keys, bitmaps, icons, string tables, fonts, and cursors. In this chapter, you'll look at three types of bitmap resources: the bitmap, the cursor, and the icon.

Windows Resources

Windows uses resources to define certain types of data for an application. Resources are read-only data stored in an application's executable file (.EXE) or in a dynamic link library (.DLL) file. Windows uses several different types of resources, including cursors, bitmaps, strings, accelerators, icons, dialog boxes, fonts, and menus. A resource typically defines a visible aspect of the application.

In general, resources are not an integral part of the application code. Therefore, you can create resources separately from the application code. This is advantageous during development because you can create resources simultaneously with the application code. Another advantage of separate resources is that, during the testing and modification of the application, you can edit and recompile resources without modifying the application code. For example, if you wanted to change the appearance of an icon or bitmap, you could simply open the icon or bitmap using a resource editor, modify it, and recompile the changes.

This chapter introduces you to three types of Windows resources: *bitmaps*, *cursors*, and *icons*. Because cursors and icons are just special kinds of bitmaps, I'll show you the bitmap first.

Bitmaps

The human eye is a bitmapped device that likes to deal with the visual universe in this format... Bitmaps [enable] you to represent reality on a computer.

—Steve Rimmer, *Supercharged Bitmapped Graphics*, 1992

A bitmap defines a graphical image for your application and is a binary representation of the image. Bitmaps have many uses in Windows applications. You can use bitmaps to create splash graphics, window backgrounds, and windows controls, just to name a few. A *bitmap* is a data series that represents a rectangular graphical object. An application uses the bitmap to draw predefined objects quickly onto the screen. The two basic types of bitmaps are the *device-dependent bitmap* and the *device-independent bitmap*.

Device-dependent bitmaps are closely tied to a particular output display device because a close correlation exists between the bits of the bitmaps and the pixels of the output display device. *Device-independent bitmaps*, on the other hand, are not closely tied to a particular display device because they represent the appearance of the image and not the correlation of the bitmap bits and the pixels of the output device.

You can create bitmap resources using almost any drawing or scanning package including Borland's Resource Workshop, which was used to create bitmap resources for the examples in this chapter. Figure 12.1 shows the Paint Editor, the part of the Resource Workshop used to create bitmaps.

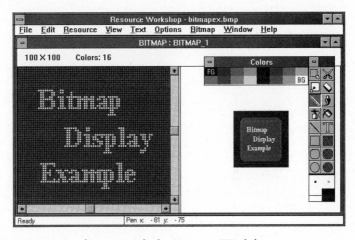

Figure 12.1. *Creating a bitmap with the Resource Workshop.*

Bitmap resources are commonly stored as binary files with the .BMP file extension. The BITMAP resource definition statement is used in the application's .RC file to define the .BMP file as an application resource. BITMAP resource definitions look like this:

```
nameID BITMAP [load-option] [mem-option] filename
```

in which

nameID is the unique name or ID that identifies the bitmap resource.

BITMAP identifies the resource as a bitmap.

[load-option] specifies when the bitmap should be loaded. Two options are supported:

LOADONCALL loads the resource when called. This is the default value.

PRELOAD loads the resource immediately.

[mem-option] specifies the memory option for the resource. Three options are supported:

FIXED—the resource is fixed at a memory location.

MOVEABLE—the resource can be moved in memory if necessary to compact memory. This is the default memory option.

DISCARDABLE—the resource can be discarded if it is not needed.

filename specifies the filename of the resource. If the specified file is not in the current directory, you should specify the full path for the file.

Windows provides several functions for creating and manipulating bitmaps. Table 12.1 lists the Windows bitmap functions.

Table 12.1. Bitmap functions.

Function	Description
BitBlt	Copies a bitmap from a source to a destination device
CreateBitmap	Creates a bitmap
CreateBitmapIndirect	Creates a bitmap described in a structure
CreateCompatibleBitmap	Creates a bitmap compatible with the specified device
CreateDIBitmap	Creates a device-specific memory bitmap from a DIB specification and initializes the bits in the bitmap
CreateDiscardableBitmap	Creates a discardable bitmap compatible with the specified device
GetBitmapBits	Gets the bits in memory for a specific bitmap
GetBitmapDimension	Gets the height and width of a bitmap
GetBitmapDimensionEx	Also retrieves the height and width of a bitmap
GetDIBits	Gets the bits in memory for a specific bitmap in device-independent form

Function	Description
PatBlt	Creates a bit pattern
SetBitmapBits	Sets the bits of a bitmap
SetBitmapDimension	Sets the height and width of a bitmap
SetBitmapDimensionEx	Also sets the height and width of a bitmap
SetDIBits	Sets the bits of a memory bitmap from a DIB
SetDIBitsToDevice	Sets the bits on a device surface directly from a DIB
StretchBlt	Copies a bitmap from a source to a destination device
StretchDIBits	Moves a DIB from a source rectangle into a destination rectangle, stretching or compressing the bitmap as required

The examples presented in this chapter use the BitBlt function to display bitmaps. This powerful function produces output that is the logical combination of three different elements: the current brush in the destination device context, the pixels in the source device context, and the pixels in the destination device context. The raster operation code (identified in the dwROP parameter of the BitBlt function) defines the way these three elements are combined. Windows and the BitBlt function support 256 different raster operation codes. Windows has assigned constants to the 15 most commonly used raster operation codes. Table 12.2 lists these 15 raster operation codes.

Table 12.2. Raster operation codes.

Value	Meaning
BLACKNESS	All output is black
DSTINVERT	The destination bitmap is inverted
MERGECOPY	Uses Boolean AND to combine the pattern and source bitmap

continues

Table 12.2. continued

Value	Meaning
MERGEPAINT	Uses Boolean OR to combine the inverted source bitmap with the destination bitmap
NOTSRCCOPY	Copies the inverted source bitmap to the destination
NOTSRCERASE	Uses Boolean OR to combine the destination and source, then inverts the combination
PATCOPY	Copies the pattern to the destination bitmap
PATINVERT	Uses Boolean XOR to combine the destination bitmap with the pattern
PATPAINT	Uses Boolean OR to combine the inverted source with the pattern, then uses Boolean OR to combine the result of the previous operation with the destination
SRCAND	Uses Boolean AND to combine the source and destination bitmaps
SRCCOPY	Copies the source bitmap to the destination
SRCERASE	Uses Boolean AND to combine the inverted destination bitmap with the source bitmap
SRCINVERT	Uses Boolean XOR to combine the source and destination bitmaps
SRCPAINT	Uses Boolean OR to combine the source and destination bitmaps
WHITENESS	All output is white

For most purposes, the SRCCOPY raster operation code is used. This code simply copies the source bitmap as is to the destination rectangle.

Now that you've gotten the bitmap basics under your belt, you need to know how to display bitmaps in the client area of the application window.

Displaying a Bitmap

I'll start with a simple bitmap demonstration. In this example, you display a bitmap in the client area of the application window. For this example, I created a 100x100 pixel bitmap with the Paint Editor of Borland's Resource Workshop, but you can use any bitmap editor to create bitmap resources. The bitmap will be positioned with its top left corner at the client coordinates (50,50). Remember that client coordinates begin at the top left corner of the client area. Because I'm using the MM_TEXT mapping mode for this example, the bitmap will be placed with its top left corner 50 pixels to the right and 50 pixels below the top left corner of the client area.

The bitmap example in the following **Working Code** section demonstrates how to load and display a bitmap in the client area of your application window. Examine a few lines of code from this example. In the bitmapex.rc file, you'll notice the following line.

```
BITDISPLAY BITMAP "bitmapex.bmp"
```

This identifies the bitmapex.bmp binary file as a bitmap resource and associates it with the BITDISPLAY resource name. No pathname for the bitmapex.bmp file is specified, so this file must be located in the current directory when building the application.

Next, take a look at a code segment from the C source file. The following code loads the bitmap resource that was associated with the resource name BITDISPLAY.

```
static HANDLE hBitDisplay;

hBitDisplay = LoadBitmap(hInstance,"BITDISPLAY");
```

Once the bitmap is loaded, the bitmap is displayed whenever the window procedure for the application window receives the WM_PAINT message. The case WM_PAINT: code segment in the following **Working Code** section carries out four steps:

1. It creates a memory device context for the bitmap. The CreateCompatibleDC function creates a memory device context compatible with the device context for the client area of the application window.

2. It selects the bitmap into the memory device context with the SelectObject function.

3. It copies the memory device context to the device context for the client area of the application window, using the BitBlt function. This actually displays the bitmap on-screen.

4. It deletes the memory device context with the `DeleteDC` function. Figure 12.2 shows the application window for the bitmap example.

Figure 12.2. *Displaying a bitmap is easy and fun for all ages. You can do it too with the* `Bitmap` *example.*

Working Code: A Bitmap Demonstration

The bitmap example in Listing 12.1 requires four files:

- The bitmapex.c file is the C source code file that contains the source code that loads and displays the bitmap resource.

- The bitmapex.rc file defines the menu resource for the application window and the bitmap resource displayed in the application window.

- The 28 file, bitmapex.def, is the module definition file for the application.

- The bitmapex.bmp file contains the bitmap resource.

If you have Turbo C++ for Windows or Borland C++, you can open bitmapex.prj from the IDE and select the Run option from the IDE's Run menu to build the application. Otherwise, create the appropriate make file or project file for your compiler to build the application using the bitmapex.c, bitmapex.rc, bitmapex.def, and bitmapex.bmp files.

As I did in the previous chapter, this is the only example with all the code listing. To save your head from spinning from all the code, I list the names of the programs as they appear on the disk. If you want to take a closer look at them, open up your editor and get to it!

Listing 12.1. The bitmap example.

```
Project Name:   bitmap.prj
Project Files:  bitmapex.c
                bitmapex.rc
                bitmapex.def
                bitmapex.bmp
```

Filename: bitmapex.c

```c
#include <windows.h>
#include <stdlib.h>
#include <string.h>

static HANDLE hBitDisplay;

long FAR PASCAL WndProc (HWND hWnd, WORD iMessage,
                WORD wParam, LONG lParam);

int PASCAL WinMain (HANDLE hInstance, HANDLE hPrevInstance,
            LPSTR lpszCmdParam, int nCmdShow)

{
HWND hWnd;
MSG Message;
WNDCLASS WndClass;

if (!hPrevInstance)
    {
    WndClass.cbClsExtra = 0;
    WndClass.cbWndExtra = 0;
    WndClass.hbrBackground = GetStockObject(WHITE_BRUSH);
    WndClass.hCursor =  LoadCursor(NULL, IDC_ARROW);
    WndClass.hIcon = LoadIcon (NULL, "END");
    WndClass.hInstance = hInstance;
    WndClass.lpfnWndProc = WndProc;
    WndClass.lpszClassName = "BITMAPWIN";
    WndClass.lpszMenuName = "MENU";
    WndClass.style = CS_HREDRAW | CS_VREDRAW;

    RegisterClass (&WndClass);
    }
```

continues

535

Listing 12.1. continued

```
hWnd = CreateWindow ("BITMAPWIN",  /* class name */
          "Bitmap Display Example",/* Caption */
          WS_OVERLAPPEDWINDOW,     /* Style */
          CW_USEDEFAULT,           /* x position */
          0,                       /* y position */
          CW_USEDEFAULT,           /* cx - size */
          0,                       /* cy - size */
          NULL,                    /* Parent window */
          NULL,                    /* Menu */
          hInstance,               /* Program Instance */
          NULL);                   /* Parameters */

hBitDisplay = LoadBitmap(hInstance,"BITDISPLAY");

ShowWindow (hWnd, nCmdShow);
while (GetMessage (&Message, 0, 0, 0))
     {
     TranslateMessage(&Message);
     DispatchMessage(&Message);
     }
return Message.wParam;
}

/***********************************************************/
/*             Window Procedure: WndProc                   */
/***********************************************************/

long FAR PASCAL WndProc (HWND hWnd, WORD iMessage,
                         WORD wParam, LONG lParam)
{
HDC hDC, hMemDC;
PAINTSTRUCT PtStr;

switch (iMessage)
     {
     case WM_COMMAND:
         switch(wParam)
         {
```

```
        case 101:
             SendMessage(hWnd, WM_CLOSE, 0, 0L);
             return 0;
        case 102:
             MessageBox(hWnd,
                "Sample Application",
                "Windows Graphics",
                MB_ICONINFORMATION¦MB_OK);
             return 0;
        }
      return 0;

   case WM_PAINT:
        hDC = BeginPaint(hWnd, &PtStr);
        hMemDC = CreateCompatibleDC(hDC);

        SelectObject(hMemDC,hBitDisplay);
        BitBlt(hDC,50,50,150,150,hMemDC,
              0,0,SRCCOPY);

        DeleteDC(hMemDC);
        EndPaint(hWnd, &PtStr);
        return 0;

   case WM_DESTROY:
        if (hBitDisplay) DeleteObject (hBitDisplay);

        PostQuitMessage(0);
        return 0;

   default:
        return(DefWindowProc(hWnd, iMessage, wParam,
              lParam));
    }
}
```

Filename: bitmapex.rc

```
MENU MENU LOADONCALL MOVEABLE PURE DISCARDABLE
BEGIN
  POPUP "File"
```

continues

Listing 12.1. continued

```
BEGIN
  MenuItem "Exit", 101
END
POPUP "Help", HELP
BEGIN
  MenuItem "About", 102
END
END
```

```
BITDISPLAY BITMAP "bitmapex.bmp"
```

Filename: bitmapex.def

```
NAME          BITMAPWIN
DESCRIPTION   'Bitmap Display Example'
EXETYPE       WINDOWS
CODE          PRELOAD MOVEABLE
DATA          PRELOAD MOVEABLE MULTIPLE
HEAPSIZE      1024
STACKSIZE     5120
EXPORTS       WndProc
```

Now that you can display a bitmap in the client area of the application window, here's another use for the bitmap—as a background for the application window.

A Bitmap in the Background

In this example, you'll use a 300×200 pixel bitmap that I created with Borland's Resource Workshop as the background for the application window. In addition, you'll make your window a specific size so that the bitmap completely fills the client area of the application window. You can do this by modifying the style attributes of the window class (more details on this later, as you examine code segments from this example). The window will be 300×240 pixels—40 pixels taller than the bitmap, to allow room for the window caption and menu bar. (Each of these is 20 pixels high when you use the standard system fonts.)

The following **Working Code** loads and displays the bitmap using the same procedure described in the bitmap example (Listing 12.1). What makes this example unique is the way the style for the application window is defined in the `CreateWindow` function call.

In all the previous examples, for your application window you've used the `WS_OVERLAPPEDWINDOW` style, which is actually an abbreviation for the following windows styles:

```
WS_OVERLAPPED
WS_CAPTION
WS_SYSMENU
WS_THICKFRAME
WS_MINIMIZEBOX
WS_MAXIMIZEBOX
```

In this example, instead of using the `WS_OVERLAPPEDWINDOW` style, you explicitly specify only the `WS_OVERLAPPED`, `WS_CAPTION`, `WS_SYSMENU`, and `WS_MINIMIZEBOX` styles. By using only these styles, your application windows cannot be sized or maximized, and your bitmap fills the entire client area. The width and height parameters of the `CreateWindow` function define the width and height of the resulting window.

The remaining code for the bitmap background example is similar to the code in the bitmap example. Figure 12.3 shows the application window for the bitmap background example.

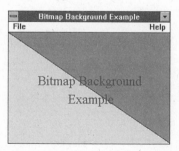

Figure 12.3. *Background bitmaps can spice up your windows.*

Working Code: Bitmapped Backdrop

The bitmap background example in Listing 12.2 requires four files.

- The bitbckex.c file is the C source code file that contains the source code that loads and displays the background bitmap resource.

- The bitbckex.rc file defines the menu resource for the application window and the bitmap resource that is displayed as the background for the application window.

- The bitbckex.def file is the module definition file for the application.

- The bitbckex.bmp file contains the background bitmap resource.

If you have Turbo C++ for Windows or Borland C++, you can open bitbckex.prj from the IDE and select the Run option from the IDE's Run menu to build the application. Otherwise, create the appropriate make file or project file for your compiler to build the application using the bitbckex.c, bitbckex.rc, bitbckex.def, and bitbckex.bmp files.

Listing 12.2. The bitmap background example.

```
Project Name:    bitbckex.prj
Project Files:   bitbckex.c
                 bitbckex.rc
                 bitbckex.def
                 bitbckex.bmp
```

Next, you'll see how to perform simple animation using two bitmaps.

Bitmap Animation

Even though Windows is a graphical environment, it doesn't really provide advanced features for animation. You can, however, easily create animation on the Windows screen using two or more bitmaps. Here's a quick example that uses two bitmaps to create a simple form of animation.

The first step is to create the two bitmaps that will be used to perform the animation. In this example, I use two balls. One ball has a stripe running northwest to southeast across the center. The other ball has a stripe extending northeast to southwest. When these two bitmaps are placed over one another, the ball appears to spin.

The bitmap animation example (presented in the next **Working Code** section) also adds another dimension to the ball's movement—the ball will appear to bounce as it spins. When the ball comes to a border of the window's client area, the ball bounces off the border and continues to move and spin.

As in the previous bitmap background example, the application window is set to a fixed size (500× 340 pixels). Therefore, the client area of the window is 500×300 pixels (remember that the window caption and menu bar each require 20 pixels). Because you know the client area of the window, you can easily determine when the spinning ball is about to bounce out of the client area.

This example introduces a new idea that I have not yet discussed—the timer. An application uses a *timer* to tell Windows that it wants to perform a particular task at predefined time intervals. In this example, you want Windows to send a WM_TIMER message every 10 milliseconds so that you can display the next bitmap in your animation sequence. To set and start the timer, call the SetTimer function when the application's window procedure receives the WM_CREATE message.

The example's animation sequence is built around the timer. Therefore, when the application's window procedure receives the WM_TIMER message, the next step in the animation sequence is performed. (Contrast this to all the previous examples that paid attention to the WM_PAINT message only.)

As shown in the following **Working Code** section, the application checks the current animation position when it receives the WM_TIMER message. If the spinning ball reaches one of the client area borders, the parameters used to control the spinning ball's direction change. Then, as in the previous bitmap examples, the application retrieves the device context of the client area, creates a compatible memory device context, selects the appropriate bitmap into the memory device context, and displays the bitmap. Figure 12.4 shows the application window for the bitmap animation example.

Working Code: Bouncing and Spinning

The bitmap animation example in Listing 12.3 requires five files.

- The bitaniex.c file is the C source code file containing the source code that loads, displays, and moves the bitmap resources to produce animation.

- The bitaniex.rc file defines the menu resource for the application window and the bitmap resources used to produce the animation.

- The bitaniex.def file is the module definition file for the application.

- The bitani1.bmp and bitani2.bmp files contain the bitmap resources used for animation.

If you have Turbo C++ for Windows or Borland C++, you can open bitaniex.prj from the IDE and select the Run option from the IDE's Run menu to build the application. Otherwise, create the appropriate make file or project file for your compiler to build the application using the files bitaniex.c, bitanex.rc, bitaniex.def, bitani1.bmp, and bitani2.bmp.

Listing 12.3. The bitmap animation example.

```
Project Name:    bitaniex.prj
Project Files:   bitaniex.c
                 bitaniex.rc
                 bitaniex.def
                 bitani1.bmp
                 bitani2.bmp
```

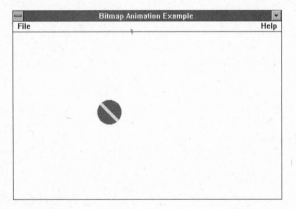

Figure 12.4. *When you run the bitmap animation example, you'll see the ball move, spin and bounce.*

Now, I'll show you a way you can use a bitmap to create a custom brush for filling objects and areas.

Bitmap Brushes

In the previous chapter, "Windows Graphics Functions," you looked at brushes, which are used to fill figures and areas of the screen. A *brush* is an 8×8 bitmap duplicated in every direction from the starting point until a figure or area is filled. Because brushes are bitmaps, you can create a custom brush using your own custom bitmap.

The following **Working Code** section presents a bitmap brush example using an 8×8 bitmap that resembles a smiling face. I created 8×8 bitmap with Borland's Resource Workshop, but you can use any bitmap editor. You'll use the smiling face bitmap to create a custom brush, which you'll then use to fill a circle. You'll draw several other ellipses on top of the first using the stock white brush. These ellipses will make the first circle resemble a face.

Creating a custom bitmap brush isn't too different from loading and displaying a bitmap. With the bitmap brush, however, you don't need to use a memory device context. First, load the bitmap you want to use as a brush. Next, use the `CreatePatternBrush` function to create a custom brush from it. Once you've called `CreatePatternBrush`, you are done with the bitmap and can delete the bitmap object. The following code segment demonstrates how to load a bitmap and create a brush that uses the bitmap pattern.

```
HBITMAP hBitBrush;
HBRUSH hBrush;

hBitBrush = LoadBitmap(hInstance,"BITBRUSH");
hBrush = CreatePatternBrush(hBitBrush);
```

Once you've created the brush, you can select the brush with the `SelectObject` function. In the portion of the following **Working Code** section that handles the `WM_PAINT` message, you use the `SelectObject` and `Ellipse` functions to select the custom brush, draw the first circle, select the stock white brush, and draw the remaining ellipses. Figure 12.5 shows the application window for the bitmap brush example.

Figure 12.5. *This smiley guy is actually a bitmap brush.*

Working Code: Smiley D. Bitmap

The bitmap brush example in Listing 12.4 requires four files.

- The bitbshex.c file is the C source code file containing the source code that creates the custom brush from the bitmap resource.

- The bitbshex.rc file defines the menu resource for the application window and the bitmap resource used to create the custom brush.

- The bitbshex.def file is the module definition file for the application.

- The bitbshex.bmp file contains the bitmap resource used to create the custom brush.

If you have Turbo C++ for Windows or Borland C++, you can open bitbshex.prj from the IDE and select the Run option from the IDE's Run menu to build the application. Otherwise, create the appropriate make file or project file for your compiler to build the application using the files bitbshex.c, bitbshex.rc, bitbshex.def, and bitbshex.bmp.

Listing 12.4. The bitmap brush example.

```
Project Name:    bitbshex.prj
Project Files:   bitbshex.c
                 bitbshex.rc
                 bitbshex.def
                 bitbshex.bmp
```

Now here are a few ways you can use a special type of bitmap, the cursor.

Cursors

Consider the mouse. Every time the mouse moves, Windows must update the on-screen position of the mouse cursor and perhaps the shape of the cursor as well. When you click a mouse button, Windows has to pass the click to the correct part of the correct window, which in turn has to process the click in some way... If the mouse moves in your client area, your window gets a WM_MOUSEMOVE *message.*

—Martin Heller, "Programming Windows,"
Windows Magazine, March 1992, p. 141-142

A *cursor* is a special 32×32 pixel bitmap that indicates the current position of the mouse. You can obtain Windows cursors from two sources, the Windows predefined cursors or your own custom cursors. Windows has several predefined cursor types, listed in Table 12.3. These predefined cursors represent the standard range of cursors required in a typical Windows application. In addition to using the predefined cursors, you can create your own cursors by using a resource editor such as the Resource Workshop. Figure 12.6 shows the Paint Editor of the Resource Workshop and the cursor resource created for the cursor example in Listing 12.5.

Table 12.3. Predefined cursor types.

Constant	Meaning
IDC_ARROW	Arrow cursor
IDC_CROSS	Crosshair cursor

continues

Table 12.3. continued

Constant	Meaning
IDC_IBEAM	I-beam text cursor
IDC_ICON	Empty icon
IDC_SIZE	Square with small square in right corner
IDC_SIZENESW	Cursor with arrows pointing northeast and southwest
IDC_SIZENS	Cursor with arrows pointing north and south
IDC_SIZENWSE	Cursor with arrows pointing northwest and southeast
IDC_SIZEWE	Cursor with arrows pointing west and east
IDC_UPARROW	Vertical arrow cursor
IDC_WAIT	Hourglass cursor

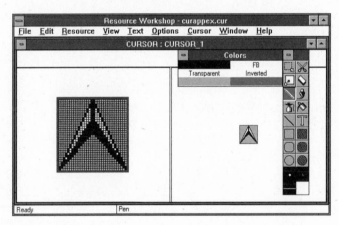

Figure 12.6. *Creating cursors with the Resource Workshop.*

Cursor resources are typically saved as binary files with the .CUR file extension. Once you've created the binary file, you must define the .CUR file as a cursor resource. The CURSOR resource statement is used in the application's .RC file to define cursor resources. The CURSOR statement associates the specified .CUR file with the specified resource name or ID. The format for the CURSOR statement follows:

```
cursorID CURSOR [load-option] [mem-option] filename
```

in which

cursorID is the unique name or integer that identifies the cursor resource.

[load-option] specifies when the cursor should be loaded. It supports two options:

LOADONCALL—the resource is loaded when called. This is the default value.

PRELOAD—the resource is loaded immediately.

[mem-option] specifies the memory option for the resource. It support three options:

FIXED—the resource is fixed at a memory location.

MOVEABLE—the resource can be moved in memory if necessary to compact memory.

DISCARDABLE—the resource can be discarded if it is not needed.

filename specifies the filename of the resource. If the specified file is not in the current directory, you should specify the full path for the file.

Windows provides several functions for creating, loading, and manipulating cursors. Table 12.4 lists these Windows cursor functions. The LoadCursor and SetCursor functions are most commonly used to define the default cursor and change the cursor shape while the application is running.

Table 12.4. Cursor functions.

Function	Description
ClipCursor	Restricts the cursor to a given rectangle
CopyCursor	Copies a cursor
CreateCursor	Creates a cursor from two bit masks
DestroyCursor	Destroys a cursor created with CreateCursor
GetClipCursor	Gets the screen coordinates of the rectangle to which the cursor has been restricted

continues

Table 12.4. continued

Function	Description
GetCursor	Gets the current cursor handle
GetCursorPos	Gets the current cursor position in screen coordinates
LoadCursor	Loads a cursor from a resource file
SetCursor	Sets the cursor shape
SetCursorPos	Sets the position of the cursor
ShowCursor	Increases or decreases the cursor display count

Now that you have reviewed the cursor basics, I'll show you a cursor example. The following example demonstrates one way that you can add a custom cursor to your application.

A Custom Cursor

Here's a quick and easy way to add a custom cursor to your application. This example, the cursor example, shows one way you can use a custom cursor resource as an application's default cursor. First, you need to create a *cursor resource.* Cursor resources can be created with most resource editors such as Borland's Resource Workshop. I used the Resource Workshop in this example to create the cursor example's custom cursor: the special arrow shown in Figure 12.6. Once you've created the cursor resource, you're ready to write your application.

Adding a custom cursor to your application is an easy two-step process:

1. Define the cursor resource saved in the binary cursor file curappex.cur as a cursor resource for the cursor example. To do this, use the CURSOR resource statement. The following CURSOR resource statement is included in the application's .RC file and associates the POINTER cursor name with the binary cursor resource in the curappex.cur file:

```
POINTER CURSOR "curappex.cur"
```

Once the cursor resource has been defined in the application's .RC file, you can begin the second step for adding a custom cursor to your application.

2. This step involves the modification of the C source code file. To assign a custom cursor for the application window, load the cursor with the LoadCursor function and set the hCursor field of the window class to the cursor handle returned by the LoadCursor function. The following code segment loads the custom cursor resource and defines the default cursor for the application window.

```
WndClass.hCursor = LoadCursor(hInstance, "POINTER");
```

When you follow these two simple steps, you can define the way the cursor looks whenever the current mouse position is within the borders of the application window. Figure 12.7 shows the application window for the cursor example.

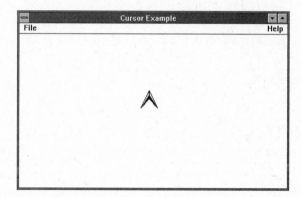

Figure 12.7. *The cursor example.*

Working Code: A "Cursory" Glance in the Window

The cursor example in Listing 12.5 requires four files.

- The curappex.c file is the C source code file containing the source code that creates the application window and loads the custom cursor for the application.

- The curappex.rc file defines the menu resource for the application window and the cursor resource used as the custom cursor for the application.

- The 28 file, curappex.def, is the module definition file for the application.

- The curappex.cur file contains the cursor resource used as the custom cursor for the application.

If you have Turbo C++ for Windows or Borland C++, you can open curappex.prj from the IDE and select the Run option from the IDE's Run menu to build the application. Otherwise, create the appropriate make file or project file for your compiler to build the application using the files curappex.c, curappex.rc, curappex.def, and curappex.cur.

Listing 12.5. The cursor example.

```
Project Name:    curappex.prj
Project Files:   curappex.c
                 curappex.rc
                 curappex.def
                 curappex.cur
```

Now, here's one way you can add multiple cursors to your application.

Multiple Cursors

Many Windows applications contain multiple cursors. The shape of the cursor often indicates the current operating mode of the software. For example, graphics applications often use the standard arrow cursor to indicate that the pointer tool is the current tool, a paintbrush cursor to indicate that the paintbrush is currently selected, and a spray can cursor to indicate that the airbrush tool is currently selected.

In the next **Working Code** section, you'll look at one way you can change the shape of the cursor as your application is running. The multiple cursor example program monitors the current mouse position and changes the shape of the cursor relative to four rectangular regions of the screen. Whenever the mouse position is outside these four rectangular regions, the standard arrow cursor displays. When the mouse position is inside one of the four rectangles, one of four different cursors displays.

As the first step, define your custom cursor resources. For this example, you need to create four different cursors—one for each rectangular region. I used the Borland Resource Workshop to create the cursors for this example, but you can use almost any resource editor. The four custom cursors for this example represent the numbers 1, 2, 3, and 4 and are saved in separate .CUR files. Once you've created the cursors, and saved them in .CUR format, you are ready to write your application.

When defining custom cursors, define the cursor resources in the application's .RC file first. In the following **Working Code** section, four CURSOR statements are used to associate the resource names POINTER1, POINTER2, POINTER3, and POINTER4 with the binary cursor files curmlt1.cur, curmlt2.cur, curmlt3.cur, and curmlt4.cur.

In order to mark the four rectangular regions of the screen where your application will display the custom cursors, you need to draw four rectangles on-screen using the Rectangle function. The rectangles are drawn when the window procedure receives the WM_PAINT message.

The last step in the multiple cursor example is to monitor the mouse position to determine the appropriate cursor to display. Use the WM_MOUSEMOVE message for this task. Each time the user moves the mouse, the WM_MOUSEMOVE message is sent to the window procedure. The lParam parameter of the WM_MOUSEMOVE message contains the mouse coordinates. The *low word* of lParam contains the horizontal mouse coordinate. The *high word* of lParam contains the vertical mouse coordinate.

The application monitors the current mouse position to determine whether that position is within one of the four rectangular regions. If it is, the appropriate cursor displays using the LoadCursor and SetCursor functions. If the current mouse position is outside the four rectangular regions, the standard arrow cursor displays. Figure 12.8 shows the application window for the multiple cursor example.

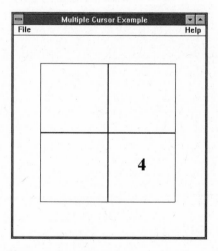

Figure 12.8. *The multiple cursor example.*

Working Code: Cursors! (Foiled Again.)

The multiple cursor example in Listing 12.6 requires seven files:

■ The curmltex.c file is the C source code file containing the source code that creates the application window and displays several different cursors depending on the current mouse position.

■ The curmltex.rc file defines the menu resource for the application window and the cursor resources displayed in the application window.

■ The curmltex.def file is the module definition file for the application.

■ The last four files, curmlt1.cur, curmlt2.cur, curmlt3.cur, and curmlt4.cur contain the cursor resources used as the custom cursors for the application.

If you have Turbo C++ for Windows or Borland C++, you can open curmltex.prj from the IDE and select the Run option from the IDE's Run menu to build the application. Otherwise, create the appropriate make file or project file for your compiler to build the application using the curmltex.c, curmltex.rc, curmltex.def, curmlt1.cur, curmlt2.cur, curmlt3.cur, and curmlt4.cur files.

Listing 12.6. The multiple cursor example.

```
Project Name:    curmltex.prj
Project Files:   curmltex.c
                 curmltex.rc
                 curmltex.def
                 curmlt1.cur
                 curmlt2.cur
                 curmlt3.cur
                 curmlt4.cur
```

Although the previous multiple cursor example demonstrates one way to change the cursor shape relative to screen position, it doesn't demonstrate the most effective way. If you study the logic, you'll notice that each time the WM_MOUSEMOVE message is received, the LoadCursor and SetCursor functions are called to define the cursor. A better way to handle cursor changes is to check exceptions. For example, instead of checking an entire rectangular region, you could limit your checks to region boundaries and change the cursor only when it crosses the boundaries between regions. By checking exceptions such as borders or boundaries, your code will be more efficient.

Now I'll show you one last type of special bitmap, the icon.

Icons

A room hung with pictures is a room hung with thoughts.

—Sir Joshua Reynolds

An *icon* is a specialized bitmap that represents a minimized application. Icons are colorful, graphical representations of the application that enable the user to quickly identify a minimized application. Double-clicking the icon that represents a minimized application opens that application window.

Icons are rectangular bitmap images, usually sized to 32×32 pixels (although you can create 32×16 and 64×64 pixel icons). You can create icons with a resource editor such as Borland's Resource Workshop. Figure 12.9 shows the Paint editor of the Resource Workshop along with the icon that I created for the icon example in Listing 12.7.

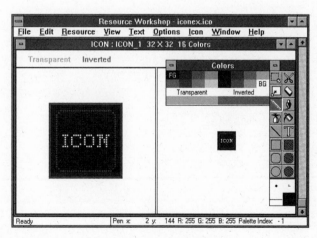

Figure 12.9. *Creating icons with the Resource Workshop.*

Icon resources are commonly stored as binary files with the .ICO file extension. You use an ICON resource definition statement in the application's .RC file to define each .ICO file as an icon resource. ICON resource definition statements follow this general format:

```
nameID ICON [load-option] [mem-option] filename
```

in which

nameID is the unique name or ID that identifies the icon resource

[load-option] specifies when the icon should be loaded. It supports two options:

LOADONCALL—the resource is loaded when called. This is the default value.

PRELOAD—the resource is loaded immediately.

[mem-option] specifies the memory option for the resource. It supports three options:

FIXED—the resource is fixed at a memory location.

MOVEABLE—the resource can be moved in memory if necessary to compact memory.

DISCARDABLE—the resource can be discarded if it is not needed.

filename specifies the filename of the resource. If the specified file is not in the current directory, you should specify the full path for the file.

Windows provides a series of icon functions that you can use to manipulate icon resources. Table 12.5 lists these functions.

Table 12.5. Icon functions.

Function	Description
CreateIcon	Creates an icon
DeleteIcon	Deletes an icon created with CreateIcon
DrawIcon	Draws an icon at the specified location in the client area
LoadIcon	Loads an icon into memory

Now that you're familiar with basics of defining icon resources, I'll show you a couple of examples that use them.

The Icon Example

Although you can use icons for several purposes, the most fundamental use for an icon is to represent the application in its minimized state. The Windows examples you have seen so far in this book do not define a custom icon. In this example, the icon example, you'll create an icon and use it to represent the minimized application.

The first step in this example is to create the icon resource. You can create icons with most resource editors. (I used the Resource Workshop to create the icon for this example.) Once you've created the icon and saved it to an .ICO file, you're ready to write the code for your application. For this example, you'll create a fundamental window and assign your icon resource as the default icon for the application.

The following **Working Code** section is almost identical to the fundamental window example presented in Chapter 10, "The Windows Graphics Device Interface." The only difference between this application and the fundamental window example is the addition of the icon.

The first step in adding the icon to the application is defining the icon resource in the application's .RC file. The following line associates a custom icon in the iconex.ico binary resource file with the MAINICON resource name.

```
MAINICON ICON "iconex.ico"
```

Once you have associated the .ICO file with a resource name, you can define the icon as the default icon for the application. The LoadIcon function is used to load the icon resource. The hIcon field of the window class is then set to the handle returned by the LoadIcon function. This line from the C program that follows defines a custom icon:

```
WndClass.hIcon = LoadIcon (hInstance, "MAINICON");
```

Once this code segment executes, the icon resource associated with the MAINICON resource name is used to represent the application when it is minimized. Figure 12.10 shows the application window for the icon example next to a second, minimized instance of the icon example.

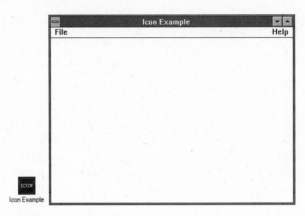

Figure 12.10. *Icons are used for many purposes, not the least of which is representing a minimized application.*

Working Code: I Think Icon, I Think Icon…

The icon example in Listing 12.7 requires four files:

■ The iconex.c file is the C source code file containing the source code that creates the application window and loads the custom icon for the application.

■ The iconex.rc file defines the menu resource for the application window and the icon resource used as the custom icon for the application.

■ The iconex.def file is the module definition file for the application.

■ The iconex.cur file contains the icon resource used as the custom icon for the application.

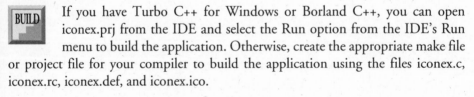 If you have Turbo C++ for Windows or Borland C++, you can open iconex.prj from the IDE and select the Run option from the IDE's Run menu to build the application. Otherwise, create the appropriate make file or project file for your compiler to build the application using the files iconex.c, iconex.rc, iconex.def, and iconex.ico.

Listing 12.7. The icon example.

```
Project Name:   iconex.prj
Project Files:  iconex.c
                iconex.rc
                iconex.def
                iconex.ico
```

Now here's a way that you can add multiple icons to an application.

The Multiple Icon Example

Windows applications are typically installed in various icon groups in the Windows *Program Manager*. Each application in the group is associated with an icon that represents the application. Most Windows applications include several icon resources so that you can specify the icon you want to represent the application. By adding multiple icons to an application, you give users the opportunity to customize their Windows environment.

The multiple icon example in the following **Working Code** section demonstrates how you can add multiple icons to the application. I created four icon resources for this example using the Resource Workshop. These icons then will be added to the source code presented in the previous example, the icon example in Listing 12.7.

Working Code: Anything You Can Do, Icons Do Better

The multiple icon example in Listing 12.8 requires eight files:

- The iconsex.c file is the C source code file containing the source code that creates the application window and loads the application icon.

- The iconsex.rc file defines the menu resource for the application window and the icon resources.

- The iconsex.def file is the module definition file for the application.

- The last five files; iconsex.ico, iconsex1.ico, iconsex2.ico, iconsex3.ico, and iconsex4.ico; contain the icon resources loaded into the application.

BUILD If you have Turbo C++ for Windows or Borland C++, you can open iconsex.prj from the IDE and select the Run option from the IDE's Run menu to build the application. Otherwise, create the appropriate make file or project file for your compiler to build the application using the files iconsex.c, iconsex.rc, iconsex.def, iconex.ico, iconsex1.ico, iconsex2.ico, iconsex3.ico, and iconsex4.ico.

Listing 12.8. The multiple icon example.

```
Project Name:    iconsex.prj
Project Files:   iconsex.c
                 iconsex.rc
                 iconsex.def
                 iconex.ico
                 iconsex1.ico
                 iconsex2.ico
                 iconsex3.ico
                 iconsex4.ico
```

The C source code file and definitions file in this example are identical to the example presented in the previous **Working Code** section.

Summary

The creative mind plays with the objects it loves.
—Karl Jung, *Psychological Types*, 1921

This chapter introduced the basics of Windows bitmaps, cursors, and icons and presented several examples that demonstrate various uses for these resources. The following examples were presented in this chapter.

- The Bitmap Example—demonstrates the procedure for loading and displaying a bitmap in the client area of the application window.

- The Bitmap Background Example—demonstrates one way to create a fixed-size application window and fill the client area with a bitmapped background.

- The Bitmap Animation Example—demonstrates the procedure for creating simple animation using two bitmaps.

- The Bitmap Brush Example—demonstrates how you can create a custom brush from a bitmap.

- The Cursor Example—demonstrates the procedure for loading and displaying a custom cursor.

- The Multiple Cursor Example—demonstrates one way you can display different cursors in the application window.

- The Icon Example—demonstrates the procedure for defining the default icon that represents the minimized application.

- The Multiple Icon Example—demonstrates how you can add multiple icons to an application.

Of course, you've only begun to scratch the surface of Windows graphics programming. The real adventure begins when you start modifying the **Working Code** presented in this chapter and the previous chapter to combine several types of graphics into a single program. You've learned how to monitor the WM_PAINT, WM_TIMER, and WM_MOUSEMOVE messages and draw a wide variety of graphics. By putting these elements together (and applying a bit of the graphics savvy you've gained throughout this book), you will quickly be on the way to your own custom interactive Windows graphics applications.

Of course, if you want to get serious about building Windows applications, you'll need to learn more about dialog boxes, menu systems, and many other aspects of Windows. As you wade in deeper, you may want to consult books dedicated entirely to Windows programming, such as *Developing Windows Applications with Borland C++* by James McCord (the author of this chapter), or *Developing Windows Applications with Microsoft C/C++* by Brent Rector. Both of these Sams titles are available where you bought this book.

V

The Graphics of Tomorrow

Image Processing

Most of this book focuses on generating sharp-looking graphics images. Often, though, you already have some scanned or computer-generated images and you want to enhance and manipulate them. Enter our next graphics guru, Spyro Gumas. You met Spyro briefly in Chapter 3, when I presented the VSA256 and TIFF256 programming libraries, which he authored. Now he's back to show you how to put those libraries to work. With his expert guidance and his IMAGEPRO software, you'll learn to beautify your snapshots and add mind-boggling special effects. Take it away, Mr. ImagePro...

Image processing is an exciting field where a few simple tricks can make you feel like a photo magician. A while ago, the only people who could play on this stage were CIA photo analysts. The memory and computational requirements of image processing could only be met with basement-sized computers that required their own personal nukes for power and icebergs for cooling. Chips shrink, memory capacity soars, prices drop...climb aboard and join the party.

We are so accustomed to accepting a failed photograph with a sigh and a shrug, but how would you feel if you could restore your favorite photos? Better yet, how about being able to perform picture enhancement that brings up detail not visible in the original photograph? (Are you a spy?) This chapter introduces you to some of the basic concepts of image processing including color lookup table manipulations, convolutions, resampling, and Fourier Transforms. Armed with these tools, you can develop your own custom image processing techniques and effects. You can thrill your friends, amaze your mom, and, yes, even get dates with the tricks you can perform with a scanned image and your personal computer.

Hardware And Software You'll Need

If the computer has bestowed one overriding blessing, it is the transformation of onerous tasks into creative experiences. Image editing belongs in this category. Gone is the gloomy darkroom with its chemical smell, gone the scissors, the exacto knife, the enlarger. In their place the luminous computer screen, the mouse, the keyboard, and with them the [capability] to make changes quickly, to play, to create.... Flaws in photos can be repaired, exposures altered, light-dark ranges modified, contrast and color saturations increased and decreased, images combined, and textures added.... These programs have not only eliminated the darkroom, but have added myriad creative options for working with images.

—Katherine Shelly Preiffer, "Alter Image,"
PC Publishing & Presentations,
February/March 1993

Almost all new computers being sold today come equipped with video adapters that support at least 256 colors. This is significant because, with so many gradations in a color sequence, the human eye starts to blur the individual steps between colors. The transitions from one color to another seem smooth and step free. Therefore, 256-color images begin to appear almost photographic in quality. Finally, you can process images to a reasonable quality level on your own PC.

I've written all the examples provided in this chapter to work with video adapters in the 256-color mode. Also, all the color lookup table routines assume a 256-entry by 18-bit wide color lookup table because this is the most common hardware being sold today. (See the next chapter for a refresher on color lookup tables). By separately treating the red, green, and blue components of an RGB image in the same manner that this chapter treats the gray-scale images, programmers with 24-bit true color hardware capability can take the concepts presented here and apply them to their own personal needs.

Obviously, this paper page is not a true color display device, either. Many of the figures in this chapter are gray-scale approximations of the corresponding color plates in the middle of this book.

The C source code examples provided in this chapter make use of the VSA256 Graphics Library and the TIFF256 Graphics Library Extensions, provided on the enclosed disk and documented in Appendices C and D. You'll need to load a VESA BIOS Extensions TSR for your video card (also provided on the disk) before running any of the examples. (Put it in your AUTOEXEC.BAT file, so you don't keep typing it. It's a harmless TSR.)

Working Code: A Little IMP

Most of the image processing (imp_*) example routines listed in this chapter work in conjunction with the IMP.H include file included on the disk. The IMP.H include file contains the required function prototypes, external declarations, and macro definitions for the imp_* routines.

Please note that the TransGraphics library is not used in this chapter. I've decided to do this in an effort to keep the size of the executable files and complexity of the source code as small as possible. Some of the VSA256 and TIFF256 routines do not map into TransGraphics library, so you still might need to link all three libraries and make vsa_* and tf_* calls directly. (vsa_* and tf_* refer to the various VSA256 and TIFF256 routines respectively).

The Color Lookup Table

One popular trick lets you dramatically increase the number of distinct colors you can display without a corresponding increase in bits per pixel. Each display is accompanied by a palette that maps the code stored in each pixel to the color you wish to display. At eight bits per pixel, you need a 256-entry palette. If each entry contains a 16-bit number, you can display 65,536 distinct colors. You just can't display all those colors at once. Instead, you choose which subset of 256 does the job well enough for each picture. That's what you store in the palette.

—P.J. Plaugher, "Technicolor and Cinemascope,"
Computer Language,
August 1990 p. 18

In Chapter 1, Guru Dick Oliver introduced you to the basic concepts of the color lookup table (or color palette). I'll summarize these concepts here because they provide a necessary foundation for understanding the following topics of image processing.

Each pixel has a *color number* that determines the color of the pixel drawn on the monitor's screen. The color number can be as simple as a 0 or 1 (Black or White), represented with one bit of information. On the other extreme, the *true color* (or RGB) pixel is represented with a 24-bit color number: 8 bits for red, 8 bits for green, and 8 bits for blue. With the true color pixel, each of the three primary colors can assume one of 256 intensity levels, resulting in a total count of 16 million color combinations.

Often, the number of bits used for the pixel's color number is decoupled from the total number of color combinations the color monitor can display, as in the case of an SVGA video adapter. This occurs with a device called a *color lookup table* (CLUT).

The CLUT is called a lookup table because that's basically how it works. You go into the CLUT with an index, the index points to one of the entries in the table, and that looked up table entry is what drives the color of the pixel on-screen. You use the pixel's N bit color number as the index into the table, and the value N determines how many entries the table has (equal to 2^N entries). The table entry indexed by the pixel's color number contains three elements: red, green, and blue. These red, green, and blue values directly drive their respective color guns on the color monitor. Even though the color number is only N bits wide, each table entry may be much wider than N bits. This explains why you can have thousands of displayable colors, on an 8-bit per pixel system. An example will help make this point.

Figure 13.1 shows an example of a CLUT implementation for the 256-color SVGA video adapter. Because each pixel color number is 8 bits, the CLUT contains 256 table entries. Each table entry stores an 18-bit value: 6 bits for red, 6 bits for green, and 6 bits for blue. When indexed by the 8-bit color number, the table outputs the respective 18-bit table entry, which drives the red, green, and blue color guns of the color monitor. Therefore, even though each pixel's color number can only be one of 256 values, each of these color values can be assigned from a "palette" of 262,144 unique colors ($262,144 = 2^{18}$).

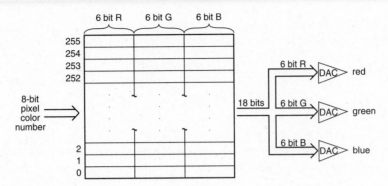

Figure 13.1. *SVGA color lookup table configuration. The 8-bit color number selects one of 256 18-bit entries.*

Reading and Writing the CLUT

CLUTs are really nifty because they enable you to manipulate your pictures in real time without having to redraw a full screen of pixels. For the example given in the last section, the CLUT contains 256 entries. For most purposes, you can reload these 256 values instantaneously. Because the screen pixel color assignments change instantaneously, this creates the impression that you redrew all the screen pixels in a flash. Many times you'll see a fractal image on some demo that seems to be growing and swimming in colors. This color animation almost always happens by continuously reloading the CLUT.

So how do you modify the values in the CLUT? Well, you could burden yourself with finding the physical address to the CLUT and writing custom code to individually rewrite these memory locations, or you could use the `vsa_write_color_block` routine provided in the VSA256 library. The source code I'll show you later in Listing 13.1 shows you how to cycle the color values in the CLUT.

What if you want to rewrite the CLUT values based on some function of their current values? For instance, you're displaying an image, such as the flowers in Figure 13.2, and for some reason you want to swap the red and blue components of the image, as in Figure 13.3. For this, you need the capability to first read out the values of the CLUT, hence `vsa_read_color_block`. Then you need to perform the swap and write the modified values back into the CLUT. See Listing 13.2 for an example of red to green, green to blue, and blue to red color swap.

Figure 13.2. *A 256-color image with reds that just won't quit.*

Figure 13.3. *Image of Figure 13.2 after swapping blues for reds. Okay, so the reds quit.*

You Can Do It: Cycling and Swapping

The IMAGEPRO program included on this book's disk demonstrates all the fancy photo footwork I'll teach you in this chapter. Each **Working Code** section discusses the part of the program that carries out the task at hand. I present the first two listings and then I refer to the others on the disk. Have a peek at the Color Cycle and Color Swap demos now.

1. Run the IMAGEPRO.EXE program.

2. Enter a value to select your screen resolution. (Try 101.)

3. Enter the number 1 to run the Color Cycle demo.

4. Enter the name of any color TIFF image. (Try MIDI.TIF.)

5. Press any key when you've had so much fun you can't stand it any more.

6. Enter the number 2 to run the Color Swap demo.

7. Enter the name of any color TIFF image. (Try MIDI.TIF.)

8. Press any key to return to the main menu.

9. Enter 18 to exit.

Working Code: Using CLUTs

Listing 13.1. The color cycling function from IMAGEPRO.C.

```
color_cycle()
{
  int i,done;
  unsigned char color_array[768];
  long long_color,temp;
/*......................................................*/
/*  Read CLUT data into color_array.  Color_array has 768   */
/*  values, where every three are an R-G-B triplet for one  */
```

continues

Listing 13.1. continued

```
/*  entry in CLUT.                                                */
/*.............................................................*/
  vsa_read_color_block(0,256,color_array);
  done = 0;
  while(!done)
    {
/*.............................................................*/
/* Perform circular shift of 18-bit CLUT entries, wait for     */
/* vertical retrace, and write them back to CLUT. Repeat until */
/* a key is pressed.                                           */
/*.............................................................*/
    for(i=1;i<256;i++)
      {
      long_color = ((unsigned long)(color_array[3*i])   << 12) +
                   ((unsigned long)(color_array[3*i+1]) << 6) +
                   (unsigned long)(color_array[3*i+2]);
      temp = (long_color & 0x00000001) << 17;
      long_color = (long_color >> 1) + temp;
      color_array[3*i]   = (unsigned char)(long_color >> 12)
                           & 0x3f;
      color_array[3*i+1] = (unsigned char)(long_color >>  6)
                           & 0x3f;
      color_array[3*i+2] = (unsigned char)long_color
                           & 0x3f;
      }
    wait_for_vert_sync();
    delay(100);
    vsa_write_color_block(0,256,color_array);
    done = _bios_keybrd(_KEYBRD_READY);
    }
  return 0;
}
```

Listing 13.2. The color swapping routine from IMAGEPRO.C.

```
color_swap()
{
  int i;
```

```
   unsigned char color_array[768];
    long long_color;
/*..........................................................*/
/*  Read CLUT data into color_array.  color_array has 768    */
/*  values, where every three are an R-G-B triplet for one   */
/*  entry in CLUT.                                           */
/*..........................................................*/
    vsa_read_color_block(0,256,color_array);
/*..........................................................*/
/* Shift red CLUT entries to green.  Green to blue, and blue to*/
/* red.  Then wait for vertical retrace and write them back to */
/* CLUT.                                                    */
/*..........................................................*/
    for(i=1;i<256;i++)
      {
        long_color = ((unsigned long)(color_array[3*i])   << 12) +
                     ((unsigned long)(color_array[3*i+1]) << 6) +
                     (unsigned long)(color_array[3*i+2]);
        color_array[3*i+1]   = (unsigned char)(long_color >> 12)
                               & 0x3f;
        color_array[3*i+2]   = (unsigned char)(long_color >>  6)
                               & 0x3f;
        color_array[3*i]     = (unsigned char)long_color
                               & 0x3f;
      }
   wait_for_vert_sync();
   vsa_write_color_block(0,256,color_array);
   return 0;
}


/*.................. WAIT_FOR_VERT_SYNC ......................*/
/*  This routine waits for a vertical retrace to begin before  */
/*  returning. You can use it to hold off an update to the CLUT*/
/*  or screen until the monitor is in vertical retrace.        */
/*..........................................................*/
wait_for_vert_sync()
{
  int vert_sync = 0;
  while(!vert_sync)
    vert_sync = inp(0x3DA) & 0x0008;
```

continues

Listing 13.1. continued

```
  return 0;
}


/*..................... DELAY .............................*/
/*  This routine waits for 'value' milliseconds.  Notice that  */
/*   it doesn't handle timer wraparound and in these cases time */
/*   delay will be short.                                       */
/*.............................................................*/
delay(value)
int value;
{
  clock_t start,end;
  start = clock();
  end = start+value;
  while(start < end)
    start = clock();
  return 0;
}
```

Brightness Adjustments

Okay, now you've got the basic ideas down. Let's put them to use first with a really basic example. To adjust the brightness of an image, such as Figure 13.4, you can manually grab onto the brightness knob of your monitor or you can be elegant and use software control (see results in Figure 13.5). To do the latter, you need to read out the values of the CLUT, add a constant offset to each of the red, green, and blue components for each CLUT entry, and write them back. Figure 13.6 shows a plot of the pixel brightness versus pixel color number before and after adding a brightness offset of 20. The brightness_cycle() function of IMAGEPRO.C uses the constant offsets of +1 and -1 to repetitively ramp the brightness of an image up and down.

Figure 13.4. *A dull (but cute) photo.*

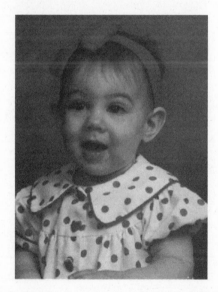

Figure 13.5. *Adjusting the brightness makes the photo less dull (and even cuter).*

Notice what happens if you don't check the results of your CLUT entry modification. For our examples, each of the red, green, and blue components is a 6-bit value ranging from 0 to 63. If you allow the modified result to exceed 63, when you go to write it back into the CLUT, anything beyond 6 bits is truncated, causing a wraparound effect where bright jumps to dark. This wrapping effect is unnatural and extremely annoying. For all the examples in this chapter, the CLUT modification routines monitor the resulting values and *clamp* them either at 0 or 63 so that wraparound does not occur in either the positive or negative direction.

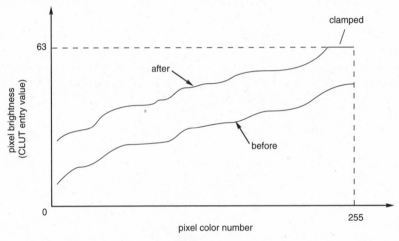

Figure 13.6. *Brightness increase: old versus new CLUT entry values.*

You Can Do It: Lighten Up!

1. Run the IMAGEPRO.EXE program.

2. Enter a value to select your screen resolution.

3. Enter the number 3 to run the Brightness Cycle demo.

4. Enter the name of any TIFF image. (Try ACG_A.TIF.)

5. Press any key to return to the main menu.

6. Enter 18 to exit.

Contrast Enhancement

Adjusting the contrast of an image is a much more useful and desirable capability in image processing. For instance, you have a wonderful image of your child, but it's all washed out (as in Figure 13.4). To enhance the contrast, you can read out the CLUT values. Then, you multiply the red, green, and blue components for each CLUT entry by a factor, but instead of just multiplying by a constant, you need to "tack" the midpoint value of the brightness curve so that it doesn't shift during the scaling. When you do this, the image average brightness remains the same before and after contrast adjustment. What changes is the dynamic range, or the extremes of brightness variation. Figure 13.8 shows a contrast enhanced kid. The `contrast_cycle()` function of IMAGEPRO.C shows an example of contrast cycling. Figure 13.7 shows a plot of pixel brightness versus pixel color number before and after contrast enhancement by a factor of 1.5. For each of the red, green, and blue components of the CLUT, the entry value is modified by the following equation:

$$NewValue = (OldValue - 32) \times 1.50 + 32$$

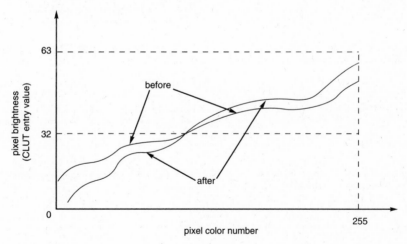

Figure 13.7. *Contrast enhancement: old versus new CLUT entry values.*

Figure 13.8. *Contrast enhanced and looking great.*

You Can Do It: Contrast and Compare

1. Run the IMAGEPRO.EXE program.

2. Enter a value to select your screen resolution.

3. Enter the number 4 to run the Contrast Enhancement demo.

4. Enter the name of any TIFF image. (Try ACG_A.TIF.)

5. Press any key to return to the main menu.

6. Enter 18 to exit.

Okay, now for the really neat part about contrast enhancement. You can perform contrast enhancement locally: only within a small range of image intensities. The other intensities of the image remain unchanged (essentially). Why would you ever want to do this? Say you have an image of Uncle Larry and yourself from when you were just three years old. You are on Uncle Larry's lap, and he is reading you a book. The brightness and contrast of the image look fine, except you can't read the title of the book. You can see the cover of the book, but it's simply too dark to make out the title.

Figure 13.9 shows how you can stretch the CLUT values locally (such as for the book cover) to bring out detail in the dark areas. The equation used to modify the CLUT is given as:

for $0 < OldValue < 10$ $NewValue = OldValue * 0.6$
for $10 < OldValue < 20$ $NewValue = OldValue * 1.9 - 13$
for $20 < OldValue < 63$ $NewValue = OldValue * 0.88 + 7.4$

The application of this simple concept can take you far into the realm of photo touch-up or photo intelligence, if you are so inclined.

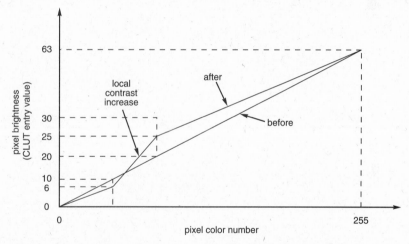

Figure 13.9. *Local contrast enhancement: old versus new CLUT entry values.*

Color Balancing

Did you ever get a set of pictures back from the lab where each photo had a reddish yellow hue? Maybe you used Daylight Film (which is color balanced for sunlight) indoors with incandescent bulbs. Yeah, it happens, especially if you're like me...too lazy to go get the flash. Well, all is not lost.

Because the CLUT stores the separate red, green, and blue components of each pixel value, you can easily adjust the relative balance of the colors within the image. In our example of the overemphasized red/yellow (orange) hues, do this. For each of the CLUT entries, read out the value, increase the blue and green components by a percentage of the current red and green components, and write the modified values back. The `color_balance()` function of IMAGEPRO.C shows you how it's done. The percentages by which you increase the blue and green components determine just how much the balance shifts away from that reddish-orange hue. As an alternate approach, reduce the red component for each CLUT entry instead of increasing the blue and green. Either way, by experimenting, you'll find that you can achieve all sorts of neat effects in addition to straight color balancing. (After a while, you might feel like a throw back to the sixties on a psychedelic journey. The heck with proper color balance, and watch out Crayola!) See Figures 13.10 and 13.11 for an example of color abuse.

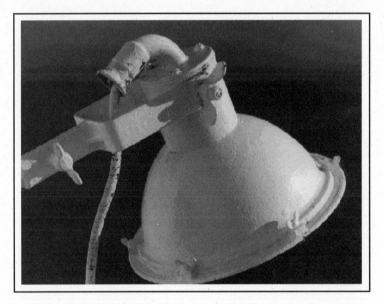

Figure 13.10. *Your basic photo.*

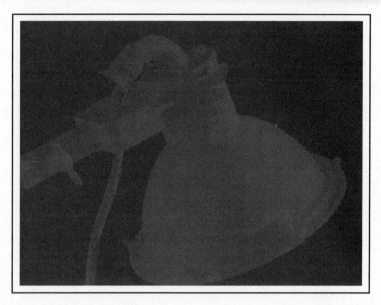

Figure 13.11. *Color abuse is fun.*

You Can Do It: The Balancing Act

With this swell demo, you get some hands-on experience at increasing and decreasing an image's blue/green color balance. Go scan yourself an image of that sun-bleached (greened out) picture of Aunt Maybelle and watch her come to life!

1. Run the IMAGEPRO.EXE program.

2. Enter a value to select your screen resolution.

3. Enter the number 5 to run the Color Balance demo.

4. Enter the name of any TIFF image. (Try ACG_A.TIF first, then try MIDI.TIF.)

5. Press any key to return to the main menu.

6. Enter 18 to exit.

Color Model Conversions

You look rather rash my dear your colors don't quite match your face.

—Daisy Ashford, "Young Visitors," 1919

With many software packages, you can display true color images on 2-, 16-, and 256-color systems. They achieve this by some form of color approximation. This section shows you how to convert 24-bit true color images, such as that of Figure 13.12, to 8-bit 256 "color" images.

Figure 13.12. *This 24-bit true color RGB image was produced with a ray-tracing program.*

The following paragraphs teach the basics of converting true color images to two different formats. Instead of learning how to traverse the intricacies of the industry standard image file formats such as TIFF, GIF, and BMP, the examples use a simple nonstandard RGB format. This way, you can concentrate on the color conversion process rather than the file traversing process. The *.RGB files contain 24-bit images and are sequential binary files with the following format:

Bytes 0-1	Image Width in Pixels
Bytes 2-3	Image Height in Pixels
Byte 4	Pixel(0,0) Red value
Byte 5	Pixel(0,0) Green value
Byte 6	Pixel(0,0) Blue value
Byte 7	Pixel(1,0) Red value
Byte 8	Pixel(1,0) Green value
Byte 9	Pixel(1,0) Blue value

.

.

.

Byte 3*width+1	Pixel(width-1,0) Red value
Byte 3*width+2	Pixel(width-1,0) Green value
Byte 3*width+3	Pixel(width-1,0) Blue value

.

.

.

Repeat for all remaining rows of pixels in image.

You Can Do It: Splitting Up

You'll find a utility on the enclosed disks called RGBSPLIT.EXE. This program asks you for the name of a standard TIFF image file (which must be 24-bit true color) and for the name of the RGB file you want to create. The program then reads the TIFF file, displays it to keep you entertained, and writes the *.RGB file to the disk. After creating the *.RGB file, you can use it as source wherever you need to access an image's red, green, and blue components.

1. Run the RGBSPLIT.EXE program.

2. Enter a value to select your screen resolution.

3. Enter the name of a 24-bit TIFF image file. (Try MIDI.TIF.)

4. Enter the name of the *.RGB file you want to create. (Try MIDI.RGB.)

5. Wait for conversion to finish, and press ESC to quit.

6. You'll use this *.RGB file in the next "You Can Do It" section.

Conversion of RGB to Gray-Scale

If you convert a true color image to 256-color using commercial software, the resulting color image is dithered (halftone) to approximate the color values that fall outside the available 256. If dithering is not used, you'll get a stepped look in the color gradations. Dithering or color stepping is not always preferred or acceptable. Many times you will want a clear gray-scale rendition of the image, as in Figure 13.13, rather than a dithered color version (especially when you start doing the image processing stuff in the next sections).

You Can Do It: Premature Gray

1. Run the IMAGEPRO.EXE program.

2. Enter a value to select your screen resolution.

3. Enter the number 6 to run the RGB to Gray-Scale Conversion demo.

4. Enter the name of an *.RGB file. (Try MIDI.RGB.)

5. The gray-scale image shows up.

6. Press any key to return to the main menu.

7. Enter 18 to exit.

Conversion to gray-scale is easy. For every 24-bit pixel in the original image, simply take the average of the pixel's red, green, and blue components. Perhaps you're interested in a specific spectral band of the image, say the greens of foliage. If so, simply discard the red and blue components and use the green component value. Save the new 8-bit pixel values for the new image.

Figure 13.13. *Gray-scale conversion of the image in Figure 13.12.*

Having converted the image, you also need to use a gray-scale CLUT, which is set up so that each CLUT entry stores the value of its index divided by 4 in each of the red, green, and blue components. It looks like Table 13.1.

Table 13.1. A Gray-Scale CLUT.

CLUT Index	CLUT Entry (R - G - B)
0	0 - 0 - 0
1	0 - 0 - 0
2	0 - 0 - 0
3	0 - 0 - 0
4	1 - 1 - 1
5	1 - 1 - 1

continues

Table 13.1. continued

CLUT Index	CLUT Entry (R - G - B)
6	1 - 1 - 1
7	1 - 1 - 1
8	2 - 2 - 2
9	2 - 2 - 2
10	2 - 2 - 2
11	2 - 2 - 2
.	
.	
.	
252	63 - 63 - 63
253	63 - 63 - 63
254	63 - 63 - 63
255	63 - 63 - 63

`imp_rgb_to_gray()` and `imp_gray_lut()` provide the code for converting an RGB file and loading the CLUT with a gray-scale.

Conversion of RGB to Indexed Color

If you want to keep the color information when converting a true color image to an 8-bit image, you must trade total shades for colors (see Figure 13.14). For instance, in the previous section an 8-bit gray-scale image has a maximum of 256 shades of gray (limited to 64 shades with our 18-bit–wide CLUT). For an 8-bit indexed color image, you can let the 8 bits represent 3 bits red, 3 bits green, and 2 bits blue. In this case, you get only 8 shades of red, 8 shades of green, and 4 shades of blue. The source code in `imp_rgb_to_indexed_color()` and `imp_true_color_lut()` show you how to convert an RGB file and load the CLUT with this general-purpose indexed color table. To use this CLUT, the code compresses the 24-bit pixels in the following fashion:

New Pixel = (*Old Pixel Red*/32) << 5

      + (*Old Pixel Green*/32) << 2

      + (*Old Pixel Blue*/64)

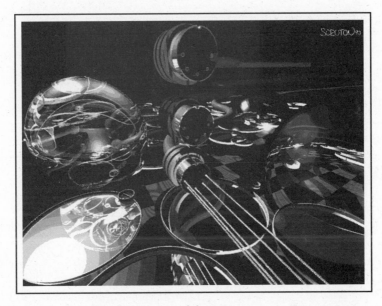

Figure 13.14. *Indexed color conversion of the RGB image in Figure 13.12.*

You Can Do It: Indexed Color Conversion

1. Run the IMAGEPRO.EXE program.

2. Enter a value to select your screen resolution.

3. Enter the number 7 to run the RGB to Indexed Color Conversion demo.

4. Enter the name of a *.RGB file. (Try MIDI.RGB.)

5. The Indexed Color image shows up.

6. Press any key to return to the main menu.

7. Enter 18 to exit.

Of course, concerning indexed color, almost an infinite number of variations exist for compressing the 24 bits of color down to 8 bits. Most of these approaches are called *adaptive color compression,* and they perform a statistical analysis on the colors present in the original true color image. Based on this analysis, they decide upon the best allocation of the 256 colors. These approaches are extremely interesting, but beyond the scope of what I can write in these pages given the existing space-time continuum.

Intermission

Photography is unreal; it alters value and perspective. Its cowlike eye stupidly registers everything that our eye first has to correct and distribute according to the needs of the case.

—Jean Cocteau,
Professional Secrets, 1922

For the remaining sections of this chapter, all discussion and examples concern gray-scale images. The CLUT is loaded as shown in the section entitled "Conversion of RGB to Gray-Scale" so that each pixel's color number is equal to the pixels brightness. I made this simplification so that you can focus your attention on the image processing concepts instead of the color conversion and interpretation details. Once you master the concepts and techniques for gray-scale images, you can apply them to color images simply by performing the image processing tasks presented here in three separate passes, one for each of the red, green, and blue image components.

Convolutions

One of the reasons for capturing an image digitally is to allow us to manipulate it to better serve our needs. Often this will include trying to improve the subjective appearance of an image through smoothing of grainy features or sharpening of indistinct features. These goals sometimes can be accomplished through the use of a discrete convolution *operation (also called* digital filtering*).*

Discrete convolution determines a new value for each pixel in an image by computing some function of that pixel and its neighbors. Often the function simply is a weighted sum of pixel values in a small neighborhood of the source pixel. These weights can be represented by a small matrix that sometimes is called a convolution kernel. *The dimensions of the matrix must be odd so there will be a central cell to represent the weight of the original value of the pixel for which we are computing a new value. The new value is computed by multiplying each pixel value in the neighborhood of the central pixel by the corresponding weight in the matrix, summing all the weighted values, and dividing by the sum of the weights in the matrix.*

—Dale A. Schumacher,
"Image Smoothing and Sharpening by Discrete Convolution,"
Graphics Gems II, 1991

Spend any amount of time in the image processing field, and you'll see the wonders of *convolution*. Convolution? Isn't that what happens to your pizza order between the time when you call in the order and the time when you pick it up? In the field of image processing, convolution has a very specific meaning that I'll explain next.

Imagine creating a template of, say, 5×5 pixels. Each of these 25 pixels has a specific brightness. (Remember, we're only talking gray-scale for now, not color.) Now, imagine passing this template across an image of 512×512 pixels, making sure to stop briefly so that the template is centered once over each and every one of the 512^2 pixels in the image. While this template is stopped over each image pixel, let's do something really weird. First, multiply the value (brightness) of each pixel in the template with the value (brightness) of the underlying pixel in the image, thus creating 25 products. Now add up these 25 products. Finally, store this result as a pixel in a new image at the same pixel coordinate as the old image where the template is centered. Are you still with me? Trust me on this, it all makes sense in the following sections.

After you finish performing this process for each pixel of the old image, you've succeeded in performing the convolution of an image (the old image) with a *kernel* (the 5×5 template) to generate another image (the new image). *That's the definition of convolution.* So what?

In the next sections, you'll see how this straightforward technique produces myriad results depending on what values you use for the kernel weights (same as the template pixels), as well as what size kernel you use (3×3, 5×5, 7×7, and so forth). After getting the basic concepts down, you'll want to experiment a bit, trying various twists on the basic kernels and watching the results. You can see what the actual code for convolutions looks like in the `imp_conv_2d` routine of IMAGEPRO.C. (See subsequent sections for routines that initialize the kernel.)

The Math Behind The Magic: Convolutions

As you might guess, doing convolutions involves some rather convoluted math. If you just want to see results, skip these **Math Behind the Magic** sections and use the **Working Code** instead.

If you're a true technophile (the kind of person who talks in technospeak and thinks formulas are fun), these sections will supply you with more thrills than a graduate-level textbook store. Stuff like this:

Convolution of an image with a kernel performs a filtering function on the image. The kernel itself defines the spatial frequency response of the filter. The frequency response can be low pass, high pass, band pass, or some combination of these. For example, the kernel may specify the filter response as low pass in the X direction and high pass in the Y direction.

$$
\text{Kernel A} =
\begin{array}{llll}
K00 & K01 & K02 & \dots\ K0M \\
K10 & K11 & K12 & \dots\ K1M \\
K20 & K21 & K22 & \dots\ K2M \\
\quad & \quad & \cdot & \\
\quad & \quad & \cdot & \\
\quad & \quad & \cdot & \\
KN0 & KN1 & KN2 & \dots\ KNM
\end{array}
$$

(Where N and M are dimensions of Kernel)

Image A = PixelA (i,j)   (Original Image)
Image B = PixelB (i,j)   (New Image)

(For $0 < i < X,\ 0 < j < Y$)

$$PixelB\,(i,j) = \sum_{p=0}^{N-1}\left[\sum_{q=0}^{M-1} K\,(p,q) * PixelA\left(i+p-\tfrac{(N-1)}{2}, j+q-\tfrac{(M-1)}{2}\right)\right]$$

(For $0 < i < X$, and $0 < j < Y$)

Blurring an Image

What happens if you take a highly detailed and intricate photograph and paint over it with a brush (maybe you're trying to get that "bumpy oil paint" look)? If the paintbrush is fatter than the size of the detail in the photo, your picture ends up with less detail—some might even call it…blurred. The degree of blurring is directly related to the size of the brush you use. A practical application of blurring in the digital image field is smoothing out the grainy noise introduced by some image scanners.

You can achieve this same effect by doing a convolution (act like you're surprised). Start with an original image (Image A) with a high level of detail, then convolve it with a convolution kernel (of the pixel spreading type) to create the blurred image (Image B). The *pixel spreading kernel* is the conceptual equivalent to the fat paintbrush. For every new pixel it creates, it spreads out and solicits contributions from the surrounding pixels, while de-emphasizing the contribution of the center pixel. Figures 13.15a and 13.15b show you an image before and after blurring. The pixel spreading kernel might look like that of Figure 13.16. The critical features of this kernel are the following:

1. N = M = odd number.

2. Weight values are symmetrical around the center pixel.

3. All weights are positive values.

4. Weights remain constant or decrease in value as they move further from the center

In technospeak parlance, convolution of an image with the pixel spreading kernel blurs an image by performing a *low-pass filter*. The low-pass filter passes the low spatial frequency components of the image while subduing or blocking the high spatial frequency components of the image.

Figure 13.15a. *A normal, and naturally cute, photo.*

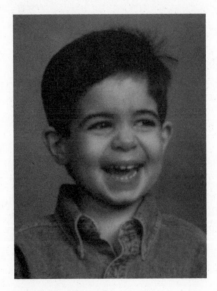

Figure 13.15b. *The same photo, blurred.*

You can increase the degree of blurring by increasing the size of the kernel (*N* and *M*). The sum of all the weights in the kernel should equal 1.0 if you don't want to increase or decrease the brightness of the image. Increasing the sum of the weights correspondingly increases the image brightness, and vice versa. Also, the "profile" of the kernel weights (pyramidal, parabolic, rectangular) gives you qualitative differences in your final image. See `imp_blur_kernel()` function of IMAGEPRO.C for code that initializes a Pixel Spreading kernel with a different profile.

0.05	0.15	0.05
0.15	0.20	0.15
0.05	0.15	0.05

Figure 13.16. *Pixel spreading 3x3 convolution kernel (blurs images).*

You Can Do It: Gimme Back My Glasses

1. Run the IMAGEPRO.EXE program.

2. Enter a value to select your screen resolution.

3. Enter the number 8 to run the Image Blurring demo.

4. Enter the name of a gray-scale TIFF image. (Try ACG_A.TIF.)

5. The original image shows up on the left; the blurred one is on the right.

6. Press any key to return to the main menu.

7. Enter 18 to exit.

Sharpening an Image

I can't conjure up with a paintbrush analogy for the image sharpening case, so I'll leave that as an exercise for the student (I've waited years for an excuse to say that!). For this one, just be brave and dive right in.

To sharpen an image, you want to perform *pixel emphasis* instead of pixel spreading. Think of pixel emphasis as a competition between each pixel of the original image and its neighboring pixels. Each pixel tries to emphasize itself while at the same time reducing the values of its neighbors. The bright pixels surrounded by relatively dim pixels can emphasize themselves more so than pixels on the same order of brightness as their neighbors. As the net result, pixel emphasis enhances the pixels in the detail areas of the image. Figure 13.17 shows you what happens when you sharpen the original image of Figure 13.15a.

Pixel emphasis convolution looks for details in an image and accentuates them. Do you buy that? If not, here's the technospeak explanation: Convolution of an image with the pixel emphasis kernel sharpens an image by performing a high-pass filter on the image. In this case, the high-pass filter enhances the high spatial frequency components of the image while subduing the low spatial frequency components of the image.

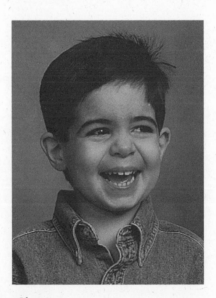

Figure 13.17. *Looking Sharp!*

To perform pixel emphasis, again, you want to do a convolution. This time, however, you want to use a pixel emphasis kernel of the type shown in Figure 13.18. The critical features of this kernel are the following:

1. $N = M$ = odd number.

2. Weight values are symmetrical around the center pixel.

3. Center weights are positive values.

4. Weights surrounding the center weights are negative.

5. Sum of weights is greater than zero.

0.0	-1.0	0.0
-1.0	5.0	-1.0
0.0	-1.0	0.0

Figure 13.18. *This pixel emphasis 3x3 convolution kernel sharpens images.*

You can increase the degree of sharpening by decreasing the number of weights in the central, positive region of the kernel and by reducing the size of the kernel (N and M). (Note that the kernel in Figure 13.18 is already at its smallest limit.) As with blurring, the sum of all the weights in the kernel should equal 1.0 if you don't want to increase or decrease the brightness of the image. Increasing the sum of the weights correspondingly increases the image brightness, and vice versa. Also the "profile" of the kernel weights gives you qualitative differences in your final image. See the `imp_sharp_kernel()` function of IMAGEPRO.C for code that initializes a slightly different pixel emphasis kernel.

You Can Do It: Looking Sharp

1. Run the program.

2. Enter a value to select your screen resolution.

3. Enter the number 9 to run the Image Sharpening demo.

4. Enter the name of a gray-scale TIFF image. (Try ACG_A.TIF.)

5. The original image shows up on the left; the sharpened one is on the right.

6. Press any key to return to the main menu.

7. Enter 18 to exit.

Edge Detection

As a kid, did you ever take a piece of paper, place it over a quarter, and rub it with a crayon? If so, an outline of George Washington popped up as if from nowhere. At this tender age, you were actually performing a highly sophisticated image processing function called *edge detection*. Figure 13.19 shows another example of tender age edge detection.

Edge detection is similar to image sharpening with the adrenaline turned on. Basically, the idea is the same except now you change the kernel so that the sum of the weights equals zero. By setting up the kernel appropriately, you can perform edge detection for vertical edges only, horizontal edges only, or both. The trick lies in setting up the kernel so that:

1. N = M = odd number.

2. Weight values are symmetrical around the center pixel (for general edge detection).

3. Center weights are positive values.

4. Weights surrounding the center weights are negative.

5. The sum of the weights equals zero.

Figure 13.19. *Edge detection is one of the most miraculous image processing stunts you can pull off.*

Performing edge detection in one orientation only is a matter of removing the symmetry from the kernel. The edge detection kernel shown in Figure 13.20 detects all edges regardless of their orientation.

0.0	-1.0	0.0
-1.0	4.0	-1.0
0.0	-1.0	0.0

Figure 13.20. *A general edge detection 3x3 convolution kernel.*

Figures 13.21 and 13.22 show the kernels for performing vertical and horizontal edge detection respectively. You can increase thickness of the edges output with edge detection by increasing the number of weights in the central, positive region of the kernel and increasing the size of the kernel (N and M). (The kernels in Figures 13.20 through 13.22 are the smallest they can get.)

0.0	0.0	0.0
-1.0	2.0	-1.0
0.0	0.0	0.0

Figure 13.21. *A vertical edge detection 3x3 convolution kernel.*

0.0	-1.0	0.0
0.0	2.0	0.0
0.0	-1.0	0.0

Figure 13.22. *A horizontal edge detection 3x3 convolution kernel.*

MATH
+ - =

The Math Behind the Magic: Higher Pass Filtering

Technically speaking, convolution of an image with the edge detection kernel performs a high-pass filter on the image—just as in image sharpening. In this case, however, the high-pass filter completely blocks the low spatial frequency components of the image.

You Can Do It: Living on the Edge

1. Run the IMAGEPRO.EXE program.

2. Enter a value to select your screen resolution.

3. Enter the number 10 to run the Edge Detection demo.

4. Enter the name of a gray-scale TIFF image. (Try ACG_A.TIF.)

5. The original image shows up on the left; the edged one is on the right.

6. Press any key to return to the main menu.

7. Enter 18 to exit.

Embossing

Embossing an image gives it that chiseled in stone look. As a key feature of an embossed image, it appears to consist of a collection of plateaus where the surface of the image rises and falls like the mesas of New Mexico. Embossing an image is a two-part process: part one is a convolution and part two is the simple addition of a constant value to the convolution's result. In Figure 13.23, you see the results of embossing the original image of Figure 13.15a.

The convolution does an edge detection, but this edge detection is different than that of the previous section. Where the edge detection scheme previously described always draws a bright line for a detected edge, the edge detection shown here will draw a bright line or a dark line depending on the direction of the brightness change (ie. from bright to dark or dark to bright) while crossing perpendicular to the edge. Thus for every part of the image which is wrapped with an edge, the embossed image will have a bright edge on one side and a dark edge on the opposite side, giving you the illusion of an elevated plateau. The Directional Edge Detection Kernel is shown in Figure 13.24, and its critical features are as follows:

1. N = M = odd number.

2. Asymmetrical weight values about the center pixel (positive/negative cancelling pairs).

597

3. Center weights are zero.

4. The sum of the weights is equal to zero.

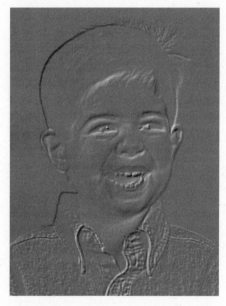

Figure 13.23. *Embossing gives you that 3-D fine art look.*

-1.0	0.0	0.0
0.0	0.0	0.0
0.0	0.0	1.0

Figure 13.24. *A directional edge detection 3x3 convolution kernel.*

See the `imp_emboss_kernel()` function of IMAGEPRO.C for code to set up this kernel. Adding a constant value to the result of the convolution simply determines the pixel brightness for the portions of the image which are flat (non edges). You must set this value bright enough so that you see the dark edge detected edges against this background (not too bright or you won't see the bright edge detected edges). A good starting point for this value is mid brightness (128 for a 256 level gray-scale image).

The Math Behind the Magic: Bipolar High-Pass Filtering

By the way, convolution of an image with the Directional Edge Detection Kernel performs a Bipolar High-Pass Filter on the image. Since the low spatial frequency components of the image are completely blocked, a DC bias is added to the convolution results to provide an image foundation from which the detected edge is added or subtracted. Just thought you'd like to know.

You Can Do It: Getting That Chiseled Look

1. Run the IMAGEPRO.EXE program.

2. Enter a value to select your screen resolution.

3. Enter the number 11 to run the Image Embossing demo.

4. Enter the name of a gray-scale TIFF image. (Try ACG_A.TIF.)

5. The original image shows up on the left; the embossed one is on the right.

6. Press any key to return to the main menu.

7. Enter 18 to exit.

Image Resampling

One pill makes you larger
One pill makes you small.
The ones that Mother gives you
Don't do anything at all.

—Jefferson Airplane, "White Rabbit"

Enlarging or reducing a bitmapped image usually results in a jaggy, ragged mess. With a quick trick called *resampling*, you can smooth out the jags and hem the seams to make your bitmaps look great at any size.

Enlargements

One day your buddy sends you an image of his new Harley so that you can admire his bike, as well as his good taste. The only problem is that he sends you a 200×150 pixel image, and you want to display it as a 800×600 image that fills your brand new high resolution monitor. How do you enlarge it?

The most common (and easiest) way to enlarge an image is to replicate each pixel in the original image an integral number of times. For instance, if you want to enlarge an image by a factor of 4, you can draw the new image by placing 4×4 pixel patches down for each pixel in the original image. The color of the 16 pixels in each 4×4 replicates the color of the respective pixel in the original image. This is usually referred to as *pixel replication*. The problem with this technique is that you can usually see the 4×4 pixel squares in the new image. The new image is bigger than the original, but it actually looks grainier or coarser.

For the budding graphics guru who seeks perfection, the better way to perform this task is through a method called *pixel interpolation*. This approach is relatively straightforward and goes like this. Say you're enlarging an image by a factor of 4. As you draw the new image, take the original pixels and space them out so that three new pixels separate each original pixel in the x and in the y dimensions. To compute the values for the new pixels, interpolate between the original pixels. Figure 13.25 shows an example of this process on a small patch of pixels as it undergoes enlargement. Since the Harley is wishful thinking, Figure 13.26 instead demonstrates image enlargement with a very nice horse, who we are free to call Harley.

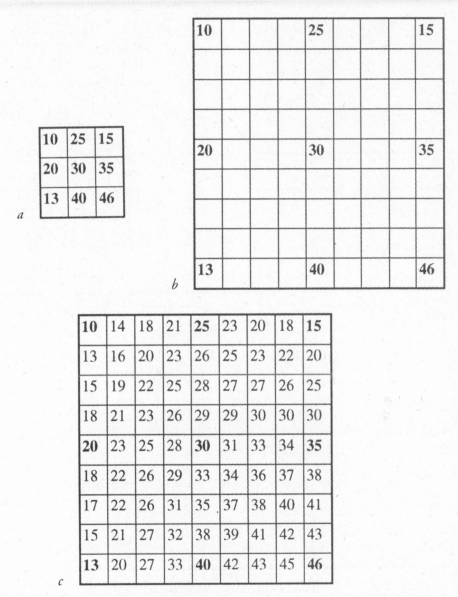

Figure 13.25. *(a) A portion of original image. Making a 4X enlargement: (b) The first step is to spread out original pixels. (c) The second step is to interpolate between original pixel values.*

Figure 13.26. *The original image (a) and two enlarged renditions: (b) a simple pixel replication and (c) a pixel interpolation.*

YOU CAN DO IT!

You Can Do It: Bigger and Better

1. Run the IMAGEPRO.EXE program.

2. Enter a value to select your screen resolution.

3. Enter the number 12 to run the Image Enlargement demo.

4. Enter the name of a gray-scale TIFF Image. (Try GROW.TIF.)

5. Enter the enlargement scale factor.

6. The original image appears at left; the pixel replicated image is in the center.

7. The interpolated image appears at right.

8. Press any key to return to the main menu.

9. Enter 18 to exit.

You can struggle through the code to actually implement a specialized pixel interpolation function, or you can be ingenious and use your convolution skills developed in this chapter. To do this, enlarge the image through the pixel replication method. Then, perform a convolution of the pixel replicated image with an averaging kernel. See the `enlarge_image` and `imp_bad_enlarge` routines of IMAGEPRO.C for the code that performs both pixel replication and pixel interpolation. The size of the averaging kernel equals the enlargement factor (in the 4X enlargement, the kernel size is 4×4). The kernel weight values are all identical and set such that the sum of all the weights is 1.0 (for the 4×4 kernel, all weights equal 0.0625).

Reductions

In the previous section, I presented an example of a Harley photograph that you wanted to enlarge. You can just as easily imagine a case where you have an image you want to reduce in size. Maybe the Harley comes as an 800×600 image, and you want to display it as one of many little postage stamp sized images on a display. Again, simple and elegant solutions exist.

The most common way to reduce the size of an image is to simply extract every Nth pixel (where N is the reduction factor) and throw out the other pixels. Enter the concept of aliasing. *Aliasing* is what happens on your TV screen when you see the grill on a car (or a pattern on a man's tie) produce those pretty moiré effects as the spacing of the grill (or the pattern) approaches the spacing of the TV's raster lines. In the case of a static image that's been reduced in size, you may either lose patterns that were present or see patterns not present in the original image. This happens because you're taking every Nth pixel and completely disregarding the image information in the other pixels.

As the guru's approach to image reduction, take a contribution from each pixel in the original image to produce those every Nth pixels. Say you want to reduce an image by a factor of 9. To do this, instead of taking just every 9th pixel, take the average of all the pixels in a 9×9 array centered on every 9th pixel. Now, no information is completely discarded. If a skinny line runs between the sampling centers, it's still visible in the reduced image because it makes a contribution via the 9×9 pixel array average. Figure 13.27 shows a test image in original form and reduced size.

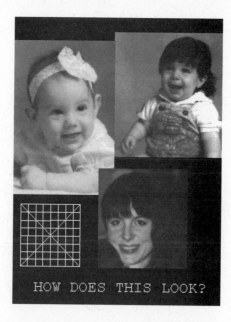

a

b

c

Figure 13.27. *An original image with high detail (a) and two size reduced renditions: one is incorrectly undersampled (b), resulting in aliasing and one is properly averaged so that aliasing is avoided (c).*

You Can Do It: Honey, I Shrank You and the Kids

1. Run the program.

2. Enter a value to select your screen resolution.

3. Enter the number 13 to run the Image Reduction demo.

4. Enter the name of a gray-scale TIFF Image. (Try SHRINK.TIF.)

5. Enter the reduction scale factor.

6. The original image appears at left; the averaged image at top right.

7. The aliased image appears on the bottom right.

8. Press any key to return to the main menu.

9. Enter 18 to exit.

The Math Behind The Magic: Avoiding Aliasing

From the mathematician's perspective, *aliasing* (or *spatial frequency aliasing*) is a phenomenon that makes one frequency look like another frequency. This is a problem whenever you undersample an image. The *Nyquist criteria* states that you must sample at least at twice the highest spatial frequency component of the image in order to faithfully capture the essence of the image and not introduce false frequencies (aliases). In the image reduction application, low-pass filter the original image so that it contains no spatial frequency components higher than 1/2 of the sampling spatial frequency. Then, sample (take every Nth pixel), and you're assured that no aliasing effects occur.

The actual implementation of this pixel averaging image reduction technique follows. If you're not in a hurry, though, as a less efficient but just as accurate approach, perform a convolution of the original image with a kernel selected for low-pass filtering. The kernel should be the size of the image reduction factor (a 9×9 kernel for a factor of 9 reduction). After performing the convolution, you can safely take every Nth (9 in this example) pixel to form the reduced image.

$$PixelB(i,j) = \sum_{p=0}^{N-1}\left[\sum_{q=0}^{M-1}K(p,q) * PixelA\left(i+p-\tfrac{(N-1)}{2}, j+q-\tfrac{(M-1)}{2}\right)\right]$$

Where:

$OldPix(i,j)$	= the original image
$NewPix(x,y)$	= the new size-reduced image
R	= the reduction scale factor
$OLDXMAX$	= the x dimension of the original image
$OLDYMAX$	= the y dimension of the original image

Working Code: Slimming Down

The code in Listing 13.3 shows two different approaches to image reduction. The nonaliasing version (imp_shrink) is written in the efficient fashion shown in the previous **Math Behind The Magic** box instead of the slower convolution approach.

Listing 13.3. Image size reduction routines (The good, the bad,...)

```
/*...................... IMP_SHRINK.C ......................*/
/* This routine performs an image size reduction by a scale    */
/* factor equal to 'factor'.  The source image is at 'x0,y0' to*/
/* 'x1,y1'.  The destination image is drawn starting at 'x2,y2'*/
/*             ---- Pixel averaging! ----                      */
/*                                                             */
/* NOTES: 1) This routine breaks if source image is greater    */
/*           than 1280 pixels wide.                            */
/*        2) The Source and destination images must not overlap*/
/*        3) Sensible values for 'factor' are 1 to 1280.       */
/*        4) The scale 'factor' is the same for width and      */
/*           height. (ie. if 'factor' = 3, the new image will  */
/*           be 1/3 as wide and 1/3 as high as the original    */
/*           image).                                           */
/*...........................................................*/
```

continues

Listing 13.3. continued

```
void imp_shrink(x0,y0,x1,y1,x2,y2,factor)
int x0,y0,x1,y1,x2,y2,factor;
{
  int i,m,n,new_width,new_height;
  int fx,fy;
  unsigned char in_array[1280],out_array[1280];
  long temp_array[1280];
/*................................................................*/
/*    Verify valid 'factor' and compute width and height.       */
/*................................................................*/
  if((factor <= 0) || (factor > 1280))
    return;
  new_width = (x1-x0+1)/factor;
  new_height = (y1-y0+1)/factor;
/*................................................................*/
/* For each line of the new image (the reduced size one) read   */
/*  out the corresponding lines from the original and average   */
/*  the appropriate pixels together.                            */
/*................................................................*/
  for(n=0;n<new_height;n++)
    {
/*................................................................*/
/*    Clear out the out_array to start new sums going.          */
/*................................................................*/
      for(i=0;i<new_width;i++)
        temp_array[i] = 0;
/*................................................................*/
/*                Compute averaged pixels.                      */
/*................................................................*/
      for(fy=0;fy<factor;fy++)
        {
          vsa_get_raster_line(x0,x1,n*factor+y0+fy,in_array);
          for(m=0;m<new_width;m++)
            {
              for(fx=0;fx<factor;fx++)
                {
                  temp_array[m] += in_array[m*factor+fx];
                }
            }
        }
/*................................................................*/
```

```
/*Now divide out_array values so that each value is an average.*/
/*Then draw the next raster line for the new reduced image.    */
/*...........................................................*/
     for(i=0;i<new_width;i++)
       out_array[i] = (unsigned char)(temp_array[i]/(factor*factor));
     vsa_raster_line(x2,x2+new_width-1,n+y2,out_array);
   }
  return;
}                              /*.... End IMP_SHRINK       .....*/




/*.................... IMP_BAD_SHRINK.C .....................*/
/* This routine performs an image size reduction by a scale     */
/* factor equal to 'factor'.  The source image is at 'x0,y0' to*/
/* 'x1,y1'.  The destination image is drawn starting at 'x2,y2'*/
/*                  — — NO PIXEL AVERAGING! — —               */
/*                                                            */
/* NOTES: 1) This routine breaks if source image is greater    */
/*            than 1280 pixels wide.                            */
/*         2) The Source and destination images must not overlap*/
/*         3) Sensible values for 'factor' are 1 to 1280.      */
/*         4) The scale 'factor' is the same for width and     */
/*            height. (ie. if 'factor' = 3, the new image will  */
/*            be 1/3 as wide and 1/3 as high as the original    */
/*            image).                                          */
/*...........................................................*/
void imp_bad_shrink(x0,y0,x1,y1,x2,y2,factor)
int x0,y0,x1,y1,x2,y2,factor;
{
  int i,m,n,new_width,new_height;
  unsigned char in_array[1280],out_array[1280];
  if((factor <= 0) ¦¦ (factor > 1280))
    return;
  new_width = (x1-x0+1)/factor;
  new_height = (y1-y0+1)/factor;
/*...........................................................*/
/*  For each line of the new image (the reduced size one) read */
/*  out the corresponding line from the original.            */
/*...........................................................*/
  for(n=0;n<new_height;n++)
    {
```

continues

609

Listing 13.3. continued

```
    vsa_get_raster_line(x0,x1,n*factor+y0,in_array);
    for(m=0;m<new_width;m++)
      out_array[m] = in_array[m*factor];
    vsa_raster_line(x2,x2+new_width-1,n+y2,out_array);
  }
  return;
}                              /*.... End IMP_BAD_SHRINK    .....*/
```

Fourier Transforms

Most of us have some intuitive feeling for the filtering of a one-dimensional wave like that in music. We turn down the treble control on our high fidelity amplifier, and we hear less of the high frequencies. What we might think of as brilliance in the music melts away, but perhaps so does some of the noise and raspiness. We end up setting the control at some compromise setting that sounds best to our learned ears. However, not many of us have the opportunity to play with the filtering of two-dimensional functions that make up pictures, so we have little feel for spatial filtering. But the same kinds of effects can be accomplished in this domain. Here the high frequencies are the fast-changing portions of the picture, like the edges of objects and the speckles of noise. By appropriate filtering we can enhance the edges and minimize noise. In addition, it is possible to do lens-like darkroom operations affecting focus and depth-of-field.

—Dr. Robert W. Lucky, *Silicon Dreams*, 1992

Now it's time to kick in the warp drives and catapult yourself into orbit around the quasar of image processing. This topic, Fourier Transforms, pulls it all together. With this technique, you can take the convolution skills you learned and generalize them to their fullest capabilities. To do this, I'll introduce some concepts that may sound as foreign to you as Moussaka (a Greek eggplant dish my mom makes...yum). After you play with the examples a few times, read this section again. It *will* start to make sense.

The Basic Idea

The Fourier Transform of an image converts that image from the *spatial domain* to the *frequency domain*—from the who to the what? I'd better explain. When you look at a computer image, it's a collection of pixels in 2-D coordinate space with the horizontal axis usually labeled x and the vertical axis usually labeled y. The units of x and y are some measure of distance. In a satellite image, perhaps the unit of measure is miles, in which case each pixel of the image represents a square mile. This image is a spatial domain representation because each pixel represents physical space.

Now, enters the concept of spatial frequency. Say that in this satellite image, some stratified clouds exist. These clouds cover a significant portion of the image and are repetitive in nature. If the cloud pattern comprises patches of white stuff repeating once every 34 pixels in the x direction, we can say that the clouds have an x dimension spatial frequency component of 0.0294 (1/34) cycles per pixel.

As a more useful system of measure, you could report the cloud frequency in terms of how many cycles fit across the full x width of the image. Therefore, if the image is 512 pixels wide, the cloud's x dimension spatial frequency component is 15.1 cycles per image width (512/34). To make it easier to talk about, I'll define μ as the x dimension spatial frequency component, in this case μ equals 15.1 cycles/image width.

If the cloud pattern's path cuts a diagonal across the image, the clouds also have a y dimension spatial frequency component. Maybe in the y dimension, the cloud patches appear once every 29 pixels. If you define ν as the y dimension spatial frequency component and if the image is also 512 pixels high, for the clouds ν equals 17.7 cycles/image height (512/29).

Having grasped the concept of spatial frequency, you now can create a new 2-D image of the satellite photograph called a *Fourier spectrum plot*. The Fourier spectrum plot shows the satellite image's energy distribution as a function of spatial frequency. Label the horizontal axis μ, and the vertical axis ν. The unit of measure for the μ axis is cycles/image width; the unit of measure for the ν axis is cycles/image height. The Fourier spectrum plot's dimensions are 512×512 (or the same as the original image), and its origin (where $\mu, \nu = 0,0$) is defined at the center of the 2-D plot. The clouds show up in this new image as a single bright pixel at μ, ν coordinate = 15,29. (In reality, the clouds are not a pure tone and contain multiple frequency components. Therefore, many pixels scattered throughout the Fourier spectrum plot would turn on due to the cloud's multifrequency content). This image is a frequency domain representation because each pixel represents a frequency component of the original image in the spatial domain.

In Figures 13.28 and 13.29, you can see how an image in the spatial domain is transformed to a Fourier spectrum plot in the frequency domain. Figure 13.28 is a spatial domain image of the Earth with noise added that consists of a 32 cycles/image width sinusoidal component (a sine wave) and a +15 DC bias component (a constant offset from pure black). Figure 13.29 is the frequency domain Fourier spectrum plot of the noisy Earth, where you can easily see the two peaks at $\mu,\nu = -32,0$ and $+32,0$. The DC bias component at $\mu,\nu = 0,0$ is hard to see because there is so much DC energy in the Earth image at the start. If you want to sneak a peak at the final, cleaned up image of the Earth, jump forward to Figure 13.31. Just remember to come back!

Figure 13.28. *An image of the Earth in spatial domain.*

Okay, you were patient and you stuck with it. You deserve a break, so go spoon up a bowl of ice cream and relax. When you come back, I'll show you how this stuff works. Go ahead, I'll wait…

Going To the Frequency Domain

Welcome back. So, you're asking, "How do I get from the spatial domain to the frequency domain?" Through a Fourier Transform, of course. Actually, because we're talking about digitally sampled data, it's really called a *Discrete Fourier Transform*. It's all math, so dive into the **Math Behind the Magic** box for the details or just use the `imp_dft_2d` routine provided in the image processing library.

Figure 13.29. *The Earth image in frequency domain.*

The Math Behind The Magic: The Discrete Fourier Transform

Because the Fourier Transform of an image contains real and imaginary data (remember from high school, anything times the square root of -1 is imaginary), you want to break the problem down into real and imaginary parts. For each pixel(m,n) of the image, compute a corresponding real $ReDFT(\mu,\nu)$ and imaginary $ImDFT(\mu,\nu)$. These values can be positive or negative and are somewhat hard to interpret if you display them as a 2-D image. You create the Fourier spectrum by computing:

$$MagDFT(\mu,\nu) = [ReDFT(\mu,\nu)^2 + ImDFT(\mu,\nu)^2]^{1/2}$$

Now you can see a nice Fourier spectrum plot by drawing a 2-D image, setting the pixels equal to $MagDFT(\mu,\nu)$ for $-X/2$ [le] $\mu < X/2$ and $-Y/2$ [le] $\nu < Y/2$, where X is the width and Y is the height of the image.

$$DFT(\mu,\nu) = x^{-1}y^{-1}\sum_{n=\frac{Y}{2}}^{\frac{Y}{2}-1}\left[\sum_{m=\frac{X}{2}}^{\frac{X}{2}-1}Pixel(m,n)\,e^{-j2\pi(\mu m/X + \nu n/Y)}\right]$$

$$\text{for}\;\; -\frac{X}{2} \le \mu < \frac{X}{2}$$

$$-\frac{Y}{2} \le \nu < \frac{Y}{2}$$

Where:

$Pixel(m,n)$ = the original image (spatial domain)

X,Y = the dimensions of the image

$DFT(\mu,\nu)$ = the Discrete Fourier Transform of the image

Implementation sequence:

$e^{-j2\pi(\mu m/X + \nu n/Y)} = \cos(2\pi(\mu m/X + \nu n/Y)) - j\sin(2\pi(\mu m/X + \nu n/Y))$

and

$DFT(\mu,\nu) = ReDFT(\mu,\nu) + jImDFT(\mu,\nu)$

so,

$$ReDFT(\mu,\nu) = X^{-1}Y^{-1}\sum_{n=-\frac{Y}{2}}^{\frac{Y}{2}-1}\left[\sum_{m=-\frac{X}{2}}^{\frac{X}{2}-1}Pixel(m,n)\cos(2\pi(\mu m/X + \nu n/Y))\right]$$

$$ImDFT(\mu,\nu) = X^{-1}Y^{-1}\sum_{n=-\frac{Y}{2}}^{\frac{Y}{2}-1}\left[\sum_{m=-\frac{X}{2}}^{\frac{X}{2}-1}-Pixel(m,n)\sin(2\pi(\mu m/X + \nu n/Y))\right]$$

Where:

$ReDFT(\mu,\nu)$ = the real component of the image's Fourier Transform

$ImDFT(\mu,\nu)$ = the imaginary component of image's Fourier Transform

I should warn you that performing a Discrete Fourier Transform (DFT) takes time. You may have noticed in **The Math Behind The Magic** section that for each pixel in the original image you compute a double summation, first across all X and then across all Y. For each pixel you perform $X*Y$ summations. Because $X*Y$ pixels are in the image, you end up doing X^2*Y^2 summations for a complete DFT of an image. For a 256×256 image, this equals 256^4 or 4.3 *billion* summations, Holy Smokes! I don't know what kind of machine you're running on, but on my 486DX33 PC clone, a 256×256 image takes about a day. (Your first hint of trouble should be when the author reports units of time in days.) So, what can you do? Well, you definitely do not have to take this kind of abuse.

A student of linear systems will tell you that you can take this type of problem and break it down into its two components or dimensions. First, compute the DFT in the X dimension, then take the results of this and perform a DFT in the Y dimension. (See the next **Math Behind The Magic** box.) Guess what? Now it only takes a total of $X^3 + Y^3$ summations. For the same 256×256 image, this equals only 34 million summations, or only about 10 minutes if you simply ratio. We're saved! Well, actually my machine takes about 30 minutes due to implementation details that you can read all about in the code listing. The `imp_dft_2d_faster` in IMAGEPRO.C provides all the necessary routines to perform a faster DFT—hence the name `imp_dft_2d_faster`.

You Can Do It: Speedy Fourier Transforms

1. Run the IMAGEPRO.EXE program.

2. Enter a value to select your screen resolution.

3. Enter the number 14 to run the 2D DFT demo.

4. Enter the name of a gray-scale TIFF image. (Try EART128.TIF.)

5. The original image shows up on the left; its DFT is on the right. (Be patient, you may not see anything happening for a minute or two DFTs are slow you know.) (Run your system with DOS SMARTDRV if you have it.)

6. Press any key to return to the main menu.

7. Enter 18 to exit.

8. IMAGE.FFT file is created for each run. Rename or copy it to EART128.FFT for the next **You Can Do It** section (Inverse DFT Demo).

The Math Behind The Magic: The DFT in Two Parts

Here's where I show you how to do a DFT in two parts. You do a 1-D DFT in the X dimension first, and then a 1-D DFT on the results in the Y dimension, as follows:

$$DFT(\mu,n) = X^{-1}\left[\sum_{m=-\frac{X}{2}}^{\frac{X}{2}-1} Pixel(m,n)\, e^{-j2\pi(\mu m/X)}\right]$$

$$\text{for} \quad -\frac{X}{2} \le \mu < \frac{X}{2}$$

Where:

Pixel(m,n) = the original image (spatial domain)

X = the X dimension of the image

DFT(μ,n) = the X dimension DFT of the image

$$DFT(\mu,v) = Y^{-1}\left[\sum_{n=-\frac{Y}{2}}^{\frac{Y}{2}-1} DFT(\mu,n)\, e^{-j2\pi(vn/Y)}\right]$$

$$\text{for} \quad -\frac{Y}{2} \le v < \frac{Y}{2}$$

Where:

Y = the Y dimension of the image.

DFT(μ,v) = the DFT of the image.

Returning to Spacial Domain

Once you have the *ReDFT*(μ,v) and *ImDFT*(μ,v) values for the image, you can compute the original image by performing the same math all over again, except now you start with real and imaginary data (because that's what the original DFT process generated). See the next **Math Behind The Magic** section or just use the `imp_inv_dft_image` routine provided in the image processing library. The results of an Inverse Fourier Transform in this case should only be real values because that's what you started with in the original image. This fact simplifies the formulas for computing the inverse transform.

The Math Behind The Magic: The Inverse Discrete Fourier Transform

$$Pixel\,(m,n) = \sum_{v=-\frac{Y}{2}}^{\frac{Y}{2}-1}\left[\,\sum_{\mu=-\frac{X}{2}}^{\frac{X}{2}-1} DFT(\mu,v)\,e^{j2\pi(\mu m/X\,+\,vn/Y)}\right.$$

$$\text{for }\; -\frac{X}{2}\le m < \frac{X}{2}$$

$$-\frac{Y}{2}\le n < \frac{Y}{2}$$

Where:

$Pixel(m,n)$ = the original image (spatial domain)

X,Y = dimensions of the image

$DFT(\mu,v)$ = the Fourier Transform of the image

Implementation sequence:

$e^{j2\pi(\mu m/X\,+\,vn/Y)} = \cos\,(2\pi(\mu m/X + v\,n/Y)) + j\sin(2\pi(\mu m/X + v\,n/Y))$

and,

$DFT(\mu,v) = ReDFT(\mu,v) + jImDFT(\mu,v)$

so,

$$Pixel\,(m,n) = \sum_{v=-\frac{Y}{2}}^{\frac{Y}{2}-1} \left[\sum_{\mu=-\frac{X}{2}}^{\frac{X}{2}-1} \left(ReDFT(\mu,v) \cos(2\pi\,(\mu m/X + vn/Y)) \right. \right.$$
$$+ jReDFT(\mu,v) \sin(2\pi\,(\mu m/X + vn/Y))$$
$$+ jImDFT(\mu,v) \cos(2\pi\,(\mu m/X + vn/Y))$$
$$\left. \left. - ImDFT(\mu,v) \sin(2\pi\,(\mu m/X + vn/Y)) \right) \right]$$

but *Pixel*(*m*,*n*) can only be real, so,

$$Pixel\,(m,n) = \sum_{v=-\frac{Y}{2}}^{\frac{Y}{2}-1} \left[\sum_{\mu=-\frac{X}{2}}^{\frac{X}{2}-1} \left(ReDFT(\mu,v) \cos(2\pi\,(\mu m/X + vn/Y)) \right. \right.$$
$$\left. \left. - ImDFT(\mu,v) \sin(2\pi\,(\mu m/X + vn/Y)) \right) \right]$$

You Can Do It: Returning to Space

This demo gives you the thrill of watching an actual image emerge from a cryptic *.FFT file. Before running it, you can create EART128.FFT by running the previous **You Can Do It** 2D DFT demo and then copying IMAGE.FFT to EART128.FFT.

1. Run the IMAGEPRO.EXE program.

2. Enter a value to select your screen resolution.

3. Enter the number 15 to run the 2-D Inverse DFT demo.

4. Enter the name of a frequency domain image. (Try EART128.FFT.)

5. The DFT image shows up on the left; the original image is on the right. (Be patient, you may not see anything happening for a minute or two. Inverse DFTs are just as slow you know.) (Run your system with DOS SMARTDRV if you have it.)

6. Press any key to return to the main menu.

7. Enter 18 to exit.

Working Code: Returning From the Fourier Domain

As you can see in the previous math section, the Forward Fourier Transform and the Inverse Fourier Transform have a slight difference between them. The Inverse Fourier Transform has a positive exponent value, and it does not divide the results by X and Y. The code in Listing 13.4 shows you how it's done. You may note that it does the inverse DFT in two parts to take advantage of the speed up realized in the previous section.

Listing 13.4. Inverse Fourier Transform (DFT in Two Parts)

```
/*.................. IMP_INV_DFT_IMAGE ......................*/
/*  This routine gets the specified FFT FILE (fft_fname) and  */
/*  computes the inverse 2-D Fourier Transform. Then the      */
/*  resulting image is displayed starting at 'x0,y0'.         */
/*          **** Uses DFT in 2 parts approach *****           */
/*..........................................................*/
void imp_inv_dft_image(fft_fname,x0,y0)
char *fft_fname;
int x0,y0;
{
  int i,j,width,height,pixel,src_file_ptr,dst_file_ptr;
  unsigned char array[1024];
  float real_array[1024],imag_array[1024],power;
  float in1_array[1024],in2_array[1024];

  src_file_ptr = imp_fft_file_open(fft_fname,&width,&height,0);
  dst_file_ptr = imp_fft_file_open("tempjunk.fft",
                                   &width,&height,1);
/*..........................................................*/
/*  Draw frame around output data area.                      */
/*..........................................................*/
  vsa_set_color(128);
  vsa_move_to(x0-1,y0-1);
  vsa_rect(x0+width,y0+height);
/*..........................................................*/
/*  For each ROW in FFT FILE, perform 1D FFT.                */
/*..........................................................*/
  for(j=0;j<height;j++)
    {
```

continues

Listing 13.4 continued

```
/*..........................................................*/
/*  Read fft data from source file one ROW at a time, and    */
/*  perform DFT in X dimension for each row. Then write results*/
/*  to temp FFT FILE (Inverse FFT data). Also Display partial  */
/*  results (amplitude only).                                  */
/*..........................................................*/
      imp_fft_file_read_row(src_file_ptr,j,in1_array,in2_array);
      imp_dft_1dc(in1_array,in2_array,real_array,imag_array,
                  width,0,0);
      imp_fft_file_write_row(dst_file_ptr,j,
                             real_array,imag_array);
      imp_draw_inv_fft_row(x0,y0+j,width,real_array);
    }
/*..........................................................*/
/*  For each COLUMN in FFT FILE, perform 1D FFT.             */
/*..........................................................*/
  for(i=0;i<width;i++)
    {
/*..........................................................*/
/*  Read fft data from temp file one COLUMN at a time, and   */
/*  perform DFT in Y dimension for each column. Then Display  */
/*  results.                                                  */
/*  Note: This routine only plots the REAL data because it    */
/*        assumes (oops) that original source for Fourier     */
/*        Transform was a Real Image.                         */
/*..........................................................*/
      imp_fft_file_read_column(dst_file_ptr,i,in1_array,
                               in2_array);
      imp_dft_1dc(in1_array,in2_array,real_array,imag_array,
                  width,0,0);
      imp_draw_inv_fft_row(x0,y0+i,height,real_array);
    }
/*..........................................................*/
/*  Close Source FFT File and Temp file and delete Temp file. */
/*..........................................................*/
  imp_fft_file_close(src_file_ptr);
  imp_fft_file_close(dst_file_ptr);
```

```
 if(remove("tempjunk.fft") == -1)
   {
     printf("ERROR: Couldn't delete TEMPJUNK.FFT file!\n");
   }
 return;
}                           /*.... End IMP_INV_DFT_IMAGE  .....*/


/*.................. IMP_FFT_FILE_READ_ROW ....................*/
/*  This routine reads a row of 2D FFT data from the file      */
/*  pointed to by 'file_ptr'.  The 'real_array' and            */
/*  'imag_array' arrays hold the floating point data which is  */
/*  read.  The data is read from 'row' of the 2-D FFT image.   */
/*                                                             */
/*  NOTE: The width and height of the 2-D FFT image are already*/
/*        stored as the first two entries in the file pointed  */
/*        to by 'file_ptr'. This routine reads those values and*/
/*        uses them in accessing 'real_array' and 'imag_array'.*/
/*        Make sure that these arrays have correct size!       */
/*...........................................................*/
void imp_fft_file_read_row(file_ptr,row,real_array,imag_array)
int file_ptr,row;
float *real_array,*imag_array;
{
  long byte_addr;
  int width,height;
  MY_LSEEK(file_ptr,0,0);
  MY_READ(file_ptr,&width,2);
  MY_READ(file_ptr,&height,2);
  if((row < 0) || (row >= height))
    {
      printf("ERROR: 'Row' out of bounds in "
             "IMP_FFT_FILE_READ_ROW!\n");
      return;
    }

  byte_addr = 4L+8L*((long)row)*((long)width);
  MY_LSEEK(file_ptr,byte_addr,0);
  MY_READ(file_ptr,real_array,4*width);
  MY_READ(file_ptr,imag_array,4*width);
  return;
}                          /*.. END imp_fft_file_read_row    ..*/
```

Things to do in the Frequency Domain

Now you know all about transforming an image to the frequency domain. You know how to interpret a Fourier spectrum plot, and you know how to transform a Fourier pattern back to a real image. You must be wondering, "Why have I bothered to learn this stuff? What good is it besides being a real CPU hog?" I don't blame you. Let's find out what you can do with this powerful stuff.

The theory goes like this. In the one-dimensional audio world, you can break down any sound pattern (voice, music, screeching brakes, and so on) into a— sometimes very large—collection of pure sine waves, each of which has a unique frequency and phase shift. Believe it or not, the exact same is true in the two-dimensional image world. You can break down any image into its various frequency components, each of which is a single frequency with a specific two-dimensional orientation and phase shift. That's exactly what you have when you perform the Fourier Transform on an image. An *M*×*N* pixel image results in an *M*×*N* array of frequency components (equal to the square root of *ReDFT* squared plus *ImDFT* squared) and associated phase shifts (equal to the arctangent of *ImDFT* divided by *ReDFT*).

Because the pixels in the frequency domain represent all the various frequency components of a spatial domain image, what do you suppose happens if you overwrite some of those frequency domain pixels with zero? If you do this, you end up removing those specific frequency components from the image. After you perform the Inverse Fourier Transform, you're back to the original image minus the missing frequency components. You've filtered the image. The filter's spatial frequency response is simply a matter of which frequencies (that is, which pixels) you mask or attenuate in the *ReDFT* and *ImDFT* arrays.

In Figure 13.30, a frequency domain mask is shown which completely blocks the $\mu,\nu = -32,0$ and $+32,0$ peaks as well as a portion (6 percent) of the $\mu,\nu = 0,0$ peak. The $-32,0$ and $+32,0$ peaks correspond to the 32 cycles/image width sinusoidal noise in the Earth image, and the $0,0$ peak corresponds to the $+15$ DC bias in the noise (refer back to Figure 13.28). Figure 13.31 shows the Earth image after the noise is filtered out of the original image.

Weren't convolutions performing some kind of spatial frequency filtering many sections back? Why, yes. *In fact, performing a convolution of an image with a kernel is equivalent to multiplying the Fourier Transform of the image with the Fourier Transform of the kernel.* Oh, oh, hot concept…read that one again! Taking this concept a little farther, the Fourier Transform of the Kernel *is* the kernel's frequency response: the effect the kernel will have on the frequency components of an image after a convolution.

Figure 13.30. *A Frequency Domain Mask.*

So, now you have a choice. You can filter an image in the spatial domain by performing convolutions or by first computing the Fourier Transform of the image, multiplying the *ReDFT* and *ImDFT* arrays with a frequency response template (or mask), and then performing the Inverse Fourier Transform on the result. (See Listing 13.5 for an example of this.) Whichever way you decide depends on the complexity of the desired frequency response. For simple 3×3, 5×5, or 7×7 kernels, just performing the convolution is faster (if you know what the kernel weights should be). For large kernels, or a frequency response more easily represented by a frequency domain mask, performing the filter is easier in the frequency domain.

What if your application requires that, for whatever reason, you filter an image with convolutions instead of Fourier Transforms? What if you also know precisely what the desired frequency response is for a certain filter function that you want to apply to an image? With these circumstances, you do the following. You generate the filter's frequency response *ReDFT* and *ImDFT* template (this is just a matter of "drawing" a mask for the various frequency components), then you perform the Inverse Fourier Transform of this data to generate the kernel for subsequent use in convolutions. Although the Inverse Fourier Transform function produces a kernel as big as your image, you can usually throw away almost everything but the central region. This is a great way to make very specific filters that do nothing but remove the obnoxious checkered pattern on Uncle Louie's tie.

Figure 13.31. *The Earth image after filtering with the mask in Figure 13.30 and then performing the Inverse Fourier Transform.*

You Can Do It: Using Frequency Masks

This demo is very "canned" in that it always works with EART128.TIF and EART128.FFT input files. You are free to experiment with your own 128×128 pixel mask files, though. Before you run this demo, however, you must first create EART128.FFT with the 2D DFT demo (two **You Can Do It** boxes ago). Otherwise, you get a free trip to PC Reset Land...an added feature.

1. Run the IMAGEPRO.EXE program.

2. Enter a value to select your screen resolution.

3. Enter the number 16 to run the DFT Custom Filter demo.

4. Enter the name of a 128×128 8-bit TIFF image. (Try MSK128.TIF.)

5. The original EART128.TIF image shows up on the top left; its DFT, EART128.FFT, is on the top right.

6. The Mask shows up on the bottom left; the filtered image is on the bottom right. (Be patient, you may not see anything happening for a minute or two. Filtering is slow you know.) (Run your system with DOS SMARTDRV if you have it.)

7. Press any key to return to the main menu.

8. Enter 18 to exit.

Math Behind The Magic: Basic Principles of Fourier Transforms

$$k(x,y) <=> K(\mu,\nu)$$

$$f(x,y) <=> F(\mu,\nu)$$

$$k(x,y) * f(x,y) <=> K(\mu,\nu) \times F(\mu,\nu)$$

$$k(x,y) \times f(x,y) <=> K(\mu,\nu) * F(\mu,\nu)$$

Where:

<=>   denotes equivalence between spatial and frequency domains

*   denotes a convolution

x   denotes a multiplication

and

$k(x,y)$ = a two dimensional function (like a convolution kernel)

$f(x,y)$ = a two dimensional function (like an image)

$K(\mu,\nu)$ = a two dimensional Fourier Transform of $k(x,y)$

$F(\mu,\nu)$ = a two dimensional Fourier Transform of $f(x,y)$

Working Code: Frequency Filtering

Listing 13.5. Functions to perform frequency filtering from IMAGEPRO.C.

```
/*................ IMP_DFT_FILTER_IMAGE ....................*/
/*  This routine reads a frequency domain mask from the 'x0,y0'*/
/*  to 'x1,y1' screen rectangle.  Then it reads in the      */
/*  'fft_fname' FFT File.  It displays the 'fft_fname' Fourier */
/*  spectrum plot starting at 'x2,y2'. The frequency domain    */
/*  mask is multipled with the 'fft_fname' FFT File and        */
/*  displayed at 'x3,y3'.  Then the Inverse Fourier Transform  */
/*  is taken of this product and displayed at 'x4,y4'.         */
/*..........................................................*/
void imp_dft_filter_image(x0,y0,x1,y1,fft_fname,
                          x2,y2,x3,y3,x4,y4)
char *fft_fname;
int x0,y0,x1,y1,x2,y2,x3,y3,x4,y4;
{
  int i,j,width,height,pixel,src_file_ptr,dst_file_ptr;
  unsigned char mask_array[1024],power_array[1024];
  float real_array[1024],imag_array[1024],power;
  float in1_array[1024],in2_array[1024];

  imp_fft_file_display(fft_fname,x2,y2);
  src_file_ptr = imp_fft_file_open(fft_fname,&width,&height,0);
  dst_file_ptr = imp_fft_file_open("tempjunk.fft",
                                   &width,&height,1);
/*..........................................................*/
/*  Draw frames around output data areas.                   */
/*..........................................................*/
```

```
    vsa_set_color(128);
    vsa_move_to(x0-1,y0-1);
    vsa_rect(x0+width,y0+height);
    vsa_move_to(x2-1,y2-1);
    vsa_rect(x2+width,y2+height);
    vsa_move_to(x3-1,y3-1);
    vsa_rect(x3+width,y3+height);
    vsa_move_to(x4-1,y4-1);
    vsa_rect(x4+width,y4+height);
/*.....................................................................*/
/*    Multiply Frequency domain mask with FFT File and display */
/*    at x3,y3.                                                 */
/*.....................................................................*/
   for(j=0;j<height;j++)
     {
       vsa_get_raster_line(x0,x0+width-1,j+y0,mask_array);
       vsa_get_raster_line(x2,x2+width-1,j+y2,power_array);
       for(i=0;i<width;i++)
         power_array[i] = ((float)mask_array[i]/255.0)*
                          power_array[i];
       vsa_raster_line(x3,x3+width-1,j+y3,power_array);
     }
/*.....................................................................*/
/*  For each ROW in FFT FILE, apply mask and perform 1D FFT.   */
/*.....................................................................*/
   for(j=0;j<height;j++)
     {
/*.....................................................................*/
/*  First read out mask columns to apply to FFT Files. Remember*/
/*  FFT File Rows are really columns!.                          */
/*.....................................................................*/
       for(i=0;i<width;i++)
         vsa_get_raster_line(x0+j,x0+j,y0+i,
                             (unsigned char *)(mask_array+i));
/*.....................................................................*/
/*  Read fft data from source file one ROW at a time, and     */
/*  multiply with mask data.                                   */
/*.....................................................................*/
       imp_fft_file_read_row(src_file_ptr,j,in1_array,in2_array);
       for(i=0;i<width;i++)
         in1_array[i] = in1_array[i]*(float)mask_array[i]/255.0;
```

continues

Listing 13.5. continued

```
      for(i=0;i<width;i++)
        in2_array[i] = in2_array[i]*(float)mask_array[i]/255.0;
/*..............................................................*/
/*  Perform DFT in X dimension for each row. Then write results*/
/*  to temp FFT FILE (Inverse FFT data), and display.          */
/*..............................................................*/
      imp_dft_1dc(in1_array,in2_array,real_array,imag_array,
                  width,0,0);
      imp_fft_file_write_row(dst_file_ptr,j,
                              real_array,imag_array);
      imp_draw_inv_fft_row(x4,y4+j,width,real_array);
    }
/*..............................................................*/
/*  For each COLUMN in FFT FILE, perform 1D FFT.               */
/*..............................................................*/
  for(i=0;i<width;i++)
    {
/*..............................................................*/
/*  Read fft data from source file one COLUMN at a time and    */
/*  perform DFT in Y dimension for each Column. Then Display    */
/*  results.                                                    */
/*..............................................................*/
      imp_fft_file_read_column(dst_file_ptr,i,
                              in1_array,in2_array);
      imp_dft_1dc(in1_array,in2_array,real_array,imag_array,
                  width,0,0);
      imp_draw_inv_fft_row(x4,y4+i,height,real_array);
    }
/*..............................................................*/
/*  Close Source FFT File and Temp file and delete Temp file.  */
/*..............................................................*/
  imp_fft_file_close(src_file_ptr);
  imp_fft_file_close(dst_file_ptr);
  if(remove("tempjunk.fft") == -1)
    {
      printf("ERROR: Couldn't delete TEMPJUNK.FFT file!\n");
    }
  return;
}                            /*... End IMP_DFT_FILTER_IMAGE ...*/
```

```
/*................. IMP_FFT_FILE_DISPLAY .................... */
/*  This routine is used to display an FFT FILE format file.   */
/*  The Power Spectrum Plot of the FFT is displayed starting at*/
/*  'x0,y0' with a width and height as defined in the file's   */
/*  header.                                                     */
/*....................................................*/
void imp_fft_file_display(fft_fname,x0,y0)
char *fft_fname;
int x0,y0;
{
  int i,j,width,height,pixel,src_file_ptr;
  unsigned char array[1024];
  float real_array[1024],imag_array[1024],power;
/*....................................................*/
/*                Open FFT File (with 'DUMP' off)          */
/*....................................................*/
  src_file_ptr = imp_fft_file_open(fft_fname,&width,&height,0);
/*....................................................*/
/*  Read out each row of FFT File and display as a COLUMN.     */
/*  Remember, FFT Files are stored inverted as far as row and  */
/*  columns go!                                                */
/*....................................................*/
  for(j=0;j<height;j++)
    {
     imp_fft_file_read_row(src_file_ptr,j,real_array,imag_array);
     for(i=0;i<width;i++)
       {
         power = width*sqrt(real_array[i]*real_array[i] +
                            imag_array[i]*imag_array[i]   );
         power = max(power,0.0);
         pixel = (unsigned char)min(power,255.0);
         vsa_set_color(pixel);
         vsa_set_pixel(x0+j,y0+i);
       }
    }
/*....................................................*/
/*                Close FFT File                          */
/*....................................................*/
  imp_fft_file_close(src_file_ptr);
  return;
}                              /*.... End IMP_FFT_FILE_DISPLAY ...*/
```

Conclusions

Filters [enable] you to quickly achieve certain effects in a production environment as well as have fun by letting you distort and modify your image. You've seen these effects in magazines and books, and now you can do it yourself. A wide variety of filters are available—depending on which application you use, you can blur, speckle, pixelize or mosaic, sharpen or soften an image, trace contours, find edges, sharpen edges, motion blur, emboss, wave, ripple, balloon or spherize, zig zag, twirl, or even create your own custom filter!

—John Stevens, "Improving Your Image,"
PC Publishing & Presentations,
August/September 1991

This chapter introduces some of the basic concepts in image processing. The examples and source code provided should help you in your trek to developing your own image processing applications. However, if you prefer to use a full-blown commercial or shareware image processing program, refer to Appendix E and the software order form in the back of the book for some recommendations.

The image processing library provided in this distribution has not been optimized for speed. A version of the IMP256 Image Processing Library is available that uses assembly code where necessary to achieve significant increases in speed. It also has a Fast Fourier Transform (FFT) routine in there that does image FFTs almost in the blink of an eye. If you would like to get your hands on this fine piece of work, please send $35 to Spyro Gumas; 1668 Shady Brook Drive; Fullerton, CA 92631. I'll gladly ship you the latest IMP256 Image Processing Library as well as the latest VSA256 Graphics Library and TIF256 Graphics Library Extensions.

Interactive Visualization

Mention the phrase computer graphics in the lobby of any corporate headquarters and you're likely to conjure up images of bar graphs from Lotus 1-2-3 made into flashy slides with Harvard Graphics or Aldus Persuasion. Those old standbys of the business world have evolved to include most of the graphics tricks covered in this book. Computer graphics, though, are also providing new ways of looking at numerical information that go far beyond even the sharpest boardroom presentation.

Interaction is the word of the day—not just for artsy types, but for bean counters and number crunchers as well. Today's speedy, graphically adept desktop PCs can display and manipulate numerical information in pictoral form, enabling you to see connections and patterns that no spreadsheet could ever reveal. New types of hands-on, visual data analysis and simulation are at your fingertips.

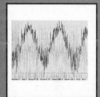

The popular buzzword for this brewing storm of graphical data analysis is *visualization.* This term and the techniques it embodies are all the rage among financial analysts, scientists, medical professionals, and almost everyone else who works with complex data sets that defy traditional analysis. This chapter applies some of the graphics techniques from previous chapters in two key areas that belong under the visualization umbrella: interactive data display and visual simulation.

Interactive Data Display

Data visualization is about comprehension, not graphics. Think of it as a range of techniques that enable you to display abstract numerical data and statistics in graphical form.

After all, you comprehend information most intuitively thorugh your visual senses. With half the neurons in the brain dedicated to visual processing, images provide the greatest mental bandwidth. Thus, by offering a picture of the data and its internal relationships, visualization makes it easier for you to understand information that's too complex to percieve numerically.

New techniques bring new possibilities. Scientists use visualization to analyze the results of experiments in fields as far-flung as pollution studies, semiconductor physics, and drug design. In engineering, visualization can provide rapid solutions in design, development, and production planning. Civic and voluntary organizations can use visualization to obtain demographic data. And in business, the use of visualization techniques can reveal buying patterns, sales penetration, or investment returns. Investors can benefit from visualization's ability to explain performance rather than just track it.

—Jack Weber, "Visualization: Seeing is Believing," *BYTE*, April 1993.

Half your brain is dedicated to processing visual information, and the optic nerves carry more information than all the rest of your senses combined. Unfortunately for businessmen and scientists, most of that visual brainpower is wasted when you're staring at a table of numbers. The official scuttlebutt from Brain Central reports that all those little black squigglies look alike.

Depict those same numbers as curves or lines, however, and Brain HQ immediately readies the pattern-recognition heavy artillery. You can almost hear those synapses click as your four-pound biological supercomputer leaps into action. "Gee, if you ignore that spike in the middle, that little twist has almost the same shape as that other piece over here. And over there—you see?—that part goes down when this part goes up." No chunk of silicon can hold its own against your carbon-based cerebrum in the multidimensional pattern analysis competition.

This helps explain the popularity of boardroom bar graphs. Somehow, though, you still find yourself nodding off at those meetings, even though the picture of Hawaii behind the graph keeps you awake a little bit longer. Why? Because presentation graphics are all one way, and total passivity isn't the key to keeping your cortex wrinkly and alert.

Most of your brain that's not connected to your eyes is hooked up to your hands. To see what's really going on in a set of data, you need to *interact* with it. When visual patterns respond to your commands with predictable movement, you can explore connections, look closer, compare, contrast, try experimental changes. In short, you can *play*. As any three-year-old can tell you, participatory play is the best—possibly the only—way that humans can develop deep understanding and expertise. (Okay, a three-year-old might phrase that a little differently. But she'd definitely agree.)

Start with the Numbers

As an example of interactive data display, you can use the following DATAVIEW program to play with some real-world numbers in visual form.

Weather and climate data prove particularly elusive when set to numerical analysis, so I've borrowed three years' worth of weather data from our local weather guru. (Every area has one. Ours is a cheerful and insightful radio weatherman named Roger Hill, who also runs a National Weather Service monitoring station from his Middlesex, Vermont home.) With the DATAVIEW program, you'll get the chance to play with the weather in ways that you could never fathom without your computer.

The forthcoming **You Can Do It** section walks you through the keystrokes, but first I'll show you some of what DATAVIEW can do.

For starters, DATAVIEW must have some numbers in a standard ASCII text file, along with some clues as to how you'd like the data displayed. The first line of a DATAVIEW-compatible file should specify the number of data points in the file. The second line tells DATAVIEW what gradations to use for the graph lines when it draws a reference grid behind the data. The rest of the file is just x and y values for the data points themselves. For example, the first few lines of the AVGTEMP.DAT file, which contains 919 data points for display over a grid of 30×10 rules, look like this:

```
919
30 10
1 30
2 35
3 28
4 38
```

```
5 40
6 44
7 34
8 35
9 33
10 41
11 41
12 35
...etc...
```

The x values represent day numbers, and the y values represent the average temperature for each day over a 919 day period in degrees Fahrenheit.

Playing with the Weather

Figure 14.1 depicts the AVGTEMP data in a variety of ways, demonstrating each of the transformations that the DATAVIEW program can perform. Although your spreadsheet software might be able to produce similar pictures, you'd need to mess with complicated menu choices each time you wanted to plot a new graph. With DATAVIEW, your display changes instantly in response to the push of a button. Note that the graph-paper grid also changes automatically when you enlarge or shrink the data, so that the horizontal increments are always 30 units (days) apart and the vertical lines always represent 10-degree increments.

Are You Serious?

If you're serious about analyzing scientific or financial data of your own, you will undoubtedly want to modify the **Working Code** for the following DATAVIEW program to add data-manipulation options specifically tailored to your needs. If the thought of doing your own programming gives you the heebie-geebies, consider buying a dedicated visualization program. Such programs are usually targeted toward a fairly narrow audience and provide custom tools just for your type of data. Therefore, I can't recommend the particular software for your particular job. The annotated bibiliography (Appendix E) in the back of this book gives you contact information for several of the general-purpose visualization tools available for PCs.

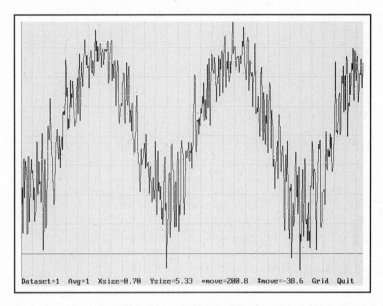

Dataset=1 Avg=1 Xsize=0.70 Ysize=5.33 ↔move=200.8 ↕move=-30.6 Grid Quit

Figure 14.1a. *When you display a data file with DATAVIEW, it automatically scales the x- and y-axes to fit the screen. Here, DATAVIEW displays the average daily temperature for a 919-day period.*

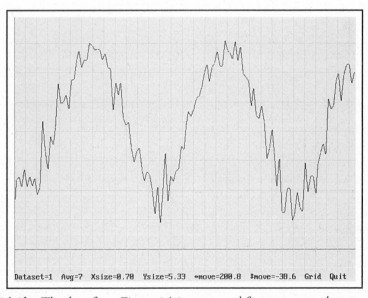

Dataset=1 Avg=7 Xsize=0.70 Ysize=5.33 ↔move=200.8 ↕move=-30.6 Grid Quit

Figure 14.1b. *The data from Figure 14.1a, averaged for every seven days. DATAVIEW enables you to dynamically average the data over any period you like and displays the results immediately.*

635

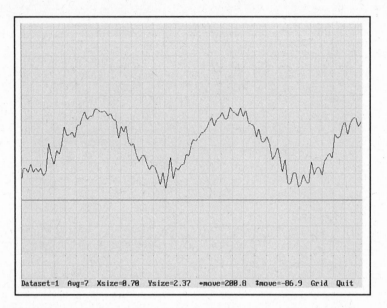

Figure 14.1c. *Often, changing the scale factor for the y-axis can make patterns easier (or more difficult) to see.*

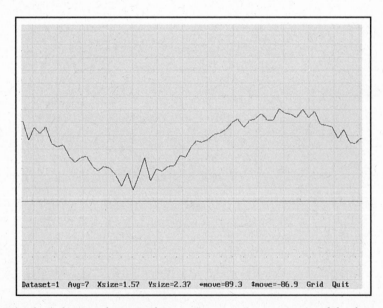

Figure 14.1d. *Enlarging the x-axis lets you "zoom in" to view part of the data more closely.*

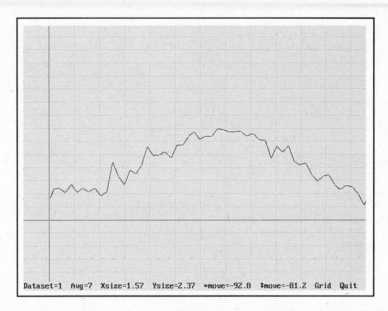

Dataset=1 Avg=7 Xsize=1.57 Ysize=2.37 *move=-92.8 $move=-81.2 Grid Quit

Figure 14.1e. *By moving the data set around, you can examine any part of it that interests you. The colored cross-hair helps you locate the origin, where x=0 and y=0.*

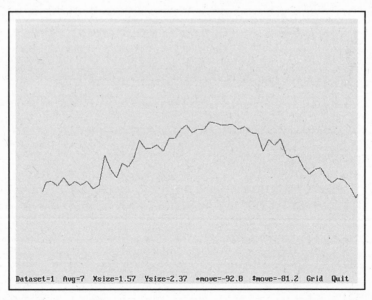

Dataset=1 Avg=7 Xsize=1.57 Ysize=2.37 *move=-92.8 $move=-81.2 Grid Quit

Figure 14.1f. *You can also turn off the graph-paper grid and origin cross-hair display to see your data more clearly.*

Meanwhile, you may find that the simple tools in DATAVIEW can actually give you enough interactive control over the display of complex data sets to let you spot many interesting patterns. The **You Can Do It** section that follows (illustrated in Figures 14.2 and 14.3) explores the Middlesex weather data and shows you how even the most basic interactive visualization can help you pick out correlations that would go completely unnoticed in a table of numbers or a static graph.

Spotting Similarities

Figures 14.2 and 14.3 show three sets of related information: the daily average temperature over a 2 1/2-year period, the deviation in temperature from the previous year for each day, and the total amount of precipitation for each day in the same period. By averaging and transforming the rather messy-looking data in various ways, connections and correspondences that were initially invisible become quite obvious.

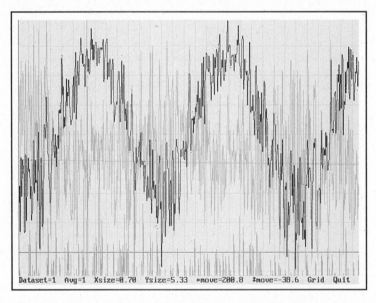

Dataset=1 Avg=1 Xsize=0.70 Ysize=5.33 *move=200.8 $move=-30.6 Grid Quit

Figure 14.2a. *Average temperature, deviation from previous year's temperature, and daily rainfall look like an incomprehensible mess when graphed in their raw form.*

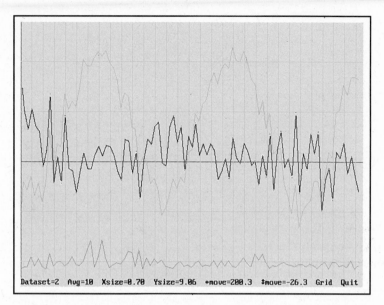

Figure 14.2b. *Displaying each curve as 10-day averages clears the mud considerably.*

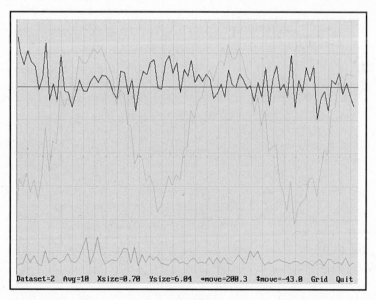

Figure 14.2c. *Moving the "deviation from previous year" curve upward makes the similarities to the summer (top) part of the average temperature curve obvious.*

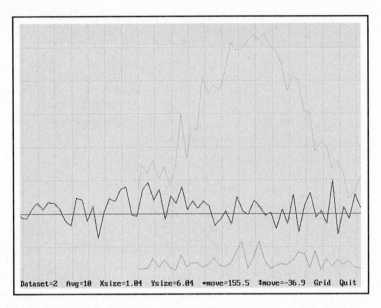

Figure 14.2d. *Move the curve down, and similarities to the winter (lower) part of the average temperature curve leap out.*

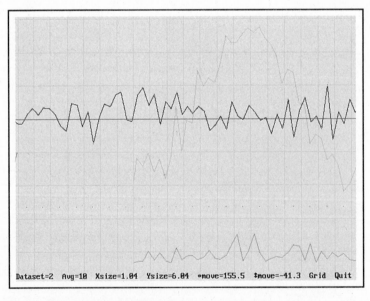

Figure 14.2e. *Because the previous year's temperature partly determines the "deviation" curve, moving the data to the left by one year should still reveal similarities.*

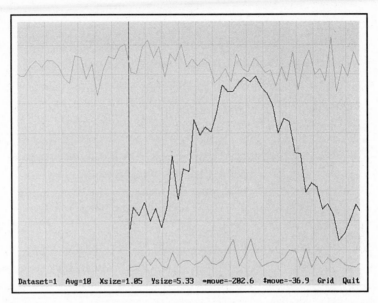

Dataset=1 Avg=10 Xsize=1.05 Ysize=5.33 ⟷move=-202.6 ↕move=-36.9 Grid Quit

Figure 14.2f. *Sure enough, the previous year's average temperature corresponds closely with the shape of the current year's "deviation from previous year."*

The similarities highlighted in Figure 14.2 are no big surprise. A moment's thought would have told you that a plot of temperature deviation from the previous year should look quite similar to both this year's and last year's average temperature data, but you can also use these average/scale/move techniques to find patterns that you didn't know about in advance. Figure 14.3 compares the deviation from previous year's temperature to the daily rainfall. Does a correlation exist? Is the correlation seasonal? I leave any conclusions up to you and your eyes.

You Can Do It: Hot and Wet, Cold and Dry?

With the DATAVIEW program included on the disk with this book, you can interactively average, scale, and move multiple graphs of data. To show you how this kind of interaction can help bring out patterns in complex data, I'll guide you through the weather experiments pictured in Figures 14.1 through 14.3.

1. To view the data in the AVGTEMP.DAT file (which represents daily average temperature), enter:

```
DATAVIEW AVGTEMP.DAT
```

2. Press V for VGA 16-color mode.

   As specified in the second text line of the AVGTEMP.DAT file (listed near the beginning of this chapter), the graph lines appear in increments of 30 units (representing days) along the x-axis and 10 units (degrees Fahrenheit) along the y-axis. The highlighted blue cross-hair along the left and near the bottom of the screen shows you where x=0 and y=0.

   Notice that DATAVIEW automatically scales and offsets the data to fit the screen and displays the scaling factors at the bottom of the screen along with the offset of the center of the data set.

   The astute observer can glean some information even from this initial pictorial representation of the data. For instance, I don't need to tell you which part of the graph is summer and which is winter. If you didn't already know, you could certainly guess the length of the time period represented from the seasonal temperature swings. What's also clear is that the variation in temperature from day to day in north-central Vermont is quite large, sometimes nearly equal to half the variation from summer to winter. Native Vermonters will be surprised at how seldom the graph dips below the 0-degree line because it sure feels like it's subzero most of the winter. (I guess my subjective thermometer reads winter minimums and summer maximums, not average temperatures.)

   Does the temperature vary from week to week as much as it does from day to day? Let's find out by telling DATAVIEW to display weekly temperature averages. You can dynamically adjust the averaging period by pressing lowercase-*a* (to increase the period) or uppercase-*A* (to decrease the period) at any time.

3. Press the letter a six times.

   Now you're looking at the 7-day averages. Though the curve appears smoother because fewer data points are displayed, the variation from one point to the next appears to be about the same as before.

Before you dive into some comparative data analysis, here's a brief overview of the tranformations that DATAVIEW can do. First, scale the data along each axis with the x and y keys.

4. Press y a couple of times, they try Y (Shift+y). Vertical scaling comes in handy when you want to compare the ups and downs of data sets with different degrees of variation.

5. Press x a few times to stretch the x axis, then try X (Shift+x). Scaling the x-axis has the effect of zooming in or out on a region of data.

   When you scale the axes, some of the data may move off the screen. To get it back in view, move the axes with the arrow keys.

6. Wander around a little bit by pressing various arrow keys. The entire data set moves just as you would expect.

7. Finally, try turning the graph-paper grid off and on by pressing the G key. (It doesn't matter if you press lowercase-g or Shift+g—either one will toggle the grid.)

8. Press Q (or press the Esc key) to quit and return to the DOS prompt.

DATAVIEW really shines when you start looking at more than one set of data at a time. The following exercise shows you how to spot some predictable correlations between related data sets and sets you up to explore possible correlations between seemingly unrelated sets.

1. Enter the following command at the DOS prompt to start DATAVIEW and display three data files. AVGTEMP.DAT is the average daily temperature, DEPTEMP.DAT is the difference between the average daily temperature and the average temperature for the same day in the previous year, and PRECIP.DAT is the daily precipitation in inches.

   ```
   DATAVIEW AVGTEMP.DAT DEPTEMP.DAT PRECIP.DAT
   ```

2. Press V to choose the VGA 16-color video mode.

   As you examine the three colored curves that pop up, keep in mind that each is scaled to fill the screen; they are not all displayed according to the same scaling factors.

3. To see the reference grid for the next data set (and the numerical scaling factors that appear at the bottom of the screen), press the letter D. Notice that the currently selected set turns white.

4. Press D again to see the third data set, then D again to return to the first set.

   (Incidentally, you can also use the Tab key to move between sets. It works just like the D key. If you've been using the programs in Chapter 7, you may have already used the Tab key to move from one item to another.)

   Every transformation you select (Xscale, Yscale, arrow key movement, and so on) is applied only to the current data set. To apply the same transformation to each data set, you must use the D (or Tab) key and give the transformation command for each set. That is done as follows:

5. Press the letter a nine times to display 10-day averages for the average temperature data (data set 1).

6. Press the letter d to move to the next data set.

7. Press the letter a nine times again to display 10-day averages for the deviation from previous year's temperature data (data set 2).

8. Press d to move to the final data set.

9. Press the letter a nine times again to display 10-day averages for the precipitation (data set 3).

   Notice that the data sets are ordered just as you specified them on the command line when you started the program.

   Averaging the temperatures this way makes it much easier to see patterns in the data. You might expect a close correlation between the average temperature and the deviation from previous year because the second data set is partially computed from the first. Such correlations are much easier to see if the curves are very close together vertically.

10. Press the d key until data set number 2, the deviation from the previous year's temperature, is selected.

11. Press the up arrow repeatedly until the curve is close to the top part of the average temperature data set.

    A correlation should be quite apparent. Your eye finds it easy to ignore the large seasonal variations in the average temperature, and the two curves tend to go up and down in roughly the same pattern during the summer months. However, it's hard to tell if the same is true for the lower (winter) part of the curve unless you move the deviation curve down near it.

12. Press the down arrow until the deviation curve comes close to the lower part of the average temperature curve.

    Again, a correlation is quite apparent.

    You would expect to see also a clear correlation between the deviation from previous year's temperature curve and the part of the average temperature curve that corresponds to the previous year. To visually verify this, you can simply move the deviation curve over one year to the left.

13. Count 12 grid lines (which, remember, represent 30-day increments) to the right from the light-blue 0 line, and keep your eye on the part of the deviation curve that crosses that one-year mark as you repeatedly press the left arrow key. Stop moving left when the one-year mark lines up with the beginning of the average temperature data at the left edge of the screen.

14. Move the deviation curve up and down with the arrow keys so you can see it close to the various parts of the average temperature curve.

    Again, you should find a close correlation in the two curves, although the two may be slightly offset horizontally due to the imprecise, large jumps that the arrow keys take.

    Visual correlations between average temperature and a deviation curve computed from the average temperature data itself don't exactly qualify as cutting-edge climatological research. Now that you've had a chance to play, you might like to see what patterns you can spot between two data sets with no obvious connection. The bottom curve on the screen represents precipitation levels for the same time period as the temperature data. Are the two related? This might certainly be possible. I'll leave it to you to play with the data and decide for yourself. (Everyone should be entitled to their own theories about the weather, and yours will now be based on hands-on interactive data visualization. Let's see your wife or fishing buddies argue with that!)

15. To line up the deviation curve with the other two again, press the right arrow key until the 0 line appears at the very left edge of the screen.

Now do your worst. Try looking at 20- or 30-day averages with the a key or zooming in on a particular region of each curve with the x key. Perhaps scaling with the y key will make the patterns more clear by emphasizing slope changes.

I've also included on the disk some additional weather data for you to explore. MINTEMP.DAT is the minimum temperature data. (If you view this along with MAXTEMP.DAT, remember that DATAVIEW positions both data sets to fit on-screen. If you want to compare the maximums to the minimums, you'll need to move the minimum data set down until the 0 line on the graph lines up with the 0 line for the maximum data set.) MAXMIN.DAT is a plot of maximum temperature versus minimum temperature—a completely different way to view the information. SAMPLE.DAT is a very small data set approximating the thickness of the polar ice caps during the last few centuries, just in case you were wondering.

Of course, you probably won't be very secure in any conclusions you draw from such simple analysis of these small data sets. You might get some hunches where no amount of statistical analysis would ever have led you, though. If weather prediction were your business, you would then want to look at more data and hone your hypotheses to the point where you could run more comprehensive analyses employing both numerical and visual methods. Meanwhile, playing with the data has given you a solid intuitive feel for its essential structure and texture that will aide you in any further explorations, and which you could never have gleaned any other way.

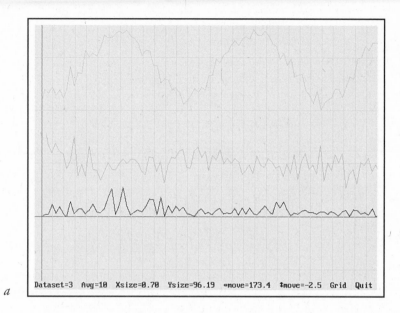

a

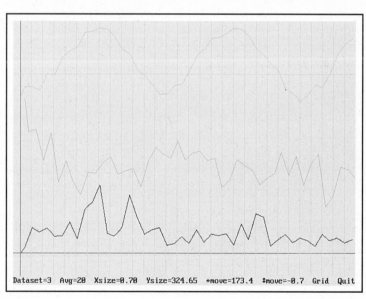

b

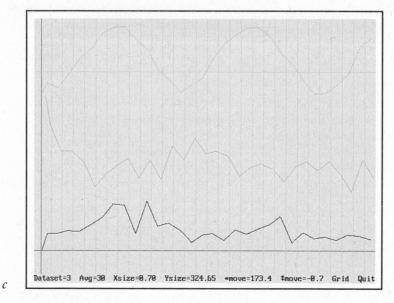

c   `Dataset=3  Avg=30  Xsize=0.70  Ysize=324.65  *move=173.4  $move=-0.7  Grid  Quit`

Figure 14.3. *Temperature, temperature deviation from previous year, and rainfall data are depicted as (a) 10-day, (b) 20-day and (c) 30-day averages.*

Working Code: Visualizing Your Data

The structure of the DATAVIEW program is quite simple: read a keystroke; change the member of the `avginc`, `xscale`, `yscale`, `midx`, or `midy` array that corresponds the current data set (specified by `set`); and display the data by drawing some lines. The only tricky trick that I use for speed is turning on the XOR mode (discussed in Chapter 2), so the current data set can be quickly erased and redisplayed without affecting the other curves on-screen.

The averaging takes place on the fly, within the `plotset()` function. You can easily add your own data-massaging code in a similar fashion. For example, you might try pulling your old statistics textbook off the shelf and tossing in a formula to plot the standard deviation, regression lines, and that sort of thing.

DATAVIEW doesn't use the fixed-point integer math used by many of the other graphics programs in the book. For scientific visualization, you often need the additional dynamic range provided by real floating-point numbers. Consequently, you'll want a math co-processor or a 486 if you're going to do much of this kind of thing. DATAVIEW and the WHEEL program presented later in this chapter are both a bit logy on an unaided 286 or 386 but will speed up significantly if you have a math-coprocessor installed.

To compile the DATAVIEW program, use the TransGraphics batch file for your compiler. For example, the Microsoft C command is:

```
TGMS DATAVIEW.C
```

and the Borland/Turbo C command is:

```
TGTC DATAVIEW.C
```

See the introduction to this book for more details on using TransGraphics.

Listing 14.1. DATAVIEW.C reads numbers from an ASCII file and enables you to interactively display them as line graphs.

```
/* DATAVIEW.C
 *
 * This program plots a set of data read from an ASCII file,
 * and allows you to interactively scale and average it.
 * See the file SAMPLE.DAT for an example of the data format.
 *
 * from Tricks of the Graphics Gurus
 */


#include <stdio.h>   /* Standard input/output and libraries */
#include <stdlib.h>
#include <math.h>                /* for float math functions */

#include "tg.h"     /* TransGraphics -- See TG.TXT for info */

/* These are the values of key bindings */

#define ENTER 13
#define ESC 27
#define TAB 9
#define UP -'H'
#define DN -'P'
```

continues

Listing 14.1. continued

```c
#define LT -'K'
#define RT -'M'

/* macro getch() replacement */

#define geta if ((a = getch()) == 0) a = -getch()

/* macros to find position on screen */

#define xposition(x) \
    (xoffset + (int) (((x) - midx[set]) * xscale[set]))
#define yposition(y) \
    (yoffset - (int) (((y) - midy[set]) * yscale[set]))

#define SCALEINC 1.5
#define OFFSETINC 16.0

#define white 15                    /* Color to make the menu */
#define axisclr 9          /* Color to make the axis lines */
#define gridclr 1          /* Color to make the graph lines */

#define NSETS 4              /* Maximum number of data sets */
#define NPOINTS 2000    /* Max number of points in each set */

int lastx[NPOINTS], lasty[NPOINTS],    /* for quick erasing */
    grid = 1,                   /* 1 = grid on, 0 = grid off */
    set = 0,                  /* currently selected data set */
    xoffset, yoffset,               /* screen positioning */
    xorigin, yorigin,            /* location of zero point */
    nsets,                           /* number of sets */
    avginc[NSETS],          /* number of points to average */
    npoints[NSETS];    /* number of data points in each set */

float midx[NSETS], midy[NSETS],      /* midpoint of each set */
    xscale[NSETS], yscale[NSETS],           /* scaling factors */
    xgridsize[NSETS], ygridsize[NSETS],  /* graph grid size */
    xgrid, ygrid,          /* graph grid size for current set */
    x[NSETS][NPOINTS], y[NSETS][NPOINTS];    /* data points */
```

```
int main(int nargs, char **arg);
void drawgrid(void);
void plotall(void);
void plotset(int set);
void printmenu(void);

int main(int nargs, char **arg)
{   int i, j;                     /* integers to use for counters */
    float xmax, xmin, ymax, ymin;  /* maximums and minimums */
    char a;                           /* for keyboard input */
    FILE *diskfile;              /* file handle and file name */
    char filename[40];
    if (nargs < 2)
    {   printf(
          "DATAVIEW -- from Tricks of the Graphics Gurus\n\n");
        printf("This program will plot data from\n");
        printf("one or more text files, and let you\n");
        printf("scale and average it interactively.\n");
        printf("Specify the data file names like this:\n\n");
        printf("DATAVIEW FILE1.DAT FILE2.DAT FILE3.DAT\n\n");
        exit(0);
    }
    nsets = nargs - 1;                /* number of data sets */
    for (i = 0; i < nsets; i++)
    {   if ((diskfile = fopen(arg[i + 1], "r")) == NULL)
        {   printf("Can't find a file named %s.", arg[i + 1]);
            exit(0);
        }

        /* read data (with almost no error checking!) */

        fscanf(diskfile, "%d", npoints + i);
        if (npoints[i] >= NPOINTS) npoints[i] = NPOINTS - 1;
        fscanf(diskfile, "%f %f",
               xgridsize + i, ygridsize + i);
        for (j = 0; j < npoints[i]; j++)
        {   fscanf(diskfile, "%f %f", &(x[i][j]), &(y[i][j]));
        }
        if (ferror(diskfile) != 0)
        {   printf("Error reading %s!", arg[i + 1]);
            fclose(diskfile);
```

continues

Listing 14.1. continued

```
            exit(0);
        }
        fclose(diskfile);
    }
    tg_pickmode();                  /* ask user for video mode */
    xoffset = tg_scrnx / 2;      /* move to center of screen */
    yoffset = (tg_scrny - tg_chary) / 2;
    for (i = 0; i < nsets; i++)
    {   xmax = xmin = x[i][0]; /* find largest and smallest */
        ymax = ymin = y[i][0];
        for (j = 1; j < npoints[i]; j++)
        {   if (x[i][j] > xmax) xmax = x[i][j];
            if (x[i][j] < xmin) xmin = x[i][j];
            if (y[i][j] > ymax) ymax = y[i][j];
            if (y[i][j] < ymin) ymin = y[i][j];
        }
        xscale[i] = ((float) tg_scrnx / (xmax - xmin));
        yscale[i] =
            ((float) (tg_scrny - tg_chary) / (ymax - ymin));
        midx[i] = (xmin + xmax) / 2;              /* place it */
        midy[i] = (ymin + ymax) / 2;
        avginc[i] = 1;                       /* don't average */
    }
    printmenu();                             /* display menu */
    plotall();                          /* plot all data sets */
    while(1)
    {   if (grid) drawgrid();              /* draw graph grid */
        tg_setcolor(white);       /* white erases in xor mode */
        tg_moveto(lastx[0], lasty[0]);       /* erase points */
        for (i = 1; i < npoints[set]; i++)
        {   tg_lineto(lastx[i], lasty[i]);
        }
        if (grid)                            /* draw new grid */
        {   xgrid = xgridsize[set] * xscale[set];
            ygrid = ygridsize[set] * yscale[set];
            xorigin = xposition(0);
            yorigin = yposition(0);
            drawgrid();
        }
```

```
printmenu();
tg_setcolor(white);                    /* plot new points */
plotset(set);
geta;
switch(a)
{   case 'x':                          /* scale x axis */
        xscale[set] *= SCALEINC;
        break;
    case 'X':
        xscale[set] /= SCALEINC;
        break;
    case 'y':                          /* scale y axis */
        yscale[set] *= SCALEINC;
        break;
    case 'Y':
        yscale[set] /= SCALEINC;
        break;
    case 'a':          /* number of points to average */
        ++avginc[set];
        break;
    case 'A':
        if (--avginc[set] < 1) avginc[set] = 1;
        break;
    case UP:                                /* move */
        midy[set] -= OFFSETINC / yscale[set];
        break;
    case DN:
        midy[set] += OFFSETINC / yscale[set];
        break;
    case LT:
        midx[set] += OFFSETINC / xscale[set];
        break;
    case RT:
        midx[set] -= OFFSETINC / xscale[set];
        break;
    case 'G':          /* toggle grid lines display */
    case 'g':
        if (grid) grid = 0;
        else grid = 1;
    case TAB:                               /* next data set */
```

continues

653

Listing 14.1. continued

```
                case 'd':
                    if ((a == TAB) || (a == 'd'))
                        if (++set >= nsets) set = 0;
                case 'D':
                    if (a == 'D')
                        if (--set < 0) set = nsets - 1;
                    tg_clearviewport();
                    plotall();
                    break;
                case ESC:                               /* fly away */
                case 'Q':
                case 'q':
                    tg_closedown();
                    printf("Solong!");   /* Hindustani for Seeya */
                    exit(0);
        }
    }
}

/* draw or erase axes and reference grid */

void drawgrid(void)
{   float x1, y1;
    tg_setcolor(axisclr);
    tg_drawline(xorigin, 0, xorigin, tg_scrny - 1);
    tg_drawline(0, yorigin, tg_scrnx - 1, yorigin);
    tg_setcolor(gridclr);
    for (x1 = xorigin - xgrid; x1 > 0; x1 -= xgrid)
    {   tg_drawline((int) x1, 0, (int) x1, tg_scrny - 1);
    }
    for (x1 = xorigin + xgrid; x1 < tg_scrnx; x1 += xgrid)
    {   tg_drawline((int) x1, 0, (int) x1, tg_scrny - 1);
    }
    for (y1 = yorigin - ygrid; y1 > 0; y1 -= ygrid)
    {   tg_drawline(0, (int) y1, tg_scrnx - 1, (int) y1);
    }
    for (y1 = yorigin + ygrid; y1 < tg_scrny; y1 += ygrid)
    {   tg_drawline(0, (int) y1, tg_scrnx - 1, (int) y1);
    }
```

```
    }

    /* plot a single data set with on-the-fly averaging */

    void plotset(int set)
    {   float x1, y1, xtotal, ytotal;
        int j, num;
        char msg[80];
        x1 = xposition(x[set][0]);
        y1 = yposition(y[set][0]);
        tg_moveto((int) x1, (int) y1);
        lastx[0] = x1, lasty[0] = y1;
        xtotal = ytotal = 0.0;
        num = 0;
        for (j = 1; j < npoints[set]; j++)
        {   xtotal += x[set][j];
            ytotal += y[set][j];
            num++;
            if (j % avginc[set] == 0)
            {   x1 = xposition((xtotal / num));
                y1 = yposition((ytotal / num));
                xtotal = ytotal = 0.0;
                num = 0;
            }
            tg_lineto((int) x1, (int) y1);
            lastx[j] = x1, lasty[j] = y1;
        }
    }

    /* plot all data sets */

    void plotall(void)
    {   int i;
        xorigin = xposition(0);
        yorigin = yposition(0);
        xgrid = xgridsize[set] * xscale[set];   /* initial grid */
        ygrid = ygridsize[set] * yscale[set];
        tg_endxor();
        if (grid) drawgrid();
        for (i = 0; i < nsets; i++)
```

continues

655

Listing 14.1. continued

```
    {   if (i != set)
        {   tg_setcolor(i + 2);
            plotset(i);
        }
    }
    tg_startxor();
    tg_setcolor(white);
    plotset(set);
}

/*  print the menu and numerical readouts */

void printmenu(void)
{   char menu[86];
    tg_setviewport(0, 0, tg_scrnx - 1, tg_scrny - 1);
    tg_endxor();
    tg_setcolor(white);
    tg_moveto(0, tg_scrny - tg_chary);
    sprintf(menu, "Dataset=%d  Avg=%d  "
        "Xsize=%3.2f  Ysize=%3.2f  "
        "move=%3.1f  move=%3.1f  Grid   Quit      ",
        set + 1, avginc[set], xscale[set], yscale[set],
        (midx[set] - xoffset) / xscale[set],
        (midy[set] - yoffset) / yscale[set]);
    tg_outtext(menu);
    tg_setviewport(0, 0,
                   tg_scrnx - 1, tg_scrny - tg_chary - 1);
    tg_startxor();
}
```

Visual Simulation

Everybody talks about the weather, but nobody does anything about it.

—Charles D. Warner, 1890

Macho mathematicians can scratch and scrawl equations all day without so much as
a glance out the window and still maintain near-religious faith in the validity of their

results. Most of us can't quite grasp that level of abstraction without seeing the equations and numbers expressed in a more visual way. Seeing may not always be believing, but believing is certainly a lot harder if you're wearing a blindfold.

You've seen how computers can help us visualize abstract information that would otherwise remain invisible, such as weather patterns over many months' time. Your PC can also simulate real-world experiments that would be much more costly and time-consuming to physically conduct than to approximate with software. Scientists, architects, and all manner of engineers now routinely begin their work by building computer-simulated models. With a visual simulation, you can play with your model, watch its behavior, change as many variables as you like, rebuild the entire structure, or even alter the laws of physics, all without investing dollar one in materials (and assuming you already have a computer). Perhaps most importantly, visual simulations give you a chance to discover which parts or behaviors of a system are worthy of further exploration.

The Lorenz Waterwheel

There are as many different techniques for visual simulation as there are subjects to simulate. To give you a feel for the benefits and drawbacks of building computer models, I've created a program that simulates a fairly simple physical system that can nonetheless exhibit extremely complex, unpredictable behavior: the Lorenz waterwheel.

Presently, I'll tell you the story of Edward Lorenz, who was a meteorologist, not an engineer. First, let me tell you how to build a replica of his peculiar waterwheel.

Take a wheel—a bicycle tire will do, or a ferris wheel if you want to go for more gradeur—and attach some buckets evenly spaced around the rim, like the chairs in a ferris wheel. The exact number of buckets doesn't matter, so long as you have at least half a dozen or so. Punch holes in the bottom of the buckets so that they leak a bit, and hook up a faucet or hose to drop a steady stream of water into the top bucket. Turn on the hose and give the wheel a little push to get things rolling. Then sit back and observe.

As the wheel turns, the water flows into each bucket as it comes around the top. The weight of the water keeps the wheel turning. If the stream of water is fairly meager, all the water leaks out of each bucket before it starts climbing back up to the top, and the wheel turns faster and faster until it reaches a steady speed. At that point, the wheel is turning just fast enough so that the buckets travel partway up the back side before all the water leaks out. The weight of that last bit of water climbing up the other side slows the rotation just enough to counterbalance the new water flowing into the buckets at the top.

Turn up the quantity of incoming water, however, and the buckets rising up the back side of the wheel may be full enough to actually reverse the rotation of the wheel. Sometimes the wheel will repeatedly reverse direction, oscillating back and forth. Other times, it just reverses direction a few times and stabilizes at a steady speed. Just when it will do which of these things is a rather complicated question—and therein lies our experiment.

Many of my readers (that's you) know the name of Edward Lorenz—and perhaps the name of Dick Oliver—well enough to suspect that some strangeness may be afoot. Chances are, you've heard rumors of something called the *Butterfly Effect*, "sensitive dependence on initial conditions," or, put more plainly, *chaos*.

Chaos is the much ballyhooed mathematical property that makes weather and stock markets hard to predict. It has turned physics and chemistry inside out in 20 years and still strikes fear in the hearts of old-school scientists everywhere. Chaos means that the flapping of a butterfly's wings in Harvard Square can radically affect the following week's weather at Princeton. It means that your heartbeat stays stable and that the solar system may not. It controls the magnificent boundaries of the Mandelbrot set and the intricate interwoven patterns of population dynamics. And it makes waterwheels act funny, too.

Betting on the Wheel

Figures 14.4 through 14.7 show screen shots from the WHEEL program presented in the following **You Can Do It** and **Working Code** sections.

On the right, you see a graphical representation of the waterwheel itself, with eight buckets and a stream of water flowing in at the top. Instead of making the buckets leak, I let you change the laws of physics so that the water evaporates quickly. (In a textbook Lorenz waterwheel, the holes in the buckets are supposed to be on the front side so the buckets don't drip into each other. Therefore, evaporation amounts to the same thing and reduces the complexity of the graphics considerably.) Text above the wheel indicates the fill rate, evaporation rate, and resistance from intertia and friction.

On the left, the rotation speed of the wheel appears as a graph and a numerical display in the top corner. The red line (dark grey in the illustrations below) shows the speed at each moment in time, whereas the green line (light grey in the illustrations) measures the speed only once each time the wheel spins around, to filter out the speed variations within each rotation. When the red trace goes all the way to the right edge of the graph, it cycles back to the left like the cardiac monitors you see in hospitals.

A blue line across the middle of the graph represents 0 speed. When the red and green traces dip below this level, the wheel is spinning counterclockwise. When the traces are above the 0 line, the wheel is spinning clockwise.

Because the simulated wheel, the short-term velocity graph, the long-term velocity graph, and numerical readouts are all on-screen at once, you can get a better mental image of what's happening than you could with only one type of display. Of course, the animated color display you'll see on your computer screen is much more informative than the following black-and-white figures. You may want to step through the next **You Can Do It** section and get the system going on your screen as you read about Figures 14.3 through 14.7. That way, you'll see much more than these few snapshots and my rambling English could describe.

Before you commence your experimental procedures, let me pose the research question clearly:

What will the long-term rotational velocity of the Lorenz waterwheel look like?

A hypothesis might be:

The wheel will reach and maintain a stable velocity.

This leads to a second question, the quantitative results of the experiment:

If our hypothesis of a stable velocity is correct, what will that velocity be?

Just to pique your curiosity, I'll tell you ahead of time that even though the aforementioned hypothesis is correct, you won't be able to get an answer to the second question, the actual stable velocity. Why not? Watch and see.

In Figure 14.4a, the wheel has just started rolling with all buckets empty at an initial speed of 34. The apparent physical speed depends on the speed of your computer, so don't worry about the physical units—call it revolutions per cyberspace minute (RPCM) if you like. A little water trickles into each bucket and the speed stays fairly steady for a while.

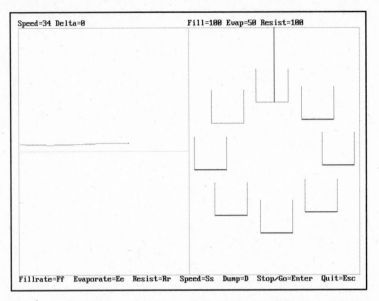

Figure 14.4a. *On the right, eight buckets spin on an (invisible) wheel while a stream of water flows into the top. On the left, a graph records rotational velocity.*

After a few revolutions, the buckets fill enough so that they start making it all the way around without emptying. This makes the speed vary, and pretty soon some buckets are more full than others, and the velocity varies rhythmically as the buckets that are more full speed down and slowly climb back up.

Eventually, the buckets that are the more full are just too heavy to make it all the way up, and the wheel starts rocking back and forth as in Figure 14.4b. Notice that the graph line has dipped above and below the zero line, indicating a change from clockwise to counterclockwise motion.

When the wheel rocks, the buckets that are more full get even more full because they pause for a long time under the spigot. Their increased weight makes the wheel rock faster and faster until the bucket that is the most full finally gets up enough speed to make it over the top. From then on, the wheel continues spinning faster and faster counterclockwise, as in Figure 14.4c and 14.4d.

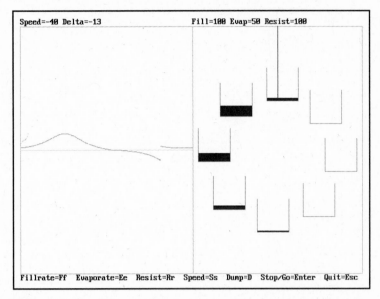

Figure 14.4b. *After a while, some buckets get too full to make it up the other side, and the wheel begins to rock back and forth.*

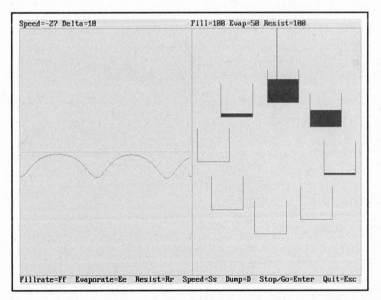

Figure 14.4c. *The bucket that's the most full fills more and more, pushing the rocking wheel faster and faster until it gets up enough speed to start spinning again.*

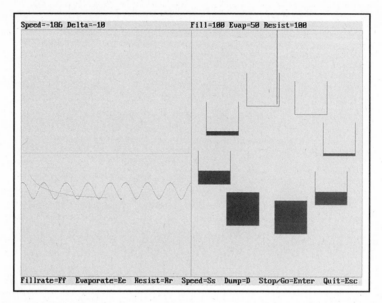

Figure 14.4d. *The wheel keeps spinning faster until it reaches an apparently stable velocity.*

At this point, you may think the experiment is over. Regardless of the rather complicated set of behaviors it took to get there, the wheel has indeed finally settled into a stable rhythmic velocity cycle. The green (or light grey) trace representing long-term velocity remains constant.

Now try to repeat the experiment. Rather than start the program over again, you can simply empty the buckets. (Of course, it would be very difficult to empty real buckets without changing the speed of the wheel. In a simulation, though, you can easily make all the water vanish into thin air at the touch of a button.) Everything except the initial speed remains the same, so you might expect the system to stabilize at the same speed it leveled off at before.

Figure 14.5a shows the wheel shortly after the buckets were emptied. The speed slowly decreases due to friction until the wheel slows down enough for the buckets to start accumulating water again, as in Figure 14.5b.

The same dance you watched before begins again. Some buckets become more full than others and eventually get so massive that they can't make it over the top. Then, the wheel starts rocking, as in Figure 14.5c.

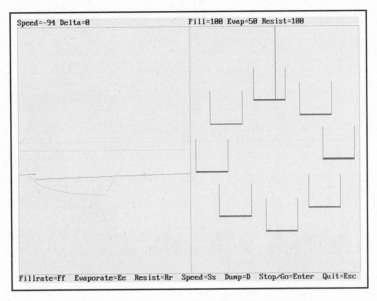

Figure 14.5a. *If you dump the buckets, the wheel gradually slows…*

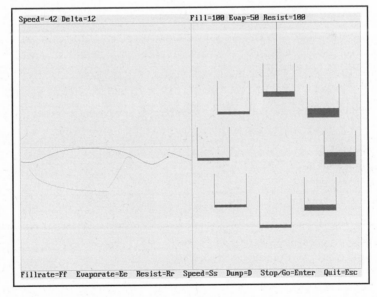

Figure 14.5b. *…until water starts accumulating again.*

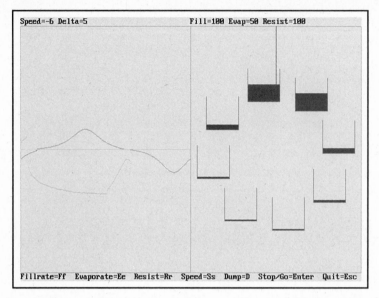

Figure 14.5c. *When a few buckets get too full to make it around, the wheel starts rocking.*

This time however, the big buckets never make it over the top again. Instead, friction stops the wheel just when the buckets are perfectly balanced. Figure 14.5d shows the wheel at rest.

If you've been following along on your computer, don't be surprised if your wheel doesn't come to a stop. (Okay, go ahead, be a little surprised. We're starting to get into that strange chaos stuff now, so a certain amount of head-scratching is in order.)

Figures 14.6 and 14.7 show two repeats of the experiment pictured previously in Figures 14.4 and 14.5. When speed stabilizes, I dumped the buckets and watched the resulting long-term behavior. In the first trial (Figure 14.6), the wheel ends up settling at a stable *clockwise* rotational speed. In the second trial, the wheel ends up settling at a stable *counterclockwise* speed.

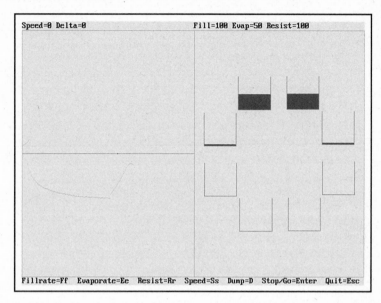

Figure 14.5d. *This time, the wheel comes to a stop as the buckets reach a balancing point.*

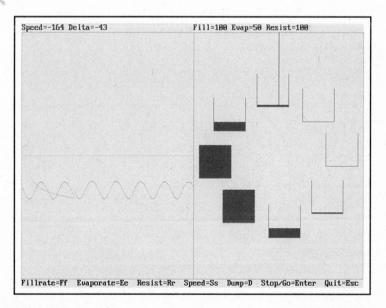

Figure 14.6a. *Repeating the same experiment as in Figure 14.5, I let the wheel find its stable velocity again.*

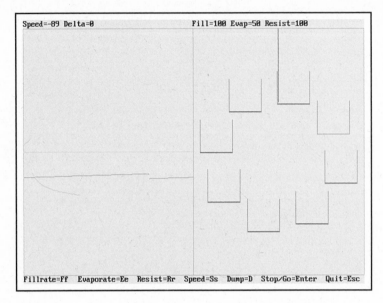

Figure 14.6b. *Then, I dump the buckets and the wheel gradually slows.*

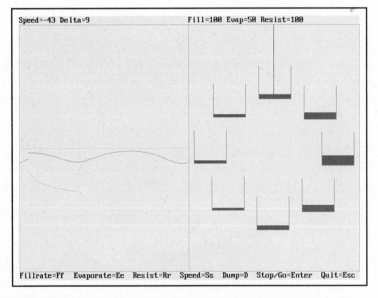

Figure 14.6c. *When the buckets start filling, the speed starts varying again.*

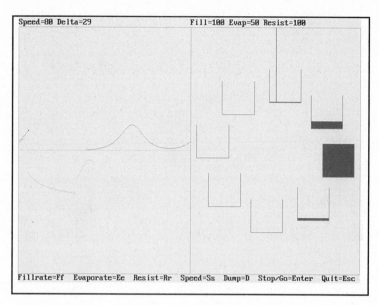

Figure 14.6d. *Full buckets make the wheel start rocking. (So far, the experiment is repeating itself perfectly.)*

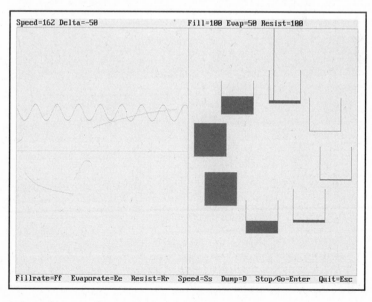

Figure 14.6e. *This time, however, the wheel doesn't stop. It stabilizes at a regular clockwise rotation pattern.*

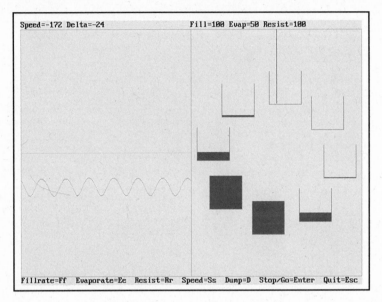

Figure 14.7a. *Let's try that again. Start over, and wait for the speed to stabilize.*

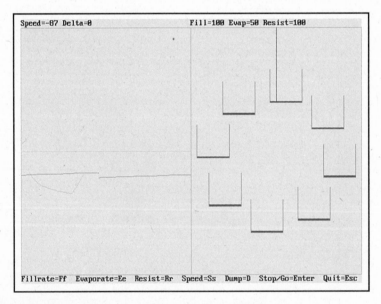

Figure 14.7b. *Dump the buckets and watch the wheel slow down.*

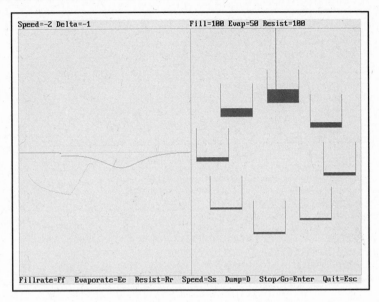

Figure 14.7c. *As the buckets accumulate water, the speed varies.*

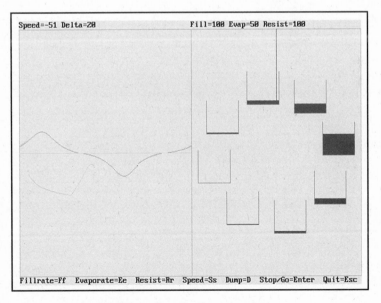

Figure 14.7d. *Just as it did before, the wheel starts rocking.*

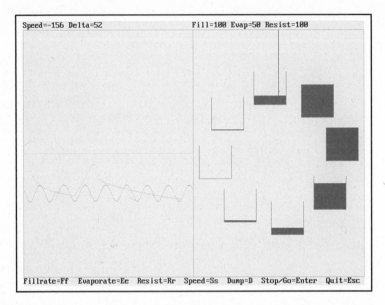

Figure 14.7e. *This time, however, it doesn't stop or end up at the same speed as in Figure 14.6. Instead, it returns to its original velocity!*

Three nearly identical experiments led to three completely different results. In each case, the wheel settled at a stable velocity, the buckets were dumped, and the wheel eventually settled again at a stable velocity. The three experiments ended up with final stable velocities of –150, 150, and 0, though. In the jargon of chaos science, you would say that the *attractor* (the final stable velocity to which the wheel is drawn) is extremely "sensitive to initial conditions."

Further experimentation would reveal that it is very difficult—theoretically impossible, in fact—to predict which of the three final velocities you'll get by measuring the exact initial velocity when you dumped the buckets. To make an accurate prediction, you would in fact need to measure that initial velocity with infinite precision.

This has some far-reaching implications, which I'll mention along with the story I promised about Edward Lorenz. First, however, you should try your own hand at this Wheel of Fort…—uh, better make that Wheel of Destiny—simulation, assuming you haven't already jumped ahead to the **You Can Do It** section.

You Can Do It: Simulating Chaos

Now that you've read the book, be sure not to miss the movie. If you have a 486 computer, the WHEEL program exposes the secret chaos inside Lorenz's waterwheel while you watch. On a 286 or 386 without a math coprocessor, you might want to grab a beer and a comfy chair to make the lengthy simulation more enjoyable. Those who still own a vintage PC or 8088 machine chained to their necks will have time to run to the computer store and shop for something speedier while the simulation runs.

1. Enter WHEEL at the DOS prompt to start the WHEEL.EXE program.

2. Press V for VGA 16-color mode.

   At this point, before the simulation starts, you could change the fill rate, evaporation rate, resistance, and initial speed with the keyboard controls at the bottom of the screen. (You can also change any of these parameters at any time during the simulation—for example, pressing s increases the speed, while S decreases the speed. Use f and F to control the fill rate, e and E for the evaporation rate, and r and R to adjust the resistance.)

   To reproduce the experiment discussed previously, just leave the parameters at their default values.

3. Press the Enter key to give the wheel a spin.

   As depicted in Figure 14.4, the wheel speeds up, rocks back and forth, and finally climbs to a stable velocity.

4. When the velocity stabilizes in a cyclic pattern between about –100 and –150, press the letter D to dump the buckets.

   As in Figures 14.5, 14.6, and 14.7, the wheel will slow and eventually start rocking. Depending on exactly (and I do mean *exactly*) when you press the D key, the wheel either ends up spinning clockwise, spinning counterclockwise, or stopping completely. (Be patient, though. Sometimes the wheel appears stopped when it is actually still moving very slowly, and it will speed up again presently.)

   What happens if you increase the fill? Can you find chaos (sensitive dependence on initial conditions) at other fill/evaporation/resistance settings besides the defaults? You may enjoy toying with this system in any number of ways. After all, that's what visual simulation is all about.

Edward Who?

I promised to tell you about Edward Lorenz, and why he invented this waterwheel in the first place. He was a meterology guru at MIT in 1961 when he first modeled a similar mathematical system—called the *Lorenz attractor*—on his Royal McBee vacuum tube computer. He discovered the unpredictability of the system quite by accident when he tried to repeat a run of his program by typing the numbers from the previous run. He only typed in four decimal places, but the computer was accurate to six decimal places internally. Much to his surprise, the difference in the tens-of-thousandths part of the numbers caused a rapid change in the behavior of the system. Thus, the study of sensitive dependence on initial conditions—now more poetically referred to as *chaos*—was born.

Interestingly enough, Lorenz' only later thought of the waterwheel as an analogy for the simple weather system he was originally trying to model. The "water" in the wheel actually represents heat, and the rotating "wheel" represents air convection currents. "Buckets" hold water and cause the wheel to spin in the same way that air holds heat and turns it into movement. The unpredictability of your simulated waterwheel is therefore a direct indication of the unpredictability of the weather.

If you'd like to find out more about the mathematics of chaos, its role in science, and its relationship to fractals, I'll be happy to send you a free newsletter with fun articles and information about related books and software. My phone number and address are on the Cedar Software order form in the back of this book.

Meanwhile, back to the primary topic at hand: interactive visualization.

Cheating the Universe

The WHEEL program exemplifies many common characteristics of simulation and visualization software in general. With it, you can locate and explore the interesting behaviors of the system. I had to go through a certain amount of trial and error to find good default parameters for fill rate, evaporation rate, and resistance. Such trial and error could have been costly and much more time consuming if I was building physical waterwheels rather than simulating the wheels in software.

The universe imposes a certain amount of hardship upon anyone who wants to assemble physical objects into any particular configuration other than a disorderly pile. (Some call it "entropy." I call it the "pick up that mess" effect.) Yet mathematical scribblings and bar charts are no substitute for hands-on interaction. Computerized visual simulation is a great way to cheat the universe into letting you play with your toys without having to clean your room.

Of course, software has an entropy of its own, and no serious simulation is complete without physical verification. Users of visualization technology must constantly be on the lookout for programming errors and mistaken assumptions that might prove downright silly in the real world. Often, simulations begin with measurement of physical models to gather the "rules of the game," move into the computer for initial exploration, and return to more detailed physical modeling and experimentation based on the results of the simulation.

No matter where you find the balance between physical construction and software simulation, software will always be far more malleable than any tangible stuff could ever be. In the Lorenz waterwheel program, for example, the object of study was actually convection and heat—not a waterwheel at all. Some of the programming shortcuts you'll find in the **Working Code** section that follows, such as the adjustable "evaporation rate" of the water, would be extremely difficult to build into a real waterwheel, even though they are perfectly appropriate for the study of convection. Building a physical convection cell—the ultimate Lorenz experiment—has been done, but it sure ain't easy to monitor those flipsy-flopsy fluids with any accuracy.

So go ahead and cheat a little—change some laws of nature in the **Working Code** for the waterwheel, or skip every other display to the screen so you can see the system evolve faster. I won't tell Mother Nature if you don't.

Working Code: Being a Big Wheel

When I designed this program, I purposely avoided referring to Lorenz's equations—or anyone elses. I wanted to see if the most obvious, straighforward implementation of a weighted spinning wheel would behave the same way that the classic Lorenz wheel did. So the "physics" is simple: each time through the main loop, the rectangular buckets move around a circle by an angular change in distance, called speed. The amount of water in each bucket is multiplied by its distance from the center of the wheel. The sum of these "weights" becomes a delta, or change in speed. The resistance of the wheel is then subtracted from the speed. The graph and numerical readouts are displayed, and the loop repeats.

A key element of any visual simulation program is speedy graphics display. A lot of stuff is moving at once here. To reduce flicker, each bucket is not erased until everything is in place to immediately redraw it. Also, I chose to make the wheel turn quite slowly so that the user can see the rotation speed clearly. Larger jumps wouldn't change the experimental results any but would reduce the spinning wheel to a flickery blur and defeat the whole purpose of having an animated display in the first place by robbing the user of a visually intuitive sense of what's happening.

You'll find the graphing functions here useful for other types of simulation as well. The white dot at the leading edge of the red trace is the only fancy touch; even a tiny moving dot makes it much easier to percieve the changing value represented by the graph.

Listing 14.2. The WHEEL.C program implements a visual simulation of the Lorenz waterwheel.

```
/* WHEEL.C
 *
 * An animated simulation of the Lorenz water wheel
 *
 * from Tricks of the Graphics Gurus
 */

#include <stdio.h>        /* Standard input/output libraries */
#include <stdlib.h>
#include <math.h>

#include "tg.h"      /* See TG.TXT for compile instructions */

#define ENTER 13                          /* Enter key */
#define ESC 27                              /* Esc key */
#define NBUCKETS 8  /* no. of buckets -- try changing this! */
#define PI 3.14159265                    /* value of pi */
#define TOPLEFT (3.0 * PI / 2.0 + PI / 16.0) /* width of   */
#define TOPRIGHT (3.0 * PI / 2.0 - PI / 16.0) /*   a bucket */
#define BUCKETCLR 5                    /* color of buckets */
#define WATERCLR 9                      /* color of water */
#define WHITE 15            /* color of menus and readouts */
#define GRAPHCLR 4              /* color of fast trace */
#define HISTCLR 2              /* color of slow trace */
#define BORDERCLR 3                /* color of borders */
#define ZEROCLR 1          /* color of zero line on graph */
```

```c
#define SPEEDSCALE 0.0000001    /* scaling factor for delta */
#define FILLINC 1          /* increment for fill rate changes */
#define EVAPINC 1          /* increment for evap. rate changes */
#define RESISTINC 0.001 /* increment for resistance changes */
#define SPEEDINC 0.001   /* increment for user speed changes */
#define INIFILL 100            /* default initial fill rate */
#define INIEVAP 50      /* default initial evaporation rate */
#define INIRESIST 100          /* default initial resistance */
#define INISPEED 0.03              /* default initial speed */
#define MAXX 514    /* maximum width of graph area in pixels */

int cx, cy,                     /* x,y center of the wheel */
    lastx[NBUCKETS],            /* previous graph values */
    lasty[NBUCKETS],                /* for quick erasing */
    level[NBUCKETS],              /* bucket water level */
    radius, size,           /* size of wheel and buckets */
    speedmax, speedmin,         /* for scaling the graph */
    histx, histy[MAXX], histmax = 0, /* history graph value */
    maxx,                       /* width of graph area */
    rotated = 0,   /* has the wheel rotated (for hist graph) */
    evaporate, fillrate,     /* evaporation and fill rates */
    speedx, speedy[MAXX],       /* speed graph values */
    streamsize,                 /* size of water stream */
    stopped = 1;                /* paused by user? */

float angle[NBUCKETS],     /* location of buckets in radians */
      scale,      /* scaling factor for bucket level display */
      delta,                      /* change in speed */
      resist,                        /* resistance */
      speed;                      /* angular speed */

char msg[60];                          /* for readouts */

void main(void);
void showspeed(void);
void showrates(void);
void drawborder(void);
void main(void)
{   int b, x, y;                 /* counters for looping */
    printf("WHEEL -- from Tricks of the Graphics Gurus\n\n");
```

continues

675

Listing 14.2. continued

```
printf("This program animates a simulation of the Lorenz"
        "water wheel, a chaotic dynamical system.\n");
tg_pickmode();                          /* confirm video mode */
tg_moveto(0, tg_scrny - tg_chary);      /* display menu */
tg_setcolor(WHITE);
tg_outtext("Fillrate=Ff  Evaporate=Ee  Resist=Rr  "
  "Speed=Ss  Dump=D  Stop/Go=Enter  Quit=Esc");
evaporate = INIEVAP;                /* initalize everything */
fillrate = INIFILL;
speed = INISPEED;
resist = INIRESIST / 1000.0;
radius = tg_scrny >> 2;
size = radius >> 2;
speedx = histx = 1;
scale = (float) size / 16192.0;
maxx = tg_scrnx / 2;
cx = tg_scrnx / 2 + tg_scrnx / 4;
cy = tg_scrny / 2;
speedmin = cy;
speedmax = cy - tg_chary - 1;
showrates();                            /* display readouts */
drawborder();                           /* display borders */
for (b = 0; b <= maxx; b++)             /* initialize graphs */
    histy[b] = speedy[b] =
        speedmin - (int) (speed * 100000.0 / speedmax);
for (b = 0; b < NBUCKETS; b++)          /* place buckets */
{   angle[b] = ((PI * 2.0) / NBUCKETS) * (b + 1);
    level[b] = 0;
    lastx[b] = cx;
    lasty[b] = cy;
}
while(1)
{   if (stopped == 0)   /* if user hasn't paused action */
    {   delta = 0.0;            /* clear delta for summing */
        streamsize = fillrate * (float) size / 4096.0;
        tg_setcolor(WATERCLR);          /* display stream */
        tg_fillrect(cx - streamsize, tg_chary,
                    cx + streamsize, cy - radius + size);
        for (b = 0; b < NBUCKETS; b++)   /* do buckets */
        {   x = cx + (int) (cos(angle[b]) * radius);
```

```
            y = cy + (int) (sin(angle[b]) * radius);
            tg_setcolor(0);
            tg_fillrect(lastx[b] - size, lasty[b] - size,
                        lastx[b] + size, lasty[b] + size);
            tg_setcolor(WATERCLR);
            tg_fillrect(x - size,
                        y + size - (int) (level[b] * scale),
                        x + size, y + size);
            tg_setcolor(BUCKETCLR);
            tg_drawline(x - size, y - size,
                        x - size, y + size);
            tg_drawline(x + size, y - size,
                        x + size, y + size);
            tg_drawline(x - size, y + size,
                        x + size, y + size);
            lastx[b] = x;
            lasty[b] = y;
            if ((angle[b] < TOPLEFT) &&    /* if at top, */
                (angle[b] > TOPRIGHT))     /* fill it up */
                if  ((level[b] += fillrate) < 0)
                    level[b] = 32767;
            angle[b] += speed;             /* move wheel */
            if (angle[b] > (PI * 2.0))  /* stay between */
            {   angle[b] -= (PI * 2.0);    /* 0 and 2pi */
                if (b == 0) rotated = 1;
            }
            else if (angle[b] < 0)
            {   angle[b] += (PI * 2.0);
                if (b == 0) rotated = 1;
            }
            level[b] -= evaporate / 10.0;  /* evaporate */
            if (level[b] < 0) level[b] = 0;
            delta += ((float) (level[b] >> 4) * SPEEDSCALE *
                    (float) (x - cx));      /* sum delta */
    }
    speed += delta / 10.0;           /* change speed */
    if (speed > 0.0)   /* resist opposite direction */
    {   speed -= resist / 1000.0;
        if (speed < 0.0) speed = 0.0;
    }
```

continues

Listing 14.2. continued

```
            else
            {   speed += resist / 1000.0;
                if (speed > 0.0) speed = 0.0;
            }
            tg_setcolor(0);                        /* erase stream */
            tg_fillrect(cx - streamsize, tg_chary,
                    cx + streamsize, cy - radius + size);
        }
        if (kbhit())                      /* process keystroke */
        {   switch(getch())
            {   case ENTER:                         /* pause */
                    if (stopped) stopped = 0;
                    else stopped = 1;
                    break;
                case 'F':                  /* fill slower */
                    fillrate -= FILLINC;
                    break;
                case 'f':                  /* fill faster */
                    fillrate += FILLINC;
                    break;
                case 'E':                  /* evaporate slower */
                    evaporate -= EVAPINC;
                    break;
                case 'e':                  /* evaporate faster */
                    evaporate += EVAPINC;
                    break;
                case 'S':                   /* less speed */
                    speed -= SPEEDINC;
                    break;
                case 's':                   /* more speed */
                    speed += SPEEDINC;
                    break;
                case 'R':                  /* less resistance */
                    resist -= RESISTINC;
                    break;
                case 'r':                  /* more resistance */
                    resist += RESISTINC;
                    break;
                case 'D':            /* dump (empty) buckets */
                case 'd':
```

```
                    for (b = 0; b < NBUCKETS; b++)
                        level[b] = 0;
                    break;
                case ESC:                          /* vamoose */
                    tg_closedown();
                    printf("Seeyanara.");   /* Japanese for */
                    exit(0);                       /* seeyalater */
            }
            showrates();          /* display fill/evap/resist */
        }
        showspeed();     /* display speed and history graphs */
    }
}

/* display numerical values for fill rate, evaporation rate,
   and resistance */

void showrates(void)
{   sprintf(msg, "Fill=%d Evap=%d Resist=%d     ",
            fillrate, evaporate, (int) (resist * 1000.0));
    tg_moveto(maxx, 0);
    tg_setcolor(WHITE);
    tg_outtext(msg);
}

/* display speed as numbers and a graph of current speed
   and speed history at each rotation */

void showspeed(void)
{   int y;
    sprintf(msg, "Speed=%d Delta=%d     ",
            (int) (speed * 1000.0), (int) (delta * 1000.0));
    tg_moveto(0, 0);
    tg_setcolor(WHITE);
    tg_outtext(msg);
    if (stopped == 0)
    {   y = speedy[speedx];
        tg_putpixel(speedx, y, GRAPHCLR);
        if (++speedx > maxx) speedx = 1;
        if (rotated)
        {   rotated = 0;
```

continues

Listing 14.2. continued

```
                tg_setcolor(ZEROCLR);
                tg_drawline(0, speedmin, maxx, speedmin);
                tg_putpixel(histx, histy[histx], HISTCLR);
                if (++histx > maxx) histx = 1;
                tg_putpixel(histx, histy[histx], 0);
                histy[histx] = y;
                tg_putpixel(histx, y, HISTCLR);
                if (histmax < histx) histmax = histx;
        }
        y = (int) (speed * 100000.0 / speedmax);
        if (abs(y) > speedmax) y = speedmax;
        tg_putpixel(speedx, speedy[speedx], 0);
        speedy[speedx] = y = speedmin - y;
        tg_putpixel(speedx, y, WHITE);
        if (speedx < histmax)
                tg_putpixel(speedx, histy[speedx], HISTCLR);
    }
}

/* draw border around the edge (no reason, just looks nice) */

void drawborder(void)
{   tg_setcolor(BORDERCLR);
    tg_drawrect(0, tg_chary, tg_scrnx - 1,
                tg_scrny - tg_chary);
    tg_drawrect(0, speedmin - speedmax - 1,
                maxx + 1, speedmin + speedmax + 1);
    tg_setcolor(ZEROCLR);
    tg_drawline(0, speedmin, maxx, speedmin);
}
```

Visualizing the Future

Computers can now create complex graphical systems that allow you to examine data in ways that never existed before.... How will all this end? When you can get the picture on your computer's screen as fast as you can imagine what you want to see.

—Peter Wayner, "Image Building," *BYTE*, April 1993.

Commercial visualization software obviously goes far beyond the rudimentary analytical tools of DATAVIEW and my simplistic WHEEL simulation. Assembling medical imaging data from NMR or CAT scans into translucent rotating brains and hearts, displaying millions of worldwide commodities exhanges as an undulating animated surface of colors, predicting the behavior of aircraft wings or global climate changes through interactive simulation—all these are still far beyond the capabilities of the average desktop PC. The price tag of most dedicated visualization software (never mind the workstation to run it on) also far exceeds the bounds of most individual PC users' budgets.

If one thing *is* predictable in the computer industry, it's that tomorrow's PCs will look an awful lot like today's high-end workstations. Although spreadsheets and bar graphs will always have their place, you can expect to interact with your data in entirely new ways. These will include interactive versions of traditional graphs as well as complete visual simulations of both physical systems and abstract data sets.

Already, a few serious visualization and simulation packages have appeared for the PC, including a $395 package called CoVis from CoHort Software (800-728-9878 or 510-524-9878). Though less sophisticated than the big-ticket packages, CoVis is one of the first serious visualization tools to work on a PC and carry a three-digit price tag. You can count on the competitive marketplace to make sure it won't be the last.

Perhaps the most popular software for visualization on any platform is Stephen Wolfram's Mathematica. Also available on the PC for under a thousand dollars (well under, if you can land an educational or student discount), Mathematica is primarily a tool for doing mathematics. As part of the bargain, you also get one of the most sophisticated animated visualization packages around. Though real-time interaction is very limited due to the speed of complex calculations on a PC, you have almost unlimited options for creating and playing back multidimensional renderings of any system you can define with mathematical equations. Mathematica's widespread success will undoubtedly bring a flock of followers into the PC visualization and simulation arena. The fact that Wolfram Research (800-441-MATH or 217-398-0700) doesn't classify Mathematica as a visualization tool is also a harbinger of things to come, when complex graphical output will be a standard component of almost every category of computer software.

Golden Technologies (800-653-2201 or 503-620-2201) offers another example of this trend in their Sliders and Dials add-on for Microsoft Excel spreadsheets. These nifty gadgets give you interactive controls and readouts for any numerical data you can put into a normal spreadsheet format—essentially turning Excel into a powerful simulation system for a meager $99. Again, the future is as clearly visible as your data.

Now that I've polished up my crystal ball, the next chapter gazes more deeply into the future of computer graphics. As you might expect, that future looks colorful, animated, and visually exciting.

The Graphics of Tomorrow

Considering the rate at which the computer-graphics industry moves, the title of this chapter could easily be "The Graphics of Tomorrow—Today." Throughout this book, we have touched on nearly every promising graphics technology and technique available today. If you think the future will just be more of the same, you're absolutely right—and completely wrong. Yes, all the essential elements of graphical computing are in place now, but as these technologies mature, they will radically alter the way we use and relate to information.

This chapter assembles the pieces of your graphical future into a solid vision of what you can expect to see on your desktop before the end of the millennium—and that's soon! I avoid fortune-telling and far-flung prognoses, focusing instead on new graphics technologies that have already begun to change the face of computing. Whenever possible, I give you contact information for the companies who are surfing the cutting edge of graphics and show you how their products may transform the way you work and play.

Hard-Hitting Hardware

It may be that within a few months, not only will you see interactive CD and TV products in almost every aspect of presentation and entertainment activities, but you will also be able to experience these events in [3-D] with very inexpensive, easy to install equipment as ubiquitous as the multimedia environment itself.

—Charles Ostman, "VR Going Mainstream," *Midnight Engineering,*
May/June 1993

The battle cry of the computer industry warlords has always been "Cheaper and Faster!" Someday that will change, as we approach the theoretical limits of information density and transfer speed. Fortunately, that day is still a long way off. As the use of graphics applications skyrockets, graphics hardware struggles to keep up with the heady demands of power-hungry software. Don't expect to find hardware that satisfies your graphics programs' lust for power any time in this decade; however, you will find cheaper, faster graphics machines with far more graphical muscle under the hood than just a new Pentium processor.

TV Color, Workstation Resolution

Everyone wants true color. We've been spoiled by TV, which displays every color our eyes can see, and we expect our $2,000 computers to match the color quality of our $200 TV sets. Naturally, the spoiled-brat consumers always get their way if they scream loud enough. This year, true color capable video cards for the PC have become widely available for under $120—cheaper than a decent TV.

As you will recall from the explanation of color models in Chapter 1, "true color" means 24 bits per pixel of graphics data sloshing around inside your computer. To pour that volume of information onto your screen any faster than cold molasses, even the fastest 486 computers need some help from a *graphics accelerator* chip—a hunk of silicon specifically optimized to toss huge 24-bit pixels around like confetti.

Furthermore, you don't really want your screen to look like a TV, which has abysmal resolution and bug-your-eyes-out image instability. (See Figure 15.1a, left half.) Better resolution alone without true color won't cut it either. (See Figure 15.1a, right half.) To look your best, you need both great resolution and great color. (See Figure 15.1b.)

Figure 15.1a. *Today, TV offers lots of colors, but lousy resolution (left). Computers offer high resolution but not enough colors (right). Neither one is very flattering.*

Figure 15.1b. *Obviously, good resolution and true color look the best. Tomorrow's computers will make you look like this.*

The VGA 640×480 resolution, updated 60 times per second, is now considered a bare minimum for true-color graphics work, and nobody really wants less than 800×600 at a flicker-free refresh rate of 70 cycles per second. (The *refresh rate* refers to the number of times per second the hardware repaints the image on your monitor, not the number of frames per second of new image data your software can put on-screen.)

A call to PC Connection (a mail-order vendor with excellent prices, selection, service and support, 800-800-0004 or 603-446-7721) in May 1993, turned up several PC video cards for under $350 that offered graphics accelerated true-color at 800×600 resolution. By the time you read this, those prices will undoubtedly be lower. Call your favorite dealer or mail-order house for quotes on the latest and greatest.

High color (15- or 16-bit color) is now quite popular, and most cheapie video boards come with a high-color chip installed. Compared to old-fashioned 8-bit VGA and Super-VGA, high color is a marvel to behold when you need to display realistic computer-generated or scanned images. Furthermore, the smaller memory requirements make it noticeably faster to work with than true color. Still, plunging prices of true-color boards and escalating demands of graphics users portend a bleak future for high color. Besides, anyone who needs high color probably really needs true color. High color will therefore continue to be a compromise technology, the role of which is to help bridge the distance from old-time VGA to the new wave of photorealism.

Ride the Local Bus

In the 1980s, the Video Electronics Standards Association (VESA) led the industry into Super-VGA resolutions by establishing and promoting software interface standards. In the 1990s, VESA has ventured into the hardware realm to promote a standard connection scheme for video cards which bypasses the *bus* (the power and data distribution system) used by standard expansion cards and communicates directly with the processor and memory of your computer.

Using a *local bus* can yield dramatic improvements in the speed of video display and graphics processing because local bus video cards can work at the full speed of your main computer board (commonly 25, 33, or 50 MHz today, though the standard imposes no restrictions on the speed of future local bus systems). Video cards that plug into ordinary expansion slots are limited to the speed of the Industry Standard Architecture (ISA) bus, which is normally only 8 MHz.

After an initial skirmish with Intel Corporation, which proposed a more universal local bus standard that would accommodate a wider variety of devices, VESA seems to have convinced the industry to adopt its less sophisticated but more stable local bus standard. Though talk of combining the Intel and VESA standards still circulates, in the meantime most new computers today have at least one VESA local bus slot on the main board.

All the major video hardware manufacturers are clambering to bring VESA local bus cards to market, and local bus video will undoubtedly become commonplace within the next year. The higher bandwidth of local bus video, combined with graphics coprocessors and ever-faster CPUs, can shuffle 24 bits per pixel fast enough to make true-color image handling downright snappy.

Local bus accelerated cards also promise to display full-motion animation in 8-bit color at speeds comparable to motion pictures. Some specialized boards can display professional-quality digital video with 30 to 60 frames per second, as well as high-color or true-color still images. Alas, these still carry four- or five-digit price tags and tax even the most advanced PC hardware to its limits. What the software gurus dream, the hardware marketing mavens will eventually sell on the cheap—and sooner than you think.

The Brick Wall

A speedy stream of gorgeous graphics isn't worth a pittance if you don't have any place to store them. Animation sequences and true-color images will slurp up memory and hard-drive space in the 1990s the way teenagers slurped up root-beer floats in the 1950s. The high cost of storage currently stands as the single largest obstacle in the way of advanced graphics on the PC.

Automatic disk compression à la Stacker or DOS 6's DoubleSpace are a long-overdue step in the right direction, but "doubling your disk capacity" is not enough to bring you into the world of serious graphics. A single true-color image (such as the ferocious hard-disk devouring beast in Figure 15.2) can easily consume 4M or more, even when compressed. Animation files can also be orders of magnitude larger than images. Spend a week working or playing with any state-of-the-art graphics software, and you'll stuff your 200-meg hard drive so full that graphics files will be bulging out of the dust seals.

Almost every graphics pro I know ran out and bought IOMEGA's new 150M removable storage drive (the Bournoulli Multi-Disk 150; call 800-456-5522 or 801-778-3000) the instant it came out—except for those folks who had already sunk $5,000 into an optical drive. At $100 a pop, though, few of us can afford to chew through 150-meg disks like candy. Regardless of any marketing hype you may hear from removable-storage vendors, nothing but a real, live hard drive is fast enough to store your working files.

Figure 15.2. *This hungry monster ate over 4 megabytes of my precious hard disk space when stored as a Windows bitmap.*

The storage crunch will only get worse in the next few years. CD-ROMs are finally starting to catch on, and a plethora of 600M graphics applications are flooding the market. Because you can't put anything on a CD-ROM except what came on it, they do nothing to alleviate the problem of where to store your own graphical creations. If anything, you're likely to copy more than a few megabytes of data from your CD-ROM collection onto your hard drive for faster access, leaving even less room for your other graphics. Until someone invents a multigigabyte storage system operating at hard-drive speeds and brings it to market for under $1,000, computer graphics capability will continue to beat its head against the brick wall of storage cost.

I don't see any such storage device on the horizon. Optical technology is the prime candidate, but researchers have yet to bring the speed up and the cost down to make optical systems viable for the growing graphics mass market. Though most of this chapter paints a rosy picture of the future, the mass-storage side of the story remains bleak.

The good news is that internal memory is now relatively cheap, after a two-year price crunch attributed largely to international politics. It's a good thing, too because you need at least 16M to run any serious graphics software these days. In the next few years, systems with 20, 32, or 48 megs of RAM will not be uncommon.

What's all that memory good for? More than you might think at first glance. Pictures, yes, but large blocks of memory called *frame buffers* can store many types of information besides the color of each dot on-screen. Some graphics applications store an *alpha channel* with transparency or other special-effect values for each pixel, multiple screens or *pages* for animation and image editing, and image *layers* that can be combined or separated at will. On your PC, frame buffers are usually stored in extended memory along with the rest of your data. Tomorrow's PCs, however, will often have frame buffers built into the video card for maximum performance, as is the norm on high-end graphics workstations today. In addition to all this image info, rendering and animation software must store mathematical descriptions of the 3-D models being rendered. For complex scenes, 3-D surface data can sop up memory in a hurry.

Often, graphics data that won't fit in memory can be stored on your hard drive, but because hard drives are much more sluggish than RAM when it comes to hauling data out of bed and sending it out into the world, such *memory swapping* severely limits the speed of your graphics programs. The moral of the story: If you're seriously involved with graphics, buy as much RAM as you can possibly afford. It's relatively cheap, and your graphics applications will perform their best tricks when they are well-fed and happy.

Multimedia and Beyond

No discussion of the future of graphics hardware would be complete without mention of the ubiquitous multimedia upgrade. Multimedia is the preeminent computer buzzword of the 1990s, though it's less sensible than it is sonorous. Intended to conjure up fantasies of multiple-information presentation machines all wrapped up in one pretty package, multimedia today actually just refers to synchronizing visual movement and sound for simultaneous playback. (Sort of like a VCR, which nobody calls multi- anything, to the best of my knowledge.)

Despite the goofy name, the promise of multimedia is enormous. Putting the image and sound-playback capabilities of a VCR into a computer that can instantly access any part of the "tape" based on the viewer's interaction is exciting in its own right. When you give that same computer the capability to generate photorealistic 3-D images of its own on the fly and combine them with the prerecorded material… the imagination reels.

According to industry pundits, every year was supposed to be the "Year of Multimedia" for the last half-decade, but the multimedia industry continues to flounder while prices of the fancy hardware to quickly display all those movie frames hover above the market playing field. In 1993, a multimedia upgrade means installing a CD-ROM reader capable of playing bad quality video in a three-inch square window, with a quarter- to half-second wait for each video access. (See Figure 15.3.) In a world where access speed is normally measured in milliseconds, a quarter-second is at least a power of ten off the mark. At least you usually do get a nice hi-fi sound card with the upgrade kits.

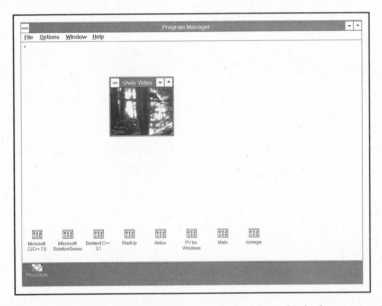

Figure 15.3. *Real-time digital video is here, but it ain't exactly the big screen. At best, you get choppy playback in a tiny window—until some new technologies make their debut.*

The less-than-thrilling state of the hardware notwithstanding, a deluge of fascinating CD-ROM titles have already made it to market. Superbly crafted interactive games, voluminous illustrated reference works, and gargantuan collections of everything from clip-art to shareware are being pumped out by the gadzillions. With titles generally priced under fifty bucks, the new generation of CD-ROM software is a steal by yesterday's pricing standards.

Is it true multimedia, though? If you accept the nonsensical moniker to mean real-time, TV-or-better-quality interactive animation with sound, even the most clever CD-ROM developers can't push the hardware hard enough to fit the bill. When they do—or when somebody gives them a rewritable optical drive with the necessary testosterone—we'll see multimedia applications that truly capture the mass-market potential of interactive graphics. In the meantime, you can get a catalog of the latest CD-ROM titles by sending $3.00 to the Multimedia PC Marketing Council (1730 M Street NW, Ste 707, Washington DC 20036); or call up your favorite mail-order source. (TigerDirect, 800-666-2562 or 305-443-8212, has most of the available titles at about the cheapest price anywhere. They'll send you enough catalogs to heat your house for free.)

Virtual Reality Gets Real

Despite the multimedia hoopla, video on a 14-inch screen with sound isn't anyone's ideal. Wouldn't you rather walk into the 3-D graphics you create, pick up your data, mull it around with your hands, and grab some interactive tools from a workbench to craft changes in your computer-generated universe? So would I. The Holy Grail of graphics is *virtual reality*, where both your eyes and both your ears (and, while we're dreaming, all your other senses) are fed high-quality digital simulations of a 3-D environment.

Virtual reality (VR) is both a distant vision of the ultimate interface and a contemporary buzzword encompassing a host of technologies aimed to help us advance towards that vision. In the sci-fi books and movies, VR is a seductive and sometimes scary place where a twisted variety of software developers have complete control over artificial universes. In *Whole Earth Review* and the popular press articles, VR is a philosophically startling new era for humankind. In the department store, VR is a weird-looking $100 glove and a $100 pair of glasses that let your kids play Super Mario Brothers in stereoscopic 3-D without a joystick.

Somewhere in the vast chasm between VR's awe-inspiring ends and its klunky beginnings lies some promising technologies that will have a major impact on PC graphics. Michael Starks at 3DTV Corporation (PO Box Q, San Rafael, CA 94913-4316, phone: 415-479-3516) now sells a low-cost stereoscopic viewing system for PCs, called PC3D. The kit includes *shutter glasses*, which look and feel like sunglasses but contain LCD panels to alternately block your view from each eye 30 times a second. The included hardware and software can interface with your PC to make your monitor display alternating left eye and right eye views in perfect synch with the shutter glasses.

The effect is full-color stereoscopic viewing on an ordinary VGA screen. The PC3D kit retails for $250, but could easily drop to $100 when manufactured in quantity. A similar kit with a data-glove interface, called PCVR, retails for $350. 3DTV Corp. also sells a PC3DTV kit, which can be used for either a PC or a video system and comes with a 3-D videotape. Says Starks, "With the breakdown of distinctions between video and graphics, I made this kit to break down that barrier."

A new category of *virtual reality software* specializes in ultrafast interactive 3-D rendering, sometimes in conjunction with stereoscopic hardware gismos like PCVR. For speed, current VR software works almost exclusively in 320x200 resolution (a.k.a. the "ug-yuk" mode). Memory constraints also limit the size and complexity of the "virtual worlds" you can create. One of the best VR programs is the Virtual Reality Development System (VRDS), available from VREAM, Inc. (312-477-0425). With VRDS, you can interactively sculpt a 3-D world with animated objects and landscapes, then jump in and explore your creation. VRDS supports a variety of input devices, including the good old-fashioned keyboard and mouse as well as the more exotic data-glove, which reads the position and posture of your hand and feeds it to the PC via a cable. VRDS costs $800, and the next cheapest VR program, World Toolkit from Sense-8 (415-331-6318) goes for a whopping $3,000. A slew of lower-priced VR packages is under development. You can enter the world of VR for next to nothing with REND386—a popular public domain along the same lines as VREAM, but with a far fewer features. REND386 is available for around $5 from most shareware dealers, or you can order a copy with the form in the back of this book. The best-selling VR program ever—and the only commercial program currently available for under $100—is VR Studio, from an English company called Domark (415-513-8929).

At the moment, multimedia and virtual reality designate completely different approaches to the vision of realistic, interactive computer graphics. When the unruly infant of today's graphics hardware grows up to embody the ideals of the software visionaries, these two "virtual worlds" will meet. (See Figure 15.4.) As computer-generated 3-D objects and prerecorded digital video mingle with stereoscopic sight and sound, cyberspace is certain to become a much more enchanting place to visit.

Graphical Operating Systems

Microsoft's robust new operating system may put DOS out to pasture someday, but not in 1993.

By now you may have heard that Windows NT is either an overpriced and hardware-intensive boondoggle or the environment that Windows, DOS, OS/2 and even UNIX should have been all along. In truth, it's a little of both. Technically, NT's a wonderful operating system that combines the familiar Windows interface with a robustness and reliability that the rickety old DOS-Windows combination can't match. But NT requires a powerful computer to work properly, and some compatibility issues still need to be worked out. In other words, don't run out and upgrade without giving it some careful thought.

—Scott Spanbaur, "Windows NT: The New DOS?" *PC World,* June 1993.

Figure 15.4. *When multimedia and virtual reality meet, you may be on the inside looking out.*

Sooner or later, DOS must die. Like many old-timers in the PC field (after all, I'm pushing 30 already), I have developed a certain affection for that familiar, unobtrusive c:> with the blinky underline tagging behind. So even though the graphics guru in me is glad to announce that the DOS prompt's days are numbered, part of me is also happy to add that millions of machines will be running good old DOS for a shamefully long time to come.

There is life beyond the command line, though, and that new life has a great many amenities and comforts for graphics developers and doodlers alike.

The Microsoft Bulldozer

Microsoft seems to be much better at holding its own against operating system imitators than IBM is at competing with clone makers. While the merits of Microsoft Windows are hotly debated, little doubt remains as to which Graphical User Interface (GUI) will dominate the market in the foreseeable future. Now that Windows NT—the GUI that's also an operating system—is (almost) here, the first truly viable replacement for DOS may have come to light.

I don't want to bet on any wrestling match between the Big Blue pinstripe-clad army and Mr. Gates' frisbie-throwing clan of software superheros, but I will report that the odds are running rather strongly in favor of the Redmond team. As much as I hate wading through my WIN.INI and SYSTEM.INI and consulting with the eccentric two-year-old with a speech impediment named Dr. Watson every time Windows crashes (which is constantly), I must admit that a mass movement to Microsoft's GUI is good news in the long run.

When you run Windows, you know that every video card will work with every program. You know that programs have access to all the memory installed in your system. You know that all your graphics software will run in your favorite high-resolution video mode. You know that all your fonts and graphics will be usable within all your programs. When you program for Windows, you know that the operating system will take care of the user interface, color mapping, and dithering, many aspects of printing and file exchange, and the nuts and bolts of reading and processing user input. You also know that you can rely on a wide selection of add-on toolkits to implement complex interface elements without reinventing everything from scratch. (See Figure 15.5.)

For the future, all this means that Windows graphics applications will be more powerful, easier to use, and quicker to develop than graphics apps for any other platform. The amenities and market opportunities that Windows and Windows NT offer to developers will ensure that most serious graphics software will be Windows software in the near future.

But not yet. Right now, power graphics need speed above all else, and DOS is currently a whole lot faster than Windows when it comes to raw display velocity. Graphics applications also need memory in giant gobs and bunches, and Windows chews up RAM like potato chips just to keep the overweight operating system alive. Don't even ask the price of a "low-end" computer system equipped to run Windows NT.

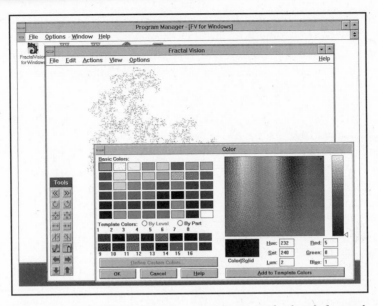

Figure 15.5. *Windows offers users and programmers standard tools for implementing complex graphics, such as this color selection dialog box from Borland's OWL interface library.*

Worst of all, the simplest Windows program is far more complex that a comparable DOS program if you're shooting for graphics splendor rather than pretty menus. As Windows-specific graphics acceleration hardware, PCs with 20+ megabytes of RAM, and a new generation of visual programming tools come to the forefront, these issues will diminish and even the die-hard DOSiers among us will take the Windows plunge. Perhaps by then Microsoft will have hammered out the major instabilities in the operating system, too. Meanwhile, be thankful that this book contains a treasure trove of good old-fashioned easy-to-read DOS programs along with the basic knowledge you need to jump over to Windows when the time comes.

Mr. X and Friends

Then there's UNIX, a loosely affiliated family of operating systems, some of which look and act alike and some of which merely stake claim to the family name for the associated wealth and power. Most (perhaps all) members of the UNIX clan share an insatiable hunger for system resources and a reputation as multiuser-ready, high-end workstation giants.

Several graphics standards have emerged in the UNIX world, including the Graphics Kernel System (GKS) and the ever-popular X-Window user interface and graphics operation protocol. Rumors occasionally spread that GKS, X-Windows, and other relics of the UNIX culture with names like PHIGS and Motif will make their way to the PC platform and then, boy, will all we DOS people realize how good life can be. If you'd like to believe that this is true, go buy Quarterdeck's X-Window version of their once-prominent Desqview windowing system. It's sure to be a collector's item someday. Otherwise, be content with the knowledge that the Computer Graphics Metafile (CGM), a somewhat rare form of vector graphics file from which the modern-day Windows CGM file evolved, originated in UNIX. So there is a "trickle-down" effect after all.

Somebody asked me to mention OS/2. It's every bit as good as Windows, except that it's usually more stable and it replaces DOS with an almost-DOS-compatible command line of its own. Lots of people use it, and if you can catch them before they replace it with Windows so they can run all the latest Windows software, you can probably make some money selling them graphics software that uses the robust multitasking features of OS/2 and the nice graphics and menuing functions. Of course, you'll have to learn to read IBMese first, or ditch the manuals and get a third-party book on OS/2 programming off the clearance shelf at your local bookstore. If you trust IBM's ability to market anything that doesn't need its own air-conditioning unit or you don't care about compatibility but you enjoy driving the luxury-car graphics technology behind OS/2, be sure to check out Mirrors, the superb Windows-to-OS/2 porting system being marketed by MicroGrafx, Inc. (214-234-1769). For more information on OS/2 graphics development tools and a lovely afternoon transferring around the Big Blue Phone Maze to get your free "call designation number," call the IBM OS/2 information line at 800-342-6672 and mention the word "graphics" to everyone you get transferred to.

There, I've mentioned OS/2. Now back to our discussion of the future of graphics on the PC.

Disclaimer: *The perspectives expressed in this chapter are the opinions of the author, and not of Sams Publishing or anybody else who has enough money to be a target for IBM's lawyers.*

A New Generation of Libraries

The TransGraphics system presented in Chapter 2 gives you an easy way to support and move freely between the major graphics libaries on the market today. Graphical operating systems like Windows have their own set of graphics functions, eliminating the need for a graphics library. Life is good.

Nonetheless there's always room for improvement. As graphics become more and more sophisticated, you'll run into one big problem with almost all the DOS and Windows graphics solutions available today: lack of speed. Windows' native graphics calls are notoriously slow even for ordinary line drawing and pixel pushing. Even the fast DOS graphics libraries slow to a crawl when you start piecing the simple line- and pixel-oriented functions together to achieve advanced effects like gradually shaded surfaces, intelligent clipping to arbitrarily shaped regions, or transparency effects with anti-aliased edges.

Faster hardware doesn't address the real issue. You want your graphics programs to perform at the best level the hardware can accomplish. In this business, fast is never quite fast enough. To answer this need, a new generation of graphics libraries will include a huge selection of specially optimized functions for advanced shading and image manipulation. Spyro Gumas' SVGA256 library included with this book foreshadows some of these advances with its speedy graduated-color line and shape drawing functions. (See Figure 15.6.)

Figure 15.6. *Sophisticated graphics require a large selection of drawing and shading tools. A new generation of graphics libraries will answer this need.*

697

Even more sophisticated libraries can take control of the graphics display within Windows and give you a host of dramatically faster and more powerful graphics functions, including the ability to intelligently query the graphics memory to find out what shapes have already been drawn. One of the first such libraries, called *Graphics Master*, is available for $149 from OHB Software (708-590-1095, 5005 Newport Dr #505, Rolling Meadows, IL 60008).

Souped-Up Software

No doubt about it, computer animation is all the rage. From feature films to commercials to music videos, computer-generated images flying around the screen are the hot ticket for grabbing an audience's attention. And since what works in Hollywood often finds its way into the corporate boardroom, animated computer images are becoming an increasingly common feature of business presentations.

Several factors are behind the growing popularity of computer animation. The last few years have seen a dramatic increase in the amount of computer power that can be assembled for a given price; and with animation's heavy requirements in terms of speed, memory and disk storage, would-be desktop animators need all the power they can get.

Animation software has also become more versatile and affordable, with a wide selection of tools available and more on the way. Many of the packages to come will be geared toward lower-end personal computer users, allowing greater numbers of business professionals to create their own animated graphics."

—John B. Callender
Presentation Products Magazine, Nov 1992

Once software developers get their hands on a new generation of graphics tools and users get the hardware upgrades to make graphics really shine, what new marvels will arise in the world of PC graphics software? Lots of 'em. Not only will traditional graphics programs gain stunning new capabilities, but programs that traditionally eschewed graphics will gradually become more and more laden with colorful, photo-quality images. This trend is unlikely to slow until all computer software becomes as visually interesting as color magazines and videos are today.

One key element in this transition will be text fonts. Earlier in the history of the PC, text and graphics were seldom seen on the screen at the same time. Now, flashy fonts have jumped the fence and escaped from "text mode" to freely cavort with graphics. Arts and letters are dancing together, and no graphics nut is happy until a corner of her hard drive is crammed with 200 spicy styles of lettering. Fortunately, all major DOS and Windows graphics programs already support both True Type and Postscript fonts. Nothing short of nuclear winter is likely to unseat either of these major players in the font marketplace. The future of font technology won't look much different than it does today.

New Dimensions

Paper is and will always be flat. Barring major breakthroughs in VR technology, most computer screens will also remain roughly two-dimensional. Almost everything else has at least three dimensions and isn't likely to give any of them up soon. No cataclysmic reality warps are scheduled for a while.

So when you want to represent anything on a piece of paper, you need to simulate three dimensions in some way or another. The artistically endowed among us have the magical ability to arrange lines, dots, and colors by hand so that they look like a 3-D object or scene. Some folks use a camera to record the patterns of light that fool our eyes into seeing 3-D on a 2-D surface. The manual approach has been around for a few millennia, while the camera has barely seen a century go by. In the last few years, both of these techniques for depicting reality have made their way to the computer screen.

As digital pens, crayons, and cameras finally catch up to the precision and flexibility of their traditional counterparts, computers themselves suggest an entirely new approach to realism. When computer-philes talk about *3-D graphics*, we don't mean 3-D-looking sketches. When we babble on about *photorealism*, we aren't talking about digitized photos. To us, *true 3-D* means mathematically simulating 3-D objects that never existed in the "real" world, and using advanced rendering techniques to make convincing 2-D representations of these objects.

This new artform has the unerring, dispassionate look of photography, but the artistic freedom of painting or drawing. With it, you can take snapshots and movies of things that never existed, or never could exist. (See Figure 15.7.) The advent of computer 3-D begins a new chapter in the history of visual expression. The resulting change in graphics will be at least as profound as the one brought on by the invention of the camera.

Figure 15.7. *Photorealistic 3-D rendering lets you take pictures of things that could never exist outside the computer. I created this shape with Fractal Grafics 3D and rendered it with Autodesk 3D Studio.*

Photorealistic 3-D is in its infancy. Watching it grow up will be thrilling indeed, and the moviegoing public will eagerly fund each stage of development with $6 donations for the chance to see it on the big screen. Whether the plot behind the 3-D graphics is sappy (*TRON*), sickening (*Terminator II*), scary (*Lawnmower Man*), or just plain silly (*The Jetsons*), fantastic computer-generated effects can be enough to draw the crowds.

In Chapters 7, 8, and 9, you learned the fundamentals of creating and rendering 3-D objects. Assuming you're not in the movie business, you probably can't afford any 3-D software that does much more than what's included with this book. But the day of low-cost 3-D animation is dawning, and the local Bijou isn't the only screen you'll be watching as the shining star of 3-D graphics rises.

Mirrored spheres and texture-mapped space stations you've seen. What's next on the 3-D thrills list? The human body is number one. Only the most sophisticated graphics systems have managed to get beyond the "mannequin" look to animate live-looking artificial actors. Every issue of *3D Artist* magazine features a better attempt at digital people puppets, and it's only a matter of time before the seamless integration of real actors and 3-D computer models we saw in *Terminator II* makes its way to the PC. (What's that? You've never heard of *3D Artist* magazine? If you're even the teensiest bit interested in low-cost 3-D on the PC, call 505-982-3532 or write to PO Box 4787, Santa Fe, NM 87502. Tell 'em I sent you and they'll give you a free sample issue within North America ($2 overseas), or a 12-issue sub for $22.)

A number of other supercool 3-D developments are beginning to make their way down to the lowly PC from their ivory workstation towers. These include *radiosity*, a subtle but dramatic technique for calculating the effects of diffuse light in a building or scene, *procedural textures*, which use a variety of algorithms to compute intricate and sometimes animated surface patterns, and *solid modeling*, which includes the ability to calculate the motion of objects based on the internal behavior of the materials they are made of. And of course you'll see ever-more-mindbending *morphing, exploding, melting, disintegrating, re-integrating*, and oodles of other special effects.

While the art and science of rendering gain maturity, thousands upon thousands of 3-D "clip-models" are being built. You can buy 3-D computer models of everything from wire-frame horses and carriages brought into cyberspace by 3-D-spacial scanners, to giant indescribable 3-D fractal constructions that could never exist outside of cyberspace. Acuris (415-329-1920) has built a thriving business by marketing animals, plants, people, machines, and even entire cities as detailed DXF files and other 3-D formats.

The only serious 3-D animation product you can buy now for under $300 is 3D Workshop, from Pacific Motion Software (415-221-5581, or 2611 Lake St., San Francisco, 94121). Though marketed less capably than more expensive packages, the latest version of 3D Workshop includes most of the fancy rendering tricks you'll ever need. It also exports models directly to the famous freeware ray-tracer, POV-Ray, for even more realistic images.

Companies to keep your eye on in the 3-D arena include CrystalGraphics (makers of TOPAS and Desktop Animator, 408-496-6175), Strata (makers of StrataVision, 800-869-6855 or 801-628-5218), Visual Software (makers of Renderize, 800-669-7318 or 818-883-7900), Impulse (makers of Imagine, 800-328-0184 or 612-425-0557), and of course the industry leader, Autodesk, which makes 3D Studio (800-879-4233 or 415-332-2344). Do yourself and all the rest of us a favor: Call these companies and tell them you'd buy their products if they were priced under $200. By 1995, somebody's bound to wake up and smell the blooming mass market for 3-D animation.

Welcome to Real Time

Animation—3-D or otherwise—is obviously where the action is. If you want to see a still image, magazines are cheaper and prettier than computer screens. The only reason to stare into a CRT instead is interactive motion. All computer software animates the screen in some form or another. (Even the word processor I'm using to write this is an interactive animation program — it's just limited to animating text.) Keeping up with contemporary computing means enhancing the animation capabilities of PC software in every way possible. Dedicated animation programs are one side of the story. But more and more software which doesn't fall in the "animation" category will include sophisticated tools for moving images as well.

Microsoft's Video for Windows, Iterated Systems' video extensions to the Fractal Image File format, and the Motion Picture Experts Group's MPEG video compression technology are three standards for adding animated video sequences to any software. At present, all of these restrict animation to a tiny window on the screen, even though all of them use state-of-the-art compression technology to speed display and reduce storage requirements. (See Figure 15.8.)

Figure 15.8. *Real-time video demands new approaches to image compression. This image was compressed with Iterated System's POEM technology to less than 1/20th of its original storage size.*

Interaction is severely limited by the fact that video sequences must be entirely prerecorded—the playback sequence can vary according to user input, but the actual content must be chosen from a set of predetermined images. You can contact Iterated Systems at 800-4-FRACTL or 404-840-0310, and if you dare to step into the tangled labyrinth Microsoft calls a phone system, you can call 800-426-9400, 206-936-8661, or almost any other number in Redmond, Washington.

Spanky new video and image compression technologies are popping up daily. Two promising, recently introduced image storage software products are MediaVision's Captain Crunch (800-845-5870) and Multimedia Imaging & Compression's Sho-Me (800-361-3202). Sho-Me is one of the first players to get Iterated Systems' to offer an image compression and display system based on fractals in a commercial Windows multimedia authoring tool. Which of these companies and the dozens to follow will ultimately fly or flounder remains to be seen. Regardless of who brings it to market first, you will undoubtedly enjoy *real-time video capture and animation* on the PC within the next five years.

As computers and 3-D rendering techniques get faster, *real-time rendering*, where photorealistic images are computed on the fly from 3-D models, also becomes viable. Once again, the preordained marriage of Prince VR and Princess Multimedia captures the popular imagination long before the ceremony can be arranged. For years to come, PC animation will be a mixed bag of compromises between prerecorded video snippets, precomputed 3-D photorealism, and rough-but-ready, real-time rendering.

Photographer Grows Up, Marries Painter

While the royal families of exotic graphics techniques carry out their elaborate courtship procedures, the peasant tools of paper and print are breaking down the gates and storming into cyberspace. One revolutionary graphics application, Fractal Design Corporation's Painter, has garnered more attention in the last two years than most other paint programs put together. Blame Fractal Design's expert marketing strategy for much of the fanfare, but give a great deal of credit to the program's authors as well. Painter is genuinely revolutionary in two ways: It is the first graphics program to successfully simulate a wide variety of traditional art tools, such as chalk, charcoal, watercolor, and oil paint, on the PC. It is also the first program to automatically apply those simulated tools to scanned photographic images. The effect, much ballyhooed by the computer press, can turn an snapshot of your daughter into an oil-painted portrait or a pastel sketch. (See Figure 15.9.)

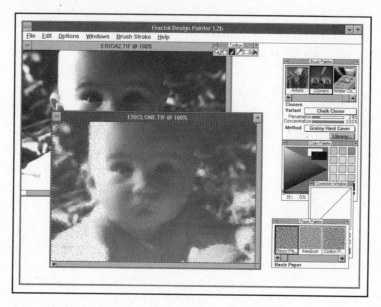

Figure 15.9. *Fractal Design Painter is the leader in a new category of photo/paint software. It can automatically simulate traditional artistic media and paper textures.*

Nobody's going to confuse *Painter's* automated "clones" with the work of a human artist, and the glut of boring fake pastel and pointillist pictures that has flooded the desktop publishing world has made many a serious artist rather queasy. But in talented hands, *Painter* and the many painterly programs that have followed in its footsteps can give artists an exciting new range of possibilities for mixing traditional, photographic, and electronic media. If you'd like to jump on the auto-Van-Gogh bandwagon, you can contact Fractal Design (who don't have much to do with fractals, by the way) at 800-647-7443 or 408-688-8800, or 335 Spreckels Dr., Aptos, CA 95003.

Developers of all the major photo-retouch and image processing software, such as Adobe (maker of Photoshop, 800-833-6687), Aldus (makers of PhotoStyler, 206-622-5500), or Ventura (makers of PicturePro, 800-822-8221) are adding a few Painter-like tools to their applications. Most of these programs also offer many unique effects of their own, such as 3-D spatial warping, ripples, whirlpools, color morphing, and all the tricks presented in Chapter 13. (Figure 15.10 shows off a few stunts in Aldus' PhotoStyler.)

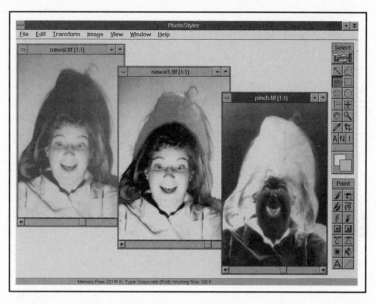

Figure 15.10. *Starting with any mediocre photo (left), you have complete artistic freedom to do good (middle) or evil (right). Though you may set out to do good, the temptation for a bit of evil-looking fun is always there.*

The future can only bring additional creative tools for electronic artists. Even if you refrain from the genuinely new art form of photorealistic 3-D simulation, you'll gain virtually limitless freedom of expression with these radical new variations on the old-fashioned canvas and camera.

The Big Picture

Realism is a corruption of reality.

—Wallace Stevens, 1957

The brave new world of computer graphics is alluring, magnificent, impressive, and more than a little bit fun. But behind the glitzy games and awesome special effects lies a more subtle, mysterious element. When we are drawn into the world behind the screen—the enchanted land of "cyberspace"—where are we actually going?

Humanity is poised on the edge of a new frontier, but the landscape we are beginning to explore is one of our own creation. The treasure that waits there, the source of that hold-your-breath-and-bite-your-lip feeling which computer-generated imagery so often inspires, is an unavoidable question: What will a world of our own creation look like? Mother Nature and whatever deity may guide human history are hurrying us toward a time when their rules are temporarily revoked, when we can freely choose to either imitate or depart from the natural world we have always inhabited. We are being set free—to create what we wish to create, to see what we want to see.

If you could build any universe you like and then jump in to explore, what would you build? If you were given the entire real world of images, along with the power to sculpt an image of any unreal world you could imagine, what would appear on your screen? That power will soon be yours.

Computers are opening the doorway to a place that looks exactly like your dreams. Yet there is always more to a dream than meets the eye. Step inside—but step with care.

Behind the Scenes: Creating the Cover Art for Tricks of the Graphics Gurus

By Katherine Hanley

This epilogue shows you step by step how the cover art for *Tricks of the Graphics Gurus* was created, and offers tips on streamlining art creation when you work electronically. The cover was created using four different types of software: a 3-D modeling package, a 2-D draw package, a paint package, and a metamorphosis package. There are many similarities between packages within the same category, so the names of specific packages used are not of primary importance. Instead, I'll focus on common features that can be used to achieve spectacular results. To get the most out of this chapter, you should be familiar with the features offered in graphics programs you own or plan to purchase.

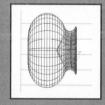

Computer Graphics Versus Conventional Methods

When it comes to creating images for print or production, there is little today that cannot be created electronically. In the early days of computer graphics, computer-generated work had a certain computerized look to it that set it apart from traditionally created art. This often evoked criticism of the methods used. Computer software options have now advanced to the point where an artist can enjoy the benefits without experiencing the drawbacks of computer-generated art. Today, it is almost impossible to point to a printed picture and know whether it was created conventionally or with the help of a computer.

Some critics contend that the electronic medium allows individuals untrained in fine art to pass themselves off as professionals. This is a ridiculous argument. The artist is always in control of the medium, not vice versa. Having the best set of oils and brushes in itself does not make a person a great painter. As with any discipline, it takes dedication, hard work, and talent to achieve mastery. Bad design done electronically is still bad design. If an electronic design touches off a negative response in the viewer, chances are that a traditionally rendered piece would have effected the same dislike. With the exception of the conceptual planning stage, the cover for this book was created electronically. If you don't like the finished product, it is the illustrator you should take issue with, not the computer.

If you often cannot tell the difference between conventional and computer-rendered art, why convince your boss to invest money in a computer system? The primary reason most companies invest in computer graphics is time savings. When an artist can create electronically in three hours what would have taken twelve to achieve conventionally, the computer pays for itself pretty quickly.

Another important benefit is the ability to experiment on a subject without risk. If an illustrator wonders what effect more wrinkles around the eyes will have on a face, or more dramatic lighting will have on an object, she can save one file of the image *as is* and then manipulate a copy of the file to her heart's content. This greatly frees up the creative process. Storage is an additional benefit: optical disks take up much less space in a studio than art boards—and a mouse or light pen won't leave paint under your fingernails.

Many companies sell their software as a complete solution to every graphics need, but often it is smarter to utilize the strengths of several packages and integrate the results. Having the choice of moving back and forth among different packages enables the illustrator to work faster and more powerfully. For example:

■ Paint packages are great for creating textures to be utilized in 3-D packages and for adding detail and blurring hard-edged images that have been created in draw packages.

■ 3-D packages are best used to create images of things that can be built, such as rooms, buildings, and mechanical objects. One of the greatest benefits of using 3-D packages is the ability to move light and camera angles, which allows you to choose perspectives that best highlight an image. Once a model has been built in a 3-D package, parts of it or even the whole thing can be saved and reused in future models.

■ Draw packages are useful for creating hard-edged images, such as the figures of the wizard. They are also great for layout purposes. Images can be moved, scaled, or rotated to achieve the best possible composition.

■ Special effects packages like the metamorphosis program add an exciting dimension by adding unusual visual effects that take an image out of the realm of the everyday.

How the Cover Art Was Created

The planning stage of this illustration was done with pencil and paper. When creating a finished piece, the idea or rough is often created traditionally because it is a quick way to record a basic idea. Once the idea is created and okayed by the client, it can be scanned in and used as a guide (See Figure 1). This conceptual stage is the time to plan out the steps to be taken throughout the creation process, either mentally or on paper. Deciding in advance how each part of the drawing will be created and in what order saves time later.

Creating the background in this picture was the first step in the process. The walls and floor were created in a 3-D package called TOPAS. Instead of drawing each brick separately in the 3-D package, it was faster to "paint" a brick texture and wrap it on the walls. The paint program Adobe PhotoShop was used to create the texture. To achieve the rough look of the brick, the feature "Add noise" was used, then the feature "Crystallize" was used to break it up further (Figure EP.1).

Figure EP.1. *The bricks in the wall are really just a 2-D image map imported from a paint program.*

The next step was to dither, or blur, the texture just a little. Then horizontal and vertical lines were added to form the brick pattern. To make the wall look very old, cracks were painted in Photoshop using a variety of different-sized brush tools. Finally, darker areas were air-brushed in to give the wall an uneven tone.

After the wall texture was saved, the shape of the room was built. A circle was built, then extended to make a 3-dimensional cylinder. Half of the cylinder was chopped off to give the appearance of an open tower room (Figure EP.2). The stored texture map was then applied to the walls. A close-up section of the same picture was projected on the floor. This made the floor bricks appear to be larger than the bricks in the wall.

The floating objects (except for the bubble-to-bear metamorphosis) were created next, also using TOPAS. To create the cauldron, a polygon was created outlining the outside of the kettle. Another polygon was created for liquid inside the cauldron. Both polygons were revolved around the same axis so the liquid would fit nicely in the pot (Figure EP.3).

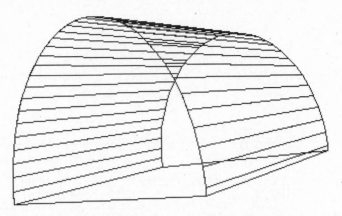

Figure EP.2. *The vaulted room started out as a simple 3-D model.*

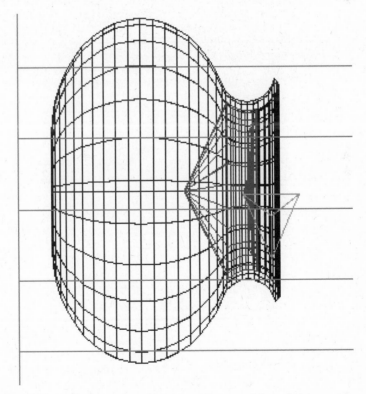

Figure EP.3. *The cauldron and its contents were created by rotating two shapes around the same axis.*

To make the bubbles, a few small spheres were added, half in and half out of the liquid. To create the background and floating objects, cubes, and spheres were created and then placed around the room. In PhotoShop, attributes of color, transparency, and metallics were added to each object to add realism. The floating objects were texture-mapped with various textures to add greater interest (Figure EP.4).

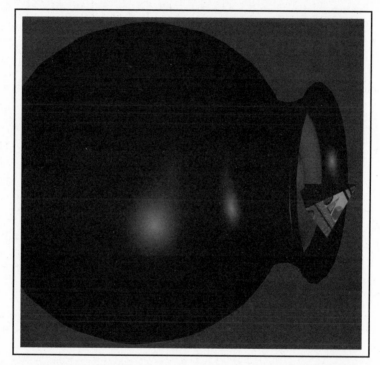

Figure EP.4. *The finished cauldron, with a texture-mapped object floating out of it.*

The image was saved as three separate pictures, so that the wizard could be placed among them once it was created. First, the room itself was saved, with all items within the room hidden. Then the room was hidden and the cauldron unhidden to be saved as an image. Lastly, the cauldron was rehidden so that the floating objects could be saved. This process would later enable all these objects to be moved around easily and allow the wizard to be placed among them, once all were imported into a 2-D draw package.

Creating and saving the images described above took just under one hour. If curved bricks had to be created instead of manipulating the precreated texture, this process would have taken far longer.

The next step of the process took place within the 2-D drawing package RIO. The room file was imported and placed in the background (Figure EP.5). Next, a scanned image of the wizard was opened as a basic template to be drawn over.

Figure EP.5. *The back wall was saved separately from the cauldron so the wizard could be placed between them.*

When rendering a figure in a drawing program it is best to start at the back and work forward. Creating a figure out of polygons, which is how the wizard was formed, is similar to working with cut paper because you are working in layers. Getting the shape of each layer right is most important. It is not important at this time to create the fine details of the image, such as facial wrinkles and clothing details. This can be done later in a paint package.

Once the wizard was drawn (Figure EP.6), it and the room were grouped together, so that they could be moved or scaled. Next the cauldron and objects were placed, and shadows were placed behind them.

Figure EP.6. *The wizard was constructed from polygons.*

Before grouping all the images together, the creation process was halted and the client consulted. This stage is a good time to bring your client into the process, because separate images can be easily manipulated to suit the client's needs. In this case the client wanted adjustments made to accommodate the title and additional text that would appear on the cover. Consequently, the number of floating objects was reduced, the wizard was shrunk in size, and the cauldron was moved down.

Once those changes were made, the different objects were all printed to one image file. Then the image was imported into PhotoShop, where final details could be added. On the wizard, facial wrinkles were painted and edges were blended. Detail was added to the wizard's face, eyebrows, and beard. The shadows on his clothes were softened using the blend tool. Smoke and bubbles were airbrushed in and around the cauldron (Figure EP.7).

Figure EP.7. *The wizard enters the room with his cauldron.*

Last of all, the bubble-to-bear metamorphosis was added to the composition. This was created using a metamorphosis project called Morph. Two equally sized files, one of the bubble and one of the bear, were imported and manipulated until the right progression of metamorphosed images was created. The images were then imported into PhotoShop and scaled over the main picture.

From conception to finished product, creating the cover art took 24 hours. It could be argued that this whole image could have been created in one software package. But to take full advantage of computer graphics, mastery of several types of programs is needed. Using only one program limits you just as much as using one conventional graphic medium, such as oil paint. The ability to work with several types of graphics programs is what enables you to create unique works of art that can be manipulated and refined with speed and ease.

VI

Appendices

Software Reference

This appendix lists all the ready-to-run programs, source code, sample images, and other files on the disks included with this book.

Manual Installation

For instructions on using the included IN-STALL program and source code compile instructions, see the Introduction in the front of this book. You can also install any of the archives by hand using LHA.EXE, a freeware compression/decompression program included on the disks. For example, to install the TG.LZH archive from floppy drive A to a directory named TRICKS on hard drive C without using the INSTALL program, enter the following commands at the DOS prompt:

```
C:
MD \TRICKS
CD \TRICKS
A:LHA X A:TG.LZH
```

If you don't have a copy of LHA.EXE on your hard drive already, you might copy it to the directory where you keep handy utility programs. LHA is a commonly used compression program, and you can use it to decompress any files that end with the .LZH extension. Should you happen to download any .LZH archives with your modem or aquire some from shareware/freeware distributors, you'll be glad you have LHA to get the files out. LHA (often called by its former name, LHARC) is similar to the more popular but slower, less efficient, and more expensive PKZIP shareware compression software. For a list of LHA command options, simply type LHA and press enter.

Archives on the Disks

Disk 1 contains eight archives, and Disk 2 contains five. The following list summarizes the general contents of each archive, and the remainder of this appendix explains each file in detail.

Disk 1

TG.LZH	TransGraphics system, MOIRE and TGDEMO programs
TGA_PCX.LZH	TGA and PCX file-handling programs and code
SVGA.LZH	Shareware Super VGA image viewer (and images)
VSA256.LZH	Shareware VESA Super VGA graphics library
TIFF256.LZH	TIFF image file functions to go with VSA256
TWEEN.LZH	Tweening, morphing, movie player, and movies
SCENE.LZH	An extraterrestrial scene generator
3D.LZH	Interactive 3-D modeling programs

Disk 2

FRACTALS.LZH	Interactive fractal animation and 3-D fractals
POLYRAY.LZH	Shareware ray tracer and scene files
WIN_GDI.LZH	Windows Graphics Device Interface examples
IMAGEPRO.LZH	Image processing program (and images)
VISUAL.LZH	Visualization and simulation programs

The following sections list all files in the order the book discusses them, with a brief description following each group of related files.

Chapter 1: Bitmapped Graphics

The TG.LZH archive contains files for Chapter 1.

MOIRE.C
MOIRE.EXE

A simple sample with some startling surprises. The program just draws lines and circles, but that's not what you'll see! These files include color animation, too.

Chapter 2: Graphics for Everyone

The TG.LZH archive contains files for Chapter 2.

TGMS.BAT	Microsoft C compiler
TGMS2.BAT	Microsoft C compiler with GRAPHICS.LIB
TGMSGX.BAT	Microsoft C with GX Graphics compiler
TGTC.BAT	Borland/Turbo C compiler
TGTCGX.BAT	Borland/Tubro C with GX Graphics compiler
EGAVGA.BGI	Borland Graphics Interface runtime
TGGX.C	GX Graphics functions
TGMS.C	Microsoft C functions
TGTC.C	BGI functions
TG.H	Master TransGraphics header
TGGX.H	GX Graphics macros
TGMS.H	Microsoft macros
TGTC.H	BGI macros
TGMOUSE.H	Mouse macros
TG.TXT	Compiler instructions and other information
READ_VSA.TXT	Notes on using TransGraphics with VSA256
TGVSA.BAT	Batch file for compiling with TG an VSA256
TGVSA.H	TransGraphics VSA256 support header
TGVSA.C	TtansGraphics VSA256 support functions

TransGraphics: A system of header files and functions to make your graphics programs compatible with all major C and C++ compilers and graphics libraries at once.

TGDEMO.C
TGDEMO.EXE

Demonstrates all the graphics functions supported by TransGraphics.

Chapter 3: Graphics File Formats

The TGA_PCX.LZH, SVGA.LZH, VSA256.LZH, and TIFF256.LZH archives contain files for Chapter 3.

The following files are in TGA_PCX.LZH:

TGA.C

Functions to read and write Targa files.

COLORTRI.C
COLORTRI.EXE

Demonstrates how to create a Targa file using the functions in TGA.C by creating a 24-bit color triangle image and saving it in a file called COLORTRI.TGA.

TGAREAD.C
TGAREAD.EXE
RAYTREE.TGA

Demonstrates how to read and display a Targa file using the functions in TGA.C. Includes a sample TGA image of a ray-traced 3-D fractal.

PCX.C

Source code functions to read and write .PCX files into a memory buffer.

The SVGA.LZH archive contains the following files:

ADAPTER.EXE	Detect and verify your Super VGA type
SVGA.EXE	Super VGA image viewer
REGISTER.FRM	Registration/Order form
SVGA.MAN	The text manual for SVGA
ADDENDUM.MAN	Addendum to SVGA.MAN
VERSION.TXT	Version history
TODO.TXT	Future update plans
CHIPSETS.TXT	List of supported Super VGA chipsets

README.TXT	Getting started notes
EDIE.PCX	Portrait of decadence and intrigue
MAN!.GIF	Man, oh, man! The Mandelbrot set
SATURN.TGA	NASA photo of Saturn and its moons

A shareware Super VGA and HiColor image viewer by John Silva that supports the .TGA, .GIF, and .PCX file formats. Some fun sample images are also provided.

The VSA256.LZH archive supplies the following files:

VSA_DEMO.C	Demo of the VSA256 library
VSA_DEMO.EXE	
VSA.H	VESA support header file
VSA256MS.LIB	Microsoft C VESA library
VSA256BC.LIB	Borland/Turbo C VESA library
READMEVS.TXT	Introductory notes
ORDERVSA.TXT	Registration/Order form
VSAWSHVS.TXT	New version wish list form for you
BUGRPTVS.TXT	List of known bugs
DRIVERS2.EXE	Verifies VESA driver

A graphics library for Super VGA support and advanced color-shaded lines and triangles. Includes a TransGraphics compatible header file. Shareware by Spyro Gumas.

The TIFF256.LZH archive contains the following files:

TIF_DEMO.C	Demo TIFF handling program
TIF_DEMO.EXE	
TIF_DATA.EXE	Displays TIFF header information
TIFF.H	Header file
TIFF_BCL.LIB	Borland/Turbo C TIFF library
TIFF_MSL.LIB	Microsoft C TIFF library
ORDERTF.TXT	Registration/Order form
VSAWSHTF.TXT	Have your wishes granted!
BUGRPTTF.TXT	List of known bugs
READMETF.TXT	Introductory notes

An extension to the VSA256 library to read and write TIFF files. Shareware by Spyro Gumas.

Chapter 4: Tweening, Morphing, and Transformations

The TWEEN.LZH archive contains files for Chapter 4.

TWEEN.H	Tweening header
TWEEN.C	General tweening functions
TWEEN1.C	Four programs to tween lines with various displays
TWEEN1.EXE	
TWEEN2.C	
TWEEN2.EXE	
TWEEN3.C	
TWEEN3.EXE	
TWEEN4.C	
TWEEN4.EXE	
TRANS.C	Program to interactively transform a shape
TRANS.EXE	

Learn to perform fast animation by creating a gradual transition beTWEEN any set of lines and any other, then add interactive spinning, zooming, leaning, and movement transformations.

PLAY.EXE	Super-fast FantaVision movie player
FANTA.SET	Used by PLAY to choose a selection of movies
WEREWOLF.MVE	Man metamorphoses into a wolf
SQUARE.MVE	Square changes into an octagon
GOODIES.MVE	Demonstration of various transformations
ZOOM.MVE	Demonstration of zoom transformation
FLYFISH.MVE	Geometric fish learns to fly
EARTH.MVE	Continental drift
CHICK.MVE	The proverbial early bird
DIVE.MVE	Stick figure goes off the high board
EVOLUT.MVE	From fish to reptile to bird
JAZZ.MVE	Big time party time
LUXO.MVE	Luxo the lamp meets his fate
MITOSIS.MVE	Reproduction the old-fashioned way
SNOWMAN.MVE	Spring fever takes its toll
FP.H	Header file for FPLAY.C

FPLAY.C	Source code for a simplified movie player
FPLAY.EXE	Works like PLAY.EXE, using the code in FPLAY.C
FPLAY.MAK	Microsoft MAKE file for FPLAY.C

Polygon morphing demo and several sample MoViE files to play. These movies were created with Scott Anderson's commercial animation software, FantaVision. (FPLAY.C requires Microsoft C to compile.)

Chapter 5: Pseudo-3-D

The SCENE.LZH archive contains files for Chapter 5.

BALL.C
BALL.EXE

Simple demonstration of super-fast shaded sphere.

FEATURES.C
GRAPHICS.C
MATH.C
MATH.H
SCENE.H
SCENE.C
SCENE.EXE
SCENE.MAK

An extraterrestrial scene generator that demonstrates a host of graphics tricks including pseudo-3-D, and anti-aliasing. (This program requires Microsoft C to compile.)

Chapter 6: Fractal Animation

The FRACTALS.LZH archive contains files for Chapter 6.

MUDI.H
MUDI.OBJ

Super-fast assembly language 32-bit multiply and divide functions for linking with the following programs. (The 3D.LZH archive also contains identical copies of these two files.)

FRAN.H
FRAN.C
FRAN.EXE

A fractal animator, which loads a fractal definition from an iterated function system (IFS) file, enables you to interactively design a new fractal and save it in a new IFS file.

FREEN.C
FREEN.EXE

A fractal tweener, which morphs any IFS fractal into any other in a given number of in-between frames.

BIGFISH.IFS
BODY.IFS
CARPET.IFS
CHAOS.IFS
CORAL.IFS
CURL.IFS
DAVIS.IFS
DRAGON.IFS
FERN.IFS
FIVE.IFS
FOUR.IFS
GALAXY.IFS
KOCH.IFS
LEAF.IFS
LEAFY.IFS
MAPLE.IFS
MOUSE.IFS
PLANT.IFS
PYRAMID.IFS
SEVEN.IFS
SHEAF.IFS
SIX.IFS
TEN.IFS
THREE.IFS
TRI.IFS
TWO.IFS

IFS fractals to be used with FRAN.EXE and FREEN.EXE.

MANIMATE.C
MANIMATE.EXE

These files generate Mandelbrot set and Julia set fractals and animate them with color cycling.

Chapter 7: Graphics in Space

The 3D.LZH archive contains files for Chapter 7.

MUDI.H
MUDI.OBJ

Super-fast assembly language 32-bit multiply and divide functions for linking with the following programs. (The FRACTALS.LZH archive contains identical copies of these two files.)

3D.H   This header is used by 3DCUBE, 3DLINES, and 3DFACES.

3DCUBE.C

3DCUBE.EXE

Animated stereoscopic, prespective view of spinning cube.

3DLINES.C
3DLINES.EXE

An interactive wireframe shape editor with which you can load a 3-D model from a drawing exchange file (DXF), rotate, scale, move, add, or delete points and lines and then save your new model to a DXF.

3DFACES.C
3DFACES.EXE

An interactive 3-D surface editor with which you can edit 3-D faces from a .DXF file or add 3-D faces to wireframe models.

DXF2PI.C
DXF2PI.EXE

A utility to translate 3DFACE entities from a DXF file into POLYRAY-compatible polygon object definitions for ray tracing.

CUBES.DXF
GEM.DXF
MYYURT.DXF
SAUCER.DXF
TETRA.DXF
TRUNK.DXF
TUBE.DXF
TUBEFACE.DXF
YURTFACE.DXF

Three-dimensional shapes in .DXF format you can use with 3DLINES.EXE, 3DFACES.EXE, and DXF2PI.EXE.

Chapter 8: 3-D Fractal Animation

The FRACTALS.LZH archive contains files for Chapter 8.

FRAN3D.H
FRAN3D.C
FRAN3D.EXE

A three-dimensional interactive fractal animator, which loads a 3-D .IFS file, enables you to edit the fractal in 3-D space and saves your new design to another .IFS file.

FREEN3D.C
FREEN3D.EXE

A three-dimensional fractal tweener, which automatically displays a given number of frames in between two 3-D .IFS fractals.

3DCUBE.IFS
3DCURL.IFS
3DFERN1.IFS
3DFERN2.IFS
3DGALAXY.IFS

3DPLANT.IFS
3DSIERP.IFS
3DTETRA.IFS
3DTREE.IFS
3DCURL.IFS

Three-dimensional IFS fractals for use with FRAN3D.EXE and FREEN3D.EXE.

IFS2DXF.C
IFS2DXF.EXE

A utility to translate IFS fractals into .DXF drawing files. You have the option of simply drawing points or placing a cube of a given size around each point.

IFS2PI.C
IFS2PI.EXE

A utility to convert IFS fractals into .PI scene description files for use with the POLYRAY ray tracer. Works just like IFS2DXF, except that it creates spheres instead of dots or cubes.

Chapter 9: Realistic Rendering with Ray Tracing

The RAYTRACE.LZH archive contains files for Chapter 9.

POLYRAY.EXE   The POLYRAY ray tracer

The POLYRAY ray tracer, a powerful 3-D rendering tool. This version requires a 386 or 486 computer, with or without a math-coprocessor. A slower 286-compatible version and a faster 486-optimized version are available using the order form in the back of this book. Note that POLYRAY is shareware. See the POLYRAY.DOC file for details on shareware registration.

READ.ME   Short note on what POLYRAY is
COLOR.DOC   Summary of built-in color names
QUICKREF.TXT   Quick reference sheet
REVISION.TXT   Revision history
TEXTURE.TXT   Notes on texture mapping
POLYRAY.DOC   The main manual
ADDENDUM   Version 1.6 addendum to the manual

Text documentation files for POLYRAY and the POLYRAY scene description language.

MAKEMAP.EXE	
GEM.PI	An example created with DXF2PI.EXE
ANIM.PI	Add this text to any .PI file to animate the scene by flying around it
SAMPLE.PI	The simple scene discussed in Chapter 9
ANIMBALL.PI	An animated bouncing ball

Sample POLYRAY scene description files from this book.

DAT

Subdirectory containing many POLYRAY example scene files and batch files to ray trace the scenes and create images. The DAT directory contains the following files and subdirectories:

MAKEALL.BAT	Batch file to ray trace all the examples (takes between a day and a week to complete them all, depending on the speed of your computer!)
COLORS.INC	Include file for standard color definitions
TEXTURE.INC	Include file for standard texture definitions
POLY	Polynomial function example scenes
MISC	Miscellaneous complex scenes
HEIGHT	Height field example scenes
SIMPLE	Quick examples of each object type
TEXTURE	Texture-mapping example scenes
ANIMATE	Several subdirectories with various animation examples
SWEEP	Sweep surface example scenes
FUNCTION	Math function example scenes
BLOBS	Blob object example scenes
GRIDDED	Grid-mapping example scenes
PERSON	"Polyray Man" and his clone
ROBARM	Animated robot arm solving a puzzle
STONES	Stone texture examples
UVMAPS	Step-map examples

Chapter 10: Windows and the Graphics Device Interface

The WIN_GDI.LZH archive contains files for Chapter 10. Due to the large size of Windows programs, ready-to-run EXE files are not provided for any of the Windows examples in this book.

FUNDWIN.C	Source code file
FUNDWIN.DEF	Definitions file
FUNDWIN.PRJ	Borland project file
FUNDWIN.RC	Resource file

A fundamental window example demonstrating the simplest possible Microsoft Windows graphics program. (Requires Borland/Turbo C version 3.0 or higher to compile.)

Chapter 11: Windows Graphics Functions

The WIN_GDI.LZH archive contains files for Chapter 11.

Due to the large size of Windows programs, ready-to-run EXE files are not provided for any of the Windows examples in this book.

POINTEX.C	Example of how to draw points
POINTEX.DEF	
POINTEX.PRJ	
POINTEX.RC	
PENSTYEX.C	Example of how to use pen styles
PENSTYEX.DEF	
PENSTYEX.PRJ	
PENSTYEX.RC	
CSTPENEX.C	Custom pen styles example
CSTPENEX.DEF	
CSTPENEX.PRJ	
CSTPENEX.RC	

STCKBREX.C   Example of how to use stock brushes
STCKBREX.DEF
STCKBREX.PRJ
STCKBREX.RC

HTCHBREX.C   Example of how to use hatch brushes
HTCHBREX.DEF
HTCHBREX.PRJ
HTCHBREX.RC

DRAWMDEX.C   Example of Windows drawing modes
DRAWMDEX.DEF
DRAWMDEX.PRJ
DRAWMDEX.RC

LINETOEX.C   MoveTo and LineTo example
LINETOEX.DEF
LINETOEX.PRJ
LINETOEX.RC

ARCEX.C   Example of how to use arcs
ARCEX.DEF
ARCEX.PRJ
ARCEX.RC

RECTEX.C   Examples of how to use rectangles
RECTEX.DEF
RECTEX.PRJ
RECTEX.RC

POLYLNEX.C   Example of how to use polylines
POLYLNEX.DEF
POLYLNEX.PRJ
POLYLNEX.RC

POLYGNEX.C   Example of how to use filled polygons
POLYGNEX.DEF
POLYGNEX.PRJ
POLYGNEX.RC

PLYPLYEX.C   Example of how to use multiple polygons
PLYPLYEX.DEF
PLYPLYEX.PRJ
PLYPLYEX.RC

ELLIPSEX.C ELLIPSEX.DEF ELLIPSEX.PRJ ELLIPSEX.RC	Example of how to use ellipses
CHORDEX.C CHORDEX.DEF CHORDEX.PRJ CHORDEX.RC	Example of how to use chorded ellipses
PIEEX.C PIEEX.DEF PIEEX.PRJ PIEEX.RC	Example of how to draw pie charts
TXTOUTEX.C TXTOUTEX.DEF TXTOUTEX.PRJ TXTOUTEX.RC	Example of how to output text with TextOut
TABTXTEX.C TABTXTEX.DEF TABTXTEX.PRJ TABTXTEX.RC	Example of how to output tabbed text
FONTSEX.C FONTSEX.DEF FONTSEX.PRJ FONTSEX.RC	Example of how to get sexy-looking fonts

Sample Windows programs demonstrating how to use the Windows GDI. (These require Borland/Turbo C Version 3.0 or higher to compile.)

Chapter 12: Bitmapped Graphics, Windows Style

The WIN_GDI.LZH archive contains files for Chapter 12.

Due to the large size of Windows programs, ready-to-run EXE files are not provided for any of the Windows examples in this book.

BITMAPEX.BMP	Sample bitmap
BITMAPEX.C BITMAPEX.DEF BITMAPEX.PRJ BITMAPEX.RC	Sample program using bitmap
BITBCKEX.BMP	Sample background bitmap
BITBCKEX.C BITBCKEX.DEF BITBCKEX.PRJ BITBCKEX.RC	Sample program using background bitmap
BITANI1.BMP BITANI2.BMP	Two sample bitmaps to be animated
BITANIEX.C BITANIEX.DEF BITANIEX.PRJ BITANIEX.RC	Sample program to animate bitmaps
BITBSHEX.BMP	Sample bitmap to be made into a brush
BITBSHEX.C BITBSHEX.DEF BITBSHEX.PRJ BITBSHEX.RC	Example of how to use bitmap brushes
CURAPPEX.CUR	Sample cursor
CURAPPEX.C CURAPPEX.DEF CURAPPEX.PRJ CURAPPEX.RC	Sample program using cursor
CURMLT1.CUR CURMLT2.CUR CURMLT3.CUR CURMLT4.CUR	Four cursors
CURMLTEX.C CURMLTEX.DEF CURMLTEX.PRJ CURMLTEX.RC	Example of how to use multiple cursors

ICONEX.ICO	Sample icon
ICONEX.C	Example of how to use an icon
ICONEX.DEF	
ICONEX.PRJ	
ICONEX.RC	

ICONSEX1.ICO	Four icons in a platonic relationship
ICONSEX2.ICO	
ICONSEX3.ICO	
ICONSEX4.ICO	

ICONSEX.C	Example of the clean, moral use of multiple icons
ICONSEX.DEF	
ICONSEX.PRJ	
ICONSEX.RC	

Sample Windows programs demonstrating how to use graphics bitmaps in Windows. (These require Borland/Turbo C version 3.0 or higher to compile.)

Chapter 13: Image Processing

The IMAGEPRO.LZH archive contains files for Chapter 13.

```
IMP.H
IMP_A.C
IMP_B.C
IMAGEPRO.C
IMAGEPRO.EXE
```

Image processing program to control brightness, contrast, and color balance of images, plus many special effects including edge detection, embossing, and advanced filtering techniques. Uses the VSA256 and TIF256 libraries presented in Chapter 3.

```
RGBSPLIT.EXE
```

Converter for turning TIF files into a simply Red/Green/Blue (RGB) format for use with some IMAGEPRO functions.

ACG_A.TIF	Portrait of Andrew Gumas, the original Mr. Cute
EART128.TIF	Our planet

MSK128.TIF	A frequency mask for Fourier transforms (two black dots on a white background)
GROW.TIF	A miniature pony for you to make into a horse
MIDI.TIF	A ray traced true color piece of visual music
SHRINK.TIF	Honey, I shrunk....

TIFF image files to be used with IMAGEPRO.EXE and RGBSPLIT.EXE.

Chapter 14: Interactive Visualization

The VISUAL.LZH archive contains files for Chapter 14.

DATAVIEW.C
DATAVIEW.EXE

Interactive plotting program for visualizing data from numerical ASCII text files and visually matching multiple data sets to find trends and similarities.

AVGTEMP.DAT	Average daily temperature in Middlesex, VT
MAXTEMP.DAT	Maximum daily temperature
MINTEMP.DAT	Minimum daily temperature
DEPTEMP.DAT	Deviation from previous year's temperature
PRECIP.DAT	Total daily precipitation
MAXMIN.DAT	Maximum versus minimum temperature

Numerical data files in ASCII text format for use with the DATAVIEW program.

WHEEL.C
WHEEL.EXE

Interactive simulation of the Lorenz water wheel with on-screen experiment monitor graphs. An example of scientific visualization will reveal unexpected chaotic behavior in a real-world system.

Chapter 15: Graphics of the Future

Chapter 15 does not include any software or code listings.

TransGraphics Unveiled

T his appendix presents and explains the complete TransGraphics source code for the Microsoft, Borland, and Genus GX Graphics library support files. First, I present generic mouse interface routines that work with any compiler and graphics library. Then, I discuss the differences among three leading graphics libraries and present the header files and .C files to support those compilers.

You'll find instructions for compiling TransGraphics programs in the introduction to this book, as well as in the TG.TXT file on the disk.

Do-It-Yourself Mouse Programming

Advanced graphics libraries (such as the GX Graphics series) usually include mouse support, and TransGraphics just calls its mouse

functions if it can. When no special mouse-handling functions are available—and they aren't available with any of the leading C or C++ compilers—TransGraphics gives you the macros you need to handle mouse access yourself. These macros call your *mouse driver*—the MOUSE.COM program installed by your AUTOEXEC.BAT file when you start up your computer. You talk to the mouse driver through a communication system called *software interrupts*. For assembly language experts and seasoned C captains, software interrupt calls are old hat. For those of you who have yet to dip your toes into the internal registers of your CPU chip, the code to access mouse interrupts reads about as clearly as ancient Dead C Scrolls.

TransGraphics does the mouse handling for you, and you can cut and paste the following **Working Code** listed in any new TransGraphics support files you create. So, you don't need to know how it works. I bet some of you are just a wee bit curious, though, so I'll dissect a few of the functions here for you. Those who can't bear the graphic details can cover their eyes and duck out for the next page or so.

In most C programming, you allocate and manipulate variables in the computer's RAM chips. Only a few key memory locations are right inside the 80×86 CPU chip itself, and your C compiler normally handles the contents of these *registers* for you automatically. To call mouse functions, however, you need to access the CPU registers directly. Most C compilers provide special data structures, usually called REGS, for accessing the registers. To get a grip on the registers, you might define two structures called iReg and oReg, one for putting data into the registers and one for getting data back out again. In C code, this looks like:

```
REGS iReg, oReg;
```

The general procedure for making a mouse call goes like this:

1. Choose the mouse function you want, using Table A.1 (or another programmer's reference book) as your menu. Put the code name of your selection into the input registers.

2. Trigger interrupt number 33h with the C function int86(). Think of this as hollering "Yo! Hey, mouse driver!" to tell it you want it to wait on you.

3. Look at the output registers to see if the driver brought you what you ordered.

I just happen to know that loading the AX register with a value of 3 and triggering 33h interrupt is the polite way to ask the BIOS to put the mouse x and y position into the CX and DX registers. In C, you would write:

Placez les positions de la souris, s'il vous plaît, dans...

Oh, sorry. That's French. In C, you would write:

```
iRegs.x.ax = 3;
int86(0x33, iRegs, oRegs);
mx = oReg.x.cx;
my = oReg.x.dx;
```

To make this more comprehensible for those of us who didn't learn C (or French) as our first language, TransGraphics defines the necessary codes with English-like names such as tg_GETSTATUS, tg_MOUSEX, and tg_MOUSEY. (Okay, I didn't say they were *English* names, I said *English-like*, which leaves a lot of leeway.) TransGraphics also defines a macro called tg_mint(), which triggers interrupt 33h. Therefore, the actual definition for the tg_getmouse() macro becomes

```
#define tg_getmousepos(mx, my); \
    {tg_mint(tg_GETSTATUS); \
    mx = tg_MOUSEX, my = tg_MOUSEY;}
```

Table A.1 lists the numerical phrases needed to issue your appeals to the mouse driver with proper etiquette.

Table B.1. Thank goodness TransGraphics handles all this BIOS-call rubbish for you, so you don't have to memorize this table.

TransGraphics definition	Interrupt 33h function number	What it does
tg_RESET	0	Resets and reports the presence of the mouse
tg_SHOWCRSR	1	Shows the mouse cursor
tg_HIDECRSR	2	Hides the mouse cursor
tg_GETSTATUS	3	Puts the button status in BX, and position in CX and DX
tg_SETPOS	4	Sets the mouse position with the contents of CX and DX

Many more mouse interrupt functions exist (31 more, to be exact) but they aren't as commonly used. For example, you can tell the mouse driver to automatically restrict mouse movement to a certain area or change the shape of the mouse cursor. If your breast burns with raging desire for all human knowledge on the subject of mouse programming, I recommend that you pick up a copy of the *Microsoft Mouse Programmer's Reference* by Microsoft Press. (But maybe you should take a cold shower first.)

The following **Working Code** section, extracted from the TGMOUSE.H file that handles TransGraphics mouse support, works with almost all C compilers and Microsoft-mouse compatible input devices. When a graphics library has its own mouse functions—as the Zortech C++ Flash Graphics and Genus GX Graphics libraries do—it's best to use those instead of BIOS calls. You may otherwise encounter some strange behavior on some Super VGA graphics cards. Generally, you can solve most compatibility problems by obtaining the latest version of your mouse manufacturer's driver. Rumor has it that you can ensure the best compatibility by using the latest Microsoft driver program, even if you don't have a genuine Microsoft mouse—though I would certainly never be caught dead recommending such a thing, what with the salary Microsoft pays its paranoid lawyers.

Working Code: Mighty Mouse Macros

Though the previous paragraphs might be a good refresher on making interrupt calls in C, you can just cut and paste these macros into any new TransGraphics headers—or, heaven forbid, non-TransGraphics programs—you write.

Because all the mouse calls are implemented as macros, they execute faster and more efficiently than function calls. Also, because the macros work with the internal CPU registers, they compile into extremely compact machine language code.

```
/* TGMOUSE.H
 *
 * TransGraphics version 1.0
 * from Tricks of the Graphics Gurus
 *
 * Generic mouse support header file
 * See the file TG.TXT for more information.
 */

/* These are the function values used by tg_mint()
   to control the mouse */
```

```
#define tg_RESET 0
#define tg_SHOWCRSR 1
#define tg_HIDECRSR 2
#define tg_GETSTATUS 3
#define tg_SETPOS 4
#define tg_GETPRESS 5
#define tg_GETRELEASE 6


/* These are the register values where returns
   from the mouse interrupt calls are stored */


#define tg_MFUNC iReg.x.ax
#define tg_MRETURN oReg.x.ax
#define tg_MOUSEX oReg.x.cx
#define tg_MOUSEY oReg.x.dx
#define tg_BUTTONS oReg.x.bx
#define tg_NEWMOUSEX iReg.x.cx
#define tg_NEWMOUSEY iReg.x.dx


#define tg_MINT 0x33            /* The mouse interrupt value */


/* Mouse interrupt macro */

#define tg_mint(m); {tg_MFUNC = (m); \
                    int86(tg_MINT, &iReg, &oReg);}


EXT union REGS iReg, oReg;             /* internal registers */


EXT int tg_mouseon;             /* Does user have a mouse? */

/* set tg_mouson to -1 if user has a mouse, 0 otherwise */

#define tg_findmouse();         \
{   tg_mint(tg_RESET);          \
    if (tg_MRETURN)             \
    {   tg_mouseon = -1;        \
        tg_mint(tg_SHOWCRSR);}  \
    else tg_mouseon = 0;}


/* show and hide  the mouse cursor */

#define tg_showmouse() tg_mint(tg_SHOWCRSR)
```

741

```
#define tg_hidemouse() tg_mint(tg_HIDECRSR)

/* get mouse button status */

#define tg_getmousebuttons(lb, rb); \
    {tg_mint(tg_GETSTATUS); \
     lb = tg_BUTTONS & 1; rb = (tg_BUTTONS & 2) >> 1;}

/* get and set mouse position */

#define tg_getmousepos(mx, my); \
    {tg_mint(tg_GETSTATUS); mx = tg_MOUSEX, my = tg_MOUSEY;}

#define tg_setmousepos(mx, my); \
    {tg_NEWMOUSEX = mx, tg_NEWMOUSEY = my; \
     tg_mint(tg_SETPOS);}

/* mouse/keyboard wait-for-something-to-happen macro */

#define tg_mousewait(); {int tg_mb; while(!kbhit())\
                { tg_mint(tg_GETSTATUS);\
                tg_mb = tg_BUTTONS;      \
                while(tg_BUTTONS != 0)   \
                {tg_mint(tg_GETSTATUS);}\
                switch(tg_mb)            \
                {   case 1: ungetch(13); break;\
                    case 2: ungetch(27); }}}

#define tg_getmouse(); {do {tg_mint(tg_GETSTATUS);} \
                while(tg_BUTTONS == 0);      \
                do {tg_mint(tg_GETSTATUS);} \
                while(tg_BUTTONS != 0);}
```

Microsoft and Borland Graphics Support

At the time of this writing—and probably for the foreseeable future—Microsoft and Borland produce the leading C/C++ compilers. Because the programming community is about evenly split between these two products, you will often want your programs to be compatible with both compilers. Nowadays, C has become a well-standardized language, so you can pretty much count on the fact that most of your C code is portable between compilers. Graphics functions are another story, however. Though advanced Windowing operating systems have standardized graphics libraries, DOS graphics calls have no standardization whatsoever. Each graphics library has it's own idiosyncrasies.

Of course, TransGraphics' raison d'être is to help you overcome these idiosyncrasies and develop graphics programs that are portable between compilers. Being the inquiring sort that buys a book like *Tricks of the Graphics Gurus*, though, I'm sure you'd like to know what kind of smoke and mirrors TransGraphics has to use in order to achieve its magic.

You've already encountered a few peculiarities of individual graphics libraries: I mentioned in Chapter 2, "Graphics for Everyone," that Microsoft C forces text output to a grid of character-sized rows and columns, whereas Borland enables you to write text to any pixel location. Also, you know that Borland and Microsoft use different storage formats for color palettes, and that each supports a different set of video modes.

In the next few sections, I explain these and other differences in detail, with side-by-side comparisons of the Microsoft and Borland TransGraphics macros and functions. The differences fall into four basic categories:

- Graphics modes and startup procedure
- Coordinate systems and clipping regions
- Function names and shape description method
- Color palette format

I'll cover each of these, with side-by-side **Working Code** comparing the Microsoft way with the Borland way. Then, I'll discuss other graphics libraries and the code for GX Graphics support.

Graphics Modes and Startup Procedure

Each compiler contains its own codes for each video mode it can access. TransGraphics calls the list of Microsoft modes `tg_msvmode`, and the list of Borland Graphics Interface (BGI) modes `tg_bgimode`. Under both compilers, TransGraphics keeps the text descriptions (displayed by `tg_pickmode()` for the user's perusal) in an array called `tg_modedesc`. The keypress codes for each mode reside in `tg_modecode`.

Setting a video mode in Microsoft Graphics is quite straightforward: you simply tell the Microsoft _setvideomode() function which mode you want. Setting a mode with the BGI is a bit more complex because Borland places its video drivers in separate files. You must distribute the appropriate .BGI driver file along with your program, and when your program runs, it must check to ensure that the .BGI file it needs is available. This is a nice idea: the sentiment being that users can update their video drivers without having to recompile or replace the graphics programs themselves. The practical reality of the situation, however, is that you usually end up with four dozen copies of the EGAVGA.BGI driver file all over your hard disk, and yet it seems to never be where you need it when you need it after you move some programs around.

Whether you're a BGI fan or foe, you'll still need to take the extra step of creating a BGI driver variable and including its address when you use the Borland initgraph() function to set a video mode.

So, setting the video mode in Turbo C isn't really much different than setting it in Microsoft C—as hardships go in life, the creation of an extra integer variable rates on the small side. When it comes to automatically detecting the best video mode available, the differences are more pronounced. The tg_detectmode() function under Microsoft C simply uses the _getvideoconfig() function and switch(vi.adapter) statement to thumb through the possibilities for video adapters and choose the best mode for each. To detect the best video mode under Turbo C, you call the detectgraph() function and check graphresult() for errors to make sure it found a valid driver. TransGraphics takes the extra step of translating the suggested video mode back into a mode number that it can use to index the tg_modecode and tg_modedesc arrays.

Once tg_setvideomode() has set up the video mode, it initializes the tg_scrnx, tg_scrny, and tg_ncolors variables. In Microsoft C, these values emerge from a structure returned by _getvideoconfig(), and in Turbo C you get the values by querying the getmaxx(), getmaxy(), and getmaxcolor() functions. The TransGraphics variables tg_charx and tg_chary are always 8 in Turbo C because the BGI uses the 8×8 system font by default. In Microsoft C, tg_charx and tg_chary are computed from the size of the screen and the number of text rows and columns.

Although Microsoft C version 6.0 and Turbo C++ Version 3.0 or earlier did not support Super VGA modes, the most recent incarnations of both compilers have added VESA Super VGA support. The following TransGraphics headers include support for Microsoft Super VGA modes up to 1280×1024 with 256 colors. However, the Borland/Turbo C support header only lists modes up to standard VGA to maintain compatibility with Turbo C++ 3.0, which is still the most inexpensive current version of the compiler. You can easily add support for other BGI drivers and modes by modifying the `tg_NMODES`, `tg_BGIMODE`, `tg_MODECODE`, and `tg_MODEDESC` definitions in TGTC.H.

Screen Control and Drawing Operations

Microsoft and Borland handle graphics screen control and drawing operations in a very similar fashion. Even the names of some functions are almost (but never completely) identical. About the biggest difference that TransGraphics must reconcile is the fact that Microsoft describes an ellipse by giving the corner points of a rectangle that just touches it on all sides, whereas Borland specifies the center, width, and height instead. TransGraphics uses the Microsoft style and uses a simple calculation in the Borland macro to compute center/width/height from the bounding box.

Microsoft and Borland also use different storage formats for polygon arrays. This time, TransGraphics uses its own storage format (borrowed from Genus GX Graphics), which eliminates the need for compiler-specific types such as Microsoft's `xycoord` and Borland's `bgi_poly`. The TransGraphics format is simply a two-dimensional array of integer, stored in the order: x1,y1; x2,y2; x3,y3; and so forth. The `tg_fillpoly()` macros translate from TransGraphics polygons into Microsoft or Borland polygons, whereas the `tg_drawpoly()` function just uses line drawing functions to play connect-the-dots without any translation at all.

A final nit-picky difference comes up in the `tg_outtext()` macros: Borland's `outtext()` function doesn't fill in the background area behind the text, so writing one text string on top of another results in gibberish on-screen. TransGraphics remedies this by using the Borland `bar()` function to paint a black rectangle behind the text. Microsoft's `_outtext()` function does this automatically.

Palette Format

The palette control macros and `tg_colorcycle()` function point up the most significant difference between Microsoft and Borland graphics. Actually, the difference is between Microsoft and the rest of the PC universe. Instead of using the standard basic input output system (BIOS) format for storing palettes, Microsoft uses a more compact format.

Furthermore, the BIOS standard has a different format for EGA and VGA palettes, whereas Microsoft uses the same format for both. (To complicate matters, Borland's EGAVGA.BGI driver treats EGA modes on a VGA as if they were VGA modes.) To point up the differences between handling palette control through the video BIOS and handling palette control through a proprietary format and library, I've used a BIOS palette and BIOS palette calls in the Borland/Turbo C support files, and Microsoft's library functions and format in the Microsoft support files. Borland does offer a (somewhat limited) selection of palette control functions, but TransGraphics ignores these and does all the palette work itself.

In case you want to manipulate the palette in unforeseen ways, you should know how each of these storage formats works.

The BIOS format for VGA and Super VGA 16- and 256-color palettes is an array of 8-bit integers (type `char`), where `tg_palette[i * 3]` is the red component of color i, `tg_palette[i * 3 + 1]` is the green component, and `tg_palette[i * 3 + 2]` is the blue component. Each component is actually a 6-bit number (value from 0 to 63), with the highest two bits always zeros.

The BIOS format for EGA palettes is simply one `char` for each color. The 8 bits of the integer are arranged like this:

00rrggbb

where *rr* means a two-bit value for the red channel, *gg* is two bits for green, and *bb* is two bits for blue. The Microsoft palettes are stored in an array of `long` (32-bit) integers, where the bits for VGA are arranged like this:

00000000 00bbbbbb 00gggggg 00rrrrrr

where *bbbbbb* is a 6-bit value for blue, *gggggg* is a 6-bit value for green, and *rrrrrr* is a 6-bit value for red. The EGA palettes are stored exactly the same way, except that only the top two bits for each color matter, and the other four bits are ignored.

The `colorcycle()` function serves as a good example of how to work with the `tg_palette` array directly to speed up palette control within your programs. If all this palette format madness seems overwhelming, remember that you can always use the BIOS routines in the TGTC.H file with any compiler. (You can even substitute them into the TransGraphics Microsoft support files if you don't care about the small speed increase offered by Microsoft's more compact format.)

Working Code: Supporting the Giants

TransGraphics uses two files to support each graphics library: a header file with variables and macro definitions and a C source code file with the functions `tg_pickmode()`, `tg_detectmode()`, `_tg_setvideomode()`, `tg_closedown()`, and `tg_colorcycle()`. (All operations except these four functions are implemented as macros.)

The TGMS.H and TGMS.C files listed first provide Microsoft support. The TGTC.H and TGTC.C files provide Borland/Turbo C/BGI support. Notice that both headers `#include TGMOUSE.H` (listed previously) for mouse support.

Listing B.1. The TransGraphics Microsoft Graphics support header.

```
/* TGMS.H
 *
 * TransGraphics version 1.0
 * from Tricks of the Graphics Gurus
 *
 * Microsoft Graphics Library support header file
 * See the file TG.TXT for more information.
 */

#include <graph.h>                         /* for graphics */
#include <dos.h>        /* for internal register definitions */

#define tg_NMODES 16             /* Number of video modes */

/* If this is the main TransGraphics module,
   define the initialization values for the arrays */

#ifdef TGMAIN
#define EXT

/* Microsoft C video mode codes */

#define tg_MSVMODE = {0, _HRESBW, _HERCMONO, \
                _MRES4COLOR, _MRES16COLOR, _MRES256COLOR, \
                             _ERESCOLOR, \
                _VRES2COLOR, _VRES16COLOR, _VRES256COLOR, \
                             _SRES16COLOR, _SRES256COLOR, \
```

continues

747

Listing B.1. continued

```
                                    _XRES16COLOR, _XRES256COLOR, \
                                    _ZRES16COLOR, _ZRES256COLOR}

/* Video mode command line switches */

#define tg_MODECODE = {' ', 'C', 'H', \
                       'L', 'O', 'A', \
                            'E', \
                       'M', 'V', '1', \
                            '2', '3', \
                            '4', '5', \
                            '6', '7'}


 /* Text descriptions of each video mode */

#define tg_MODEDESC = {"NONE", \
                       "CGA mono    640x200    2-color",    \
                       "Hercules    720x348    2-color",    \
                                                            \
                       "CGA lo-res  320x200    4-color",    \
                       "EGA lo-res  320x200    16-color",   \
                       "VGA lo-res  320x200    256-color",  \
                                                            \
                       "EGA hi-res  640x350    16-color",   \
                                                            \
                       "VGA mono    640x480    2-color",    \
                       "VGA hi-res  640x480    16-color",   \
                       "VESA 101h   640x480    256-color",  \
                                                            \
                       "VESA 102h   800x600    16-color",   \
                       "VESA 103h   800x600    256-color",  \
                                                            \
                       "VESA 104h   1024x768   16-color",   \
                       "VESA 105h   1024x768   256-color",  \
                                                            \
                       "VESA 106h   1280x1024 16-color",    \
                       "VESA 107h   1280x1024 256-color"}
#endif
```

```
/* If this is not the main TransGraphics module,
   reference all variables as extern */

#ifndef TGMAIN
#define EXT extern
#define tg_MSVMODE
#define tg_MODECODE
#define tg_MODEDESC
#endif

#include "tgmouse.h"              /* for generic mouse macros */

EXT int tg_scrnx, tg_scrny, /* size of the screen in pixels */
    tg_viewx, tg_viewy,    /* size of the viewport in pixels */
    tg_charx, tg_chary,    /* width and height of text chars */
    tg_ncolors,            /* number of colors in the palette */
    tg_videomode;              /* just what you think it is */

/* Video mode codes and descriptions */

EXT int tg_msvmode[] tg_MSVMODE;
EXT char tg_modecode[tg_NMODES + 1] tg_MODECODE,
         tg_modedesc[tg_NMODES + 1][32] tg_MODEDESC;

/* function prototypes */

EXT int tg_setvideomode(int vmode);        /* set video mode */
EXT int tg_detectmode(void);        /* detect best video mode */
EXT void tg_pickmode(void);      /* ask user to confirm mode */
EXT void tg_closedown(void);             /* die gracefully */
EXT void tg_colorcycle(int step);    /* animate the palette */

/*************************************************************/
/* Graphics Screen Control                                 */

/* go back to text mode */

#define tg_settextmode() _setvideomode(_DEFAULTMODE)

/* set and get the viewport corners */
```

continues

749

Listing B.1. continued

```
EXT int tg_vx1, tg_vy1, tg_vx2, tg_vy2;

#define tg_setviewport(x1, y1, x2, y2); \
     {_setviewport(x1, y1, x2, y2); \
      tg_vx1 = x1; tg_vy1 = y1; tg_vx2 = x2; tg_vy2 = y2; \
      tg_viewx = tg_vx2 - tg_vx1; tg_viewy = tg_vy2 - tg_vy1;}

#define tg_getviewport(x1, y1, x2, y2) \
     (x1 = tg_vx1, y1 = tg_vy1, \
      x2 = tg_vx2, y2 = tg_vy2)

/* clear the viewport */

#define tg_clearviewport() _clearscreen(_GVIEWPORT)

/* clear the screen */

#define tg_clearscreen() _clearscreen(_GCLEARSCREEN)

/***************************************************************/
/* Drawing Operations                                        */

/* set or recall the current color for drawing and text */

#define tg_setcolor(x); {_setcolor(x); _settextcolor(x);}

#define tg_getcolor()   _getcolor()

/* read or write the color of one pixel */

#define tg_getpixel(x1, y1)    _getpixel(x1, y1)

#define tg_putpixel(x1, y1, c) \
    {int tempc; tempc = _getcolor(); \
     _setcolor(c); _setpixel(x1, y1); _setcolor(tempc);}

/* draw a line */

#define tg_drawline(x1, y1, x2, y2)  \
    _moveto(x1, y1), _lineto(x2, y2)
```

```
/* output one line of text to current position */

#define tg_outtext(x)   _outtext(x)

/* move current drawing and text cursor position */

#define tg_moveto(x1, y1) \
    {_moveto(x1, y1); \
     _settextposition((y1)/tg_chary+1, (x1)/tg_charx+1);}

/* draw a line from the current position to a new position */

#define tg_lineto(x1, y1) _lineto(x1, y1)

/* draw outlined rectangle */

#define tg_drawrect(x1, y1, x2, y2) \
    _rectangle(_GBORDER, x1, y1, x2, y2)

/* fill a rectangle */

#define tg_fillrect(x1, y1, x2, y2) \
     _rectangle(_GFILLINTERIOR, x1, y1, x2, y2)

/* draw a filled polygon */

#define tg_NPTS  64     /* Maximum number of polygon points */
EXT struct xycoord tg_op[tg_NPTS];   /* for polygon filling */

#define tg_fillpoly(poly, n) \
    {int tg_i; for (tg_i = 0; tg_i < n; tg_i++)  \
     tg_op[tg_i].xcoord = poly[tg_i][0], \
     tg_op[tg_i].ycoord = poly[tg_i][1]; \
     _polygon(_GFILLINTERIOR, tg_op, n);}

/* draw a polygon outline */

#define tg_drawpoly(poly, n); \
    {int i; \
     _moveto(poly[n - 1][0], poly[n - 1][1]); \
     if (n > 2) for(i = 0; i <= n - 1; i++) \
```

continues

Listing B.1. continued

```
    _lineto(poly[i][0], poly[i][1]);}

/* draw a filled ellipse */

#define tg_fillellipse(x1, y1, x2, y2) \
    _ellipse(_GFILLINTERIOR, x1, y1, x2, y2)

/* draw an outlined ellipse */

#define tg_drawellipse(x1, y1, x2, y2) \
    _ellipse(_GBORDER, x1, y1, x2, y2)

/* fill a region bounded by a color */

#define tg_floodfill(x, y, c) _floodfill(x, y, c)

/**************************************************************/
/* Bitmaps and Animation                                    */

/* store images in char buffers */

typedef char far *IMAGEBUFFER;

/* allocate an image buffer */

#define tg_makeimagebuffer(img, x, y) \
    (img = (char far *) \
        malloc((size_t) _imagesize(0, 0, x, y)))

/* store the screen into the picture buffer */

#define tg_getimage(img, x1, y1, x2, y2) \
    _getimage(x1, y1, x2, y2, img)

/* display the picture from the buffer to the screen */

#define tg_putimage(img, x, y) \
    _putimage(x, y, img, _getwritemode())

/* free up an image buffer */
```

```
#define tg_freeimagebuffer(img) free((void *) img)

/* turn XOR mode on and off */

#define tg_startxor() _setwritemode(_GXOR)
#define tg_endxor()   _setwritemode(_GPSET)

/***************************************************************/
/* Color Palette Control                                    */

/* Make a MS format palette big enough for 256 VGA colors    */

EXT long tg_palette[256];

EXT union REGS xregs;          /* registers for BIOS access */
EXT struct SREGS sregs;

/* Are we in an EGA 16-color mode? */

#define tg_egamode() ((tg_videomode == _ERESCOLOR) || \
                      (tg_videomode == _MRES16COLOR))
#define tg_vgamode() (!(tg_egamode()) && (tg_ncolors >= 16))

/* set one color value in the palette */

#define tg_setpalcolor(iclr); \
    {outp(0x3C8, iclr); \
    outp(0x3C9, (tg_palette[iclr]) & 0x3F); \
    outp(0x3C9, (tg_palette[iclr] >> 8) & 0x3F); \
    outp(0x3C9, (tg_palette[iclr] >> 16) & 0x3F);}

/* set the whole palette all at once
   NOTE: The Microsoft _remapallpalette() function is
   incredibly, unbelievably, excruciatingly slow! */

#define tg_setallpalcolors() \
    {int i; long *tg_p; tg_p = tg_palette; \
     for (i = 0; i < tg_ncolors; i++) \
     {   outp(0x3C8, i); \
         outp(0x3C9, (*tg_p) & 0x3F); \
         outp(0x3C9, (*tg_p >> 8) & 0x3F); \
```

continues

753

Listing B.1. continued

```
            outp(0x3C9, (*tg_p >> 16) & 0x3F); \
            tg_p++;}}

#define tg_getallpalcolors() \
    { int gapi; \
      for (gapi = 0; gapi < tg_ncolors; gapi++) \
          tg_getpalcolor(gapi); }

/* read one color value in the palette
   Microsoft C doesn't have a function to do it, so use
   the BIOS interrupt 10H, function 10H
   (WARNING: this does not work on some EGA systems!) */

#define tg_getpalcolor(iclr) \
    {   if (tg_egamode()) \
        {   xregs.x.ax = 0x1000; \
            xregs.h.bh = tg_palette[iclr]; \
            xregs.h.bl = iclr; \
            int86(0x10, &xregs, &xregs); \
        } \
        else if (tg_vgamode()) \
        {   if (tg_ncolors == 16) \
            {   xregs.x.ax  = 0x1007; \
                xregs.h.bl = iclr; \
                int86(0x10, &xregs, &xregs); \
                xregs.x.bx = xregs.h.bh & 0x03F; \
            } \
            else xregs.x.bx = iclr; \
            xregs.x.ax = 0x1015; \
            int86(0x10, &xregs, &xregs); \
            tg_palette[iclr] = (((long) \
                        ((xregs.h.cl) << 8 \
                        ¦ (xregs.h.ch)) << 8) \
                        ¦ (xregs.h.dh)); \
        } \
    }

/* make a palette color from red, green, and blue values */
```

```
#define tg_makepalcolor(iclr, red, green, blue) \
    {   tg_palette[iclr] = (((long) ((blue) << 8 \
                        ¦ (green)) << 8) \
                        ¦ (red)); \
        tg_setpalcolor(iclr); \
    }

/* split a palette color into red, green, and blue values */

#define tg_splitpalcolor(iclr, red, green, blue) \
    {   red = tg_palette[iclr] & 0x3F; \
        green = (tg_palette[iclr] >> 8) & 0x3F; \
        blue = (tg_palette[iclr] >> 16) & 0x3F; \
    }
```

Listing B.2. The TransGraphics Microsoft Graphics support functions.

```
/* TGMS.C
 *
 * TransGraphics
 * from Tricks of the Graphics Gurus
 *
 * Microsoft Graphics Library support functions
 * See the file TG.TXT for more information.
 */

#define TGMAIN        /* Tell TGMS.H this is the main module */
#include "tgms.h"         /* Microsoft support header file */
#undef TGMAIN

/* automatically detect the best video mode */

int tg_detectmode(void)
{   int i;
    struct videoconfig vi;
    _getvideoconfig(&vi);
    switch(vi.adapter)
```

continues

755

Listing B.2. continued

```
{   case _MDPA: i = 0;
               break;
    case _CGA:  i = 1;
               break;
    case _HGC:  i = 2;
               break;
    case _MCGA: i = 5;
               break;
    case _EGA:  i = 6;
               break;
    case _VGA:  i = 8;
               break;
    case _SVGA: i = 9;
               break;
}
    return i;
}

/* Set the video mode and get the video configuration */

int tg_setvideomode(int vmode)
{   int i;
    struct videoconfig vc;
    if (vmode != 0)        /* if vmode isn't 0, use new mode */
        tg_videomode = tg_msvmode[vmode];
    if (_setvideomode(tg_videomode) == 0) return(0);
    _getvideoconfig(&vc);   /* get video configuration data */
    tg_scrnx = vc.numxpixels;
    tg_scrny = vc.numypixels;
    tg_ncolors = vc.numcolors;

    /* calculate text width and height */

    tg_charx = vc.numxpixels / vc.numtextcols;
    tg_chary = vc.numypixels / vc.numtextrows;

    /* set the viewport to the whole screen */

    tg_setviewport(0, 0, tg_scrnx - 1, tg_scrny - 1);
    tg_setcolor(15 % tg_ncolors);
```

```c
        if (tg_ncolors >= 16)          /* get the palette colors */
            tg_getallpalcolors();
        _wrapon(_GWRAPOFF);        /* turn text line wrapping off */
     return(1);
}

/* Ask user to pick a video mode
   (this routine works unmodified for all
   libraries and compilers as long as tg_modecode[]
   and tg_modedesc[] are defined) */

void tg_pickmode(void)
{   int i, a, trythis;
    printf("\nPlease choose a video mode, "
           "or press Q to quit.\n");
    trythis = tg_detectmode();
    for (i = 1; i <= tg_NMODES; i++)
    {   if (i == trythis) printf("\nTRY THIS ONE -->");
        else printf("\n                 ");
        printf(" %c    %s", tg_modecode[i], tg_modedesc[i]);
    }
    printf("\nYour choice: ");
    while(1)
    {   a = toupper(getch());
        if ((a == 'Q') || (a == 27))
        {   printf("Quit\n\n");
            exit(0);
        }
        for (i = 1; i <= tg_NMODES; i++)
        {   if (tg_modecode[i] == a)
            {   printf("%c", a);
                if (tg_setvideomode(i) != 1)
                {   printf("\nUnable to set graphics mode:"
                           " %s\n", tg_modedesc[i]);
                    exit(0);
                }
                return;
            }
        }
    }
}
```

continues

Listing B.2. continued

```
/* shut down MS Graphics */

void tg_closedown(void)
{   if (tg_mouseon) tg_hidemouse();    /* hide mouse cursor */
    tg_settextmode();                  /* go back to text mode */
}

/* animate the screen by rotating the palette colors
   until a key is hit (NOTE: Microsoft palettes are different
   than anyone else's, so this routine is different than
   the BIOS-compatible one used for other libraries.) */

void tg_colorcycle(int step)
{   int last,                    /* location of last color(s) */
        nbytes;                  /* number of bytes in each step */
    long *firstbuf,           /* buffer to hold first color(s) */
        *pfirst, *psecond;      /* first and second color */
    nbytes = sizeof(long) * step;
    firstbuf = (long *) malloc(nbytes);  /* allocate buffer */
    pfirst = tg_palette;      /* precompute these for speed */
    psecond = tg_palette + step;

    /* don't rotate the background color in VGA modes */

    if (tg_vgamode()) ++pfirst, ++psecond;
    last = tg_ncolors - step;
    while(!kbhit())        /* Keep rotating until a keypress */
    {
        /* copy the first colors(s) into firstbuf */

        memcpy(firstbuf, pfirst, nbytes);

        /* move each color in the palette down one position */

        memmove(pfirst, psecond, sizeof(long) * last);

        /* copy firstbuf into the last part of the palette */

        memcpy(tg_palette + last, firstbuf, nbytes);
```

```
        /* change all the colors on the screen at once */

        tg_setallpalcolors();
    }
    free((void *) firstbuf);          /* free up the buffer */
}
```

Listing B.3. The TransGraphics Borland Graphics Interface support header.

```
/* TGTC.H
 *
 * TransGraphics
 * from Tricks of the Graphics Gurus
 *
 * Borland BGI Library support header file
 * See the file TG.TXT for more information.
 */

#include <graphics.h>  /* for graphics */
#include <alloc.h>      /* for memory allocation */
#include <dos.h>        /* for internal register access */

#define tg_NMODES 6     /* Number of video modes */

/* If this is the main TransGraphics module,
   define the initialization values for the arrays */

#ifdef TGMAIN
#define EXT

/* BGI video mode codes */

#define tg_BGIMODE = {0, CGAHI, HERCMONOHI, \
                   CGAC0, EGAHI, \
                   MCGAHI, VGAHI}

/* Video mode command line switches */

#define tg_MODECODE = {' ', 'C', 'H', 'O', 'E', 'M', 'V'}

/* Text descriptions of video modes */
```

continues

Listing B.3. continued

```
#define tg_MODEDESC = {"NONE", \
                        "CGA mono    640x200    2-color",   \
                        "Hercules    720x348    2-color",   \
                                                            \
                        "EGA lo-res  320x200    16-color",  \
                                                            \
                        "EGA hi-res  640x350    16-color",  \
                                                            \
                        "VGA mono    640x480    2-color",   \
                        "VGA hi-res  640x480    16-color"}
#endif

/* If this is not the main TransGraphics module,
   reference all variables as extern */


#ifndef TGMAIN
#define EXT extern
#define tg_BGIMODE
#define tg_MODECODE
#define tg_MODEDESC
#endif

#include "tgmouse.h"        /* for generic mouse macros */

/* create and initialize the video mode stuff defined above */

EXT int tg_bgimode[tg_NMODES + 1] tg_BGIMODE;
EXT char tg_modecode[tg_NMODES + 1] tg_MODECODE,
         tg_modedesc[tg_NMODES + 1][32] tg_MODEDESC;

EXT int tg_scrnx, tg_scrny,      .  /* resolution in pixels */
    tg_viewx, tg_viewy,             /* viewport size in pixels */
    tg_charx, tg_chary,             /* size of a text character */
    tg_ncolors,                 /* number of colors in the palette */
    tg_bgidriver,                   /* BGI driver identifier */
    tg_videomode,               /* guess. -- yep, you're right */
    tg_ret;                     /* return code for BGI functions */

/* functions prototypes -- for that squeaky clean ANSI look */
```

```
EXT int tg_setvideomode(int vmode);        /* set video mode */
EXT int tg_detectmode(void);        /* detect best video mode */
EXT void tg_pickmode(void);        /* ask user to confirm mode */
EXT void tg_closedown(void);              /* die gracefully */
EXT void tg_colorcycle(int step);          /* animate palette */

/*************************************************************/
/* Graphics Screen Control                                  */

/* go back to text mode */

#define tg_settextmode() restorecrtmode()

/* set and get the viewport corners */

#define tg_setviewport(x1, y1, x2, y2); \
    {setviewport(x1, y1, x2, y2, 1); \
     tg_viewx = (x2) - (x1); tg_viewy = (y2) - (y1);}

#define tg_getviewport(x1, y1, x2, y2); \
    {struct viewporttype tg_vi; \
     getviewsettings(&tg_vi); \
     x1 = tg_vi.left, y1 = tg_vi.top, \
     x2 = tg_vi.right, y2 = tg_vi.bottom;}

/* clear the viewport */

#define tg_clearviewport() clearviewport()

/*  clear the screen */

#define tg_clearscreen()  cleardevice()

/*************************************************************/
/* Drawing Operations                                       */

/* set and get the current color */

#define tg_setcolor(x);  {setcolor(x), setfillstyle(1, x);}
#define tg_getcolor() getcolor()
```

continues

761

Listing B.3. continued

```
/* read and write the color of a pixel */

#define tg_getpixel(x1, y1)      getpixel(x1, y1)
#define tg_putpixel(x1, y1, c)  putpixel(x1, y1, c)

/* draw a line */

#define tg_drawline(x1, y1, x2, y2) line(x1, y1, x2, y2)

/* draw outlined rectangle */

#define tg_drawrect(x1, y1, x2, y2) rectangle(x1, y1, x2, y2)

/* output one line of text to current position
   (the bar() function is used to clear the area where text
   would go first, since BGI doesn't do this automatically) */

#define tg_outtext(x)  {int xnow, ynow, cnow; \
                        xnow = getx(); ynow = gety(); \
                        cnow = getcolor(); \
                        setfillstyle(1, 0); \
                        bar(xnow, ynow,           \
                        xnow + textwidth(x), \
                        ynow + textheight(x));\
                        setfillstyle(1, cnow); \
                        outtext(x);}

/* move current drawing and text cursor position */

#define tg_moveto(x1, y1) moveto(x1, y1)

/* draw a line from the current position to a new position */

#define tg_lineto(x1, y1) lineto(x1, y1)

/* draw a filled polygon */

#define tg_NPTS 64      /* Max number of points in a polygon */
EXT int tg_bgipoly[tg_NPTS];          /* for polygon filling */
```

```
#define tg_fillpoly(poly, n) \
        {int i, j; \
         for (i = 0, j = 0; i < n; i++)  \
         tg_bgipoly[j++] = poly[i][0], \
         tg_bgipoly[j++] = poly[i][1]; \
         fillpoly(n, tg_bgipoly);}

/* draw a polygon outline */

#define tg_drawpoly(poly, n); \
    {int i; \
     if (n > 2) \
     for(i = 0; i < n - 1; i++) \
     line(poly[i][0], poly[i][1], \
     poly[i + 1][0], poly[i + 1][1]); \
     line(poly[0][0], poly[0][1], \
     poly[n - 1][0], poly[n - 1][1]);}

/* draw a filled ellipse
   (The calculations translate the TransGraphics
   "bounding box" coordinates into BGI center/height/width) */

#define tg_fillellipse(x1, y1, x2, y2) \
   fillellipse(((x1) + (x2)) / 2, ((y1) + (y2)) /2, \
               ((x2) - (x1)) / 2, ((y2) - (y1)) /2)

/* fill a region bounded by a color */

#define tg_floodfill(x, y, c) floodfill(x, y, c)

/* draw an outlined ellipse */

#define tg_drawellipse(x1, y1, x2, y2) \
    ellipse(((x1) + (x2)) / 2, ((y1) + (y2)) /2, 0, 360, \
            ((x2) - (x1)) / 2, ((y2) - (y1)) /2)

/* fill a rectangle, or outline if bkgd color */

#define tg_fillrect(x1, y1, x2, y2) bar(x1, y1, x2, y2)
```

continues

763

Listing B.3. continued

```
/*****************************************************************/
/* Bitmaps and Animation                                        */

/* store images in untyped buffers */

#define IMAGEBUFFER void *

/* allocate an image buffer */

#define tg_makeimagebuffer(img, x, y) \
     (img = (void *) malloc((size_t) imagesize(0, 0, x, y)))

/* store the screen into the picture buffer */

#define tg_getimage(img, x1, y1, x2, y2) \
    getimage(x1, y1, x2, y2, img)

/* display the picture from the buffer to the screen */

#define tg_putimage(img, x, y) \
    putimage(x, y, img, tg_writemode)

/* free up an image buffer */

#define tg_freeimagebuffer(img) free(img)

/* turn XOR mode on and off */

EXT int tg_writemode;               /* keep track of XOR mode */

#define tg_startxor() setwritemode(tg_writemode = XOR_PUT)
#define tg_endxor()   setwritemode(tg_writemode = COPY_PUT)


/*****************************************************************/
/* Color Palette Control                                        */

/* Are we in an EGA 16-color mode? */
/* Because of a strange quirk (we won't use the "B" word)
 * in the EGAVGA.BGI driver, EGA palettes act like VGA
 * palettes on VGA systems. If you have a true EGA, add
 * the next line and comment out the one after it. */
```

```
/* #define tg_egamode() (tg_videomode == EGAHI) */
#define tg_egamode() (tg_videomode == 0)

/* Are we in a VGA mode? */

#define tg_vgamode() (!(tg_egamode()) && (tg_ncolors >= 16))

/* A BIOS format palette big enough for 256 colors */

EXT unsigned char tg_palette[256 * 3];

EXT union REGS xregs;            /* registers for BIOS access */
EXT struct SREGS sregs;

/* set one color value in the palette */

/* Borland provides palette control functions, but
   we'll use the BIOS instead, since the BGI doesn't
   have all the functions we need and uses a slightly
   different palette format. Note that you can do this
   faster with the outp() call exemplified in TGMS.H
   by simply cutting and pasting the #define from that
   file into this file. I put this slower way here
   because I thought you'd like to see both ways. */

#define tg_setpalcolor(iclr) \
    {   if (tg_vgamode())\
        {   xregs.x.ax = 0x1007;\
            xregs.h.bl = iclr;\
            int86(0x10, &xregs, &xregs);\
            xregs.x.ax = 0x1010;\
            xregs.x.bx = xregs.h.bh & 0x03F;\
            xregs.h.dh = tg_palette[iclr * 3];\
            xregs.h.ch = tg_palette[iclr * 3 + 1];\
            xregs.h.cl = tg_palette[iclr * 3 + 2];\
            int86(0x10, &xregs, &xregs);\
        }\
        if (tg_egamode())\
        {   xregs.x.ax = 0x1000;\
            xregs.h.bh = tg_palette[iclr];\
            xregs.h.bl = iclr;\
            int86(0x10, &xregs, &xregs);\
```

continues

Listing B.3. continued

```
        }\
    }

/* set the whole palette all at once */

#define tg_setallpalcolors() \
{   int i, j; \
    for (j = 0, i = 0; j < 16; j++) \
    {   if (tg_vgamode()) \
        {   xregs.x.ax = 0x1007; \
            xregs.h.bl = j;                    \
            int86(0x10, &xregs, &xregs);   \
            xregs.x.ax = 0x1010;             \
            xregs.x.bx = xregs.h.bh & 0x03F; \
            xregs.h.dh = tg_palette[i++]; \
            xregs.h.ch = tg_palette[i++]; \
            xregs.h.cl = tg_palette[i++]; \
            int86(0x10, &xregs, &xregs);   \
        }                                    \
        if (tg_egamode())                    \
        {   xregs.x.ax = 0x1000;             \
            xregs.h.bh = tg_palette[j];      \
            xregs.h.bl = j;                  \
            int86(0x10, &xregs, &xregs);     \
        }                                    \
    }                                        \
}

#define tg_getallpalcolors() \
    { int gapi; \
      for (gapi = 0; gapi < tg_ncolors; gapi++) \
        tg_getpalcolor(gapi); }

/* read one color value in the palette
   (WARNING: this does not work on some EGA systems!) */

#define tg_getpalcolor(iclr) \
    {   if (tg_egamode()) \
        {   xregs.x.ax = 0x1000; \
            xregs.h.bh = tg_palette[iclr]; \
```

```
                xregs.h.bl = iclr; \
                int86(0x10, &xregs, &xregs); \
            } \
            else if (tg_vgamode()) \
            {   if (tg_ncolors == 16) \
                {   xregs.x.ax  = 0x1007; \
                    xregs.h.bl = iclr; \
                    int86(0x10, &xregs, &xregs); \
                    xregs.x.bx = xregs.h.bh & 0x03F; \
                } \
                else xregs.x.bx = iclr; \
                xregs.x.ax = 0x1015; \
                int86(0x10, &xregs, &xregs); \
                tg_palette[iclr * 3] = xregs.h.dh; \
                tg_palette[iclr * 3 + 1] = xregs.h.ch; \
                tg_palette[iclr * 3 + 2] = xregs.h.cl; \
            } \
    }

/* make a palette color from red, green, and blue values */

#define tg_makepalcolor(iclr, red, green, blue) \
    {if (tg_egamode()) \
        tg_palette[iclr] = ((red & 0x20) >> 3) +\
                        ((red & 0x10) << 1) +\
                        ((green & 0x20) >> 4)+\
                        (green & 0x10) +\
                        ((blue & 0x20) >> 5) +\
                        ((blue & 0x10) >> 1); \
    else if (tg_vgamode()) \
        tg_palette[(iclr) * 3] = red, \
        tg_palette[(iclr) * 3 + 1] = green, \
        tg_palette[(iclr) * 3 + 2] = blue;  \
    tg_setpalcolor((iclr));}

/* split a palette color into red, green, and blue values */

#define tg_splitpalcolor(iclr, red, green, blue) \
    {   tg_getpalcolor(iclr);        \
        if (tg_egamode())    \
        {   int k;           \
```

continues

767

Listing B.3. continued

```
            k = tg_palette[iclr]; \
            red = ((k & 0x04) << 3) + ((k & 0x20) >> 1); \
            green = ((k & 0x02) << 4) + (k & 0x10);       \
            blue = ((k & 0x01) << 5) + ((k & 0x08) << 1); \
        }                                                 \
        else if (tg_vgamode())       \
            blue = tg_palette[(iclr) * 3], \
            green = tg_palette[(iclr) * 3 + 1], \
            red = tg_palette[(iclr) * 3 + 2]; \
    }
```

Listing B.4. The TransGraphics Borland Graphics Interface support functions.

```
/* TGTC.C
 *
 * TransGraphics
 * from Tricks of the Graphics Gurus
 *
 * Borland BGI Library support functions
 * See the file TG.TXT for more information.
 */

#define TGMAIN
#include "tgtc.h"
#undef TGMAIN

/* automatically detect best video mode */

int tg_detectmode(void)
{   int i, suggestmode;

  /* detect graphics hardware available */
   detectgraph(&tg_bgidriver, &suggestmode);

   /* read result of detectgraph call */
   tg_ret = graphresult();
   if (tg_ret != grOk)   /* an error occurred */
```

```
    { printf("Graphics error: %s\n", grapherrormsg(tg_ret));
      printf("Press any key to continue.");
      getch();
      return(0); /* terminate with an error code */
    }
    for (i = 1; i <= tg_NMODES; i++)
        if (tg_bgimode[i] == suggestmode) break;
    if (i > tg_NMODES) i = 0;
    return i;
}

/* Set video mode and get video configuration information */

int tg_setvideomode(int vmode)
{   int i;
    if (vmode != 0) /* unless reset current mode (vmode==0) */
    {  tg_videomode = tg_bgimode[vmode];    /* set new mode */
       initgraph(&tg_bgidriver, &tg_videomode, "");
    }
    else
    {   closegraph();                    /* set same old mode */
        initgraph(&tg_bgidriver, &tg_videomode, "");
    }
    tg_ret = graphresult();     /* result of initialization */
    if( tg_ret != grOk )        /* Error occurred during init */
    {   printf(" Graphics System Error: %s\n",
            grapherrormsg(tg_ret) );
        return(0);
    }
    tg_ncolors = getmaxcolor() + 1;     /* number of colors */
    tg_scrnx = getmaxx() + 1;
    tg_scrny = getmaxy() + 1;                /* size of screen */
    tg_charx = 8, tg_chary = 8;      /* text character size */
    tg_endxor();                      /* turn off XOR mode */

    /* set the viewport to the whole screen */

    tg_setviewport(0, 0, tg_scrnx - 1, tg_scrny - 1);
    tg_setcolor(15 % tg_ncolors);
    if (tg_ncolors >= 16)
    {   tg_getallpalcolors();    /* get the default palette */
```

continues

Listing B.4. continued

```c
    }
    return(1);
}

/* Ask user to pick a video mode
   (this routine works unmodified for all
   libraries and compilers as long as tg_modecode[]
   and tg_modedesc[] are defined) */

void tg_pickmode(void)
{   int i, a, trythis;
    printf("\nPlease choose a video mode, "
            "or press Q to quit.\n");
    trythis = tg_detectmode();
    for (i = 1; i <= tg_NMODES; i++)
    {   if (i == trythis) printf("\nTRY THIS ONE -->");
        else printf("\n                ");
        printf(" %c    %s", tg_modecode[i], tg_modedesc[i]);
    }
    printf("\nYour choice: ");
    while(1)
    {   a = toupper(getch());
        if ((a == 'Q') || (a == 27))
        {   printf("Quit\n\n");
            exit(0);
        }
        for (i = 1; i <= tg_NMODES; i++)
        {   if (tg_modecode[i] == a)
            {   printf("%c", a);
                if (tg_setvideomode(i) != 1)
                {   printf("\nUnable to set graphics mode:"
                            " %s\n", tg_modedesc[i]);
                    exit(0);
                }
                return;
            }
        }
    }
}
```

```c
/* shut down BGI and free up the buffers it used */

void tg_closedown(void)
{   if (tg_mouseon) tg_hidemouse();     /* hide mouse cursor */
    closegraph();                        /* tally me bananas */
}


/* animate the screen by rotating the palette colors
   until a key is hit
   (Since we're using BIOS format palettes, this routine
   will work with most compilers and graphics libraries) */

void tg_colorcycle(int step)
{   int last,                    /* location of last color(s) */
        nbytes;                  /* number of bytes in each step */
    char *firstbuf,              /* buffer to hold first color(s) */
         *pfirst, *psecond;      /* first and second color */
    if (tg_egamode())            /* EGA has one byte per color */
    {   firstbuf = malloc(step);
        pfirst = tg_palette;
        psecond = tg_palette + 1;
        last = 16 - step;
        nbytes = step;
    }
    else
    {   if (tg_vgamode())    /* VGA has three bytes per color */
        {   firstbuf = malloc(step * 3);
            pfirst = tg_palette + 3;
            psecond = tg_palette + 3 * (step + 1);
            last = (tg_ncolors - step) * 3;
            nbytes = step * 3;
        }
        else return;    /* If not EGA or VGA, don't even try */
    }
    while(!kbhit())          /* Keep rotating until a keypress */
    {
        /* copy the first colors(s) into firstbuf */

        memcpy(firstbuf, pfirst, nbytes);

        /* move each color in the palette down one position */
```

continues

Listing B.4. continued

```
        memmove(pfirst, psecond, last);

        /* copy firstbuf into the last part of the palette */

        memcpy(tg_palette + last, firstbuf, nbytes);

        /* Zap! change all the colors on the screen at once */

        tg_setallpalcolors();
    }
    free((void *) firstbuf);            /* free up the buffer */
}
```

GX Graphics Support

Many people are more than happy using the graphics libraries that came with their C or C++ compilers, but if you've recompiled some of the C programs in this book and compared the performance of your EXEs with the performance of the EXEs included on the disk, you know why many programmers go the extra mile and get an add-on graphics library. For all my serious development work, including the ready-to-run programs that came with this book, I use the GX Graphics toolkit from Genus Microprogramming (1155 Dairy Ashford, Suite 200, Houston, TX 77079-3012; or 1-800-227-0918).

GX Graphics offers faster, smoother operations (you'll really notice the difference with 256-color palette animation), more robust support for Super VGA cards, and many advanced features such as drawing to multiple offscreen bitmaps. Several other excellent graphics libraries that offer similar features to GX Graphics are on the market. In particular, MetaWindow from MetaGraphics (269 Mount Hermon Road, PO Box 66779, Scotts Valley, CA 95066; or 1-800-332-1550) offers a wider selection of Super VGA adapter and video mode support than GX Graphics, for a similar price.

One of the main reasons I've chosen to include GX Graphics support with TransGraphics is that you don't need to buy the full GX Graphics package to enjoy many of its benefits. The book/software bundle *Graphics Programming PowerPack* from Sams Publishing contains most of the GX Graphics' functions along with complete reference material by Michael Jones. You can pick up the *Graphics Programming PowerPack* wherever you purchased this book for about $25—one tenth the price of any other professional-quality graphics library.

Other Compilers and Libraries

The TransGraphics GX Graphics support files TGGX.H and TGGX.C give you an example of how you can create your own TransGraphics files to support any graphics library. The tg_printerr() function and gxerr array also demonstrate how you can implement sophisticated error handling while still maintaining full compatibility with the other graphics libraries that TransGraphics supports.

With three versions of the TransGraphics support files (Microsoft, Borland, and Genus GX Graphics) for reference, you should find it easy to produce additional files to support any graphics library or compiler that I've left out, or the latest graphics goody that comes along.

C

VSA256 Graphics Library

For C Programmers

Version 2.0b
November 15, 1992

© Spyro Gumas, 1992.
All Rights Reserved

Introduction

The Video Electronics Standards Association (VESA) has developed a set of BIOS extensions which standardize the Super VGA (SVGA) graphics environment. The VSA256 Graphics Library provides a C programmer with the tools necessary to drive a video adapter running with the VESA version 2.0 BIOS extensions. The name "VSA256" reflects the fact that this library is primarily aimed at supporting the 256 color video modes 100h, 101h, 103h, 105h, and 107h defined within the VESA standard (See table in section 3.1.1).

Version 2.0b is the REGISTERED version of the VSA256 Graphics Library. Whereas the VSA256 Graphics Library Version 1.x is shareware, Version 2.0b **IS NOT** shareware and may only be used in accordance with the terms of the purchase agreement. The major changes between version 1.1 and 2.0b are listed below:

- 3 to 1 speed up of `vsa_line_to`

- 2 to 1 speed up of `vsa_raster_line`

- 3 to 1 speed up of `vsa_h_line`

- New routine, `vsa_get_raster_line`

- New routine, `vsa_gouraud_line`

- New routine, `vsa_triangle_fill`

- New routine, `vsa_shaded_triangle` (Gouraud)

The distribution of the VSA256 Graphics Library consists of the 7 files listed below plus the drivers listed in Section 2.1. These files are archived in the self extracting file VSA256_2.EXE. To extract, just type VSA256_2 in the directory that you want the files extracted to.

VSA_DEMO.C	Demonstration program (Source Code).
VSA_DEMO.EXE	Demonstration program (Executable).
VSA256MS.LIB	VSA256 Graphics Library (Microsoft C compatible).
VSA256BC.LIB	VSA256 Graphics Library (Borland C Compatible).
VSA.H	Include file required in your program.
VSA256.DOC	This text document in Word For Windows 1.0 format.
ORDER.TXT	A text file order form for upgrades and registration.

The Programming Environment

Setting Up The VESA Environment

The VSA256 Graphics Library works with any (any?) IBM PC, XT, AT or compatible computer equipped with an SVGA video adapter card capable of 256 colors and a suitable VESA BIOS Extensions Driver. A math coprocessor chip is not required; however if it exists, this library will take advantage of it.

Before using the VSA256 Graphics Library, the VESA BIOS Extensions must be loaded. This is accomplished by executing the appropriate driver or adding it to your AUTOEXEC.BAT file. If your video adapter card came with a VESA driver, use it. Otherwise use one of the drivers provided depending on the video adapter card installed in the PC as follows:

APPIAN	\APPIAN\APVESA.EXE
ATI	\ATI\VESA.COM
C&T	\C&T\VESA451.COM (or VESA452.COM)
CIRRUS	\CIRRUS\CRUSVESA.COM
EVEREX	\EVEREX\EVRXVESA.COM
GENOA	\GENOA\VESA.COM
OAK	\OAK\37VESA.COM (or67VESA.COM)
ORCHID	\ORCHID\ORCHDVSA.COM
PARADISE	\PARADISE\VESA.EXE
SIGMA	\SIGMA\SIGVESA.COM
STB	\STB\STB-VESA.COM
TECMAR	\TECMAR\VGAVESA.COM
TRIDENT	\TRIDENT\VESA.EXE
VIDEO7	\VIDEO7\V7VESA.COM

Global Graphics Parameters

The file VSA.H is used as an include file during program development. This file includes all of the function prototypes and it defines the global graphics parameters that describe the specific video adapter installed in the PC (See Section 6.1). The global graphics parameters are initialized by the vsa_init function and are described below:

XResolution: Unsigned, the number of screen pixels across (x dimension).

YResolution: Unsigned, the number of screen pixels high (y dimension).

XCharResolution: Unsigned, the number of screen characters across (x dimension).

YCharResolution: Unsigned, the number of screen characters high (y dimension).

XCharSize: Unsigned char, the character cell width.

YCharSize: Unsigned char, the character cell height.

BitsPerPixel: Unsigned char, the number of bits per pixel.

Function Descriptions

This section describes the functions supported in the VSA256 Graphics Library. To use these functions, link your program with the appropriate library listed below depending on the compiler being used.

Borland C++ or Turbo C   -   VSA256BC.LIB
Microsoft C or Quick C   -   VSA256MS.LIB

In the following sections each function is listed along with a definition of its inputs and return values. A description is provided followed by comments on the compatibility of the function with various video modes. Although many functions can drive non-VESA and non-256 color video modes, predictable operation requires that this software be used with the 256 color VESA modes only.

VESA Configuration Functions

vsa_set_svga_mode(video_mode)

Inputs: unsigned video_mode;

Returns: unsigned fail_flag;

Description: This routine sets the video mode. The mode number may be any of the standard VESA SVGA mode numbers as defined in the tables below. The mode is passed to this routine through the video_mode parameter. This routine returns 0 if the call was a success (a 1 for failure). It should be noted that this routine will also work with standard MDA, CGA, EGA, and VGA mode numbers; however, the rest of the VSA256 functions will not necessarily work.

Comments: Works in all VESA video modes.

Also works in MDA, CGA, EGA and VGA Modes.

WARNING: Use `vsa_init` instead (Section 3.1.3)! If you don't use `vsa_int`, then the rest of the routines won't work because they depend on the global parameters initialized by `vsa_init`;

Table C.1. VESA SVGA VIDEO MODES.

GRAPHICS	Mode	Resolution	Colors
	100h	640x400	256
	101h	640x480	256
	102h	800x600	16
	103h	800x600	256
	104h	1024x768	16
	105h	1024x768	256
	106h	1280x1024	16
	107h	1280x1024	256

TEXT	Mode	Columns	Rows
	108h	80	60
	109h	132	25
	10Ah	132	43
	10Bh	132	50
	10Ch	132	60

vsa_get_svga_mode(video_mode)

Inputs:	`unsigned far *video_mode;`
Returns:	`unsigned fail_flag;`

Description: This routine gets the current video mode. The mode is returned to the calling routine via the `video_mode` pointer. The mode number may be any of the standard VESA SVGA mode numbers as defined in Section 3.1.1. This routine returns 0 if the call was a success (a 1 for failure).

Comments: Works in all VESA video modes.

Also works in MDA, CGA, EGA and VGA Modes.

vsa_init(video_mode)

Inputs:	`unsigned video_mode;`
Returns:	`unsigned fail_flag;`

Description: This routine sets the video mode and initializes the VESA graphics environment. This routine must be called prior to the use of any of the routines in Sections 3.4 through 3.7. The mode number may be any of the standard VESA SVGA mode numbers as defined in Section 3.1.1. If the mode number is not a VESA SVGA mode number, this routine will still set the desired video mode, however, the VESA graphics environment will not be initialized and subsequent calls to drawing routines will produce unpredictable results. The mode is passed to this routine through the `video_mode` parameter. This routine returns 0 if the call was a success (a 1 for failure).

Comments: Works in all VESA video modes.

Also works in MDA, CGA, EGA and VGA Modes.

Miscellaneous Functions

vsa_set_display_start(x_strt,y_strt)

Inputs: `unsigned x_strt,y_strt;`

Returns: `unsigned fail_flag;`

Description: This routine sets the current start pixel address which is mapped to the upper left corner of the display. This routine returns 0 if the call was a success (a 1 for failure).

Comments: Works in all VESA video modes.

Also works in MDA, CGA, EGA and VGA Modes.

vsa_get_display_start(x_strt,y_strt)

Inputs: `unsigned far *x_strt, far *y_strt;`

Returns: `unsigned fail_flag;`

Description: This routine gets the current start pixel address which is mapped to the upper left corner of the display. This routine returns 0 if the call was a success (a 1 for failure).

Comments: Works in all VESA video modes.

Also works in MDA, CGA, EGA and VGA Modes.

Attribute Functions

vsa_set_color(color)

Inputs: `unsigned color;`

Returns: Nothing

Description: This routine sets the current drawing color which is used in drawing pixels, lines, and rectangles. The "color" is an 8-bit value from 0 to 255 which is used to index in to the Color Look Up Table (see Section 3.4).

Comments: Works only in 256 color VESA video modes.

vsa_set_text_color(color)

Inputs:	`unsigned color;`
Returns:	Nothing
Description:	This routine sets the current text color which is used in drawing text. `color` is an 8-bit value from 0 to 255 which is used to index into the Color Look Up Table (see Section 3.4). In 16 color SVGA modes, the 4 LSBs define text color. In 256 color SVGA modes, the 8 bits define text color.
Comments:	Works in all VESA video modes.
	Also works in EGA and VGA Modes.

Color Look Up Table Functions

The Color Look Up Table consists of 256 registers and each register stores an 18-bit value defining 6-bit levels for each of red, green, and blue. The drawing functions index into the Color Look Up Table with an 8-bit value (usually set with `vsa_set_color`) to determine the drawing color. With the following functions, the Color Look Up Table can be read or modified one register at a time or all at once in a block operation.

vsa_read_color_register(index,redptr,grnptr,bluptr)

Inputs:	`unsigned index;`
	`unsigned char far *redptr, far *grnptr, far *bluptr;`
Returns:	Nothing
Description:	This routine reads the value of one of the 256 color registers as defined by `index`. Pointers to the red, green, and blue components of the color are returned (6 bits each for red, green, and blue).
Comments:	Works in all VESA video modes.
	Also works in EGA and VGA Modes.

vsa_write_color_register(index,red,green,blue)

Inputs:	`unsigned index;`
	`unsigned char red,green,blue;`
Returns:	Nothing
Description:	This routine writes the value of one of the 256 color registers as defined by `index`. The calling routine provides `red`, `green`, and `blue` components of the color (6 bits each for red, green, and blue).
Comments:	Works in all VESA video modes.
	Also works in EGA and VGA Modes.

vsa_read_color_block(start,count,array)

Inputs:	`unsigned start,count;`
	`unsigned char far array[];`
Returns:	Nothing
Description:	This routine reads count (Range: 1 to 256) consecutive color registers starting at `start` (Range: 0 to 255) within the Color Look Up Table. The `count` must be less than or equal to 256—`start`. The values read from the color registers are returned from this routine in `array[]`. Each element of `array[]` is a byte, and the size of `array[]` is equal to three times `count`. Every three bytes in `array[]` represents the red, green, and blue color values respectively for one color register. Each color component (`red`, `green`, or `blue`) is a byte value but only ranges from 0 to 63.
Comments:	Works in all VESA video modes.
	Also works in EGA and VGA Modes.

vsa_write_color_block(start,count,array)

Inputs:	`unsigned start, count;`
	`unsigned char far array[];`
Returns:	Nothing

Description: This routine writes count (Range: 1 to 256) consecutive color registers starting at start (Range: 0 to 255) within the Color Look Up Table. The count must be less than or equal to 256—start. The values loaded into the color registers are passed to this routine in array[]. Each element of array[] is a byte, and the size of array[] is equal to three times count. Every three bytes in array[] represents the red, green, and blue color values respectively for one color register. Each color component (red, green, or blue) is a byte value but only ranges from 0 to 63.

Comments: Works in all VESA video modes.

Also works in EGA and VGA Modes.

Text Functions

vsa_set_text_cursor(row,col)

Inputs: unsigned row, col;

Returns: Nothing

Description: This routine sets the current text cursor position to row, col in character coordinates (not pixel coordinates). The current text cursor position is only used by vsa_write_string_alt.

Comments: Works in all VESA video modes.

Also works in EGA and VGA Modes.

vsa_set_text_cursor_mode(mode)

Inuts: unsigned mode;

Returns: Nothing

Description: This routine determines the mode of the text cursor operation. If mode is 0 (the default after calling vsa_init), the text cursor is not updated after a new text string is written with vsa_write_string or vsa_write_string_alt. If mode is 1, then the text cursor is moved to the end of the text string after executing vsa_write_string or vsa_write_string_alt.

Comments: Works in all VESA video modes.

                        Also works in EGA and VGA Modes.

vsa_write_char(row,col,alpha)

Inputs: `unsigned row, col;`

                        `char alpha;`

Returns: Nothing

Description: This routine writes a the single character `alpha` at position (`row`, `col`). The character is written with the current text color. After execution, the current text cursor position remains set to (`row`, `col`).

Comments: Works in all VESA video modes.

                        Also works in EGA and VGA Modes.

vsa_write_string(row,col,color,string)

Inputs: `unsigned row, col, color;`

                        `char far string[];`

Returns: Nothing

Description: This routine writes a null terminated text string `string` at position (`row`, `col`). The text is written with the `color` passed to this routine. After execution, if the text cursor mode is `0`, the text cursor remains at `row`, `col`, otherwise it is set to the end of the text string just written.

Comments: Works in all VESA video modes.

                        Also works in EGA and VGA Modes.

vsa_write_string_alt(string)

Inputs: `char far string[];`

Returns: Nothing

Description: This routine writes a null terminated text string string at the current text cursor position as determined by vsa_set_text_cursor. The text is written with the current text color. After execution, if the text cursor mode is 0, the current text cursor remains unchanged, otherwise it is set to the end of the text string just written.

Comments: Works in all VESA video modes.

                Also works in EGA and VGA Modes.

Basic Drawing Functions

vsa_move_to(x,y)

Inputs: unsigned x, y;

Returns: Nothing

Description: This routine sets the current cursor position to x, y. The current cursor position is used by the vsa_line_to, vsa_rect_fill, and vsa_rect functions.

Comments: none

vsa_set_pixel(x,y)

Inputs: unsigned x, y;

Returns: Nothing

Description: This routine draws a single pixel at x, y with the current drawing color.

Comments: Works in all VESA 256 color video modes.

vsa_line_to(x,y)

Inputs: unsigned x, y;

Returns: Nothing

Description: This routine draws a line from the current cursor position to x, y with the current drawing color. Then the current cursor position is moved to x, y.

The drawing speed of this routine is up to 3 times faster than that of the vsa_line_to() function in VSA256 Graphics Library Version 1.1.

Comments: Works in all VESA 256 color video modes.

vsa_gouraud_line(x0,c0,x1,c1,y)

Inputs: unsigned x0,c0,x1,c1,y

Returns: Nothing

Description: This routine draws a color interpolated line from the x0, y to x1, y1. The pixel color value is linearly varied from a starting value of c0 at x0, y to an ending value of c1 at x1, y. This technique of color interpolation is named Gouraud shading after the famous Joe-Bob Gouraud... a French guy. Valid values for c0 and c1 are 0 through 255 and serve as indexes into the Color Look Up Table. Gouraud-shaded lines serve as a fundamental drawing element for realistic 3-D graphics. The current cursor position remains unaffected by this routine.

This is a new routine not provided in the shareware VSA256 Graphics Library Version 1.1.

Comments: Works in all VESA 256 color video modes.

vsa_rect_fill(x,y)

Inputs: unsigned x, y;

Returns: Nothing

Description: This routine draws a filled rectangle from the current cursor position to the rectangles diagonal position x, y with the current color.

Comments: Works in all VESA 256 color video modes.

vsa_rect(x,y)

Inputs:	`unsigned x, y;`
Returns:	Nothing
Description:	This routine draws a rectangle from the current cursor position to the rectangles diagonal position x, y with the current color.
Comments:	Works in all VESA 256 color video modes.

vsa_triangle_fill(x0,y0,x1,y1,x2,y2)

Inputs:	`unsigned x0, y0, x1, y1, x2, y2`
Returns:	Nothing
Description:	This routine draws a filled triangle defined by the 3 vertices (x0, y0), (x1, y1), and (x2, y2). The triangle is drawn with the current drawing color. The current cursor position remains unaffected by this routine.
	This is a new routine not provided in the shareware VSA256 Graphics Library Version 1.1.
Comments:	Works in all VESA 256 color video modes.

vsa_shaded_triangle(x0,y0,c0,x1,y1,c1,x2,y2,c2)

Inputs:	`unsigned x0, y0, c0, x1, y1, c1, x2, c2, y2`
Returns:	Nothing
Description:	This routine draws a color interpolated triangle defined by the 3 vertices (x0, y0), (x1, y1), and (x2, y2). The pixel color value is linearly varied in 2 dimensions across the surface of the triangle using the values c0, c1, and c2 as the starting colors at the respective vertices. This technique of color interpolation is named Gouraud shading after the famous Joe-Bob Gouraud... a French guy. Valid values for c0, c1, and c2 are 0 through 255 and serve as indexes into the Color Look Up Table. Gouraud-shaded triangles

serve as a fundamental drawing element for realistic 3-D graphics. (Basically, most 3-D surfaces can be constructed out of shaded triangles.) The current cursor position remains unaffected by this routine.

This is a new routine not provided in the shareware VSA256 Graphics Library Version 1.1.

Comments: Works in all VESA 256 color video modes.

vsa_h_line(y,x0,x1)

Inputs: `unsigned y, x0, x1;`

Returns: Nothing

Description: This routine draws a horizontal line from (`x0`, `y`) to (`x1`, `y`). The line is drawn with the current drawing color. For horizontal lines this function is quicker than the `vsa_line_to` function.

The drawing speed of this routine is up to three times faster than that of the `vsa_h_line()` function in VSA256 Graphics Library Version 1.1.

Comments: Works in all VESA 256 color video modes.

vsa_v_line(x,y0,y1)

Inputs: `unsigned x, y0, y1;`

Returns: Nothing

Description: This routine draws a vertical line from (`x`, `y0`) to (`x`, `y1`). The line is drawn with the current drawing color. For vertical lines this function is quicker than the `vsa_line_to` function.

Comments: Works in all VESA 256 color video modes.

Specialized Drawing Functions

vsa_raster_line(x0,x1,y,array)

Inputs: unsigned x0, x1, y;

                     unsigned char far array[];

Returns: Nothing

Description: This routine draws a horizontal raster line from (x0, y) to (x1, y). The array[] values specify each pixel's color value. If x0 <= x1, then array[0] defines the color of the first pixel in the line at x0, y. If x1 < x0, then array[0] defines the color of the first pixel in the line at x1, y. The vsa_raster_line() routine is typically used to draw images on the display one raster line at a time.

                     The drawing speed of this routine is up to 2 times faster than that of the vsa_raster_line() function in VSA256 Graphics Library Version 1.1.

Comments: Works in all VESA 256 color video modes.

vsa_get_raster_line(x0,x1,y,array)

Inputs: unsigned x0, x1, y;

                     unsigned char far array[];

Returns: Nothing

Description: This routine gets a horizontal raster line from (x0, y) to (x1, y). The array[] is loaded with each pixel's color value. If x0 <= x1, then array[0] defines the color of the first pixel in the line at x0, y. If x1 < x0, then array[0] defines the color of the first pixel in the line at x1, y. The vsa_get_raster_line() routine is typically used to read back images already drawn on the display one raster line at a time.

                     This is a new routine not provided in the shareware VSA256 Graphics Library Version 1.1.

Comments: Works in all VESA 256 color video modes.

790

Nitty Gritties

Registration Information

THANK YOU FOR REGISTERING!

If you received the VSA256 Graphics Library Version 2.0b through unscrupulous means, a registration fee of $20 would be appreciated. This version of the VSA256 Graphics Library is copyrighted commercial software and **IS NOT** shareware. If you register, you will receive a diskette and manual for the next upgrade of the software.

Please state the version number of the software you are presently using. Send check or money order to:

Spyro Gumas
1668 Shady Brook Drive
Fullerton, CA 92631

Software License

VSA256 Graphics Library, Version 2.0b
Copyright Spyro Gumas, 1992. All Rights Reserved.

Legitimate use of the VSA256 Graphics Library Version 2.0b is governed through the options which were paid for in your purchase order. You may not copy or distribute the VSA256 Graphics Library Version 2.0b without the written permission of the author.

Disclaimer

This software is provided "as is." All warranties relating to this software are disclaimed, whether expressed or implied, including without limitation any implied warranties of merchantability or fitness for a particular purpose. Neither the author nor an agent of the author will be liable for any special, incidental, consequential, indirect or similar damages due to loss of data or any other reason, even if the author or an agent of the author has been advised of the possibility of such damages. In no event shall the author's or an agent of the author's liability for any damages ever exceed the price paid for the license to use software, regardless of the form of the claim. The person using the software bears all risk as to the quality and performance of the software.

Technical Support

If you have any questions or comments about the VSA256 Graphics Library, please write me at:

Spyro Gumas
1668 Shady Brook Drive
Fullerton, CA 92631

Or, contact me on CompuServe. My address is 71064,1571.

Graphics Library Extensions

The VSA256 Graphics Library (Version 1.1 or higher) is a base library which is supported by library extensions for more specialized tasks. New extensions will be developed periodically. The current extensions are:

TIFF256 Graphics Library Extension 1.0—This library extension provides functions which operate with Tagged Image File Format (TIFF) images. With these functions, you can traverse the image file, extract image information, and display the images as part of your own program. The image types supported include Bilevel, Grayscale, Palette Color and RGB True Color. This is shareware software available from the same place that you got the VSA256 Graphics Library.

TIFF256 Graphics Library Extension 2.0—This is the registered version of the TIFF256 Graphics Library Extension. In addition to the capabilities provided by the version 1.0, version 2.0 lets you modify the TIFF images and write them back to TIFF files. Furthermore, any image that you generate with VSA256 can be saved as a TIFF file. You can get your legal fingers on this with a $20 registration fee, or get both VSA256 Ver. 2.0 and TIFF256 Ver 2.0 for the highly discounted price of $25. See the ORDER.TXT for ordering information.

Appendix

VSA.H Include File

```
/*.............................. VSA.H .............. 11-8-92 .......*/
/* This file declares the VSA256 Graphics Library functions and global   */
/* parameters used throughout the graphics routines.                     */
/*                                                                       */
/*                      VERSION 2.0b.                                    */
/*                                                                       */
/*        Copyright Spyro Gumas, 1992.  All Rights Reserved.            */
/*.....................................................................*/
/*.....................................................................*/
/*                      Function Prototypes                              */
/*.....................................................................*/
unsigned  _far _cdecl vsa_set_svga_mode( unsigned );
unsigned  _far _cdecl vsa_get_svga_mode( unsigned _far * );
unsigned  _far _cdecl vsa_set_display_start( unsigned, unsigned );
unsigned  _far _cdecl vsa_get_display_start( unsigned _far *,
                                  unsigned _far * );
unsigned  _far _cdecl vsa_init( unsigned );
void _far _cdecl vsa_set_color( unsigned );
void _far _cdecl vsa_set_text_color( unsigned );
void _far _cdecl vsa_set_text_cursor_mode( unsigned );
void _far _cdecl vsa_set_text_cursor( unsigned, unsigned );
void _far _cdecl vsa_write_char( unsigned, unsigned, char );
void _far _cdecl vsa_write_string( unsigned, unsigned, unsigned, char _far
                    * );
void _far _cdecl vsa_write_string_alt( char _far * );
void _far _cdecl vsa_read_color_register( unsigned, unsigned char _far *,
                unsigned char _far *, unsigned char _far *);
void _far _cdecl vsa_write_color_register( unsigned, unsigned char,
                          unsigned char, unsigned char );
void _far _cdecl vsa_read_color_block( unsigned, unsigned,
                          unsigned char _far * );
void _far _cdecl vsa_write_color_block( unsigned, unsigned,
                            unsigned char _far * );
void _far _cdecl vsa_move_to( unsigned, unsigned );
void _far _cdecl vsa_set_pixel( unsigned, unsigned );
void _far _cdecl vsa_line_to( unsigned, unsigned );
```

```
void _far _cdecl vsa_triangle_fill(unsigned,unsigned,unsigned,unsigned,
                            unsigned,unsigned);
void _far _cdecl vsa_rect_fill( unsigned, unsigned );
void _far _cdecl vsa_rect( unsigned, unsigned );
void _far _cdecl vsa_h_line( unsigned, unsigned, unsigned );
void _far _cdecl vsa_v_line( unsigned, unsigned, unsigned );
void _far _cdecl vsa_raster_line( unsigned, unsigned,unsigned,
                        unsigned char _far *);
void _far _cdecl vsa_get_raster_line( unsigned, unsigned,unsigned,
                            unsigned char _far *);
void _far _cdecl vsa_gouraud_line(unsigned,unsigned,unsigned,unsigned,
                            unsigned);
void _far _cdecl vsa_shaded_triangle(unsigned,unsigned,unsigned,unsigned,
                        unsigned,unsigned,unsigned,unsigned,unsigned);
void _far _cdecl vsa_about( void );
/*.......................................................................*/
/*                    External Parameter Declarations                   */
/*.......................................................................*/
unsigned XResolution, YResolution, XCharResolution, YCharResolution;
unsigned char XCharSize, YCharSize;
unsigned char BitsPerPixel;
```

TIFF256 Graphics Library Extensions

For C Programmers

Version 2.0b
November 15, 1992

© Spyro Gumas, 1992.
All Rights Reserved

Introduction

The TIFF256 Graphics Library Extensions Version 2.0b is a library of C routines which enhance the VSA256 Graphics Library to provide a C programmer with the tools necessary to display Tagged Image File Format (TIFF) images using a video adapter running with the VESA BIOS Extensions, Version 2.0. Support is provided for both Microsoft C and Borland C products. The name "TIFF256" reflects the fact that this library supports the 256-color video modes defined within the VESA standard.

Version 2.0b is the REGISTERED version of the TIFF256 Graphics Library Extensions. Whereas the TIFF256 Graphics Library Extensions Version 1.0 is shareware, Version 2.0b **IS NOT** shareware and may only be used in accordance with the terms of the purchase agreement.

The major change between version 1.0 and 2.0b is the addition of the routine called `tf_save_file`. With this one new routine, the programmer may now create a TIFF file from any image generated using the VSA256 Graphics Library and the TIFF256 Graphics Library Extensions.

The distribution of the TIFF256 Extensions consists of the 8 files listed below. These files are archived in the self extracting file TIF256.EXE. To extract, just type TIF256 in the directory that you want the files extracted to.

TIF_DEMO.C	Demonstration program (Source Code).
TIF_DEMO.EXE	Demonstration program (Executable).
TIF_DATA.EXE	TIFF file analysis program (Executable).
TIFFMSL.LIB	TIFF256 Extensions, Large Memory Model (Microsoft C).
TIFFBCL.LIB	TIFF256 Extensions, Large Memory Model (Borland C).
TIFF.H	Include file required in your program.
TIFF256.DOC	This text document in Word For Windows 1.0 format.
ORDER.TXT	A text file order form for upgrades and registration.

Some TIFF Insight

A TIFF file can contain one or more images. Each of these images is stored in the file as an "Image File Directory" (an IFD). Each IFD consists of numerous fields or "tags."

Each tag defines a particular aspect of the image (ie. color model, width, length, resolution, etc.). With the TIFF256 Extensions, a programmer can find out how many IFDs are contained within a TIFF file, jump to the desired IFD, read all of the tags within the IFD, and display the IFD's image.

The TIFF256 Extensions Environment

Using The TIFF256 Extensions

The TIFF256 Extensions work with any (any?) IBM PC, XT, AT or compatible computer equipped with an SVGA video adapter card capable of 256 colors and a suitable VESA BIOS Extensions Driver. A math coprocessor chip is not required, however if it exists, this library will take advantage of it. The TIFF256 Extensions are distributed as a Large Memory Model library for either Microsoft C or Borland C. If other memory models are required, contact me.

The TIFF256 Extensions are used in conjunction with the VSA256 Graphics Library Version 1.1 or higher (Version 1.0 Won't Work, Find V1.1 in same place you got TIFF256 Extensions). The following discussion assumes that you are adding TIFF capability to an existing program which already uses the VSA256 Graphics Library. To use the TIFF256 Extensions, add the file TIFF.H to your C compiler's default directory for INCLUDE files, add the statement:

```
#include<tiff.h>;
```

to your program, and add the file TIFFBCL.LIB or TIFFMSL.LIB to the list of files that your program is linked with.

Support of TIFF 5.0

For the programmer familiar with the TIFF 5.0 Technical Memorandum, the following list indicates which and to what degree the defined tags are supported by the TIFF256 Extensions. The tags supported provide functionality with most images. When in doubt, run the provided TIF_DATA program to determine the characteristics of a given TIFF file.

TAGS SUPPORTED:

Basic Tags

BitsPerSample = 8,8,8 (for RGB or True Color Images)
BitsPerSample <= 8 (for Bilevel, Grayscale, or Palette images)
ColorMap
Compression = none
ImageLength
ImageWidth
NewSubFileType
PhotometricInterpretation = Bilevel and Grayscale
PhotometricInterpretation = RGB (True Color)
PhotometricInterpretation = Palette Color
PlanarConfiguration = 1
ResolutionUnit
RowsPerStrip
SamplesPerPixel
StripByteCounts
StripOffsets
XResolution
YResolution

TAGS NOT SUPPORTED (Maybe Next Revision):

Basic Tags

BitsPerSample != 8,8,8 (for RGB or True Color Images)
BitsPerSample > 8 (for Bilevel, Grayscale, or Palette images)
ColorResponseCurves
Compression = CCITT Group 3 1-Dimensional Modified Huffman RLE
Compression = LZW Compression
Compression = PackBits Compression
GrayResponseCurve
GrayResponseUnit
PhotometricInterpretation = Transparency Mask
PlanarConfiguration = 2
Predictor

TAGS NOT SUPPORTED (continued):

Informational Tags

Artist
DateTime
HostComputer
ImageDescription
Make
Model
Software

Facsimile Tags

Group3Options
Group4Options

Document Storage and Retrieval Tags

DocumentName
PageName
PageNumber
XPosition
YPosition

Obsolete Tags

CellLength
CellWidth
FillOrder
FreeByteCounts
FreeOffsets
MaxSampleValue
MinSampleValue
SubFileType
Orientation
Thresholding

Global Graphics Parameters

The file TIFF.H is used as an include file during program development. This file includes all of the extension's function prototypes and it defines the global parameters that describe the TIFF File and individual IFDs. The global graphics parameters are initialized by the `tf_get_file_info()` and `tf_read_ifd()` functions and are described below:

TF_Num_Ifd:
Unsigned, the number of IFDs in the TIFF file.

TF_ImageWidth:
Unsigned `long`, the image width in pixels.

TF_ImageLength:
Unsigned `long`, the image length in pixels.

TF_BitsPerSample[3]:
Unsigned, the number of bits per sample. For Bilevel, grayscale, or Palette Color, pixel size = `TF_BitsPerSample[0]`. For True Color, pixel Red Component = `TF_BitsPerSample[0]`, pixel Green component = `TF_BitsPerSample[1]`, pixel Blue component = `TF_BitsPerSample[2]`.

TF_ResolutionUnit:
Unsigned, 1 = Not specified, 2 = Inch, 3 = Centimeter.

TF_SamplesPerPixel:
Unsigned, the number of samples per pixel.

TF_PhotometricInterpretation:
Unsigned, 1 = Bilevel or Grayscale, 2 = RGB (True Color) image, 3 = Palette Color Image.

TF_XResolution_int:
Unsigned `long`, the integral number of pixels in the x dimension per `TF_Resolution` Unit

TF_XResolution_frac:
Unsigned `long`, the fractional number of pixels in the x dimension per `TF_Resolution` Unit

TF_YResolution_int:
Unsigned `long`, the integral number of pixels in the y dimension per `TF_Resolution` Unit

TF_YResolution_frac: Unsigned long, the fractional number of
                            pixels in the y dimension per
                            TF_Resolution Unit

TF_Black: Unsigned, index into CLUT for color
                            nearest to Black.

TF_Red: Unsigned, index into CLUT for color
                            nearest to Red.

TF_Orange: Unsigned, index into CLUT for color
                            nearest to Orange.

TF_Yellow: Unsigned, index into CLUT for color
                            nearest to Yellow.

TF_Green: Unsigned, index into CLUT for color
                            nearest to Green.

TF_Aqua: Unsigned, index into CLUT for color
                            nearest to Aqua.

TF_Blue: Unsigned, index into CLUT for color
                            nearest to Blue.

TF_Violet: Unsigned, index into CLUT for color
                            nearest to Violet.

TF_White: Unsigned, index into CLUT for color
                            nearest to White.

TIFF256 Extensions Functionality

This section describes the operation of the TIFF256 Extensions. To use the functions
in this library, compile your program using the **Large Memory Model** and link your
program with the appropriate librarys listed below depending on the compiler being
used.

Microsoft C or Quick C   -   VSA256MS.LIB and TIFFMSL.LIB
Borland C++ or Turbo C   -   VSA256BC.LIB and TIFFBCL.LIB

Function Descriptions

In the following sections each function is listed along with a definition of its inputs and return values. A description is provided followed by any relevant comments.

tf_open_file(filename)

Inputs:	`char far filename[];`
Returns:	`int fail_flag;`
Description:	This routine opens the TIFF file specified by the character string `filename[]` for use by the TIFF256 Extensions. Only one file can be opened at a time. The file is opened as 'Read Only.' If the file is successfully opened, this routine returns `0`. Otherwise, it returns `-1`. This routine must be called before calling `tf_get_file_info()`.

Comments:

tf_close_file()

Inputs:	Nothing
Returns:	Nothing
Description:	This routine closes the currently open TIFF file. This routine must be called before opening a new TIFF file with `tf_open_file()`. This routine should be called before exiting your program.

Comments:

tf_get_file_info()

Inputs:	Nothing
Returns:	`int fail_flag;`
Description:	This routine verifies that the selected file is a TIFF format file. Then it initializes the TIFF256 environment for this file. The global parameter `TF_Num_Ifd` is set to the number

of Image File Directories (IFDs) existing within the file. An IFD is one 'picture,' and multiple IFDs can exist within one TIFF file. The TIFF file pointer is set to point to the first IFD in the file. This routine is typically called after `tf_open_file()`. If an error occurs, this routine returns 1, otherwise it returns 0.

Comments:

tf_skip_ifd(count)

Inputs: `unsigned count;`

Returns: `int reached_end;`

Description: This routine moves the TIFF file pointer ahead `count` IFDs. Typically, this routine is called after `tf_get_file_info()` to index the TIFF file pointer to the desired IFD. For example, if `tf_get_file_info()` sets `TF_Num_Ifd` to 5, calling this routine immediately after `tf_get_file_info()` with `count = 3`, will cause the TIFF file pointer to skip over the first 3 IFDs and point to the 4th IFD. If `count` equals or exceeds the number of remaining IFDs, this routine returns 1, and the TIFF file pointer is set to point to the last IFD. Otherwise it returns 0.

Comments:

tf_set_defaults()

Inputs: Nothing

Returns: Nothing

Description: This routine sets the default values for all of the global parameters which are modified by TIFF `Tags`. TIFF files may not include data for all of the parameters used by the TIFF256 environment, and therefore the defaults should be set. This routine should be called at the beginning of each new IFD, prior to calling `tf_read_ifd()`. The default values are listed below:

```
TF_ImageWidth  =                             0
TF_ImageLength =                             0
TF_BitsPerSample[0]    =                     1
TF_BitsPerSample[1]    =                     1
TF_BitsPerSample[2]    =                     1
TF_ResolutionUnit      =                     2
TF_SamplesPerPixel     =                     1
TF_PhotometricInterpretation  =              1
TF_XResolution_int     =                   300
TF_XResolution_frac    =                     1
TF_YResolution_int     =                   300
TF_YResolution_frac    =                     1
```

Comments:

tf_read_ifd()

Inputs: Nothing

Returns: `int fail_flag;`

Description: This routine reads the data from the IFD currently pointed to by the TIFF file pointer. The TIFF file pointer must be pointing to a valid IFD prior to calling this routine. (This routine is typically called after `tf_open_file()` or `tf_skip_ifd()` which initialize the pointer.) After reading the data from the current IFD, the TIFF file pointer is set to point to the next IFD. If the TIFF file pointer points to the last IFD in the TIFF file and this routine is executed, the IFD is read, and then the TIFF file pointer is set with a null value. After calling this routine, `tf_display_image` can be called to display the IFD's image. If an error occurs, or this routine is called with the TIFF file pointer set to a null value, `fail_flag` is returned set to 1, otherwise it is returned set to 0. The following global parameters are set by this routine:

```
TF_ImageWidth
TF_ImageLength
TF_BitsPerSample[3]
```

```
TF_ResolutionUnit
TF_SamplesPerPixel
TF_PhotometricInterpretation
TF_XResolution_int
TF_XResolution_frac
TF_YResolution_int
TF_YResolution_frac
```

Comments:

tf_display_image(x0,y0)

Inputs: Unsigned x0;

Unsigned y0;

Returns: Nothing

Description: This routine displays the image that is defined in the IFD read by the most recent call to tf_read_ifd(). The image is drawn with its top left corner at screen coordinates x0, y0. The Color Look Up Table (CLUT) is not modified until this routine is executed. When executed, this routine prepares the CLUT as defined by the IFD being displayed. Before calling this routine, tf_read_ifd() must be called to initialize all of the required parameters.

Comments: This routine may be called more than once per tf_read_ifd() call. Please **DO NOT** call this routine if tf_read_ifd() returns an error (return value = 1).

tf_set_prime_colors()

Inputs: Nothing

Returns: Nothing

Description: This routine updates the prime color global parameters: TF_Black, TF_Red, TF_Orange, TF_Yellow, TF_Green, TF_Aqua, TF_Blue, TF_Violet, and TF_White. It does this by scanning the CLUT and loading each parameter with the CLUT index for the brightest color nearest to the color specified by the parameter name. This routine should be called following any operation which modifies the CLUT (such as `tf_display_image`).

The prime color global parameters are provided in an attempt to give the user access to a standard set of colors (for use with text, borders, etc.) regardless of CLUT operations. However, the color must exist in the CLUT for this routine to find it.

Comments:

tf_save_file(x0,y0,x1,y1,filename)

Inputs: `unsigned x0, y0, x1, y1;`

                    `char far filename[];`

Returns: Nothing

Description: This routine saves the portion of the screen image defined by `(x0, y0) (x1, y1)` to the TIFF file `filename`. The image is saved as an 8-bit Palette Color image (ie. 8 bits/pixel). This routine may be called at anytime after `vsa_init` is called.

The TIFF image file saved as a result of this routine has the following characteristics, as defined by the TIFF specification:

Intel Byte Ordering
SamplesPerPixel = 1
BitsPerSample = 8 (ie. 8 bits per pixel)
ColorMap (ie. CLUT stored within TIFF file)
PhotometricInterpretation = Palette Color
PlanarConfiguration = 1
RowsPerStrip = 1
ImageWidth = |x1-x0|+1 (pixels)
ImageLength = |y1-y0|+1 (pixels)
Resolution Unit = 2 (inches)

XResolution = 100 (Dots Per Inch)
YResolution = 100 (Dots Per Inch)
Compression = none

Comments: This is a new routine not provided in the shareware TIFF256 Graphics Library Extensions Version 1.0.

Handling The Color Look Up Table

The TIFF256 Extensions supports Bilevel and 8-bit or less Grayscale (`TF_PhotometricInterpretation` = 1), 24-bit True Color (`TF_PhotometricInterpretation` = 2) and 8-bit or less Palette Color (`TF_PhotometricInterpretation` = 3) image types. Since this library is specifically designed for 256 entry Color Look Up Tables (CLUTs), for True Color images, the Red, Green, and Blue color components are compressed to 8-bit pixels consisting of 3 bits Red, 3 bits Green, and 2 bits Blue, and the CLUT is loaded with a compressed True Color table. For Palette color images, the IFD comes with its own values which are directly loaded into the CLUT. Regardless of image type, the CLUT is not loaded until `tf_display_image` is called, even though the IFD may have already been read by `tf_read_ifd()`. This means that the previously loaded CLUT (typically from previously displayed IFD) remains in force until `tf_display_image()` is called.

Nitty Gritties

Registration Information

THANK YOU FOR REGISTERING!

If you received the TIFF256 Graphics Library Extensions Version 2.0b through unscrupulous means, a registration fee of $20 would be appreciated. This version of the TIFF256 Graphics Library Extensions is copyrighted commercial software and **IS NOT** shareware. If you register, you will receive a diskette and manual for the next upgrade of the software.

Please state the version number of the software you are presently using. Send check or money order to:

Spyro Gumas
1668 Shady Brook Drive
Fullerton, CA 92631

Software License

TIFF256 Extensions, Version 2.0b
Copyright Spyro Gumas, 1992. All Rights Reserved.

Legitimate use of the TIFF256 Graphics Library Extensions Version 2.0b is governed through the options which were paid for in your purchase order. You may not copy or distribute the TIFF256 Graphics Library Extensions Version 2.0b with out the written permission of the author.

Disclaimer

This software is provided "as is." All warranties relating to this software are disclaimed, whether expressed or implied, including without limitation any implied warranties of merchantability or fitness for a particular purpose. Neither the author nor an agent of the author will be liable for any special, incidental, consequential, indirect or similar damages due to loss of data or any other reason, even if the author or an agent of the author has been advised of the possibility of such damages. In no event shall the author's or an agent of the author's liability for any damages ever exceed the price paid for the license to use software, regardless of the form of the claim. The person using the software bears all risk as to the quality and performance of the software.

Technical Support

If you have any questions or comments about the TIFF256 Extensions, please write me at:

Spyro Gumas
1668 Shady Brook Drive
Fullerton, CA 92631

Or, contact me on CompuServe. My address is 71064,1571.

TIFF.H Include File

```
/*.....\..................... TIFF.H ................ 11-14-92 .......*/
/* This file declares the TIFFLB library functions and global parameters   */
/* used throughout the graphics routines (Version 2.0b).                    */
/*                                                                          */
/*          Copyright Spyro Gumas, 1992.  All Rights Reserved.              */
/*..........................................................................*/


/*..........................................................................*/
/*                        Function Prototypes                               */
/*..........................................................................*/
int  _far _cdecl tf_open_file(char _far *);
void _far _cdecl tf_close_file(void);
int  _far _cdecl tf_get_file_info(void);
int  _far _cdecl tf_skip_ifd(unsigned);
void _far _cdecl tf_set_defaults(void);
int  _far _cdecl tf_read_ifd(void);
void _far _cdecl tf_display_image(unsigned,unsigned);
void _far _cdecl tf_set_prime_colors(void);
int _far _cdecl tf_save_file(unsigned,unsigned,unsigned,unsigned,char _far *);


/*..........................................................................*/
/*                        Parameter Declarations                            */
/*..........................................................................*/

unsigned char _far TF_Byte_Buf[4096];
unsigned long TF_ImageWidth, TF_ImageLength;
unsigned _far TF_BitsPerSample[3],TF_Num_Ifd;
unsigned TF_ResolutionUnit,TF_SamplesPerPixel;
unsigned TF_PhotometricInterpretation;
unsigned long TF_XResolution_int,TF_XResolution_frac;
unsigned long TF_YResolution_int,TF_YResolution_frac;
unsigned TF_Black,TF_Red,TF_Orange,TF_Yellow,TF_Green;
unsigned TF_Aqua,TF_Blue,TF_Violet,TF_White;
```

Annotated Bibliography

What? You've gone through 800 pages and 30 graphics programs, and you're still hungry for more? Good. An expanding universe of spectacular graphics lies out there. This appendix will help you embark on further graphics adventures.

This bibliography isn't a mammoth alphabetical list of authors and titles. Instead, I've selected a few outstanding books, software programs, and other resources. I've grouped them by subject. The brief description that follows each listing gives you enough information to enable you to know whether that reference is up your alley.

Mail-Order Resources

Michael Strasmich is the high-exalted marketing guru of all things computer-graphical. His mail-order company, Media Magic, offers a

staggering selection of books, software, videotapes, unique graphics hardware gadgets, CD-ROMs, laser disks, periodicals, posters, cards, and calendars—all of which are specifically focused on "computers in science and art." (Media Magic doesn't sell graphics hardware—except for a few state-of-the-art gizmos that are hard to find elsewhere.) The free 120-page catalogue should be your first stop when you search for anything and everything dealing with computer graphics, animation, 3-D modeling, scientific visualization, fractals and chaos, image processing, simulation, and other related topics.

Because Michael sells *everything*, his detailed catalog descriptions contain no competitive hype. This makes the catalog itself the best, most up-to-date bibliography on computer graphics that you'll find. By putting his 800 order number and an order form in the back and letting you order it all at lower-than-retail prices, Michael can actually give this phenomenal research tool away for free. Get one.

Media Magic
Post Office Box 598
Nicasio, CA 94946
Telephone: (415) 662-2426
Fax: (415) 662-2225

You might have a favorite supplier, but I personally recommend PC Connection in Marlow, New Hampshire. Although I usually don't like big, industry-leading companies, PC Connection has consistently impressed me with its knowledgeable sales and support staff, rock-bottom prices, huge selection, and big-hearted return policies. Having wrestled with dozens of companies over returns and support—with varying degrees of success—I have yet to encounter a company in any part of the industry that is more willing to pay special attention to the picayune whims of a fickle, unruly customer like me. (They never knew I was an author and journalist, but they always treated me like one anyway.)

If you want to know what's new in graphics cards, printers, mass storage, and commercial software, call PC Connection (or your favorite mail-order house), ask for Sales Support, and grill the people about feature comparisons and pricing. It's a great way to get an up-to-the-minute survey of the industry in one telephone call.

PC Connection
6 Mill Street
Marlow, NH 03456
Telephone: (800) 800-0004 or (603) 446-0004

Magazines and Newsletters

The Media Magic catalogue offers one-stop shopping for all the best computer graphics magazines, including *Computer Graphics World, High Color, Virtual Reality News,* and *Computer Artist.* Several specialty magazines explore particular regions of the graphics countryside. Here are five of them.

New Media
Hypermedia Communications, Inc.
901 Mariner's Island Boulevard, Suite 365
San Mateo, CA 94404

New Media is a surprisingly informative and attractive trade magazine that covers multimedia, CD-ROM, and that sort of thing. Best of all, if you "specify, recommend, buy, or approve the purchase of" multimedia equipment for a company—which you do, right?—you can qualify for a free subscription by filling out a short questionnaire. (The questionnaire ensures *New Media* advertisers that you are rich and influential enough that they should pay to send you a free magazine with their ads in it.) Unlike most freebie ad rags, *New Media* includes much more than sensationalist product hype—although that's in there, too.

3D Artist
Columbine, Inc.
Post Office Box 4787
Santa Fe, NM 87502
Telephone: (505) 982-3532

3D Artist is the only magazine dedicated to low-cost 3-D modeling, design, rendering, animation, and virtual reality on the PC. *Low-cost* means everything from 3D Studio and TOPAS to freeware ray-tracers such as POV-Ray. If you mention *Tricks of the Graphics Gurus,* the publisher, Bill Allen, will give you a free sample issue (within North America, that is. Send $2 for postage overseas). A 12-issue subscription costs $22.

Algorithm
c/o A.K. Dewdney
Westmount Postal Outlet
Post Office Box 29237
785 Wonderland Road South
London, Ontario N6K 1M6
CANADA
Telephone: (519) 432-8042

Algorithm is a delightful quarterly dedicated to "personal programming." Its editor is A.K. Dewdney, who did the "Computer Recreations" column in *Scientific American* for years. Almost every issue explores several fascinating graphics algorithms. A one-year, four-issue subscription costs $20.

Aldus Magazine
Aldus Corporation
411 First Avenue South
Seattle, WA 98104-2871
Telephone: (206) 628-2321

You don't need to be using Aldus products (see the section on software in this appendix) to get a lot out of this beautifully produced in-house journal. Of course, all the step-by-step tutorials refer to only Aldus software, but anyone who works with desktop publishing, photo-retouch, or graphics arts will benefit from the outstanding design examples. If only the other desktop publishing magazines were this good! A one-year, six-issue subscription costs $20 or is free with many Aldus products.

Dick Oliver's Nonlinear Nonsense
Cedar Software
RR 1, Box 5140
Morrisville, VT 05661
Telephone: (802) 888-5275

Dick Oliver's Nonlinear Nonsense is my own quarterly-ish newsletter about fractals, chaos, and creative graphics. In the back, there's sales hype and an order form for my software. I'll send the newsletter free to anyone who asks for it.

Books

In the introduction to this book, I mentioned that each chapter could easily be a Sams book of its own. Here's a list of my favorite books that expand on the topics in each chapter. (Of course, they're not all from Sams, but some of the best ones are.)

Chapters 1, 2, and 3: More Than Just Pretty Pictures

If you need more hand-holding than I've provided in this book, the *Windows Graphics FunPack* (Sams, 1993) book and software bundle gets you up to speed on graphics without mucking about in source code or advanced topics.

Roy Plastock's *Theory and Problems of Computer Graphics* (Schaum's Outline Series/McGraw-Hill, 1986) is an equation-packed reference book that succintly explains all the basic principles of computer graphics—from the definition of a pixel to 3-D viewing transformations and clipping—and hands you the algorithms to play with. It costs only $13!

If your C is rusty, brush up with Stephen Kochan's *Programming in C* (Sams, 1990). If your C is non-existent, pick up a copy of Peter Aiken's and Brad Jones' *Teach Yourself C in 21 Days* (Sams, 1993).

For all those nitty-gritty details that you need to program video memory and registers—if that's your thing, and you don't care about SVGA—refer to Richard Wilton's *Programmer's Guide to PC & PS/2 Video Systems* (Microsoft Press, 1987) or Roger Stevens' *Graphics Programming in C* (M&T Press, 1989).

You won't need either of the previous two books if you get Michael Jones' *Graphics Programming Power Pack* (Sams, 1992), which includes a disk with a top-notch programmer's graphics library.

You can find everything you ever wanted to know about programming a mouse (but had no reason to ask) in the *Microsoft Mouse Programmer's Reference* (Microsoft Press, 1989).

The authoritative references on bitmapped graphics file formats are Steven Rimmer's *Bitmapped Graphics* (Windcrest/McGraw-Hill, 2d ed. 1993), which covers the most common formats, and *Supercharged Bitmapped Graphics* (Windcrest/McGraw-Hill, 1992), which covers some 24-bit formats and other fancy stuff.

If you use the Borland C/C++ compiler, James McCord's *Borland C++ Programmer's Guide to Graphics* (Sams, 1991) leads you through all the functions and graphics operations that you must be familiar with. Microsoft C or C++ fans can refer to the graphics section in Naba Barkakati's *The Waite Group's Microsoft C Bible* (Sams, 1988).

Chapters 4, 5, and 6: Setting Things in Motion

Scott Anderson's new book, *Morphing Magic* (Sams, 1993), takes tweening ten steps further to create full-color morph effects like those you've seen in the movies.

Tony White's *Animator's Workbook* (Watson-Guptill Publications, 1986) has nothing to do with computer graphics, but would-be computer animators can learn a great deal by studing the old-fashioned way.

For a friendly and thorough introduction to all aspects of fractals and chaos theory written by a charming and good-looking guy with virtually no vices except for a slight lack of humility, don't miss my *Fractal Vision* book and software bundle (Sams, 1992).

Anyone who wants to delve deeper into the math or image compression algorithms behind two-dimensional iterated function systems should get copies of Michael Barnsley's *Fractals Everywhere* (Academic Press, 1988) and *Fractal Image Compression* (Academic Press, 1993).

Chapters 7, 8, and 9: The Third Dimension

Leendert Ammeraal's *Programming Principles in Computer Graphics* has much neat and clean C code for 3-D model definition, hidden-line removal, and hidden surface/light source rendering. Although they are less spectacular visually than ray-tracing, these 3-D rendering algorithms are much faster.

There is no such thing as a book about 3-D fractals—yet. The closest thing you'll find is Tim Wegner's *Fractal Creations* (Waite Group Press, 1992), which briefly describes how the freeware program FRACTINT (included with the book) does several types of 3-D projections of 2-D fractals and even a few true 3-D and 4-D fractal types. Roger Stevens' *Fractal Programming and Ray-Tracing with C++* (M&T Books, 1992) takes a stab at the subject, although the coverage of 3-D fractals is slimmer than its title suggests.

Craig Lindley's *Practical Ray-Tracing in C* (Wiley, 1992) will be remembered as *the* classic exposition of the secrets of ray-tracing. The DKB ray-tracer source code that comes with the book has since evolved into the famous POV-Ray freeware program. The POV-Ray program is included in Drew Well's fun and fanciful *Ray-Tracing Creations* (Waite Group Press, 1992).

Chapters 10, 11, and 12: Graphics in Microsoft Windows

James McCord—who wishes that we would stop calling him a guru and just respect him for his clean, thorough, "explain the topic, give 'em the code, and get out of the way" style—has written several authoritative books on Windows programming. They include *Developing Windows Applications with Borland C++ 3.1* (Sams, 2d ed. 1992), *Windows 3.1 Programmer's Reference* (Que, 1992), and *Windows Programmer's Guide to Borland C++ Tools* (Sams, 1992). His *Windows Developer's Treasure Chest* (Sams, 1993) includes a CD-ROM disk stuffed with Windows programming tools.

If you prefer BASIC—or no programming at all—you will enjoy Ed Tiley's *Tricks of the Windows 3.1 Masters* (Sams, 1992), which comes with three disks packed with Windows shareware and utilities.

Chapter 13, 14, and 15: The Graphics of the Future

Craig Lindley's *Practical Image Processing in C* (Wiley, 1991) covers all the essentials of image processing and illustrates the techniques with lots of C code. Tim Wegner's *Image Lab* (Waite Group Press, 1992) and Mike Morrison's *The Magic of Image Processing* (Sams, 1993) are less technical and include oodles of image processing software on disks.

Visualization is a giant topic; you could easily read thousands of pages on the subject without repetition. A good overview is Richard Mark Friedhoff's delightfully philosophical *Visualization* (Harry N. Abrams, 1989). Another book—more academically oriented—is R. A. Earnshaw's and N. Wiseman's *Introductory Guide to Scientific Visualization* (Springer-Verlag, 1992).

Gleick's best-seller *Chaos* (Viking Penguin, 1986) is a thoroughly enjoyable exposition of the history and theory behind chaos science. It discusses the work of Edward Lorenz (whose water wheel you explored in Chapter 15 of this book) in painstaking detail. Gleick uses masterful storytelling narratives to bring this new science to life.

To explore the multimedia world of digital video and sound, check out Roger Jennings' *Discover Windows 3.1 Multimedia* (Que, 1992) or Ron Wodaski's *Multimedia Madness* (Sams, 1993). Wodaski's book includes a CD-ROM and lots of juicy stuff for techies and programmers. Nathan and Ori Gurewich's *Programming Sound with DOS and Windows* (Sams, 1993) helps you integrate sound with animated graphics.

Howard Rheingold's *Virtual Reality* (Simon and Schuster, 1992) contains deeply philosophical musings on VR and its role in society. If you're more interested in today's VR toys than in tomorrow's VR worlds, check out Nicholas Lavroff's *Virtual Reality Playhouse* (Waite Group Press, 1992); it comes with a disk of software goodies. Ken Pimental's and Kevin Teixeira's *Virtual Reality: Through the New Looking Glass* (Windcrest/McGraw-Hill, 1992) focuses on the history and development of VR technology.

For a revealing glimpse at the big picture of where computers and computer graphics are taking us, ponder Robert Lucky's *Silicon Dreams* (St. Martin's, 1989). Clifford Pickover takes a more whimsical, but no less profound, approach to computer graphics in *Computers and the Imagination* (St. Martin's, 1991).

Software

Some of the software included with this book—the SVGA image viewer and the VSA256 and TIFF256 programming libraries—are shareware evaluation copies. This means that you are politely requested—and legally required—to send a registration fee directly to their authors if you continue to use the programs.

For the SVGA image viewer, send $15 to

John P. Silva
3429 Maywood Drive
Richmond, CA 94803

The $15 covers use of the version of SVGA that comes with this book. For an additional $10, John will send you a printed manual and a disk containing an update to the latest version.

For the VSA256 and TIFF256 programming libraries, send $25 to

Spyro Gumas
1668 Shady Brook Drive
Fullerton, CA 92631

This special $25 offer covers use of both the VSA256 and TIFF256 libraries, which normally cost $20 each. Your registration entitles you to a free update to the next version, which includes dramatic speed-up tricks and other enhancements.

Many other excellent shareware, freeware, and public domain graphics programs are available. I have sifted through hundreds of them and selected a few exceptional programs which work especially well with the topics covered in this book. You can use the form in the back to order these for $5 per disk. The order form also includes a special discount offer for my fractal software.

If you'd like to see a more extensive list of all types of shareware, freeware and public domain software, I recommend Public Brand Software. They are more thorough than most distributors in carrying only the latest versions of top-quality programs. Ask for their free catalog.

Public Brand Software
PO Box 51315
Indianapolis, IN 46251
Telephone: (800) 426-DISK or (317) 856-7571

This book mentions several commercial software packages. Information on their publishers is listed below. I recommend these packages. They are the most promising—although inevitably imperfect—graphics products of the ones that I've evaluated. However, don't take omission from this list as a mark against any product or company. There are thousands of fine products that I've never tried, and many top-quality products that I have seen didn't make it onto this list.

Graphics File Conversion and Processing Software

Conversion Artist
$149 from North Coast Software
18A Shipley Road
Post Office Box 459,
Barrington, NH 03825
Telephone: (603) 664-7871

HiJaak for Windows
$249 from Inset Systems
71 Commerce Drive
Brookfield, CT 06804
Telephone: (203) 740-2400

Image Pals
$249 from U-Lead Systems
970 West 190 Street, Suite 520
Torrance, CA 90502
Telephone: (310) 523-9393

Graphic Workshop
$40 from Alchemy Mindworks
Post Office Box 500
Beeton, Ontario
CANADA L0G 1A0

Graphic Workshop is also available as shareware. You can get a complete working copy to evaluate for $5. Use the order form at the back of this book.

Paintshop Pro
$49 from JASC, Inc.
10901 Red Circle Drive, Suite 340
Minnetonka, MN 55343
Telephone: (612) 930-9171

If you have an image editing program that supports multiple file formats—such as the shareware Paintshop Pro—you can convert among them by loading an image from one type of file and saving it to another. You can get a fully functional shareware evaluation copy of Paintshop Pro for $5 using the order form in the back of this book.

POEM/ColorBox Fractal Image Compression SDK
$499 or $750 from Iterated Systems, Inc.
5550-A Peachtree Parkway
Norcross, GA 30092
Telephone: (800) 4-FRACTL or (404) 840-0310

3-D Rendering and Animation Software

3D Studio
$2,995 from dealers
Autodesk
2320 Marinship Way
Sausalito, CA 94965
Telephone: (800) 879-4233 or (415) 332-2344

Contact Autodesk for the name of a dealer near you.

Acuris 3D Clip-Models
Sets of 25 models for $295 from Acuris
125 University Avenue, Suite 125
Palo Alto, CA 94301
Telephone: (415) 329-1920

3D Workshop
$300 from Pacific Motion Software
2611 Lake St.
San Francisco, CA 94121
Telephone: (415) 221-5581

Desktop Animator/TOPAS
$1995 or $3995 from CrystalGraphics
3110 Patrick Henry Drive
Santa Clara, CA 95054
Telephone: (408) 496-6175

StrataVision
$995 from Strata, Inc.
2 West St. George Boulevard, Number 200
St. George, UT 84770
Telephone: (800) 869-6855 or (801) 628-5218

Renderize
$495 from Visual Software
21731 Ventura Boulevard, Number 310
Woodland Hills, CA 91364
Telephone: (800) 669-7318 or (818) 883-7900

Imagine
$495 from Impulse
8416 Xerxes Avenue North
Brooklyn Park, MN 55444
Telephone: (800) 328-0184 or (612) 425-0557

Fractal Grafics 3D
$149 from Cedar Software
RR 1, Box 5140, Garfield Rd
Morrisville, VT 05661
Telephone: (802) 888-5275

Visualization Software

CoVis (animated 3-D graphing software)
$395 from CoHort Software
Post Office Box 1149
Berkeley, CA 94701
Telephone: (800) 728-9878 or (510) 524-9878

Mathematica
$495 and up (price depends on the configuration) from Wolfram Research
100 Trade Center Drive
Champaign, IL 61820-7237
Telephone: (800) 441-MATH or (217) 398-0700

Sliders and Dials (add-on for Microsoft Excel spreadsheets)
$99 from Golden Technologies
14251 Camden Lane
Lake Oswego, OR 97035
Telephone: (800) 653-2201 or (503) 620-2201

Virtual Reality Software

Virtual Reality Development System
$795 from VREAM, Inc.
2568 North Clark, Number 250
Chicago, IL 60614
Telephone: (312) 477-0425

World Toolkit
$2,900 from Sense-8
4000 Bridgeway, Suite 101
Sausalito, CA 94965
Telephone: (415) 331-6318

VR Studio
$95 from Domark Software
1900 South Norfolk Street, Suite 202
San Mateo, CA 954403
Telephone: (415) 513-8929

Image Processing and Photo Manipulation Software

Painter
$495 from Fractal Design Corp.
335 Spreckels Drive, Suite F
Aptos, CA 95003
Telephone: (800) 647-7443 or (408) 688-8800

Photoshop and **Illustrator**
$895 and $695 from Adobe Systems
1585 Charleston Road
Post Office Box 7900
Mountain View, CA 94039-7900
Telephone: (800) 833-6687 or (415) 961-4400

Photostyler, **PageMaker**, **Freehand**, and **Gallery Effects**
$549, $549, $399, and $139 from Aldus, Inc.
411 First Avenue South
Seattle, WA 98104
Telephone: (206) 622-5500

PicturePro
$795 from Ventura, Inc.
15175 Innovation Drive
San Diego, CA 92128
Telephone: (800) 822-8221 or (619) 673-0172

Additional References

Bellin, Adam, and Pier Del Frate. "True Color for Windows." *BYTE* (December 1990): 284.

Bonner, Paul. "Windows 3.1: Popular and Compelling." *PC Magazine* (10 November 1992): 216.

Caffery, William J. "The Visual Revolution." Gartner Group's *Managing Advanced Technology Transfer Evaluation Review* (Fall 1992): 13.

Callender, John B. "Animation Software: Breathing Life into Computer-Based Presentations." *Presentation Products Magazine* (November 1992): 50.

Clark, Jim. "Roots and Branches of 3-D." *BYTE* (May 1992): 164.

Derfler, Frank J., Jr. "Solutions: Graphics." *PC Magazine* (16 March 1993): 373.

Dewdney, A.K. "Computer Recreations." *Scientific American.*

Duncan, Ray. "Power Programming: Mastering the Complexity of the Windows API." *PC Magazine* (11 June 1991): 390.

————. "Programmer's Bookshelf." *Dr. Dobb's Journal* (August 1991): 171.

Dunteman, Jeff. "Windows Outlook." *PC Techniques* (February-March 1992): 48.

Floyd, Michael. "What? Me Worry About Windows Programming?" *Dr. Dobb's Journal* (December 1991): 4.

Graef, Gerald L. "Graphics Formats." *BYTE* (September 1989): 305.

Lancaster, Don. "Hardware Hacker." *Radio Electronics* (January 1990): 70.

Miastkowski, Stan. "Windowing: Not by DOS Alone." *BYTE* (Outlook 1992 special edition): 172.

Nassar, Dale. "Three-Dimensional Graphics by Computer: Computer-Generated Anaglyphs." *Circuit Cellar Ink* (December 1991): 16-19.

Ostman, Charles. "VR Going Mainstream." *Midnight Engineering* (May-June 1993): 16.

Petzold, Charles, and Richard Hale Shaw. "The Windows Programming Experience." *PC Magazine* (10 November 1992): 230.

Pietgen, H.O., et al. *The Beauty of Fractals.* New York: Springer-Verlag, 1986.

Plaugher, P.J. "Technicolor and Cinemascope." *Computer Language* (August 1990): 18.

Porter, Kent. "Graphics Programming." *Dr. Dobb's Journal* (February 1989): 121.

Schumacher, Dale A. "Image Smoothing and Sharpening by Discrete Convolution." In *Graphics Gems II.* San Diego: Academic Press, 1991.

Spanbaur, Scott. "Windows NT: The New DOS?" *PC World* (June 1993): 161.

Tazelaar, Jane Morrill. "State of the Art: Advanced Graphics." *BYTE* (December 1990): 250.

Urlocker, Zack. "Polymorphism Unbound." *Windows Tech Journal* (March 1992): 16-17.

Wayner, Peter. "Image Building." *BYTE* (April 1993): 141.

Weber, Jack. "Visualization: Seeing Is Believing." *BYTE* (April 1993): 121.

Yares, Evan. "Photo-Realism: Computing Images That Look Like Real Objects and Scenes." *BYTE* (May 1992): 167.

Glossary

286—Commonly used abbreviation for any computer using the Intel 80286 or a comparable chip as its central processing unit.

2-D—Two-dimensional, flat. Like paper, computer screens, and cartoon characters who've been run over by a steam roller.

386—Commonly used abbreviation for any computer using the Intel 80386 or a comparable chip as its central processing unit.

3-D—Three-dimensional, not flat. Like the room you're in, or space before Einstein got hold of it.

3-D face—Short for three-dimensional surface. Usually 3-D faces are defined by three or four points that all fall on the same plane.

3-D graphics—Computer-graphics representations of 3-D objects. Usually implies that the objects themselves are mathematically defined in the computer, as opposed to digitized photographic pictures of real 3-D objects.

3-D space—Any part of a universe having three dimensions. Where we all hang out all the time.

3DFACE entities—What you call 3-D faces when you put them into a .DXF file.

3DLINE entities—What you call line segments in 3-D space when you put them into a .DXF file.

486—The 80486, Intel's most popular computer chip as of this writing. Also used to mean any computer containing an 80486.

8086—The ancestor of the 286, 386, and 486. Mostly seen in garage sales and accountant's offices these days. Same as the 8088 for all practical purposes today.

Adapters—The hardware expansion cards that allow your computer to display graphics are often called "adapters." (See also: **CGA**, **EGA**, **VGA**, **Hercules**, and **Super VGA**.)

Adaptive Color Compression—The process of performing a statistical analysis on the colors present in an original true color image and, based on this analysis, deciding upon the best allocation of 256 colors for a palette-based image.

Additive color model—Red, green, and blue are called the additive colors (also, primary colors) because you can add various intensities of these three colors together to form any other color.

AI—Adobe Illustrator PostScript (vector) drawing (a valid EPS file in disguise).

Algorithm—A procedure, a way of doing things.

Aliasing—The effect that makes jagged "stair-stepping" in computer pictures of low resolution. Comes from the square shape of the pixels and is actually a moiré effect. You can correct it with a technique called anti-aliasing, which blends the colors on the jaggy edges to make them look smoother.

Alpha channel—A fourth "color channel" besides red, green, and blue. Often used for special effects, especially transparencies.

Ambient light—Light that appears to come from everywhere at once. Rendering programs use this to approximate the small amount of stray light that is always bouncing around between objects, but which would be very difficult to compute exactly.

American National Standards Institute (ANSI)—A standards-setting institute. The folks who brought us ASCII and ANSI-standard C.

Anaglyphic stereoscopy—The art of making 3-D images by wearing goofy-looking but fun red/blue glasses and displaying a red image for one eye and a blue image for the other.

Anaglyphs—Pictures made for viewing with red/blue 3-D glasses.

Anchor points—Used in morphing to determine which parts of the original picture should "turn into" corresponding parts of the final picture.

Animation—Simulating motion by displaying a sequence of images in rapid succession.

ANSI—See **American National Standards Institute**.

Anti-aliasing—See **Aliasing**.

Application programming interface (API)—The standard way for programmers to use functions of an operating system (such as Windows) in their own programs.

Application queue—In Windows, the dispatching system that sends messages to the functions that need to pay attention to them.

Application window—In Windows, the main screen window for a program.

Arc—A part of a circle.

ASCII text—The American Standard Code for Information Interchange defined a standard for representing text on computers a long time ago, and everyone uses it now whether they know it or not. A normal text file is therefore often called an ASCII file. Pronounced "ass-key."

Attractor—When the results of a mathematical function are fed back into the same function repeatedly, the result often settles down to a stable value or set of values no matter what value you started with. This stable set is called the attractor of the function. Attractors of complex functions are often fractals.

AutoCAD—A popular computer-aided design program from Autodesk, Inc. The original source of the .DXF file format.

Automatic disk compression—The process of removing extra spaces and repetitive patterns from data as it's written on a hard disk and restoring the data to its original form when it's read from the disk. Compression saves a lot of space and can be done invisibly by programs like Stac Electronic's Stacker and Microsoft's DoubleSpace.

Axis—A dimension, often represented by a line passing through the zero-point on another perpendicular axis. The x- and y-axes represented by a cross hair through the origin are a familiar example.

Background—The image or color that occupies most of the screen and appears to be behind everything else.

Binary—A numbering system based on only two possible values for each digit. In binary, you count 0, 1, 10, 11, 100, and so forth.

Binary digit—A variable that can store one of two possible values, usually represented by 0 or 1. Usually called a "bit." The fundamental unit of information.

Binary files—Any file other than an ASCII text file.

Binary number—Any number can be represented by a sequence of ones and zeros. For example, the binary representation of the decimal number 255 is 11111111, and decimal 256 is 100000000 in binary.

Bipolar high pass filter—See **Filter**.

Bit—See **Binary digit**.

Bit planes—A way of organizing video memory so that all the "first bits" of all the pixels are consecutive, then all the "second bits" and so on.

Bitmap—Because computer graphics images are made by mapping binary digits onto the monitor screen and interpreting the binary numbers as colors, images are called *bitmaps*.

Bitmap brush—A drawing tool (within Windows and other graphics systems) that uses a bitmapped pattern to fill a region.

Bitmapped graphics—Computer graphics images that are stored pixel by pixel, as they appear on the screen. (Contrast with **Vector graphics**.)

Bitmapped image—See **Bitmap** and **Bitmap graphics**.

Bitmapped program—A program that stores and edits bitmapped graphics, as opposed to vector graphics.

Block—Jargon used in certain file formats to mean a section of data.

Blur—The process of averaging adjacent colors in an image to make it look more blurry.

BMP—Microsoft Windows bitmap (can be used for Windows wallpaper).

Bounding box—Ellipses and circles are often defined by specifying the corner points of a bounding box, the rectangle that just touches their top, bottom, and side edges.

Brightness—The apparent lightness of an image or part of an image.

Brush—A shape used to draw or fill a region.

Bus—The power and data distribution system of a computer.

Butterfly Effect—See **Chaos**.

Byte—Eight bits, which can store 256 possible values.

CAD—Computer-aided drafting, or computer-aided design, depending on whom you ask. Sometimes called CADD, to mean computer-aided drafting and design.

Cathode ray tube (CRT)—The name for the display technology used in most computer monitors and televisions.

CD-ROM—Compact disk read-only memory. Up to 680 megabytes can be stored on the same type of CD that commonly holds music.

CDR—CorelDRAW vector drawing file

Cedar Software—The author, Dick Oliver's, sole proprietorship. A Cedar Software order form is located in the back of this book.

CGA—Computer Graphics Array, an early PC graphics adapter capable of 4 colors at 320x200 resolution or 2 colors at 640×200 resolution.

CGM—Computer Graphics Metafile, another "universal standard" that never caught on. The Windows metafile is a more well-known variation on the same theme.

Chaos—When any system displays "sensitive dependence on initial conditions," it becomes impossible to predict its behavior reliably even with very precise measurement. This is also known as *chaos*, or the *butterfly effect* because a butterfly flapping its wings today could effect tomorrow's weather. The study of chaos has far-reaching consequences in almost all branches of science. Intimately related to the fields of fractals and complexity.

Chaos game—Another name for the random iteration algorithm for drawing an iterated function system fractal.

Chip—Integrated circuits, especially the ones that make your computer work. Examples: The 386 chip, the VGA chip.

Chorded ellipse—An ellipse with sections cut out so that only a portion appears on the screen.

CIS—CompuServe Information Service, the world's largest on-line service and electronic bulletin board service (BBS).

Clamp—Normally, when a computer counts past the highest number that can be stored in a variable, it returns to zero and keeps counting. In image processing, this can lead to weird effects unless you *clamp* the image at the maximum value instead.

Clear codes—Used in GIF files and other LZW compression schemes to clear the string table and start building it over again when you run out of memory to store more pattern strings.

Client area—In Windows, the region of a window where the application is allowed to draw.

Clip-models—Prebuilt mathematical descriptions of 3-D objects.

Clipping plane—In 3-D rendering, objects beyond the clipping plane are considered to be behind the viewer's head and are not displayed.

CLUT—See **Color look up table**.

CMYK color model—Cyan-Magenta-Yellow-Black color model, used when printing on paper. The opposite of the RGB color model.

Coastline—Sometimes used to refer to any fractal curve that weaves in and out like a real coastline.

Coefficients—Generally, any number that gets multiplied by a variable in an equation.

Color balance—The relative intensities of red, green, and blue in a computer image or cyan, magenta, and yellow in a printed picture.

Color cycling—The process of rapidly rotating the values in the palette (color lookup table) to animate the entire screen at once.

Color look up table (CLUT)—Also called a palette or color palette, CLUT is used in video systems where only 8 bits or less are available for each pixel. A color number is stored for each pixel, and an 18-bit or 24-bit color value is stored in the CLUT, which determines the actual color of a pixel on the screen.

Color number—See **Color look up table**.

Color palette—See **Color look up table**.

Color plane—Colors are usually stored as red, green, and blue component values. The collection of all the red component values are called the "red color plane," and so forth.

Color resolution—The number of colors that can be displayed on the screen at once. For example, standard VGA has a maximum color resolution of 256 colors, which requires 8 bits per pixel to store the color number.

Color space—An abstract 3-D space where the three dimensions are red, green, and blue (or cyan, magenta, yellow, or hue, saturation, lightness, depending on the color model you choose). The set of colors visible by the eye or displayable by a monitor can be represented as a region in color space.

Color stepping—See **Color cycle**.

Color triangle—A slice of color space, where each corner of the triangle represents red, green, or blue. The region within the triangle shows all possible mixtures of the three component colors at a particular lightness value.

Color values—The actual numerical description of the intensities of red, green, and blue light to be displayed at a particular point on the screen.

Command-line arguments—When you type a command to run a program from the DOS prompt, you can type filenames or other parameters after the command itself, before you press enter. How these command-line arguments are interpreted depends on the program.

Compiler—A program to translate a human-readable language like C or BASIC into the native instruction code of a particular CPU.

Complex numbers—Numbers with two parts, called the real part and the imaginary part, or simply x and y. Used to perform computations on a two-dimensional surface.

Complex plane—The abstract space represented by complex numbers. In computer graphics, the complex plane usually represents the two-dimensional computer screen.

Component—(1) The red, green, or blue part of a color. (2) The x or y part of a complex number. (3) Any part of anything.

Compression—The act of removing repetitive patterns from data so that it can be stored using fewer bits.

CompuServe Information Service (CIS)—See **CIS**.

Computer-aided drafting or Computer-aided design (CAD)—See **CAD**.

Computer graphics—Visual images made on or with a computer.

Computer Graphics Adapter (CGA)—See **CGA**.

Computer Graphics Metafile (CGM)—See **CGM**.

Contrast enhancement—The act of amplifying color differences in an image to improve the apparent contrast.

Control block—Used in some graphics file formats to mean data which describes how the image should be displayed rather than actual pixel-by-pixel coloring information.

Control menu—The leftmost menu in a Windows application menu bar.

Control points—(1) Points in any graphics or CAD image that allow you to control some part of the image with the mouse. (2) See **Anchor points**.

Controller register—A storage location within a video chip that controls various display functions.

Convolution—A mathematical technique for image processing.

Coordinate—A numerical location along an axis.

Coordinate system—The reference system for locating points on the screen. Windows has several options: the screen coordinate system, whole-window Coordinate system, or client area coordinate system.

CRT—See **Cathode ray tube**.

CRT gun—The electron gun within a CRT. Color CRTs have separate electron guns for red, green, and blue light.

CUR—A Windows cursor bitmap file.

Cursor—The little icon that shows you where your mouse or text editing point is on the screen. The mouse cursor is usually arrow-shaped.

Cyan—Bluish-green.

Cyberspace—(1) The abstract universe on the other side of the computer screen. (2) The worldwide network of digital telecommunications interconnections.

Data blocks—Used in some file formats to mean the pixel-by-pixel color data, as opposed to control blocks.

Data stream—The incoming stream of data when reading a file from a disk.

Data-glove—An inexpensive glove with motion detection and position sensors attached; Marketed by Sega-Genesis, Inc.

DCX—A bunch of PCX images all crammed into one file (thank Intel for it).

Decimal—The ten-valued numbering system we normally use for counting money and almost everything else.

Decode—To read a file and translate the data back into the original form it had before it was stored in the file.

Default—The value something has if you don't bother to change it.

Delta—The amount to change something (from the Greek letter, which mathematicians often use to stand for an amount of change).

Depth cue—Visual information that helps your brain decipher two-dimensional images into a mental image of 3-D space.

Device context—Windows programming jargon meaning the state the display (or another device) is in.

Device driver—A small software program to interface with a physical piece of hardware.

Device-dependent bitmap (BMP)—Windows storage format that stores images in a format similar to the way they are stored on the PC.

Device independent—Software that can be used without change on a wide variety of hardware.

Device-indepentent bitmap (DIB) Windows storage format that stores images in a form that can be used on any type of computer (very theoretically).

DFT—Discrete Fourier transform, a mathematical technique used in image processing.

DIB—See **Microsoft Windows Device Independant Bitmap**.

Diffuse light—Light that is widely scattered by an object's surface. In rendering, diffuse light depends only on the orientation of the surface relative to the light source and does not show reflections or highlights.

Digital—In a form that can be stored as a collection of bits. The opposite of analog, which is stored as a continuously varying voltage or magnetic strength.

Digital video—Motion pictures stored as bits, as opposed to analog video tape or physical film.

Direct color—Video hardware that stores the actual color values for each pixel, as opposed to palette-based color.

Discrete Fourier transform (DFT)—See **DFT**.

Disintegrating—Pfffzzz...

Displacement—Translation, or movement from one location to another without rotation.

Dither—To approximate more colors than you can actually display or print by mixing small dots of more than one color very close together.

DLL—Dynamic link library, and file used by Windows programmers to store parts of a program.

DOS—Disk operating system. Used to mean the MS-DOS, PC DOS, DR DOS, and compatible operating systems, or the computers that run them.

DOS prompt—The prompt displayed by DOS when it's ready for you to type a command. Usually looks like C:> or C:\TGG> where TGG is the name of the current directory.

Draw programs—Programs that work with vector data, as opposed to paint programs, which work with bitmapped images only.

Drawing exchange file (DXF)—A popular file format originally developed by Autodesk, Inc. for exchanging vector data between CAD programs.

Drawing modes—In Windows, how the drawing operations decide what color to put on the screen, based on the color of the object being drawn and the color that is already on the screen at the location being drawn over.

Drawing operation—A procedure that draws something on the screen, such as a line, a circle, and so on.

DRW—Micrografx Designer vector drawing file

DXF—AutoCAD vector drawing exchange file

Dynamic link library (.DLL)—See **DLL**.

Edge Detection—The process of recognizing and highlighting regions of rapid color transition in an image.

EGA—See **Enhanced graphics adapter**.

Ellipses—Elongated circles.

Embossing—The process of coloring edges in an image to look as though the picture consists of 3-D layers of metal or stone.

Encode—To compress or otherwise process an image as you save it to disk.

Enhanced graphics adapter (EGA)—An aging standard for PC graphics display, which supports up to 640×350 resolution with 16 colors.

Enlargement—Making an image bigger by adding more pixels than in the original.

ENTITIES—Shapes are called ENTITIES when stored in a DXF file.

Entropy—The tendency for rooms to be messy shortly after you tidy them up. The same principle applies to life in general.

EPS—Encapsulated PostScript file, can be printed or read by most PostScript-compatible programs.

Escape-time algorithm—A way of drawing fractals such as the Mandelbrot set and Julia sets.

Event-driven—A way of organizing a program so that functions are initiated by the user or hardware input. The opposite of procedure-driven, where functions are generally executed in a fixed order no matter what the user says.

Exceptions—Problems, errors, or urgent events that must be attended to by a program. (Going back to fix a mistake in an earlier test grade or the occurrence of a hard-disk error during data entry, for example.)

EXE—The file extension of an executable file.

Executable file—A file containing instructions to be run by the computer, a program file.

Exploding—Kaboom!

Eye—(1) One of your peepers. (2) The theoretical point in 3-D space where the observer is located in a computer-generated scene.

Eye ray—An artificial ray of light that travels from the eye back into the scene, bouncing off objects until it either encounters a light source or zooms off to infinity.

Face—See **3-D face**.

Fast Fourier transform (FFT)—See **FFT**.

FAX—Short for facsimile transmission. As in "FAX machine".

FFT—(1) A super-quick way of doing a Fourier transform, not covered in this book. (2) A file extension used by the IMAGEPRO program for Fourier file transfers.

Field—A variable or set of variables.

FIF—See **Fractal image format**.

Fractal image format (FIF)—A highly compressed bitmapped image stored as fractals.

Filter—The technical term for many image processing operations. Examples: a high pass filter eliminates rapidly changing colors, blurring the image; a low pass filter eliminates slow-changing colors, sharpening the image.

Fixed-point—A way of storing numbers so that calculations can be significantly sped up as compared to normal, floating-point number calculations.

Flavors—Variations on a file format. Example: there are many incompatible flavors of TIFF.

FLC—Autodesk Animator Pro high-resolution bitmapped animation file.

FLI—Autodesk Animator low-resolution (320×200 256-color) animation file.

Flicker—Any visible or subliminally visible shimmering or flashing caused by repeatedly erasing and redrawing images.

Floating-point—A way of storing numbers inside the computer. (See also: **Fixed-point**.)

Fonts—Typefaces; The actual shapes that are displayed or printed to represent characters of the alphabet, numbers, and punctuation.

Forward Fourier transform—Transformation from the spacial domain into the frequency domain. See **Fourier transformation**.

Fourier spectrum plot—A picture of the frequency domain laid out as if it were the spatial domain. See **Fourier transformation**.

Fourier transformation—The translation of an image from the spatial domain, where each pixel represents a location in two-dimensional space, into the frequency domain, where each pixel represents a particular period of repetition. Fourier transformations (also called Fourier transforms) are useful in image processing for filtering out repetitive noise.

Fractal image file (FIF)—A file format for highly compressed images stored as fractals.

Fractal—An infinitely detailed shape. Generally, each part of a fractal resembles the whole. (See also: **Iterated function systems**.)

FRACTINT—A famous freeware program to generate many different kinds of fractal images.

Frame—Another name for a picture. Usually used only when the image is part of an animated sequence of images.

Frame buffers—Memory set aside for storing images and pixel-by-pixel information about how to process images.

Freeware—Copyrighted software whose authors expicitly permit free distribution as long as no fee is charged beyond materials, duplication, shipping, and handling. Compare to: Shareware.

Frequency Domain—See **Fourier transformations**.

Function—A computer-language procedure or mathematical formula that may take in and/or return a value or set of values.

Functionality—The capability to get some work done. (As opposed to **User interface**.)

Fundamental window—The simpest possible Windows program: includes a menu bar, scroll bars, and a blank client area.

Gamma correction—The process of changing the balance of red, green, and blue light in an image to correct for the sensitivity of our eyes to different colors, or the capability of a monitor or printer to display or print different colors.

Gate—One junction within a chip.

GDI—See **Graphics device interface**.

GIF—CompuServe Graphics Interchange Format compressed bitmap.

Gigabyte—Approximately one billion bytes. Can mean exactly 1,000,000,000 bytes or exactly 1,073,741,824 (two to the thirtieth power (2^{30}), the highest number you can count to with 30 bits), depending on who you ask.

Graphic-rendering blocks—Regions of a GIF file where instructions for displaying images are stored.

Graphical user interface (GUI)—Any convention for the appearance and use of a program that uses graphical elements such as icons, pretty fonts, and/or a mouse.

Graphics accelerator—Hardware to take on some of the graphics calculations normally done by the CPU, thus speeding up the display of complex graphics.

Graphics device interface (GDI)—The name for Windows' graphics programming library.

Graphics interchange format (GIF)—A standard for compressed image storage.

Graphics kernel system (GKS)—A popular graphics programming system on UNIX platforms.

Graphics mode—Most PC video adapters have special display modes for text, where fonts are handled by the hardware itself. All other video modes are called graphics modes.

Gray scale—Several shades of gray.

GUI—See **Graphical user interface**.

Guru—(1) Somebody who apparently knows quite a bit about a particular subject and probably knows more than they're letting on. (2) A humble religious leader (generally wearing a turban and/or loincloth and sitting on a mountain, patiently waiting for disciples to clamber up).

Handle—(1) When programming, a pointer to information identifying a file or object. (2) When using a graphics program, any point or shape that can be grabbed with the mouse to control the placement or configuration of a larger shape.

Hardware—Physical machines or parts, as opposed to software.

Hatched brush—In Windows, a brush that fills with a hatched pattern when drawing.

Header—A standard arrangement of data items found at the beginning of a file.

Heighway's Dragon—A famous fractal shaped (sort of) like a dragon.

Hercules graphics adapter—(HGA, or HGC for Hercules Graphics Card) The first graphics card with better resolution than CGA. Still a low-end monochrome graphics standard.

Hexagon—A six-sided figure.

HGA—See **Hercules graphics adapter**.

HGC—See **Hercules graphics adapter**.

HiColor—Sierra Designs' brand name for their high color (15- color) RAMDAC chips.

Hidden surfaces—Surfaces that wouldn't be visible if you were looking at a real 3-D object, but which need to be purposefully hidden when displaying a computerized rendering of a 3-D model.

High color—15-bit color, which uses 5 bits each for red, green, and blue. 15 bits can display 32,768 distinct colors.

High pass filter—See **Filter**.

High word—The most significant 16 bits of a 32-bit number.

Highlights—The shiny parts of a partially reflective surface, also called *specular highlights*.

Horizontal resolution—The number of pixels across the screen in the x direction.

Horizontal scroll bar—The bar at the bottom of a Windows window that allows you to move the window view back and forth horizontally.

HPG—Hewlett Packard Plotter Graphics Language (used by vector printing devices).

HSV model—The hue/saturation/ value color model, an alternative to red/green/ blue or cyan/magenta/yellow for describing colors.

Hue—(1) In the HSV model, the location in the rainbow spectrum where a color would be found. (2) Generally, a synonym for color.

ICO—A Windows icon file.

Icon—A little picture, used in Windows to represent a program or document.

IDE—Integrated development environment. A programmer's workplace where you can edit, compile, and test your programs without returning to the command line or Program Manager window.

IFD—See **Image file directory**.

IFF—A graphics file that snuck onto your machine from an Amiga (also called HAM).

IFS—See **Iterated function system**.

IFS Codes—See **Iterated function system**.

IGES—Initial graphics exchange specification, a standard file format for exchanging drawings and images between CAD programs.

Illumination—Simulated lighting, when rendering an image of a 3-D model.

Image buffer—The memory where an image is stored.

Image file directory (IFD)—The part of a TIFF file that records which parts of which images go where in the file.

Image plane—In 3-D rendering, the plane in theoretical 3-D space that corresponds to the display screen.

Image processing—A general term refering to any digital manipulation of scanned photographs or computer-generated pictures.

Imaginary—An antiquated term for the y coordinate in two-dimensional numbering systems.

Indexed color—See **Palette-based color**.

Industry standard architecture (ISA)—The expansion bus in an AT-compatible computer. Almost all PCs have ISA buses.

Initial graphics exchange specification (IGES)—See **IGES**.

Integers—Counting numbers (1, 2, 3...), negative numbers (-1, -2, -3...) and, of course, zero.

Intensity—The amount of light, or the amount of a particular color.

Interaction—Two-way communication (often, between a computer and a person—though sometimes two people can interact, too). Also, the "interaction of light" with a model produces highlights and shadows.

Interactive—Involving interaction.

Inverse Fourier transform—Going from the frequency domain back to the spatial domain. See **Fourier transformations**.

ISA—See **Industry standard architecture**.

Iterate—To feed the results of an operation back into the same operation again. See **Chaos** and **Iterated function system**.

Iterated function system (IFS)—A set of numbers, called IFS Codes, which defines a set of geometric tranformation to be performed repeatedly. The result, when displayed visually, looks like a fractal.

Iterative—Involving iteration.

Jaggy—Having jagged edges. See **Aliasing**.

JPEG—(1) The Joint Photographic Experts Group. (2) An image file compression standard defined by JPEG, which achieves very high compression ratios with some loss of image quality.

JPG—Highly compressed format design by the Joint Photographic Experts Group (JPEG).

Julia set—A type of fractal, similar to the Mandelbrot set.

Kernel—(1) The central, essential part of anything. (2) The array of numbers that defines the effect of an image-processing convolution.

Kilobyte—1,024 bytes.

Latch bits —Part of the innards of video chips that you may be grateful you don't need to worry about.

Layers —Independant parts of a drawing or image.

Lean—Tilt sideways, keeping the top and bottom parallel to the ground. Similar to shear and skew.

Library—(1) A collection of common programming functions to be used in many different programs. Example: a graphics library. (2) Any large collection of similar items. Example: an image library. (3) A place where you can borrow old-fashioned books to read for free.

Limpel-Ziv & Welch (LZW)—A very efficient, lossless image compression algorithm used in GIF and some varieties of TIFF files.

Lines —Theoretically, infinitely long, invisible straightnesses. Often used to mean visible approximations of line segments.

Local bus—A special connection within some new PCs that allows the video card to send and receive data at CPU speeds.

Lorenz attractor—A simple mathematical model of a weather system that shows chaotic behavior. See **Attractor** and **Chaos**.

Lorenz Water Wheel—A water wheel with leaky buckets—a direct analogy to the Lorenz attractor.

Low word—The least significant 16 bits of a 32-bit number.

Low-pass filter—See **Filter**.

LZW compression—See **Limpel-Ziv & Welch compression**.

MAC—MacPaint format from the Apple Macintosh computer.

Macro—A definition of a sequence of commands or instructions. Once defined, the name of the macro can be inserted in place of the entire sequence to save typing.

Magenta—Bright purplish-pink.

Mandelbrot set—A famous mathematical fractal popularized by the French mathematician Benoit Mandelbrot. Most of the fractal pictures you see in magazines, with the pretty colored spirals within spirals, are parts of the infinitely detailed Mandelbrot set.

Mapping mode—In Windows, a setting that determines where and how graphics are drawn in a window.

Mask bits—A pattern used to select only certain bits from a binary number.

Matrix—An array of numbers, often representing coefficients in a transformation formula.

Maximize box—In Windows, the part of a window that makes the window grow to fill the entire screen when you click it with the mouse.

Meg—Short for Megabyte.

Megabyte—Approximately a million bytes. Either 1,000,000 bytes, 1,024,000 bytes (1,000 Kilobytes), or 1,048,576 bytes (1,024 Kilobytes), depending on whom you ask and what they're trying to sell you.

Melting—Aaaaahhhwwwwwmmmmmmrrrrr...

Memory—(1) The chips in your computer that store bits. As in random-access memory, or RAM. (2) Anything that stores bits. (As in compact disk read-only memory, or CD-ROM.)

Memory—(1) The chips in your...wait a minute, didn't I just define memory?

Memory swapping—Copying a part of the computer's internal memory to a hard drive to make more room for other data, and then copying it back into internal memory when needed. Gives the appearance of nearly unlimited memory capacity, at the price of speed.

Menu bar—In Windows (and most commercial programs for DOS nowadays), the area at the top of the screen or top of a window where the menu choices are.

Mesh entity—A compact way of describing a complex surface with a grid of connected 3-D faces.

Message—In Windows (or almost any other object-oriented programming system), a signal that tells parts of the program that an event has occurred.

Message loop—The part of a Windows program that checks for messages and takes the appropriate action to deal with the messages it receives.

Minimize box—In Windows, the little square that turns the window into an icon when you click it.

Module definition file—In Windows programming, a file describing the various component parts of a windows program.

Module name—The name of a file containing part of a Windows program.

Moiré patterns—Ripply interference patterns, popular in the 18th century and still enjoyed in moiré fabric. Sometimes lovely, sometimes bothersome when they appear on a computer screen. Moiré means "watery" in French. (See also: **Aliasing**.)

Monitor—The big box on top of your computer that you probably stare into all day.

Mono—Short for monochrome graphics.

Monochrome graphics—Graphics with only two colors (black and white, or sometimes green or amber if you have an "ergonomic" monitor), or shades of gray.

Morphing—(1) Tweening; Gradually metamorphosing a shape into another shape. (2) Specifically, tweening full color pictures, as opposed to simple lines and polygon shapes.

Motif—A graphical user interface for UNIX systems, championed by the Open Look Foundation.

Motion cues—Visual information that helps you tell how objects are moving relative to one another.

Mouse—(1) The pointing device on your desk (2) The pointy-tailed fellow peeking out from under your desk.

Mouse cursor—See **Cursor**.

MPEG—The Motion Picture Experts Group's MPEG video compression technology, a standards for adding animated video sequences to any software using JPEG compression.

MPG—File extension for an MPEG file.

MS-DOS—Microsoft Disk Operating System. See **DOS**.

Multimedia—Buzzword for anything that combines digital video and sound, usually on a CD-ROM.

Multitasking—Doing more than one thing at a time. Most "multitasking" environments, including Windows, just fake it by slicing up their time between multiple tasks.

NAPLPS—North American Presentation-Level Protocol Syntax, a graphics standard of days gone by.

Negative—(1) In image processing, just as in photography, the inversion of the intensities of red, green, and blue light or grayscale intensities. (2) Mathematically, less than zero.

Normal—The direction the top of your head would be pointing if you stood on a 3-D face. Used to compute the interaction of light rays with models. See **Right hand rule**.

North American Presentation-level Protocol Syntax (NAPLPS) See **NAPLPS**.

Nyquist criteria—States that you must sample at least twice the highest spatial frequency component of the image if you are to faithfully capture the essence of the image and not introduce false frequencies (aliases).

Object—(1) In programming, a procedure that contains its own data and responds to messages telling it what to do with that data. (2) In 3-D graphics, a mathematical model of a real object. (3) In ordinary English, any old thing.

Operating system (OS)—The program that starts when you start your computer and that launches other programs. Most OSes handle disk operations and other low-level housekeeping so the application programs don't have to.

Optical—(1) Dealing with light, as in the optical properties of an object to be rendered. (2) Mass storage that uses laser light to read and/or write information, as in optical disks.

OS—See **Operating system**.

Pages—(1) Additional video memory for storing off-screen images. Used in animation to prepare the next frame while the current frame is still being displayed. (2) Pieces of paper.

Paint programs—Programs that edit bitmapped images pixel-by-pixel. Contrast with **Drawing programs**.

Palette—See **Color look up table (CLUT)**.

Palette rotation—Another word for **Color cycling**.

Palette-based mode—Video modes where color numbers are stored for each pixel, and a palette or color look up table is used to determine the actual color value that corresponds to each color number. See **Color look up table**.

PC—(1) Any IBM-PC or IBM-AT compatible personal computer (2) Any personal computer or microcomputer.

PCL—Hewlett Packard Printer Control Language (for LaserJet-compatible printers).

PCs—More than one PC.

PCT—Apple MacIntosh PICT format bitmap (also sometimes given the PIC extension).

PCX—ZSoft's PC Paintbrush bitmap format.

Pel—IBM's goofy word for pixel.

Pen—A pointing-device that resembles an ordinary desk pen, but contains electronics allowing the computer to tell where it is relative to the screen or a digitizing pad.

Pentium—The name Intel chose for their next CPU chip when they found out they couldn't buy all worldwide rights to the digits 5, 8, and 6.

Perspective—The effect that makes distant objects look smaller than close objects.

Perspective distance—The simulated distance between your eyes and the object you're rendering in 3-D.

PHIGS—An old UNIX graphics standard. The letters stand for something-something-graphics standard, I suppose.

Photo CD—Kodak's attempt at mass-marketing a service to digitize 35mm film photos and put them on a CD-ROM for you.

Photorealism—The appearance that something looks so real it could be a photo. Implies that the subject never existed except as a mathematical model in a computer.

Photorealistic—Possessing the quality of photorealism.

PIC—Could be a picture from Pictor/PC Paint or from Lotus 1-2-3 charting (several other programs also use this extension for incompatible file formats).

PICT—An Apple Macintosh graphics file format.

Pie piece—A wedge-shape. (You need six of them to win at Trivial Pursuit.)

Pixel—The smallest dot on your computer screen. See **Resolution**.

Pixel Emphasis—Another word for **Sharpening**.

Pixel Interpolation—An image processing technique for enlarging an image without making it look all jaggy.

Pixel Replication—An image processing technique for enlarging an image that makes it look all jaggy.

Pixel Spreading—Another word for **Blur**.

Play—Whooppeee!! Interaction at its best.

Point clouds—A bunch of points in 3-D space. Many of the fractals presented in this book are point clouds.

POINT entities—A point in 3-D space, when written to a DXF file.

Pointer—A variable that contains the location of another variable in the computer's memory.

Pointillism—The practice of prepresenting pictures with a large number of tiny dots or pixels.

Points—In theory, zero-dimensional locations. In practice, a small region surrounding a point is illuminated so we can see it.

Point light—A light source that radiates light in all directions. Contrast with **Spotlight**.

Polygon—A two-dimensional closed figure with line segments as its edges. For example, triangles, squares, pentagons, and hexagons are all polygons.

Polyline—The outline of a polygon.

POLYLINE entities—Polylines in a DXF file.

Polypolygon—Multiple polygons defined in one big array.

Positive—(1) In image processing or photography, an image with the original coloring of the subject is called a *positive*. The opposite of a **Negative**. (2) Mathematically, greater than zero.

PostScript—A computer language specifically designed to describe graphics images and text fonts. Unlike most languages, PostScript is usually interpreted by a processor in the printer, not the CPU.

Primary colors—Red, Green, and Blue. See **RGB color model**.

Primitives—Simple shapes, just as lines, polygons, circles, tetrahedra, cubes, and so on.

Probability—The likelihood of something happening.

Procedural—See **Procedure-driven**.

Procedural texture—The use of a variety of algorithms to compute intricate and sometimes animated surface patterns

Procedure—(1) A set of instructions for doing something. (2) In Windows, a function that responds to a message.

Procedure declaration—The part of a C program that indicates the input and output types of a procedure.

Procedure-driven—A program that carries out tasks in a specific order, rather than allowing the user to initiate events and then respond to them. Contrast with **Event-driven**.

Processor—The "brain" of your computer, which carries out all the instructions in a program. The CPU.

Program initialization—Any necessary housekeeping tasks to be carried out once at the beginning of a program.

Programmer—The guy or gal who types the instructions that compose a computer program.

Projection—A simple way of representing 3-D objects in 2-D by dropping a coordinate. Essentially, casting a shadow of the 3-D object on a 2-D plane.

PUB—Used by a number of desktop publishing programs, including Microsoft Publisher and PFS:First Publisher.

Radiosity—A subtle but dramatic technique for calculating the effects of diffuse light in a building or scene.

RAM—Random-access memory, the main memory chips inside your computer. Unlike read-only memory (ROM) or disk drives, RAM forgets everything when you turn the computer off.

RAMDAC—Random-access memory digital analog converter. (1) The circuits that convert color values into actual voltages to go to the monitor. (2) Specifically, a chip that allows your computer to display 15-bit or 24-bit color.

Random iteration algorithm—A technique for drawing iterated function system fractals by randomly hopping around on a fractal and lighting up dots as it goes. See **Attractor** and **IFS**.

Raster—(1) The scanning electron gun inside a CRT. (2) A horizontal line across the screen, a scanline. (3) A general term referring to any bitmapped graphics, as opposed to vector graphics.

Raster operation—A way of combining the color of pixels to be drawn with the pixel colors already on the screen. The most commonly used "raster-ops" are XOR and simple replacement, sometimes called SET or PUT.

Ray tracer—A program that generates photorealistic images by calculating the interaction of light rays with a 3-D model.

Ray tracing—The act of using a ray tracer, or the calculations that the ray tracer carries out.

Resampling—Enlarging or shrinking an image by interpolating or averaging the values of each pixel.

Resizing—Enlarging or shrinking.

Real—(1) Existing in the physical world outside the computer. (2) See **Real time**.

Real time—The time scale we experience, as opposed to the internal rhythm of the computer or the painstakingly slow frame-by-frame calculation of extremely complex images

Red/blue glasses—The 3-D glasses that came with this book. See **Anaglyphic stereoscopy**.

Reduction—Shrinking, making smaller.

Reflection—The effect you see when light bounces off something and the image of the surrounding environment appears in that thing. Easy to simulate on a computer with ray tracing.

Refraction—The bending of light as it passes through a transparent or translucent object.

Register—(1) A few key memory storage locations within the CPU or video chips themselves. (2) To pay for shareware that you have evaluated and decided you want to continue using.

Render—To produce a two-dimensional picture of a 3-D object by calculating what it would look like from a particular angle.

Resolution—(1) The number of pixels in an image. (2) The amount of memory required to store an image. This includes color resolution, which is the number of bits required to store the color number of a pixel.

Resource—The visual element of a Windows program, such as bitmaps, icons, and cursors.

Resource editor—A program to create and edit Windows bitmaps, icons, and cursors.

Resource file—A file containing the visual elements of a Windows program, such as bitmaps, icons, and cursors.

RGB color model—The method of describing colors by specifying the intensities of red, green, and blue light to be added together.

Right-hand rule—A way of relating rotation to a direction in space. Hold your right hand with the fingers slightly curled and the thumb sticking out. The direction of your thumb tells you that direction is positive, assuming that the rotation from your palm to your fingertips is considered clockwise.

RLE—(1) An old CompuServe bitmap from before GIF was invented. (2) A Microsoft Windows run-length encoded bitmap. (3) See **Run length encoding**.

Routine—Another name for a function or procedure.

Run length encoding (RLE)—A way of compressing image data that replaces long sequences ("runs") of identical values with a code followed by the number of times the value is repeated.

Saturation—The overall amount of light or pigment in a color or an entire image.

Scanline—One horizontal line of pixels all the way across the screen.

Screen—The display part of a computer monitor—where the image shows up.

Secondary colors—Cyan, Magenta, and Yellow. See **CMYK color model**.

Self-similar—Having parts that resemble the whole.

"Sensitive dependence on initial conditions"—See **Chaos**.

Sequential—Occuring in a specific, fixed order. A synonym for **Procedural**.

Shadows—The darkness cast by the light. Each day hides a small patch of night.

Shareware—Software that is freely distributed for evaluation purposes. You are legally required to pay a registration fee to the author if you continue to use the software, although nobody's going to come and bust your door down. This honor system for software distribution saves tons of wasted money on marketing and packaging, allowing authors to focus on quality and low prices. Also called "try before you buy" software.

Sharpen—To enhance the quality of an image by accentuating color changes.

Shear—A synonym for **Tilt**. Contrast with **Skew**.

Shutter glasses—Glasses that have LCD panels in each eye opening. By alternately blocking each eye opening 30 times a second and simultaneously flipping between left and right eye views on a computer monitor, the shutter glasses enable you to see color stereo pictures.

Sierpiński's Triangle—A famous fractal consisting of triangles within triangles within triangles on down to infinity.

Simulation—Faking something on a computer.

Skew—To rotate one axis only, causing an object to appear to twist in a way that couldn't happen with real physical objects. Contrast with **Tilt**.

Software—Instructions and data structures, as opposed to physical hardware.

Solid modeling—Representing the insides of 3-D objects as well as their surfaces. Sometimes includes the capability to calculate the motion of objects based on the internal behavior of the materials that compose them.

Source code file—A file that contains the instructions that make up a computer program, written in C, C++, BASIC, or another human-readable computer language.

Spatial Domain—The normal way of representing an image, where the x and y axes correspond to horizontal and vertical dimensions in ordinary space. See **Fourier transformation**.

Spatial frequency aliasing—Means the same thing as **Aliasing**.

Spatial frequency components—Specific periodic repetitions in a pattern. See **Fourier transformation**.

Special purpose blocks—Parts of a GIF file that contain program-specific information.

Specular light—Highlights on shiny objects, which come from scattering of imperfectly reflected light.

Speed—More, more, more! Whizzzz…

Spin—Your run-of-the-mill rotation. Turning, tumbling, that sort of thing.

Spotlight—A directional light source that casts shadows. Contrast with **Point light**.

Spreadsheet—A program that lays out a grid of numbers and text, enabling you to enter formulas instead of a number for any square in the grid. Handy tool for simple number-crunching and accounting tasks as well as "what-if" numerical analysis.

Square root—The number that, when multiplied by itself, produces a given value.

Squashing—Resizing one axis only, so that an object appears to elongate or smush in one direction.

Stereo pairs—A left-eye view and a right-eye view of the same scene or object. Often placed side by side for viewing.

Stereo vision—The ability to judge the relative distance of things from the differences between what you see with your left eye and what you see with your right eye.

Stereoscopic—Involving stereo vision.

Stock brush—In Windows, one of a few standard brush fill patterns.

String table—A record of the patterns found in a file, used for compression and decompression of images with the Limpel-Ziv & Welsh algorithm.

Strip—Part of an images. Used in TIFF files.

Subtractive color model—A way of describing any color by specifying the amount of Cyan, Magenta, and Yellow pigments. Called subtractive because the pigments create color by absorbing (subtracting) light instead of emitting (adding) it. Contrast with **Additive color model**.

Successive approximation algorithm—A way of drawing a fractal by making more and more detailed approximations of it.

Super VGA—(1) Any video adapter with higher resolution than VGA's 640×480 by 16 colors. (2) Specifically, 800×600 by 16-color resolution, or 640×480 by 256 colors.

Super VGA+—Video adapters with resolutions beyond 800×600 and/or more than 256 colors.

Surface—Two-dimensional plane or curve in 3-D space. See **3-D face**.

SVGA, or SVG for short—See **Super VGA**.

System font—A standard typeface that comes built into an operating system.

System queue—In Windows, the main message dispatch system. See **Message queue**.

Tabbed text—Text arranged in columns. Also called tabulated text.

TABLES—A section of a DXF file that contains CAD data on colors, shape types, and other advanced stuff.

Tag—A label that tells what type of data follows it in an image file.

Tagged image file format (TIFF)—See **TIFF**.

Targa—(1) A high-end line of graphics hardware manufactured by TrueVision, Inc. (2) See **TGA**.

Text mode—Most PC video adapters have special display modes for text, where fonts are handled by the hardware itself.

Text—Letters and numbers.

TGA—Bitmap format originally created for Truevision Targa boards.

TIF—Three-letter extension for TIFF files.

TIFF—Tagged image file format used by many graphics programs.

Title bar—In Windows, the very top part of a window, that contains the title of the window.

Transform—(1) To change from one thing into another. (2) Short for Transformation.

Transformation—A mathematical description of how to change one thing into another, or move something from one place to another.

TransGraphics—A system of header s and functions that make graphics programs compatible with multiple compilers and grpahics libraries. (Included with this book.)

Translation—(1) Displacement, movement from one place to another without rotation. (2) The re-expression of words from one language into another.

Transparency masks—In many photo-editing programs, a shape that covers part of the image and lets the rest show through. See also **Alpha channel**.

True 3-D—Rendering three-dimensional models, as opposed to pseudo-3-D, which simply fakes 3-D lighting and perspective effects without using a 3-D model at all.

True color—24-bit-per-pixel color, with 8 bits each for red, green, and blue. Better color resolution than your eye can distinguish!

TrueType—A font description language recently introduced by Apple and Microsoft to compete with PostScript. Unlike PostScript, TrueType is generally used only for text and not for illustrations.

TSR—A terminate-and-stay-resident program. TSRs are usually loaded when your computer starts and remain in memory to carry out their tasks whenever they are called or automatically triggered by some event. Because DOS was not originally designed to support them, they are sometimes a cause of problems when they conflict with one another or other programs.

TV—If you don't know what TV is, you got off on the wrong planet.

Tweening—Automatically calculating several images between key frames in an animation.

Unifying normals—Making sure the outsides of all faces on an object point out, and the insides all point in.

UNIX—A loosely standardized group of operating systems and communications protocols used by all major universities and colleges, as well as many large corporations.

User interface—The appearance and conventions for using a program.

Value—An amount, quantity, or other specific piece of data, such as 6 or 2.3 or "Fred" or whatever.

Variables—Memory locations that store values.

VCR—Videocassette recorder. See **TV**.

Vector data—See **Vector graphics**.

Vector graphics—Mathematical descriptions of shapes, as opposed to pixel-by-pixel representations of images. Contrast with **Bitmapped graphics**.

Vector-based programs—Software that uses vector graphics.

Vertical resolution—The number of pixels in the y direction.

Vertical scroll bar—The bar at the right side of a Windows window that allows you to move the window view up and down.

VESA—(1) The Video Electronics Standards Association, a standard-setting consortium consisting of big graphics hardware and software companies. (2) The Super VGA modes standardized by VESA. (3) The local bus specification proposed by VESA.

VGA—Video graphics array, the current low-end standard for color graphics hardware on the PC. Capable of 640×480 with 16 colors or 320×200 with 256 colors.

Video—(1) Moving pictures stored electronically. (2) Anything to do with visual displays or computer graphics.

Video capture—The capability to digitize video and store it on a computer.

Video cards—Computer graphics adapter hardware (not necessarily capable of dealing with video capture or digital video).

Video Electronics Standards Association (VESA)—See **VESA**.

Video for Windows—A new standard for displaying digitized motion pictures within Microsoft Windows. Uses a tiny 160×120 pixel window for speed.

Video Graphics Array—See **VGA**.

Video hardware—See **Video cards**.

Video memory—Memory within a computer used only for storing and displaying images.

Video modes—All video cards support many different operational modes, called video modes. These include text modes and graphics modes of various resolutions.

Viewing frustrum—In 3-D rendering, the area of space that is visible in an image.

Viewpoint—The point in space where the observer or camera is located when computing a 3-D rendering.

Viewport—A region of the screen to which all output is temporarily restricted. Usually, the top left corner of the viewport becomes the 0,0 coordinate from which all locations are measured.

Virtual reality (VR)—A buzzword for a variety of 3-D computer graphics developments. Ideally, VR implies total immersion in a simulated world, with stereoscopic wraparound head-mounted displays and stereo sound.

Virtual reality software—Software that supports real time 3-D rendering, preferably with stereoscopic display. Most VR software enables you to create a virtual world and then interactively explore it.

Virtual worlds—See **Virtual reality software**.

Visual simulation—Modeling something in a way that makes its essential components visible while the dynamics of the system do their thing.

Visualization—A broad label for any visual representation of data. Usually implies that some or all of the data would have been invisible or too abstract to understand without computer-graphics representations.

VR—See **Virtual reality**.

What-you-see-is-what-you-get (WYSIWYG)—Pronounced "Wizzy-wig" or "Wizzy-wiggy." Means that printed output of a program looks nearly identical to the screen display you saw before you printed it.

Window border—In Windows, the edge around a window. You can grab the border with the mouse and resize the window.

Windows—When capitalized, the Microsoft Windows (Trademark, Registered, Copyright, bow-when-you-say-that, and so on) graphical user interface operating system. When not capitalized, a rectangular region of the screen that contains the graphics output of a program or function.

Windows CGM—See **Windows metafile**.

Windows function—In Windows programming, a function that does some calculation or display task. Called by other functions or procedures, but not initiated directly by a message. Contrast with **Windows procedure**.

Windows metafile—A special type of graphics file that can be a device independent bitmap, a series of vector drawing commands, or just a link to the application that created the graphic.

Windows NT—The newest version of Windows, which can run on several different types of computers and does not require DOS.

Windows procedure—In Windows programming, a function that is initiated by and responds to a message. Contrast with **Windows function**.

Wizzy-wiggy—See **What-you-see-is-what-you-get**.

WMF—Microsoft Windows MetaFile (either a DIB image or a just a link to the drawing application).

Word—(1) Two bytes. (2) The number of bits that a particular computer handles most efficiently (on a 286, 16 bits; on a 386, 32 bits).

Workstation—A powerful microcomputer, usually, but not necessarily, running UNIX.

WPG—WordPerfect vector drawing or bitmap image.

WYSIWYG—See **What-you-see-is-what-you-get**.

X—Usually used to represent a horizontal location coordinate.

X-Window—User interface and graphics operation protocol.

XOR—Exclusive-Or, a raster operation that allows graphics to be drawn over a complex background and then erased without damaging the background image by drawing with XOR again.

Y—Usually used to stand for a vertical location coordinate. Sometimes implies the in-and-out location coordinate in 3-D space instead.

Yurt—A round Himalayan hut.

Z—Usually used to represent an in-and-out location coordinate (perpendicular to the screen) in 3-D space. Sometimes used as the vertical coordinate instead. Other times, Z means a complex number that includes both x and y coordinate values.

Zoom—Resizing with pizzazz.

Index

B

C

C programming language source code files, 469
see also source code files
C++ programming language source code files, 469
see also source code files
CAD (computer-aided drafting), 5, 829
calculating tweening points, 143-144
calling functions, 738-739
cameras, ray tracer relationships, 412-415
Captain Crunch (MediaVision), 703
cathode ray tube (CRT), 829
CD-ROM, 688, 829
Cedar Software, 829
CGA (Color Graphics Array), 9, 829
CGM (Computer Graphics Metafile), 829
chaos, 829
Lorenz waterwheel, 658-680
Chaos, 817
chaos game, 222-223, 829
chips, 829
gates, 837
Chord function (Windows), 513-516
chorded ellipses, 829
drawing, 513-516
chordex.c source code file, 516
chordex.def module definition file, 516
chordex.prj project file, 516
chordex.rc resource file, 516
circles, drawing, 26-34, 513-515
CIS (CompuServe Information Service), 829
clamping, 830
clear codes, 830
client area, 456, 830
client area coordinate system, 481
clip-models, 830

clipping plane, 414, 830
closedown( ) function, 27
CLUT, *see* color look up table
CMYK color model, 68-69, 830
coastline, 830
coefficients, 830
color balance, 577-579, 830
color cycling, 569-570, 830
color image conversions, 580-586
RGB to gray-scale, 582-584
RGB to indexed colors, 584-586
color interpolated lines, drawing, 787
color interpolated triangles, drawing, 788
color lookup table (CLUT), 565-579, 830
brightness adjustments, 572-574
color balancing, 577-579
contrast of images, enhancing, 575-577
functions (VESA), 782-784
gray-scale, 583-584
reading, 567-572
TIFF 256 Extension, 807
writing, 567-572
color numbers, 14, 566
color palettes, *see* color look up table
color planes, 830
color resolution, 7, 830
color space, 831
color triangle, 831
color values, 15-17, 831
color_balance( ) function, 577-579
color_cycle( ) function, 569
color_swap( ) function, 570-572
colorcyle( ) function, 27
colors, 14
1-bit, 14
4-bit, 15
24-bit, 18
32-bit, 19

H

load3difs() function, 390

LoadCursor function (Windows), 547

LoadIcon function (Windows), 554

loadifs() function, 230-242

loading

    BIOS extensions, 777

    bitmaps, 533

    cursors, 548

    icons, 554

local bus, 686-687, 841

logical coordinate system, 480-481

logical units, 481

Lorenz attractor, 841

Lorenz, Edward, 657-680, 817

Lorenz waterwheel, 657-680, 841

low word, 841

Lucky, Robert, 818

LZW compression utility, 84

M

MAC format (MacPaint), 841

Macintosh PCT bitmap, 844

MacPaint, 841

magazines, 813-814

The Magic of Image Processing, 817

mail-order resources, 811-812

main() function, 45

Mandelbrot set, 253-267, 727, 841

    MANIMATE.C program, 261-267

MANIMATE.C program, 261-267

mapping texture/bump, 346-347

mapping modes, 478-480, 841

mask bits, 842

MATH.C (Scene Generator) file, 213-215

MATH.H (Scene Generator) file, 213-215

Mathematica visualization software, 681, 822

matrices, 842

    transformation

        3-D IFS files, 386

        editing, 354-355

matrix algebra, 228

    3-D transformations, 353-356

Maximize box, 842

Maximize button, 457

maximizing windows, 457

MAXTEMP.DAT file, 646

McCord, James, 815-817

Media Magic mail-order company, 811-812

megabytes, 842

memory, 842

    swapping, 842

    video memory, 854

mental triangulation, 276-277

menu bar, 457, 842

menus

    control, 832

    System, 456

MERGECOPY raster operation code, 531

MERGEPAINT raster operation code, 532

mesh entity, 842

message loops, 463-464, 842

messages, 842

    status, 3DFACES program, 327

    WM_COMMAND, 475

    WM_DESTROY, 475

N

O

P

Q–R

W

X

Y–Z

Add to Your Sams Library Today with the Best Books for Programming, Operating Systems, and New Technologies

The easiest way to order is to pick up the phone and call

1-800-428-5331

between 9:00 a.m. and 5:00 p.m. EST.
For faster service please have your credit card available.

ISBN	Quantity	Description of Item	Unit Cost	Total Cost
0-672-30318-3		Windows Sound FunPack (Book/Disk)	$19.95	
0-672-30310-8		Windows Graphics FunPack (Book/Disk)	$19.95	
0-672-30249-7		Multimedia Madness! (Book/Disk CD-ROM)	$44.95	
0-672-30248-9		FractalVision (Book/Disk)	$39.95	
0-672-30305-1		Computer Graphics Environments (Book/Disk)	$34.95	
0-672-30361-2		Virtual Reality and the Exploration of Cyberspace (Book/Disk)	$26.95	
0-672-30322-1		PC Video Madness! (Book/Disk CD-ROM)	$39.95	
0-672-30315-9		The Magic of Image Processing (Book/Disk)	$39.95	
0-672-30345-0		Wasting Time with Windows (Book/Disk)	$19.95	
0-672-30301-9		Artificial Life Explorer's Kit (Book/Disk)	$29.95	
0-672-30352-3		Blaster Mastery (Book/Disk CD-ROM)	$34.95	
0-672-30320-5		Morphing Magic (Book/Disk)	$29.95	

❏ 3 ½" Disk

❏ 5 ¼" Disk

Shipping and Handling: See information below.		
TOTAL		

Shipping and Handling: $4.00 for the first book, and $1.75 for each additional book. Floppy disk: add $1.75 for shipping and handling. If you need to have it NOW, we can ship product to you in 24 hours for an additional charge of approximately $18.00, and you will receive your item overnight or in two days. Overseas shipping and handling: add $2.00 per book and $8.00 for up to three disks. Prices subject to change. Call for availability and pricing information on latest editions.

11711 N. College Avenue, Suite 140, Carmel, Indiana 46032

1-800-428-5331 — Orders   1-800-835-3202 — FAX   1-800-858-7674 — Customer Service

Book ISBN 0-672-30308-6

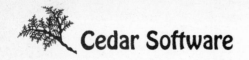

Cedar Software

Order Form

___ Please send me a free copy of *Dick Oliver's Nonlinear Nonsense*, **an 8-page illustrated newsletter of fractals, chaos, and creative graphics.** And while you're at it, Dick, send me some sales hype about your *Fractal Grafics 3D* program and a coupon for $50 off the normal $149 price in case I decide to buy it.

___ **I don't have a 3.5" disk drive.** Please send the software included with this book on 5.25" 1.2Mb disks. (I've enclosed a $5 handling fee.)

___ **Please send me the disks selected below on:**

   ___ 5.25" 1.2Mb disks

   ___ 3.5" 1.44Mb disks

Total number of disks _____ x $5 each = _____

(Overseas, add $10 shipping. In VT, add 5% tax.)

| Name: _____ |
| Phone: _____ |
| Address: _____ |
| _____ |

Visa/Mastercard or US check #: _____ Exp. Date: _____ Sign: _____

___ **Polyray ray tracer, math coprocessor versions.** The version of the Polyray shareware ray tracer included with this book runs on any 386 or 486, with or without a math coprocessor. This extra disk contains a faster version requiring a 387 or 486DX math coprocessor, as well as a version for 286/287 users.

___ **Utilities which work great with Polyray.** Includes Dave Mason's Targa Animator, which creates FLI animations from Polyray TGA files, Alfonso Hermida's POVCAD interactive modeling program with Polyray output, and other utilities to make ray tracing more fun. Some shareware, some freeware.

___ **Ray tracing C source code.** Mark VandeWettering's MTV ray tracer (a simpler predecessor to Polyray) with full C source code, plus several C programs by Eric Haines to produce complex ray-trace scenes in MTV and Polyray format. Also includes ready-to-run EXE files. Public domain.

___ **Graphic Workshop** from Alchemy Mindworks. This shareware utility converts between many graphics file formats, prints graphics to a wide variety of printers, displays, crops, dithers, rotates, re-sizes and more.

___ **Paintshop Pro** from JSAC Software. A shareware image processing program with oodles of filters and special effects, plus support for all major graphics file formats. Requires Microsoft Windows.

___ **REND386 Virtual Reality Kit** by Dave Stampe and Bernie Roehl. A freeware development kit for ultra-fast real-time 3D rendering. Libraries for C programmers and ready-to-explore "virtual worlds."

___ **FRACTINT Fractal Generator** by the Stone Soup Group. Freeware program to draw over 70 types of mathematical fractals, *fast*. With color cycling, 3-D projection, mountains, planets and much more.

___ **FRACTINT source code.** Complete C and assembler code for this giant program. Contains a wealth of graphics programming tricks, including direct support for nearly every video card in existence.

___ **3D Fractal Demos** by Dick Oliver. Fun animations show what you can do with *Fractal Grafics 3D*.

Send this page to:
Dick Oliver, Cedar Software, RR 1 Box 5140, Morrisville, VT 05661

Or call: 802-888-5275
FAX: 802-888-3009

What's on the Disks

- *TransGraphics System*, which makes your graphics programs compatible with all major C and C++ compilers and graphics libraries.
- *PolyRay* raytracing program
- *SVGA* Super VGA image viewer
- *VSA256* VESA Super VGA graphics library
- *ImagePro* image processing program
- *FantaVision* movie player and sample movies
- Tweening and morphing examples
- 2-D and 3-D Fractal animation and tweening programs
- 3-D surfaces editor and 3-D programming examples
- Interactive visualization program
- Examples of Windows GDI functions
- Sample graphics files

Installing the Floppy Disks

The software included with this book is stored in a compressed form. You cannot use the software without first installing it to your hard drive.

> **Note:** To install all the files, you need at least 6.6M of free space on your hard drive.

1. From a DOS prompt, change to the drive that contains the first installation disk. For example, if the disk is in drive A:, type A: and press Enter.

2. Type INSTALL and press Enter.

3. You will see a menu giving you the choice of installing a single program archive, or installing the entire disk. Use the arrow keys to highlight a choice and press Enter. Unless you do not have enough hard disk space, choose **INSTALL ENTIRE DISK**.

4. After you make a choice on the menu, you will be prompted to type in the drive letter of your hard drive.

5. When the files for this menu choice have been installed, the program will pause and ask you to press any key.

6. You will be returned to the installation menu, where you can choose another archive to install, or exit the program.

Repeat this procedure for Disk 2. The files will be installed to a directory named \TGG on your hard drive. Be sure to read the README file—it contains important information about the files and compiling the programs.